Evidence–Based Faculty Development Through the Scholarship of Teaching and Learning (SoTL)

Rachel C. Plews
Haute école pédagogique du canton de Vaud, Switzerland

Michelle L. Amos
University of Central Missouri, USA

A volume in the Advances in Educational
Marketing, Administration, and Leadership
(AEMAL) Book Series

Published in the United States of America by
IGI Global
Information Science Reference (an imprint of IGI Global)
701 E. Chocolate Avenue
Hershey PA, USA 17033
Tel: 717-533-8845
Fax: 717-533-8661
E-mail: cust@igi-global.com
Web site: http://www.igi-global.com

Library of Congress Cataloging-in-Publication Data

Names: Plews, Rachel C., 1981- editor. | Amos, Michelle L., 1971- editor.
Title: Evidence-based faculty development through the scholarship of
 teaching and learning (SoTL) / Rachel C. Plews and Michelle L. Amos,
 editors.
Description: Hershey, PA : Information Science Reference, 2020. | Includes
 bibliographical references and index. | Summary: "This book examines the
 role of the educational developer in promoting and supporting the
 Scholarship of Teaching and Learning (SoTL) as part of a professional
 development program"-- Provided by publisher.
Identifiers: LCCN 2019037706 (print) | LCCN 2019037707 (ebook) | ISBN
 9781799822127 (hardcover) | ISBN 9781799822134 (paperback) | ISBN
 9781799822141 (ebook)
Subjects: LCSH: Education--Research. | Learning--Research. |
 Teaching--Research. | Learning and scholarship--Research. | Reflective
 teaching.
Classification: LCC LB1028 .E948 2020 (print) | LCC LB1028 (ebook) | DDC
 370.71/1--dc23
LC record available at https://lccn.loc.gov/2019037706
LC ebook record available at https://lccn.loc.gov/2019037707

This book is published in the IGI Global book series Advances in Educational Marketing, Administration, and Leadership (AEMAL) (ISSN: 2326-9022; eISSN: 2326-9030)

British Cataloguing in Publication Data
A Cataloguing in Publication record for this book is available from the British Library.

For electronic access to this publication, please contact: eresources@igi-global.com.

Advances in Educational Marketing, Administration, and Leadership (AEMAL) Book Series

Siran Mukerji
IGNOU, India
Purnendu Tripathi
IGNOU, India

ISSN:2326-9022
EISSN:2326-9030

MISSION

With more educational institutions entering into public, higher, and professional education, the educational environment has grown increasingly competitive. With this increase in competitiveness has come the need for a greater focus on leadership within the institutions, on administrative handling of educational matters, and on the marketing of the services offered.

The **Advances in Educational Marketing, Administration, & Leadership (AEMAL) Book Series** strives to provide publications that address all these areas and present trending, current research to assist professionals, administrators, and others involved in the education sector in making their decisions.

COVERAGE

- Marketing Theories within Education
- Academic Administration
- Direct marketing of educational programs
- Advertising and Promotion of Academic Programs and Institutions
- Educational Leadership
- Educational Marketing Campaigns
- Educational Management
- Enrollment Management
- Technologies and Educational Marketing
- Governance in P-12 and Higher Education

IGI Global is currently accepting manuscripts for publication within this series. To submit a proposal for a volume in this series, please contact our Acquisition Editors at Acquisitions@igi-global.com or visit: http://www.igi-global.com/publish/.

Titles in this Series

For a list of additional titles in this series, please visit: www.igi-global.com/book-series

Utilizing Technology, Knowledge, and Smart Systems in Educational Administration and Leadership
Mehmet Durnali (Ereğli Faculty of Education, Zonguldak Bülent Ecevit University, Turkey)
Information Science Reference • © 2020 • 364pp • H/C (ISBN: 9781799814085) • US $195.00

Handbook of Research on Literacy and Digital Technology Integration in Teacher Education
Jared Keengwe (University of North Dakota, USA) and Grace Onchwari (University of North Dakota, USA)
Information Science Reference • © 2020 • 442pp • H/C (ISBN: 9781799814610) • US $245.00

Enhancing Teaching and Leadership Initiatives With Teacherpreneurs Emerging Research and Opportunities
Pam Epler (Youngstown State University, USA)
Information Science Reference • © 2020 • 150pp • H/C (ISBN: 9781799820741) • US $165.00

Collaborative Strategies for Implementing Equitable Learning Opportunities
Jason Jolicoeur (Washburn University, USA) and Binh Bui (University of Houston, USA)
Information Science Reference • © 2020 • 300pp • H/C (ISBN: 9781522593355) • US $185.00

Leveraging Technology to Improve School Safety and Student Wellbeing
Stephanie P. Huffman (Missouri State University, USA) Stacey Loyless (University of Central Arkansas, USA)
Shelly Albritton (University of Central Arkansas, USA) and Charlotte Green (University of Central Arkansas, USA)
Information Science Reference • © 2020 • 329pp • H/C (ISBN: 9781799817666) • US $195.00

Addressing Multicultural Needs in School Guidance and Counseling
Simon George Taukeni (University of Namibia, Namibia)
Information Science Reference • © 2020 • 402pp • H/C (ISBN: 9781799803195) • US $185.00

Emerging Methods and Paradigms in Scholarship and Education Research
Lorraine Ling (La Trobe University, Australia) and Peter Ling (Swinburne University of Technology, Australia)
Information Science Reference • © 2020 • 330pp • H/C (ISBN: 9781799810018) • US $195.00

Cases on Global Leadership in the Contemporary Economy
Ivonne Chirino-Klevans (Kenan-Flagler Business School, University of North Carolina, Chapel Hill, USA & International School of Management, Paris, France)
Business Science Reference • © 2020 • 187pp • H/C (ISBN: 9781522580881) • US $195.00

701 East Chocolate Avenue, Hershey, PA 17033, USA
Tel: 717-533-8845 x100 • Fax: 717-533-8661
E-Mail: cust@igi-global.com • www.igi-global.com

Table of Contents

Section 1
Introduction to SoTL and Faculty Development

Section 2
SoTL as a Form of Professional Development

Section 4
SoTL in Action: Case Studies From the Field

Section 5
Addressing the Challenges and Assessing the Impact of SoTL

Detailed Table of Contents

Section 1
Introduction to SoTL and Faculty Development

The first chapter of this publication is dedicated to an examination of the evolution of SoTL from Boyer's Scholarship of Teaching to the present "fourth wave" of SoTL in higher education decades later. After this introduction, the next chapter moves into a discussion of how SoTL can be embedded into institutional culture to help change thinking about and discussions around teaching and learning.

The Scholarship of Teaching and Learning (SoTL) is an important international movement in higher education. It is a continuously developing field that is traced back to Ernest Boyer's 1990 report, "Scholarship Reconsidered: Priorities of the Professoriate," which outlines his argument for an understanding of scholarship that includes a scholarship of teaching. This chapter traces the history and development of SoTL as a research domain since 1990. It includes specific attention to the rationale and dimensions, the debates and critiques of the field, as well as the potential future directions

This chapter charts how in England, Scholarship of Teaching and Learning (SoTL) activities that may until recently have been seen as 'marginal' or 'added' value are increasingly viewed as strategic enablers. This is of potential interest to international audiences due to the growing and, arguably, unprecedented expectations placed on English universities to evidence the impact of their education through the Teaching Excellence and Student Outcomes Framework. However, if SoTL is to become a fully functioning enabler of strategic transformation—rather than simply a cited exemplar or initiative—it needs to be systematically coordinated and evidenced. Drawing on a recently developed conceptual model—'the enquiring university'—the chapter charts how the role and impact of SoTL can be coordinated, recorded, and evaluated through an emergent SoTL Strategic Implementation and Impact Framework. Finally, the authors illustrate its application through reference to an example of a SoTL activity aligned to two key elements of the framework.

Section 2
SoTL as a Form of Professional Development

This section is dedicated to chapters reflecting how SoTL is practiced as a form of faculty professional development. Chapter 3 focuses on how educational development can take place in different contexts and, subsequently, how SoTL is integrated into these different structures. Chapters 4 and 5 focus on the collaborative nature of SoTL inquiry as a form of faculty co-development. The following chapter focuses on reflection, specifically how reflection is used prior to and during a SoTL inquiry. Finally, this section concludes with a chapter that specifically explores the role of non-standard faculty and how SoTL can help them better their practice.

Chapter 3
Jennifer C. Friberg, Illinois State University, USA
Lauren Scharff, U.S. Air Force Academy, USA

Colleges and universities around the world share a broad focus on education. However, unique characteristics and priorities across institutions may lead to vastly different educational development opportunities for the Scholarship of Teaching and Learning (SoTL) and levels of impact for the SoTL efforts (e.g., micro, meso, macro, mega). This chapter is organized in two distinct parts. Part 1 examines five different structures typical for SoTL educational development with a focus on their organizational structure within the institution and the SoTL expertise of individuals who that lead these efforts. Strengths and limitations of each structure are presented. Part 2 provides a discussion of critical considerations that impact all SoTL educational development efforts regardless of the type of structure that exists within an institution.

Chapter 4
Mandy Frake-Mistak, York University, Canada
Heidi L. Marsh, Humber College Institute of Technology and Advanced Learning, Canada
Geneviève Maheux-Pelletier, York University, Canada
Siobhan Williams, Humber College Institute of Technology and Advanced Learning, Canada

In this chapter, the authors share their reflections on the practice of using a community-based approach to doing SoTL research. They examine two professional development programs at their respective institutions—York University and Humber College in Ontario, Canada—that support faculty members' engagement in SoTL research. EduCATE and the Teaching Innovation Fund are two variations of SoTL programs in which participants come together to engage in and support each other through the process of doing SoTL research and are organized around participants' individual goals rather than a predetermined set of outcomes. The authors provide a fulsome narrative and reflective account of the EduCATE and

Teaching Innovation Fund programs with a particular focus on each program's development and relative success. Throughout, the impact of SoTL as a form of professional development is emphasized.

Chapter 5
    Sandra Sgoutas-Emch, University of San Diego, USA
    Judith Liu, University of San Diego, USA
    Moriah Meyskens, University of San Diego, USA
    Tara Ceranic Salinas, University of San Diego, USA
    Jane Friedman, University of San Diego, USA
    Perla Myers, University of San Diego, USA

Cultivating a community of faculty to support Scholarship of Teaching and Learning (SoTL) work at universities can be challenging. There are many obstacles to overcome—obstacles such as how to sustain such efforts over time. The Center for Educational Excellence set out to design a strategic plan designed to address certain barriers to SoTL work and to create a long-standing community of practice for a SoTL group of faculty members—a group that has lasted over nine years to date. This chapter outlines strategies employed over the years and the evolution of the interdisciplinary group from a learning community to community of practice. The stories of past and present members are included along with advice on how others may have successful programs at their universities.

Chapter 6
    Laura Zizka, Ecole hoteliere de Lausanne, Switzerland & HES-SO University of Applied
        Sciences and Arts of Western Switzerland, Switzerland

Reflection was introduced into educational institutions to encourage students to seek beyond the descriptive and simple response toward critical, deep thinking, and effectively make better choices. It is also an integral part of the structured inquiry of one's teaching through the Scholarship of Teaching and Learning (SoTL). Based on Dewey and Schön's foundation of reflection as linked to actions undertaken in apprentices' daily tasks, this chapter attempts to dispel common misconceptions related to reflection to show that reflection can and should be encouraged by all stakeholders in educational programs regardless of the discipline, level, or type of study. A Reflection Radar has been created to identify reflective practices in teaching and learning. The chapter concludes with how reflection through SoTL can and should be implemented as a solid, formative pedagogical tool at all levels of education and contribute to the scholarship of teaching and learning for all educators.

Chapter 7
    Lauren Hays, University of Central Missouri, USA
    Lindsay McNiff, Dalhousie University, Canada

Non-standard faculty are individuals with faculty appointments, but whose responsibilities fall outside the traditional faculty role. Non-standard faculty are often overlooked in conversations about SoTL, but they play an integral part in the teaching and learning that occurs on post-secondary campuses. Due to the focus on local context within SoTL, non-standard faculty greatly benefit from this type of professional development. Using the micro, meso, macro, and mega framework, the authors of this chapter describe how educational developers can support non-standard faculty in using SoTL for professional development. This common SoTL framework helps educational developers bring non-standard faculty into SoTL conversations while also recognizing the unique teaching environments in which they work.

Section 3
Faculty Developers as Partners in SoTL

This section is dedicated to the role of the faculty developer and his or her role in supporting and promoting a culture of SoTL across an institution. Despite the competing commitments that faculty members face, faculty developers are in a role that contributes to teaching excellence, and one way to do this is through SoTL. The first part of this section shares scenarios and case studies which illustrate the nature of these relationships through the perspectives of both faculty members and faculty developers. The section concludes with a chapter discussing research ethics and implications for SoTL with an emphasis on the role of the faculty developer.

Chapter 8

Erik Brogt, University of Canterbury, New Zealand
Kerry Shephard, University of Otago, New Zealand
Bernadette Knewstubb, Victoria University of Wellington, New Zealand
Tracy Leigh Rogers, University of Otago, New Zealand

This chapter discusses how Scholarship of Teaching and Learning (SoTL) can be used to foster a research approach to teaching and learning and how faculty development that supports colleagues to engage in SoTL can support the development of scholarly faculty. Both the process and the product of SoTL are discussed, conceptualised as different levels of SoTL engagement. The role of the faculty developer in such scholarship is discussed, drawing on Pedagogical Content Knowledge as a framework for engagement in SoTL projects. Last, implications for the work of a faculty developer are drawn and future avenues of research in faculty development proposed.

Chapter 9

Kathryn Janet Meldrum, James Cook University, Australia
Kristi Giselsson, James Cook University, Australia

The Scholarship of Teaching and Learning (SoTL) has been suggested as an ideal vehicle for engaging faculty with professional development for teaching in higher education. However, previous authors have identified that faculty find writing about SoTL difficult. The aim of this chapter is to support educational developers (EDs) to collaborate with faculty to support writing. Two theoretical frameworks to support collaboration are proposed: the first, the Knowledge Transforming Model of Writing, to assist with the process of writing; the second, an adaptation of Brigugilio's working in the third space framework to support collaboration. The authors utilise both frameworks to reflect on their own SoTL collaboration and subsequently pose questions to support faculty and EDs to do the same. Ultimately, it is proposed that collaboration not only enhances the practices of faculty and EDs but improves what should be an important priority for the wider academy: the learning outcomes of students.

Mid-Semester Assessment Programs (MAPs) have been successfully utilized as a professional development tool for faculty interested in improving their teaching in the context of higher education by assessing voluntary formative student feedback that guides changes instructors make in the classroom. Faculty centers and educational developers have the unique opportunity to recruit instructors via MAPs who have participated in these programs to promote and support the scholarship of teaching and learning (SoTL) among faculty who already display an innate interest in best teaching practices and are open to advancing their own teaching in order to improve student learning and to propel student success. This chapter provides a guide for educational developers who seek to become active partners for faculty to become interested and engaged in the scholarship of teaching and learning through a unique recruitment mechanism that serves as a natural steppingstone for faculty not having engaged with SoTL yet.

This chapter explores the ongoing collaboration between an educational developer and a faculty member at a university of teacher education in Switzerland as an inquiry into one's teaching practice to improve the implementation of the flipped classroom approach. Through the lens of transformative learning theory, the chapter examines how SoTL can serve as faculty enrichment in addition to an approach for systematic reflection on practice. Special attention is paid to the role of the educational developer as a mentor throughout the inquiry. The chapter concludes with practical strategies for developing a productive SoTL relationship between educational developers and faculty member, as well as visibility across an institution.

This chapter stems from popular misconceptions demonstrated by educators who lack familiarity with the significance and necessity of honoring ethical guidelines and practices when conducting SoTL research. The authors articulate the value of incorporating ethical principles and practices in research design and provide educational developers with much needed critical information about ethical considerations when conducting SoTL research. An overview of the purpose and functions of review ethics boards is included, along with common scenarios involving ethical dilemmas educators may encounter when embarking on a SoTL research study. Reflective questions to contemplate and strategies about how ethical practices can and should be embedded into SoTL research planning and design are explained. A framework and applicable resource are provided so that educational developers may guide and support instructor/researchers through safe and ethical SoTL inquires.

Section 4
SoTL in Action: Case Studies From the Field

In this section, examples of SoTL inquiries across diverse contexts and disciplines are presented. The aim is to showcase individual work in the field that represents strong practical examples of SoTL. While these studies are rooted in different literature and take on different methodological approaches, they all have the common goal of improving student learning.

Chapter 13

Michelle L. Amos, University of Central Missouri, USA
Morgan Ely, University of Central Missouri, USA

Using the SoTL framework provides students with an accessible, relevant model of professional and critical reflection on practice. Explicit participation in this research can benefit students with scaffolded practice applying reflection to instruction. Guiding students in examining assumptions around literacy supports meaningful integration of these skills in instructional design. This transformation of students' frames of reference requires meaningful reflection and a challenge to their current beliefs about disciplinary literacy. This study uses Reading/Writing Workshop format to individualize instruction, engage students in self-directed learning, and facilitate differentiation and formative assessment. This redesigned course used experiential learning and a social constructivist model to build collaboration and real-world communication skills. Transformation is supported through structured reflection. Thus, a data collection instrument was adapted from Brookfield's Critical Incident Questionnaire to guide students with specific, practiced, and meaningful reflection.

Chapter 14

Rob Hallis, University of Central Missouri, USA

The Scholarship of Teaching and Learning nurtures an academic discussion of best instructional practices. This case study examines the role domain knowledge plays in determining extent to which students can effectively analyze an opinion piece from a major news organization, locate a relevant source to support their view of the issue, and reflect on the quality of their work. The goal of analyzing an opinion piece is twofold: it fosters critical thinking in analyzing the strength of an argument and it promotes information management skills in locating and incorporating relevant sources in a real-world scenario. Students, however, exhibited difficulties in accurately completing the assignment and usually overestimated their expertise. This chapter traces how each step in the process of making this study public clarifies the issues encountered. The focus here, however, centers on the context within which the study was formulated, those issues that contributed to framing the research question, and how the context of inquiry served to deepen insights in interpreting the results.

Chapter 15

Maurizio Costabile, University of South Australia, Australia
Hayley Timms, University of South Australia, Australia

One approach used in teaching scientific principles is laboratory practical classes. However, it can be challenging to teach concepts prior to their introduction in lectures. Academic teaching staff that wish to use alternative approaches to bridge this gap and, in turn, enhance student learning, often require help from their local Educational Developers (EDs). This chapter outlines the process of identifying a problem and then developing, implementing, and evaluating an online interactive simulation to teach enzyme kinetics to undergraduate students at the University of South Australia (UniSA). The challenges faced by the academic and ED in developing the simulation are covered. By the end of the chapter, the reader (academic or ED) will have a better appreciation of the challenges faced in developing a new teaching approach as well as the strategies that can be used to address these challenges.

Chapter 16

Namala Lakshmi Tilakaratna, National University of Singapore, Singapore
Mark Brooke, National University of Singapore, Singapore
Laetitia Monbec, National University of Singapore, Singapore
Siew Tiang Lau, National University of Singapore, Singapore
Vivien Xi Wu, National University of Singapore, Singapore
Yah Shih Chan, National University of Singapore, Singapore

The chapter provides a description of the first stage of an SoTL project consisting of an interdisciplinary research collaboration between nursing disciplinary experts from the Alice Lee Centre for Nursing Studies (ALCNS) and academic literacy experts from the Centre for English Language Communication (CELC) at the National University of Singapore (NUS). This stage includes the creation of appropriate lesson material for teaching critical reflection drawing on Focus Group Discussions (FGDs) with nursing lecturers and the use of 'model' reflective writing texts from high-scoring students in past cohorts analysed using Systemic Functional linguistic frameworks such as genre pedagogy, appraisal, The Legitimation Code Theory tool of semantic waves. The intervention was designed to improve the highly valued skill of 'critical reflection' in nursing undergraduate clinical modules drawing on the use of rigorous theoretical frameworks that make visible salient linguistics resources and knowledge practices drawing on SFL and LCT.

Chapter 17

Jenna Kammer, University of Central Missouri, USA

Transformative learning can be used as a strategy for measuring teacher effectiveness in online courses. By measuring the transformations that occur within their courses, instructors can understand more about the activities and experiences that are the most impactful for students. In addition, instructors can create opportunities for transformation by designing learning experiences that encourage students to critically self-reflect. This chapter presents an exploratory study that examined instructor and student perceptions of transformation in an online school library graduate program. The data was used to redesign one unit in a course on reference and information services to create opportunities for students to experience transformation with the content.

Chapter 18

Deanna Meth, Queensland University of Technology, Australia
Holly R. Russell, Queensland University of Technology, Australia
Rachel Fitzgerald, Queensland University of Technology, Australia
Henk Huijser, Queensland University of Technology, Australia

This chapter outlines the multiple ways in which Scholarship of Teaching and Learning (SoTL) activities might be activated and/or realized through the processes of curriculum and learning design of a degree program. Key dual enablers for these activities are an underpinning curriculum framework, bringing a series of defined developmental steps each underpinned by SoTL, and the Curriculum Design Studio construct as a vehicle for collaborative ways of working between staff, including academics and curriculum designers and students. Drawing on evidence from the practices of four curriculum designers, examples are presented across a wide range of disciplinary areas. In many instances, SoTL not only brings an evidence base to the work, but also the potential for research outputs, thus becoming a useful lever for academic staff to engage in ongoing curriculum design discussions and evidence-informed practice. Such activities serve to mitigate against acknowledged challenges faced by academics such as lack of adequate time for such activities and the pressure to produce research outputs.

Section 5
Addressing the Challenges and Assessing the Impact of SoTL

This final section of the book discusses common challenges faced by faculty and faculty developers with SoTL before moving into a chapter highlighting an example of the impact of SoTL on both professional development and educational quality improvement. Chapter 19 looks at the challenges encountered when implementing a SoTL program as an ongoing faculty development initiative. The final chapter presents one practice example, which could provide a basis for discussion focused more on the impact of SoTL to combat the potential barriers or challenges often encountered.

Chapter 19

Sherry Fukuzawa, University of Toronto, Mississauga, Canada
Dianne Ashbourne, University of Toronto, Mississauga, Canada
Fiona Rawle, University of Toronto, Mississauga, Canada

In order for teaching and learning to improve throughout an institution, the Scholarship of Teaching and Learning (SoTL) must be valued within institutional culture and contribute to the scholarly identity of researchers. This chapter emphasizes some of the challenges for SoTL researchers, whether educational developers or faculty members, to consider as they begin their foray into educational research. SoTL challenges are divided into four inter-related themes: (1) scholarly identity, (2) institutional challenges, (3) accessing and searching the SoTL literature, and (4) conducting SoTL research (SoTL research design, methodology, funding and time commitments, and ethical considerations). The chapter includes a series of opportunities and resources to help SoTL researchers reframe these challenges into opportunities for their institutions.

The Curriculum Evaluation Research (CER) Framework was developed as a response to increasing scrutiny and expectations of the higher education sector, including legislated standards for curriculum and professional teachers that explicitly require a systematic and comprehensive approach to evaluating curriculum. The CER Framework is designed to facilitate a scholarly environment to drive and assure the quality of a curriculum and the capabilities of its teaching team. It stems from a synthesis of teacher as action researcher (TAAR), quality improvement (QI), quality assurance (QA), and the Scholarship of Teaching and Learning (SoTL) applied to the curriculum as it is designed, taught, and revised. In this chapter, the implementation of the CER Framework to the University College is reviewed and evaluated. The University College is an organisational unit comprises approximately 600 students and 80 staff. This chapter includes a reflection on the barriers and enablers of implementing the CER Framework.

Preface

In his 2019 article, "Expertise in University Teaching & the Implications for Teaching Effectiveness, Evaluation & Training," renowned Stanford scholar Carl Wieman encourages us to reflect on what it means to be considered an expert in university teaching, and why such experts are needed across institutions in higher education. Faculty developers, particularly those with current and previous teaching experience, can be considered such experts, serving to guide discipline-focused faculty members on their continued path of professional development. Faculty learning, or faculty professional development, can be unconscious, multi-dimensional, and multi-level, occurring in the connection among theory, practice, and person (Korthagen, 2017).

To support this learning, faculty development programs should aim to address the challenges and opportunities of the individual within the context of the elements of theory and practice fundamental to the ideals of an "effective educator." One way to make this connection is through structured inquiry into one's teaching, known as the Scholarship of Teaching and Learning (SoTL). SoTL can be presented as a form of action research; Lewin (1948) framed action research as a paradigm of inquiry where the researcher's primary purpose is to improve the capacity and subsequent practices of the researcher rather than to produce theoretical knowledge (Morales, 2016, p.158). SoTL provides a platform for faculty members to reflect on their own teaching with the overall goal of improving their practice. Through this research process and subsequent outcomes, teaching strategies are challenged, existing ideas may shift or expand, and evidence is secured to inform future pedagogical decisions (Phung, Cole, & Zarestky, 2017).

PURPOSE

SoTL presents an opportunity for faculty professional development that is action-oriented, evidence-based, and engaging for faculty members at any stage in their academic career. Educational developers play a central role in supporting faculty members through the research process and in using the results to inform their ongoing professional development programming. The main aims of this publication are to introduce SoTL and its role in educational development and to provide practical support for both educational developers and faculty members looking to engage, and perhaps collaborate, in this type of inquiry.

TERMINOLOGY

Mueller and Schroeder (2018) define teaching development as "a developmental process in which an individual engages for the purpose of improving teaching and learning effectiveness (p.399)." These authors also address the different terms commonly used around the world to describe this definition - *faculty development* in the United States, *academic development* in Australia and New Zealand, and *educational development* in Canada and the United Kingdom. Other terms with more precise elements within the field include curriculum development, instructional development, and organizational development. This difference in terminology itself can be complex, so the authors of this publication have decided to use the terms *faculty development* and *educational development* interchangeably throughout the work.

As the contributors for each chapter are from around the world, there is terminology used that might be unfamiliar or used differently in another region. At the end of each chapter, readers will find a section with key terms or phrases for that chapter, helping to address these differences. Many authors also have paid special detail to this in their work to guide the reader through each chapter. In addition, readers may find a few instances where the spelling of a particular word is inconsistent with the spelling of that word in a different chapter. The Editors recognize this and wish to allow each chapter to be grounded in its own context; for example, the word program, when used in the US context, might read as programme when used in other contexts. In contrast, punctuation has been standardized to American English usage; for example, terminology may be set off with double quotation marks rather than single quotes.

AUDIENCE

This book is designed to be a reference for faculty developers and faculty members in higher education. It is particularly suited towards these individuals who are called to collaborate on a SoTL initiative at a course, program, or institutional level. For this reason, higher education administrators will also find the content useful in working to promote a culture of SoTL across the institution.

OVERVIEW OF CONTENTS

The 20 chapters are grouped into five sections. These include "An Introduction to SoTL and Faculty Development," "SoTL as a Form of Professional Development," "Faculty Developers as Partners in SoTL," "SoTL in Action: Case Studies From the Field," and "Addressing the Challenges and Assessing the Impact of SoTL." Readers will find introductions at the start of each section to guide them through the chapters.

Chapter 1, "Riding the Fourth Wave: An Introduction to the Scholarship of Teaching and Learning," provides the reader with an in-depth overview of the evolution of SoTL during the past twenty years from the 1990s work of Ernest Boyer with the introduction of the idea of scholarly teaching, to an era focused on priorities and assessment, to Hutching's (2000) work on the types of SoTL, to Huber & Hutching's (2005) concept of the SoTL commons, and finally to recent developments in the field including discussion on the levels of SoTL (Simmons, 2016) and the public dissemination of this work, including the *Teaching & Learning Inquiry* journal by the International Society for the Scholarship of Teaching and Learning (ISSOTL).

In Chapter 2, "The Enquiring University: The Scholarship of Teaching and Learning as a Foundation for Strategic Educational Transformation," the authors illustrate a shift in thinking from SoTL as a "value-added" for faculty members to a "strategic enabler" that is developed, managed, supported, and evaluated. Written in the form of a case study from an English university, this work focuses on a conceptual framework called the "enquiring university" and its application, making it a nice follow-up to Chapter 1.

As the reader continues into the second section of the book, "SoTL as a Tool for Professional Development," Chapter 3, "Structures and Consideration for SoTL Educational Development," addresses five types of structures for SoTL based on the overall institutional structure and the key individuals involved. The authors then move into a discussion of critical considerations for SoTL in any structure. From a practice-oriented perspective, this Chapter can be particularly useful to administrators and teaching center directors who are implementing a new or evaluating an existing SoTL program.

Chapter 4, "Making SoTL Stick: Using a Community-Based Approach to Engage Faculty in the Scholarship of Teaching and Learning," highlights the element of collaboration and discourse as a significant element of SoTL for professional development. The authors share two different institutional programs - York University's EduCATE and Humber College's Teaching Innovation Fund - to highlight how participants collaborate and support one another through a SoTL project. This chapter discusses the development, implementation, and evaluation of the programs from an objective standpoint, as well as from the reflective perspectives of those involved.

Chapter 5, "Building Faculty SoTL Skills Through a Multi- and Interdisciplinary Writing and Learning Community," continues in the discussion of the significance of collaborative efforts in SoTL. The authors discuss an ongoing strategy of using a Community of Practice (CoP) to bring SoTL to the forefront of university initiatives as well as to support faculty members working on SoTL projects. This chapter provides first-hand accounts of experiences from different participants in the CoP and practical advice for launching a similar program in another context.

Chapter 6, "Reflection and SoTL: Putting Reflection (Back) on the Faculty Radar," brings the reader back into a more personal account of SoTL, emphasizing the role of reflection. The author presents a tool called the Reflection Radar which helps faculty members to think about their teaching, in particular the elements of a course that encourage reflective activities for deeper learning for students. Various examples are shared, along with practical suggestions for implementation for ongoing faculty professional development.

In Chapter 7, "SoTL as a Professional Development Tool for Non-Standard Faculty," the authors discuss how SoTL can be used as a professional development tool for staff members who are classified as faculty members but whose main role does not center around the traditional activities of teaching, research, and service. This includes academic librarians, academic advisors, and others in roles concentrated on institutional support services.

As the reader moves into the third section of the book, "Faculty Developers as Partners in SoTL," the chapters have a focus on the specific nature of the role of the faculty developer and his or her role in SoTL from an individual to an institutional level. Chapter 8, "Using SoTL to Foster a Research Approach to Teaching," explores how educational developers can work with faculty members to develop the posture of scholarly teaching. Using the Pedagogical Content Knowledge framework, practical examples are illustrated as are implications for research in the field.

Chapter 9, "Writing Into the Scholarship of Teaching and Learning: Approaches to Supporting Faculty to Find Their 'Voice,'" presents two frameworks to guide faculty developers in collaborating with faculty members for SoTL projects - the Knowledge Transforming Model of Writing and an adaptation of Carmela Brigugilio's working in the third space to support collaboration. The emphasis is on the nature of and the ongoing opportunities and challenges inherent with this collaborative work with the overall objective remaining improved student learning outcomes.

Chapter 10, "Using Mid-Semester Assessment Programs (MAPs) as a Catalyst for the Scholarship of Teaching and Learning (SoTL)," discusses the development and implementation of one specific method for collaboration among faculty developers and faculty members. The authors present the program as an entry point to introduce faculty members to the philosophy and methods of SoTL and engage them in this work. The program focuses on a commitment to improving teaching methods and activities with the student at the center of the work.

Chapter 11, "At the Intersection of Transformative Learning and SoTL: A Collaborative Project Exploring the Flipped Classroom in Teacher Education," discusses the role of an educational developer from the lens of a SoTL inquiry and as a champion of faculty learning. Readers learn about the phases of a SoTL project through the voices of both the faculty developer and the faculty member. Lessons learned and practical implications for working collaboratively on SoTL initiatives are shared.

Chapter 12, "The Role of Educational Developers in Supporting Research Ethics in SoTL," concludes this section with a discussion of the role of the faculty developer and research ethics that can be generalized to any research context, but that focuses on the nuances of SoTL inquiries. While this subject can be specific to departments, institutions, countries, and contexts, awareness is central for faculty developers when guiding SoTL work.

In the third section of this book, "SoTL in Action: Case Studies From the Field," examples of SoTL inquiries from different disciplines around the world are presented from the perspective of faculty members, faculty developers, or both. In Chapter 13, "Practicing What We Teach: Using SoTL to Challenge Preservice Teachers' Assumptions With the Reading/Writing Workshop Model," the authors redesigned a course using experiential learning and a social constructivist model to build collaboration and real-world communication skills. The students recorded their reflections during the course using an adaptation of Stephen Brookfield's critical incident questionnaire. The results of this change in teaching methods are shared in this collaborative initiative.

A second SoTL project focused on writing initiatives, this time in an academic writing course, is presented in Chapter 14, "Scholarly Rigor: Focusing Reflection Through Engaging in an Academic Dialogue." Written by an academic librarian who is also an active teaching faculty member, the SoTL project focuses on a threshold concept in the course--the analysis of an opinion piece. Through a change in his teaching practice through the introduction of a scaffolded activity, the author aims to analyze the effectiveness of this approach in terms of student learning.

Chapter 15, "Developing an Online Interactive Simulation to Teaching Enzyme Kinetics to Undergraduate Biochemistry Students: Analysis From an Educational Designer and an Academic's Perspective," moves the reader into a SoTL project in the sciences disciplines. The topic of enzyme kinetics is typically taught using a traditional lecture style method. The authors sought to teach this topic in a new way--with an online simulation. This work discusses the development, implementation, and evaluation of this new teaching method.

In Chapter 16, "Insights Into an Interdisciplinary Project on Critical Reflection in Nursing: Using Systemic Functional Linguistic and Legitimation Code Theory to Enhance SoTL Research and Practice," the authors present the development of a SoTL inquiry to teach critical reflection to nursing students. Drawing on Systemic Functional Linguistic frameworks and Legitimation Code Theory tools, new course materials were developed and student reflections were analyzed to assess the effectiveness of student learning.

Chapter 17, "A Case Study in the Application of Transformative Learning Theory: The Redesign of an Online Course in Order to Achieve Deep Learning," presents an exploratory study that examined instructor and student perceptions of transformation in an online school library science graduate program. This SoTL inquiry focuses on instructional design in the online learning environment and how the various online teaching methods used may be effective in helping students learn.

The last chapter in this section, Chapter 18, "Embracing and Enabling Scholarship of Teaching and Learning Activities Across a Curriculum Design Framework: A Lever for Faculty Engagement," shares the perspectives of faculty members and curriculum designers about using SoTL to design the curriculum across different disciplines. By using SoTL as a driver for engagement, some of the traditional challenges associated with having the capacity for change in terms of time and resources are addressed within this approach.

In the final section of the book, challenges often experienced when assimilating SoTL into an institutional culture are addressed, a topic that is then followed by concrete examples of assessing the impact of SoTL. In Chapter 19, "Overcoming Challenges to Impactful SoTL: Considerations for Professional Development Programs," the authors discuss the factors that may lead to a resistance for engagement in SoTL. These four areas include an individual faculty member's scholarly identity, institutional challenges, the ability to access and search the SoTL Literature, and knowledge about how to design and conduct a SoTL project. The authors share practical considerations to enable educational developers to help faculty members overcome these challenges.

Finally, this publication concludes with Chapter 20, "Exploring the Impact of SoTL on Day-to-Day Learning and Teaching: A Conceptual Framework for Professional Development and Quality Improvement." The authors present their work on the development and implementation of a framework with SoTL as a primary indicator to assess curriculum and quality across an institution. The topic of assessing impact of SoTL is complex, and this chapter presents one way to view impact, with an invitation to consider adaptations and other ideas for future ways to assess SoTL activities at different levels.

CONCLUSION

This publication presents SoTL and faculty development practices through the perspectives and experiences of authors from around the world. While striving to address specifically how faculty developers can contribute to an institutional culture of SoTL, the book has elements of collaborative work embedded throughout each section. We believe that building from these resources can help bring faculty development practices into the next decade, riding the fourth wave of SoTL with a continued and elevated focus on co-development.

REFERENCES

Bishop, J. L., & Verleger, M. A. (2013, June). The flipped classroom: A survey of the research. *ASEE National Conference Proceedings*, 30(9), 1-18.

Huber, M. T., & Hutchings, P. (2006). Building the teaching commons. *Change: The Magazine of Higher Learning, 38*(3), 24–31. doi:10.3200/CHNG.38.3.24-31

Hutchings, M., & Quinney, A. (2015). The flipped classroom, disruptive pedagogies, enabling technologies, and wicked problems: Responding to "the bomb in the basement". *Electronic Journal of E-Learning, 13*(2), 106-119.

Hutchings, P. (2000). Approaching the Scholarship of Teaching and Learning. In *Opening lines: Approaches to the Scholarship of Teaching and Learning*. Retrieved from http://www.carnegiefoundation.org/elibrary/approaching-scholarship-teaching-and-learning

Morales, M. P. E. (2016). Participatory action research (PAR) cum action research (AR) in teacher professional development: A literature review. *International Journal of Research in Education and Science, 2*(1), 156–165. doi:10.21890/ijres.01395

Mueller, R., & Schroeder, M. (2018). From seeing to doing: Examining the impact of non-evaluative classroom observation on teaching development. *Innovative Higher Education, 43*(5), 397–410. doi:10.100710755-018-9436-0

Simmons, N. (Ed.). (2016). *The scholarship of teaching and learning in Canada: Institutional impact. New Directions in Teaching and Learning, 146.* San Francisco, CA: Jossey-Bass.

Wieman, C. E. (2019). Expertise in University Teaching & the Implications for Teaching Effectiveness, Evaluation & Training. *Daedalus, 148*(4), 47–78. doi:10.1162/daed_a_01760

Acknowledgment

The editors would like to express their sincere thanks to everyone who has contributed to the success of this publication. To our chapter authors, thank you for sharing your expertise and experience in the diverse areas of SoTL from conceptual frameworks to concrete SoTL project examples, and finally to practical implications for faculty developers, faculty members, and university administrators. To our Advisory Board, thank you for being with us from the initial stages of the project to help shape a publication that will contribute to the field. To our reviewers, thank you for spending the time to provide constructive feedback to the various chapter authors to improve their manuscripts; we appreciate your time and thoughtful work. We would also like to acknowledge the AEGIS (Adult Education Guided Intensive Study) program at Teachers College, Columbia University (with special appreciation to Dr. Lyle Yorks, Dr. Victoria Marsick, and Dr. Jeanne Bitterman) where our collaborative initiatives began. Finally, we want to thank our families for their continued support during all of our academic and professional adventures; their constant love, support, and patience helps us to achieve our goals.

Section 1
Introduction to SoTL and Faculty Development

The first chapter of this publication is dedicated to an examination of the evolution of SoTL from Boyer's Scholarship of Teaching to the present "fourth wave" of SoTL in higher education decades later. After this introduction, the next chapter moves into a discussion of how SoTL can be embedded into institutional culture to help change thinking about and discussions around teaching and learning.

Chapter 1
Riding the Fourth Wave:
An Introduction to the Scholarship of Teaching and Learning

Andrea S. Webb

https://orcid.org/0000-0003-3963-5057

The University of British Columbia, Canada

ABSTRACT

The Scholarship of Teaching and Learning (SoTL) is an important international movement in higher education. It is a continuously developing field that is traced back to Ernest Boyer's 1990 report, "Scholarship Reconsidered: Priorities of the Professoriate," which outlines his argument for an understanding of scholarship that includes a scholarship of teaching. This chapter traces the history and development of SoTL as a research domain since 1990. It includes specific attention to the rationale and dimensions, the debates and critiques of the field, as well as the potential future directions

INTRODUCTION

Societal, economic, and political influences have drawn attention to teaching and learning in higher education. In reaction, institutions of higher education are shifting from an instructional paradigm to a learning-centered approach (Barr & Tagg, 1995). No longer is the transfer of knowledge from master to acolyte sufficient. In order to function in today's professional culture, graduates of higher education require adaptive skills to assist them as they navigate diverse international contexts and changing technology in a rapidly shifting employment market. In response, institutions of higher education are creating environments where students discover and construct knowledge for themselves through initiatives on flexible learning and the individualization of curriculum.

The Scholarship of Teaching and Learning (SoTL) is an international movement, coming into maturity in the 21st century, which contributes to the quality of teaching and learning in higher education as well as a growing body of educational literature (Hubball, Pearson, & Clarke, 2013). Operating under "the big tent" (D'Andrea, 2006; Gilpin, 2011; Huber & Hutchings, 2005, p. 4), SoTL is accessible to

DOI: 10.4018/978-1-7998-2212-7.ch001

all disciplines, including inter- and intra-disciplinary inquiry. Through literature-informed, rigorous methodological inquiry, and peer-disseminated findings, SoTL provides a practical and complementary undergirding for research into learning, regardless of the theoretical positions from which inquirers come (Gilpin, 2011; Hubball, Clarke, Webb, & Johnson, 2015). This chapter traces the development of SoTL as a research domain. It includes specific attention to the history of SoTL and its dimensions, including the critiques of the field, and suggests potential directions for the next wave of SoTL.

TEACHING AND LEARNING IN HIGHER EDUCATION: THE CONTEXT

Given the importance, and challenges, of the teaching–research nexus, this paper traces the history and development of the field of SoTL since 1990. The landscape of teaching and learning in higher education is complex, with increasing student diversity, the development of niche programs, the use of technology to enhance flexible learning, and highly specialized disciplinary knowledge butting up against institutional and public accountability. Into this landscape, the Scholarship of Teaching and Learning offers a way for higher education institutions to encourage faculty to engage with research, teaching, and innovation through proactive faculty development and supportive institutional governance.

The Scholarship of Teaching (SoT) arose out of the fertile ground of previous work in the educative practices of disciplines. During the first decades of the 20th century, a small number of disciplinary societies sponsored specialized journals (i.e., the American Society for Engineering Education, starting in 1910, and the Division of Chemical Education of the American Chemical Society published the *Journal of Chemical Education*, starting in 1924) (Huber & Hutchings, 2005, p. 9). The 1960s saw an explosive growth in the discussion and debate in the wider higher education community, coinciding with the massification of higher education in North America (Glassick, Huber, & Maeroff, 1997). The *Chronicle of Higher Education* and *Change* both began publishing in 1969, and in 1972, the United States Department of Education began providing financial support for the Fund for the Improvement of Postsecondary Education. Around the same time, the National Science Foundation introduced new initiatives to improve education practices in science, technology, engineering, and mathematics (STEM).

However, it is hard to underestimate the influence of the Carnegie Foundation in furthering the study of higher education. Founded in 1905, it has a long history of involvement in educational policy and research (Carnegie Foundation for the Advancement of Teaching, n.d.); however, it was Ernest Boyer's appointment as president that initiated the separation of the Carnegie Corporation and the Carnegie Foundation. The newly separated Foundation's interest in higher education was broadened to include all levels of the educational experience, not just politics and policies.

In his influential work, *Scholarship Reconsidered: Priorities of the Professoriate*, Ernest Boyer (1990) suggested that the 1990s would become the decade of undergraduate education. But at the center of this debate, he predicted, would be the issue of faculty time, as stakeholders debated the primacy of the professoriate's activities. For what activity do institutions of higher education engage professors? Is it possible to have fruitful discussions about the importance of teaching in higher education if professors are not recognized or compensated for the improvements in this area? This tension still exists; however, a number of institutions are recognizing this tension and addressing teaching and learning in higher education as an area worthy of scholarship. It is not "an intriguing aside, or an add-on, but an essential facet of good teaching—built into the expected repertoire of scholarly practice" (Shulman, 2000, n.p.).

The Scholarship of Teaching

According to Boyer (1990), institutions of higher education had, at the time, adopted too narrow a view of scholarship, "one that limits it to a hierarchy of functions" (p. 15), with basic research as the first and foremost scholarly activity. However, Boyer went on to suggest that "causality can, and frequently does, point in both directions" (p. 16). Teaching, research, and service are actually intertwined into a comprehensive, dynamic relationship where they are continuously influencing and overlapping with each other. Good teaching is a scholarly, dynamic endeavor undertaken by faculty as learners (Boyer, 1990). It transforms and extends knowledge as well as transmitting it. There is also a key place for the learner in Boyer's definition of good teaching; classroom discussion, comments, and questions push professors in new and generative directions. The application of knowledge should be understood as an act of scholarship on par with the discovery of knowledge through research, the integration of knowledge, and the sharing of knowledge through teaching (Boyer, 1990). Therefore, Boyer concluded that what is needed in higher education is a more inclusive view of what it means to be a scholar—"a recognition that knowledge is acquired through research, through synthesis, through practice, and through teaching" (Boyer, 1990, p. 24). Boyer highlighted four keys to scholarship: discovery (research), integration (moving outside the disciplinary silos), application (bringing knowledge to bear on consequential problems), and teaching (initiating students into the best values of the academy). At the crux of *Scholarship Reconsidered* is the assertion that the academy needs to avoid a narrow definition of scholarship and to recognize and reward all four categories of scholarship.

The SoTL movement has incited the academy to reconceptualize the place of teaching and learning within tertiary education. Making teaching "community property" (Shulman, 1993) has gone a long way toward moving beyond the teaching-versus-research debate and giving a broader, more valuable meaning to classroom practice (Boyer, 1990). This is a more inclusive view of what it means to be a scholar, bringing "legitimacy to the full scope of academic work" (Boyer, 1990).

THE WAVES OF SoTL

The Scholarship of Teaching and Learning can be divided into three waves or phases (Gurung & Schwartz, 2010), although the borders of these phases could be debated. While the early phases were concerned with definition and theorization, it is the opening up of the third wave that has included and invited a broad array of practitioners into the "big tent." This third phase has been particularly generative, as it has featured the maturation of the field, with rich dialogue and debate through international journals and conferences.

Priorities and Assessment (1990–1998)

The first 10 years of SoTL were taken up with definitions (Huber, 2010). Between Boyer's definition of a Scholarship of Teaching to Shulman's of teaching as a public act, early SoTL scholars were concerned with conceptualizing a Scholarship of Teaching with value to institutions of higher education.

Utilizing its position as an external driver of change, The Carnegie Foundation continued to advocate for recognition of a scholarship of teaching. In *Scholarship Assessed: A Special Report on Faculty Evaluation* (later published widely as *Scholarship Assessed: Evaluation of the Professoriate*), Glassick, Huber, and Maeroff (1997) consider the standards that might be used in assessing scholarship in all its forms. They suggest that in the narrow definition of scholarship focused on discovery/research, the sharing of knowledge through teaching and the application of knowledge through service have suffered. The reward structure in higher education continues to be a challenge, and there is little consensus on how to move forward. They note that scholars seeking promotion and tenure present a long list of publications and numerically validated student evaluations of teaching with scant acknowledgement of academic values like integration, application, and teaching. Based on a broad conceptualization of scholarship across many disciplines, the authors define scholarly work based on six qualitative standards: clear goals, adequate preparation, appropriate methods, significant results, effective preparation, and reflective critique. They also suggest that documenting this scholarship requires "rich and varied materials that the scholar and others assemble over time to make a case" (Glassick, Huber, & Maeroff, 1997, p. 37). The qualities of a scholar extend beyond, but are connected to, a body of knowledge and include personal characteristics such as integrity, perseverance, reason, courage, humility, and honesty. This key publication articulates a possible path for institutions of higher education to explore in order to recognize scholarship in teaching as a rigorous academic pursuit.

Following Boyer's death in 1997, Lee Shulman became the president of the Carnegie Foundation. Shulman's vision was to create a center for advanced study for teachers of all levels. This marked a major turning point for the Scholarship of Teaching, as Shulman worked with the American Association for Higher Education on the concept of teaching as community property and as a scholarly practice in a community of peers. This led to the launch of The Carnegie Academy for the Scholarship of Teaching and Learning (CASTL) in 1998, as a major initiative to bring about change in pedagogical research. The program

sought to support the development of a Scholarship of Teaching and Learning that: fosters significant, long-lasting learning for all students; enhances the practice and profession of teaching, and; brings to faculty members' work as teachers the recognition and reward afforded to other forms of scholarly work (Carnegie Foundation for the Advancement of Teaching, n.d.),

building upon *Scholarship Reconsidered* (Boyer, 1990) and *Scholarship Assessed* (Glassick, Huber, & Maeroff, 1997). The intention of CASTL was to make teaching public to a scholarly and general community and to subject it to critical peer review. This move reinforces the public, pedagogical role of the Scholarship of Teaching.

Widening the Field (1998–2004)

A key characteristic of the second wave or phase is the ongoing theoretical development of SoTL. By 1999, Hutchings and Shulman (1999) have characterized SoTL as a catalyst for change. They have also extended the Scholarship of Teaching to include learning as foundational to the definition. Marking the division between Boyer's SoT and the new SoTL, Hutchings and Shulman suggest that all faculties have an obligation to excellence in teaching. This is echoed by Huber and Morreale (2002) as "across the academy, "regular" faculty are taking systematic interest in curriculum, classroom teaching, and the quality of student learning" (p. 1). However, the Scholarship of Teaching and Learning must take up four additional challenges: beginning the conversation about credible methods of inquiry, keeping SoTL open to a wide set of inquiries, making a commitment to publicly share research (Shulman, 1993), and creating sustainable change. In this phase, SoTL seeks to facilitate change by bringing rigor and rich research to investigations of a pedagogical and curricular nature.

Hutchings (2000) describes SoTL as "not yet fully defined or conceptualized" (p. 2). Drawing from the taxonomy of research questions from CASTL institutes, she identifies the research questions as divided into four categories: what works?, what is?, visions of the possible, and new conceptual frameworks. Identifying theory building as important to the development of SoTL, Hutchings suggests that the last category of questions is where the field can be enriched—especially through cross-disciplinary collaboration.

The second wave of SoTL's development also highlights the methodological flexibility of faculty members engaging in inter- and intra-disciplinary research. Recognizing that each discipline has its "own intellectual history, agreements, and disputes about subject matter and methods," Huber and Morreale (2002) acknowledge that SoTL scholars "must address field-specific issues if they are going to be heard in their own disciplines, and they must speak in a language that their colleagues understand" (p. 2). This second phase of SoTL acknowledges disciplinary difference, but heeds Boyer's scholarship of integration; "growth in knowledge also comes at the borders of disciplinary imagination" (Huber & Morreale, 2002, p. 2). As interdisciplinary conversations and collaborations become more frequent and substantial, SoTL widens the "trading zone" (Gallison, 1997, as cited in Huber & Morreale, 2002, p. 2), where meanings and methods may vary but contributes to the intellectual discourse and debate on teaching and learning in higher education (Shulman, 2000).

When studying the domains of knowledge about teaching, Kreber and Cranton (2000) contend, "the scholarship of teaching includes both ongoing learning about teaching and the demonstration of teaching knowledge" (p. 478). They utilize Mezirow's concepts of content, process, and premise reflection as a framework from which to derive instructional, pedagogical, and curricular knowledge about teaching. In each of these domains, knowledge is created through three forms of reflection, leading to nine components of a Scholarship of Teaching (See Kreber & Cranton, 2000, for a visual model of the Scholarship of Teaching [p. 485] and a table of examples of indicators of the Scholarship of Teaching [p. 488]). They state that faculty members who commit to the Scholarship of Teaching engage in three different kinds of reflection on both theory-based and experience-based knowledge as it relates to questions of instructional design, pedagogy, and the broader curriculum. These nine components could then serve to inform new ways of documenting how learning and knowledge about teaching could be demonstrated.

Shulman (2000) concludes *Opening Lines* with a chapter entitled, "Inventing the Future." He advocates for the role of professor to include teacher, mentor, steward, and public servant and calls for institutional support with formal structures that merge institutional commitments to both teaching and inquiry. Ultimately, SoTL cannot be sustained in isolation, and professors must create intellectual communities that transcend institutional boundaries (Shulman, 2000).

SoTL Under the Big Tent (2004–2011)

The conclusion of CASTL in 2010 (Huber, 2010) would have been a logical place to launch the third wave of SoTL (Gurung & Schwartz, 2010), with a smooth transition buoyed by optimism for the Scholarship of Teaching and Learning. However, the concept of the SoTL commons (Huber & Hutchings, 2005, 2006) is the defining feature of the transition to the third phase of the development of the Scholarship of Teaching and Learning. The SoTL commons, also called the teaching commons, is "an emergent conceptual space for exchange and community among faculty, students, administrators, and all others committed to learning as an essential activity" (Huber & Hutchings, 2005). It is an intellectual space where a diversity of SoTL scholars can engage with others and judiciously borrow practices and insights from various communities. They can adapt them for new purposes in order to capture, and build upon, the intellectual work being done in teaching and learning.

The establishment of the International Society for the Scholarship of Teaching and Learning (ISSoTL) and its international conference in 2004 demonstrate the interest and inclusion of an international community focused on dialogue and debate in SoTL. The culmination of the transition to the third phase is the publication of the International Journal for the Scholarship of Teaching and Learning (IJSoTL) in 2007. While the journal is not officially affiliated with ISSoTL, the first issue of IJSoTL included invited articles by Pat Hutchings and Carolin Kreber, founding members of ISSoTL.

Hutchings (2007) highlights the tension in SoTL between theory and practice, with the ultimate application in the classroom. There is so much diversity by personal approach, department, and faculty that it is challenging to create links across SoTL through the disciplines, but she asserts that looking for common themes and aims is essential to continuing the work of SoTL. Kreber (2007) focuses on authenticity in SoTL practice. As practitioners, "an important question we need to address is whether the 'Scholarship of Teaching and Learning' is in the important interest of students" (Kreber, 2007, p. 3). An ethical dimension of SoTL means taking great care with our subject matter and our students (MacLean & Poole, 2010), and reviews of the SoTL literature suggest that the foundational dialogue supports responsiveness to educational contexts and responsibility to changing demographics in higher education. The third wave is also characterized by an emphasis on the transformational agenda of SoTL (Gilpin & Liston, 2009).

The third wave of SoTL culminates in *The Scholarship of Teaching and Learning Reconsidered: Institutional Integration and Impact* (Hutchings, Huber, & Ciccone, 2011). In it, the authors reflect on the expansion of the teaching commons to the core areas of higher education work. Speaking specifically to campus leaders, in order to situate SoTL as a set of principles and practices that are central to institutions' goals for student learning, the authors attempt to guide future phases of SoTL work in classroom teaching, professional development, institutional assessment, and the recognition and reward for pedagogical work. This call marks a new direction for SoTL. As representatives of the third phase in SoTL, all these authors bring attention to the integration of research, practice, and teaching by SoTL scholars within and across many disciplines.

CRITIQUES OF THE SoTL

Throughout the three decades of SoTL work, there have been several enduring critiques, which are addressed within the literature.

Localized, Classroom-Based Research

Specific critiques of SoTL have tended to focus on its localized, classroom-based research (Haigh, 2012). Many scholarly teaching projects are undertaken to address a personal or situationally specific issue (Haigh, 2012) and are therefore not seen as applicable outside of the specific locale as the projects are undertaken to address local and institutional contexts. Stierer and Antoniou (2004) note that much of the pedagogic research in the UK is conducted by researchers from disciplines other than education.

These practitioner-researchers are mainly concerned about issues within their own disciplinary and professional contexts, rather than with the nuances of educational research methodology. This approach to pedagogic research could either be criticized as 'amateurish' and 'parochial', or applauded as relevant to the needs and local circumstances of practitioners, and reflecting emerging syntheses of educational research methodologies and the research traditions from practitioners' own subjects and disciplines. (Stierer & Antoniou, 2004, p. 283)

A similar challenge exists in North American higher education (Chick, 2014). As this research reflects concerns from within a community, the outcomes or recommendations are thought to be transitory or limited in their persuasiveness. Generalization across disciplinary contexts is impeded by epistemological and ontological differences across disciplines. Tight (2018) continues this critique in a systematic review of academic research in SoTL. However, McKinney and Jarvis (2009) reject the dismissal of SoTL work, emphasizing the value of the SoTL commons and applying the SoTL work of others. Additionally, Chick and Poole (2018) argue that studying learning at the micro level provides a detailed examination of the building blocks of learning in higher education. This long-standing critique continues to be debated and discussed in SoTL journals and at conferences.

Theoretical and Practical SoTL Research

While the debate over the definition of SoTL continues (Chick, 2014; Felten & Chick, 2018; Potter & Kustra, 2011), the field is moving forward to consider the practical and the theoretical in SoTL research, including the differing conceptions of the place of educational theory in the SoTL (Geertsema, 2016; Huber, 2010; Kanuka, 2011; Svinicki, 2012; Parker, 2008).

The Place of Education Theory in SoTL

The relationship between educational research and SoTL is longstanding and often fraught with tension (Larsson, Mårtensson, Price, & Roxå, 2017). Parker (2008) discusses the differing conceptions of the place of educational theory in North American and European SoTL. As the Carnegie roots of SoTL are in the disciplines (Huber & Morreale, 2002), many SoTL scholars tend to work within their discipline, taking on the most common methodologies of their field. Essentially, Parker is arguing that SoTL needs more education theory to legitimize its application in an educational space. Kanuka (2011) and Svinicki (2012) both weigh in on this pivotal debate. Focusing on the place of educational research within SoTL, Kanuka (2011) questions whether it is enough to take teaching public through peer review and critique. She suggests that it is necessary to use educational research frameworks when approaching SoTL research. Credibility as a researcher comes from knowledge in the theory of the content area and their educative practices:

academics engaged in SoTL whose expertise falls outside of the field of higher education will take time to learn about education research traditions, the extensive corpus literature in teaching and learning in higher education that exist – not the least of which are theories of learning. (Kanuka, 2011, p. 9)

Svinicki (2012) also tackles the challenging question of "how well someone needs to understand both the discipline and the theories and methods of educational research to be entitled to engage in SoTL"

(p. 1). However, rather than requiring expertise in educational theory, Svinicki advocates for the SoTL community to encourage teams of researchers working together over time to produce deep scholarship of high rigor. Svinicki further identify two models for conducting SoTL research. First, the research team utilizes distributed expertise where no one researcher is expected to know everything, and all can contribute their expertise. The teaching commons (Huber & Hutchings, 2005, 2006) is one form of this collaboration. Second, Svinicki argues for programs of research rather than single studies. In reaction to early SoTL research targeted at a single semester, course, or constrained time-period (i.e., during a sabbatical), she suggests longitudinal research in order for the study to develop over time.

Approaches to SoTL Research

Building upon the theory debate, another productive tension is the debate over the epistemological and methodological approaches, which mark the Scholarship of Teaching and Learning (Thomas, 2011). Huber (2010, p. 7) delineates two camps: the narrow constructionists, who emphasize SoTL's affinity with conventional research, and the broad constructionists, who are happy to use the "big tent" to cover a wider range of work in greater or lesser degrees of polish and make it public in forums with local and far reaches.

As a distinctive form of research (Hubball & Clarke, 2010), SoTL research is within the "broad umbrella for many different disciplines and interdisciplinary approaches" (p. 8). It is impossible to prescribe quantitative or qualitative methods, as the research will be driven by the nature of the research question. Therefore, Danielson (2012) proposes that we consider SoTL as a methodology, or a "a philosophical study of plurality of methods" (Watzlawick, Weakland, & Fisch, 1974, p. 8, as cited in Danielson, 2012, p. 2), and build learning communities through the generative, heuristic methodology of SoTL. If researchers adopt the concept of a safe trading zone for boundary-crossing research, then SoTL research can be a rich forum where scholars from different fields, interests, and philosophical orientations find space, and thrive, as their work seeks to change the landscape of teaching and learning at the classroom, institutional, national, or international level (Danielson, 2012; Gurung, 2014; Hubball & Clarke, 2010; Huber & Morreale, 2002; Miller-Young, Yeo, & Manarin, 2018).

Lack of Training in Educational Research

Additionally, faculty members in most disciplines have no formal training in the kind of multi-disciplinary research that SoTL encompasses. Indeed, they often have no training in teaching itself (Huber & Hutchings, 2005, p. 30). Therefore, through mobilization of the SoTL commons, campuses need to become or support places where this work can take place through programs, structures, and rewards. Activating SoTL research teams (Svinicki, 2012) brings together differing academic expertise and educational development in the pursuit of credible and significant teaching and learning research. Different disciplines bring different rules and assumptions about what constitutes credible evidence and what kind of methods yield scholarly results. Differences of opinion in this area can make it hard for SoTL to be valued across disciplines, yet disciplines can borrow and learn from one another. This borrowing may enrich the lessons learned and make the work more broadly significant (Huber & Hutchings, 2005; McKinney & Jarvis, 2009). Yet, interdisciplinary structures entail both strengths and weaknesses. Interdisciplinary research is more likely to innovate from cross-pollination, but institutional reward structures continue to flow through departments.

Institutional Barriers

Institutionally, there are still many barriers to change (Hubball & Pearson, 2010; Webb, Wong, & Hubball, 2013), including entrenched systems of credit hours, scheduling, methods of teaching and assessment, departmental or disciplinary silos, administration systems, and reward systems that value research over pedagogical or curricular leadership. The policies and practices that are designed to improve standards and efficiency in higher education are often at odds with those designed to improve student learning (Hockings, 2005; Young 2006). A personal commitment to teaching and to students is identified as the primary motivation for improving teaching, yet a commitment to be an exceptional instructor may mean sacrificing possibilities for promotion (Young, 2006). The unanimously acknowledged low status of teaching (Young, 2006), despite new developments to enhance teaching and learning at post-secondary institutions, combined with a lack of reward for exceptional teaching, are identified as the major barriers to developing teaching and learning in higher education (Dobbins, 2008; Young, 2006). As argued by Elen, Lindblom-Ylanne, and Clement (2007), academic developers at research-intensive universities have to work within the institutional mandate through the development of "research-intensive teaching" (p. 125).

Nevertheless, while these critiques identify some of the long-standing challenges to SoTL research, current SoTL scholars are working to address many of these barriers and to push SoTL in new directions.

SoTL IN THE FOURTH WAVE (2012–PRESENT)

At the close of its third decade, the field of SoTL has matured to address many of its critiques and explore new areas of teaching and learning in higher education. Some SoTL scholars would argue that SoTL is comfortably in the "big tent," and the creation of *Teaching and Learning Inquiry*, the official journal of ISSOTL, marks a clear movement into the current wave of SoTL. So, where does SoTL go now? Where is the fourth wave?

SoTL in the fourth wave is addressing new challenges and following new paths. The current landscape of practice includes a diverse number of faculty, educational/academic developers, and students engaging in sustained, collaborative investigation into teaching and learning in higher education. Informed by past critiques, the SoTL community is focused on sustained involvement of academics and the identity of SoTL scholars, who are often outside of traditional faculty positions.

As mentioned previously, the transition out of the third wave includes a renewed focus on institutional support and challenges to SoTL. The micro, meso, and macro levels of SoTL work (Simmons, 2016) include collaborative teams connecting institutional centers for teaching and learning with disciplinary researchers. SoTL scholars are no longer just disciplinary researchers exploring teaching and learning within their discipline; they include educational developers, students, and administration.

Bolstered by the expanding scope of SoTL research, many SoTL scholars are looking beyond their institutional context (micro, meso, and macro) to consider the mega, global engagement with SoTL. Increasing internationalization, including regional conferences (e.g., EuroSoTL) and journals (e.g., *Asian Journal of the Scholarship of Teaching and Learning* and *SoTL in the South*), is supporting the development of SoTL within local educational contexts. However, there are debates as to how SoTL could be taken up around the world.

The next section of the chapter will discuss some of the current directions in SoTL, opportunities for SoTL scholars, and the potential for these areas to be the foci of the fourth wave of SoTL.

Addressing New Challenges

Sustained Faculty Engagement

Encouraging tenure track and sessional (adjunct) faculty members to engage in SoTL is still a challenge. Bortolini's 2018 article, "SoTL: The Party That No One Really Wants to Go to," highlights the ongoing challenges of buy-in and sustained engagement among faculty members. While SoTL research is rigorous, has an active community, and adds credence to educational endeavors in higher education, there is a need to build capacity amongst faculty members in order to develop and initiate impactful SoTL projects (Simmons, 2016). Understanding and addressing the intellectual and institutional challenges identified by academics in higher education can support the SoTL work of faculty members. Yet, the constraints to navigating SoTL hinder sustained engagement by faculty and staff in a variety of contexts. Identifying and understanding these constraints is of particular importance to instructional teams facilitating professional development programs in the Scholarship of Teaching and Learning (Webb, 2019). There have been two directions to support faculty in SoTL: threshold concepts and decoding the disciplines.

It is often taken for granted that academics are excellent researchers; even so, they are not always familiar or comfortable with SoTL research, and faculty members need to be guided through the language and research conventions of SoTL (Chick, 2014, 2018). The Decoding the Disciplines approach (Middendorf & Pace, 2008) supports the shift from reflective teaching to SoTL by helping faculty identify the researchable questions that align with the interests of their discipline. While research into the threshold concepts in SoTL (Tierney, 2016; Webb, 2019) highlights the places where those new to SoTL get stuck and which concepts constrain faculty members from sustained engagement in SoTL. In order to support ongoing engagement with SoTL, it is important that this topic continues to be investigated.

Identity of SoTL Scholars

SoTL scholars are often betwixt and between; they identify with their disciplinary background, but have also developed a new identity as a SoTL scholar (Kensington-Miller, Renc-Roe, & Moron-Garcia, 2015; Miller-Young et al., 2018; Simmons et al., 2013). Ingrained disciplinary cultures often slow scholars' enculturation into SoTL and often leave some academics unable or unwilling to let go of specific disciplinary ways of thinking (Bunnell & Bernstein, 2012). There is a tension between their responsibility to the discipline and their personal responsibility to scholarly curiosity and the students they teach (Webb, 2019). But this either/or dichotomy misses the fundamental issue that SoTL research is an intertwining of teaching and learning within a disciplinary or institutional context (Felten & Chick, 2018). At the same time, a lack of professional incentives (often related to merit or tenure and promotion criteria) discourages participants from ongoing engagement with SoTL (Webb et al., 2013).

The changing nature of employment in higher education may also impact SoTL scholars' identities (Miller-Young, Yeo, & Manarin, 2018). As Kensington-Miller, Renc-Roe, and Moron-Garcia (2015) and Bennett et al. (2016) discuss, the position of academic developer often places SoTL scholars in the liminal space: betwixt and between disciplinary cultures and educational research.

Issues for Teaching Focused Faculty (TFF), for whom teaching and learning scholarship, and SoTL specifically, may or may not be considered part of their workload, are particularly challenging. Rawn and Fox (2017) examine the position and perceptions of TFF in a recent study. Increasingly, TFF are permanent positions with allocations for service, but include inconsistent requirements for scholarly activities. Nonetheless, a large number of their study participants report being active in teaching, service, scholarly teaching, and curriculum leadership. The interconnected areas of SoTL engagement and identity have proved generative for further investigation.

Additionally, continued theorizing on the nature of an educational leader (Fields, Kenny, & Mueller, 2019; Hubball et al., 2015; Miller-Young et al., 2017) can help to characterize SoTL leadership, as the identity of SoTL scholars can also be connected to their position as pedagogical or curriculum leaders within their institution or discipline.

Following New Paths

Global SoTL

SoTL in the "big tent" praises the methodological and theoretical pluralism of SoTL, but how is cultural pluralism represented (Chng & Looker, 2013)? As SoTL knowledge is conceptualized as relational—it connects SoTL practitioners with the work they disseminate to the community—local recommendations require a localized understanding of SoTL (Booth & Woollacott, 2018, p. 537), attending to the generative potential of reconsidering SoTL in context (Liebowitz, 2017). Instead of attempting to promote a global uptake of SoTL, SoTL leaders and advocates could be promoting "glocal" understanding of SoTL programs: global in principles, but local in situation (Patel & Lynch, 2013). Glocalization of the curriculum is an attempt to balance the driving forces of contemporary curriculum practice, namely localization, internationalization, and globalization. With a focus on glocalization, global SoTL positions itself as promoting SoTL diversity through curriculum reform (Fanghanel et al., 2015). Glocal philosophies encourage SoTL research and programs that are aligned with SoTL principles (like Felten, 2013), but with curriculum practices that are locally mediated.

Program-Level Assessments

While the third wave of SoTL was concerned with pedagogical insights, the fourth wave has turned its attention to program-level assessment (Hubball & Burt, 2004; Hubball et al., 2013; Hubball & Gold, 2007). This means encouraging SoTL scholars to move beyond individual classroom research to program and curricular change (Hubball & Burt, 2004; Gilpin, 2011). Bringing curriculum assessment under the umbrella of SoTL means responding to the call by Hutchings, Huber, and Ciccone (2011) and further widening the shelter of the "big tent" to institutional-level examination.

Curriculum reform is often a complex process shaped by social, political, economic, organizational, and cultural factors (Hubball & Burt, 2004). The Scholarship of Curriculum Practice (SoCP) focuses on investigating scholarly approaches to curricula change in higher education. As higher education contexts demand empirical evidence to support program reform, there is urgency for SoCP in order to enhance learning-centered curricula (Hubball & Gold, 2007). SoCP involves a systematic, rigorous, and cyclical process of inquiry, shaped by diverse learning contexts. SoCP recognizes that curriculum practice is inherently situated, socially mediated, and locally implemented (Hubball et al., 2013). It recognizes that the development, implementation, and evaluation of curricula are situated within a context and may be rooted in "signature pedagogies" (Shulman, 2005) of the discipline. Hubball and Gold (2007) suggest that critical examinations of an undergraduate curriculum should not be relegated to the five-year cycle of data-gathering for institutional and/or accreditation reviews. Rather, constructing and revising undergraduate curricula should be considered as scholarly, formative, and developmental review processes for all stakeholders in the program learning community.

Applying a scholarship approach to curriculum decisions can inform individual decisions and bring the findings to a peer review for a formalized sharing. This more expansive view of SoTL, a rigorous and robust evaluation of undergraduate and graduate programs through SoCP, has a strong strategic value to research intensive universities making high-stakes curriculum decisions (Hubball et al., 2013; Hubball, Lamberson, & Kindler, 2012; Hubball & Pearson, 2010).

Students as Partners

In his principles for good practice in SoTL, Peter Felten proposed that SoTL should be conducted with students (Felten, 2013). This echoed a growing interest in exploring student engagement as a joint venture to shape teaching and learning in higher education (Bovill, Bulley, & Moss, 2011; Healey, Flint, & Harrington, 2014; Matthews, 2016; Werder, Thibou, & Kaufer, 2012).

Students as Partners (SaP) proposes that the relationship between student and professor be developed through partnership as one based on respect, responsibility, and reciprocity (Cook-Sather, Bovill, & Felten, 2014). The relationship is dialogic, in which the learning and teaching are co-conceptualized and co-created between equal partners. A systematic review of the literature highlights four themes: the importance of reciprocity; the need to make space for sharing the realities of partnership; a focus on partnership activities that are small scale, at the undergraduate level, extracurricular, and focused on teaching and learning enhancement; and the need to move toward inclusive, partnered learning communities (Mercer-Mapstone et al., 2017).

Recently, Felten's principles have been adopted as the guidelines for ISSoTL conference pedagogy (Moore, 2019), and there has been significant interest in engaging SaP in pedagogical and curricular research. Matthews (2017) has proposed principles for good practice in SaP, and an international journal was created in 2017.

CONCLUSION

The Scholarship of Teaching and Learning provides a vehicle to engage educators as advocates for our disciplines, as well as for teaching and learning in higher education. Lee Shulman (2000) reminds us, "a professor is a member of a learned profession" (p.103), who has a responsibility to serve as a steward of his/her discipline or profession. So, rather than decide between doctor as researcher and doctor as teacher, those who engage in SoTL are both researcher and teacher, as many of the chapters in this volume attest. But the world of work in higher education is no longer the same landscape that Shulman mapped in 2000. Is SoTL moving beyond the "big tent"? Do the past metaphors for SoTL engagement still ring true? In the evolving world of higher education, frequently, hiring is not happening in traditional, disciplinary appointments. Instead, there is an increasing number of positions as Teaching-Focused Faculty or positions as educational developers or curriculum leaders in para-academic positions. This change increases both the complexity and the opportunity in the work of SoTL scholars.

The future of SoTL is firmly connected to the evolving state of higher education. As institutions reflect on the educational experience of students and respond to the needs of accrediting organizations and employers, it behooves them to demonstrate program, curriculum, and pedagogy changes that are connected to rigorous empirical research. Conducting and disseminating SoTL research operates as a bridge between excellence in teaching and excellent research on teaching. The ongoing reconceptualization of Boyer's Scholarship of Teaching serves as a valuable addition to the teaching–research nexus of higher education. It provides the possibility for encouraging dynamic advancement within institutions. The Scholarship of Teaching and Learning, both in its programs and practice, provides a compatible way for higher education to support and engage in research, teaching, and innovation.

ACKNOWLEDGMENT

This research received no specific grant from any funding agency in the public, commercial, or not-for-profit sectors.

REFERENCES

Barr, R. B. & Tagg, J. (1995). From teaching to learning: A new paradigm for undergraduate education. *Change: The Magazine of Higher Learning, 27*(6), 12-26.

Bennett, R., Hobson, J., Jones, A., Martin-Lynch, P., Scutt, C., Strehlow, K., & Veitch, S. (2016). Being chimaera: A monstrous identity for SoTL academics. *Higher Education Research & Development, 35*(2), 217–228. doi:10.1080/07294360.2015.1087473

Booth, S., & Woollacott, L. C. (2018). On the constitution of SoTL: Its domains and contexts. *Higher Education, 75*(3), 537–551. doi:10.100710734-017-0156-7

Bortolini, K. (2018, November 29). SoTL: The party that no one really wants to go to. *University Affairs*. Retrieved from https://www.universityaffairs.ca/opinion/in-my-opinion/sotl-the-party-that-no-one-really-wants-to-go-to/

Bovill, C., Bulley, C. J., & Moss, K. (2011). Engaging and empowering first-year students through curriculum design: Perspectives from the literature. *Teaching in Higher Education, 16*(2), 197–209. doi:10.1080/13562517.2010.515024

Boyer, E. (1990). *Scholarship reconsidered: Priorities of the professoriate*. Princeton, NJ: Carnegie Foundation for the Advancement of Teaching.

Bunnell, S. L., & Bernstein, D. J. (2012). Overcoming some threshold concepts in scholarly teaching. *Journal of Faculty Development, 23*(3), 14–18.

Carnegie Foundation for the Advancement of Teaching. (n.d.). *Foundation history*. Retrieved from http://www.carnegiefoundation.org/about-us/foundation-history

Chick, N., & Poole, G. (2018). Editors' introduction: In defense of microscopes. *Teaching & Learning Inquiry, 6*(1), 1–2. doi:10.20343/teachlearninqu.6.1.1

Chick, N. L. (2014). 'Methodologically sound' under the 'big tent': An ongoing conversation. *International Journal for the Scholarship of Teaching and Learning, 8*(2). doi:10.20429/ijsotl.2014.080201

Chick, N. L. (Ed.). (2018). *SoTL in action: Illuminating critical moments of practice*. Sterling, VA: Stylus.

Chng, H. H., & Looker, P. (2013). On the margins of SoTL discourse: An Asian perspective. *Teaching & Learning Inquiry, 1*(1), 131–145. doi:10.20343/teachlearninqu.1.1.131

Cook-Sather, A., Bovill, C., & Felten, P. (2014). *Engaging students as partners in learning and teaching: A guide for faculty*. San Francisco, CA: Jossey-Bass.

D'Andrea, V. (2006). Exploring the methodological issues related to pedagogical inquiry in Higher Education. *New Directions for Teaching and Learning, 107*, 89–98. doi:10.1002/tl.247

Danielson, M. A. (2012). SoTL as a generative heuristic methodology for building learning communities. *International Journal for the Scholarship of Teaching and Learning, 6*(2). doi:10.20429/ijsotl.2012.060204

Dobbins, K. (2008). Enhancing the Scholarship of Teaching and Learning: A study of factors identified as promoting and hindering the scholarly activities of academics in one faculty. *International Journal for the Scholarship of Teaching and Learning, 2*(2). doi:10.20429/ijsotl.2008.020217

Elen, J., Lindblom-Ylanne, S., & Clement, M. (2007). Faculty development in research-intensive universities: The role of academics' conceptions on the relationship between research and teaching. *The International Journal for Academic Development, 12*(2), 123–139. doi:10.1080/13601440701604948

Fanghanel, J., McGowan, S., Parker, P., McConnell, C., Potter, J., Locke, W., & Healey, M. (2015). *Literature review. In Defining and supporting the Scholarship of Teaching and Learning (SoTL): A sector-wide study*. York, UK: Higher Education Academy.

Felten, P. (2013). Principles of good practice in SoTL. *Teaching & Learning Inquiry, 1*(1), 121–125. doi:10.20343/teachlearninqu.1.1.121

Felten, P., & Chick, N. (2018). Is SoTL a signature pedagogy of educational development? *To Improve the Academy, 37*(1), 4-16. doi:10.002/tia2.20077

Fields, J., Kenny, N. A., & Mueller, R. A. (2019). Conceptualizing educational leadership in an academic development program. *The International Journal for Academic Development, 24*(3), 218–231. doi:10.1080/1360144X.2019.1570211

Geertsema, J. (2016). Academic development, SoTL, and educational research. *The International Journal for Academic Development, 21*(2), 122–134. doi:10.1080/1360144X.2016.1175144

Gilpin, L. (2011). Scholarship of Teaching and Learning trades. *International Journal for the Scholarship of Teaching and Learning, 5*(2). doi:10.20429/ijsotl.2011.050204

Gilpin, L., & Liston, D. (2009). Transformative education in the Scholarship of Teaching and Learning: An analysis of SoTL literature. *International Journal for the Scholarship of Teaching and Learning, 3*(2). doi:10.20429/ijsotl.2009.030211

Glassick, C. E., Huber, M. T., & Maeroff, G. I. (1997). *Scholarship assessed: Evaluation of the professoriate*. San Francisco, CA: Jossey-Bass.

Gurung, R. A. R. (2014). Getting foxy: Invoking different magesteria in the Scholarship of Teaching and Learning. *Teaching & Learning Inquiry, 2*(2), 109–114. doi:10.20343/teachlearninqu.2.2.109

Gurung, R. A. R., & Schwartz, B. M. (2010). Riding the third wave of SoTL. *International Journal for the Scholarship of Teaching and Learning, 4*(2). doi:10.20429/ijsotl.2010.040205

Haigh, N. J. (2012). Sustaining and spreading the positive outcomes of SoTL projects: Issues, insights, and strategies. *The International Journal for Academic Development, 17*(1), 19–31. doi:10.1080/1360 144X.2011.586462

Healey, M., Flint, A., & Harrington, K. (2014). *Engagement through partnership: Students as partners in learning and teaching in higher education.* York, UK: Higher Education Academy. Retrieved from https://www.heacademy.ac.uk/engagement-through-partnership-students-partners-learning-and-teaching-higher-education

Hockings, C. (2005). Removing barriers? A study of the conditions affecting teaching innovation. *Teaching in Higher Education, 10*(3), 313–326. doi:10.1080/13562510500122149

Hubball, H. T., & Burt, H. (2004). An integrated approach to developing and implementing learning-centred curricula. *The International Journal for Academic Development, 9*(1), 51–65. doi:10.1080/1360144042000296053

Hubball, H. T., & Clarke, A. (2010). Diverse methodological approaches and considerations for SoTL in higher education. *The Canadian Journal for the Scholarship of Teaching and Learning, 1*(1). doi:10.5206/cjsotl-rcacea.2010.1.2

Hubball, H. T., Clarke, A. C., Webb, A. S., & Johnson, B. (2015). Developing institutional leadership for the Scholarship of Teaching and Learning: Lessons learned with senior educational leaders in multi-national research-intensive university contexts. *International Journal of University Teaching and Faculty Development, 4*(4). Retrieved from https://www.novapublishers.com/catalog/product_info.php?products_id=53411

Hubball, H. T., & Gold, N. (2007). The scholarship of curriculum practice and undergraduate program reform: Integrating theory into practice. *New Directions for Teaching and Learning, 112*(112), 5–14. doi:10.1002/tl.293

Hubball, H. T., Lamberson, M., & Kindler, A. (2012). Strategic restructuring of a centre for teaching and learning in a research-intensive university: Institutional engagement in scholarly approaches to curriculum renewal and pedagogical practices. *International Journal for University Teaching and Faculty Development, 3*(2), 95–110.

Hubball, H. T., & Pearson, M. (2010). Grappling with the complexity of undergraduate degree program reform: Critical barriers and emergent strategies. *Transformative Dialogues: Teaching & Learning Journal, 3*(3). Retrieved from http://kwantlen.ca/TD/TD.3.3/TD.3.3_Hubball&Pearson_Undergraduate_Degree_Program_Reform.pdf

Hubball, H. T., Pearson, M., & Clarke, A. (2013). SoTL inquiry in broader curricula and institutional contexts: Theoretical underpinnings and emerging trends. Invited peer-reviewed essay for inaugural issue. *International Journal for Inquiry in Teaching and Learning, 1*(1), 41–57. doi:10.1353/iss.2013.0009

Huber, M. T. (2010). Editorial: CASTL has concluded. Long live the Scholarship of Teaching and Learning. *Arts and Humanities in Higher Education, 9*(1), 5–8. doi:10.1177/1474022209357660

Huber, M. T., & Hutchings, P. (2005). *The advancement of learning: Building the teaching commons.* San Francisco, CA: Jossey-Bass.

Huber, M. T., & Hutchings, P. (2006). Building the teaching commons. *Change: The Magazine of Higher Learning, 38*(3), 24-31. Doi:10.3200/CHNG.38.3.24-31

Huber, M. T., & Morreale, S. P. (2002). Situating the Scholarship of Teaching and Learning. In M. T. Huber & S. P. Morreale (Eds.), *Disciplinary styles in the scholarship of teaching: Exploring common ground* (pp. 1–24). Washington, DC: American Association for Higher Education and the Carnegie Foundation for the Advancement of Teaching.

Hutchings, P. (2000). Approaching the Scholarship of Teaching and Learning. In P. Hutchings (Ed.), *Opening lines: Approaches to the Scholarship of Teaching and Learning.* Retrieved from http://www. carnegiefoundation.org/elibrary/approaching-scholarship-teaching-and-learning

Hutchings, P. (2007). Theory: The elephant in the Scholarship of Teaching and Learning room. *International Journal for the Scholarship of Teaching and Learning, 1*(1). doi:10.20429/ijsotl.2007.010102

Hutchings, P., Huber, M. T., & Ciccone, A. (2011). *The Scholarship of Teaching and Learning reconsidered: Institutional integration and impact.* San Francisco, CA: Jossey-Bass.

Hutchings, P., & Shulman, L. (1999). The Scholarship of Teaching: New elaborations, new developments. *Change: The Magazine of Higher Learning, 31*(5), 10-15. Doi:10.1080/00091389909604218

Kanuka, H. (2011). Keeping the scholarship in the Scholarship of Teaching and Learning. *International Journal for the Scholarship of Teaching and Learning, 5*(1). doi:10.20429/ijsotl.2011.050103

Kensington-Miller, B., Renc-Roe, J., & Moron-Garcia, S. (2015). The chameleon on a tartan rug: Adaptations of three academic developers' professional identities. *The International Journal for Academic Development, 20*(3), 279–290. doi:10.1080/1360144X.2015.1047373

Kreber, C. (2007). What's it really all about? The Scholarship of Teaching and Learning as an authentic practice. *International Journal for the Scholarship of Teaching and Learning, 1*(1). doi:10.20429/ ijsotl.2007.010103

Kreber, C., & Cranton, P. (2000). Exploring the Scholarship of Teaching. *The Journal of Higher Education, 71*(4), 476–495. doi:10.2307/2649149

Larsson, M., Mårtensson, K., Price, L., & Roxå, T. (2017). Constructive friction? Exploring patterns between educational research and the scholarship of teaching and learning. *Proceedings of the EuroSoTL, 2017,* 161–165.

Liebowitz, B. (2017). The significance of SoTL in the South. *SoTL in the South, 1*(1), 1–3.

MacLean, M., & Poole, G. (2010). An introduction to ethical considerations for novices to research in teaching and learning in Canada. *The Canadian Journal for the Scholarship of Teaching and Learning, 1*(2). doi:10.5206/cjsotl-rcacea.2010.2.7

Matthews, K. E. (2016). Students as partners as the future of student engagement. *Student Engagement in Higher Education Journal, 1*(1), 1-5. Retrieved from https://journals.gre.ac.uk/index.php/raise

Matthews, K. E. (2017). Five propositions for genuine students as partners practice. *International Journal for Students as Partners, 1*(2). doi:10.15173/ijsap.v1i2.3315

McKinney, K., & Jarvis, P. (2009). Beyond lines on the CV: Faculty applications of their Scholarship of Teaching and Learning research. *International Journal for the Scholarship of Teaching and Learning, 3*(1). doi:10.20429/ijsotl.2009.030107

Mercer-Mapstone, L., Dvorakova, S. L., Matthews, K., Abbot, S., Cheng, B., Felten, P., & Swaim, K. (2017). A Systematic Literature Review of Students as Partners in Higher Education. *International Journal for Students As Partners, 1*(1). doi:10.15173/ijsap.v1i1.3119

Middendorf, J., & Pace, D. (2008). Easing entry into the Scholarship of Teaching and Learning through focused assessments: The "Decoding the Disciplines" approach. *To Improve the Academy, 26*(1), 53-67.

Miller-Young, J. E., Anderson, C., Kiceniuk, D., Mooney, J., Riddell, J., Schmidt Hanbidge, A., & Chick, N. (2017). Leading up in the Scholarship of Teaching and Learning. *The Canadian Journal for the Scholarship of Teaching and Learning, 8*(2). doi:10.5206/cjsotl-rcacea.2017.2.4

Miller-Young, J. E., Yeo, M., & Manarin, K. (2018). Challenges to disciplinary knowing and identity: Experiences of scholars in a SoTL development program. *International Journal for the Scholarship of Teaching and Learning, 12*(1). doi:10.20429/ijsotl.2018.120103

Moore, J. (2019, March 23). ISSoTL Conference Pedagogy [Web post]. Retrieved from https://www.issotl.com/issotl-conference-pedagogy

Parker, J. (2008). Theory of SoTL: Translating international perspectives. In *Proceedings of The London Scholarship of Teaching and Learning 7th International Conference 2008* (pp. 171-176). London: City University London.

Patel, F., & Lynch, H. (2013). Glocalization as an alternative to internationalization in higher education: Embedding positive glocal learning perspectives. *International Journal on Teaching and Learning in Higher Education, 25*(2), 223–230. Retrieved from https://eric.ed.gov/?id=EJ1016539

Potter, M., & Kustra, E. (2011). The relationship between scholarly teaching and SoTL: Models, distinctions, and clarifications. *International Journal for the Scholarship of Teaching and Learning, 5*(1). doi:10.20429/ijsotl.2011.050123

Rawn, C. D., & Fox, J. A. (2017). Understanding the work and perceptions of teaching-focused faculty in a changing academic landscape. *Research in Higher Education, 59*(5), 591–622. doi:10.100711162-017-9479-6

Shulman, L. S. (1993). Teaching as community property: Putting an end to pedagogical solitude. *Change: The Magazine of Higher Education, 25*(6), 6-7. Doi:10.1080/00091383.1993.9938465

Shulman, L. S. (2000). Inventing the future. In P. Hutchings (Ed.), *Opening lines: Approaches to the Scholarship of Teaching and Learning.* Retrieved from http://www.carnegiefoundation.org/elibrary/inventing-future-opening-lines-approaches-scholarship-teaching-and-learning

Shulman, L. S. (2005). Signature pedagogies in the professions. *Daedalus, 134*(3), 52–59. doi:10.1162/0011526054622015

Simmons, N. (Ed.). (2016). *The Scholarship of Teaching and Learning in Canada: Institutional impact. New Directions in Teaching and Learning, 146.* San Francisco, CA: Jossey-Bass; doi:10.1002/tl.20192

Simmons, N., Abrahamson, E., Deschler, J. X., Kensington-Miller, B., Manarin, K., Morón-García, S., & Renc-Roe, J. (2013). Conflicts and configurations in a liminal space: SoTL scholars' identity development. *Teaching & Learning Inquiry, 1*(2), 9–21. Retrieved from https://journalhosting.ucalgary.ca/index.php/TLI/article/view/57382/43155

Stierer, B., & Antoniou, M. (2004). Are there distinctive methodologies for pedagogic research in higher education? *Teaching in Higher Education, 9*(3), 275–285. doi:10.1080/1356251042000216606

Svinicki, M. D. (2012). Who is entitled to do SoTL? *International Journal for the Scholarship of Teaching and Learning, 6*(2). doi:10.20429/ijsotl.2012.060202

Thomas, S. (2011). Broadening conceptions of what constitutes knowledge and evidence in SoTL. *International Journal for the Scholarship of Teaching and Learning, 5*(1). doi:10.20429/ijsotl.2011.050125

Tierney, A. M. (2016). *More than just a teaching fellow: The impact of REF and implications of TEF on life science teaching-focused academics in UK HEIs (Unpublished doctoral dissertation).* Durham, UK: University of Durham. Retrieved from http://etheses.dur.ac.uk/11826/

Tight, M. (2018). Tracking the Scholarship of Teaching and Learning. *Policy Reviews in Higher Education, 2*(1), 61–78. doi:10.1080/23322969.2017.1390690

Webb, A., Wong, T., & Hubball, H. T. (2013). Professional development for adjunct teaching faculty in a research-intensive university: Engagement in scholarly approaches to teaching and learning. *International Journal on Teaching and Learning in Higher Education, 25*(2), 231–238. Retrieved from http://www.isetl.org/ijtlhe/index.cfm

Webb, A. S. (2019). Navigating the lows to gain new heights: Constraints to SoTL engagement. *The Canadian Journal for the Scholarship of Teaching and Learning, 10*(2). doi:10.5206/cjsotl-rcacea.2019.2.8173

Werder, C., Thibou, S., & Kaufer, B. (2012). Students as co-inquirers: A requisite threshold concept in educational development. *Journal of Faculty Development, 26*(3), 34–38.

Young, P. (2006). Out of balance: Lecturer's perceptions of differential status and rewards in relation to teaching and research. *Teaching in Higher Education, 11*(2), 191–202. doi:10.1080/13562510500527727

ADDITIONAL READING

Bishop-Clark, C., & Dietz-Uhler, B. (2012). *Engaging in the Scholarship of Teaching and Learning: A guide to the process, and how to develop a project from start to finish.* Sterling, VA: Stylus.

Hubball, H. T., & Clarke, A. (2010). Diverse methodological approaches and considerations for SoTL in higher education. *The Canadian Journal for the Scholarship of Teaching and Learning, 1*(1). doi:10.5206/cjsotl-rcacea.2010.1.2

Hubball, H. T., Clarke, A., Chng, H. H., & Grimmett, P. (2015). The scholarship of educational leadership in research-intensive university contexts: Implications for promotion and tenure supervision. *Asian Journal for the Scholarship of Teaching and Learning*, 5(2), 92–107. Retrieved from http://www.cdtl.nus.edu.sg/ajsotl/article/the-scholarship-of-educational-leadership-in-research-intensive-university-contexts-implications-for-promotion-and-tenure-supervision/index.html

O'Brien, M. (2008). Navigating the SoTL landscape: A compass, map and some tools for getting started. *International Journal for the Scholarship of Teaching and Learning*, 2(2). doi:10.20429/ijsotl.2008.020215

Poole, G. (2010, March 2). The promises and potential of the Scholarship of Teaching and Learning: Moving slowly along a fascinating path. *Academic Matters*. Retrieved from http://www.academicmatters.ca/2010/03/the-promises-and-potential-of-the-scholarship-of-teaching-and-learning-moving-slowly-along-a-fascinating-path/

KEY TERMS AND DEFINITIONS

Curriculum: Curriculum refers to a particular course of study. It is often a selection of relevant content structured according to the learning context and organized to guide learners through a process.

Educational Leader: An educational leader is a faculty member whose employment involves high-stakes decisions regarding curricular and pedagogical initiatives at a departmental, faculty, or institutional level.

Faculty Member: A faculty member is an individual who belongs to a faculty or department in higher education. They are appointed to permanent employment in frequently tenure, tenure-track, or instructor positions.

Higher Education: Post-secondary education, especially at a college or university.

Interdisciplinary: Combining two or more academic disciplines or fields of study. Biochemistry represents an interdisciplinary approach to a field.

Intradisciplinary: Being within the scope of a single academic discipline.

Multidisciplinary: Composed of several, usually separate, fields of study or expertise. A multidisciplinary cohort brings together faculty members from diverse academic disciplines.

Pedagogy: The art and science of teaching, pedagogy is the methods of lesson, course, and program delivery.

Scholarship of Teaching and Learning: The Scholarship of Teaching and Learning is a rigorous, literature-informed, and peer-reviewed framework for investigating teaching and learning in higher education. It is methodologically flexible and open to many types of inquiries into pedagogical, curricular, disciplinary, and institutional contexts.

Teaching–Research Nexus: The interrelated links between teaching and research in higher education.

Chapter 2
The Enquiring University:
The Scholarship of Teaching and Learning as a Foundation for Strategic Educational Transformation

Elizabeth Cleaver
University of the West of England, Bristol, UK

Mike Mclinden
University of Birmingham, UK

Maxine Lintern
https://orcid.org/0000-0003-3358-8077
Birmingham City University, UK

Andy Birch
University of the West of England, Bristol, UK

ABSTRACT

This chapter charts how in England, Scholarship of Teaching and Learning (SoTL) activities that may until recently have been seen as 'marginal' or 'added' value are increasingly viewed as strategic enablers. This is of potential interest to international audiences due to the growing and, arguably, unprecedented expectations placed on English universities to evidence the impact of their education through the Teaching Excellence and Student Outcomes Framework. However, if SoTL is to become a fully functioning enabler of strategic transformation—rather than simply a cited exemplar or initiative—it needs to be systematically coordinated and evidenced. Drawing on a recently developed conceptual model—'the enquiring university'—the chapter charts how the role and impact of SoTL can be coordinated, recorded, and evaluated through an emergent SoTL Strategic Implementation and Impact Framework. Finally, the authors illustrate its application through reference to an example of a SoTL activity aligned to two key elements of the framework.

DOI: 10.4018/978-1-7998-2212-7.ch002

INTRODUCTION

This chapter builds on many of the varied ideas and evidence presented in this text, to propose a framework and methodology for higher education providers (HEPs) to harness, enhance, and evaluate the impact of Scholarship of Teaching and Learning (SoTL) activities at the macro-institutional (e.g. university or college) or meso-institutional (e.g. faculty[1], school, or department) levels. Recent changes in the policy and regulatory landscape in England (one of four home nations that make up the United Kingdom) provide the backdrop for the development of our framework. In this fast-changing national context, it is clear that there is increasing focus on enhancements in learning and teaching. This is primarily through the expectation that all registered HEPs will submit a return to the Teaching Excellence and Student Outcomes Framework (TEF), and that SoTL has real potential to become a fully-embedded and strategic aspect of institutional enhancement activities. Following an outline of the shifting policy landscape that has given rise to TEF and its associated provider submissions (OfS, 2019a) and the potential of SoTL-based activities to contribute to institutional TEF evidence bases, we present an emergent framework and methodology to support institutions to systematically embed SoTL activities and evidence the difference they have made.

While there is no one clear definition of SoTL, and its methods and approaches remain the focus of ongoing discussion and debate (Fanghanel et al., 2016), for the purposes of this chapter, we have drawn on a definition provided by Healey (2003). Healey identifies SoTL as educational or pedagogic research or evaluation activities, undertaken by staff within a HEP and which are explicitly designed to build, synthesise, or apply evidence to enhance and improve student learning and outcomes. Like other scholarship, McKinney (2006) reminds us that we should also engage in the "public sharing and review of such work through presentations, performance, or publications" (p. 39). By sharing in such a way, and seeing our "teaching as community property" (Shulman, 1993), SoTL has real potential to improve student learning and to enhance the quality of our learning and teaching both within and beyond our own classrooms.

Our starting point, then, is the assumption that SoTL is already undertaken and shared in this way in some institutions, particularly those whose strategic leaders recognise the benefits of centrally-coordinated and strategically-aligned critical enquiry into teaching and learning practices. However, we argue that without a clear strategically aligned institutional framework to support it, SoTL can be in danger of remaining no more than an individual academic endeavour (or a collection of these), and it is unlikely to become a fully functioning strategic enabler for the transformation of contemporary HEPs.

To support HEPs in developing their approach to the strategic embedding and evaluation of teaching and learning through the lens of SoTL, we draw on a recently developed conceptual model of the "enquiring university" (see McLinden, Cleaver, & Lintern, 2018, Figure 16.2, p.273). This model, which outlines four nested levels of enquiry, helps us to consider the various institutional layers in which HEPs can actively and systematically chart, build, and evidence the impact of SoTL-based activities, in connected ways, to greater strategic advantage. With reference to this model, we outline the parameters of an emergent SoTL Strategic Implementation and Impact Framework to support the development and use of SoTL as a foundation for strategic educational transformation. We illustrate its application through reference to an example of a SoTL activity aligned to two key elements of the framework.

POSITIONING SoTL WITHIN THE CHANGING ENGLISH HE LANDSCAPE

Compulsory for all registered English higher education providers (HEPs), and available as an opt-in for HEPs in Scotland and Wales, the TEF is presented by the new regulator for higher education in England, the Office for Students (OfS) as "a national exercise... [which] assesses excellence in teaching at universities and colleges and how well they ensure excellent outcomes for their students in terms of graduate-level employment or further study" (OfS, 2019c).

The introduction of the TEF needs to be positioned within the new regulatory landscape for English HE that came into effect following the Higher Education and Research Act (HM Government, 2017) where HEPs are now primarily judged on the principle of "value for money". This means ensuring that students can gain "the full benefits of higher education in exchange for the effort, time and money they invest" (OfS, 2019b). In turn, students have gained associated consumer rights (Competition and Markets Authority, 2015).

The introduction of the TEF also forms the latest in a long line of governmental attempts to promote excellence in, and to raise esteem for, teaching in English HEPs. The focus on teaching as a core and important academic endeavour had arguably lost ground in the face of the UK's Research Excellence Framework (REF, 2019) and a series of other policy decisions; these have resulted in separate national funding and governance structures for research and teaching, despite both aspects of work being core to most institutional missions. This has arguably bolstered divisions between research and teaching and contributed to the development of what has been termed the "prestige economy" in UK HE (Blackmore, 2016a; 2016b), where research appears in many HEPs to hold the highest prestige or value of all academic activities and is perceived as the primary promotional route for academics.

So, what does TEF mean for HEPs in practice? All registered HEPs in England are presented with evidence that has been collected by central agencies against core metrics under the three broad headings of Teaching Quality, Learning Environment, and Student Outcomes and Learning Gain. This data indicates an initial award category:

- TEF Gold for "delivering consistently outstanding teaching, learning, and outcomes for its students. It is of the highest quality found in the UK"
- TEF Silver "for delivering high quality teaching, learning, and outcomes for its students. It consistently exceeds rigorous national quality requirements for UK higher education"
- TEF Bronze "for delivering teaching, learning, and outcomes for its students that meet rigorous national quality requirements for UK higher education"
- TEF Provisional if a provider meets national quality requirements and "is taking part in the TEF, but does not yet have sufficient data to be fully assessed" (OfS, 2019d).

The metrics include National Student Survey scores, data from the Destination of Leavers in Higher Education survey[2], the learning environment, and earnings on graduation amongst other things and are benchmarked against similar institutions. HEPs are able to supplement this data with a written provider statement (up to 15 pages long[3]) in which further quantitative and qualitative evidence is provided to support and contextualise the claim for a given level of award. These submissions are made available in full, to assist in ensuring a transparency of outcomes, through a publicly accessible database. In his review of the first TEF written submissions, the Chair of the first TEF Assessment Panel indicated the types of evidence that panels found useful: "...the best provider submissions did not describe initiatives—of which no institution is short – but *systematically demonstrated* the difference they had made" (Husbands, 2017. p.6: our emphasis). This clearly paves the way for a role for SoTL as an approach to achieve this institutional evidence base.

Whilst there is a wealth of literature that examines and reports on SoTL at discipline, programme, and individual teacher/classroom levels (see dedicated journals such as the *International Journal for the Scholarship of Teaching and Learning,* and dedicated conferences such as the *International Society for the Scholarship of Teaching and Learning* annual conference*)*, access to consistent information on institutionally-coordinated and aligned SoTL investments and activities has been limited. This is perhaps unsurprising given the increasingly competitive landscape that higher education operates within. However, within the recent developments in England outlined above, the TEF has begun to provide the sector with an unprecedented opportunity—at a national level—to consider the ways in which HEPs describe their SOTL-based activities in relation to the TEF categories of activity, within their written provider submissions.

Moore et al.'s (2017) analysis of a sample of TEF Year 2[4] Provider Written Statements provides a helpful starting point for our own thinking in this area. Significant in the context of this chapter, the authors state that within their sample, "there were relatively few explicit narratives on the Scholarship of Teaching and Learning (SoTL), although it was implicit in some of the accounts within submissions" (Moore et al., 2017, p. 55). In total, they found that SoTL-type activities were explicitly and/or implicitly included in around half of the provider statements, in what Moore et al. (2017) term "narratives of innovation in pedagogy". Of the statements that made reference to such innovation, they noted the following process to support SoTL-type activities (pp. 55-58):

- funding arrangements to fund ideas and testing (mentioned by 29%), which included student-led projects which focus on impacting directly on students' programmes as well as staff-led projects
- support provided by dedicated *individuals* or teams (mentioned by 20%)
- opportunities for sharing practice and research (mentioned by 14%)
- mechanisms for staff reward including institutional teaching fellowships (mentioned by 14%)
- drawing on staff expertise to promote pedagogical development (mentioned by 11%)
- offering sabbatical or secondment opportunities (mentioned by 5%)
- fostering external partnerships and collaboration (mentioned by 3%)

The conclusions of the report are clear: "generally, the submissions *describe* processes for supporting innovation rather than examining the impact that they have had" (Moore et al., 2017, p. 56). The authors, therefore, argue that the effective development of institutional approaches to teaching excellence could be further enhanced by embedded whole institution approaches to "developing, implementing and evaluating strategies and processes which support excellence", which draw on "evidence-based approaches for achieving the best student outcomes" through investment in "evaluation mechanisms in order to establish the impact at the institutional level", and "mechanisms for assuring competency of staff beyond the achievement of qualifications" (p. 106).

What the project does not offer—justifiably, given its purpose and focus—is an approach for embedding and structurally supporting such activities and mechanisms, in order to develop and create a whole institutional approach, and the impact, that it advocates. With this in mind, in the next section of the chapter we outline our emergent Strategic Implementation and Impact Framework to support the development and use of SoTL as a foundation for strategic educational transformation.

OUR EMERGENT APPROACH

The starting point for building our Strategic Implementation and Impact Framework is insight provided by Blackmore and Kandiko (2012). Reporting on the findings of a survey of curriculum change in HEPs, they argue that HEPs often reported that *"making the change was in itself so difficult that implementing it was often seen as success enough"* (p.176), rather than success judgements deriving from evidence of real improvements for students. Blackmore and Kandiko therefore recommend that "careful attention be paid to evaluation, from the beginning of the initiative, and that flexible and practical evaluation approaches should be built in throughout, at all levels, to maximise the possibilities that learning will take place speedily within the organisation as a result of experience" (p. 177).

In many ways, this finding is surprising, particularly given that the capacity to build a whole-institution culture of integrated critical enquiry—"the enquiring university"—is unique to HEPs that engage in both research and teaching, where staff, students, and other stakeholders, as part of an enquiring community, can harness their knowledge and skills for institutional benefit (McLinden, Cleaver, & Lintern, 2018, p.275). However, like Moore et al. (2017), we recognise that much of this activity is in reality happening, but it often takes place in discrete pockets, associated with particular funding streams and groups of individuals or projects, rather than as an embedded and connected strategic institutional endeavour. As such we have argued,

...what is less known or understood is how far the varying aspects of this activity are nested, connected and embedded within the culture of each institution and the extent to which they are each supported, celebrated and, indeed, rewarded. (McLinden, Cleaver, & Lintern, 2018, p.274)

Our earlier consideration of this problem ended with the conclusion that the particular shape that a given "enquiring university" is likely to adopt will necessarily reflect its complex and distinctive institutional ethos, cultures, and staff and student skills-sets. We therefore encouraged HEPs to undertake a meta-analysis of critical enquiry (including SoTL) activities at a number of levels as seen in Figure 1, to highlight strengths, gaps in activity, and whether such activities were interconnected or discrete. We now turn toward an emergent framework through which this meta-analysis can be undertaken.

Developing Our Framework

To develop our own framework for the meta-analysis of SoTL activities as part of the enquiring university, we have drawn on and adapted an existing framework—the McKinsey 7 S (M7S) Framework—which was originally designed to help organizations seek "harmony" in their activities to ensure optimum performance. The architects of this framework argue that for an organization to perform effectively, there needs to be alignment and coherence between each of seven interdependent elements, which together contribute to overall organisational effectiveness (Pascale & Athos, 1981; see Figure 2).

In application, the seven elements are often broken down into "hard" (strategy, structure, and systems) and "soft" (staff, style, and skills) elements, with the final element—shared values—sitting at the heart of the approach and central to the "harmony" that it seeks to build. A brief summary of each element is presented below:

Figure 1. Integrated critical enquiry in the enquiring university. This illustrates the potential alignment between students, academic staff, the discipline, the institution and sectoral practices placing "learning through critical enquiry" at the heart of all activity.
(*adapted from McLinden, Cleaver, & Lintern, 2018, p. 273*)

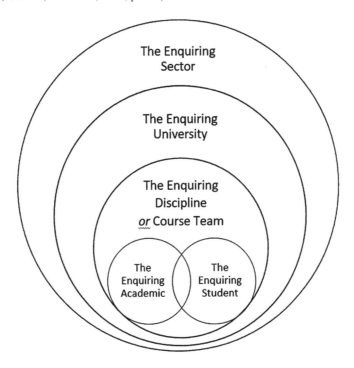

- Strategy – the strategic "plans" drawn upon by the institution to guide its future direction.
- Structure – how the institution is organized.
- Systems – the activities, procedures, and processes that staff within the institution draw upon to undertake their jobs.

Figure 2. Overview of the original M7S Framework and its seven elements

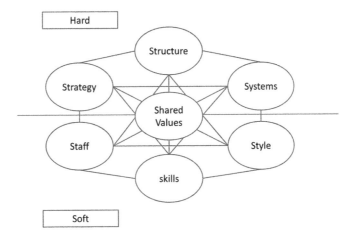

Figure 3. The SoTL Strategic Implementation and Impact Framework, adapted from the M7S framework (Pascale & Athos, 1981)

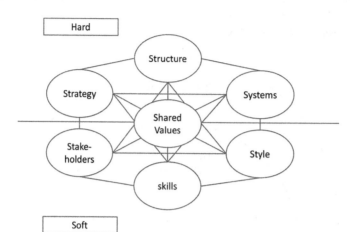

- Style – the style of leadership that is used within the institution.
- Staff – the background of the employees and their capabilities.
- Skills – the skills and competencies of the staff within the institution.
- Shared Values – the core values of the institution that underpin, and are reflected by, all other elements.

The M7S framework highlights the fact that, in creating any type of organisational impact or change, attention must be paid to all seven organisational elements and their inter-relationships. It illustrates how these factors work together to support institutional effectiveness and shows how changes in one area can affect others. In its application in organizational settings, it demonstrates the benefits of any proposed change (however local in its focus) must be considered in relation to the whole. The framework therefore offers the opportunity to gauge the effectiveness of any change made within a particular element, in relation to the other elements, by considering the various inter-relationships and the impacts that may occur. Usefully, for the purposes of this chapter and our developing approach to planning for integrated critical enquiry in "the enquiring university", the M7S Framework was also designed to allow organisations to create an evidence baseline, to plan, and then to monitor potential changes in line with agreed success criteria across all seven elements (as appropriate).

There is already some evidence to show how the M7S Framework can be employed within the HE sector to audit, embed, and promote cultural change in the area of inclusive policy and practice (see, for example, May & Bridger, 2010; McLinden et al., 2019). To adapt the model to contemporary HEP settings, McLinden et al. (2019) additionally included "students" in addition to the original "staff" element. We have also adapted the model. To ensure fitness for purpose, we have augmented the "Staff/Students" element further, in recognition that SoTL engages a range of other relevant parties (e.g., professional bodies, partners from other organizations or industry, etc.). We have therefore changed the staff element to "Stakeholders" in our adapted model (see Figure 3).

Below, we outline the parameters of our emergent framework and illustrate its application through reference to a worked example of a SoTL activity.

OUTLINING THE PARAMETERS OF OUR EMERGENT SOTL STRATEGIC IMPLEMENTATION & IMPACT FRAMEWORK

Introduction: The Stages of the Framework

The purpose of the *SoTL Implementation and Impact Framework* is to provide a planning tool to help those who work in HEPs to purposefully align new and existing SoTL activities to broader strategic priorities and, in doing so, to support the development and use of SoTL activities as a foundation for, and enabler of, strategic educational transformation. By including a series of short, structured reflective prompts and questions associated with each of the seven elements, the framework is designed to afford HEPs a way of identifying, auditing, planning, and evidencing SoTL systematically, strategically, and as part of a connected whole. As such, it can be used as an initial audit tool (which we refer to as a *Baseline Snapshot*), as well as a means of identifying and reviewing progress toward agreed priorities within later stages (which we refer to as a *Review Snapshot* and an *Endpoint Snapshot*).

We illustrate its application by taking the reader through a worked example of a SoTL activity in relation to one element: adopting the role of a prospective review team who are seeking to undertake a planned SoTL activity in a fictional HEP (which we refer to as institution A). The SoTL activity is designed to identify evidence of the benefits of students working in closer collaboration with staff—captured succinctly as *"Evidencing the Benefits of Students as Partners"*. We have selected this topic as it is currently of relevance within each of our respective HEPs and has been identified as an issue that resonates globally (see Cooke-Sather, Bovill, & Felten, 2014; Healey, Flint, & Harrington, 2014). Further, it can be considered at a range of different organisational levels (e.g., at the module or unit level, at the course or departmental level, or at the institutional level). A summary of the "review brief" that we designed to produce the worked example as a prospective review team is presented in Table 1.

The Framework supports the reviewer or review team to produce a series of snapshots at various points in the process of implementing changes or undertaking an activity. This is to determine to what extent the change or activity, once embedded in each of the relevant interdependent elements, is working (alongside other activities) to contribute to the overall effectiveness of the institution and enhancement of the student experience. As you begin the process, it is important to be fully aware of the *level* at which the planned SoTL activity is operating: the enquiring academic and/or student, the enquiring course-team or discipline, or the enquiring university (see Figure 1). This level will determine the kind of information that you gather, and from whom, at each of the evidence gathering stages.

Stage 1: *the SoTL Activity Descriptor*–forms an initial project overview, aimed at ensuring a collective understanding of the purpose of the planned activity, where it sits within the institutional direction of travel, at what level it is operating, and how it is planned to demonstrate impact.

Stage 2: *the Baseline Snapshot*—intended to map the planned SoTL activity—whatever its level of operation—to strategic priorities. For each of the seven elements of the Framework, we offer a brief set of prompt questions to help gather information.

Stage 3: the Baseline Snapshot provides the reference point for a series of review or progress points—*the Snapshot Reviews* at which the questions are asked again, to ensure that the project or activity remains on track and organizationally-aligned. Where the activity did not fully align to an element of the Framework, these *Snapshot Reviews* offer up an opportunity to showcase if alignment has improved and how this has been achieved.

Table 1. Summary of review brief to guide the production of a SoTL Implementation and Impact Framework worked example

---

Setting the Scene - Evidencing the Benefits of Students as Partners Project – Institution A

Institution A is a university in England, offering a range of first/undergraduate degree courses as well as post-graduate teaching and post-graduate research awards. A recent institutional strategic review, in line with preparations for Subject-Level TEF, identified the need for greater evidence-based practice. It has invited programmes and departments to apply for Enhancement Funding around a number of themes that reflect institutional strategic priorities: *research informed teaching,* students *as partners, decolonizing the curriculum, inclusive assessment,* and *work-integrated learning.*

Department Y made a successful application for a small development grant to evidence practice and value of students as partners across a cluster of courses in the area of Computer Science and Cyber Security. The team has been actively working to engage students, ensure that they have a voice in a range of forums, and are involved in the co-creation of their curriculum for some time.

However, Department Y does not have local expertise in or experience of qualitative research approaches. As a result, they have been uncertain as to how to collect evidence of students' engagement with or perceptions of these activities, beyond using quotations from free text comments in end of module feedback surveys (which are limited, as they are not collected for this purpose), and anecdotal comments gathered from informal discussions with students.

The call for funding has prompted Department Y to seek out support from their Psychology colleagues, with whom they work on elements of the cyber security courses. The Psychology team has suggested that Department Y employ some of their post-graduate taught (PGT) students. They have also suggested that each PGT student from Psychology who is involved is paired up with one from Department Y, so that they can engage in peer learning about research approaches and paradigms throughout the project. The Psychology team have committed independently to evaluating the peer-learning aspect of the project.

The project is planned over a 12-month period from September 2019 to August 2020 with the main data gathering points completed by May 2020, and analysis and reporting taking place from June-August 2020.

Stage 4: at the end of the project or activity, the team completes a final snapshot review—*the Endpoint Snapshot,* where the questions are asked a final time before the project concludes. By this point, although ideally at an earlier Snapshot Review, alignment across all relevant elements of the Framework should be fully achieved.

In the next section of the chapter, we offer up a series of prompt questions associated with each stage and/or organisational element. These are addressed to readers in the first person to support active engagement with and use of the Framework. In addition (see Tables 1 and 2 below), we provide two worked examples of how, acting as the review team in Department Y of Institution A, we have used the Framework to evidence the organisational alignment of the *Evidencing the Benefits of Students as Partners* project (outlined in Table 1). Following this guide may be useful to support and develop staff experience and confidence in leading strategically aligned SoTL activities.

Stage 1: Completing the SoTL Activity Descriptor

Before you begin the mapping process, it is useful to have a brief overview of the planned SoTL activity or project you are undertaking, so that it is clear what is being mapped, who it is designed to affect, when it has taken or is planned to take place, and how you will gather evidence and disseminate it. This not only creates a shared team understanding of the project but additionally provides information for a department or institutional database of SoTL activities that, in turn, can support the identification of synergies, overlaps, and gaps. The following reflective prompts are designed to help with this process. A short worked example of this stage of the process in relation to our *Evidencing the Benefits of Students as Partners* project is included in Table 2.

1. What is the provisional title of the planned SoTL activity?
2. What is the broad nature of the planned SoTL activity?
3. Why is the activity planned; what is the problem or enhancement it is aiming to address?
4. How would you describe the level at which the planned SoTL activity is operating?
   a. Micro-level—e.g., the enquiring academic, in collaboration with students in one particular unit or module at one level of study.
   b. meso-level—e.g., the enquiring course team/discipline in collaboration with students across a whole course or department at all levels of study.
   c. macro-level—e.g., the enquiring university in collaboration with lead students representing broad groups of students in the HEP.
5. What is the proposed benefit or impact, and for whom?
6. Who will be involved in supporting the activity through to completion?
7. When will the activity take place?
8. How will you communicate or disseminate your aims, project, and any outcomes?
9. Is this first time this kind of activity has been undertaken within the institution? Does it connect with or follow on from any other SoTL projects you or others have undertaken?
10. Outline up to three overall success measures. How will you know you have achieved them?

Stage 2: Prompts for Creating the Baseline Snapshot

Once project information has been recorded in the SoTL Activity Descriptor, you can use the Framework to create a *Baseline Snapshot*. This maps your SoTL activity to the seven organisational elements and is your starting point for its development as an enabler for strategic transformation. For each of the seven elements of the Framework, we ask a series of prompt questions to help gather this baseline snapshot. This snapshot then provides the starting point for your *Snapshot Review* and *Endpoint Snapshot* points where the questions are asked again/adapted in the light of activity developments and insights. These review points might be at six monthly intervals for a two year project or quarterly for a one year project.

The core purpose of this mapping activity is to ensure that you initially and continually align your activity to the broader organisational vision, goals, priorities, and activities of your HEP against the seven organizational elements. Not all elements of the framework will necessarily be relevant to every one of your SoTL activities. However where there are gaps, or where your activity is not fully aligned, it is important to be able to explain why this is, whether it should remain the case or, if not, to think of plans for clearer alignment as you progress through the stages of the Framework. Importantly, this ensures that any local positive outcomes can be simultaneously mapped to organisational level outcomes and activities as the activity project progresses to showcase its relevance to this bigger strategic picture.

We suggest you provide a brief answer to each of the questions—approximately 50 words—in the form of short sentences or bullet points. This makes the record easy to complete, read, share and maintain.

Table 2. Worked example of SoTL Activity Descriptor

Reflective Prompts	Response
What is the provisional title of the planned SoTL activity?	Evidencing the benefits of student as partners in their learning
What is the broad nature of the planned SoTL activity?	We wish to find out the best ways to involve students in enhancing their learning, to ensure that they can be fully engaged as active change agents and not just consulted about change, at all relevant points in their learning journey at the University.
Why is the activity planned; what is the problem or enhancement it is aiming to address?	At present we make claims about the benefits of our students being partners in learning in our departmental and course advertising documents. However, to date we have very little evidence to support this.
How would you describe the level at which the planned SoTL activity is operating?	We are looking at this at the meso-level, from the whole course perspective, as a course team, to ensure that we can foster, embed, and evidence partnership activities and outcomes at regular and appropriate points within the course.
What is the proposed benefit or impact and for whom?	Students will be the primary beneficiaries, as they will have the opportunity to highlight and explore issues and practice that they believe are important, contribute towards solutions, and bring about change. Other stakeholders include current and future employers, who will gain benefits from students learning to identify problems and solutions, work as part of a team, and take a partnership approach. The University, will also benefit as it can harness the ideas and energies of its core stakeholders—students—to effect transformation and change in the areas that matter most to them.
Who will be involved in supporting the activity through to completion?	The course and module/unit leaders with students from all years of study within the course.
When will the activity take place?	Semesters 1 and 2—Academic Year 2019-2020.
How will you communicate or disseminate your aims, project, and any outcomes?	A call for student participation from Psychology and Computer Science will be made at the beginning of Semester 1, to alert students to the project and ask for volunteers as lead student partners. All students from across the programme will have an opportunity to learn more about the project and engage during formal study time. A regular update will be posted in the online learning environment course pages of each programme involved, with opportunities to engage online as well as face-to-face. The project will be presented in partnership with students to the Faculty Forum during Second Semester, at the Students' Union Conference in May 2020 and at the University's Festival of Learning in July 2020. We will co-create a case study about the project, with resources, to upload to our University Good Practice Portal.
Is this first time this kind of activity has been undertaken within the institution? Does it connect with or follow on from any other SoTL projects you or others have undertaken?	We are aware of other pockets of good practice in other parts of the University, and we will be inviting staff and students to form a Community of Practice where we can join up, learn from, and disseminate to each other as the project progresses.
Outline up to three overall success measures. How will you know you have achieved them?	By the end of the year, our course students will identify themselves as partners in their learning and will be able to identify real examples of where this partnership has occurred in practice. We intend to put a focused question about this into our end-of-year student survey as well as hold focus groups with students from each year (by July 2020). The Students as Partners Community of Practice is thriving—and we are regularly meeting with and learning from others who are engaged in similar activities (by July 2020). Our employers and placement providers are note a difference in our graduates' engagement with team-work, problem-solving, and change. We will actively seek feedback on this six months after the project ends and a further six months later (by July 2021).

Element 1: Strategy

This element allows you to audit/review your planned activity in relation to the strategic priorities and/ or goals at the relevant level of your institution. These could be programme level, department level, faculty level, or institutional. A worked example in relation to our *Evidencing the Benefits of Students as Partners* project is included in Table 3.

1. Outline any strategic priorities and/or goals that are relevant to your SoTL activity. Please indicate the *level* of these strategic priorities or goals (e.g., programme, department, faculty, or institution).
2. Are you aware of any issues in relation to this element that may positively or negatively impact or affect your SoTL activity?
3. What will success look like, in relation to this element, for your planned SoTL activity?
4. Please indicate using a Red/Amber/Green or Not Applicable (N/A) rating, the extent to which at the beginning of your project, your work aligns to this organisational element:
   a. Red = does not currently align
   b. Amber = some alignment
   c. Green = fully aligns
   d. N/A = this element is not applicable to the project
5. Please indicate why you have made this judgement.
6. What will you need to do to create greater alignment of your planned SoTL activity to this element or to maintain current alignment levels?
7. Do you have any other comments about your planned SoTL activity in relation to this element?

Element 2: Structures

This element allows you to audit/review your planned activity in relation to the structures that exist (ways of organizing, making decisions, and doing things) at the levels that your project is operating and impacting in the institution. These could be programme level, department level, faculty level, and/or institutional level structures.

1. What are the key management and leadership structures of the organization (or its relevant constituent part) that frame your SoTL?
2. What are the reporting arrangements and decision-making structures of the aspect of the organization that relate to your SoTL activity?
3. Are you aware of any structural issues that may positively or negatively impact or affect your SoTL activity?
4. What will success look like for this element in relation to your planned SoTL activity?
5. Please indicate using a Red/Amber/Green or Not Applicable (N/A) rating, the extent to which at the beginning of your project, your work aligns to this organisational element and explain why you have made this judgement:
   a. Red = does not currently align
   b. Amber = some alignment
   c. Green = fully aligns

Table 3. Baseline Snapshot worked example for Element 1: Strategy

Organisational Element	Strategy
Title of Project or Planned Activity	Evidencing the Benefits of Students as Partners
Baseline Snapshot Date	September 2019
Outline any strategic priorities and/or goals that are relevant to your SoTL activity. Please indicate the *level* of these strategic priorities or goals (e.g., programme, department, faculty, or institution).	Currently we claim students are "partners in learning" in our institutional strategy. This is also highlighted in strategies at faculty and departmental level and is mentioned in open day presentations.
Are you aware of any issues in relation to this element that may positively or negatively impact or affect your SoTL activity?	The institutional strategy is reviewed and revised on a five-year basis. This project will report just after the strategy is refreshed. It is therefore important to ensure that alignment to the new strategy is undertaken in the endpoint snapshot if this information is available.
What will success look like, in relation to this element, for your planned SoTL activity?	That we can confidently claim in our strategy and our TEF statement that we have strong and sustained evidence of our partnerships with students rather than using anecdotes and partial evidence.
Please indicate using a Red/Amber/Green or Not Applicable (N/A) rating, the extent to which at the beginning of your activity, your work aligns to this organisational element: • Red = does not currently align • Amber = some alignment • Green = fully aligns • N/A = this element is not applicable to the project Please explain why you have made this judgement.	• Amber This is a key strategic priority for the institution and the department, and we currently know that we are doing a number of things to meet it. However, we have no real evidence of the extent of these activities or their impact. Moreover, when we discuss these activities we don't always align them with the strategy. This would need to be done in meaningful ways for different audiences.
What will you need to do to create greater alignment of your SoTL activity with this element or to maintain current alignment levels?	Maintain a watching brief on the strategy as it emerges and ensure that we are collecting information that relates to any new strategic priorities. Ensure that any documents and dissemination about the project as it progresses use strategically relevant language in appropriate ways for particular audiences.
Do you have any other comments about your planned SoTL activity in relation to this element?	A key issue is how we cascade our findings throughout the institution and meet with others who are undertaking similar activities. We need to ensure alignment at different levels if we are to systematically evidence our strategic commitments and share our successes. It may be useful to structure the recommendations of our report for these different audiences

  d. N/A = this element is not applicable to the project

6. What will you need to do to create greater alignment of your SoTL activity to this element or to maintain current alignment levels?

7. Do you have any other comments about your planned SoTL activity in relation to this element?

Element 3: Systems

This element allows you to audit/review your planned SoTL activity in relation to the activities, procedures, and processes that staff and students within your institution draw upon to undertake their jobs and to support their studies. These could be operating at, and impacting on, the programme level, the department level, the faculty level, and/or the institutional level.

1. What daily activities, processes and procedures that staff and students operate and interact with for their studies or jobs to progress relate to your planned SoTL activity?

2. Are there any less formal internal rules and processes that the team uses to keep on track that will impact your planned SoTL activity?

3. Which individuals or groups have access to and maintain/operate these processes and procedures? How might you need to alert them to the fact that you are undertaking your SoTL activity? How could they support you in this activity?

4. Are you aware of any other issues or concerns with respect to this element and your planned SoTL activity?

5. What will success look like for this element in relation to your planned SoTL activity?

6. Please indicate using a Red/Amber/Green or Not Applicable (N/A) rating, the extent to which at the beginning of your SoTL activity, your work aligns to this organisational element and explain why you have made this judgement:
   a. Red = does not currently align
   b. Amber = some alignment
   c. Green = fully aligns
   d. N/A = this element is not applicable to the project

7. What will you need to do to create greater alignment of your SoTL activity to this element or to maintain current alignment levels?

8. Do you have any other comments about the planned SoTL activity in relation to this element?

Element 4: Style

This element allows you to audit/review your planned SoTL activity in relation to the dominant styles and forms of leadership and management within your institution, identify how you could draw on these to support your activity, and navigate any issues that might arise. Leadership and management may be operating at the programme level, the department level, the faculty level, and/or the institutional level, all of which may impact your particular SoTL activity.

1. Who are the leaders and managers who are likely to be engaged with or impacted by your SoTL activity? What forms of leadership and management approaches and styles to they advocate and use?

2. How will you engage with or draw on this resource to support you in this activity and how will you influence this?

3. Are you aware of any issues or concerns with respect to this element and your planned SoTL activity?

4. What will success look like for this element in relation to your planned SoTL activity?

5. Please indicate using a Red/Amber/Green or Not Applicable (N/A) rating, the extent to which at the beginning of your SoTL activity, your work aligns to this organisational element and explain why you have made this judgement:
   a. Red = does not currently align
   b. Amber = some alignment
   c. Green = fully aligns
   d. N/A = this element is not applicable to the project

6. What will you need to do to create greater alignment of your SoTL activity to this element or to maintain current alignment levels?

7. Do you have any other comments about the planned SoTL activity in relation to this element?

Element 5: Stakeholders (e.g., Staff/Students/Partners)

This element allows you identify a range of stakeholders who will be engaged in the activity, how you will work to prepare them for this engagement, and how you will communicate the benefits to them. We encourage you to think broadly in relation to this element, as often the obvious and direct beneficiaries are only one of a series of core stakeholders. It is worth ensuring that any opportunities for stakeholder preparation, involvement, and dissemination are taken up at the earliest opportunity, as this can significantly augment the impact of your activity.

1. Who are the key beneficiaries from and contributors to the success of your SoTL activity?
2. How will you ensure that they are made fully aware of the purpose and scope of the activity and are ready to support you to take it forward?
3. How will you engage them at different points of the activity as it progresses?
4. Are you aware of any issues or concerns with respect to this element and your planned SoTL activity?
5. What will success look like for this element in relation to your planned SoTL activity?
6. Please indicate using a Red/Amber/Green or Not Applicable (N/A) rating, the extent to which at the beginning of your SoTL activity, your work aligns to this organisational element and explain why you have made this judgement:
    a. Red = does not currently align
    b. Amber = some alignment
    c. Green = fully aligns
    d. N/A = this element is not applicable to the project
7. What will you need to do to create greater alignment of your SoTL activity to this element or to maintain current alignment levels?
8. Do you have any other comments about the planned SoTL activity in relation to this element?

Element 6: Skills

This element allows you identify whether those who are involved in the activity, and others who are likely to hear about it, are suitably skilled to fully engage. How you will work to prepare those who may need upskilling to do so, and how you will make certain that members of your team are skilled in translating the outcomes of the activity for broader dissemination to non-experts. It is worth ensuring that any appropriate opportunities for skills development are designed into the activity at the earliest opportunity, as this can support its smooth progress and help to augment its impact.

1. What core skills and understandings are needed to progress, complete, and disseminate your SoTL activity?
2. Do the current team members have the necessary skills and competences to support the planned activity? Are there any skills gaps? How will you address these?

3. Will information about the project be accessible and understandable to all stakeholders? Are you likely to use any jargon or a particular methodology or methods that may be unfamiliar for others and will need interpretation and translation?
4. Are there any other issues or concerns that you can identify with respect to this element and your planned SoTL activity?
5. What will success look like for this element in relation to your planned SoTL activity?
6. Please indicate using a Red/Amber/Green or Not Applicable (N/A) rating, the extent to which at the beginning of your SoTL activity, your work aligns to this organisational element and explain why you have made this judgement:
    a. Red = does not currently align
    b. Amber = some alignment
    c. Green = fully aligns
    d. N/A = this element is not applicable to the project
7. What will you need to do to create greater alignment of your planned SoTL activity to this element or to maintain current alignment levels?
8. Do you have any other comments about the planned SoTL activity in relation to this element?

Element 7: Shared Values

This final element sits at the centre of the mapping process and forms one of the key ways in which the "harmony" of your SoTL activity with the organization and its elements can be judged and evidenced. Not all HEPs, faculties, departments, or course-teams will have explicit shared values, so if you cannot agree and evidence these, you may want to substitute this element for "Shared Vision" or "Shared Mission". Be careful to ensure that your answers to these questions recognise and reflect the difference between values and vision and "Strategy" (Element 1).

1. Outline any shared and agreed values that are relevant to your SoTL activity. Please indicate the *level* of these shared values (e.g. programme, department, faculty, or institution) and how they relate to your activity.
2. How will you ensure that these values are reflected in and supported by your SoTL activity moving forward?
3. Are you aware of any issues in relation to this element that may positively or negatively impact or affect your SoTL activity?
4. What will success look like, in relation to this element, for your planned SoTL activity?
5. Please indicate using a Red/Amber/Green or Not Applicable (N/A) rating, the extent to which at the beginning of your project, your work aligns to this organisational element:
    a. Red = does not currently align
    b. Amber = some alignment
    c. Green = fully aligns
    d. N/A = this element is not applicable to the project

Please explain why you have made this judgement.

6.   What will you need to do to create greater alignment of your planned SoTL activity to this element or to maintain current alignment levels?

7.   Do you have any other comments about your planned SoTL activity in relation to this element?

Stage 2: Reflections

The Stage 2 questions and prompts outlined above provide the starting point for a series of review or progress points at which your project and its outputs can be assessed against each of the seven organisational elements. However, this is an important staging post in its own right, as it may represent the first time such an analysis has been conducted within your HEP. We recommend, at this point, that you ask a series of questions to help you to reflect on what you have learned so far and whether any changes need to be made to your activity or project as a result:

- What does this initial review tell us about the way in which our project or activity is organizationally aligned?
- Are there any obvious misalignments, gaps, or areas of over-focus?
- How does the information gathered so far impact upon the next stages of my planned activity?

Take, for example, a stage two analysis that indicates the following: In relation to Element 1, "Strategy", your HEP espouses that *Students as Partners* is a central institutional commitment and aligns to core institutional values "enabling" and "inclusive". In contrast, your analysis of Elements 2 and 3—"Structures" and "Systems"—indicates that there is a predominant focus on knowledge transmission and didactic style teaching and on using Virtual Learning Environments (VLEs) as repositories for the sharing of information and documents. Further, your analysis of Element 6, "Skills", indicates that staff are typically engaged in didactic styles of learning and teaching and are not confident in engaging in enquiry-based learning approaches.

You may wish to recalibrate your SoTL activity to address some of these misaligned elements as soon as possible. While you may be unable to influence "Structures" or "Systems" in their widest sense, you are likely to be able to argue the case to for more interactive rooms to be timetabled for your activities. You may, further, decide that an intervention in relation to "Skills" is more important and to ensure that this is fully embedded as part of your SoTL activity so that, irrespective of the timetabled room, staff and students have the skills and confidence to be able to engage in active learning.

Stages 3 and 4—Planning and Completing the Snapshot Reviews, Endpoint Snapshot, and Alignment Overview Table

The Stage 2 questions should be repeated at appropriate intervals until the project completes. Where the planned SoTL activity is found not to fully align to an element of the Framework at any stage, and actions have taken place to remedy this (see Stage 2 Reflections), the review points offer up an opportunity to check whether alignment has improved, how this has been achieved, and whether there is room for further improvement. At the end of the project, the team can complete a final snapshot review—*the Endpoint Snapshot*, where all questions are considered a final time before the project concludes. At this point, although potentially at an earlier Snapshot Review, alignment across all relevant elements of the Framework should be fully evidenced.

Table 4. Example Activity Rag Overview Table which evidences growing alignment and harmony with all organisational elements

SoTL Activity	Evidencing the Benefits of Students as Partners						
	S1	S2	S3	S4	S5	S6	S7
Baseline Review September 2020	Amber	Red	Green	Red	Amber	Amber	Red
Snapshot Review 1 December 2020	Amber	Amber	Green	Red	Amber	Green	Amber
Snapshot Review 2 March 2021	Green	Amber	Green	Amber	Green	Green	Amber
Snapshot Review 2 June 2021	Green	Green	Green	Amber	Green	Green	Amber
Endpoint Review August 2021	Green	Green	Green	Amber	Green	Green	Green

For example, you have observed that through adapting your SoTL activity that "Skills" are now supporting "Strategy", even though the "Structures" and "Systems" that they are bound by do not facilitate this approach. You will now be able to focus your evaluation and reporting activities on "skills" development. Further, while the SoTL activity that you are undertaking may well be focused initially at the micro level, your work may help to evidence a misalignment between elements at the meso or macro levels. And while we acknowledge that no HEP would or should seek to change its "Structure" or "Systems" based on one localised piece of evidence, if the framework is adopted at an institutional or wider level and analysis of all of the available evidence through the baseline, snapshot, and endpoint reviews are considered together, there is potential for more *systematic* demonstration of and evidence for this misalignment.

During each review stage, we recommend that an overview table is completed to showcase gaps in alignment, progress, and final outcomes using the Red/Amber/Green (RAG) ratings that you have recorded. This helps track progress and to show where any priority actions need to be taken. An annotated exemplar of this Activity RAG Overview Table is presented in relation to our *Evidencing the Benefits of Students as Partners Project* in Table 4.

SUMMARY AND FUTURE RESEARCH DIRECTIONS

In this chapter, we have outlined the issues identified in the literature and offered an emergent framework as a conceptual and practical response, illustrated with reference to a composite exemplar activity to demonstrate how this could manifest in practice.

Our framework, which results from an adaptation of the M7S framework, is designed to evidence and align the benefits of any proposed change (however local in its focus) in relation to the whole organization: its purpose, its values, and its structures. The framework therefore offers those engaged in SoTL activities an opportunity to consider and develop their inter-relationship with key organisational elements and the ways in which each of these intersects and interrelates to create indirect impact. We argue that if all SoTL activities, however localized, were to actively seek to align to each of these interrelated organisational elements, this has the potential to ensure that they can have the maximum positive impact beyond their immediate and planned context, and they can be actively employed as evidence for broader strategic change. Further, the evidence-base created by this process forms an institutional database of evidence that is consistently collected, aligned to each of the seven organisational elements.

We recognise that the approach presented here is emergent, and while piloted conceptually, it has not been fully tested on SoTL activities in an institutional setting. To do this, we will be working to field test the approach within our respective institutions and will work with colleagues in other HEPs to hone and develop our *SoTL Implementation and Impact Framework*. We therefore welcome interest from others who wish to be involved in this process. While our focus has been primarily in the English sector, we understand that the issues that we have raised and discussed have global relevance. The requirement for evidence of impact is at the heart of effective SoTL, and in this chapter we have offered a potential map to support these future developments for the wider benefits of SoTL and of learning and teaching.

CONCLUSION

To conclude, we return to the recommendations of Blackmore and Kandiko (2012) who noted the need to ensure that flexible and practical evaluation approaches are built in from the beginning of any project or change initiative. We acknowledge that there are always challenges in adopting a holistic approach to evaluating change, at a range of levels, in large and complex organisations. One key challenge can be the lack of a suitable generic framework with which to identify factors that can influence success and through which organisational alignment and impact can be evidenced.

The pilot Framework presented in this chapter can help to fill this gap. It offers a consistent approach that can be employed at a range of small scale and cross-institutional levels—with each responding to a consistent set of prompts and questions. As such, each SoTL project would not have to develop its own methodologies for demonstrating impact and change but would use an agreed approach (and templates) which would ensure alignment with strategic priorities across all elements of the HEP. This has the added benefit of efficiencies with respect to time and communication and provides a wealth of ready and consistently-aligned evidence for a range of internal and external reporting processes.

While there is limited literature to date reporting on how the M7S framework can be applied in the context of institutional change within HEPs (McLinden et al., 2019), this chapter indicates how a slightly adapted version offers an opportunity to evidence alignment among a project and the respective elements of an organisation. Our emergent *SoTL Strategic Implementation and Impact Framework* illustrates how, in explicitly aligning to all seven elements of the M7S framework over time, any research, evaluation, or development activities—even those that appear very localised and small scale—can quickly demonstrate (and grow) their alignment with, connection to, and importance for, the HEP as a whole. In doing so, they can additionally become part of a growing map of SoTL-based evidence for, strategically aligned educational transformation.

REFERENCES

Blackmore, P. (2016a) Why research trumps teaching and what can be done about it. In P. Blackmore, R. Blackwell & M. Edmondson (Eds.), *Tackling wicked issues: Prestige, employment outcomes, and the Teaching Excellence Framework*. HEPI Occasional Paper 14. Retrieved from http://www.hepi.ac.uk/wp-content/uploads/2016/09/Hepi_TTWI-Web.pdf

Blackmore, P. (2016b). *Prestige in academic life: Excellence and exclusion*. London: Routledge.

Blackmore, P., & Kandiko, C. (2012). *Strategic curriculum change in universities: Global trends*. London: Routledge / SRHE. doi:10.4324/9780203111628

Competition & Markets Authority. (2015). *Undergraduate students: Your consumer rights*. Retrieved from: https://assets.publishing.service.gov.uk/government/uploads/system/uploads/attachment_data/file/411288/Students_consumer_rights_60ss.pdf

Conservative Party. (2015). *Strong leadership. A clear economic plan. A brighter, more secure future*. Retrieved from https://www.conservatives.com/manifesto2015

Cooke-Sather, A., Bovill, C., & Felten, P. (2014). *Engaging students as partners in learning and teaching: A guide for faculty*. San Francisco, CA: Jossey-Bass.

Fanghanel, J., Prichard, J., Potter, J., & Wisker, G. (2016). *Defining and supporting the Scholarship of Teaching and Learning (SoTL): A sector-wide study. Executive summary*. Retrieved from: https://www.heacademy.ac.uk/knowledge-hub/defining-and-supporting-scholarship-teaching-and-learning-sotl-sector-wide-study

Government, H. M. (2017). *Higher Education and Research Act*. Retrieved from http://www.legislation.gov.uk/ukpga/2017/29/contents/enacted

Graduate Outcomes. (2019). *About the survey*. Retrieved from: https://www.graduateoutcomes.ac.uk/about-survey

Healey, M. (2003). The scholarship of teaching: Issues around an evolving concept. *Journal on Excellence in College Teaching, 14*(2/3), 5–26.

Healey, M., Flint, A., & Harrington, K. (2014). *Engagement through partnership: Students as partners in learning and teaching in higher education*. York, UK: HEA. Retrieved from https://www.heacademy.ac.uk/knowledge-hub/engagement-through-partnership-students-partners-learning-and-teaching-higher

Husbands, C. (2017). Foreword: Ten TEF Lessons. In *Going for gold: Lessons from the TEF provider submissions*. Higher Education Policy Institute Report 99. Retrieved from: https://www.hepi.ac.uk/wp-content/uploads/2017/10/FINAL-HEPI-Going-for-Gold-Report-99-04_10_17-Screen.pdf

Institute for Apprenticeships. (2018). *Academic professional standard*. Retrieved from: https://www.instituteforapprenticeships.org/apprenticeship-standards/academic-professional/

May, H., & Bridger, K. (2010). *Developing and embedding inclusive policy and practice in higher education*. York, UK: The Higher Education Academy.

McKinney, K. (2006). Attitudinal and structural factors contributing to challenges in the work of the Scholarship of Teaching and Learning. *New Directions for Institutional Research, 2006*(129), 37–50. doi:10.1002/ir.170

McLinden, M., Cleaver, E., & Lintern, M. (2018). Developing and promoting a culture of critical enquiry within higher education: some final reflections. In E. Cleaver, M. Lintern, & M. McLinden (Eds.), *Teaching and Learning in Higher Education: Disciplinary Approaches to Educational Enquiry.* London: Sage.

McLinden, M., Grove, M., Green, J., & Birch, A. (2019). Developing and embedding inclusive policy and practice within higher-education institutions. In K. M. Krcmar (Ed.), *The inclusivity gap: Expectations and delivery in higher education.* Aberdeen, UK: Inspired by Learning.

Moore, J., Highham, L., & Sanders, J. (2017). *Evidencing teaching excellence analysis of the Teaching Excellence Framework (TEF2) provider submissions.* York, UK: HEA. Retrieved from: https://www.heacademy.ac.uk/system/files/hub/download/TEF2%20Provider%20Submissions%20Review_2.pdf

Morgan, H., & Houghton, A. (2011). *Inclusive curriculum design in higher education. Considerations for effective practice across and within subject areas.* York, UK: HEA. Retrieved from https://www.heacademy.ac.uk/system/files/resources/introduction_and_overview.pdf

OfS. (2019a). *TEF outcomes.* Retrieved from https://www.officeforstudents.org.uk/advice-and-guidance/teaching/tef-outcomes/#/tefoutcomes/

OfS. (2019b). *Value for money.* Retrieved from https://www.officeforstudents.org.uk/advice-and-guidance/student-wellbeing-and-protection/value-for-money/

OfS. (2019c). *What is the TEF?* Retrieved from https://www.officeforstudents.org.uk/advice-and-guidance/teaching/what-is-the-tef/

OfS. (2019d). *Guidance for providers for TEF year four. Video 1: What is the Teaching Excellence and Student Outcomes Framework.* Retrieved from: https://www.officeforstudents.org.uk/advice-and-guidance/teaching/tef-year-four/guidance-for-providers/

OfS. (2019e). *Graduate earnings data on Unistats from the Longitudinal Education Outcomes (LEO) data.* Retrieved from: https://www.officeforstudents.org.uk/data-and-analysis/graduate-earnings-data-on-unistats/

OfS. (2019f). *TEF Outcomes: The Conservertoire for Dance and Drama.* Retrieved from: https://apps.officeforstudents.org.uk/tefoutcomes2019/docs/submissions/Submission_10001653.pdf

Pascale, R. T., & Athos, A. G. (1981). *The art of Japanese management.* London: Allen Lane. doi:10.1016/0007-6813(81)90032-X

REF. (2019). *What is the REF?* Retrieved from https://www.ref.ac.uk/about/what-is-the-ref/

Shulman, L. S. (1993). Teaching as community property: Putting an end to pedagogical solitude. *Change, 25*(6), 6–7. doi:10.1080/00091383.1993.9938465

ADDITIONAL READING

McLinden, M., Grove, M., Green, J., & Birch, A. (2019). Developing and embedding inclusive policy and practice within higher-education institutions. In K. M. Krcmar (Ed.), *The inclusivity gap: Expectations and delivery in higher education*. Aberdeen, UK: Inspired by Learning.

KEY TERMS AND DEFINITIONS

Higher Education Provider (HEP): The current collective terminology for universities and other institutions that provide forms of higher education in England, used by the Office for Students.

Office for Students: The national regulator for English higher education, formed following the dissolution of the Higher Education Funding Council for England (HEFCE) as a result of the Higher Education and Research Act (HM Government, 2017).

Research Excellence Framework or REF: An exercise assessing the quality of research in the UK which aims to provide accountability for public investment in research and produce evidence of the benefits of this investment, to provide benchmarking information, and to establish reputational yardsticks for use within the HE sector and for public information and to inform the selective allocation of funding for research (REF, 2019).

Teaching Excellence and Student Outcomes Framework or TEF: A national exercise run by England's Office for Students, created to assess excellence in teaching at universities and colleges and how well they ensure excellent outcomes for their students in terms of graduate-level employment or further study.

ENDNOTES

[1] In this chapter we use the English meaning of the term faculty (a meso-level organisational structure within an HEP e.g. the Faculty of Arts and Social Sciences) rather than the American English meaning (i.e. faculty as a descriptor of instructional staff members of the HEP).

[2] The Destination of Leavers from Higher Education Survey data is soon to be replaced by the Graduate Outcomes Survey (Graduate Outcomes, 2019) and further experimental work is being undertaken with regard to a study of Longitudinal Educational Outcomes (OfS, 2019e).

[3] Importantly, the layout and length of the institutional written submission is the choice of each institution. Some are very succinct, some contain images, and others fill the full fifteen pages with text. For example the Conservertoire for Dance and Drama chose to submit a descriptive half page submission (see OfS, 2019f).

[4] TEF Year 2 was the first year in which HEPs completed written provider statements. At this point HEPs were not required to participate. TEF submissions are now a compulsory condition of registration with the Office for Students in England.

Section 2
SoTL as a Form of Professional Development

This section is dedicated to chapters reflecting how SoTL is practiced as a form of faculty professional development. Chapter 3 focuses on how educational development can take place in different contexts and, subsequently, how SoTL is integrated into these different structures. Chapters 4 and 5 focus on the collaborative nature of SoTL inquiry as a form of faculty co-development. The following chapter focuses on reflection, specifically how reflection is used prior to and during a SoTL inquiry. Finally, this section concludes with a chapter that specifically explores the role of non-standard faculty and how SoTL can help them better their practice.

Chapter 3
Structures and Considerations for SoTL Educational Development

Jennifer C. Friberg
Illinois State University, USA

Lauren Scharff
iD https://orcid.org/0000-0003-4961-6538
U.S. Air Force Academy, USA

ABSTRACT

Colleges and universities around the world share a broad focus on education. However, unique characteristics and priorities across institutions may lead to vastly different educational development opportunities for the Scholarship of Teaching and Learning (SoTL) and levels of impact for the SoTL efforts (e.g., micro, meso, macro, mega). This chapter is organized in two distinct parts. Part 1 examines five different structures typical for SoTL educational development with a focus on their organizational structure within the institution and the SoTL expertise of individuals who that lead these efforts. Strengths and limitations of each structure are presented. Part 2 provides a discussion of critical considerations that impact all SoTL educational development efforts regardless of the type of structure that exists within an institution.

INTRODUCTION

Educational development—and educational developers—can be viewed from a variety of perspectives and are impacted by numerous variables. Considered leaders in understanding teaching and learning in higher education, most educational developers work interactively with individual course instructors, academic departments, and other institutional groups or units to facilitate the use and understanding of effective pedagogical approaches. To accomplish this, educational developers represent a wide range of topic area specialties (i.e., online learning, culturally responsive teaching and learning, instructional design, embedded assessment) within the areas of teaching and learning. Increasingly across institu-

DOI: 10.4018/978-1-7998-2212-7.ch003

tions, some specialize in the Scholarship of Teaching and Learning (SoTL), developing programs to support research on teaching and learning. This chapter presents possible organizational structures for SoTL-focused educational development, along with important considerations for stakeholder groups with an interest in SoTL.

Unique characteristics and priorities across colleges and universities around the globe may lead to vastly different ways of doing the business of educational development. Many institutions have established structures for educational development that involve teaching and learning centers (TLCs) where students, staff, and faculty might learn about a variety of teaching and/or learning topics. Other institutions have smaller units or single individuals tasked with providing educational development to those interested in such opportunities. Lee (2010, p. 23) proposed a list of five basic organizational structures for educational development in higher education:

1. Centralized TLCs
2. An individual faculty member-leader, with or without a physical center
3. A committee that supports faculty development
4. A clearinghouse for programs and offerings
5. Structures that encompass more than one institution (system-wide offices)

Across each of these organizational structures, similar work occurs. Educational developers design and/or engage in workshops, consultations, classroom observations, orientations, grants/funding, faculty fellows, teaching circles, learning communities, research centered on teaching and learning, and external projects or collaborations. It should be noted, however, that the breadth and depth of programming these structures may offer to stakeholders varies depending on several factors: the institution type (e.g., comprehensive, research, liberal arts), the mission of the institution, resources allocated to the educational development unit (e.g., personnel, financial, space), and the interests and experiences of those affiliated with each structure (Lee, 2010).

Scholarship of Teaching and Learning as Part of Educational Development

SoTL both provides a foundation for many other education development efforts and receives inspiration from those other efforts. However, SoTL educational developers do not simply engage in SoTL research or serve as research mentors for others who engage in SoTL research. Specifically, Simmons and Taylor (2019) identify the primary work of SoTL educational developers as consisting of efforts to increase stakeholder interest in four distinct areas of focus: engagement, connection building, collaboration, and advocacy. Therefore, a SoTL educational developer might build capacity for SoTL through making connections with other institutional stakeholders to support SoTL work, providing resources for individuals/groups engaged in SoTL (e.g., consultations, trainings, support for travel/presentations/publication), developing small and large scale communities of stakeholders to support engagement in SoTL, and building a culture for SoTL across their institution. Cruz, Cunningham, Smentkowski, and Steiner (2019) developed a scaffold to extend the conventional work of SoTL educational developers to include mentorship in a developmental manner, arguing that in addition to the traditional roles of SoTL educational developers, it is incumbent upon individuals in such roles to provide scaffolded support to those engaged in SoTL, both novice and more veteran. Thus, the role of the SoTL educational developer encompasses a wide array of duties, and educational developers specializing in SoTL work with myriad

Table 1. Levels of impact, contexts, and routine activities of SoTL educational developers

Level of SoTL Impact	Context of SoTL Work	Routine Activities of SoTL Educational Developers
Micro	Individual or single course (potentially with multiple instructors)	• Assist in searching for sources of evidence to support specific pedagogical approaches. • Consult with faculty to develop and implement a research project to study teaching and/or learning in a particular context. • Assist in the ethics review process.
Meso	Academic department or program	• Provide resources and support to aid in curriculum development or redesign. • Support SoTL work at the program level or across sequential courses. • Integrate SoTL into departmental culture as a meaningful formative assessment. • Promote the value of SoTL as a meritorious form of scholarship, similar to disciplinary research.
Macro	Institution	• Provide workshops and resources available to stakeholders across the institution. • Encourage faculty/staff to include and engage students as partners in SoTL work. • Explain SoTL's potential applications for program review, accreditation, and institutional assessment efforts. • Advocate for SoTL as a meritorious form of scholarship in the processes of promotion and tenure. • Create venues for recognition of SoTL research at the institutional level (research presentations, awards, other highlights).
Mega	Beyond the single institution	• Volunteer for roles in SoTL professional societies and organizations. • Collaborate with other educational developers to develop programming and other resources. • Aid in the establishment of multi-institutional SoTL projects and initiatives.

stakeholders to mentor, engage in, and advocate for SoTL. As with the other areas of educational development, how SoTL is situated and supported within an institution will directly impact the breadth and depth of the SoTL educational development effort.

A variety of scholars have discussed the "4M" framework for conceptualizing the impact of SoTL work across different contexts: micro (individual/classroom), meso (department/ program), macro (institutional), and mega (beyond a single institution) (Poole & Simmons, 2013; Simmons, 2016). Primarily, these levels of impact have been applied to the research of SoTL scholars themselves, rather than to broader array of efforts in which SoTL educational developers routinely engage (Simmons & Taylor, 2019). That said, the 4M model is a framework that can easily describe the multitude of ways in which a SoTL educational developer might impact various contexts. Table 1 provides several examples of the potential impact of SoTL educational development.

Recognizing the potential impact of SoTL educational developers, it is important to understand the various structures wherein SoTL educational development might occur. The following section of this chapter will examine five different structures typical for SoTL educational development, with a focus on the individuals and campus units that might lead these efforts. Subsequently, a discussion related to critical factors that impact all SoTL educational development structures will be undertaken to identify uniform considerations for all SoTL educational development.

Figure 1. Structures for SoTL educational development

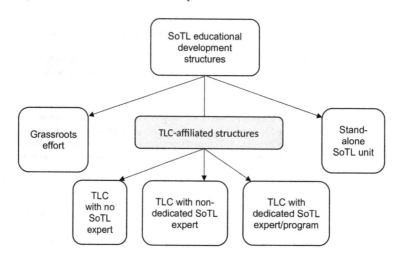

POTENTIAL STRUCTURES FOR SoTL EDUCATIONAL DEVELOPMENT

At the core of the broad range of activities given for SoTL educational developers in Table 1 is a focus on research on teaching and learning; however, as mentioned previously, the size and impact of SoTL educational development at any institution is tied directly to its priorities, values, and needs. Institutions that value teaching and learning scholarship tend to allocate more resources to SoTL educational development efforts than those that either place less importance on such endeavors or that have not yet explicitly established an institutional priority for such work. To that end, some institutions offer a robust SoTL educational development presence, while others have none or are in the process of developing such units/efforts.

Across institutions engaged in SoTL educational development, there are a collection of specific structures that characterize the ways in which this work is being done, each of which has the potential to impact SoTL across a variety of stakeholders and levels (micro, meso, macro, mega). These are organized differently within each institution and may exist within or outside of a TLC. Figure 1 presents five structures that describe the bulk of SoTL educational development routinely observed in higher education. Two exist separately from a TLC: Grassroots efforts and stand-alone SoTL units. The remaining three, TLC with no SoTL expert, TLC with non-dedicated SoTL expert, and TLC with dedicated SoTL expert/program, are collaborations with campus TLCs, which for the purposes of this work, we define as having at least one full-time staff member tasked with educational development responsibilities.

Below we describe how an institution might structure or grow each of these types of SoTL educational development unit, from the most informal (grassroots effort) to the most formal (stand-alone SoTL unit). Descriptions for each structure explain its organization, necessary personnel, and processes inherent to that structure. Note that when the term "SoTL expert" is used, it refers to someone who, in addition to possessing knowledge of evidence-based pedagogies, also has a broad understanding of different research designs, methods, data sources, and analysis schemes.

Grassroots Effort not Tied to Institutional Structure

Most typically seen at institutions with an emerging interest in SoTL, this educational development structure might be best characterized as a grassroots effort, with faculty and/or staff seeking like-minded stakeholders to identify resources for learning about and supporting SoTL within that institution's context. Typically, these individuals are not trained as educational developers, but rather, have a deep interest in learning more about evidence-based teaching and learning that guides their efforts. They might have been inspired by SoTL research they saw presented at a conference or by efforts they've heard about from colleagues at other institutions. Although a unit or center related to teaching and learning or faculty-development might exist at their institution, its mission would not provide any clear connection to SoTL efforts. For instance, a teaching and learning resource center might exist on a campus with a relatively narrow mission to support those using online course management systems or diversity and inclusive-instruction.

In the absence of an institutional structure, individuals or groups of SoTL-interested stakeholders take the lead to form informal Communities of Practice to provide support and peer mentorship for applying SoTL or to develop individual or collaborative SoTL projects. These types of efforts operate predominantly at the micro level of impact. However, it might also reach into the mega level as well, as it is common for faculty/staff engaged in grassroots SoTL efforts to seek support from two groups of individuals external to their institution: 1) broad-based educational developers with expertise in supporting teaching and learning, or 2) SoTL experts identified through professional societies, conferences, or social media who provide mentorship to sustain and extend the SoTL work being initiated on campus. Those leading the grassroots efforts might also engage in SoTL professional development opportunities at nearby institutions or online.

Strengths and Limitations of This Type of Structure

The hallmark strength of this type of SoTL educational development structure lies in its genesis: stakeholder excitement and engagement in research on teaching and learning. Grassroots efforts can be very successful in initiating institutional innovations, with faculty, staff, and/or students adopting the role of change agent, demonstrating "passion and on-the-ground substantive knowledge to move SoTL forward" (Ginsberg & Bernstein, 2011, p. 4). Leaders in this type of SoTL educational development structure become mentors to other faculty, staff, and students, in turn growing the SoTL culture within an institution. Over time, those engaged in this work gradually build the capacity for SoTL to become more visible on their campuses, leading to a variety of potentially positive outcomes: use of evidence-based pedagogies to support student learning, increased administrative support for SoTL, expanded faculty/staff/student engagement in SoTL, potential partnerships with institutional partners to seek sources of support for SoTL work, or even the establishment of a more formal institutional SoTL support structure.

The fact that this structure for SoTL educational development is a grassroots movement and not driven by administrative initiative may be its biggest challenge. Loose structures such as these generally offer limited programming and reach due to a lack of personnel and/or financial resources. However, they can increase offerings and impact by seeking out sources of support for their efforts, perhaps by aligning with other campus partners or initiatives to encourage stakeholder buy-in, completion of SoTL projects, and the attainment of additional resources to support future SoTL initiatives. Unfortunately, the long-term sustainability of this type of SoTL educational development structure is questionable, as the stakeholder leaders of such groups generally engage in these efforts on top of their regular work duties and without tangible support from the institution.

Teaching and Learning Center (TLC) Structures

This type of educational development structure places all programming within one broad campus unit with oversight for multiple aspects of educational development for that institution (e.g., educational technology, instructional design, embedded assessment). Typically led by a director or coordinator with expertise in pedagogy as well as adult education/professional development, TLCs may employ additional personnel for program planning and instructional technology development/maintenance, though the number and types of employees varies widely based on institutional context and priorities. While not all TLCs provide educational development opportunities focused on SoTL, many do, and this can be viewed as a strength for SoTL across an institution in a variety of ways. We identify three subtypes of this structure with respect to how SoTL educational development is housed within the existing TLC: no SoTL expert, non-dedicated SoTL expert, and dedicated SoTL expert/program.

Regardless of subtype, the biggest benefit to SoTL educational development structures housed within a TLC is their affiliation with a formally recognized and institutionally-supported entity. The importance of partnership with a TLC is directly tied to the availability of resources that promote SoTL across an institution. In some cases, TLCs offering SoTL educational development have resources to provide grants or small stipends to faculty, staff, or students engaged in SoTL work. In terms of visibility, an established campus unit such as a TLC generally has ways to communicate with faculty, staff, and students across the institution to bring awareness of SoTL opportunities and appeal to a wide variety of individuals who might be interested in SoTL educational development. Finally, as TLC staff have interactions with administration, program directors, and leaders of other campus units, discussions about the value of SoTL work can be integrated more easily into important conversations about teaching, learning, and research, with the potential to positively impact perceptions of faculty productivity and student engagement in SoTL research. Thus, TLC-based SoTL educational development is able to operate at the micro, meso, and macro levels, and depending upon the SoTL effort leader's initiative, can also operate at the mega level. However, the availability of these potential benefits of being housed within a TLC and the direct support for SoTL researchers (e.g., mentoring with research design and ethics review) will vary based on the subtype of structure, as described below.

TLC Without a SoTL Expert

With this institutional structure, SoTL educational development is housed within a TLC, but lacks coordination by a SoTL expert. Rather, educational developers with expertise in other aspects of teaching and learning provide general support for SoTL to interested stakeholders. Institutions with these SoTL educational development structures indicate some value for SoTL and find it important to share with their campus stakeholders; however, allocating resources to employ a SoTL expert is not possible due to TLC or institutional priorities, lack of financial resources to hire a specialized educational developer, or an inability to secure an individual to fill that role on a given campus.

In the absence of a SoTL expert within the TLC, educational development efforts centered on SoTL typically focus on facilitating efforts to find and locate resources that support SoTL-involved stakeholders, rather than directly guiding and mentoring SoTL research. This general approach for support is largely due to the fact that, while non-SoTL-expert educational developers demonstrate a broad understanding of evidence-based teaching and learning and use SoTL to inform their work with faculty and staff engaged in course design and implementation, they often have not personally engaged in an active SoTL research agenda nor do they have foundational expertise in research methodology and data analysis. Thus, their efforts might be limited to providing introductory workshops about SoTL, sponsoring of teaching/learning communities for SoTL scholars, and providing assistance in establishing connections to other campus units that might support the work of SoTL scholars (e.g., research units, ethics review, libraries, student groups, and administration).

It is not uncommon for external SoTL experts to help provide or design SoTL programming in this subtype of TLC-housed SoTL educational development. External experts can extend the general SoTL support that non-expert educational developers provide, especially with respect to the more direct research design and analysis. However, their ability to help with ethics review is limited, as ethics review processes are typically idiosyncratic to individual institutions. External SoTL experts can also assist with ideas for sharing SoTL and engaging in SoTL advocacy to further support SoTL-involved campus stakeholders that might be less intuitive to non-SoTL educational developers.

Strengths and Limitations of this Type of Structure

The primary strength of this subtype of TLC-housed SoTL educational development is that SoTL is a recognized effort within an institutionally supported structure, which indicates that the TLC (and perhaps the institution at large) recognizes the merits of encouraging faculty, staff, and students to be active researchers in teaching and learning. While the programming might be limited to more general aspects of support, even that can be enough to facilitate interest and initial efforts in SoTL. Further, the center likely has broader formal reach and communication channels than grassroots efforts structures are able to access. Finally, SoTL researchers may also have access to funding from a TLC's budget to conduct and present SoTL research or to partner with external SoTL experts to design and promote more advanced programming in SoTL.

The fundamental weakness of this model is that when SoTL educational development is implemented by an individual without expertise this type of scholarship, there is the potential for programming and/ or mentoring to lack the complexity needed to adequately support those engaged in learning about or conducting SoTL. Added to that, an institution's non-expert SoTL educational developers will have competing professional responsibilities within a TLC separate from SoTL, which may limit the reach and impact of SoTL programming offered. These weakness can be partially alleviated with the help of external SoTL experts; however, such individuals are situated outside of the institutional context and may not be readily accessible when needed. Additionally, external SoTL experts may not be attuned to aspects of institutional culture (e.g., perceptions of SoTL, institutional mission/strategic objectives) that might impact the SoTL work done on a specific campus.

TLC with a Non-dedicated SoTL Expert

It is not uncommon for TLCs to have at least one educational developer with expertise in SoTL as well as in other areas of teaching/learning pedagogy. As these individuals serve a variety of programming needs within a TLC, they are not able to serve solely in the role of SoTL educational developer. However, in addition to the general SoTL support that could be provided by the non-SoTL expert, these individuals can also provide more direct mentoring in research development and analysis of data. Because of their expertise with SoTL, they are also better equipped to advocate for SoTL within the broader institutional context.

Strengths and Limitations of this Type of Structure

Having the knowledge and skills of an "in house" SoTL expert is a tremendous strength of this educational development structure, as faculty, staff, and students seeking support for any aspect of SoTL have access to an individual capable of providing such services within their own institution. As SoTL experts possess a broad understanding of different research designs, methods, data sources, analysis schemes, and ways to share scholarly work that a non-expert might lack, SoTL stakeholders with access to an expert in SoTL educational development have an advantage in understanding SoTL and developing high quality scholarship focused on issues germane to teaching and learning. Additionally, a SoTL expert understands needs for advocacy for SoTL work that non-experts might lack. For these reasons, a SoTL expert within a TLC can be an active voice to support the value of the SoTL work being conducted on a campus.

The main limitation of a SoTL educational development structure with a non-dedicated SoTL expert is that programming and support for SoTL stakeholders might be constrained by competing responsibilities. The role of an educational developer is complex and time consuming, with each responsibility requiring non-trivial amounts of time and focus to detail. SoTL experts with other duties have to juggle tasks and projects, which might limit the scope of support they can provide for SoTL-related work. For this reason, campuses with greater demand for SoTL support might struggle with the limitations inherent to this structure.

TLC with a Dedicated SoTL Expert/Program

In this structure, a dedicated SoTL expert housed within the TLC is available to work with individuals interested in engaging in SoTL as well as to coordinate all aspects of SoTL programming and advocacy. SoTL-focused support and programming are clearly apparent in the center offerings and part of the center's strategic planning. Two variations of this subtype exist: 1) the SoTL expert may lead all these efforts as part of their named position, with programming and research completely reliant on TLC budget and resources, or 2) they may be the director of a more formally established program under the TLC umbrella that has its own budget and resources for at least some aspects of the SoTL programming/work. The latter subtype might come about due to external donations specifically targeting SoTL work, or to recognition by the TLC or institutional leadership that SoTL might require ongoing, dedicated funding to provide opportunities such as yearly research fellowships.

Strengths and Limitations of this Type of Structure

There are several strengths to having a dedicated SoTL expert/program within a TLC. The dedicated nature of the expert/program sends a clear message regarding the positive value of SoTL at that institution. These SoTL experts are less likely to have major job responsibilities in other areas of educational development, which will decrease interference with their ability to provide support for SoTL programming and research. Because they are housed within a TLC, dedicated SoTL experts can still be part of the overall TLC team, which is comprised of other teaching and learning professionals who can help brainstorm ideas for programming and provide logistical support at SoTL events. The TLC infrastructure itself can provide access to established institutional communication channels to promote SoTL events and awareness, and to senior leadership to advocate for TLC programs, including SoTL. If the program has some level of independent funding, the impact of the typical fluctuations in budget that may occur across fiscal years in higher education can be reduced and give the program greater autonomy.

On the less positive side, although not as demanding as when there is no dedicated SoTL expert, dedicated SoTL experts within a TLC are expected to be part of the overall TLC team, which means there are some general TLC responsibilities that would pull time or resources from SoTL efforts (e.g., providing reciprocal support for other TLC events, de-conflicting with other TLC programming). Further, due to the embedded nature of SoTL within the TLC, the SoTL planning will be shaped by the strategic initiatives of the TLC at large and potentially be limited by the sharing of resources and monies.

Stand-alone SoTL Unit

Though not as common, there are institutions that have established campus units to provide SoTL educational development separate from any existing TLC or other campus entity. These SoTL units are typically independent in budget (often due to an endowment) and leadership, and are developed to focus solely on fostering, scaffolding, and advocating for SoTL within (and sometimes beyond) that institution. SoTL educational developers with this type of structure are likely to operate at all levels of the 4Ms, especially if part of the mission of the center is to build external engagement and reputation as well as internal responsibilities.

Stand-alone SoTL educational development units offer programming similar to TLCs, but with all programming targeting SoTL-focused topics. One important advantage to having an established stand-alone SoTL unit is the ability to create and operationalize strategic objectives focused exclusively on SoTL, largely eliminating competing priorities for other areas of educational development that might adversely impact the delivery of SoTL-focused opportunities for campus stakeholders. Due to this sole attention on research on teaching and learning, some stand-alone SoTL educational development units are able to benefit from an advantageous administrative reporting structure that can bolster the perceptions of SoTL on a given campus. For example, SoTL educational development units that report to an institution's chief research officer or vice provost for research benefit from the clear recognition of SoTL as a valued form of research.

Many of the opportunities offered within stand-alone SoTL educational development units mirror those outlined above for dedicated SoTL expert/program (e.g., establishment of named awards, robust trainings, involvement in a campus teaching/learning symposium). That said, with the ability to focus exclusively -- and with autonomy -- on SoTL educational development, many stand-alone SoTL units have the capacity to develop initiatives for SoTL scholars that other structures may lack the resources to offer, such as large-scale research grants, internal peer-reviewed publications, incentives for presenting/publishing SoTL work, creation of a SoTL resource group to serve as advisors for the unit and peer mentors for novice SoTL scholars, development of a certificate program for graduate students interested in SoTL, and so forth. There is always at least one SoTL expert connected with a stand-alone SoTL unit, typically as the leader. Beyond that, stand-alone SoTL units may employ additional SoTL experts as educational developers, depending on the unique contexts and priorities within an institution.

Strengths and Limitations of this Type of Structure

The presence of a stand-alone SoTL unit has several notable benefits. Primary amongst these is that its presence signals strong institutional support for SoTL, as resources (e.g., budget and multiple personnel) have been allocated to the facilitation of SoTL educational development. The value of autonomy cannot be overlooked as a huge strength of this structure. The ability for a SoTL unit to exist apart from other campus entities provides freedom that cannot be realized within other structures, as combining SoTL educational development with broader teaching/learning support offered by a TLC results in the need to share personnel, budget, and other resources. Further, integration with a TLC can sometimes dilute the felt presence of SoTL, as stakeholders often inadvertently mesh SoTL with other aspects of faculty development.

Ironically, one of the main limitations of having a stand-alone SoTL unit is the flip side of the strengths listed in the previous paragraph: autonomy means that SoTL educational development leaders cannot easily leverage resources from a TLC to support their work. TLCs, as broad specialists in teaching and learning, generally enjoy a larger clientele for trainings and workshops. Thus, SoTL educational developers who are affiliated with TLCs have the ability to reach those who access the TLC for other programming by being part of the same unit. In contrast, stand-alone SoTL units must develop their own unique ways of reaching stakeholders who have not chosen to interact with their SoTL center. Additionally, while programming collaborations are possible between TLCs and stand-alone SoTL educational units, these become more complex with issues of leadership, budget, and responsibility for administrative duties to consider.

Considerations Across SoTL Educational Development Structures

The above descriptions differentiate five types of SoTL educational development structures. While it is evident that each shares a focus on providing support to encourage and promote SoTL within an institutional context, obvious differences exist across each structure type that may affect the depth, breadth, and impact of work that is able to be accomplished. That said, SoTL educational developers, no matter the structure or organization of their efforts, may benefit from examining the following considerations in order to maximize the impact of their work:

Promoting SoTL as Meritorious Work

As SoTL leaders in higher education, SoTL educational developers can impact how campus stakeholders perceive SoTL and its contributions to an institution, primarily through formal and informal conversations with individuals and groups who influence campus culture. As stated previously, SoTL is considered differently across institutional contexts. Many believe that variances in perception of and value for SoTL occur because scholarly work in teaching and learning often looks different than research that many academics are accustomed to producing or reading within their disciplines (Poole, 2013). SoTL is conducted across disciplines using a multitude of methodologies. Further, in doing SoTL, course instructors often study their own students, leading some who are unfamiliar with SoTL to question its rigor (McKinney, 2015).

Evidence of how perceptions of SoTL vacillate from one institution to the next can be seen by looking at reward structures for engaging in SoTL. For example, in making promotion and tenure determinations, some institutions consider SoTL to be an example of teaching productivity, while others count it as meritorious scholarship. Consider the following statement from Iowa State University's Faculty Handbook (2016) that clearly acknowledges the expectation of evidence-informed (scholarly) teaching and the value placed on SoTL as meritorious research:

While SoTL may be an important part of the promotion and tenure process, it should not displace high quality scholarly teaching in annual performance reviews and in promotion and tenure decisions. Although faculty should engage in scholarly teaching, not all faculty need to engage in SoTL...If a faculty member chooses to pursue SoTL, this work is part of their scholarship/creative activity/research responsibilities. (p. 62)

Statements such as these position SoTL well within an institutional context and clearly place merit on research on teaching and learning. Similar positive and negative messages are conveyed to the campus community based on how SoTL is or is not recognized beyond being part of tenure and promotion. For example, the existence of SoTL-related campus-wide awards, research showcase events such as institution-wide poster sessions and presentations, research/travel grants, research fellowships, and so forth send a clear message of value and support. The explicitly communicated support of SoTL by senior leaders and department heads also sends powerful messages of value and encouragement for engagement in SoTL.

Understanding that the way SoTL is recognized will impact its perceived value, advocacy for SoTL becomes an important function of SoTL educational development (McKinney, 2007; Friberg & McKinney, 2019). SoTL educational developers are amongst the most qualified individuals on any campus to provide institutional-wide advocacy for SoTL and for SoTL scholars. They can affect change by systematically educating relevant stakeholders as to what SoTL is, the purpose it serves, and its potential positive impact for students and faculty on campus. Therefore, SoTL educational development is not limited to the practice of supporting interested stakeholders who wish to engage in SoTL, it also subsumes educating those not yet aware of SoTL, as well. The next section, focused on the development of strategic internal partnerships, explores this notion in greater depth.

Development of Strategic Internal Partnerships

Often, SoTL educational development units function quietly within an institution, providing opportunities for SoTL-interested faculty, staff, and students to engage in and share their work with others, but in a manner that is disconnected with the larger campus community. While this approach to educational development may be effective in supporting small groups of stakeholders who have sought out SoTL on their own, it fails to take advantage of opportunities to bring awareness of SoTL to new potential SoTL stakeholders, which limits growth of SoTL-related efforts. Key to broadening participation in and appreciation for SoTL within an institution are collaborations with other campus groups and/or units.

Consider the following examples of internal strategic partnerships for the SoTL educational developer:

- **Individual academic programs' promotion and tenure committees**. Consultation with such groups about the purpose, nature, and rigor of SoTL can promote SoTL being viewed positively, even though the methods used, variables studied, and outcomes might look very different from traditional disciplinary research. Every conversation a SoTL educational developer has with a member of a promotion and tenure committee is an opportunity for strategic advocacy to support the SoTL scholars within an institution.

- **Academic Senates**. These groups are considered to be the governing academic body in institutions with systems of shared faculty governance. Academic Senates maintain faculty handbooks that delineate expectations for faculty productivity in terms of teaching, service, and scholarship. The voice of a SoTL educational developer in such a body has the potential to broadly advocate for SoTL to be viewed with merit and as scholarly work.

- **Strategic planning committees**. Most colleges and universities have developed and implemented a strategic plan outlining the mission, vision, values, and next steps for an institution. The explicit mention of SoTL or evidence-based teaching in a strategic plan sends an important message related to the value of SoTL to the campus community, which might lead to increased interest in SoTL educational development opportunities. Such mentions are more likely to occur if SoTL educational developers participate in or collaborate with these committees.

- **Research ethics boards**. Active engagement with this institutional group helps implement review processes supportive of SoTL research, which tends to fall in the low-risk category, while still being protective of human subjects. Additionally, SoTL educational developer input into ethics processes also further legitimizes SoTL as rigorous research following similar oversight processes required for disciplinary research.

- **Research and grants office**. This office has broad reach and typically is associated with traditionally-valued, disciplinary research endeavors. Working with this office to have SoTL included as part of the institution's recognized research centers and programs will increase SoTL's legitimacy alongside disciplinary research.

- **Assessment and accreditation committees**. Assessment and SoTL can be distinguished by how their data are used (to support internal program review and improvements versus to contribute to the broader literature and understanding about teaching and learning, respectively). However, the underlying data can often be the same for the two efforts (e.g., measures of student performance and attitudes) and the goals for both relate to understanding teaching and learning. Thus, in some cases SoTL and assessment efforts can be collaborative and beneficial with respect to shared effort, resources, and the promotion of perceived value for SoTL work (Hutchings, et al., 2013).

- **Administrative search committees**. Service on search committees for campus administration allows SoTL educational developers to advocate for the hiring of individuals who support SoTL and see value in its role within an institution.

- **Award review committees**. SoTL educational developers serving on institutional teaching or research award review committees can advocate for recognition of SoTL-productive faculty who have pursued work that improved not only their own teaching and research skills but also student learning.

- **New faculty orientation committees**. Sharing information about SoTL and SoTL opportunities with incoming new faculty represents an opportunity to not only grow the number of those engaged in SoTL, but to establish a foundational understanding of and appreciation for SoTL prior to faculty becoming embedded in their new disciplinary department. Further, early exposure to SoTL allows new faculty to understand how SoTL fits into an institution's culture.

- **Student programs**. Opportunities for SoTL exist outside the traditional disciplinary classroom, as learning is not isolated to a single context. There may be beneficial partnerships with campus units such as study abroad, honors programs, or other registered student organizations to engage in the study of student learning. These units can also share with students the benefits of involvement in SoTL experiences.

- **Student research coordinators**. In order to promote student participation in research as scholars, rather than just participants, SoTL educational developers can make connections to promote SoTL research for undergraduate and graduate research projects, including independent studies, capstones, theses, and dissertations (Felten et al., 2013; Cook-Sather, Bovill, & Felten, 2014).

Overall, any campus partnership that yields greater understanding of SoTL should be considered strategic and important because work towards building such relationships has the potential to improve the visibility of SoTL, stakeholder engagement in SoTL, and positive perceptions of SoTL across and beyond an institution.

Development of Strategic External Partnerships

Creating SoTL partnerships and networks external to the institution can advance the work of a SoTL educational development unit by providing new ideas, resources, and collaborations. While strategic external partnerships are typically established with other SoTL educational developers or with other SoTL scholars (e.g., at other higher education institutions or even in K-12 schools), they might include work with local civic units or businesses to support institutional SoTL efforts and develop collaborative projects and experiences for faculty and students. Sometimes external groups have funding to support specific types of efforts such as higher education STEM outreach with public schools, which could provide opportunities for SoTL in new contexts.

The most typical source of external partnerships stems from connections formed at professional conferences with faculty and staff from other institutions or through committee work for SoTL-related professional societies. SoTL educational developers might attend a wide spectrum of conferences, from smaller, regional SoTL conferences to large, international SoTL events. These SoTL conferences are typically cross-disciplinary in nature; however, SoTL educational developers also often attend disciplinary research or practice conferences, where conversations about SoTL focus around work in a single, professional area. External partnerships might also form with neighboring institutions due to geographical proximity, which makes it feasible for site visits and the sharing of invited speakers. Regardless of how the connections are formed, partnerships established from interactions with individuals external to a SoTL educational developer's own institution can lead to networking opportunities for sharing of ideas and resources or for future collaborations based on common interests and objectives (Draeger & Scharff, 2019). As indicated above, partnerships with external SoTL entities can be especially helpful for SoTL educational development structures that do not have access to a dedicated SoTL expert at their institution.

Disseminating SoTL

Ways of sharing SoTL are numerous and include a variety of possibilities: peer reviewed journal articles, books, edited volumes, conference presentations (internal or external), blogs, wikis, workshops, and other forms of creative representation. These latter forms of dissemination fall outside the conventional realm of scholarly publishing but represent a more public form of scholarship that is being championed by the International Society for the Scholarship of Teaching and Learning (Chick, 2019). Because SoTL scholars have so many possible venues for sharing their work, SoTL educational developers often provide support in a variety of ways to facilitate work towards dissemination, recognizing that there is no "right" way for SoTL to be shared. SoTL educational developers might consult with SoTL scholars to examine potential outlets for a given project, considering the scope of the project being shared as well as a range of possibilities and the positives and negatives of each. Those conversations may include reminders to consider disciplinary expectations for sharing research when disseminating SoTL, as recognition and reward structures for faculty tend to honor dissemination practices similar to those common to their disciplinary scholarship. Beyond this, SoTL educational developers might act as preliminary reviewers for SoTL work or suggest ways in which projects might be shared through more than one venue to extend the impact of a project beyond a single outlet.

Linked with considerations regarding type of dissemination are considerations regarding the audience. Typically, researchers' primary audience are fellow researchers. However, there are also audiences with whom SoTL can be shared that can provide an important form of visibility and advocacy for the SoTL work. Thus, SoTL educational developers should also consider ways SoTL might be disseminated more informally with internal and external stakeholders who might find SoTL useful, interesting, or valuable to their own roles and responsibilities on campus. The following represent a few possible audiences that move beyond that of other SoTL scholars:

- **Students**. SoTL research is conducted to better understand how or what students learn in particular teaching or learning contexts. Necessarily, students serve as participants for these projects; however, outcomes from these studies are rarely shared with students. This lack of communication constitutes a missed opportunity that would allow students to understand the project they were a part of (if participants), conceptualize outcomes that might help encourage their own evidence-based learning, or consider the possibility of involvement in SoTL as scholars rather than only as participants (Felten et al., 2019).
- **TLC-based educational developers**. Course instructors interact routinely with TLC-based educational developers to understand ways by which improvements in teaching might maximize student learning. To this end, the work done in most TLCs is centered on encouraging the application of already-published SoTL outcomes to inform the use of evidence-based pedagogies in the college classroom. By sharing ongoing, local SoTL research, outcomes, and trends with TLC personnel, SoTL educational developers help to bridge the theory-to-practice gap in the college classroom (Friberg, 2016).
- **Stakeholders not yet involved in SoTL**. SoTL educational developers have the opportunity to bring awareness of SoTL to individuals across an institution who are unaware of its existence, utility, or applications. Efforts to share SoTL outcomes or opportunities for SoTL via social media, print newsletters, listservs, and formal/informal conversations or presentations can bring a focus to SoTL that might not otherwise develop.
- **Interested community groups**. Individuals external to the institutional context may have unrealized interests in SoTL that could be uncovered through interaction with a SoTL educational developer/expert. Alumni groups are often excited to hear of campus initiatives focused on improving the student experience. Local business owners often have a vested interest in student learning, as new graduates become their future employees. Bringing SoTL to these external groups might encourage donors to come forward to sponsor awards, grants, gifts, or endowed chair positions to benefit SoTL educational development efforts.

CONCLUDING THOUGHTS AND CONSIDERATIONS FOR THE FUTURE

Every institution of higher education represents a unique SoTL context, with individual and varied missions, values, and priorities. SoTL educational development efforts are no less varied. This chapter identified five SoTL educational development structures and the impacts they might have across the 4M framework. It is important to note, however, that these structures are presented as organizational frameworks. In fact, the ways in which educational developers engage with SoTL-interested stakeholders varies greatly within these structure types, largely due to differences in priorities, programming, resources, and perceptions of value for SoTL. For that reason, what might be possible within one SoTL educational development structure might be impossible within another, a notion evident considering the strengths and weaknesses for each structure presented in this chapter.

Some may ask whether an optimal structure for SoTL educational development exists. The answer to this question is not entirely clear. What does seem evident is that having a dedicated SoTL expert, whether connected to a TLC or a stand-alone SoTL educational development unit, is most ideal for growing a strong, visible, and sustainable SoTL program within an institution. That said, any SoTL educational development efforts have the potential to make a positive impact. SoTL educational development -- and advocacy -- need to start somewhere. Grassroots efforts to grow a SoTL program have been the genesis of many formally established and institutionally encultured SoTL units that currently exist. In truth, grassroots efforts to build a foundation for SoTL may be more meaningful than if a SoTL educational development unit is suddenly dropped into an institutional context with little expressed interest or buy-in from relevant stakeholders.

Beyond the ideas already presented in this chapter is one final consideration. A variety of stakeholders take part in SoTL across institutional types and contexts. Typically, faculty have primarily been engaged in SoTL work, and they will continue to do so. However, there are changes in the SoTL movement that have brought new voices to research on teaching and learning. Students are now considered strategic partners in SoTL as co-inquirers rather than solely as subjects of SoTL research (Felten et al., 2013; Cook-Sather, Bovill, & Felten, 2014). Thus, SoTL educational developers must consider ways in which students -- as scholars -- can be part of their efforts to support SoTL within their institutions. Additionally, opportunities to build new and different strategic external partnerships are growing. Two-year colleges and other vocational programs are encouraging instructors to engage in SoTL (Ford & Peaslee, 2018). Cross-institutional SoTL collaborations are becoming more commonplace (Felten, Moore, & Peeples, 2019). SoTL educational developers within each of the various structures have the responsibility of responding to these changes and developing partnerships to support a broadening group of potential SoTL scholars.

REFERENCES

Chick, N. (2019). *SoTL as public scholarship*. Keynote address at the annual meeting of the International Society for the Scholarship of Teaching and Learning, Atlanta, GA.

Cook-Sather, A., Bovill, C., & Felten, P. (2014). *Engaging students as partners in learning and teaching*. San Francisco, CA: Jossey-Bass.

Cruz, L., Cunningham, K., Smentkowski, B., & Steiner, H. (2019). The SoTL scaffold: Supporting evidence-based teaching practice in educational development. *To Improve the Academy, 38*(1).

Draeger, J., & Scharff, L. (2019). Catalyzing the exchange and application of SoTL beyond the classroom: An analysis of two types of community spaces. In J. C. Friberg & K. McKinney (Eds.), *Applying SoTL beyond the individual classroom*. Bloomington, IN: Indiana University Press. doi:10.2307/j.ctvpb3w0t.10

Felten, P., Abbot, S., Kirkwood, J., Long, A., Lubicz-Nawrocka, T., Mercer-Mapstone, L., & Verwoord, R. (2019). Reimagining the place of students in academic development. *The International Journal for Academic Development*, 24(2), 192–203. doi:10.1080/1360144X.2019.1594235

Felten, P., Bagg, J., Bumbry, M., Hill, J., Hornsby, K., Pratt, M., & Weller, S. (2013). A call for expanding inclusive student engagement in SoTL. *Teaching & Learning Inquiry*, 1(2), 63–74. doi:10.20343/teachlearninqu.1.2.63

Felten, P., Moore, J. L., & Peeples, T. (2019). Multi-institutional SoTL: A case study of practices and outcomes. In J. C. Friberg & K. McKinney (Eds.), *Applying SoTL beyond the individual classroom*. Bloomington, IN: Indiana University Press. doi:10.2307/j.ctvpb3w0t.11

Ford, C., & Peaslee, D. (2018, February 26). A community college perspective on creating a SoTL scholars program [web log post]. Retrieved from https://illinoisstateuniversitysotl.wordpress.com/2018/02/26/a-community-college-perspective-on-creating-a-sotl-scholars-program/

Friberg, J. (2016, July 25). Knowing who we are [web log post]. Retrieved from https://illinoisstateuniversitysotl.wordpress.com/2016/07/25/knowing-who-we-are/

Friberg, J. C., & McKinney, K. (Eds.). (2019). *Applying SoTL beyond the individual classroom*. Bloomington, IN: Indiana University Press.

Ginsberg, S. M., & Bernstein, J. L. (2011, January). Growing the Scholarship of Teaching and Learning through institutional culture change. *The Journal of Scholarship of Teaching and Learning*, 11(1), 1–12.

Hutchings, P., Borin, P., Keesing-Styles, L., Martin, L., Michael, R., Scharff, L., ... Ismail, A. (2013). The Scholarship of Teaching and Learning in an age of accountability: Building bridges. *Teaching & Learning Inquiry*, 1(2), 35–47. doi:10.20343/teachlearninqu.1.2.35

Lee, V. S. (2010). Program types and prototypes. In K. J. Gillespie & D. L. Robertson (Eds.), *A guide to faculty development* (2nd ed.). San Francisco, CA: Jossey-Bass.

McKinney, K. (2007). *Enhancing learning through the Scholarship of Teaching and Learning: The challenges and joys of juggling*. Boston, MA: Anker.

McKinney, K. (2015, December 7). Is SoTL 'less rigorous' or simply 'different' than other research? The SoTL Advocate [weblog]. Downloaded from https://illinoisstateuniversitysotl.wordpress.com/2015/12/07/is-sotl-less-rigorous-or-simply-different-than-other-research/

Poole, G. (2013). Square one: What is research? In K. McKinney (Ed.), *The Scholarship of Teaching and Learning in and across the disciplines*. Bloomington, IN: Indiana University Press.

Poole, G., & Simmons, N. (2013). The contributions of the Scholarship of Teaching and Learning to quality enhancement in Canada. In G. Gordon & R. Land (Eds.), *Quality enhancement in higher education: International perspectives* (pp. 118–128). London: Routledge.

Simmons, N. (2016). The Scholarship of Teaching and Learning in Canada: Institutional impact. *New Directions for Teaching and Learning*, *146*, 95–102. doi:10.1002/tl.20192

Simmons, N., & Taylor, K. L. (2019). Leadership for the Scholarship of Teaching and Learning: Understanding bridges and gaps in practice. *The Canadian Journal for the Scholarship of Teaching and Learning*, *10*(1), 2. doi:10.5206/cjsotl-rcacea.2019.1.7995

Wuetherick, B., & Yu, S. (2016). The Canadian teaching commons: The Scholarship of Teaching and Learning in Canadian higher education. *New Directions for Teaching and Learning*, *2016*(146), 23–30. doi:10.1002/tl.20183

KEY TERMS AND DEFINITIONS

4M Framework: A scaffold for conceptualizing the impact of SoTL work across different contexts, including micro (individual/classroom), meso (department/program), macro (institutional), and mega (beyond a single institution).

Grassroots Effort: An informal SoTL educational development structure directed by volunteer faculty and/or staff to identify resources for learning about and supporting SoTL within that institution's context.

SoTL Expert: An individual who, in addition to possessing knowledge of evidence-based pedagogies, has a broad understanding of different research designs, methods, data sources, analysis schemes, etc.

Stand-Alone SoTL Unit: A SoTL educational development structure wherein a SoTL educational development unit exists separately from a teaching or learning center or other campus entity.

Teaching and Learning Center: Centers within an institution where students, staff, and faculty engage with educational developers to learn about a variety of teaching and/or learning topics including evidence-based pedagogies.

Teaching and Learning Center Structure With a Dedicated SoTL Expert/Program: A SoTL educational development structure led by a SoTL expert serving either as a full-time SoTL educational developer affiliated with a teaching and learning center or as the director of a more formally established SoTL program within the teaching and learning center.

Teaching and Learning Center Structure With a Non-Dedicated SoTL Expert: A SoTL educational development structure led by an educational developer with expertise in SoTL who does not serve solely in the role of SoTL educational developer.

Teaching and Learning Center Structure With No SoTL Expert: A SoTL educational development structure housed within a TLC coordinated by a non-expert educational developer who provides general support for SoTL to interested stakeholders.

Chapter 4
Making SoTL Stick:
Using a Community-Based Approach to Engage Faculty in the Scholarship of Teaching and Learning

Mandy Frake-Mistak
York University, Canada

Heidi L. Marsh
Humber College Institute of Technology and Advanced Learning, Canada

Geneviève Maheux-Pelletier
York University, Canada

Siobhan Williams
Humber College Institute of Technology and Advanced Learning, Canada

ABSTRACT

In this chapter, the authors share their reflections on the practice of using a community-based approach to doing SoTL research. They examine two professional development programs at their respective institutions—York University and Humber College in Ontario, Canada—that support faculty members' engagement in SoTL research. EduCATE and the Teaching Innovation Fund are two variations of SoTL programs in which participants come together to engage in and support each other through the process of doing SoTL research and are organized around participants' individual goals rather than a predetermined set of outcomes. The authors provide a fulsome narrative and reflective account of the EduCATE and Teaching Innovation Fund programs with a particular focus on each program's development and relative success. Throughout, the impact of SoTL as a form of professional development is emphasized.

INTRODUCTION

DOI: 10.4018/978-1-7998-2212-7.ch004

Now that educational development grounds itself in practice-based scholarship (Geertsema, 2016; Gibbs, 2013), much of this work is about generating knowledge that informs teaching and learning practices and about supporting faculty as they adopt more evidence-based, learning-centred approaches to their teaching. Because "academic teachers are better teachers if they pay close attention to their students' learning and reflect about and design teaching with the students' learning in focus" (Roxå & Mårtensson, 2009, p. 547), the Scholarship of Teaching and Learning (SoTL) has gained momentum in higher education. SoTL works double duty: it is a systematic, iterative, and reflective approach to teaching that ultimately contributes to improving student learning and provides an exciting path to explore new scholarly horizons that can lead to external recognition and career advancement. Hence, meaningfully supporting the Scholarship of Teaching and Learning is both tremendously important and daunting.

In their practice, educational developers deploy a wide range of strategies to support SoTL, from one-off workshops to informal small-group discussions and peer-based learning. When immediately relevant and practical, these strategies yield positive outcomes in overall participant satisfaction and self-reported changes in understanding, and, to various degrees, in attitudes and future intentions (Steinert et al., 2006). The question often becomes one of balance: how can educational developers offer context-rich and ambitious programs (Bamber, 2008) without overextending themselves, or creating "unrealistic demands on faculty already immersed in their discipline, already short on time" (Geertsema, 2016, p. 127)? It is the authors' belief that a sustainable way forward exists in adopting a peer-based approach to supporting and doing SoTL research.

In this chapter, reflections are offered of and on the practice of using a peer-based approach to doing SoTL research. In their respective institutions, the authors strive to engage faculty continuously with their own questions and interests (not predesigned workshops/events) and believe that using a peer-based approach can help them to achieve this. The authors examine two professional development programs that support faculty members' engagement in SoTL research, which they spearheaded at their respective institutions, York University and Humber College, both located in South-Western Ontario, Canada. These initiatives include the Education, Curriculum And Teaching Excellence Course, heretofore referred to as EduCATE, a one-year program for faculty to explore any aspect of teaching and learning by engaging in action research at York University, and the Teaching Innovation Fund, a developmental support framework for faculty to develop, conduct, and disseminate SoTL research at Humber College. These two variations of "SoTL courses", in which faculty, professional staff, and graduate students come together to engage in and support the process of SoTL research, are organized around participants' individual goals rather than a predetermined set of outcomes. Provided is a fulsome narrative and reflective account of the EduCATE and Teaching Innovation Fund programs with a particular focus on each program's development and relative success. Throughout, the impact of SoTL as a form of professional development is emphasized.

As in Hum, Amundsen, and Emmioglu (2015), each of these courses has been developed using an intentional, scholarly approach, with direct consideration to the goals of the programs as well as the populations that they serve. The authors aim herein to 1) describe the broader context within which the courses exist, and the processes that evolved in the program development stage, 2) detail the structure of each of the programs and their accompanying metrics of success, and 3) identify the challenges that remain with respect to maximizing the impact of these forms of SoTL support, in terms of longer-term, sustained opportunities for professional development.

SoTL AS A FORM OF PROFESSIONAL DEVELOPMENT

While many attribute the conception of SoTL to Boyer's (1990) seminal work, conversations around the definition and meaning of SoTL grew exponentially in the decade that followed (Hutchings & Shulman, 1999). Many of these early conceptions situated SoTL within the conventional bastions of academia, stipulating that SoTL should be subject to traditional forms of peer review and disseminated in scholarly formats, including international journals and conferences (Buffalo State College, 2003; Carroll, 2004, as cited in McKinney, 2007; Kern, Mettetal, Dixson, & Morgan, 2015; Richlin, 2001; Secret, Leisey, Lanning, Polich, & Schaub, 2011; Shulman, 2000; Ashwin & Trigwell, 2004). These definitions appeal to the aspirational notion that SoTL improves our generalized professional understanding of student learning and situate SoTL as a form of educational research, traditionally conceived (Geertsema, 2016).

SoTL undertaken as educational research mandates scholarly publications in peer-reviewed journals as its main outcome (Trigwell, 2013). It demands "distinctive protocols, methods, conventions, and literatures [that] will have damaging consequences for academic development in that it cannot but create unrealistic demands on faculty already immersed in their discipline, already short of time" (Geertsema, 2016, p.127). To counterbalance this perspective, Geertsema (2016) has advocated for a re-oriented conception of SoTL as a developmental enterprise, with emphasis at the individual and local community level (2016). Indeed, as definitions of SoTL have evolved, it is now recognized that SoTL can be shared in ways that are "appropriately public" (Felten, 2013). In particular, Felten observed that SoTL is often "iterative and highly contextual" (p. 123), and as such might not be properly situated in traditional academic journals, explicitly stating that SoTL "should not rely exclusively on the typical method of judging scholarly quality, publication in top-tier peer-reviewed journals" (p. 122). Instead, he - along with others (Huber, 2009) - emphasizes the impact that both engaging in and sharing SoTL has among more local, informal networks. Recently, Booth and Woollacott (2018) also recognized that "SoTL embodies a range of aims, activities and contexts and any particular piece of SoTL work occupies only part of the terrain and may transcend whatever boundary is drawn" (p. 538). It seems clear that context is central to much of the existing SoTL landscape; although it is grounded in theory and literature, it is enacted in individual classrooms, and institutional and cultural contexts. To this end, many have recognized the value of alternative and more local forms of dissemination (Cambridge, 2000; Edgerton et al., 1991; Kreber, 2001; Weston & McAlpine, 2001), a theme that is returned to later in the discussion.

Part of the role of the educational developer is to help others do research into their teaching and learning. The convergence between academic development and SoTL should not be surprising "...for although their histories differ, the Scholarship of Teaching and Learning and faculty development have long shared at least one common purpose - transforming teaching and learning for the better" (Hutchings, Huber, & Ciccone 2011, n.p.). Indeed, the primary role of educational developers is to support faculty in improving student learning. At the institutions highlighted within this chapter, the authors have adopted the view that SoTL is a productive way to engage in a systematic process of decision making and reflection about teaching, an approach widely agreed upon in the literature (Bass, 1999; Hutchings, 2000; Potter & Kustra, 2011). However, the SoTL initiatives described herein have been intentionally designed and delivered with care, noting the realistic limitations of the participants that they serve; in particular, the developers have been cognisant of the fact that promoting SoTL comes with the risk of overextending faculty members - especially those for whom teaching is their primary or only responsibility: college professors; university teaching stream faculty; and those who teach on a contractual basis, among others (Vander Kloet et al., 2017). In these instances, research is not a formal part of their professional role.

Table 1. Ashwin & Trigwell's (2004) Levels of investigation

Level	Purpose of Investigation	Evidence Gatherings Methods and Conclusions Will Be	Investigation Results in
1	To inform oneself	Verified by self	Personal knowledge
2	To inform a group within a shared context	Verified by those within the same context	Local knowledge
3	To inform a wider audience	Verified by those outside of that context	Public knowledge

With this in mind, Geertsema (2016) aptly points out, "academic development units should think carefully about the most effective ways to encourage SoTL as a means of changing institutional culture to strengthen teaching and learning" (p. 130). SoTL can generally serve two purposes: it is either a means of development or a form of research. While both involve rigorous investigations into teaching practices and seek evidence in student learning, they "are associated with different standards of evidence and ways of collecting that evidence, and they will have a different range of implications" (Ashwin & Trigwell, 2004, p. 118). For example, when SoTL is framed as a means of development, it is aimed at enhancing student learning through scholarly investigations performed by the instructor in their own classroom. As "academic practice on the ground" (Geerstema, 2016, p. 127), it is appropriate to focus on SoTL inquiry on the immediate context to serve the needs and aspirations of the practitioner and their students.

In the context of SoTL as professional development, it is helpful to examine how the authors of this chapter frame its primary purposes. Borrowed are ideas presented by Ashwin and Trigwell (2004), whose pleas for adopting a scholarly approach to educational development find a parallel to Boyer's Scholarship of Teaching. As seen in Table 1, Ashwin and Trigwell (2004) have described three "Levels of investigation", illustrating the relations between the purpose, process, and outcomes of each level (Ashwin & Trigwell, 2004, p. 122). They draw useful distinctions between the three qualitatively different levels of investigation, based on the kind of knowledge or resources "that academics draw upon in learning about their teaching" (p. 122).

At the most informal level, SoTL serves to enhance personal knowledge and inform individual practice, which is primarily informed by the relevant literature, the academic's experience, and evidence verified by self. When an investigation serves to inform a group within a limited context, it produces local knowledge authenticated by members of that shared context. Lastly, SoTL may serve a broader audience and result in public knowledge verified by outsiders; Ashwin and Trigwell (2004) argue that the wider the audience (e.g., peer-reviewed journal readers), the less relevant it is to the local context, but the more status it gains as a legitimate body of knowledge.

In both courses explored in this chapter, the role of context is significant not only given the widely different institutions but, within each, the diverse range of experiences and expertise among the professoriate (Maheux-Pelletier, Marsh, & Frake-Mistak, 2019). The contexts surrounding these faculty members influence their approach to teaching and learning irrespective of their own beliefs about teaching: as "knowledgeable agents, [academic teachers] are also placed in a dialectical relation with the surrounding world" (Roxå & Mårtensson, 2009, p. 548). Yet, as they immerse themselves in the peer-based context through which they engage with SoTL, they start having "sincere conversations about teaching with a few specific colleagues" (Roxå & Mårtensson, 2009, p. 554). By aiming to provide a space where it is welcome and safe to have reflective conversations about teaching and learning, the aim is not only to help co-construct a microculture (Roxå & Mårtensson, 2015) that places high value in their students' learning, but also a means to develop significant networks where private conversations form the basis of their learning (Roxå & Mårtensson, 2009).

As will be evidenced in this chapter, the impact of the initiatives described here has been greatest at the micro level (Ashwin & Trigwell's Level One): the outcome is often most obvious in the realm of personal and professional development - as teachers and/or researchers. Many of the projects being supported are as much about personal goals/understanding as they are about advancing the knowledge of the field in general; the process is often as valuable as the product. As well, the authors see their work aligning with Ashwin and Trigwell's (2004) Level Two "to inform a group within a shared context" (p.122). Sharing SoTL research at the local/community level further aligns with Simmons' (2009) work, that this particular context is operating within the "meso" level. Indeed, the strategies used to support SoTL have emphasized the local, community level, both in supporting research in action and disseminating this work primarily among colleagues.

Hence, it is our contention that the most impact occurs within Levels One and Two of Ashwin and Trigwell's (2004) framework. The authors perceive this framework as legitimizing experience as an appropriate form of evidence. Furthermore, taking a peer-to-peer approach to course design has further assisted course participants in their SoTL research and dissemination. Measuring impact beyond the institution, or Level 3, is outside the scope of the initiatives described in this chapter, but as evidenced through the courses' evaluation procedures, some participants have disseminated their work to wider, more public audiences.

In this context, the work of educational developers may be understood as that of a broker. Wenger (2000), cited by Geertsema (2016), states that academic developers can connect diverse communities "... in the institution so that the scholarly project on teaching and learning becomes useful to others" (p. 130). Of critical importance to this process is the making public of the product of SoTL inquiry, thus resulting in the sharing of work on a local level (Level Two of Ashwin & Trigwell's framework). Geertsema suggests that "making public locally provides solutions to issues other colleagues may experience in their teaching" (p. 130). We turn to the community that is both fostered and the instrument through which professional development happens in the next section.

PEER-TO-PEER FOCUSED SOTL SUPPORT

Taking a peer-based approach to educational development, and to SoTL initiatives in particular, is not unique. There is widespread literature that advocates for this kind of practice (Babmer 2008; Cambridge 2004, 2001; Geertsema, 2013; Gibbs, 2013). The courses described in this chapter offer a formal way for faculty across the respective institutions to engage in SoTL research and serve as a lever to improve teaching and student learning (Geertsema, 2013). It may be, over time, a means to changing teaching and learning culture across the institution, if not across the sector. While the leads of EduCATE and the Teaching Innovation Fund share this optimism, they understand that community building at the local level is the cornerstone of a strong and growing SoTL culture.

Because professional development initiatives are often offered in group settings, participants tend to represent different disciplines, faculties, and departments, providing wide scope to new ways of thinking and approaches to teaching. Of particular note, providing space for a cross-section of faculty to come together further allows for a breaking down of institutional and programmatic silos. By engaging in "sincere conversations" (Roxå & Mårtensson, 2009, p. 554) beyond their immediate surroundings, they may indeed be contributing ever so slightly but significantly to possible shifts in localized or siloed teaching and learning cultures. Consistent with the approach taken by the academic developers in the design of their courses, Roxå and Mårtensson (2009) advocate that most educators are likely to rely on a small group of individuals, or significant networks, where conversations provide opportunities for conceptual development on learning and reflection. Sorcinelli (2002) includes "encourage collegiality and community" as one of ten principles of good practice in creating and sustaining teaching and learning centres. This work cites studies stating that faculty need each other's support and report a desire to work with other faculty within and outside their discipline. Although a number of themes are identified in the literature with respect to supporting SoTL, (e.g., value placed on SoTL by faculties, departments, and the institution; through tenure and promotion; and the use of awards), Cambridge (2004, 2001) identifies benefits of working in groups with colleagues.

This was validated in the author's local context in a recent study by Kim et al. (Under Review), who investigated faculty experiences and challenges faced when engaging in SoTL research. Within the article, faculty are commonly cited as stating that working with colleagues and building a community were significant in the process of completing their projects. Specifically, they refer to the supportive environment created amongst their peers, peer-to-peer support, encouragement, and a shared understanding of the significance of SoTL research. Similarly, Albers (2008), who explores the role of communities in SoTL and how institutions can further work to support SoTL, advises that conversations within small networks may be more impactful when they are informed by and contribute to scholarship - features which are a purposeful design of EduCATE and the Teaching Innovation Fund.

This approach emerged from a recognition that those engaging within the courses bring diverse ways of knowing and understanding and different approaches to learning and teaching, and that this diversity has the mass potential to enrich the collective experiences when engaged with SoTL. Furthermore, the approach values participant experiences as it shifts from an expert model to one that encourages the co-construction of knowledge through ongoing dialogue, in that the course lead (educational developers) do not direct and inform.

The idea that SoTL, as a form of scholarship, might have equal or even greater impact at the "local" or "meso" level, makes it somewhat unique among scholarly disciplines. It is to this idea that we return as we describe the two initiatives introduced in this chapter, two examples of SoTL as a form of professional development at the individual and community levels.

SITUATING SOTL SUPPORT AS PROFESSIONAL DEVELOPMENT

In the sections that follow, scope and breadth is given to each of the SoTL support initiatives - EduCATE at York University and the Teaching Innovation Fund at Humber College. For each course, an institutional context is provided, and the process involved in developing the programs, goals, outcome measures, and ongoing challenges are detailed. Although there are similarities in approaches to course delivery and facilitation, the authors interrogate both the similarities and differences in the features of the courses and sustainability of the initiatives across our campuses. Connectedly, the role of the educational developer in promoting and supporting SoTL throughout these courses/programs is described.

Institutional Context at York University - EduCATE

York University, located just outside of Toronto, Ontario, is the second largest university in Ontario and third largest in Canada. It is diverse both in terms of its interdisciplinarity (with 11 faculties) and its student body of 55,000 undergraduate and graduate students, 8,500 of whom are international students representing over 178 countries worldwide (about.yorku.ca). York University employs approximately 1600 full-time faculty (OIPA, 2019a). Of significance to the context of this chapter, York has adopted a tenurable teaching stream characterized by an increased teaching load with no research expectations. Teaching stream roles are parallel to conventional tenure stream roles with a heavy research-orientation, resulting in a diverse professoriate with divergent agendas, and very few in either capacity prioritize SoTL as a form of academic practice. In addition to full-time faculty are the 1800 contract faculty and teaching assistants (OIPA, 2019b) employed at York University. While graduate students are most often employed as teaching assistants, those employed contractually largely hold doctoral degrees and are seeking active employment within a professoriate. In an effort to demonstrate their academic inclinations, it is common for these individuals to conduct research over and above their heavy teaching load, although it is not considered part of their job tasks (Vander Kloet et al., 2017).

Bearing in mind the diverse professoriate and the diverging agendas of our full-time faculty (teaching and research stream) and contract faculty at York University, it was important to recognize within the teaching and learning centre that SoTL support across our institution was imperative. Having previously offered no formal support, a course known as EduCATE was developed as a small step towards building an institutional framework for SoTL research. Moreover, our aim was to begin connecting individuals who were already engaging and those who wished to engage in SoTL inquiry to build a community of SoTL scholars. While workshops about SoTL were offered as a generic introduction to its methods and ethics, ultimately, it was decided that a more sustainable and meaningful support framework was needed for those who wished to explore an area of their teaching using a form of action research.

Description of the Program

The first iteration of the Education, Curriculum, And, Teaching Excellence course, fondly called EduCATE, was launched in 2015-2016. It is a one-year program for faculty to explore any aspect of teaching and learning by engaging in action research and contributing to SoTL literature. The course is informed by Peter Felten's (2013) five principles of doing SoTL research and Pat Hutchings' (2000) taxonomy of SoTL questions. These perspectives facilitate the process for course participants as they design their own SoTL projects and begin to methodically explore questions they may not have necessarily formulated explicitly before enrolling in the course.

EduCATE is structured in such a way that participants meet on select dates as a cohort where SoTL as a field of inquiry is broadly explored and ethical practices in conducting SoTL research are considered. Time is spent with course participants reviewing the institutional policies of the research ethics board and the human participant research committee in an effort to provide support on all aspects of their research process and levels of experience in doing research.

In addition to this formal learning, course participants come together monthly as a small group comprised of peers from across campus in varying disciplines and with diverse experiences and interests, as shown in Figure 2, a schematic of the EduCATE course. Through this process they begin forging a community of SoTL practice as they engage in the small group sessions known as Action Learning

Sets (McGill & Brockbank, 2004). Action Learning Sets are small structured groups where participants come together to discuss an area of common interest. During each session, EduCATE participants take turns discussing questions, challenges, or problems related to their SoTL research project with their groups to collectively develop solutions or areas of further inquiry in a supportive environment. Each Action Learning Set concludes with participants committing to a deliverable for the next session. This commitment to action will be the starting point for dialogue in the next set. An Action Learning Set is usually supported by a facilitator, but over time may become self-facilitating.

The course has two formal assessments for participants to have successfully completed the EduCATE course. The first is to present their research at the institution's annual teaching and learning conference, known as Teaching in Focus. Each participant will present in

Pecha Kucha style—this presentation format requires speakers to be concise and focus on the most important aspects of their work as they must complete their presentation in a predetermined number of slides and brief time allocation for each. This presentation gives course participants the opportunity to share their work with the wider York Community as well as to further invite others into dialogue about teaching and learning and about SoTL research. This is consistent with Peter Felten's (2013) last principle of sharing one's SoTL research publicly.

The final assessment in the course is a written piece. Course participants have a choice between two written assessments. The first is a reflective piece that will detail an overview of their work in the course, and what they have learned through this experience and by connecting with their peers through this intensive process. The second option is a more formal piece for those whose research is nearing completion. The objective here is to continue in the provision of support as participants selecting this option will write their research in the format of a journal article. In doing so, participants are provided with a zero-risk submission to the educational developer. They will receive feedback on the paper and have an opportunity to revise before submission for publication.

Figure 1. Schematic of the EduCATE Course Process

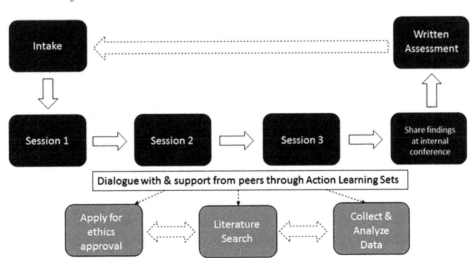

Evaluation of the Program

Upon completion of the EduCATE course, participants are required to complete an online evaluation which includes questions about their perceived benefits and challenges; changes they are considering making to their courses and/or teaching as a result of their engagement in the course; and how in-class activities and their research contributed to their approaches to course design, assessment, active learning, and talking about teaching with their colleagues. The course lead, an educational developer, also tracks the number of hours spent with course participants beyond core sessions and Action Learning Sets, completed projects, and where possible, proposals to conferences and journal submissions beyond the scope of EduCATE.

Since the first iteration of EduCATE in 2015, 32 participants including research and teaching stream professors (tenured and tenure-stream), contract faculty, librarians, professional staff, post-doctoral fellows, and graduate students completed the course (the impact of a long labour disruption accounts for a lower than expected completion rate). The 2019-2020 cohort includes an additional eleven participants. Of note, two faculty have opted to repeat the course as they were seeking additional support for new SoTL projects. Participants in the course have a range of research experience prior to entry, some with no research experience in their professional careers, and a large majority with little conceptual understanding of SoTL. What prompts them to enroll, however, is that they have a question pertaining to their teaching and are seeking additional support to be able to answer it. To date, the course has supported its participants in presenting at the internal teaching and learning conference, presentating at national and international conferences, designing a Teaching Assistant development program, providing educational resources, informing a needs analysis for a programmatic review, and publishing their work in academic journals.

Of significance in 2018, York University's Academic Innovation Fund (AIF) launched a funding stream for SoTL research. The purpose of the AIF is to provide seed grants that will support faculty in a range of projects promoting teaching and learning and the student experience. Recipients of the AIF (SoTL stream) are now required to participate in the EduCATE course. This decision was made by the Office of the Vice-President, Teaching and Learning in order to ensure that successful proposals received targeted support, thus instituting EduCATE as part of a formal strategic initiative to support SoTL at York University.

In a study with EduCATE participants, Kim et al. (Under Review) found widespread acknowledgment that the peer-based approach to the course was instrumental in overcoming the challenges of doing SoTL research, particularly because they felt accountable not only to themselves but to their immediate community. This speaks to levels one and two of Ashwin and Trigwell's (2004) framework. While impact at the third level is neither the aim nor an obvious outcome of EduCATE, the first cohort of the course benefited from a small fund for conference travel that enabled a few participants to present at a national teaching and learning conference that took place within drivable distance that year. Looking forward, the AIF combined with EduCATE should yield greater impact at the third level of investigation, hence generating public knowledge without minimizing contributions to personal and local growth.

Next Steps and Remaining Challenges

What remains a challenge is lack of participants' knowledge of SoTL research prior to commencing their own research. Consequently, the course has been revised significantly for the upcoming iteration to try to fill in some of these gaps. One such attempt is to meet with individuals prior to the first large group session to discuss their proposal, research questions, and their definition of SoTL. Scholarly articles have been circulated in advance in an effort to create common ground and common language about SoTL as a field of inquiry as well as to encourage participants to become more familiar with SoTL scholarly literature.

Another challenge is in providing support beyond the EduCATE course. Aside from participants having to repeat the course in its entirety, Action Learning Sets are now being offered as a stand-alone initiative without mandatory attendance at the large group sessions for those who have participated in EduCATE since 2015. Because they are structured as Action Learning Sets, a familiar and successful structure for past participants, there is optimism that co-mentoring relationships will thrive and sustain themselves.

Institutional Context at Humber College - Teaching Innovation Fund

Humber College, located in Toronto, Ontario, is one of the largest polytechnic institutes in Canada, with approximately 28,000 full- and part-time students. The college is characterized by the range of credentials offered, with approximately 180 programs including apprenticeships, two- and three- year diplomas, four-year undergraduate degrees, and post-graduate certificates. Accompanying this variety is the range of research experience that the faculty at the college have. Some are doctorally-prepared, while others have never conducted research professionally. The focus of the college is on teaching excellence; research (of any nature) is not mandated, although it is encouraged. Faculty typically teach the equivalent of about five courses per semester. Thus, the educational development unit serves a population of educators who have a heavy teaching load, have varied research experience, and have no formal requirement for research.

Given this context, the SoTL support framework was built around a developmental fund, adapted from Hum et al. (2015). Although competitive funds, in which a selection of "successful" SoTL proposals are granted funding, routinely serve as the foundation for SoTL support frameworks, they are not necessarily effective or even appropriate at all types of institutions. Given their very nature, they are exclusionary to some, and therefore may serve as a barrier to engagement with SoTL. Recognizing this, Hum et al. (2015) took a different approach, and developed a fund that was "formative" in nature. In their framework, applicants work with colleagues and SoTL facilitators to develop a proposal until it is finalized to a satisfactory level; all proposals that reach this point are given funding. A similar structure was adopted with the Teaching Innovation Fund at Humber.

The Teaching Innovation Fund is formative, rather than competitive, and aims to build capacity—both in terms of research and in terms of scholarly teaching—among its participants, regardless of the amount of research experience they have had. It is deployed within a peer-based context, with proposal development and project deployment situated within an ongoing conversation among each cohort of fund-recipients and the SoTL facilitators. By embedding a SoTL fund within a community, the goal is to provide participants with social accountability and support across all phases of the project. It also allows for a safe space for faculty to engage in peer review of scholarly work, which is a new process for many. Indeed, the framework is fundamentally developmental; every project is as much about a faculty member's own professional development as it is about contributing to our knowledge of student learning (Felten, 2013). The educational developers who designed and facilitate the course aspire to strike a balance between building confidence and research capacity and ensuring that each SoTL project has an appropriate level of rigour. In this way, the goal of the fund is not only to increase the amount of SoTL engagement at the institution, but to build an accompanying community of SoTL practitioners. The particular features of the process are outlined in more detail, below.

Description of the Program

Application to the fund requires only an articulation of an idea or area of inquiry; this might consist of a few written sentences. Faculty attend two proposal development workshops, during which SoTL facilitators share instruction around SoTL methodology, and participants engage in dialogue and peer review of one another's ideas, as they further develop and articulate a research question and accompanying research plan. The dialogue continues between participants and the SoTL facilitators between and following the workshops, as they go through several iterations of revision and conversation to finalize their research proposals. Once finalized, all proposals are granted funding (currently $1400 per investigator; investigators may team up with one or two others, to pool their funding up to $4200).

During the data collection phase of their projects, the SoTL facilitation team continues to support participants, including activities such as helping with the ethics review process, and developing, building, and deploying research instruments (e.g., surveys, focus groups). Cohorts of fund-recipients also regroup approximately twice per year for informal lunches to chat about their progress and maintain a Community of Practice. The final deliverable for the fund consists of a presentation (either a poster or a workshop) at the institution's annual teaching and learning conference. In this way, participants spread institutionally-relevant SoTL findings broadly among their colleagues. Following project completion, all cohorts are invited to participate in other SoTL initiatives, such as sharing their research at lunch and learn sessions, taking part in writing retreats to publish their findings, and, of course, reapplying for further funding to continue their scholarly pursuits. Should fund-recipients choose to engage further with subsequent projects, they are not required to attend the proposal development workshops but continue to participate in the other peer-to-peer aspects, including the check-in lunches and institutional conference presentations. See Figure 2 below for a schematic of the Teaching Innovation Fund course.

Figure 2. Schematic of the Teaching Innovation Fund processEvaluation of the Program

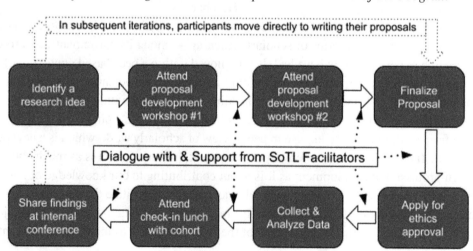

To evaluate the extent to which the Teaching Innovation Fund is fulfilling its goals of professional development (as teachers and researchers) and community-building, course leads routinely examine a number of sources of evidence. With respect to professional development, the number of applications, proposals that are successfully developed and submitted, and completed projects are tracked. Additionally, the number of hours of training, consultation, and additional support that are provided by the SoTL facilitation team are recorded. Upon completion of projects, an in-depth survey to fund-recipients is administered, which includes questions about the impact of the experience, the level of support, the role of the community, and barriers to success.

Since its inception in 2015, the Teaching Innovation Fund has supported fifty-one completed projects, with an additional fifteen currently under development. Twenty-one faculty have engaged with the fund multiple times. Through the proposal development workshops, 144 faculty have received formal training in SoTL methodology and ethics, in addition to approximately 450 one-on-one consultations with the SoTL facilitation team. Of the fund-recipients who responded to the survey (n = 63), more than one-third (36.5%) had never conducted research of any kind in their professional careers. Based on the survey data, the vast majority of faculty (between 80-90%, depending on the item) reported increased confidence as researchers and as teachers, respectively, and felt that their engagement with SoTL had led to an improvement in their teaching approach. Almost all survey respondents (96.3%) felt that they had received adequate support from the SoTL facilitation team throughout the process.

With respect to the second goal of developing a community of SoTL practitioners, course leads have found similar although somewhat weaker evidence of success. 86.9% of participants met faculty they might otherwise not have met through the fund, and 70.0% felt a sense of community with the other faculty engaged in the Teaching Innovation Fund. 81.7% enjoyed meeting other faculty through the fund , but only 58.5% enjoyed updating others about their project at the check-in lunches. With respect to local dissemination, Teaching Innovation Fund projects have led to 16 "lunch and learn" sessions at the institution and 40 presentations at Humber's institutional teaching and learning conference since 2015. However, survey respondents did not as frequently perceive an impact within their own departments; 74.5% felt that their involvement in SoTL was visible to their program/school colleagues, and 31.7% of participants believed that others in their department had changed their teaching in some way as a result of their SoTL project.

Although the focus of the fund is at the individual and local level, a selection of projects has reached Ashwin and Trigwell's third level of investigation (2004). In particular, three projects have resulted in publications in scholarly journals, and 38 presentations have been given at national and international teaching and learning conferences. Thus, while the majority of the impact has occurred at the micro and meso levels, there has been some impact beyond the institution, into the broader SoTL community.

Taken together, these metrics suggest that the fund is making progress toward both goals in its mandate. Nonetheless, the process of evaluation and reflection is ongoing. Ongoing challenges are discussed below.

Next Steps and Remaining Challenges

One issue that the authors encountered speaks to the hazard of placing unrealistic demands on faculty who are already limited in time (Ashwin and Trigwell, 2004). In the first few cohorts of the fund, it became clear that flexibility would need to become a feature of the process. Unavoidable features of the academic semester, such as exams and work placements, meant that progress on SoTL proposals and/or projects could not always proceed along the anticipated timelines. As a practice, timelines (and expectations therein) have become more fluid; faculty may begin with one cohort of colleagues, then have to put their project on hiatus for a period of time, only to return and rejoin with a different cohort. This flexibility aligns with the fund's emphasis on professional development and process, as opposed to "SoTL as research" and scholarly products.

Similar to our colleagues at York, a second and ongoing challenge is to find ways of fostering mentorship within our SoTL community. Although past fund-recipients take part in some of the community activities in subsequent projects (e.g., check-in lunches, institutional conference presentations), they are not enmeshed within the community in the same way. This may be attributed to the fact that the SoTL support framework has fixed beginning and end points that unintentionally also serve as "exit" points from the community. In the coming year, course leads are exploring ways to entrench mentors in the proposal development process, through increased peer review and conversation. We envision adding more extensive peer review to the proposal development sessions, with both new and seasoned SoTL scholars, allowing participants to critically appraise their peers' research plans. Furthermore, consideration of more formal mentoring partnerships, with regular check-ins and support between new fund-recipients and those with previous experience will be given.

DISCUSSION AND ANALYSIS

The two SoTL courses discussed in this chapter share a great deal in common despite their differing contexts. Both take a developmental approach in the provision of support to faculty engaging in them. In each course, support is provided throughout the entire research process, through the design and deployment of measurement tools, research methodologies, the research ethics process, and data analysis. Furthermore, although the area of SoTL inquiry is driven by individual faculty members, ideas are co-developed over time with a community of peers who are also participating in the course (Action Learning Sets in EduCATE and the proposal development workshops in the Teaching Innovation Fund). A major endeavour shared by both initiatives is the minimization of barriers to participants, in an effort to broaden the accessibility of engagement with SoTL as a field of inquiry; all faculty are eligible to take part, regardless of their previous experience with research and scholarship.

Connectedly, because of the developmental approaches of these courses, an additional distinguishing feature is the prolonged nature of the support. In contrast to "just-in-time" training sessions, workshops, and individual consultations that often characterize the work of educational developers (Gibbs, 2013), each of these programs recognized the need for and potential impact of continued support to foster sustainable action (Bamber, 2008; Gibbs, 2013). In both courses, the metrics shared suggest that each initiative is meaningfully contributing to professional development at the micro level, supporting individual participants' teaching and learning practices, and aligning with Level One of Ashwin and Trigwell's (2004) Levels of Investigation.

In addition, these programs share the purpose of providing a protected time and space for faculty to engage in SoTL projects and initiatives with a cohort of peers. At the core of the courses, a peer-to-peer approach has been adopted whereby participant experiences are not only enriched through increased social contributions and accountability, but also by the knowledge shared amongst the group through diversity of thought, perspectives, and experiences. The authors suggest that intentionally focusing on community-building strengthens the outcomes and overall success for the participants, the credibility of the associated teaching and learning centres, and the contributions to scholarship. And while the community of course participants is a critical component of the courses themselves, the larger, local community is also the focus of dissemination. In particular, the final deliverable for both courses is a presentation at the institutions' respective teaching and learning conferences, thus making public the SoTL investigations within the local contexts (Felten, 2013). In this way, both courses inform and enrich not only the community of faculty that are directly enrolled, but also the larger institutional teaching and learning community, aligning with Level Two of Ashwin and Trigwell's (2004) framework.

In some cases, although it is not a focus of either course, individuals have also extended into Ashwin and Trigwell's (2004) third Level of Investigation, with presentations at national and international conferences, and occasional publication in scholarly journals. Because this is not a required outcome of the courses (although it is welcomed), as reflected in the frameworks presented above, the authors view this extension as significant.

Given the two distinct institutional designations, these initiatives have different starting points. EduCATE is a program that aligns with research intensification efforts put forth at York University, while Humber College has traditionally focused on applied research opportunities for students, with faculty dedicated entirely to teaching and learning. Despite this obvious difference, the authors speculate that the initiatives—while developed independently—have converged in mission and structure because they serve similar populations of non-traditional academics. In particular, both York and Humber have diverse professoriates, with divergent teaching and research agendas, and as a result, both the SoTL courses serve academics who may not have prioritized or engaged in scholarly pursuits.

A final point of similarity is that the relative success of each of these initiatives has led the educational development teams at each institution to re-examine other programming within their respective departments to identify further opportunities for prolonged, peer-to-peer initiatives. At York for example, the peer-based approach applied in EduCATE has been adapted to other initiatives offered through the teaching and learning centre. Active Learning Sets are used widely as they enable those involved to bring and apply their own lived experiences to the context. Course leads see evidence of this working as participants return to engage with the centre at many levels.

Similarly, this trend can be seen in the writing-support programs at Humber, such as the Scholarly Writing Boot Camps and on-campus "Writers' Collective" writing club, both of which bring together groups of faculty, on an ongoing basis, to support scholarly writing and dissemination (Maheux-Pelletier et al., 2019). This move from the support of the individual to the support of communities, and from small, one-time offerings to longer-term, integrated initiatives aligns with observations found elsewhere in the educational development landscape (Gibbs, 2013).

RECOMMENDATIONS FOR FUTURE PROGRAMMING

Having developed two distinct but similar processes of peer-based program development, there are several recommendations that we would apply to future initiatives. These are described in the following bulleted points:

- Start small and strong: A structure needs to be in place first even when awareness about SoTL is scarce. Once there is a solid program, faculty will start coming, with incremental impact taking place over time.

- Provide incentives and recognition: The Teaching Innovation Fund at Humber College began with a funding mechanism whereas EduCATE is tied to a credential. Moreover, faculty at Humber are incentivized further after the fact through conference sponsorship for those who have been good "ambassadors" of the fund by sharing extensively at the local level.
- Be flexible in the design and delivery of the program: Both EduCATE and the Teaching Innovation Fund have relaxed the rules and timelines for faculty. At Humber, some participants begin with one cohort, but for any number of reasons must temporarily put their project on hold and are able to rejoin with a different cohort at a later point. In EduCATE, participants schedule the date and time of their Action Learning Sets when it is mutually convenient to the small group as opposed to a mandated time designated by the course facilitator.
- Prioritize informal learning and support through peers: Common to both structures is the peer-review component. This an ongoing learning process through which one learns about SoTL by doing SoTL is embedded within a peer-to-peer context.
- Embrace varying definitions of success that make sense to the participants: Ultimately, the authors have embraced varying definitions of success based on the groups they work with, recognizing that for some, the goal will be a scholarly contribution to the literature, whereas for others, this work will serve to develop their own personal professional practice. The authors believe that a learner-centred process where the measure of success is not predetermined is what has led to deep and long-standing participant engagement.

CONCLUSION

As a preliminary analysis, the authors observe varying definitions of success in the SoTL courses described in this chapter. While for one participant, learning how to do SoTL research and forming a simple research design may be a meaningful milestone, for another with a great deal of knowledge and experience with research methodologies and analysis, the completion of a SoTL project may result in publication. Using a peer-based approach allows for both outcomes and multiple notions of success - in any instance, transformation is possible. The authors believe that taking a peer-to-peer approach provides strength and foundation and allows participants to be engaged and successful in their SoTL experience. This structured approach provides numerous benefits to course participants learning to do SoTL, to the greater institutional community where SoTL is used as a tool to build/extend teaching and learning capacity, as well as in the contribution to scholarship.

In a context where the Scholarship of Teaching and Learning is relatively new to most academic environments, the authors conclude by suggesting that prolonged, developmental programs allow for participant-defined success, and the authors see this as a strength of the programs. From an educational development perspective, the success of these initiatives is brought about by a peer-based approach to SoTL, which has offered our communities a practical and sustainable model for engaging faculty members from any "walk of academic life" and at any stage of their academic career. In this process, competent facilitation is a necessary skill that educational developers are uniquely positioned to provide to both forge community and support a research process that feels uncomfortable to most of the participants, regardless of their level of competence with disciplinary research. Despite this tension, and despite the many demands on a faculty member's time, the authors notice continued engagement and growth stemming from the programs described in this chapter. This gives the authors reason to think that the communities fostered are the glue that make participants stick to their SoTL commitment. The SoTL culture thus created lays the foundation for a renewed teaching and learning institutional culture, one that places high value on the student experience, not only in discourse but also, and more importantly, in practice.

At both institutions, this revelation has transformed how the authors, course leads, and educational developers approach their work. More peer-based learning opportunities are offered that expand over time. Not only are they better attended than traditional workshops with punctual commitment, they foster one's critical engagement with teaching and learning that a one-off workshop cannot. Hence, it appears that despite being over-extended, faculty will invest themselves when there are genuine opportunities for personal growth leading to a greater sense of belonging.

REFERENCES

Albers, C. (2008). Improving pedagogy through action learning and Scholarship of Teaching and Learning. *Teaching Sociology*, *36*(1), 79–86. doi:10.1177/0092055X0803600110

Ashwin, P., & Trigwell, K. (2004). Investigating staff and educational development. In D. Baume & P. Kahn (Eds.), *Enhancing staff and educational development* (pp. 117–131). London: Routledge. doi:10.4324/9780203416228_chapter_7

Bamber, V. (2008). Evaluating lecturer development programmes: Received wisdom or self-knowledge? *The International Journal for Academic Development*, *13*(2), 107–116. doi:10.1080/13601440802076541

Bass, R. (1999). The scholarship of teaching: What's the problem? *Inventio, 1*(1).

Booth, S., & Woollacott, L. C. (2018). On the constitution of SoTL: Its domains and contexts. *Higher Education*, *75*(3), 537–551. doi:10.100710734-017-0156-7

Boyer, E. L. (1990). *Scholarship reconsidered: Priorities of the professoriate*. Princeton, NJ: Carnegie Foundation for the Advancement of Teaching.

Buffalo State College. (2003). *Supplemental directory of policy statements (DOPS) policy on scholarship encompassing applied research and the scholarship of teaching*. Retrieved July 10, 2019, from http://bscintra.buffalostate.edu/dops/policysect6/060405.pdf

Cambridge, B. L. (2001). Fostering the Scholarship of Teaching and Learning: Communities of Practice. In D. Lieberman & C. Wehlburg (Eds.), *To Improve the Academy* (pp. 3–16). Bolton, MA: Anker. doi:10.1002/j.2334-4822.2001.tb00521.x

Cambridge, B. L. (Ed.). (2004). *Campus progress: Supporting the Scholarship of Teaching and Learning*. Washington, DC: American Association for Higher Education.

Felten, P. (2013). Principles of good practice in SoTL. *Teaching & Learning Inquiry*, *1*(1), 121–125. doi:10.20343/teachlearninqu.1.1.121

Geertsema, J. (2016). Academic development, SoTL, and educational research. *The International Journal for Academic Development*, *21*(2), 122–134. doi:10.1080/1360144X.2016.1175144

Gibbs, G. (2013). Reflections on the changing nature of educational development. *The International Journal for Academic Development, 18*(1), 4–14. doi:10.1080/1360144X.2013.751691

Huber, M. T. (2009). Teaching travels: Reflections on the social life of classroom inquiry and innovation. *International Journal for the Scholarship of Teaching and Learning, 3*(2), 2. doi:10.20429/ijsotl.2009.030202

Hum, G., Amundsen, C., & Emmioglu, E. (2015). Evaluating a teaching development grants program: Our framework, process, initial findings, and reflections. *Studies in Educational Evaluation, 46*, 29–38. doi:10.1016/j.stueduc.2015.02.004

Hutchings, P. (2000). *Opening lines: Approaches to the Scholarship of Teaching and Learning*. Menlo Park, CA: Carnegie Publications.

Hutchings, P., Huber, M. T., & Ciccone, A. (2011). *The Scholarship of Teaching and Learning reconsidered: Institutional integration and impact*. San Francisco, CA: Josey-Bass.

Hutchings, P., & Shulman, L. S. (1999). The scholarship of teaching: New elaborations, new developments. *Change: The Magazine of Higher Learning, 31*(5), 10–15. doi:10.1080/00091389909604218

Kern, B., Mettetal, G., Dixson, M., & Morgan, R. K. (2015). The role of SoTL in the academy: Upon the 25th anniversary of Boyer's Scholarship Reconsidered. *The Journal of Scholarship of Teaching and Learning*, 1–14. doi:10.14434/josotl.v15i3.13623

Kim, A., Popovic, C., Farrugia, L., Saleh, S., Maheux-Pelletier, G., & Frake-Mistak, M. (2019, July). On nurturing the emergent SoTL researcher: Responding to challenges and opportunities. *The International Journal for Academic Development*, 8.

Maheux-Pelletier, G., Marsh, H., & Frake-Mistak, M. (2019). The benefits of writing retreats revisited. In N. Simmons (Ed.), *Critical collaboration communities: Academic writing partnerships, groups, and retreats* (pp. 92–105). Rotterdam: Brill-Sense Publishers.

McGill, I., & Brockbank, A. (2004). *The action learning handbook: Powerful techniques for education, professional development and training*. New York: Routledge Falmer.

McKinney, K. (2007). *Enhancing learning through the Scholarship of Teaching and Learning: The challenges and joys of juggling*. Anker Publishing.

Office of Institutional Planning and Analysis (OIPA). (2019a). *Contract faculty and teaching assistants headcount*. Retrieved from http://oipa.info.yorku.ca/data-hub/quick-facts/quick-facts-contract-faculty-and-tas/

Office of Institutional Planning and Analysis (OIPA). (2019b). *Full-time faculty headcount*. Retrieved from http://oipa.info.yorku.ca/data-hub/quick-facts/quick-facts-full-time-faculty-headcount/

Potter, M. K., & Kustra, E. D. H. (2011). The relationship between scholarly teaching and SoTL: Models, distinctions, and clarifications. *International Journal for the Scholarship of Teaching and Learning, 5*(1), 23. doi:10.20429/ijsotl.2011.050123

Richlin, L. (2001). Scholarly teaching and the scholarship of teaching. *New Directions for Teaching and Learning, 2001*(86), 57–68. doi:10.1002/tl.16

Roxå, T., & Mårtensson, K. (2009). Significant conversations and significant networks—Exploring the backstage of the teaching arena. *Studies in Higher Education, 34*(5), 547–559. doi:10.1080/03075070802597200

Roxå, T., & Mårtensson, K. (2015). Microcultures and informal learning: A heuristic guiding analysis of conditions for informal learning in local higher education workplaces. *The International Journal for Academic Development, 20*(2), 193–205. doi:10.1080/1360144X.2015.1029929

Secret, M., Leisey, M., Lanning, S., Polich, S., & Schaub, J. (2011). Faculty perceptions of the Scholarship of Teaching and Learning: Definition, activity level and merit considerations at one university. *The Journal of Scholarship of Teaching and Learning, 11*(3), 1–20.

Shulman, L. (2001). From Minsk to Pinsk: Why a Scholarship of Teaching and Learning? *The Journal of Scholarship of Teaching and Learning,* 48–53.

Simmons, N. (2009). Personal reflection: Playing for SoTL impact: A personal reflection. *International Journal for the Scholarship of Teaching and Learning, 3*(2), 30. doi:10.20429/ijsotl.2009.030230

Sorcinelli, M. D. (2002). Ten principles of good practice in creating and sustaining teaching and learning centers. *A guide to faculty development: Practical advice, examples, and resources,* 9-23.

Steinert, Y., Mann, K., Centeno, A., Dolmans, D., Spencer, J., Gulula, M., & Prideaux, D. (2006). A systematic review of faculty development initiatives designed to improve teaching effectiveness in medical education: BEME Guide No. 8. *Medical Teacher, 8*(6), 497–526. doi:10.1080/01421590600902976 PMID:17074699

Trigwell, K. (2013). Evidence of the impact of Scholarship of Teaching and Learning purposes. *Teaching & Learning Inquiry, 1*(1), 95–105. doi:10.20343/teachlearninqu.1.1.95

Vander Kloet, M., Frake-Mistak, M., McGinn, M. K., Caldecott, M., Aspenlieder, E. D., Beres, J. L., ... Gill, A. (2017). Conditions for contingent instructors engaged in the Scholarship of Teaching and Learning. *The Canadian Journal for the Scholarship of Teaching and Learning, 8*(2). doi:10.5206/cjsotl-rcacea.2017.2.9

Wenger, E. (2000). Communities of Practice and social learning systems. *Organization, 7*(2), 225–246. doi:10.1177/135050840072002

Chapter 5

Building Faculty SoTL Skills Through a Multi- and Interdisciplinary Writing Community of Practice

Sandra Sgoutas-Emch
University of San Diego, USA

Judith Liu
University of San Diego, USA

Moriah Meyskens
University of San Diego, USA

Tara Ceranic Salinas
University of San Diego, USA

Jane Friedman
University of San Diego, USA

Perla Myers
University of San Diego, USA

ABSTRACT

Cultivating a community of faculty to support Scholarship of Teaching and Learning (SoTL) work at universities can be challenging. There are many obstacles to overcome—obstacles such as how to sustain such efforts over time. The Center for Educational Excellence set out to design a strategic plan designed to address certain barriers to SoTL work and to create a long-standing community of practice for a SoTL group of faculty members—a group that has lasted over nine years to date. This chapter outlines strategies employed over the years and the evolution of the interdisciplinary group from a learning community to community of practice. The stories of past and present members are included along with advice on how others may have successful programs at their universities.

DOI: 10.4018/978-1-7998-2212-7.ch005

INTRODUCTION

Can you imagine a mathematician reading and providing valuable feedback on a piece of theater peda-gogy—or a sociologist truly engaging with physics education work? That is exactly what we experience as members of a Scholarship of Teaching and Learning (SoTL) community. What started as a series of workshops designed to help faculty members think about assessing student learning and designing SoTL research transformed into a sustained and vibrant writing and learning community that has stood the test of time.

Being part of the SoTL group gave me an opportunity to learn about this area of scholarship through reading and providing feedback on the work of the other group members. I was able to see how to imple-ment research projects in the classroom. I was motivated not only to continue my work on my first SoTL project but to also try new techniques in the classroom. (Associate Professor in Mathematics)

The statement above is from a member of a long-running (since 2010) multi- and interdisciplinary SoTL writing community of faculty members that was organized by the Center for Educational Excel-lence (CEE), the development center for faculty across campus. This community meets monthly dur-ing the academic year to discuss its members' SoTL project development and writing projects, and the output of the group has resulted in dozens of scholarly papers, presentations, chapters, and proposals (see Appendix 1 for a sample list of publications resulting from the SoTL group). This chapter provides a glimpse into the origins of the community; a detailed description of how the multi and interdisciplin-ary writing process functions; insights into how this community has evolved over the years to support sustainability; and a list of suggestions for other teaching and learning centers or institutions that would like to pursue similar initiatives on their campuses. The chapter is divided into major themes highlighting faculty members' stories of their experiences and the writing group's impact both on the participants' scholarship and the participants' professional development. We also discuss the numerous opportunities that have evolved as a result of an initiative that started with just a few workshops ten years ago.

CREATING A SoTL SPACE

This fruitful collaborative group started as an effort to generate interest in teaching and learning research at the university. The University of San Diego (USD) is an independent, medium-sized Catholic institution that is primarily focused on undergraduate programs in Arts and Sciences, Business, and Engineering. USD also has several graduate programs including Peace Studies, Leadership and Educational Sciences, Nursing, and Law. As with many primarily undergraduate institutions, faculty members spend a large percentage of their time teaching, and they put an emphasis on innovation in the classroom. At the same time, demands for scholarship and academic excellence are steadily increasing. So, why is SoTL work not associated with necessary professional development for all faculty members? Why do so few institu-tions and faculty members see the value of supporting and investing resources in SoTL (Chick, 2018)?

Often, the answer is that there is simply a lack support to pursue SoTL or insufficient understanding of pedagogical research (Lueddeke, 2003). It is an unfortunate truth that SoTL work is often not highlighted or is seen as less impactful than more "traditional" disciplinary scholarship (McKinney, 2006; Webb, 2019). Pedagogy journals, despite being peer-reviewed and rigorous, do not typically appear on the lists provided by rank and tenure committees of what constitutes research publication leading to tenure and promotion (Segalla, 2008). Often junior faculty are discouraged from this type of research, and those that do want to engage in SoTL work do not necessarily have the training on SoTL or on how to apply for Human Subjects approval when the research subjects are their students. This potential lack of skills and awareness to take on SoTL projects (Weimer, 2006) can be a deterrent to the pursuit of SoTL work, but this is where the SoTL writing community comes in. The SoTL writing group provides a supportive community with opportunities for faculty members to develop an understanding of SoTL research and to engage in innovative and high-impact teaching and much-valued research (Gilpin & Liston, 2009). Furthermore, others have documented the potential for SoTL work to transform institutions and elevate the learning environment (Hutching, Huber, & Ciccone, 2011).

To specifically address the need for support and guidance in SoTL work, the CEE implemented a three-tiered strategy over ten years ago. The first tier consisted of holding open discussions and panels featuring faculty members who were already engaged in various types of SoTL work and who had a track record of publishing in reputable outlets. Events were well-attended and generated interest among several faculty members. These events helped raise awareness on campus and stimulated interest in SoTL, but raising awareness was often not enough to propel change in the culture and behavior (Christiano & Neimand, 2017). The CEE staff knew that more needed to be done in order to move the needle on what was happening on campus to provide faculty members with the skills, motivation, and efficacy necessary in order to move forward with SoTL.

To address the gaps in knowledge concerning research methodology and project development, the second level of the strategy was designed to train faculty members in how to do SoTL work. The CEE invited experts in the field to come to campus and assist faculty members in their professional development. Several day-long workshops on topics ranging from project design, to assessment of student learning (Welch, 1999), to the creation of critical reflection assignments (Ash & Clayton, 2004) were organized. The CEE also collaborated with other campus units to bring in scholars from particular areas that aligned with the values of our institution—areas including Catholic social teaching, course-based community engagement, and contemplative pedagogy.

Following these training efforts, as the third step, the CEE invited faculty members to be a part of a SoTL learning and writing community facilitated by the CEE. The CEE chose the learning community approach as faculty learning communities and writing groups have been found to have a profound impact (Moore, 2018; McKinney, 2013) on supporting faculty members' success (Heinrich & Oberleitner, 2012; Lancaster et al., 2014; Lee & Boud, 2003; Nugent et al., 2008). Interested faculty members from a variety of disciplines and levels of experience across campus signed up to be part of the group, which started as a cohort-based faculty learning community. This specific formulation was the result of an initial plan to meet for the year as a multi-disciplinary peer-led group who would provide structured feedback and support to one another to combat what Cox (2004) described as the "isolation, fragmentation, stress, neglect, or chilly climate in the academy" (p. 8) experienced by many in the group. Over time, this group offered support and strategies that went beyond research feedback.

The initial call for participation for this SoTL group included the following intended goals of the writing/learning community:

1. To gather a group of faculty members interested in learning more about SoTL and methodologies;
2. To provide a supportive space for exchange of ideas around student learning and teaching;
3. To have structured review of faculty members' work products related to SoTL;

4. To offer accountability to help reach individual goals for productivity; and
5. To educate ourselves in the basic tenets of SoTL—and to help mentor and educate other faculty members in this area.

Most of these goals still guide the work of the group today, but they have been modified through the years to meet the needs of the group's individual members and the type of diverse materials we examine. The flexibility also supports the work of faculty members according to their own development and status and contributes to the sustainability of the community. Below is a quote from a faculty member which outlines some of the specific development needs addressed by the SoTL group:

When I joined the SoTL writing group, I was a pre-tenure faculty member in a department known for its dysfunction. I was becoming more confident as a teacher, and yet I did not have formal spaces for discussing the craft of pedagogy with colleagues in my field. The SoTL group was a wonderful opportunity for me to learn about teaching tactics in other disciplines, to discuss the highs and lows of teaching, and to become exposed to the journals publishing in the scholarship of teaching, including those within and outside my field of theology/ethics. The SoTL group modeled inclusive community and fostered the leadership development of women on campus, building networks of support that helped me navigate department politics. (Assistant Professor of Theology and Religious Studies, now Associate Professor)

EVOLUTION FROM LEARNING COMMUNITY TO COMMUNITY OF PRACTICE

I am not sure that I would have been as successful or as motivated to think about my teaching in the way that SoTL pushes me to do. This group has been such a supportive and welcoming experience. I can't say enough about how I have grown. (Professor of Psychological Sciences)

Initially, the SoTL group was organized specifically for faculty members with interests in pedagogical scholarship (Richlin & Cox, 2004) to network with colleagues and provide and receive feedback on SoTL work. The community evolved into so much more than a typical writing group. For example, many of the individuals in the group became involved in interdisciplinary projects because of their exposure to each other's work. The development of courses, scholarly presentations and publications, grant proposals, collaborative projects with community partners, and international outreach initiatives are some examples of work generated over the years. Members have come and gone (for various reasons), but a core group of faculty members continue to meet and critique, support, and assist in the creation, execution, and dissemination of SoTL projects. To date, around 60% of members are from the original cohort.

Following the knowledge-building of the learning community, the SoTL group intentionally evolved into a Community of Practice. Communities of Practice (CoP) are defined as "groups of people who share a concern or a passion for something they do and learn how to do it better as they interact regularly" (Wenger, 2011, pg.1). CoP are rooted in learning theory and are comprised of practitioners who are actively engaged in a particular exploration to help spread knowledge and innovation (Wenger, 1999). The SoTL group scheduled regular monthly meetings, set ground rules and expectations, and documented individual goals for the academic year. The CoP ranged from 6 - 12 people at any given time with a total of 30 faculty and their collaborators participating over the years. At the beginning, the group was comprised of an even balance of pre-tenured, associate, and full professors from the College of Arts and Sciences and the School of Business. Through the years, the group included non-tenure track faculty as well.

The process was simple, and accountability measures were designed to be lighthearted to help build a sense of collegiality and cooperation rather than one of competition and criticism. Individuals signed up to present their work, and everyone was responsible for coming prepared by reading the work and preparing written feedback. This feedback was then discussed in a round-table format to be sure that the author got the full range of suggestions and often new ideas surfaced from the general discussion. If a member could not attend, they would send the feedback over email. Over the years, the group added celebrations including end-of-semester white elephant gift exchanges and potluck meals to build a true sense of community. The quotes presented throughout this chapter exemplify the value and impact on teaching approaches this CoP has had for the individuals involved. The group members share their personal growth and increased awareness of various pedagogical approaches.

Researchers have found that CoPs can help to shift the culture within institutions particularly with regard to teaching and learning (Foulger, 2005; Gannon-Leary & Fontainha, 2007). Since this group is a CoP instead of a more traditional writing group, it has helped to support faculty members' development efforts in SoTL across campus. Members have been part of trainings, panels, and workshops designed to build capacity and to spread the word on the mechanics and importance of research in teaching and learning. This chapter is illustrative of such a collaborative effort to disseminate the group's work to the larger community. Another interesting aspect of this group is that most of the members implement community engagement work in their courses, and, therefore, a lot of what is discussed focuses on the intersection of community-based research and SoTL.

I love learning about the work my SoTL colleagues are doing in other departments around campus. The group inspires me! I have received wonderful feedback on projects that definitely enhanced the final products. (Professor in Mathematics)

CHARACTERISTICS AND GOALS FOR SUCCESS

I would say that having interdisciplinary feedback helps me/us find the "holes" in our work. Having eyes on what we are writing from outside our own discipline allows us to write better and more nuanced cases/papers/presentations. As a result of my time in SoTL (since May 2010), I have received invaluable feedback and have published many cases with teaching notes and articles. (Professor of Management)

This quote is just one of the many examples of how, from the beginning, this group was designed to be unique. Faculty members come from a diversity of disciplines and types of SoTL projects. Faculty members from Science, Technology, Engineering and Mathematics (STEM), Theater, Community Engagement, Theology and Religious Studies, Social Sciences, and Business have been a part of this community. The multidisciplinary nature of the group provides interesting opportunities to learn about a wide range of research methods and pedagogical approaches used in various disciplines (Moore, 2018). The knowledge gained from learning multiple approaches across disciplines allows members the ability to communicate to a larger audience of readers and scholars than just those within their own areas of expertise (Baskerville & Goldblatt, 2009).

Flexibility is key in this CoP. We have seen members leave and return over the years, and we are always eager to welcome new people. These transitions, although they change the composition of the group, have consistently been beneficial. Members who leave often do so as a result of changing commitments, but they always express how much they miss the group and still show up at our celebrations when possible. Their absence allows for someone new to join, and this benefits us all with new insights. No matter who is currently participating, the group remains strong and committed. This sustainability is partially due to the productivity of the group but is also in part due to the celebrations and collegiality built over the years. Members have also become each other's supporters and champions. For example, they have become mentors for the tenure process, references for applications, sounding boards to address challenges, and nominators for awards.

Having an entity that oversees, organizes, and schedules the SoTL meetings is crucial to help make things easier for very busy faculty. Although the nature of the CoP includes a lot of flexibility, incorporating some structure and leadership is essential for success and sustainability (Muller, 2006; Wenger & Synder, 2000). The CEE provided the resources, space, logistics, and environment to ensure the continuation and success of this community in accomplishing collective and personal goals year after year.

BRIDGING THE SILOS: COLLECTIVE COLLABORATION

This SoTL CoP was able to bring faculty from disparate disciplines together to address both teaching practice and writing. Below we offer examples from business and sociology to highlight the myriad benefits this group provides.

School of Business Perspective

Similar to most universities, in the School of Business, we operate in silos. The SoTL Community of Practice provides a means to bridge these silos and work together in a collaborative manner. At the same time, we have created a community of people who support each other in their academic, professional, and personal achievements and frustrations. I love meeting with this community to get constructive feedback on my work and to get perspectives from different disciplines. We also each have our strengths that we contribute to the group. (Clinical Professor of Management)

In the field of business, many active research-focused faculty members participate in groups with individuals from a similar discipline and meet on a regular basis to get feedback and constructive criticism on their research. For example, an entrepreneurship faculty member might present research on innovation and get feedback from faculty members in accounting, finance, international business, and operations. This provides a means to bridge the silos in the areas of business and subsequently improve the ultimate research product. Both the discipline-focused peer-mentoring groups, and the broader business-focused research forums (inter-professional mentoring) provide excellent methods to exchange ideas and feedback for discipline-focused research (Lait, 2011). These groups are in line with research that suggests that participation in peer mentoring groups helps forge scholarly identify, which leads to learning by all engaged (Driscoll et al., 2009; Mullen, 2005).

Case studies with teaching notes are often used as pedagogical tools to enhance learning (Hammond, 1976) in the business classroom. Case writing can be challenging for a variety of reasons. First, it is essential to tell a story of interest to the students. The best cases engage the students in a nuanced discussion by offering unique situations faced by businesses with challenges that have a variety of potential solutions. Second, the writer must ensure that sufficient information is presented in the body of the case so that students can answer the discussion questions. Third, and perhaps most challenging, is writing the teaching note. This is a completely separate document that not only offers potential answers to all discussion questions, but also a list of all courses and topics where the case may work; suggested readings and multimedia resources; class activities; and a timeline for how to approach the case in the context of a course.

SoTL is especially helpful in the tricky process of case writing. The SoTL CoP provides a means to get feedback and incorporate ideas from different disciplines (Gannon-Leary & Fontainha, 2007). This ultimately enhances the final product and improves learning outcomes (Lowry, Curtis, & Lowry, 2004). The suggestions of a theater faculty member to tell a good story, combined with having a sociologist who consistently helps come up with "sexy" titles, allow us to implement different approaches to writing that we simply do not have access to in a school of business. The group also allows us to see what is missing and what is superfluous in our case writing. Cases are all about balance, and providing too much information in a case can take away from the learning potential. The SoTL group helps shine a light on where there is too much information and where the case is underdeveloped. Additionally, SoTL can help create novel ways of exploring a case with students. Since each teaching note requires the inclusion of some sort of class activity to help students engage with the case material, the group can generate insightful activities that students truly enjoy. The different ways of thinking offered by each member create an invaluable contribution to the cases.

Sociology Perspective

Writing is initially a solitary endeavor. As an art and a craft, pieces of writing can convey so much more than content—they also convey meaning, emotion, and style. As contemporary writers such as Stephen King and Anne Lamott so eloquently share, writing is a process that demands dedication, commitment, and fearlessness in perfecting the craft (King, 2000; Lamott, 1994). Writing can be as intimidating as it can be liberating because in the end, it requires the writer to actually produce something tangible. That production also necessitates writing again and again: As you write, so shall you rewrite; for even the most prolific and gifted writer cannot do a "one-off". Good writing entails taking a great idea and turning it into a compelling story that can impart knowledge and wisdom while captivating the reader's attention. Writers must consider for what audience they are writing, including the publication parameters as well as the reader. These requirements, then, in some sense, dictate the style of writing needed.

In academia, writing that results in publication is a measure of one's professionalism by contributing to a field of discipline. For the sociologist, writing entails using research skills, evoking a "sociological imagination", and deepening a field of study. The process begins with an inspiration that sparks the writer to delve deeper into a topic by searching for materials that support that nascent idea. Once written, however, that piece must go through a cycle of review, feedback, revision, and editing in order to hone the piece into something that is much better than the original. Finally, what began as a solitary endeavor ends as a more collaborative effort.

As such, writing is both personal and public. Writing takes courage in that it must be put out for public review, and it places us in the vulnerable position of being judged by strangers. Having a SoTL group serves an important function by providing invaluable feedback on a piece prior to sending it off to a potential publisher. Our group's diverse disciplines allow us to be "naïve" but intelligent readers. This multidisciplinary, multi-dimensional group provides insightful comments, suggestions, and genuine support for all of us, helping to remove disciplinary blinders we may not be aware we have. Having reviewers from outside one's discipline truly helps us refine our work because the suggestions and feedback result in much stronger pieces of writing.

LESSONS LEARNED: STRATEGIES FOR DEVELOPING A SUSTAINABLE AND PRODUCTIVE COMMUNITY OF PRACTICE IN SoTL

Below, we outline strategies that others can use when establishing a SoTL group. Our approach and suggestions stem from our own evolution from a learning community to a CoP and are based in the literature as well as our experiences over the years. An important note is that participants are not paid, so funding requirements are minimal. There is the time of staff in the CEE to organize meetings and some minor funding for food at times. The group meets in the CEE conference room, so there is not a lot of coordination for space that needs to take place.

For more detailed notes on our specific approach, please see Table 1.

The Bigger Strategic Picture

Targeted Faculty Development

Taking a developmental approach to achieving goals and launching outreach initiatives across campus is key, but raising awareness was not enough to change the culture of the institution. It is also important to have champions and influencers on the side of SoTL. When other faculty members see people they admire and view as mentors giving testament about how participation in a learning community serves as a professional development opportunity and provides academic success supporters (Hutchings, Huber, & Ciccone, 2011), their interest is piqued and they see the potential in engaging in this type of work.

Alignment With Mission and Value

It is imperative that SoTL work is aligned with your institute's mission and values (Holland, 2005). This is especially true if your institution is undergoing a new strategic planning process. Examine how engaged scholarship and SoTL development might align with these new plans. How does the context of your institution support SoTL work, or do you need to do some work beforehand to get buy-in?

SoTL in the Retention, Promotion, and Tenure Process

Despite the fact that every national academic organization has a section on pedagogy, writing about teaching and learning is not uniformly valued (Webb, 2019). Academic units frequently determine whether or not scholarly works on pedagogy "count" towards retention, promotion, and tenure (Reinke, Muraco, & Maurer, 2016). Department chairs and deans of academic units may need to be convinced that SoTL publications should count and that they are indeed an important aspect of our professional lives. However,

Table 1. How we developed the SoTL CoP

Remember the Big Strategic Picture
Targeted Faculty Development: Through a three-step process, we launched outreach initiatives across campus. A large part of this strategy was to raise awareness of what SoTL work looks like and why the research in this area should be supported as other research agendas are. Bringing noted scholars such as Patti Clayton and Marshall Welch to campus to share their work was an excellent first step, but more support was necessary. Through targeted outreach, the CEE recruited faculty already working in SoTL to speak at various events across campus. This helped raise the awareness of and respect for this type of work.
Alignment with Mission and Values: Our university has a new strategic plan that included "engaged scholarship" as one of the pillars. Striking while the iron is hot can produce momentum in shifting culture. Therefore, the SoTL group is currently reengaging with the broader community about SoTL in order to align with the new strategic plan and build momentum.
SoTL in the retention, promotion, and tenure process: Although SoTL work on our campus is inconsistently supported across the university, the two largest units, the College of Arts and Sciences and the School of Business, have recently rewritten tenure and promotion policies to include SoTL work as valued and encouraged.
Highlight SoTL work on campus: Ensuring that SoTL faculty are consistently mentioned in university-wide publications goes a long way. This practice has helped our university become a Carnegie-classified as well as an Ashoka change-making designated institution.
The Community of Practice
Make it multidisciplinary: Including a diversity of disciplines in the group was absolutely crucial to enhancing broader engagement and understanding of SoTL work. The opportunity to break down silos is one that many faculty members appreciated the most about the community.
Nurture a non-competitive, cooperative, and caring environment: We achieved building a supportive environment through a number of ways. First, we had a schedule of whose work would be presented with the expectation that the piece would be sent to all members of the SoTL group at least one week prior to the scheduled meeting so that all would be prepared for the discussion. If a scheduled presenter was unable to keep to the schedule, the penalty exacted was to bring something sweet to eat. Instead of reviewing a written piece, the presenter was encouraged to verbally discuss the proposed piece of writing and was provided feedback nonetheless. Second, coffee and snacks were always available during the meeting time to help stave off any caffeine deprivation and/or hunger pangs; this helped brighten the mood. Providing feedback in person not only gave the presenter an opportunity to practice presenting ideas but it also created a synergetic space for reviewers to add new comments, insights, and suggestions for revision. Titles for the work frequently emerged during these sessions. Presenting the work live also helped the writer consider other forms of disseminating the information—such as proposing a conference panel, being a conference presenter, or participating in an on-campus lecture series. Several conference papers, panels, poster presentations and workshops were launched as a result of the initial SoTL review.
Be flexible about the writing: We reviewed many "non-traditional" works including a proposal for a new major in Behavioral Neuroscience. We also opened up the meeting to non-community members, on occasion, when there were co-authors who were interested in hearing the group's feedback. These opportunities exposed other faculty members, students, and community partners to the community and created a collaborative spirit of all being "in this together". *Our group morphed from being solely focused on reviewing articles or chapters on pedagogy to covering all aspects of academic writing. Thus, we reviewed grant proposals, conference abstracts, theoretical treatises, book and article proposals, revise and resubmit suggestions, keynote speeches, and conference presentations. This flexibility enormously expanded my field of knowledge by exposing me to aspects of other disciplines, which I would never have had otherwise. Younger colleagues may feel intimidated by or a burden to more senior faculty members by asking them to review their work. Creating a space for genuine collaboration can help all writers become bold not only in their writing but also in their presenting skills and teaching. The process of providing constructive criticism helps writers become more reflective on what they are doing. This, in turn, expands our abilities to imagine better ways of conveying our ideas.* (Professor of Sociology)
Leadership and Ownership
Have a convener: Our group tried several methods—each member taking responsibility to organize one meeting; one member taking responsibility for an entire semester; a rotation system amongst the members; and the presenter organizing the meeting. This somewhat willy-nilly approach proved to be untenable in actual practice. In the end, what worked best was when the convener was the director of the CEE who was not only competent but also efficient and organized. Not only did she have the staff to help organize the schedules, but we also met in the center's meeting space. She took the lead to gather the data to create a schedule for the entire semester. Setting such a specific schedule ensured that we had a time and place to meet and fostered a sense of commitment to the group. Ideally, members of the group should be prepared to present during each semester. The CEE has also set up a literature review of SoTL references from across disciplines to help support faculty members scholarship in this area; all faculty members can use this for their research.
Promote love of learning and development of knowledge: During some meetings, we didn't have any SoTL work to review from the group. We would still meet to discuss other projects we were working on and to bounce ideas about future research off of one another.

continued on following page

Table 1 continued

Find a mentor/Be a mentor: The CoP model has been particularly useful for mentoring junior faculty. Several faculty members were lucky enough to form mentoring relationships that went beyond SoTL. They met regularly outside of the SoTL gatherings. These productive meetings took place off-hours at the university and at our homes. The senior faculty member provided feedback for potential submissions to scholarly journals as part of tenure review, as well as written comments on the junior faculty members' actual tenure materials
Accountability: It is required that the assigned person submit their work a week prior to our meetings in order to give time for people to review it. We also expect people to come prepared to critique and give input. However, as mentioned earlier, we have created a "punishment" of having to bring baked goods to the group. We have rarely had anyone miss their deadlines over the nine years since the group's inception. This may be because of the feeling of community that has been developed so that we hold each other accountable and want to make sure we are there for each member.
Recognition
Celebrate: Over the years, we have added fun elements to build collegiality and support the non-competitive environment of the group. The "punishment clause" for not presenting during one's "turn" morphed into a once-a-semester "White Elephant" gift exchange and potluck celebration—one in December and one in May. Not only are they fun, but they also serve to celebrate our efforts and successes during the year. These celebrations also inspire us to continue in the group and to rededicate ourselves to the writing process. Our celebrations have brought much-needed relief to our usually serious and stress-filled professions. And although each member, over time, has been productive because of the work of this Community of Practice, these moments of celebration are keys to its longevity and success.
Compile and maintain a list of all publications: Not only does this show us exactly what we have accomplished, but it is a way to show others what is possible via SoTL work.

increasingly, chairs and deans across the country are counting SoTL publications, and individual rank and tenure committees are increasingly acknowledging the importance of this type of work.

Highlighting SoTL Work on Campus

Publicizing SoTL work in university-wide publications is an important means of highlighting faculty members who are dedicated to honing their teaching. Additionally, it puts the institution in a good light—especially when it is recognized as being a leader in teaching as well as in research. It is important to cultivate a good working relationship with those on campus responsible for publications that highlight faculty members' achievements. Featuring faculty members who have received awards for their pedagogical pursuits and publications places an institution in the positive limelight it desires.

The Community of Practice

Make It Multidisciplinary

Having a multidisciplinary CoP can provide faculty with a learning opportunity that expands the knowledge base and encourages the formation of collaborative teaching and research projects (Oborn & Dawson, 2010; Stevenson, Duran, Barrett & Colarulli, 2005). Learning different methodologies and approaches to research and pedagogy helps to expand one's skills and broaden one's ways of knowing. Having a diverse group also allows for the creation of interdisciplinary projects that may not happen organically.

Nurture a Non-Competitive, Cooperative, and Caring Environment

Rooted in the literature about CoP is the fact that such approaches to faculty development can provide a nurturing and cooperative environment to support faculty success and institutional change (Klein & Connell, 2008; O'Sullivan, 2007). Create a laid-back atmosphere that includes snacks, if possible, and leave time for conversation about non-research life. Having members really know one another helps develop a stronger sense of community.

Be Flexible About the Writing

SoTL work can occur in a variety of contexts: conference presentations, cases, grant proposals, institutional review board proposals, chapters, and book proposals are all potential outlets so be willing to stray from "typical" journal articles in the context of the group. The most productive SoTL groups deal with faculty members with many different types of projects, at different stages of their careers, and in different disciplines (Weimer, 2006).

Leadership and Ownership

Have a Convener

Having some leadership structure is essential for success (Wenger & Synder, 2000). Using an established organization on campus (like the CEE) with someone specifically in charge of the SoTL planning will yield the best results. If your institution does not have a faculty development or teaching and learning center to assist, see if there is an equivalent administrator who would be willing to organize things, or whether members of the community could rotate duties. Setting dates ahead of time, designating space, and setting personal goals at the beginning of each academic year ensures that there will always be something to review and that people looked at their schedules to see what works. Sending reminder emails is also important and falls under the umbrella of the convener. Members of the community turn to this individual for leadership and support.

Promote Love of Learning and Development of Knowledge

Many academics became professors because they love to learn. Operating in a discipline, academics become experts in a particular subject area. However, a Community of Practice bridging silos across campus provides an opportunity to not only create a community but also to continue that exploration and journey of learning (Wenger, 1999). A SoTL CoP provides an opportunity to be continually reminded of the benefits and joys of learning from different perspectives.

Find a Mentor/Be a Mentor

Mentoring relationships are only natural in CoP (Heinrich & Attebury, 2010). Working closely with a group fosters professional and personal relationships that go a long way to breaking traditional disciplinary and academic divisions. Ensuring that there is a diversity of levels of experience allows more senior faculty to gravitate towards mentorship of the more junior faculty. These relationships can also make junior faculty aware of the opportunities they did not know existed such as the high-impact practice of incorporating community service-learning.

Accountability

At the beginning of each semester, assign people to present what they are working on based on their writing goals. Ensure a specific schedule is established and maintained for meetings and feedback so authors get comments in a timely manner. Should members be unable to meet in person, establish alternative ways to send feedback.

Recognition

Celebrate

Building community is more than having a set of common goals. Encourage a few times a year where members can come together to enjoy each other's company and acknowledge the work that was done. Recognizing each other and providing a break from the grind of academic life is part of creating a successful SoTL group.

Compile and Maintain a List of All Publications

Keeping a complete list of all publications that emerge from the SoTL community can serve not only as a historical record but also as a continuously evolving document as new publications are added. This helps when making the case for the viability of SoTL research across a multitude of disciplines.

OUR CHALLENGES AND YOUR FUTURE DIRECTIONS

As our group continues to evolve we have faced particular challenges. Scheduling meetings has become more challenging, so the group reduced the number of meetings to once a month (for the first six years the group met every three weeks). Additionally, we have adapted to include online feedback via Google Docs for those occasions when we cannot find a time that everyone can meet. The online platform allows us to continue critiquing and giving input even when one or more members cannot physically be present. The group has also grown smaller, and efforts to bring in a new generation of scholars into the fold are underway. It has been challenging to recruit and raise interest in this area because of changes in administration and the expectations for faculty members. Newer faculty members come in with greater demands for scholarship in their disciplines, including finding money to support their work. This takes time away from engaging in what is still often seen as being "less" important work.

Members today tend to be post-tenure or adjunct/ non-tenure-based faculty members. Targeting non-tenure-track faculty members is important to the success of any program, given the rising number of these faculty members in our ranks. Moreover, this population of faculty members tends to do the bulk of teaching, especially in general education areas. Yet, as our group keeps looking to engage new members, going back to our roots by starting from the beginning and training a whole new set of individuals who are interested in SoTL work is of paramount importance.

A key initiative is elevating mentors to help train new faculty members and to reach out to departments and schools that have not had members participate. In several ways, we have taken many steps forward but need to go back to our roots in order to outreach to a broader audience. This next academic year, the CEE will sponsor a new SoTL learning community as a means to find other academics on campus who are interested in pedagogical research and who might potentially be interested in becoming a part of the existing Community of Practice. After all, the CEE started this group almost ten years ago through a similar initiative with great success, and any challenges are well worth the struggle—considering the accomplishments we have made on our own and collectively as a group.

Challenges aside, this group has been truly transformational for past and present members. We encourage you to pick the elements of what we have done that will work at your institution and start your own SoTL Community of Practice. Be prepared to read and learn things far outside of your discipline and enjoy the amazing supportive community that develops as a result.

REFERENCES

Ash, S. L., & Clayton, P. H. (2004). The articulated learning: An approach to guided reflection and assessment. *Innovative Higher Education, 29*(2), 137–154. doi:10.1023/B:IHIE.0000048795.84634.4a

Baskerville, D., & Goldblatt, H. (2009). Learning to be a critical friend: From professional indifference through challenge to unguarded conversations. *Cambridge Journal of Education, 39*(2), 205–221. doi:10.1080/03057640902902260

Chick, N. L. (2018). *SoTL in action: Illuminating critical moments of practice.* Sterling, VA: Stylus.

Christiano, A., & Neimand, A. (2017). Stop raising awareness already. *Stanford Social Innovation Review,* 33–41. Retrieved from https://ssir.org/articles/entry/stop_raising_awareness_already

Cox, M. D. (2004). Introduction to faculty learning communities. *New Directions for Teaching and Learning, 97,* 5–23. doi:10.1002/tl.129

Driscoll, L. G., Parkes, K. A., Tilley-Lubbs, G. A., Brill, J. M., & Bannister, V. R. P. (2009). Navigating the lonely sea: Peer mentoring and collaboration among aspiring women scholars. *Mentoring & Tutoring, 17*(1), 5–21. doi:10.1080/13611260802699532

Foulger, T. (2005). Innovating professional development standards: A shift to utilize Communities of Practice. *Essays in Education, 14*(1), Article 1. Retrieved from https://openriver.winona.edu/eie/vol14/iss1/1

Gannon-Leary, P., & Fontainha, E. (2007). Communities of Practice and virtual learning communities: Benefits, barriers and success factors. *eLearning Papers, 5,* 20-29.

Gilpin, L. S., & Liston, D. (2009). Transformative education in the Scholarship of Teaching and Learning: An analysis of SoTL literature. *International Journal for the Scholarship of Teaching and Learning, 3*(2), 11. doi:10.20429/ijsotl.2009.030211

Hammond, J. S. (1976). *Learning by the case method.* Harvard Business School. Case 9-376-241. Retrieved from http://projects.iq.harvard.edu/files/sdpfellowship/files/hbs_casemethod_overview.pdf

Heinrich, K. T., & Oberleitner, M. G. (2012). How a faculty group's peer mentoring of each other's scholarship can enhance retention and recruitment. *Journal of Professional Nursing, 28*(1), 5–12. doi:10.1016/j.profnurs.2011.06.002 PMID:22261599

Henrich, K. J., & Attebury, R. (2010). Communities of practice at an academic library: A new approach to mentoring at the University of Idaho. *Journal of Academic Librarianship, 36*(2), 158–165. doi:10.1016/j.acalib.2010.01.007

Holland, B. (2005, July). Scholarship and mission in the 21st century university: The role of engagement. In *Proceedings of the Australian Universities Quality Forum* (pp. 11-17). Academic Press.

Hutchings, P., Huber, M. T., & Ciccone, A. (2011). *The Scholarship of Teaching and Learning reconsidered: Institutional integration and impact.* San Francisco, CA: Jossey-Bass.

King, S. (2000). *On writing: A memoir of the craft.* New York, NY: Scribner.

Klein, J. H., & Connell, N. A. (2008). The identification and cultivation of appropriate Communities of Practice in higher education. *Communities of Practice: Creating Learning Environments for Educators, 1*, 65-81.

Lait, J., Suter, E., Arthur, N., & Deutschlander, S. (2011). Interprofessional mentoring: Enhancing students' clinical learning. *Nurse Education in Practice, 11*(3), 211–215. doi:10.1016/j.nepr.2010.10.005 PMID:21093376

Lamott, A. (1994). *Bird by bird: Some instructions on writing and life.* New York, NY: Pantheon Books.

Lancaster, J. W., Stein, S. M., MacLean, L. G., Van Amburgh, J., & Persky, A. M. (2014). Faculty development program models to advance teaching and learning within health science programs. *American Journal of Pharmaceutical Education, 78*(5), 99. doi:10.5688/ajpe78599 PMID:24954939

Lee, A., & Boud, D. (2003). Writing groups, change, and academic identity: Research development as local practice. *Studies in Higher Education, 28*(2), 187–200. doi:10.1080/0307507032000058109

Lowry, P. B., Curtis, A., & Lowry, M. R. (2004). Building a taxonomy and nomenclature of collaborative writing to improve interdisciplinary research and practice. *The Journal of Business Communication, 41*(1), 66-99.

Lueddeke, G. R. (2003). Professionalising teaching practice in higher education: A study of disciplinary variation and 'teaching-scholarship'. *Studies in Higher Education, 28*(2), 213–288. doi:10.1080/0307507032000058082

McKinney, K. (2006). Attitudinal and structural factors contributing to challenges in the work of the Scholarship of Teaching and Learning. *New Directions for Institutional Research, 2006*(129), 37–50. doi:10.1002/ir.170

McKinney, K. (2007). *Enhancing learning through the Scholarship of Teaching and Learning: The challenges and joys of juggling.* San Francisco, CA: Anker.

Moore, J. L. (2018). Writing SoTL: Going public for an extended audience. In N. L. Chick (Ed.), *SoTL in action: Illuminating critical moments of practice* (pp. 119–126). Sterling, VA: Stylus.

Mullen, C. A. (2005). *The mentorship primer*. New York, NY: Peter Lang.

Muller, P. (2006). Reputation, trust, and the dynamics of leadership in Communities of Practice. *The Journal of Management and Governance, 10*(4), 381–400. doi:10.100710997-006-9007-0

Nugent, J. S., Reardon, R. M., Smith, F. G., Rhodes, J. A., Zander, M. J., & Carter, T. J. (2008). Exploring faculty learning communities: Building connections among teaching, learning, and technology. *International Journal on Teaching and Learning in Higher Education, 20*(1), 51–58.

O'Sullivan, M. (2007). Creating and sustaining Communities of Practice among physical education professionals. *New Zealand Physical Educator, 40*(1), 10–13.

Oborn, E., & Dawson, S. (2010). Learning across Communities of Practice: An examination of multidisciplinary work. *British Journal of Management, 21*(4), 843–858. doi:10.1111/j.1467-8551.2009.00684.x

Reinke, J., Muraco, J., & Maurer, T. W. (2016). The state of the Scholarship of Teaching and Learning in family science. *Family Science Review*, 10; Advance online publication.

Richlin, L., & Cox, M. D. (2004). Developing scholarly teaching and the Scholarship of Teaching and Learning through faculty learning communities. *New Directions for Teaching and Learning, 2004*(97), 127–135. doi:10.1002/tl.139

Segalla, M. (2008). Publishing in the right place or publishing the right thing: Journal targeting and citations' strategies for promotion and tenure committees. *European Journal of International Management, 2*(2), 122–127. doi:10.1504/EJIM.2008.017765

Stevenson, C. B., Duran, R. L., Barrett, K. A., & Colarulli, G. C. (2005). Fostering faculty collaboration in learning communities: A developmental approach. *Innovative Higher Education, 30*(1), 23–36. doi:10.100710755-005-3293-3

Webb, A. S. (2019). Navigating the lows to gain new heights: Constraints to SoTL engagement. *The Canadian Journal for the Scholarship of Teaching and Learning, 10*(2). doi:10.5206/cjsotl-rcacea.2019.2.8173

Weimer, M. (2006). *Enhancing scholarly work on teaching and learning: Professional literature that makes a difference*. San Francisco, CA: Jossey-Bass.

Welch, M. (1999). The ABCs of reflection: A template for students and instructors to implement written reflection in service-learning. *NSEE Quarterly, 25*(2), 1, 23–25. Retrieved from https://digitalcommons.unomaha.edu/slceeval/16

Wenger, E. (1999). *Communities of Practice: Learning, meaning, and identity*. Oxford, UK: Cambridge University Press.

Wenger, E. (2011). *Communities of Practice: A brief introduction*. Academic Press.

Wenger, E. C., & Snyder, W. M. (2000). Communities of Practice: The organizational frontier. *Harvard Business Review, 78*(1), 139–146. PMID:11184968

KEY TERMS AND DEFINITIONS

Case Study: A process or record of research in which detailed consideration is given to the development of a particular person, group, or situation over a period of time.

Center for Educational Excellence (CEE): The CEE is the faculty development center at the University of San Diego.

Community of Practice: A Community of Practice is a group of people who share a concern or a passion for something they dd and learn how to do it better as they interact regularly.

Faculty Learning Community (FLC): FLCs are is a group of trans-disciplinary faculty of size 6-15 or more (8 to 12 is the recommended size) engaging in an active, collaborative, yearlong program with a curriculum about enhancing teaching and learning and with frequent seminars and activities that provide learning, development, transdisciplinarity, the Scholarship of Teaching and Learning, and community building.

Interdisciplinary: Relating to more than one branch of knowledge.

Multidisciplinary: A group of people who share a concern or a passion for something they do and learn how to do it better as they interact regularly.

Scholarship of Teaching and Learning (SoTL): A systematic inquiry into student learning which advances the practice of **teaching** in higher education by making inquiry findings public.

APPENDIX 1

Sample References From Some Members of SoTL Group (in Descending Order)

Interdisciplinary Collaborative Efforts Within the Group

Sgoutas-Emch, S. A., Baird, L., Camacho, M., Friedman, J., & Lord, S. (2016). Fostering success to support a cohort /cluster of women in STEM at the University of San Diego. NSF ADVANCE/ GSE Program Workshop.

Sgoutas-Emch, S. A., Nayve, C., Liu, J., & Loggins, J. (2016). Supporting seasoned practitioners by bridging community engagement, social change and scholarship. New Orleans, LA: IARSLCE.

Sgoutas-Emch, S. A., Baird, L., Myers, P. Camacho, M., & Lord, S. (2016). We're not all white men: Using a cohort/cluster approach to diversify faculty hiring in STEM. *Journal of Thought and Action, 32*(1), 91–107.

Advancement of female faculty: Institutional climate, recruitment, and mentoring (AFFIRM), National Science Foundation. $599,414 awarded during the 8/15/11–7/31/16 period.

Ehrich, K., Ceranic, T., & Liu, J. (2014). Business unusual: Transforming business school curricula through community engagement. *Metropolitan Universities Journal, 25*, 111–124.

Sgoutas-Emch, S., Ceranic, T., Liu, J., & Zarate, S. (2014). Preparing faculty for the scholarly work of civic engagement. New Orleans, LA: International Association for Research on Service Learning and Community Engagement Conference.

Lord. S., Camacho. M., Myers, P. Sgoutas-Emch, S., Baird, L., & Friedman, J. (2014). Interactive theatre to engage faculty in difficult dialogs: First implementation. Madrid, Spain: Frontiers in Education (FIE) conference.

Baird, L., Friedman, J., Lord, S., Camacho, M, Myers, P., & Sgoutas-Emch, S. (2014). Using mixed methods to assess campus climate for faculty and develop programming for retention. Washington D.C: ADVANCE NSF conference.

Baird, L., Boyd, M., Friedman, J., Hubbard, L., Lord, S., Myers, P., & Sgoutas-Emch, S. (2013). AFFIRM's mentoring inside out: A pilot project for early career female faculty. Washington D.C: ADVANCE NSF conference.

Ehrich, K., Ceranic, T., & Liu, J. (2012). Business unusual: Transforming business school curricula through community engagement. Chattanooga, TN: Paper presented at the Coalition of Urban and Metropolitan Universities.

Ehrich, K., Ceranic, T., & Liu, J. (2012). Business unusual: Transforming business school curricula through community service-learning. Seattle, WA: Workshop at the 15th Annual Continuums of Service Conference.

Ehrich, K., Ceranic, T., & Liu, J. (2011). Beyond the bottom line: Incorporating service learning in a business school. Poster presentation. San Diego, CA: 14th Annual Continuums of Service Conference.

Psychological Sciences

Sumner, S., Sgoutas-Emch, S. A., Nunn, L., & Kirkley, E. (2017). Implementing innovative pedagogy and a rainbow curriculum to expand learning on diversity. *InSight: A Journal for Scholarly Teaching, 12*, 94–119.

Guerrieri, K., & Sgoutas-Emch, S. (2016). Immersions in global equality and social justice: A model of change. *Engaging Pedagogies in Catholic Higher Education, 2*(1), Article 4.

Sgoutas-Emch, S. A. (2011). Dilemmas working on the politics of community: Lessons from community service learning and health psychology. In C. Cress and D. M. Donahue, *Democratic dilemmas of teaching service learning: Tensions, trials, and triumphs*. Sterling, VA: Stylus Press.

Business Management

Meyskens, M., Shi, Ruixia, & Munshi, A. (Submitted). JD.com. International expansion of the Chinese e-commerce powerhouse. Case study.

Meyskens, M., Christensen, R., & Marquez, P. (2019). Social entrepreneurship competitions: Hoping for funding and gaining valuable experience in the process—An exploratory study. *New frontiers in entrepreneurial finance research*. New Jersey: World Scientific Publishing.

Meyskens, M., & Auch, N. (2013). An exploratory study of social venture competitions: Value creation at the individual, venture and societal levels. *Theory and Empirical Research in Social Entrepreneurship*. Northhampton, MA: Edward Elgar Publishing.

Sociology

Liu, J. (2016). Reflections on skipping stones to diving deep: The process of immersion as a practice. *Engaging Pedagogies in Catholic Higher Education, 2*(1). Retrieved from http://dx.doi.org/10.18263/2379-920X.1011

Liu, J. (2016). Supporting seasoned practitioners by bridging community engagement, social change and scholarship. Presentation at the International Association for Research on Service Learning and Community Engagement (IARSLCE) Conference. New Orleans, LA: IARSLCE.

Liu, J., Darby, M., & Leppard, E. (2019). Learning by growing: The promise of public sociology. Panel at the Pacific Sociological Association (PSA). Oakland, CA: PSA.

Theology and Religious Studies

Browning, M., & Reimer-Barry, E. (2013). Preaching, sexuality, and women religious: Listening to prophetic voices at the margins of religious life. *Theology and Sexuality, 19*(1), 69–88.

Reimer-Barry, E. (2013). Reflecting on fieldwork in Tijuana: Embodied ethnography and lingering concerns [roundtable discussion]. *Practical Matters: A Transdisciplinary Multimedia Journal of Religious Practices and Practical Theology, 6*(Spring 2013). Retrieved from http://www.practicalmattersjournal.org/issue/6/centerpieces/reflecting-on-fieldwork-in-tijuana

Reimer-Barry, E. (2013). Changemaker in the making? Moral development in the college classroom. Action Research Conference. University of San Diego: School of Leadership and Educational Sciences.

Reimer-Barry, E. Faculty Innovation in Teaching Grant, 2014–2015.

Reimer-Barry, E. Center for Educational Excellence Travel Grant, 2014.

Chapter 6
Reflection and SoTL:
Putting Reflection (Back) on Faculty Radar

Laura Zizka

ⓘ https://orcid.org/0000-0001-5835-685X

Ecole hoteliere de Lausanne, Switzerland & HES-SO University of Applied Sciences and Arts of Western Switzerland, Switzerland

ABSTRACT

Reflection was introduced into educational institutions to encourage students to seek beyond the descriptive and simple response toward critical, deep thinking, and effectively make better choices. It is also an integral part of the structured inquiry of one's teaching through the Scholarship of Teaching and Learning (SoTL). Based on Dewey and Schön's foundation of reflection as linked to actions undertaken in apprentices' daily tasks, this chapter attempts to dispel common misconceptions related to reflection to show that reflection can and should be encouraged by all stakeholders in educational programs regardless of the discipline, level, or type of study. A Reflection Radar has been created to identify reflective practices in teaching and learning. The chapter concludes with how reflection through SoTL can and should be implemented as a solid, formative pedagogical tool at all levels of education and contribute to the scholarship of teaching and learning for all educators.

INTRODUCTION

Reflection has been effectively used in educational institutions to encourage students to seek beyond the descriptive and simple response to critical, deep thinking and, effectively, make better choices. It has been used as part of the structured inquiry of one's teaching through the Scholarship of Teaching and Learning (SoTL). SoTL has been defined as scholarship in education that involves new and critical interpretations of what is already known about teaching and learning (Healey, 2000). SoTL promotes a professional engagement with teaching and learning through formal, informal, or critically reflective inquiry to support teachers and students at various moments in their learning journeys (Kreber, 2015). A scholarly approach to teaching and learning through SoTL involves, amongst other elements, evaluating, reflecting, and, subsequently, disseminating these reflections on teaching and learning practices.

DOI: 10.4018/978-1-7998-2212-7.ch006

Reflection and critical reflection that SoTL encourages leads to transformation in teaching and learning (Liu, 2015). Nonetheless, to effectively reflect on how SoTL is informing teaching practices, teachers must understand the theoretical underpinnings of reflection and critical reflection. According to Cranton (2011), "learning about teaching is to learn about supporting students' learning of the discipline in the best possible way, or, in other words, the Scholarship of Teaching and Learning" (p. 81).

Based on Dewey and Schön's foundation of reflection as linked to specific actions which apprentices or workers undertake in their daily tasks, i.e., reflection-in-action and reflection-on-action, this chapter attempts to dispel common misconceptions related to reflection to show that reflection can and should be encouraged in all educational institutions regardless of the discipline, level, or type of study. Reflection through SoTL should be a positive opportunity for faculty developers and educators to inform their academic career development. This reflection offers opportunities in the classroom setting where critical thinking skills are addressed, and authentic learning is/should be taking place.

The purpose of this chapter is to encourage all educators and faculty developers to consider reflection as a significant tool to create authentic teaching and learning practices both inside and outside the classroom. In today's educational system, it is important for students to transfer problems across educational and workplace contexts (Tanggaard, 2007) and address real-world problems. Real life problems rarely have a quick fix or simple answer as they necessarily entail the data or description the student has gathered (Rodgers, 2002) as well as their existing beliefs, heuristics, theory, knowledge, experience, etc. which each student will rely upon to decipher what the data or description is actually saying (Hebert, 2015). Learning then is transformed by the experiences in which the student participates (Miettinen, 2000). However, two students can look at the same event and see it differently, and different cultures may interpret the same stimulus in different ways (Miettinen, 2000). In many instances, there may not be one straightforward "right" answer but a need to have alternative ways of seeing things (Thompson & Pascal, 2012). Thus, "reflection itself becomes not a means to an end or something to perform, but rather a way of being in the world" (Hebert, 2015, p. 369).

The Reflection Radar can be used to stimulate inquiry into one's own teaching practice and student learning. The underlying premise is that this project could be implemented in any school, regardless of level or area of studies. It begins by identifying the four levels of activities frequently implemented in the classroom, i.e., habitual actions, understanding, reflection, and critical reflection and differentiates between reflection and critical reflection. It continues with the four common misconceptions about reflection, i.e., elitist, asocial, disruptive, and unreal, and attempts to dispel these misconceptions to offer a healthier and more positive version of reflection in education. A first attempt at a Reflection Radar based on reflection has been provided to help educational institutions at all levels to visualize the effectiveness and depth of reflection within their existing programs. Clearly, faculty developers need to understand how teachers *think* learning occurs (Grant & Hurd, 2010) and why they have chosen one task or pedagogy over another to impart content-specific knowledge. This Reflection Radar can offer an opportunity for educators and faculty developers to learn from each other in a collaborative process. The chapter concludes with how reflection through SoTL can and should be implemented as a solid, formative pedagogical tool at all levels of education and contribute to the Scholarship of Teaching and Learning for all educators.

BACKGROUND

The use of reflection as initially defined by Dewey and adapted by Schön for apprentices or workers will be elaborated upon and applied to higher education settings. The concept of reflection was the subject of pedagogical importance for Dewey, often referred to as the founding father of the concept of reflection, early in the 20th century (Van Beveren, Roets, Buysse, & Rutten, 2018). Dewey (1933) defined reflection as "active, persistent and careful consideration of any belief or supposed form of knowledge in the light of the grounds that support it and further conclusion to which it tends" (p. 9). For Dewey, reflection was difficult to assess, difficult to talk about, and difficult to research effects on education and professional development (Rodgers, 2002). Perhaps, for this reason, he focused on systematic, rigorous, and disciplined reflection deeply rooted in scientific inquiry (Rodgers, 2002). While reflecting on making sense of the world and questioning any belief or supposed form of knowledge through "active, persistent, and careful consideration" (Dewey, 1938, p. 9) was admirable, not all problems are, strictly speaking, scientific. For that reason, Schön's elaboration on Dewey's reflection and reflective thinking and his terms of reflection-in-action and reflection-on-action have been adopted and adapted and remain the reference used in reflection research today. Schön's reflection-in-action, or thinking while doing the task, involves being mindful of and in the moment while reflection-on-action entails thinking after the event or action is completed (Hebert, 2015; Hickson, 2011; Johnston & Fells, 2017; Thompson & Pascal, 2012; Van Beveren et al., 2018; Wopereis, Sloep, & Poortman., 2010; Yanow & Tsoukas, 2009). Reflection-in-action is based on routinized action, the encounter of surprise, and reflection leading to new action and is often an improvised response which allows the participant to reflect while amid the action without interrupting what one is doing (Yanow & Tsoukas, 2009). This is most commonly referred to as 'thinking on your feet'. After a task is complete, the reflection-on-action begins where students "explore the understanding they have brought to the handling of the case" (Schön, 1983, p. 61).

Reflection is multi-faceted, complex, rigorous, intellectual, and emotional (Ryan & Ryan, 2012) and is often based on ill-defined or wicked problems that are dealt with in professional practice or real life. In fact, reflection itself can be considered a 'wicked' problem in its own right (Harvey, Coulson, Mackaway, & Winchester-Seeto, 2010). While Schön argued that professional education courses could use a rational approach to solve well-defined problems with unique solutions, this is rarely the case in most higher education settings (Kember et al., 2000). Problems are ambiguous, solutions are varied, and the context may constantly be changing.

Before focusing on this chapter's topic of reflection, it is important to understand the range of tasks that students are expected to complete and the teaching that prepares them to do so. There are four categories commonly employed in teaching and learning in traditional classrooms: Habit, understanding, reflection, and critical reflection (Kember et al., 2000; Kember, McKay, Sinclair, & Wong, 2008). Within the classroom setting, a mix of all four categories is common, and, some would argue, necessary. Habitual actions also referred to as 'non-reflection,' are characterized by responding to a task without trying to understand it, i.e., surface learning (Kember et al., 2008), and can be practiced until it is performed automatically, like riding a bike (Kember et al., 2000). In the next stage, understanding, students are expected to search for underlying meanings often learned from books or lectures (Kember et al., 2008). While students provide evidence of understanding, they are not obliged to reflect upon its significance in personal or practical situations (Kember et al., 2000). The third category and the purpose of this chapter is reflection. Reflection happens when students take a concept they have learned and relate it to personal experience to make stronger connections between theory and practice (Harvey et al., 2010). Students make sense of experiences in relation to self, others, and specific contexts (Wong, 2016). Reflection includes both intellectual and affective activities (Kember et al., 2000). The final stage and the one that is rarely reached is that of critical reflection. Critical reflection is defined as a deeper, more thoughtful, and profound reflection (Kember et al., 2000) that results in deep, active learning (Ryan & Ryan, 2012). In examining all possible outcomes before taking a decision, students undergo a transformation of perspective (Kember et al., 2000) guided by transformative learning (Harvey et al., 2010) or through a transformative approach (Ryan & Ryan, 2012). But critical reflection is time-consuming as it necessitates considering all potential outcomes before reacting and relies on practice and feedback (Harvey et al., 2010) to reap the full benefits of this reflection. In the real world and within the restraints of an overloaded scholastic schedule, time is a luxury that most programs cannot allow.

REFLECTION IN EDUCATIONAL INSTITUTIONS

In educational institutions of all levels, reflection has been categorized as elitist, asocial, disruptive, and unreal. The four misconceptions related to reflection will be addressed and redefined as seen below:

1. From reflection is elitist to reflection is democratic.
2. From reflection is asocial to reflection is collective.
3. From reflection is disruptive to reflection is constructive.
4. From reflection is unreal to reflection is authentic.

Elitist to Democratic

There is a long tradition of elitism in education, beginning with the economically elite. In the past, the opportunity to be educated was a privilege accessible only by the top economic tier of society who had the money and time to be educated. Education offered opportunities to the ruling classes and promoted a culture that served their interests and needs (Rowland, 2001), including the continuation of their accumulated wealth and status. The second wave of elitism derived from identifying the talent elite. As the centuries moved on, a talent for learning, great intelligence, or an "exceptional mind" was also recognized as a golden ticket to enter into university. Access to education evolved from an economic advantage to a talent advantage, but some advantage was necessary nonetheless. In China, for example, a college degree has become the "golden ticket" into the elite group, although access to elite universities with ample resources and renowned teaching staff allocated by the government remains restrictive (Wu, 2017) and the concept of elite education still exists despite advances in accessibility to higher education for all. The "best" students continue to attend the "best schools", which are predominantly expensive, private institutions (Bergh & Fink, 2009), and the vicious cycle of elitism continues. The most powerful elite voices continue to be heard but not those of the old elite, the wealthy or most talented; rather, the voices of the marketplace (Rowland, 2001). Elitism, in this manner, is linked to the business and quantitative value of education, which is standardized and measured, but to what end? Embracing the same logic, then, the opportunity to be educated is elitist, learning is elitist, research is elitist, and academia, in general, is elitist as long as the results can be quantified through the number of student graduates, course evaluation scores, number of publications in high ranked reviews, and the ranking of the school on a global scale.

Nonetheless, in the last century, education has shifted from an elite privilege to an opportunity for the masses. While some would argue that education should be accessible to all and has reduced social inequality (Wu, 2017), others argue that this has led to a "dumbing down" of the curriculum (Rowland, 2001), a lowering of standards, and a devaluation of college credentials (Wu, 2017) resulting in a less educated and less prepared mass of graduates on the work market. Rowland (2001) suggested that higher education today is little more than "preparation for the job market" (p. 1).

Reflection for All

Reflection "involves understanding one's own process of learning in various contexts" (Wopereis et al., 2010, p. 246) and "thinking deeply or carefully about something" (Hebert, 2015, p. 361) which is valuable for professional practice and lifelong learning (Van Beveren et al., 2018). Reflection is about engaging otherness and enacting connectedness (Hibbert, Sillince, Diefenbach, & Cunliffe, 2014) across the disciplines and education as a whole through multidisciplinary conversations and "notice the noticing" in relationships with others (p. 286). It is useful when developing an awareness of others in the school and work context (Van Beveren, 2018). While distinctions still exist between the levels or types of reflection, ranging from technical and practical to more critical forms (Van Beveren et al., 2018), reflection is, in fact, the antithesis of elitism. Levels or types of reflection may exist, but the potential to reflect remains constant regardless of education. Thus, reflection is appropriate and accessible for all regardless of educational level or degree program. In SoTL projects, researchers are engaged in the same activity as their students, i.e., learning (Healey, 2000). Both teachers and students benefit from this relationship. For example, an Academic Writing teacher uses academic writing principles when writing journal articles and is faced with the same challenges when receiving feedback from reviewer critiques. In this way, this teacher plays the triple role of teacher and researcher and learner. These teachers/researchers/learners have more credibility in the eyes of the students compared to a teacher who simply studied academic writing back in university as they can empathize with students' struggles when trying to write a paper.

SoTL research remains a victim of elitism in educational institutions where there are "written and unwritten, articulated and invisible, and open and hidden ideologies related to teaching and learning" (Cranton, 2011, p. 78). While it is more difficult to "identify excellence in teaching compared to excellence in research" (Healey, 2000, p. 176), there is no guarantee that being a productive researcher also means being a good teacher. At present, researchers choose to conduct research that is discipline-specific as it will lead to more recognition within their area of expertise at the price of conducting SoTL projects to advance the knowledge on teaching and learning. For most academics, "their primary allegiance is to their subject or profession" (Healey, 2000, p. 173). They fear losing the power of their expertise by spreading their research too thin. Further, in the ever competitive "publish-or-perish" mentality encouraged in many institutions, researchers seeks publication in the highest ranking journals in their area of expertise rather than more general SoTL journals. At present, then, it is more advantageous to be a successful researcher in one's area of expertise as opposed to collaborating with colleagues in other areas to publish in lower-tiered journals. Often, teachers are placed in categories such as research predominant, teaching only, or a combination of research and teaching. Teaching must be recognized as inquiry that is relevant to research and a scholarly endeavor in its own right (Gilpin & Liston, 2009). Educators need to be aware of the value of their content-specific knowledge and critical of the knowledge produced by researchers (Liu, 2015). Educational institutions continue to proliferate this elitism by openly acknowledging the success of research professors while struggling with ways to give the same attention to recognize good teachers and good teaching. Nonetheless, 'if teaching is to be valued equally with research, then, like research, teaching must open itself up to the scrutiny of theoretical perspectives, methods, evidence, and results" (Healey, 2000, p. 176).

Asocial to Collective

While reflection was initially portrayed as a quiet, internal process, reflection today is seen as a collective practice that only has meaning when shared with others. This is done most commonly in groups called Communities of Practice or COPs.

Reflection as a Solitary Activity

Education was initially constructed as an individual activity which focused on the learner as an individual (Roth & Lee, 2006). Historically, for those who could afford it, private tutors were employed to impart knowledge on the child or children in the home. In early schools, children were grouped together often in one room, regardless of age or previous knowledge. The concept of learning in a group as a group was born, only to be replaced by a new set of divisive criteria. As the school system evolved and grew, students were divided into grade levels, and further divided based on reading and math levels as well. Remedial courses, "standard" courses, and honors courses joined the divisions. Regardless of the school setting, students worked toward specific targets or grades and compared themselves to others rarely in the process, albeit to establish their ranking as a "better" student than the others.

Collective/Social Side of Reflection

Reflecting individually can lead students and faculty down the wrong road; reflection needs to be compared by and to others as an "active, intentional, and purposeful process of exploration, discovery, and learning" (Lin, Hmelo, Kinzer, & Secules, 1999, p. 46). As people learn as members of society and the larger world (Tanggaard, 2007) and "human existence is fundamentally social" (Thompson & Pascal, 2012, p. 318), there is a need for support to engage in the process of reflection based on inquiry (Rodgers, 2002) as "one has to assimilate, imaginatively, something of another's experience in order to tell him intelligently of one's own experience" (See Dewey, 1916/1944, p. 6). Traditionally, reflection was seen as an individual learning experience which neglected the emotional dimension of learning (Kember et al., 2000; Thompson & Pascal, 2012). However, humans interact with their own thoughts and those of others as a means of constantly interacting and accommodating new experiences and actors to make new connections (Tsoukas & Chia, 2002). Reflection necessitates consideration of the emotional aspects of an experience (de la Croix & Veen, 2018; Harvey et al., 2010). According to Orlikowski (2002), "knowing is ongoing social accomplishment, constituted and reconstituted as actors engage the world in practice" (p. 249). For this reason, reflection has been accepted as a collective and social practice (Johnston & Fells, 2017) and the practice leading to that reflection has been referred to as 'social' (Yanow, 2014).

Communities of Practice

One crucial aspect of the collective side of reflection derives from its innate ability to encourage groups of people with common goals to join together as communities of learners, knowledge-building communities, pedagogic hubs (Ryan & Ryan, 2012), or, most commonly referred to as Communities of Practice (Hibbert, 2012; Roth & Lee, 2006). According to Tanggaard (2007), "learning is about becoming a member of certain practices and gaining access to valuable learning, leading to a form of belonging to and being accepted into these practices" (p. 465). Yet simply putting students into the same classroom does not constitute a Community of Practice; rather, this supposition proliferates the fallacy whereby "individual learning is said to constitute the basis for collective learning" (Roth & Lee, 2006, p. 28) and, by grouping individuals together, a genuine collective is formed. Rather, a Community of Practice involves "individuals who have the same object of activity—producing identical or similar objects act in analogous ways" (Roth & Lee, 2006, p. 28). Following this logic, then, a group of service apprentices could form a Community of Practice; they have the same training, learn identical skills, and are expected to contribute to one goal, i.e., ensuring the overall success of that service and, subsequently, guarding the reputation of the establishment.

The community environment cannot be created without established ground rules that encourage maximum participation from all members of the group through participant comfort, engagement, and empowerment (Beaudoin, 2012). In this manner, a 'safe' place is established where participants, both students, and faculty, can share knowledge and experiences without the risk of judgment or disdain. When participants can share freely without fear, the process of lifelong learning has begun. Participants can question their beliefs, philosophies, and practices in an open and trusting climate (Beaudoin, 2012; Harvey et al., 2010; Ryan & Ryan, 2012; Wong, 2016). They will soon realize that they learn as much through the sharing of their own experiences as the experiences of others and will be surprised that so much learning can and will be done outside of the traditional classroom setting. In fact, more learning may take place within their community.

In SoTL projects, Communities of Practice encourage critical conversations between like-minded individuals, not judgments on individual practices (Lui, 2015). Educators are encouraged to reflect on an on-going basis in a collaborative manner in a community setting (Benade, 2015). As a community, educators need to "scaffold, promote, and value each other's teaching, research, writing, and professional development" (Swanson & Kayler, 2010, p. 3). Educators seek out structured opportunities for dialogue that encourages collective learning. Unfortunately, though, many conversations and Communities of Practice revolve around specific content areas and the specificities of each (Swanson & Kayler, 2010) rather than encouraging dissemination of findings with the larger community.

Disruptive to Constructive

Reflection as Disruptive

Previous literature examined the disruptive effect of reasoning and deliberation that could be explained by several specificities related to reflection in itself. One aspect of reflection which could potentially be disruptive is the surprise or puzzle which interrupts the regular, stable action and leads to adjustments in the action (Yanow, 2014). A second disruptive aspect leading to reflection is the unexpected backtalk (Yanow, 2014) or backchat (Johnston & Fells, 2017). The third element derives from the critical nature of reflection, that is, the ability to accept criticism and justify the assumptions on which beliefs and values have developed (Hickson, 2011). Finally, reflection has a dark side where participants either believe their own stories or are unable to be critical about their assumptions or focus uniquely on the weaknesses and mistakes (Hickson, 2011). In short, reflective practices are intellectually unsettling (Benade, 2015).

Further, educators may revert to "shortcutting" or using the same solutions regardless of the context or actors involved or show signs of "evidence blindness", that is the inability to accept evidence that impugns one's beliefs despite the compelling character of that evidence" (Yanow, 2014, p. 30) as they may lack the necessary body of rich experiences to make appropriate changes to the surprise they encounter (Hibbert, 2012) and lack appropriate theoretical background to address these issues in their reflections. Further, teachers may become reflective zombies, defined by de la Croix and Veen (2018) as those "who have been conditioned to follow prescribed steps rather than engaging in truly reflective behavior" (p. 394). These zombies have learned how to replicate certain phrases and expressions that emulate reflection without actually having reflected at all (de la Croix & Veen, 2018). It would only be through interrogation that these individuals would be caught out and their sham would be exposed. These examples of the "dark" side of reflection can be destructive or harmful (Hickson, 2011) and disrupt authentic reflection from taking place.

Building Courses From the Rubble

Disruption often occurs as a result of untrained and inexperienced educators embarking on actions for which they lack knowledge and expertise (Holt, 1999). Thus, there is a clear need for knowledge, training, and practice to fill the gaps and reduce or eliminate the disruptive effects of reflection. One such way is through educational programs that embolden teachers at all levels to learn from experts, i.e., more experienced colleagues, who encourage them to perform expert tasks as if they knew what they were doing, followed by reflection and feedback. The benefit of learning from their actions, right or wrong, could be catalysts to inspire the need for more theoretical learning.

Yet disruption to one is construction for another; it is all about finding a common language or meaningful dialogue where ideas and issues can be discussed freely to move forward toward shared progress (Beaudoin, 2012). Dialogue and collaboration bring new ideas and structure to "messy" problems (Dickerson et al., 2016; Ryan & Ryan, 2012) by offering a richer understanding of the existing phenomenon (Beaudoin, 2012). As the participants never know where the conversation will lead, the potential is unlimited. Nonetheless, this exciting opportunity of collaborative and rich dialogue does have its drawbacks: Collaboration can be complex and needs respect and trust to work (Dickerson et al., 2016).

SoTL is an advocate of transformative learning (Cranton, 2011; Lundgren & Poell, 2016), or education that helps individuals see themselves as relative to larger social structures (Gilpin & Listor, 2009, p. 8), as posited by Mezirow. This type of learning requires critical reflection and questioning the validity of long taken-for-granted meaning in regard to oneself (Liu, 2015). Learning becomes, in a sense, emancipatory (Gilpin & Listor, 2016) as imaginative speculation explores new ways of thinking to challenge our current ways of knowing (Liu, 2015). Reflection, a cornerstone of SoTL and teacher-conducted research, is "foundational for transformative education" (Gilpin & Listor, 2009, p. 6). In transformative education, there is a deep shift in perspective, making the mind more open to new learning experiences. The educator's role is to "recognize the need for change and be willing to break with the past" (Benade, 2015, p. 45). The experience of conducting research such as the SoTL project expanded upon in this chapter is transformative in nature for the individual educator and researcher (Cranton, 2011).

Unreal to Authentic

Reflection as Unreal

During their educational experience, students and faculty are faced with a mix of familiarity (and legitimacy) and strangeness and with an environment which is constantly changing, evolving, and adapting based on different objects and participation across contexts (Tanggaard, 2007). For example, students are asked to assimilate information for many courses simultaneously while focusing on their own learning styles and place in society (Ryan & Ryan, 2012). Further, they are asked to provide feedback to others, i.e., their peers, on this same learning process. Even further, just when students think they have understood a topic, a new element or concept is introduced. For some students, adding reflection to changing contexts complicates the learning process, and these students fail to see the legitimacy or relevance of reflection. After all, how can one reflect on a context that has changed since the student experienced it? For this reason, when faced with a reflective task, students may revert to superficial interpretations of complex issues (Ash & Clayton, 2004; Ryan & Ryan, 2012) or long descriptive prose of what they have seen; neither being a reflection. Educators need to be aware of these legitimate student concerns in regards to reflection and address them in an honest and safe classroom setting before asking students to just reflect.

Through partnerships with others, innovative solutions to existing problems can be found (Acai et al., 2017; Dickerson, Jarvis, & Stockwell, 2016). In today's educational institutions, student roles can shift from passive consumers to "prosumers" who produce specific content to partners or co-produces of knowledge (Dickerson et al., 2016) to "co-sumers" who co-create all elements of the learning experience with the faculty and staff. There is a need for educational institutions to move from research-led to research-based teaching that supports student inquiry (Jenkins & Healey, 2015) and encourages a question-asking environment. The SoTL environment is ideal for promoting this shift in student and faculty attitudes toward a positive and productive relationship.

There is one further element to making the reflection more authentic, that of emotions. Emotion resides at the heart of transformation (Cranton, 2011) as emotion-laden experiences lead to greater personal development and growth (Lundgren & Poell, 2016). As seen earlier, SoTL projects encourage transformative education where trying new learning experiences is seen as an advantage, not a mistake. Learning to reflect and the reflections themselves involve a continuing process that is both individual and social. Nonetheless, it is often a messy process (de la Croix & Veen, 2018) filled with perplexity, hesitation, and doubt (Ash & Clayton, 2004) with no clear cut responses or correct answers. Authentic reflection involves emotions and entails finding the meaning of an event in relation to one's inner and outer worlds (de la Croix & Veen, 2018). Emotion must play a more integral, central, and holistic role in reasoning or meaning making (Lundgren & Poell, 2016). For a reflective approach to have meaning, it must include intent, expectations, authenticity, alignment, and transparency (Harvey et al., 2010). Anything less is unreal, unemotional, and, frankly, un-authentic. Thus, there is a clear need to raise awareness of the implications and potential opportunities of emotions in reflection and critical reflection (Lundgren & Poell, 2016).

Reflection on Scholarship of Teaching and Learning

There's no doubt that personal reflection strengthens professional practice (Young, James, & Noy, 2016), for both students and faculty, but there are numerous challenges to face. Not all students and faculty wish to share their harshest critiques or strongest emotions with others. Further, many educators cannot articulate what reflection means from a teaching or learning perspective (Wong, 2016). Can one person's reflective progress, even if it is a faculty member, drive all reflections from the students that suffer through it? As seen earlier, education should be a safe haven for exploring new ideas and making mistakes. Is every classroom a safe haven that encourages reflection? At present, it seems not. Students are afraid of making mistakes that could lead to failing courses; faculty are afraid of making mistakes that could lead to poor evaluations and affect their professional career progression within the school. To address these challenges, educators must be prepared to consider reflection through a different lens, potentially for each course and, ideally, for each student.

Nevertheless, like their students, educators experience teaching and learning in different ways. They need to evaluate what is going well and what is not going well in the teaching and learning process. For Healey (2000), their teaching scholarship is a balance between instructional knowledge (i.e., knowledge in instructional design), pedagogical knowledge (i.e., what is known about how students learn), and curricular knowledge (i.e., the goals, purposes, and rationale of the course or program). These three types of knowledge are gained through a process elaborated by Mezirow (1991) of content, process, and premise reflection (Healey, 2000; Kreber, 2006; Lundgren & Poell, 2016). Content reflection is an examination of the content of the problem; process reflection focuses on problem-solving strategies; and premise reflection takes place when underlying assumptions are questioned (ibid). Some teachers learn through theory while others learn through examining their own processes and reporting them in a scholarly manner, i.e., research projects. According to Healey (2000), some teachers are intuitively excellent in practice but have never studied theory whereas others have studied theory extensively but never gotten better at teaching. These are the two extremes, and the majority of faculty falls between the two. Clearly, there is place to incorporate theory into teaching practices, but that cannot be the only way to encourage reflection on teaching and learning in schools.

The Reflection Radar which will be explained in detail in the next section, can be used to complement existing traditional portfolios used to evaluate teaching and learning in the classroom. While traditional portfolios are useful in demonstrating teacher effectiveness to some extent, the Reflection Radar was created to provide a supplementary element on which discussions with colleagues, peer pedagogical coaches, faculty developers, or critical friends can be based. In this way, faculty can provide further evidence to support the teaching and learning within their classrooms. Simply speaking, the Reflection Radar offers another way of measuring or self-measuring teacher effectiveness and student learning. For faculty developers, any tools that encourage reflection and critical reflection can be useful to provide appropriate support to educators who strive for excellence in teaching and learning.

SOLUTION—THE REFLECTION RADAR

Reflection Radar: This section begins with a table of reflection questions and Reflection Radar as applied to one undergraduate program at an international hospitality management school in Switzerland. The questions are divided into four categories of activities/tasks (habits, understanding, reflection, and

Table 1. Reflection radar

Category/Criteria	Scale			
Learning **You Expect Students to:**				
Take notes during lectures (H)	1	2	3	4
Write the description of a company (H)	1	2	3	4
Answer simple questions to show they have understood (U)	1	2	3	4
Learn course concepts from books or articles (U)	1	2	3	4
Apply theory to practice (R)	1	2	3	4
Share personal experience/previous knowledge in class (R)	1	2	3	4
Take a position on a topic (CR)	1	2	3	4
Peer assess (CR)	1	2	3	4
Teaching				
The majority of class time is lecture (H)	1	2	3	4
Your role is to impart knowledge (H)	1	2	3	4
You attempt to elicit active responses (U)	1	2	3	4
You use course text to prepare assignments/assessments (U)	1	2	3	4
Problem-based learning is used in class (R)	1	2	3	4
Assignments encourage group or team work (R)	1	2	3	4
Assignments develop students' capacity to self-assess (CR)	1	2	3	4
You include students in the future development of the course (CR)	1	2	3	4
Assessment/Evaluation				
Evaluations ask students to recall specific information (H)	1	2	3	4
Evaluations derive from previous exams (H)	1	2	3	4
Evaluations require students to explain a concept (U)	1	2	3	4
Evaluations have verifiable right/wrong answers (U)	1	2	3	4
Evaluations ask students to transfer knowledge from one context to another (R)	1	2	3	4
Evaluations ask students to include emotion/personal experience (R)	1	2	3	4
Evaluations oblige students to provide original/creative solutions (CR)	1	2	3	4
Evaluations oblige students to question their existing beliefs, habits, and heuristics and/or consider how their actions affect the world's resources (CR)	1	2	3	4
Professional Development/Faculty Development				
You read articles/resources on your area of expertise (H)	1	2	3	4
You attend conferences/symposiums in your subject area (H)	1	2	3	4
You present original work at conferences/symposiums in your area of expertise (U)	1	2	3	4
You explain teaching philosophy/objectives to other teachers (sharing with a "critical friend") (U)	1	2	3	4
You transfer subject knowledge to other areas of expertise and/or into other contexts (R)	1	2	3	4
You adopt teaching methods to different learning styles (R)	1	2	3	4
You critique own practices, habits, and techniques (CR)	1	2	3	4
You seek/invent innovative methods/techniques in teaching (CR)	1	2	3	4

continued on following page

Table 1 continued

Key for Reflection Radar (frequency OR importance):

1 – Never/Not at all

2 - Occasionally/Somewhat

3 - Often/Very

4 – Always/Extremely

Source: Adapted from Gershan, M. (2013). *How to use questioning in the classroom: The complete guide.* Germany: Amazon Distribution and Ashwin, P., & Boud, D. (2015). *Reflective teaching in higher education.* London: Bloomsburg Academic.

critical reflection) to assess student learning, teaching, assessment/evaluation, and personal development. Each of the statements is followed by a 4-point scale that could be measured for importance or frequency. A third example is a weighted average by a simple yes/no response to each of the statements. Examples are provided below to demonstrate three different measures. Nonetheless, the final decision on how the Reflection Radar can be adapted for your faculty and to your programs is up to you.

NOTE: While these questions derive from previous work conducted by Gershan (2013) and Ashwin and Boud (2015), my contribution is the visual representation of the results through the Reflection Radar which can be used to spark discussion on practices in and outside the classroom. The selected questions used for this chapter and as an example for the reader were chosen specifically for their courses, level, and program (See Table 1). Supplementary questions can be found in the Appendix.

In the next paragraph, faculty developers and the faculty themselves will be provided with concrete recommendations on how to apply the Reflection Radar to their courses and academic programs to gauge critical (and deep) teaching and learning. To do so, faculty developers can use this table of reflection categories or consult a further, although non-exhaustive, list provided at the end of the chapter (See Appendix). For authentic reflection to take place, faculty developers as a group or inclusive of other faculty members need to define the most relevant criteria for their programs of study and type of students. No one Reflection Radar nor one set of reflection criteria could or should be imposed across all education levels.

Directions: Use one course you are comfortable teaching. Using the 4-point Likert scale, rate each of the following phrases for frequency of activity or importance in your classroom.

A third potential weighted rating for these questions is based on the following:

Process: Faculty will be given a list of statements regarding teaching, learning, assessment, and research. They will respond yes/no to each. Each section will include habit tasks, understanding tasks, reflection tasks, and critical reflection tasks. The score will be calculated based on the following logic.

Tentative scoring:

Habit tasks= no= 0 yes = -1

Understanding tasks= no= 0 yes= 1

Reflection tasks= no= 0 yes= 2

Critical reflection tasks= no= 0 yes= 3

Two examples have been provided in Figures 1 and 2 to show the results of an Academic Writing and Crisis/Strategic Communication course respectively. The results derived from responding to the criteria in three ways: A Likert scale for importance of the task; a Likert scale for frequency of the task; and a weighted score based on the level of reflection for each task.

As seen in Figures 1 and 2, there is little difference between what a teacher deems as important and the frequency with which they implement that task. In following the line for importance for the learn-

Figure 1. Reflection Radar for Academic Writing course all tasks combined

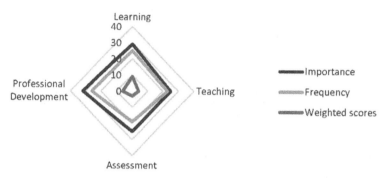

ing, teaching, assessment, and professional development, the radar is quite similar. Further, when the weighted averages for all types of tasks for all four categories are tabulated, the radar shows slightly different results, although not significantly different to question the radar's effectiveness.

Figures 3 and 4, however, show how one measure, frequency, can be scored when applied to all four tasks in all four categories. Here, the differences are much more substantial, and the radars are much more significant. For this reason, frequency has been chosen as the most effective method to represent the actual situation of a teacher in the categories that affect them most: Student learning, teaching, assessment, and professional development. A teacher who received a Reflection Radar such as the one shown in Figure 3 could reflect on each of their core categories, i.e., learning, teaching, assessment, and professional development, and make strategic decisions on how to change these scores to optimize reflection in both their courses and their careers.

Figure 2. Reflection Radar for Crisis Communication course all tasks combined

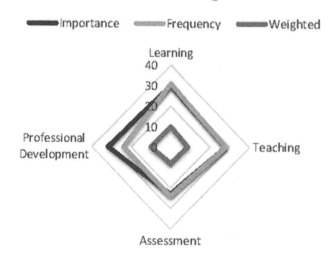

Figure 3. Reflection Radar for Academic Writing based on frequency

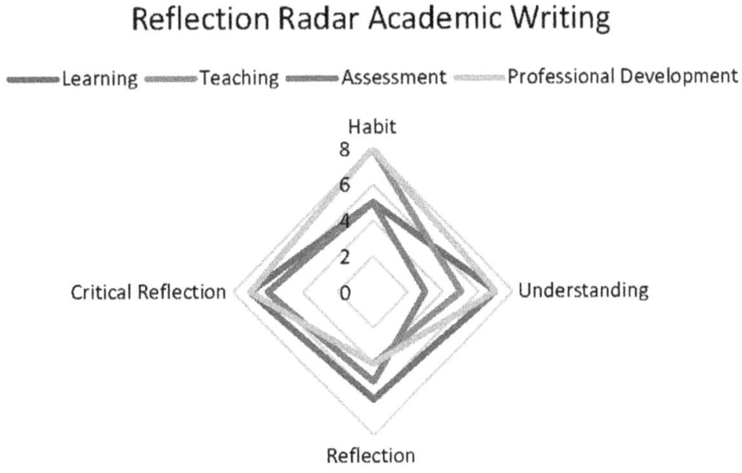

Reflection Radar Academic Writing

══Learning ══Teaching ══Assessment ══Professional Development

In Figure 3, the results for this Academic Writing teacher demonstrate higher levels of reflection and critical reflection in learning, teaching, and professional development, but less so in assessment. For this teacher in a second-semester course in a Bachelor's Degree program, habitual tasks are reported most often in the teaching and professional development categories yet less so for the learning and assessment categories. Understanding tasks are implemented most often in the learning and professional development categories than in the teaching and even less so in the assessment category.

However, in Figure 4, the Reflection Radar for a higher level Crisis/Strategic Communication course taught to final-year students shows a different picture. Compared to the Academic Writing course radar, the learning line for Crisis/Strategic Communication shows an almost equally spread balance between all four types of tasks, while the teaching line includes many more reflective elements. The assessment

Figure 4. Reflection Radar for Crisis Communication course based on frequency

Reflection Radar Crisis/Strategic
Communication

══Learning ══Teaching ══Assessment ══Professional Development

Figure 5. Reflection Radar for Human Behavior and Performance course based frequency

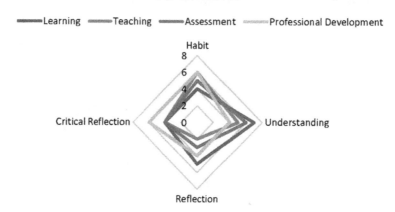

is broader, as well. Interestingly, the professional development for the Crisis/Strategic Communication course is broader as well, showing that more reflection is used for this course.

As seen in Figure 5, the teacher relies heavily on understanding tasks in learning, teaching and assessment. There is little critical reflection in the class, but there is high critical reflection in his/her professional development category. Students taking this course are in their first semester of their Bachelor's Degree which could explain why understanding is so important and ranked so highly.

The Reflection Radar in Figure 6 demonstrates that all four categories of tasks are heavily rated for professional development while habit tasks are rated least for learning, teaching, and assessment. This suggests that the faculty member is engaged with their topic and makes concerted efforts to improve their knowledge in their area of expertise. But it also indicates that this specific course, Technology in Education, may be more hands-on where students are asked to apply what they are learning to one

Figure 6. Reflection Radar for Technology in Education course based on frequency

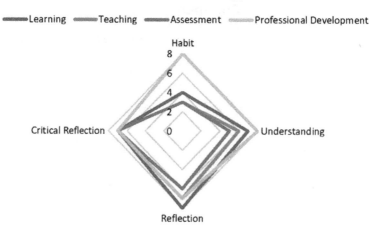

Figure 7. Reflection Radar for Introduction to Business English course based on frequency

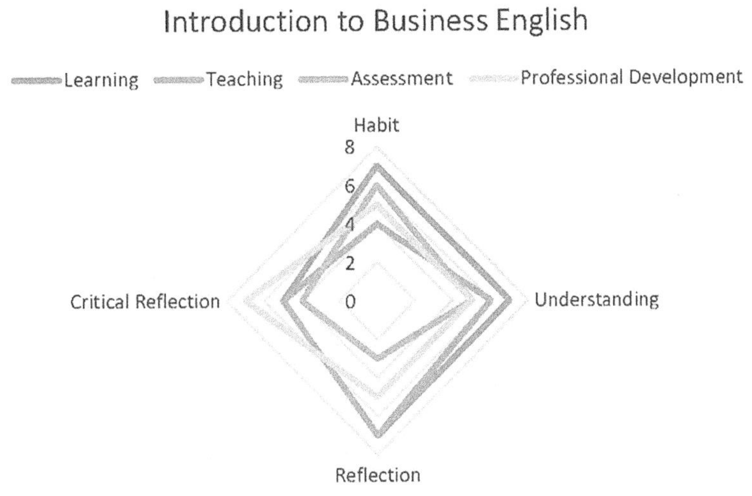

Introduction to Business English

Learning Teaching Assessment Professional Development

Habit

8

6

4

2

Critical Reflection   0   Understanding

Reflection

context or numerous contexts thus leading to higher scores for reflection and even critical reflection. Thus, both the faculty member (i.e., his/her experience and attitude toward teaching) and the type of course (i.e., one that is more practical in application) can also affect the results of the Reflection Radar.

In the final example presented in this chapter (Figure 7), the teacher rates high habit, understanding, and reflection tasks for learning and teaching, but only habit and understanding dominate the assessment criteria.

The Reflection Radar in Figure 7 is based on a course given to students before entering the Bachelor's Program, i.e., between secondary school and higher education. The semester prepares students for the courses that will follow. It is logical, then, that little critical reflection would be expected at this stage for learning, teaching, or assessment.

As all of the above examples are based on different types of courses, student levels, and teacher profiles, you can already start to see the potential of using Reflection Radars in your various courses and with faculty members. It is a personalized way of seeing the tasks they do as linked to the core elements of being a teacher.

RECOMMENDATIONS AND FUTURE RESEARCH DIRECTIONS

To the best of this author's knowledge, the Reflection Radar (presented in this manner) as linked to education and SoTL, in particular, has not been used in other research projects or contexts. This chapter could be the beginning of future SoTL research projects implementing and expanding upon this tool both to assess reflection within courses and programs and to improve critical thinking skills in educators, faculty developers, and students. Nonetheless, the Reflection Radar in this chapter has yet to succumb to any rigorous testing for robustness. It has been proposed as a starting place for faculty developers to adapt to their own needs and programs. The original questions have been offered in Table 1, but many more questions are also available in the appendices. Faculty developers or interested faculty members could choose the questions that are most relevant to their level of teaching or type of program. This could be a great opportunity for a Community of Practice based on reflection to be formed to create the criteria for their faculty. Similar to the debate on whether reflection can be assessed and, if so, how, this Reflection Radar attempts to provide one tool that could be used and adapted for all levels of education regardless of the discipline or degree.

These Reflection Radars offer a discussion platform between teachers and faculty developers based on the most common tasks and their teaching/professional development activities. Should all faculty members strive for the "perfect" radar? Of course not; that doesn't exist. But the Reflection Radar should incite reflection on the part of the faculty member. Is the course based too heavily on memorization or simply repeating what the teacher said? Is the level of reflection aligned with the level of students or where the course is placed in the greater curriculum? Is there a place for more targeted professional development through conferences or training? These questions and many more should arise when examining the results of the Reflection Radar.

A faculty member who is teaching in the first semester or first-year course could be expected to demonstrate more habit and understanding tasks in student learning and teaching than a faculty member who is teaching on a higher level course to students who are closer to graduation. In the latter case, one would expect to see more emphasis on reflection and critical reflection in learning, teaching, and assessment. Faculty developers need to compare what is comparable. For example, the Reflection Radars of all faculty members in the first year could be created to examine if the overall learning, teaching, and assessment are aligned with the learning outcomes. Through dialogue with faculty developers, educators can be validated in their choices or begin the discussion and process of finding new ways to teach.

However, while different faculty members within the same semester or level could be compared, it is not advised here. If reflection in an overall program is to be encouraged, it must be in a safe environment. Comparing one faculty member to another could prove to be demotivating or divisive. Reflection Radars should be used as the tool they intended to be, that is, a means to reflect on what faculty are doing in their own courses and for their own personal development.

CONCLUSION

This chapter dispels the four common misconceptions about reflection in educational institutions, both for educators and students. As seen in the chapter, reflection is not elitist; rather, it is for everyone and every type of student at every level. Reflection is not a solitary activity; rather, it is a social, collective process which involves other apprentices and the masters/mentors. Reflection may begin as a solitary activity, but it is only validated once it is shared with a master, a group, a team, or an authentic Community of Practice. Reflection is not disruptive in the workplace; rather, it is an asset for ensuring more efficient practice each new time the action is completed. Reflection is not unreal; rather, it is steeped in reality when based on actions that one could encounter in the "real" workplace with the same contexts and results.

For Ash and Clayton (2004), reflection can only be assessed when based on the articulation of purposeful, strategic, and rigorous reflection. While I agree that having a common language to discuss reflection is a positive step, it is not the only one to take. This language may need to be flexible and adaptable depending on the course and program. A student's reflection may not fit into strict guidelines or checklists, but that does not constitute a lack of reflection. As critical reflection is complex, perhaps there is no one clear way to articulate it, teach it, learn it, or live it!

As an ongoing SoTL project, the initial findings and Reflection Radar tool presented in this chapter are subject to critique and improvement. The very process of writing this chapter was an example of research (or scholarship) of teaching and learning and the future use of this Reflection Radar should continue to contribute to SoTL research in the future by myself or others. Further, this SoTL project is not only interdisciplinary in nature; it is also interdepartmental as both faculty members from all disciplines and faculty developers are joining as one to create more rewarding teaching and learning experiences in educational institutions. In the future, the Reflection Radar will need to be adapted, deconstructed, and reconstructed as faculty developers see fit. While critical reflection is the highest or deepest level of reflection, it does not infer that other types of knowledge or reflection are unimportant (Liu, 2015). Many educators have a penchant for utilizing habit tasks in their classrooms and may have solid reasons for doing so. When used parsimoniously, habitual tasks are necessary as they are tasks we face in our daily lives. For examples, we cannot theorize about why we performed a mathematical operation if we have not learned (through habitual practice) to apply it. By reflecting through the Reflection Radar, educators can questions why they do the tasks they do and how effective these tasks are to further student learning.

Not everyone can be reflective at a said time or at said times. One cannot be told to "go and reflect" (Ash & Clayton, 2014). Students or educators who struggle to see the relevance of reflection may refuse or resent the process (Wong, 2016). Further, not all communities will be functional ones. In this chapter, the sense of community has been stressed as paramount to the success of reflection in and outside the classroom. While I believe this is true, it only works when the community realizes they have something to learn from each other and are ready to embrace the opportunity to be uncomfortable in front of others. The concept of creating safe spaces based on deeper awareness, understanding, and growth, bathing in a climate of openness and intellectual rigor and focused on participant comfort, engagement, and empowerment (Beaudoin, 2012) is the crucial element to authentic reflection and, in the most effective communities, critical reflection that is transformative and wholesome.

As educators, we can only reflect on what we can do to make teaching and learning more effective and rewarding for the students and ourselves. We cannot stop reflecting on potential best practices or new constructs. In fact, if we are to become critical reflectors in our own right, we need the time to reflect and try new things. We need to read the literature to gain a theoretical base, conduct our own research projects (alone or with other disciplines), attend conferences (in our area of expertise or that of others), and share our reflections with our critical friends or Communities of Practice. If we want to question our own practices and experience our own perspective transformation, we need to put reflection back on our radar…

ACKNOWLEDGMENT

This research received no specific grant from any funding agency in the public, commercial, or not-for-profit sectors. The author would like to thank the colleagues who gave feedback and participated in completing the Reflection Radars used in this chapter.

REFERENCES

Acai, A., Akesson, B., Allen, M., Chen, V., Mathany, C., McCollum, B., & Verwoord, R. E. M. (2017). Conceptualizations of success in student-faculty/staff SoTL partnerships: Motivations, challenges, power, and definitions. *The Canadian Journal for the Scholarship of Teaching and Learning, 8*(2), 1–15. doi:10.5206/cjsotl-rcacea.2017.2.8

Ash, S. L., & Clayton, P. H. (2004). The articulated learner: An approach to guided reflection and assessment. *Innovative Higher Education, 29*(2), 137–154. doi:10.1023/B:IHIE.0000048795.84634.4a

Ashwin, P., & Boud, D. (2015). *Reflective teaching in higher education.* London: Bloomsburg Academic.

Beaudoin, B. (2012). Creating community: From individual reflection to SoTL transformation. *International Journal for the Scholarship of Teaching and Learning, 6*(1), 1–10. doi:10.20429/ijsotl.2012.060117

Benade, L. (2015). Teachers' critical reflective practice in the context of twenty-first century learning. *Open Review of Educational Research, 2*(1), 42–54. doi:10.1080/23265507.2014.998159

Bergh, A., & Fink, G. (2009). Higher education, elite institutions, and inequality. *European Economic Review, 53*(3), 376–384. doi:10.1016/j.euroecorev.2008.06.002

Cranton, P. (2011). A transformative perspective on the Scholarship of Teaching and Learning. *Higher Education Research & Development, 30*(1), 75–86. doi:10.1080/07294360.2011.536974

de la Croix, A., & Veen, M. (2018). The reflective zombie: Problematizing the conceptual framework of reflection in medical education. *Perspectives on Medical Education, 7*(6), 394–400. https://doi.org. doi:10.100740037-018-0479-9 PMID:30353284

Dewey, J. (1933). *How we think.* Buffalo, N.Y.: Prometheus Books.

Dewey, J. (1938). *Experience and education.* New York, NY: Collier Books, Macmillan.

Gershan, M. (2013). *How to use questioning in the classroom: The complete guide.* Germany: Amazon Distribution.

Gilpin, L. S., & Liston, D. (2009). Transformative education in the Scholarship of Teaching and Learning: An analysis of SoTL literature. *International Journal for the Scholarship of Teaching and Learning, 3*(2). doi:10.20429/ijsotl.2009.030211

Grant, S., & Hurd, F. (2010). Incorporating critical pedagogy into the Scholarship of Teaching and Learning: Making the journey alongside our students. *International Journal for the Scholarship of Teaching and Learning, 4*(2). doi:10.20429/ijsotl.2010.040220

Harvey, M., Coulson, D., Mackaway, J., & Winchester-Seeto, T. (2010). Aligning reflection in the cooperative education curriculum. *Asia Pacific Journal of Cooperative Education, 11*(3), 137–152. Retrieved from https://pdfs.semanticscholar.org/04f4/b126ef8af981e73f765118a2e036fe55c74b.pdf

Healey, M. (2000). Developing the scholarship of teaching in higher education: A discipline-based approach. *Higher Education Research & Development, 19*(2), 169–189. doi:10.1080/072943600445637

Hebert, C. (2015). Knowing and/or experiencing: A critical examination of the reflective models of John Dewey and Donald Schön. *Reflective Practice, 16*(3), 361–371. doi:10.1080/14623943.2015.1023281

Hibbert, P., Sillince, J., Diefenbach, T., & Cunliffe, A. L. (2014). Relationally reflexive practice: A generative approach to theory development in qualitative research. *Organizational Research Methods, 17*(3), 278–298. doi:10.1177/1094428114524829

Jenkins, A., & Healey, M. (2015). International perspectives on strategies to support faculty who teach students via research and inquiry. *Council on Undergraduate Research Quarterly, 35*(3), 31–37. Retrieved from https://www.cur.org/download.aspx?id=3147

Kember, D., Leung, D. Y. P., Jones, A., Loke, A. Y., McKay, J., Sinclair, K., ... Yeung, E. (2000). Development of a questionnaire to measure the level of reflective thinking. *Assessment & Evaluation in Higher Education, 25*(4), 381–395. doi:10.1080/713611442

Kember, D., McKay, J., Sinclair, K., & Wong, F. K. Y. (2008). A four-category scheme for coding and assessing the level of reflection in written work. *Assessment & Evaluation in Higher Education, 33*(4), 369–379. doi:10.1080/02602930701293355

Kreber, C. (2006). Developing the scholarship of teaching through transformative learning. *The Journal of Scholarship of Teaching and Learning, 6*(1), 88–109. Retrieved from https://pdfs.semanticscholar.org/ab6d/0db0049f0468bee87ad2b27ce4a20abfda92.pdf

Liu, K. (2015). Critical reflection as a framework for transformative learning in teacher education. *Educational Review, 67*(2), 145–157. doi:10.1080/00131911.2013.839546

Lundgren, H., & Poell, R. F. (2016). On critical reflection: A review of Mezirow's theory and its operationalization. *Human Resource Development Review, 15*(1), 3–28. doi:10.1177/1534484315622735

Miettinen, R. (2000). The concept of experiential learning and John Dewey's theory of reflective thought and action. *International Journal of Lifelong Education, 19*(1), 54–72. doi:10.1080/026013700293458

Orlikowski, W. J. (2002). Knowing in practice: Enacting a collective capability in distributed organizing. *Organization Science, 13*(3), 249–273. doi:10.1287/orsc.13.3.249.2776

Rodgers, C. (2002). Defining reflection: Another look at John Dewey and reflective thinking. *Teachers College Record, 104*(4), 842–866. doi:10.1111/1467-9620.00181

Roth, W.-M., & Lee, Y.-J. (2006). Contradictions in theorizing and implementing communities in education. *Educational Research Review, 1*(1), 27–40. doi:10.1016/j.edurev.2006.01.002

Rowland, S. (2001). *Higher education: Purposes and roles.* Conference paper: British Educational Research Association Annual Conference, University of Leeds. Retrieved from www.leeds.ac.uk/educol/documents/00001915.doc

Ryan, M. E., & Ryan, M. (2012). Theorising a model for teaching and assessing reflective learning in higher education. *Higher Education Research & Development,* 1–20. doi:10.1080/07294360.2012.661704

Schön, D. A. (1983). *The reflective practitioner: How professionals think in action.* New York, NY: Basic Books.

Swanson, K. W., & Kayler, M. (2010). Faculty development and adult learning: A model for transforming higher education. *International Journal for the Scholarship of Teaching and Learning, 4*(1). doi:10.20429/ijsotl.2010.040116

Tanggaard, L. (2007). Learning at trade vocational school and learning at work: Boundary crossing in apprentices' everyday life. *Journal of Education and Work, 20*(5), 453–466. doi:10.1080/13639080701814414

Thompson, N., & Pascal, J. (2012). Developing critically reflective practice. *Reflective Practice, 13*(2), 311–325. doi:10.1080/14623943.2012.657795

Tsoukas, H., & Chia, R. (2002). On organizational becoming: Rethinking organizational change. *Organization Science, 13*(5), 567–582. doi:10.1287/orsc.13.5.567.7810

Van Beveren, L., Roets, G., Buysse, A., & Rutten, K. (2018). We all reflect, but why? A systematic review of the purposes of reflection in higher education in social and behavioral sciences. *Educational Research Review, 24*, 1–9. doi:10.1016/j.edurev.2018.01.002

Wong, A. C. K. (2016). Considering reflection from the student perspective in higher education. *SAGE Open*, 1–9. doi:10.1177/2158244016638706

Wu, X. (2017). Higher education, elite formation, and social stratification in contemporary China: Preliminary findings from the Beijing College students panel survey. *Chinese Journal of Sociology, 3*(1), 3–31. doi:10.1177/2057150X16688144

Young, K., James, K., & Noy, S. (2016). Exploration of a reflective practice rubric. *Asia Pacific Journal of Cooperative Education, 17*(2), 135–147. Retrieved from https://www.ijwil.org/files/APJCE_17_2_135_147.pdf

ADDITIONAL READING

Adachi, C., Tai, J. H.-M., & Dawson, P. (2018). Academics' perceptions of the benefits and challenges of self and peer assessment in higher education. *Assessment & Evaluation in Higher Education, 43*(2), 294–306. doi:10.1080/02602938.2017.1339775

Bruno, A., & Dell'Alversana, G. (2018). Reflective practicum in higher education: The influence of the learning environment on the quality of learning. *Assessment & Evaluation in Higher Education, 43*(3), 345–358. doi:10.1080/02602938.2017.1344823

Chia, R. (2014). Reflections: In praise of silent transformation—Allowing change through "Letting Happen". *Journal of Change Management, 14*(1), 8–27. doi:10.1080/14697017.2013.841006

Clark, J. L., & Boud, D. (2018). Refocusing portfolio assessment: Curating for feedback and portrayal. *Innovations in Education and Teaching International, 55*(4), 479–486. doi:10.1080/14703297.2016.1250664

Harrison, N. (2018). Using the lens of "Possible Selves" to explore access to higher education: A new conceptual model for practice, policy, and research. *Social Sciences, 7*(10), 1–21. doi:10.3390ocsci7100209

Hibbert, P. (2013). Approaching reflexivity through critical reflection: Issues for critical management education. *Journal of Management Education*, *37*(6), 803–827. doi:10.1177/1052562912467757

Wanner, T., & Palmer, E. (2018). Formative self-and peer assessment for improved student learning: The crucial factors of design, teacher participation, and feedback. *Assessment & Evaluation in Higher Education*, *43*(7), 1032–1047. doi:10.1080/02602938.2018.1427698

KEY TERMS AND DEFINITIONS

Co-Sumers: Students co-create all elements of an effective course in collaboration with the teacher.

Communities of Practice (COPs): Groups of likeminded individuals who share a common goal or interest and work together to thrive.

Critical Reflection: A deeper and more profound reflection based on active learning.

Reflection: Relating a concept to personal experience and applying it in practical situations.

Reflective Zombie: Students who learn how to repeat specific words or phrases to sound reflective when little reflection has actually occurred.

Transformative Learning: The slow and infrequent process of changing one's assumptions or beliefs.

Wicked Problems: Problems that are ill-defined, unique, and dynamic with no answer and no clear solution.

APPENDIX

Learning

- Students take notes during lectures (H)
- Students listen to lecture (H)
- Students repeat the same formula with different numbers (H)
- Students write the description of a company (H)
- Students are asked to read articles outside of class (H)
- Students answer simple questions to show they have understood (U)
- Students search for underlying meaning in what they have read (U)
- Students learn material for a mid-term or final exam only (U)
- Students learn course concepts from books, articles, or the professor (U)
- Students write assignments based on a textbook or lecture notes only (U)
- Students are encouraged to add their personal experience/opinion in their writing (R)
- Students find their own sources to respond to questions (R)
- Students apply theory to practice (R)
- Students share personal experience or previous knowledge in class (R)
- Student written responses include personal insights beyond book/lecture theory (R)
- Students are expected to take a position on a topic (CR)
- Students create rubrics (CR)
- Students peer assess (CR)
- Students self-assess in class (CR)
- Students lead class discussions (CR)
- Students propose new solutions/materials/resources (CR)

Teaching

- The majority of class time is lecture (H)
- Teacher's assistant runs tutorials (H)
- Teacher's role is to impart knowledge (H)
- Teacher attempts to elicit active responses (U)
- Teacher ensures participation from the majority of the students (U)
- Teacher creates a positive atmosphere for learning (U)
- Teacher team-teaches with a colleague (U)
- Case-based approach is used in class (U)
- Teacher encourages questions in and outside the classroom (R)
- Coursework is adapted to different levels (R)
- Coursework is adapted to different learning styles (R)
- Assignments encourage students to work with others (R)
- Student feedback is considered in grading rubrics (R)
- Assistant feedback is solicited to improve courses (R)
- Teacher encourages peer tutorials (R)

- After each class, teacher reflects on what worked/didn't work (R)
- Problem-based learning is used in class (R)
- Teaching method is adapted to different learning styles (R)
- Creativity and risk-taking is encouraged in class (CR)
- Teacher shares reflection/critique of self with "critical friend" (CR)
- Students give input for course design/activities (CR)
- Students are involved in future development of course (CR)
- Assignments develop students' capacity to self-assess (CR)
- Tasks develop students' capacity to peer-assess (CR)
- Teacher co-teaches with students (CR)
- Teacher co-creates materials with students (CR)
- Lifelong learning activities are proposed (CR)

Assessment

- Exam questions ask students to recall specific information (H)
- Exam questions ask students to define key concepts (H)
- Exam answers derive directly from lecturer's slides/notes (H)
- Exam questions derive from previous exams (H)
- Exam questions focus on comprehension of key concepts (U)
- Exam questions require descriptive responses (U)
- Exam questions require students to explain a concept (U)
- Exam questions have verifiable right/wrong answers (U)
- Exam questions ask students to transfer knowledge from one context to another (R)
- Exam questions ask students to include emotion/personal experience (R)
- Exam questions ask student to choose between several viable options (R)
- Exam questions ask students to explain how they solved the problem (R)
- Exam responses include analysis of a concept/phenomena (CR)
- Exam questions oblige students to provide original/creative solutions (CR)
- Exam questions ask students to forecast or predict future outcomes (CR)
- Exam questions oblige students to question their existing beliefs, habits, heuristics (CR)
- Exam questions ask students to assess validity/reliability of responses (CR+)
- Exam questions ask students to critique existing concepts/theories (CR+)
- Exam questions ask students to make judgments and justify the responses (CR+)
- Exam questions ask students to consider the morality of their choices (CR++)
- Exam questions ask students to consider how their actions affect the world's resources (CR++)
- Exam questions have no right/wrong answers (i.e. wicked problems) (CR++)

NOTE: CR+ is a higher level of CR, that of evaluation

    CR++ is the highest level of CR, that of philosophical reflection

Professional Development

- You read articles/resources in your area of expertise (H)
- You attend conferences/symposiums in your subject area (H)
- You write opinion pieces on topics in your subject area (H)
- You observe other teachers in the classroom (H)
- You follow training/courses when told by your superior (H)
- You present original work at conferences/symposiums in your area of expertise (U)
- You describe your teaching philosophy/objectives to other teachers (U)
- You give workshops to colleagues on topics in your area of expertise (U)
- You take courses to improve your skills in your area of expertise (U)
- You ask others to assist at your courses (U)
- You speak with colleagues about your research projects (R)
- You collaborate with colleagues to produce research (R)
- You take courses outside of your area of expertise (R)
- You transfer knowledge to other areas of expertise and/or into other contexts (R)
- You consider emotion/personal experience when choosing courses/training/workshops (R)
- Your role as a teacher/faculty developer is in constant evolution (CR)
- You critique your own practices, habits, and techniques (CR)
- You justify why you need further training/improvement (CR)
- You seek /invent innovative methods/techniques to advance your professional development (CR)

Source: Adapted from Gershan, M. (2013). *How to use questioning in the classroom: The complete guide*. Germany: Amazon Distribution and Ashwin, P., & Boud, D. (2015). *Reflective teaching in higher education*. London: Bloomsburg Academic.

Chapter 7
SoTL as a Professional Development Tool for Non-Standard Faculty

Lauren Hays
https://orcid.org/0000-0002-0985-987X
University of Central Missouri, USA

Lindsay McNiff
https://orcid.org/0000-0001-5070-7635
Dalhousie University, Canada

ABSTRACT

Non-standard faculty are individuals with faculty appointments, but whose responsibilities fall outside the traditional faculty role. Non-standard faculty are often overlooked in conversations about SoTL, but they play an integral part in the teaching and learning that occurs on post-secondary campuses. Due to the focus on local context within SoTL, non-standard faculty greatly benefit from this type of professional development. Using the micro, meso, macro, and mega framework, the authors of this chapter describe how educational developers can support non-standard faculty in using SoTL for professional development. This common SoTL framework helps educational developers bring non-standard faculty into SoTL conversations while also recognizing the unique teaching environments in which they work.

INTRODUCTION

Institutions of higher education are inherently learning organizations. Everyone who works with students is responsible for helping them gain new knowledge, grow, and learn. While academic teaching faculty are primarily responsible for teaching and learning, faculty whose responsibilities include instructing outside the traditional class setting also have a great deal to learn from SoTL. In the absence of a generally-accepted term for faculty in these roles, the term "non-standard" faculty will be used for the purposes of this chapter. Non-standard faculty may be faculty members who are expected to produce scholarship

DOI: 10.4018/978-1-7998-2212-7.ch007

and engage in professional development, and who may teach or interact with students in a way that could benefit from closer scholarly inquiry, but whose responsibilities do not primarily involve teaching full credit courses. In Canada and the United States, these non-standard faculty include librarians, clinical faculty, counselors, and learning specialists. Each of these positions supports the academic institution's instructional mission. The non-standard faculty role is in contrast to the standard faculty role. In this chapter, a standard faculty role is defined as a faculty member whose primary responsibilities include teaching, service, and scholarship. Their teaching is conducted in for-credit course settings where they are the principal instructor.

Librarians in the majority of Canadian academic institutions have academic status, defined as "recognition that the duties performed are integral to the academic mission of the institution, but that all the rights and responsibilities associated with faculty status are not necessarily to be expected" (Jacobs, 2013, pp. 9-10). Academic status approximates faculty status to different degrees depending on the institution. Many academic librarians in Canada are expected to engage in teaching, research, and service in order to achieve the equivalent of tenure at their institutions. Walters (2016) found that librarians at 52% of American research universities have faculty status. Dalhousie University in Nova Scotia, Canada also includes counselors in their faculty collective agreement, while other institutions have expanded their scope even further. Grant MacEwan University (2017) in Alberta, Canada, for example, includes "Professional Resource Faculty members" in their collective agreement, and these include counselors, learning specialists, librarians, Nursing Laboratory Resource Professionals, and Writing and Learning Consultants. Similarly, Antelope Valley College (2017) in Lancaster, California includes "counselors, librarians, transfer center coordinator, writing center specialist, learning disabilities specialist, math learning specialist, and any other regular, contract, or temporary faculty employees who are non-administrative academic personnel" (p. 4) in their faculty agreement. Likewise, Lakeland College (2016) in Canada includes counselors, public services librarians, learner success strategists, and the Faculty Development Coordinator or Researcher in their collective agreement.

At many schools, clinical faculty primarily have responsibilities for clinical supervision and direction outside of the traditional classroom. Individuals falling into these categories often work very closely with students in a variety of capacities and are also expected to produce scholarly work. They may not be aware of SoTL as a potential avenue for this, or they may need support as one of the few, if not the only person in their unit, who is working in this area.

The mission of university teaching centers is to support faculty in their teaching (Wright, Lohe, & Little, 2018). Instructional development programs have aided in the growth of teaching and learning on many college campuses. However, due to the focus on learning outcomes, many non-standard faculty may be unintentionally excluded from professional development opportunities hosted by educational developers because the teaching role of non-standard faculty is not as clearly aligned with institutional learning outcomes. Due to institutional shifts in teaching cultures to decentralized models (Wright et al., 2018), all individuals who impact learning need to be involved in professional development.

Educational developers who are responsible for assisting the professional growth of faculty in the area of teaching and learning also need to be aware that studies have shown a persisting need for more practical research development (Cilliers & Herman, 2010; Stes & Van Petegem, 2011). Typically, SoTL is thought of as a movement focused on teaching and learning within the classroom. However, SoTL has implications for the broad institutional teaching culture (Schroeder, 2007). For faculty whose responsibilities fall outside the norm, using SoTL as a professional development tool can help foster growth in all facets of teaching and learning.

The purpose of this chapter is to describe considerations for professional development that educational developers can use to support non-standard faculty in using SoTL for professional development. "Micro-teaching cultures" (Mårtensson, 2014, p. 3) exist on all campuses. Roxå and Mårtensson (2013) define microcultures as "strong academic contexts" (p. 3) where the faculty is primarily responsible for teaching and learning in their area. In most institutions, a small group of faculty members are responsible for the teaching and learning that occurs in their academic discipline (Roxå & Mårtensson, 2013). These micro-teaching cultures also exist for non-standard faculty. Librarians, counselors, clinical faculty, and learning specialists are all part of an academic discipline that has its own teaching and learning literature. Furthermore, many non-standard faculty work closely with other non-standard faculty at their respective institutions to create learning environments, develop curriculum, and discuss teaching strategies.

SoTL frameworks (e.g., Hutchings' four questions, O'Brien's Compass) can be used to establish a common language around teaching and learning across micro-teaching cultures, or academic silos, while still acknowledging the differences in teaching conducted by standard and non-standard faculty. Additionally, SoTL is a platform that "examines processes that [have an] impact on the learning experience rather than seeing teaching as a self-contained context-free action" (Fanghanel, 2013, p. 61). When non-standard faculty teach, they are often instructing in a context not solely established by them. Instead, non-standard faculty teach in an environment impacted by departmental cultures and, in the case of learning specialists and librarians, cultures established by the faculty whose students they are supporting. Using the micro, meso, macro, and mega levels of SoTL (Table 1) helps to include all instructors (Simmons, 2016; Wuetherick, & Yu, 2016).

Table 1. Levels of SoTL; opportunities for educational developers and non-standard faculty

	Micro	**Meso/Macro**	**Mega**
Level	Individual	Departmental/Institutional	Beyond institution
Opportunities for educational developers	Focus on local teaching contexts (such as clinical/lab setting, library, writing center); Encourage non-standard faculty to ask questions about their students; Encourage students as partners in SoTL work	Gain awareness of the specific types of teaching that non-standard faculty are involved with and the unique perspectives they bring; Encourage non-standard faculty to be a part of faculty learning communities	Encourage non-standard faculty to attend conferences and join organizations such as ISSOTL; Gain a better understanding of their needs and communicate this to conference organizers
Challenges	Non-standard faculty may have limited or mitigated access to students	Non-standard faculty may feel outside of the teaching culture of their universities or struggle with their teacher identity	Non-standard faculty may gravitate toward the research methods with which they are familiar
Practical examples	Lesson study	Faculty learning communities	Offer workshops on research methodologies; Connect individuals from different disciplines; Recommend SoTL articles that use different methods

SOTL FOR PROFESSIONAL DEVELOPMENT FOR NON-STANDARD FACULTY

Asking good questions about teaching and learning is the hallmark of SoTL (Hutchings, 2000). It is also a fundamental aspect of educational development. As Felten, Kalish, Pingree, and Plank (2007) describe, educational developers seek to assist their institutions to be effective teaching and learning communities, which often includes asking questions about the teaching and learning that occurs campuswide. The campus community served by educational developers includes non-standard faculty who work closely with students in a variety of capacities. For educational developers, there may be many questions about the type of teaching and learning with which non-standard faculty are involved. Remembering the purposes of SoTL, including "professionalism, pragmatism, and policy" (Shulman, 2000, p. 49), and the primary goals of enhancing student learning and making teaching and learning public (Huber & Hutchings, 2006), educational developers can create professional development opportunities for non-standard faculty and promote SoTL as a professional development tool.

FOCUS ON PROFESSIONAL DEVELOPMENT AND COLLABORATION

Professional development for non-standard faculty includes development of pedagogy, but does not always require growth in the area of research. Frequently, non-standard faculty have different requirements for promotion and rank advancement that may include a reduced number of required publications. With this reduced publication requirement often comes an expectation of service and professional development in order to maintain and update skills. Although recertification is not a factor for many non-standard faculty including academic librarians, for example, they are generally involved in some degree of professional education (Mitchell & Mitchell, 2015). Due to this, educational developers need to frame SoTL as a professional development tool that "provides a space for dialogic critique.... into practice that contribute(s) to advancing individual and collective knowledge of the field of higher education" (Fanghanel, 2013, p. 59). Instead of exclusively positioning SoTL as a research strategy, highlighting SoTL as a "form of inquiry that focuses on processes, boundary-crossing, and making public its findings" (Fanghanel, 2013, p. 60) can be an effective hook. Furthermore, participation in professional development activities has been shown to motivate teachers to seek out more professional development opportunities (Karabenick & Conley, 2011).

Isolation negatively impacts engagement in SoTL. Similar to contingent faculty, non-standard faculty may be unfamiliar with departmental teaching and learning cultures. Some non-standard faculty, although full-time in their roles, may be contingent instructors themselves. Vander Kloet and co-authors (2017) described contingent faculty with outside professional employment as "classic" contingent instructors. Academic librarians, for example, sometimes have the opportunity to expand their teaching role to teach credit-bearing courses (Kemp, 2006; Raven & Rodrigues, 2017); for example, librarians might teach undergraduate research courses offered by the library (Raven & Rodrigues, 2017) or they might teach as an adjunct instructor in a Master of Library and Information Studies program. In either case, they might experience the same unfamiliarity with the teaching and learning culture of the department or faculty, and may not be privy to conversations about curricula. This unfamiliarity poses barriers for engagement with SoTL research (Vander Kloet et al., 2017). Therefore, using SoTL as a professional development tool to foster collaboration and the public sharing of teaching and learning can greatly benefit non-standard faculty when they are purposefully included.

Furthermore, due to the various contexts in which non-standard faculty work, their identities as faculty and disciplinarians may be complicated. Miller-Young, Yeo, and Manarin (2018) found that traditional faculty struggled with the interdisciplinary nature of SoTL because it did not align with their discipline's epistemology and because they were unfamiliar with some of the research methods used within SoTL and that lack of expertise caused discomfort. Many faculty members find balancing the identities of SoTL scholar, disciplinary-scholar, and teacher to be a challenging endeavor. Faculty are often seen as experts within their field and assume that identity. SoTL pushes faculty to closely examine their teaching and to engage with new disciplines, which can lead to identity discomfort (Bennett, 2016; Miller-Young et al., 2018). Acknowledging and anticipating the discomfort SoTL can bring is necessary for educational developers. When working with all faculty, and particularly with non-standard faculty whose roles are often less clearly defined, educational developers must attend to group dynamics, create space for conversations about professional identity, and foster a sense of belonging for all (Miller-Young et al., 2018).

EXAMPLES OF NON-STANDARD FACULTY AND SOTL

Each institution includes different non-standard faculty in their collective agreement. For non-standard faculty, the roles and responsibilities that make up their work are shaped by the higher education institution and by the discipline in which they were trained. For educational developers, it is important to learn about both the institutional and disciplinary contexts when working with non-standard faculty. Relatedly, non-standard faculty may or may not be familiar with SoTL. Non-standard faculty members' knowledge of SoTL is impacted more often by their institutional affiliations than their disciplinary training. In this section, the authors highlight common non-standard faculty and their disciplines' engagement with SoTL.

Academic Librarians

Academic librarians are aware of SoTL, but in general this might be considered, at the professional level, a burgeoning awareness. Many academic librarians are practicing elements of SoTL without realizing it (MacMillan, 2015) by testing new teaching strategies in their classrooms and presenting at conferences or publishing in journals dedicated to academic librarianship or information literacy. Others practice program or information literacy assessment regularly to gather evidence of the efficacy of their teaching strategies for self-improvement only without ever publishing. SoTL has been discussed directly in the library literature, often in an introductory or persuasive way to raise awareness of the opportunities available to librarians with SoTL and to make connections between SoTL and the work librarians are already doing (Bradley, 2009). Other discussions have centered around the potential of SoTL to strengthen librarians' understanding of curriculum and pedagogy (McNeill & Haines, 2003). Similar to some of the challenges faced by contingent faculty (Vander Kloet et al, 2017), librarians are often excluded from discussions of curricula and, despite acting in liaison roles with departments, many librarians are not regularly invited to departmental meetings where issues of curricula and pedagogy are discussed. Some publications have been reflective, such as Otto's (2014) discussion of signature pedagogies in librarianship and McNiff and Hays' (2017) reflection on incorporating SoTL into Library and Information Studies graduate curricula. A recently published monograph by the Association of College and Research Libraries (ACRL) is the first book-length volume offering case studies and viewpoints on SoTL and librarianship (*The Grounded Instruction Librarian: Participating in The Scholarship of Teaching and*

Learning, Eds. Mallon, Huisman, Hays, Bradley, & Belanger, 2019). Educational developers can help librarians, particularly those who already have an interest in the topic, frame SoTL within the context of librarian teaching, strengthen the connections that already exist, and provide guidance on communicating about SoTL within their cohort of colleagues. Research has shown that although not all librarians see themselves as teachers (Houtman, 2010; Weaver, 2019), SoTL can have a positive impact on librarians' teacher identity (Hays & Studebaker, 2019).

Faculty members in traditional teaching positions have dual roles as teachers and researchers, and they must consider professional ethics and the power dynamic between instructors and their students in tandem with the research ethics process (Felten et al., 2007). This power dynamic is usually character-ized, in part, by the grading relationship that exists between professors and students. As instructors who support the curriculum and student learning, librarians, for example, do not generally assign grades to the work students complete in a library classroom. Thus, their relationships with students, while still involving a power dynamic, do not do so to the same degree, and students would not feel compelled to participate in the research in order to preserve their grade in a course. In this way, instructors such as librarians, for whom the dual role of instructor and researcher is short-lived and of less impact on students, are positioned to richly observe and describe the processes of student learning and improve their own teaching. Many librarians who see assessment as an important part of their instruction and who routinely modify their instruction based on the evidence they have gathered are already engaged in informal work that is similar to SoTL (MacMillan, 2015).

Clinical Faculty

For this chapter, clinical faculty members are identified as practicing health professionals who also teach and contribute to the research output of a university. They provide a much-needed experiential dimension to the learning of medical students. Simpson et al. (2007) are considered to have defined the relationship between SoTL and academic medicine, and their work is seen as foundational to defining how educational scholarship can be evaluated in the tenure and promotion process (Grigsby & Thorn-dyke, 2011). For clinical faculty members, SoTL is often one of the types of non-traditional scholarship that addresses a specific need. Although many clinical faculty members are evaluated for promotion and tenure, their service work as practitioners is not generally considered as part of the promotion and tenure process (Grigsby & Thorndyke, 2011). Thus, clinical faculty members often face a challenge in documenting their contribution to the university in a way that can be evaluated. Because of their impor-tant role as educators to educators to future practitioners, clinical faculty can benefit from involvement with SoTL. Morahan and Fleetwood (2008) discussed the challenges of developing scholarship through educational and clinical activities and outlined non-traditional methods of scholarship to help faculty develop educational scholarship. With respect to SoTL, the authors noted that "such collective and collaborative scholarship is essential in academic medicine if educational activity is to be rigorously assessed and dispersed" (p. 37). They outlined a step-by-step process for turning educational activities into scholarship, specifically with junior clinical faculty in mind.

Counselors

Counselors generally work with psychological and/or medical services at a university and are often con-sidered faculty. While these faculty members are likely to be actively publishing in their specific areas of scholarship, much of this work might directly intersect with matters of interest to the teaching and learning community (such as research about students' cognitive processes and stressors, procrastination, and the first-year experience, to name just a few). Much of the Scholarship of Teaching and Learning in the counseling field relates to counselor education, and trends in these publications between 2001 and 2010 were outlined by Barrio Minton, Wachter Morris, and Yaites (2013). The articles analyzed in their review were concerned mainly with teaching techniques and were written to suit all levels of curricula. Interestingly, they found that only 14.78% of the articles analyzed were clearly grounded in learning theory and research and another 12% were minimally grounded (p. 170). A much larger portion of the articles were grounded instead in counseling literature and research. This finding may suggest that although the interest is there, counselors publishing SoTL research may need a firmer foundation in instructional research to ground their studies, and this would be fruitful ground for educational developers to play a role.

Learning Specialists

Learning specialists encompass a range of roles including writing specialist, learner success strategist, and math specialist. These individuals often conduct one-on-one consultations and tutoring sessions with students. They may also teach remedial-level courses. Very little has been written about SoTL in a tutoring environment. Even less has been written about SoTL from the perspective of learning specialists. Writing centers have seen their profile expand in recent decades due to programs such as writing across the curriculum, but writing centers have existed in various forms since the 1930s (North, 1984). Writing specialists teach writing concepts and help students understand various disciplinary writing requirements (Harris, 1995; Mackiewicz & Thompson, 2015; Savini, 2011). Smetkowski, Conway, and Starrett (2009) found the writing center at their institution to be a place where SoTL work could expand and flourish. At other institutions "writing centers are increasingly places where people take research seriously, assuming it be as essential as keeping records or training tutors" (Harris, 2001, p. 663). However, this research has not fully extended into SoTL where much knowledge could be gained and shared.

Learning success strategists, or academic learning strategists, work with college students on learning plans and learning strategies. Their primary responsibilities include work that leads to student retention and academic success. In a review of the literature, the authors of this chapter could not locate any articles specifically addressing SoTL work by learning success strategists. Additionally, SoTL has been slow to expand into the field of mathematics education; however, there have been promising developments (Dewar & Bennett, 2010). Very little has been written about SoTL and math specialists, who work as tutors and support student learning outside the classroom. Overall, learning specialists have minimally engaged in SoTL, based on published literature to date.

SOTL PROFESSIONAL DEVELOPMENT AT THE MICRO LEVEL

The micro level of SoTL is particularly useful as a professional development tool for non-standard faculty (Simmons, 2016). Professional development for non-standard faculty must account for the context of any teaching and learning research or discussion that includes non-standard faculty. Therefore, SoTL is an excellent professional development tool for non-standard faculty because of its focus on the local context. One of the principles of good SoTL practice is that it is "grounded in context" (Felten, 2013, p. 122), which includes the local context where the teaching and learning occurs. Huber and Hutchings (2005) listed numerous contexts to consider when engaged in SoTL work: the "discipline, student demographics, institutional type, pedagogical approach, and curricular goals" (p. 35). For non-standard faculty, teaching takes place in a variety of settings and can include additional contexts that must be considered such as the location where the class is held (e.g., clinical setting, library, computer lab, or writing center), the relationship between the non-standard faculty member and the faculty member whose students they are assisting, and the length of the learning opportunity (e.g., semester, one class session).

Educational developers can encourage non-standard faculty to ask good questions about their teaching and their students' learning. Hutchings' (2000) taxonomy of questions translates well to teaching in any setting. Similarly, O'Brien (2008) identified four questions in The SoTL Compass that non-standard faculty can use as easily as faculty in more traditional teaching roles. In fact, the question "Who are my students and how will they learn effectively?" (O'Brien, 2008, p. 4) is particularly applicable for non-standard faculty whose students and their characteristics may not be as readily apparent. By asking the question "who are my students?," non-standard faculty seek to understand the many factors that impact the students they teach. These factors may include the discipline in which the student is majoring, student backgrounds, course load, the point at which the student is in their sequence of studies, co-curricular involvement, or career goals, among others.

Students as Partners

At the micro level, educational developers can also support non-standard faculty in their professional development by advocating for students as partners in SoTL work and hosting programming on this topic. When describing the principles of good SoTL practice, Felten (2013) stated that SoTL should be "conducted in partnership with students" (p. 123). Non-standard faculty should also consider how they can work with students in SoTL research and not solely engage in SoTL without student partnerships. Similar to standard faculty, non-standard faculty have much to learn about the student experience both in and outside of the classroom, and students can provide both groups with insight into many of the contexts that impact learning. This practice of students as partners can help non-standard faculty answer questions about students' learning that would not be fully possible without the students' insights into the totality of their educational experience.

Non-standard faculty may not have ready access to or established relationships with students that would be the best partners in SoTL work. Educational developers can foster this relationship for non-standard faculty. Additionally, educational developers are in a key position to help ensure the quality of the students-as-partners experience through aiding in the research design and by educating both the non-standard faculty and the student on the broader educational context in which the research is taking place. The perspective of the educational developer is particularly useful in ensuring a thorough SoTL project.

Lesson Study

Non-standard faculty may not have consistent contact with students over the course of a semester, which poses a challenge when trying to determine what teaching methods worked well and where improvement is needed. Models such as Lesson Study provide a framework to study the efficacy of individual lessons (Cerbin & Kopp, 2006; Wood & Cajkler, 2018), which are often the mode in which faculty who do not teach full-credit courses instruct. According to Wood and Cajkler (2018),

Lesson study is a long established teacher-led collaborative approach which focuses on improving both the professional learning of teachers and student learning. The approach is founded on the principle that a collaborative process between teachers has the potential to bring new insights and professional development to their work. (p. 5)

Lesson study is typically divided into eight steps (Stigler & Heibert, 1999). However, for higher education, Wood and Cajkler (2018) suggest a six-step model that includes a research seminar or course session where the lesson is taught. The six steps are as follows:

1. *Teacher group identifies an issue focusing on student difficulty to investigate a "learning challenge".*
2. *The Lesson Study group plans a "research seminar" to meet the learning challenge, focusing on case student reactions.*
3. *The seminar is taught by one member whilst others observe student reactions/learning.*
4. *Members of the Lesson Study group complete student interviews to gain insights into learning experiences.*
5. *The Lesson Study group evaluates the observation and interview evidence to consider the extent to which they have met the challenge.*
6. *Summative interviews and focus groups are completed and general insights drawn to feed into new practice and learning challenges.* (Wood & Cajkler, 2018, p. 11)

For educational developers, the Lesson Study model lends itself well to including non-standard faculty in the teacher group. Non-standard faculty could participate in one of two ways. First, they could be part of the teacher group that discusses and observes student learning. This would be an opportunity for non-standard faculty to familiarize themselves with common teaching practices at the institution as well as help non-standard faculty gain a deeper understanding of student learning challenges. This opportunity supports non-standard faculty in developing their own teaching through observation, reflection, and discussion. A second way non-standard faculty could participate in Lesson Study is to be the seminar instructor. This type of SoTL study is particularly useful for non-standard faculty because it focuses on the type and length of teaching many non-standard faculty conduct. In this role, the non-standard faculty may identify a challenge from their own teaching and student learning. The Lesson Study collaborative group could consist of standard teaching faculty and other non-standard faculty. Standard faculty would benefit from the opportunity to observe and discuss the teaching and learning that occurs outside of traditional contexts while the non-standard faculty may benefit from the reflections of standard faculty on student behaviors. Often, non-standard faculty does not have the ongoing history with a group of students to understand how factors like group dynamics impact course engagement and learning.

Educational developers can encourage non-standard faculty to participate in Lesson Study by emphasizing the value of it, facilitating workshops on how to conduct a Lesson Study, and facilitating Lesson Study groups with standard and non-standard faculty. Given the contexts in which non-standard faculty often teach, Lesson Study is one micro-level SoTL practice that fits well as a professional development tool.

SOTL PROFESSIONAL DEVELOPMENT AT THE MESO AND MACRO LEVELS

Geertsema (2016) argued that SoTL can be impactful on university campuses at the meso level and encouraged educational developers to focus on promoting SoTL as a means to enhancing the teaching and learning at the institution by working directly with academic departments. To fully realize this vision, non-standard faculty must be considered in their unique institutional contexts and not solely as one group of faculty outside the norm. Academic librarians, learning specialists, counselors, and clinical faculty all work in contexts that are unique unto themselves. It would behoove educational developers to provide support to each individual group of non-standard faculty. This does not negate the need to include non-standard faculty in professional development opportunities with standard faculty nor the need to promote the collaboration of non-standard faculty with each other.

Many non-standard faculty often work across departments and see a large picture of teaching and learning at their institution (Handler & Hays, 2019). At the meso level/department level and macro level/institutional level, non-standard faculty are valuable members of Communities of Practice and research teams studying the teaching and learning that occurs more broadly than within an individual classroom. For educational developers who are looking to foster collaborative SoTL work, the meso level and macro levels are rife with opportunities for non-standard faculty. By bringing non-standard faculty into SoTL communities, educational developers can further support the growth of a SoTL culture on their campuses.

The work of non-standard faculty is impacted by higher education contexts. Working at the macro level demands the acknowledgement of historical and current contexts in which students learn. This includes recognizing the socio-economic and political forces at play in higher education as well as the use of technology as the medium for many learning opportunities (Atkinson, 2014). Non-standard faculty often use technology to meet with students, conduct observations, complete a coaching session, and to develop learning modules. Understanding the higher education landscape can help non-standard faculty select the best technology for their students. Additionally, an understanding of the higher education landscape can inform the design of SoTL projects and be a lens through which SoTL study results are filtered, thus leading to more informed professional growth for non-standard faculty. Educational developers are in a position to shed light on various higher education learning contexts for all faculty, but particularly for non-standard faculty who may not be part of traditional faculty discussions.

Faculty learning communities, as they are often referred to in the literature, are a "group of cross-disciplinary faculty and staff...who engage in an active, collaborative, yearlong program with a curriculum about enhancing teaching and learning" (Cox, 2004, p. 8). They are a type of Community of Practice (CoP), described by Wenger, McDermott, and Snyder (2002) as groups that meet or interact on a regular basis to share their interest and expertise on a topic, and to strengthen or renew their knowledge. As a type of CoP, Cox (2013) identified faculty learning communities as one "structured... voluntary, and of size 8-12, meeting tri-weekly with a focus on building community and developing a scholarly product, usually Scholarship of Teaching and Learning" (p. 18). The benefits of faculty learning communities (FLCs) are well-documented, and these benefits have implications for both faculty members and students. Participants report feeling reduced stress, a sense of togetherness, and appreciation for the benefit of regular check-ins and opportunities for mentoring (Smith et al., 2016).

Although student learning communities themselves are common initiatives, faculty learning communities also have an impact on student outcomes. While the goal of FLCs is to increase faculty engagement in a group and with a topic, the topic often stems from some effort to improve teaching practices, which should logically extend positive benefits to students. Vescio, Ross, and Adams (2008) used ten studies of professional learning communities (PLCs) in schools to determine how teaching practices had changed, and whether the literature pointed to an increase in student learning outcomes when teachers engage in a PLC. The authors found that all of the studies in their sample that investigated the impact of PLCs on student achievement documented an increase.

Learning communities that are open to faculty in non-standard teaching roles also support the development of an institution-wide professional development program with SoTL at the core (Fanghanel, 2013), and can foster better support for instructors' intellectual and emotional needs (Bond, 2015). Non-standard faculty bring a unique perspective to the teaching and learning process. Their interactions with students outside the classroom can reveal much about the affective aspects of learning as well as student barriers that may not be as obvious to the traditional faculty member. As Cox (2004) noted, one of the goals of a faculty learning community is to "create an awareness of the complexity of teaching and learning" (p. 10). Counselors, for example, may have a deeper insight into the cognitive changes at work in a first-year university student, and how mental health issues such as depression can impact a student's learning (Rosslyn, 2004). Many academic librarians report anecdotally that students seem comfortable speaking openly with them about some of the difficulties they are having in their courses; without the power dynamic in place that exists between professors and students, students can approach librarians for help with their coursework with, for some, fewer feelings of intimidation.

Topic-Based Faculty Learning Communities

Educational developers can encourage participation by non-standard faculty in learning communities. In topic-based faculty learning communities, members address a particular teaching and learning topic as a group (Cox, 2004). In this model, educational developers can encourage the call for participants to specifically include non-standard faculty. Furthermore, non-standard faculty may be the ones to propose a topic and educational developers assist in recruiting a wider membership.

Cohort-Based Faculty Learning Communities

The second type of learning community is cohort-based. In these groups, the membership is comprised of individuals who may experience a particularly difficult time in the teaching and learning culture of the institution. According to Cox (2004), cohort-based faculty learning communities "address the teaching, learning, and developmental needs of an important group of faculty or staff that has been particularly affected by the isolation, fragmentation, stress, neglect, or chilly climate of the academy" (p. 8). Examples include junior faculty and graduate students. Non-standard faculty is another group that fits the description written by Cox. Therefore, educational developers have an opportunity to foster cohort-based learning communities of non-standard faculty.

Librarians in particular, who teach regularly as part of their jobs but face specific challenges with respect to teaching, their sense of themselves as teachers, and their sense of connection to a teaching community fit well into Cox's description of marginalized faculty (Weaver, 2019). At this point, it may be helpful to describe briefly the kind of teaching that academic librarians generally do in order to clarify why this is so. While some academic librarians do teach semester-long credit-bearing courses, whether these be research- and information-focused library-based courses (Raven & Rodrigues, 2017) or courses in schools of Library and Information Studies, most librarians teach what is commonly referred to the library literature as the "one-shot." The one-shot model earned its name because the instructor librarian is typically invited to a class once as a guest lecturer, sees the students once, and has literally "one shot" at teaching the students how to do research. "[B]orn of necessity," (Bowles-Terry & Donovan, 2016, p. 137), this model has left many dissatisfied for obvious reasons. Defining what should be taught in a single hour (or worse, half an hour) is difficult, which can leave librarians feeling like they have wasted their and the students' time. The content is often repetitious (Bowles-Terry & Donovan, 2016; Sheesley, 2001) and students are often uninterested (Sheesley, 2001). A quick scan of the literature around the "one-shot" reveals much discussion of "revitalizing," "revising," "transforming," and "moving beyond," while other articles wish to dispense with the model altogether (Mery, Newby, & Peng, 2012). However, for many academic librarians, this is the primary mode in which they teach (Black & Allen, 2019; Bryan, Asher, & Karshmer, 2018; Cox, 2019; Julien, Gross, & Latham. 2018).

Burnout is a factor for academic librarians (Nardine, 2019; Sheesley, 2001) and counselors (Wardle & Mayorgo, 2016). As Cox (2004) noted, Karpkia's 1997 study of mid-career faculty, many of whom were experiencing malaise and burnout, included recommendations that were, in essence, for creating learning communities. For academic instruction librarians, the causes of burnout are not difficult to guess: content repetition, lack of audience interest, staff shortages, lack of teaching training or experience, a sense of disconnect from the final outcomes of library instruction (for example, most librarians do not get a chance to see students' assignments to determine whether their instruction had any impact), lack of feedback, and a sense of isolation from other academics on campus (Sheesley, 2001).

DeLathouwer and co-authors (2012) explored how learning communities can help to level traditional hierarchies that can impact anxiety levels within academic communities. For non-standard faculty who may be feeling burnout, isolation, and a sense of disconnectedness from other faculty members involved in teaching, the opportunity to collaborate in a setting that positions all involved as learners could be of great benefit.

SOTL PROFESSIONAL DEVELOPMENT AT THE MEGA LEVEL

Disciplinary and interdisciplinary contexts provide non-standard faculty with opportunities to bring their unique perspectives. The mega level can be easily used by educational developers to promote professional development. Organizations such as the International Society for the Scholarship of Teaching and Learning, the Professional and Organizational Development Network, and discipline-specific associations provide opportunities for non-standard faculty to learn and present their knowledge.

Haley, Wiessner, and Robinson (2009) studied learning at a SoTL conference. Their findings indicated the importance for conference organizers to understand adult learning theory and to create opportunities for "inclusion and connectedness" (p. 79). The authors also encouraged conference organizers to intentionally include time for reflection (Haley et al., 2009). These findings have direct implications for educational developers who seek to support non-standard faculty's professional development through SoTL. At a minimum, educational developers can encourage SoTL conference attendance. For further engagement, educational developers can work with non-standard faculty to understand their professional development needs and then relay that information to conference organizers, or work on conference planning committees themselves. Providing intentional opportunities for non-standard faculty to engage, discuss, reflect, and plan new teaching and learning undergirds their growth.

Supporting non-standard faculty in research methods is another way educational developers can encourage non-standard faculty in using SoTL as a professional development tool at the mega level.

This can be done through programming or individual consultations. SoTL often relies on the use of social science research methods (Felten, 2013); however, other research methodologies drawing from the arts, humanities, physical sciences, and education fields are equally valid in SoTL (Bass & Linkon, 2008; Felten, 2013; Potter & Wuetherick, 2015). Most non-standard faculty will gravitate towards the research methods they studied while in graduate school. These methods may work well for SoTL studies, but they may not explore the breadth of knowledge that can be gained from using a variety of traditionally discipline-specific research methodologies. By conducting workshops on research methodologies, partnering individuals from different disciplines, and by recommending SoTL articles that use different methods, educational developers can introduce non-standard faculty to ways of research they might not have previously considered, thus expanding the insights they can gain. At the mega level, this support by educational developers can have far-reaching implications for the SoTL research strategies non-standard faculty members use in their studies.

EDUCATIONAL DEVELOPERS AND NON-STANDARD FACULTY: SIMILARITIES AND OPPORTUNITIES

Others have argued that educational developers themselves should go beyond supporting SoTL at their institutions and take a SoTL approach to their own work (Felten et al., 2007; Hoessler, Britnell, & Stockley, 2010). Many of the challenges and opportunities for educational developers engaging in their own inquiry can be mapped onto the argument for educational developers supporting non-standard faculty members who are involved in teaching. For example, Felten and co-authors (2007) framed participating in SoTL as a way for educational developers to "look through a scholarly lens at the outcomes of [their] own practice" (p. 93). Many non-standard faculty members described in this chapter also play a largely supportive role in teaching. In the case of librarians, support for the SoTL work of their faculty colleagues might also extend to assisting with or advising on literature searches, whether as part of a team of researchers or as a consultant, or creating guides and other resources to assist faculty members with SoTL research, which for many faculty members is outside of their regular domain of research.

Much knowledge about the work of educational developers comes from program assessment and sharing best practices (Felten et al., 2007). Although instruction librarians publish scholarship, often in journals devoted to matters in academic librarianship and information literacy, much of their other work follows a similar path. While sharing knowledge within the field is crucial to the evolution of library instruction, librarians and other non-standard faculty also have much insight to offer about student learning to instructors in the larger academic environment. One of the three key components of SoTL (Hutchings & Schulman, 1999) is the public sharing of research findings—public, in this case, extending to the wider academic community beyond the discipline of, for example, librarianship.

Felten and co-authors (2007) acknowledged the challenges for educational developers who do not have the benefit of enough continuous contact with students to find meaningful conclusions about the impact of their interventions. Non-standard faculty are often in the same position, encountering students on a more short-term basis. This challenge nonetheless presents an opportunity for educational developers to partner with or invite faculty members to be co-investigators (Felten et al., 2007); the same is also true for non-standard faculty, who can also look for opportunities to work more closely with instructors on SoTL projects. Partnerships like these can form organically through the work of teaching faculty, librarians, or counselors, but could also develop through better integration of non-standard faculty members in multidisciplinary learning communities, as previously discussed.

An institution's culture around teaching and learning, and faculty members' awareness of that culture, may influence instructors' engagement with SoTL (Vander Kloet et al., 2017). Some faculty associations have taken steps to protect SoTL and other non-traditional forms of scholarship in their collective agreements. For example, Dalhousie University (2018) draws on the Boyer model and cites it specifically in the collective agreement to define scholarship at that institution as including the scholarship of discovery, application, and/or teaching. The University of Central Missouri (2018) also includes SoTL as a form of scholarship acceptable for tenure in the College of Education. Likewise, national associations have endorsed the Boyer model, such as the Canadian Association of Schools of Nursing (CASN, previously Canadian Association of University Schools of Nursing), which has done so since 2001 (Dick, 2006). Collective agreements between other universities and their faculty associations also mention the Scholarship of Teaching and Learning, such as that of Western University in Ontario (2014), which includes SoTL as an optional component of the Professional Development section of a teaching dossier (along with professional associations and relevant research publications); others, such as Mount Royal University (2016), mention SoTL as a type of research eligible for relief from their teaching workload along with other traditional scholarship and artistic work; while still others, such as the University of British Columbia Faculty Association (2017), are explicit about the ways in which SoTL is recognized to be scholarly achievement. The University of British Columbia (2017) articulates SoTL activity as "evidenced by originality or innovation, demonstrable impact in a particular field or discipline, peer reviews, dissemination in the public domain, or substantial and sustained use by others," (p. 65). This is not an exhaustive list of examples.

As SoTL becomes increasingly accepted as a form of scholarship appropriate to tenure and promotion, faculty members who work outside of the classroom but for whom improving student learning and student success outcomes is their primary focus could be early adopters and advocates for SoTL at their institutions (Gubbins, 2014). Even at schools that support SoTL in the tenure and promotion process, there remains a need for educational developers to work on shifting institutional cultures to embrace SoTL (Marcketti & Freeman, 2016). This needed cultural shift highlights the value of non-standard faculty involvement in SoTL.

CONCLUSION

Each institution has non-standard faculty who perform different roles and responsibilities. Those roles and responsibilities are shaped by the institution, but also by the disciplinary context in which the non-standard faculty member is trained. Just as educational developers strive to understand how the disciplinary contexts impact how standard faculty members engage with their work (Taylor, 2010), educational developers must also recognize and learn the job duties and disciplinary contexts of non-standard faculty. This knowledge will help educational developers identify how SoTL can be effectively incorporated into professional development. As Bath and Smith (2004) argued, educational developers are disciplinarians in their own right. They study higher education, and much of the work done by educational developers is to support and grow higher education. To comprehensively undertake the work of developing higher education, educational developers must support all those involved in the teaching and learning that occurs at their institution.

SoTL is a useful professional development tool for non-standard faculty. Its focus on the local context and supports the unique teaching environments non-standard faculty typically inhabit. As Schroeder (2007) wrote, SoTL has implications for all members of an academic institution involved in teaching and learning. To fully encourage SoTL as a professional development tool for faculty outside of traditional teaching roles, educational developers should use the micro, meso, macro, and mega framework to identify the best areas of fit. Despite different work settings, the work of non-standard faculty is still the work of teaching and learning. Therefore, using common SoTL language, frameworks, and taxonomies encourages non-standard faculty to see themselves as part of the learning culture. At the same time, because of SoTL's focus on the local context, using SoTL as a professional development tool also allows for non-standard faculty to remain unique and embrace their own disciplinary backgrounds.

REFERENCES

Antelope Valley College Federation of Teachers. (2017). *Collective bargaining agreement between Antelope Valley Community College District and Antelope Valley College Federation of Teachers, July 1, 2015 - June 30, 2018.* Retrieved from https://www.avc.edu/sites/default/files/administration/hr/cert-contract/Certificated%20Agreement%2C%207-1-15%20-%206-30-18%20%282%29.pdf

Atkinson, M. P. (2014). Context matters for teaching and SoTL: Economic constraints, contingent faculty, and technology. *International Journal for the Scholarship of Teaching and Learning, 8*(2). doi:10.20429/ijsotl.2014.080202

Barrio Minton, C. A., Wachter Morris, C. A., & Yaites, L. D. (2014). Pedagogy in counselor education: A 10-year content analysis of journals. *Counselor Education and Supervision, 53*(3), 162–177. doi:10.1002/j.1556-6978.2014.00055.x

Bass, R., & Linkon, S. L. (2008). On the evidence of theory: Close reading as a disciplinary model for writing about teaching and learning. *Arts and Humanities in Higher Education, 7*(3), 245–261. doi:10.1177/1474022208094410

Bath, D., & Smith, C. (2004). Academic developers: An academic tribe claiming their territory in higher education. *The International Journal for Academic Development, 9*(1), 9–27. doi:10.1080/1360144042000296035

Bennett, R., Hobson, J., Jones, A., Martin-Lynch, P., Scutt, C., Strehlow, K., & Veitch, S. (2016). Being chimaera: A monstrous identity for SoTL academics. *Higher Education Research & Development, 35*(2), 217–228. doi:10.1080/07294360.2015.1087473

Black, S., & Allen, J. D. (2019). Part 9: Planning instruction. *The Reference Librarian, 60*(2), 93–108. doi:10.1080/02763877.2019.1571469

Bond, N. (2015). Developing a faculty learning community for non-tenure track professors. *International Journal of Higher Education, 4*(4), 1–12. doi:10.5430/ijhe.v4n4p1

Bowles-Terry, M., & Donovan, C. (2016). Serving notice on the one-shot: Changing roles for instruction librarians. *The International Information & Library Review, 48*(2), 137–142. doi:10.1080/105723 17.2016.1176457

Bradley, C. (2009). The Scholarship of Teaching and Learning: Opportunities for librarians. *College & Research Libraries News*, *70*(5), 276–278. doi:10.5860/crln.70.5.8181

Bryan, J. E., Asher, D., & Karshmer, E. D. (2018). Assessing librarians' teaching of one-shot sessions: A new model for evaluating instructional performance. *College & Undergraduate Libraries*, *25*(4), 350–371. doi:10.1080/10691316.2018.1527268

Cerbin, W., & Kopp, B. (2006). Lesson study as a model for building pedagogical knowledge and improving teaching. *International Journal on Teaching and Learning in Higher Education*, *18*(3), 250–257.

Cilliers, F. J., & Herman, N. (2010). Impact of an educational development programme on teaching practice of academics at a research-intensive university. *The International Journal for Academic Development*, *15*(3), 253–267. doi:10.1080/1360144X.2010.497698

Cox, C. (2019). Becoming part of the course: Using Blackboard to extend one-shot library instruction. *College & Research Libraries News*, *63*(1), 11–39. doi:10.5860/crln.63.1.11

Cox, M. D. (2004). Introduction to faculty learning communities. *New Directions for Teaching and Learning*, *97*(97), 5–23. doi:10.1002/tl.129

Cox, M. D. (2013). The impact of Communities of Practice in support of early-career academics. *The International Journal for Academic Development*, *18*(1), 18–30. doi:10.1080/1360144X.2011.599600

Dalhousie Faculty Association. (2018). *A collective agreement between the Board of Governors of Dalhousie University and the Dalhousie Faculty Association, 2017 - 2020*. Retrieved from https://cdn.dal.ca/content/dam/dalhousie/pdf/dept/hr/Academic-Staff-Relations/DFA-2017-20-Collective-Agreement.pdf

DeLathouwer, E., Roy, W., Martin, A., & Liska, J. (2012). Multidisciplinary collaboration through learning communities: Navigating anxiety. *Collected Essays on Learning and Teaching*, *5*, 27–32. doi:10.22329/celt.v5i0.3443

Dewar, J., & Bennett, C. (2010). Situating SoTL within the disciplines: Mathematics in the United States as a case study. *International Journal for the Scholarship of Teaching and Learning*, *4*(1). doi:10.20429/ijsotl.2010.040114

Dick, D. D. (2006). Options and possibility: Scholarship in the SIAST nursing division--An example of advancing scholarship in the polytechnic environment. *The College Quarterly*, *9*(3).

Faculty Association of Grant MacEwan University. (2017). *Collective agreement between the Board of Governors of Grant MacEwan University and the Faculty Association of Grant MacEwan University, July 1, 2017 - June 30, 2019*. Retrieved from https://www.macewanfa.ca/public/download/documents/42611

Faculty Association of the University of British Columbia. (2017). *Collective agreement between the University of British Columbia and the Faculty Association of the University of British Columbia, July 1, 2016 - June 30, 2019*. Retrieved from https://www.facultyassociation.ubc.ca/assets/media/Faculty-CA-2016-to-2019_V_6July2018.pdf

Fanghanel, J. (2013). Going public with pedagogical inquiries: SoTL as a methodology for faculty professional development. *Teaching & Learning Inquiry*, *1*(1), 59–70. doi:10.20343/teachlearninqu.1.1.59

Felten, P. (2013). Principles of good practice in SoTL. *Teaching & Learning Inquiry, 1*(1), 121–125. doi:10.20343/teachlearninqu.1.1.121

Felten, P., Kalish, A., Pingree, A., & Plank, K. M. (2007). Toward a Scholarship of Teaching and Learning in educational development. *To Improve the Academy: A Journal of Educational Development, 25*(1), 93-108.

Geertsema, J. (2016). Academic development, SoTL and educational research. *The International Journal for Academic Development, 21*(2), 122–134. doi:10.1080/1360144X.2016.1175144

Grigsby, R. K., & Thorndyke, L. (2011). Perspective: Recognizing and rewarding clinical scholarship. *Academic Medicine, 86*(1), 127–131. doi:10.1097/ACM.0b013e3181ffae5e PMID:21099387

Gubbins, P. O. (2014). The Scholarship of Teaching and Learning: An opportunity for clinical faculty members in academic pharmacy and other health professions to develop a program of scholarship. *International Journal for the Scholarship of Teaching and Learning, 8*(1). doi:10.20429/ijsotl.2014.080103

Haley, K., Wiessner, C., & Robinson, E. E. (2009). Encountering new information and perspectives: Constructing knowledge in conference contexts. *Journal of Continuing Higher Education, 57*(2), 72–82. doi:10.1080/07377360902964384

Handler, K., & Hays, L. (2019). Librarians as faculty developers: Leading educational development initiatives. *College & Research Libraries News, 80*(4), 220–235. doi:10.5860/crln.80.4.220

Harris, J., Podis, L. A., Podis, J. A. M., Rafoth, B., Inman, J. A., Sewell, D. N., ... Grimm, N. M. (2001). Reaffirming, reflecting, reforming: Writing center scholarship comes of age. *College English, 63*(5), 662–668. doi:10.2307/379050

Harris, M. (1995). Talking in the middle: Why writers need writing tutors. *College English, 57*(1), 27–42. doi:10.2307/378348

Hays, L., & Studebaker, B. (2019). Academic instruction librarians' teacher identity development through participation in the Scholarship of Teaching and Learning. *International Journal for the Scholarship of Teaching and Learning, 13*(2), 4. doi:10.20429/ijsotl.2019.130204

Hoessler, C., Britnell, J., & Stockley, D. (2010). Assessing the impact of educational development through the lens of the Scholarship of Teaching and Learning. *New Directions for Teaching and Learning, 122*(122), 81–89. doi:10.1002/tl.400

Houtman, E. (2010). "Trying to figure it out": Academic librarians talk about learning to teach. *Library and Information Research, 34*(107), 18–40. doi:10.29173/lirg246

Huber, M. T., & Hutchings, P. (2005). *The advancement of learning: Building the teaching commons.* San Francisco: Jossey-Bass.

Huber, M. T., & Hutchings, P. (2006). Building the teaching commons. *Change: The Magazine of Higher Learning, 38*(3), 24–31. doi:10.3200/CHNG.38.3.24-31

Hutchings, P. (2000). *Opening lines: Approaches to the Scholarship of Teaching and Learning.* Menlo Park, CA: Carnegie Publications.

Jacobs, L. (2013). Academic status for Canadian academic librarians: A brief history. In J. Dekker & M. Kandiuk (Eds.), *In solidarity: Academic librarians labour activism and union participation in Canada* (pp. 9–37). Sacramento, CA: Library Juice Press.

Julien, H., Gross, M., & Latham, D. (2018). Survey of information literacy instructional practices in U.S. academic libraries. *College & Research Libraries*, *79*(2), 179–199. doi:10.5860/crl.79.2.179

Karabenick, S. A., & Conley, A. (2011). *Teacher motivation for professional development.* Retrieved from http://hub.mspnet.org/media/data/Teacher_PDM.pdf?media_000000007652.pdf

Kemp, J. (2006). Isn't being a librarian enough? Librarians as classroom teachers. *College & Undergraduate Libraries*, *13*(3), 3–23. doi:10.1300/J106v13n03_02

Lakeland College Faculty Association. (2016). *Collective agreement between the Board of Governors of Lakeland College and the Lakeland College Faculty Association, July 1, 2016 - June 30, 2018.* Retrieved from https://issuu.com/lakelandcw/docs/faculty_collective_agreement_2016-2

Mackiewicz, J., & Thompson, I. K. (2015). *Talk about writing: The tutoring strategies of experienced writing center tutors.* New York, NY: Routledge.

MacMillan, M. (2015). EBLIP + IL = SoTL. *Brain-work: The C-EBLIP blog.* Retrieved from https://words.usask.ca/ceblipblog/2015/03/24/eblip-il-sotl/

Marcketti, S. B., & Freeman, S. A. (2016). SoTL evidence on promotion and tenure vitas at a research university. *The Journal of Scholarship of Teaching and Learning*, *16*(5), 19–31. doi:10.14434//josotl.v16i5.21152

Mårtensson, K. (2014). *Influencing teaching and learning microcultures: Academic development in a research intensive university.* Retrieved from http://lup.lub.lu.se/search/ws/files/3403041/4438677.pdf

McNeill, K., & Haines, B. (2003). Scholarship of teaching and librarians: Building successful partnerships with faculty. *Georgia Library Quarterly*, *39*(4), 4–8.

McNiff, L., & Hays, L. (2017). SoTL in the LIS classroom: Helping future academic librarians become more engaged teachers. *Communications in Information Literacy*, *11*(2), 366–377. doi:10.15760/comminfolit.2017.11.2.8

Mery, Y., Newby, J., & Peng, K. (2012). Why one-shot information literacy sessions are not the future of instruction: A case for online credit courses. *College & Research Libraries*, *73*(4), 366–377. doi:10.5860/crl-271

Miller-Young, J. E., Yeo, M., & Manarin, K. (2018). Challenges to disciplinary knowing and identity: Experiences of scholars in a SoTL development program. *International Journal for the Scholarship of Teaching and Learning*, *12*(1), 3. doi:10.20429/ijsotl.2018.120103

Mitchell, L. N., & Mitchell, E. T. (2015). Using SoTL as a lens to reflect and explore for innovation in education and librarianship. *Technical Services Quarterly*, *32*(1), 46–58. doi:10.1080/07317131.2015.972876

Morahan, P. S., & Fleetwood, J. (2008). The double helix of activity and scholarship: Building a medical education career with limited resources. *Medical Education, 42*(1), 34–44. doi:10.1111/j.1365-2923.2007.02976.x PMID:18181845

Mount Royal Faculty Association. (2016). *Collective agreement between Mount Royal Faculty Association and the Board of Governors of Mount Royal University, July 1, 2016 - June 30, 2018.* Retrieved from https://mrfa.net/wp-content/uploads/2019/01/MRFA-Collective-Agreement-July-1-2016-to-June-30-2018.pdf

Nardine, J. (2019). The state of academic liaison librarian burnout in ARL libraries in the United States. *College & Research Libraries, 80*(4), 508–524. doi:10.5860/crl.80.4.508

North, S. M. (1984). The idea of a writing center. *College English, 46*(5), 433–446. doi:10.2307/377047

O'Brien, M. (2008). Navigating the SoTL landscape: A compass, map and some tools for getting started. *International Journal for the Scholarship of Teaching and Learning, 2*(2), 15.

Otto, P. (2014). Librarians, libraries, and the Scholarship of Teaching and Learning. *New Directions for Teaching and Learning, 2014*(139), 77–93. doi:10.1002/tl.20106

Potter, M. K., & Wuetherick, B. (2015). Who is represented in the teaching commons?: SoTL through the lenses of the arts and humanities. *The Canadian Journal for the Scholarship of Teaching and Learning, 6*(2), 2. doi:10.5206/cjsotl-rcacea.2015.2.2

Raven, M., & Rodrigues, D. (2017). A course of our own: Taking an information literacy credit course from inception to reality. *Partnership. The Canadian Journal of Library and Information Practice and Research, 12*(1).

Rosslyn, F. (2004). The emotional background to learning: A university experience. *Emotional & Behavioural Difficulties, 9*(1), 70–76. doi:10.1177/1363275204041964

Roxå, T., & Mårtensson, K. (2013). *Understanding strong academic microcultures: An exploratory study.* Retrieved from https://www.lunduniversity.lu.se/lup/publication/246cf361-3a33-47df-8fad-c21ec704fb4d

Savini, C. (2011). An alternative approach to bridging disciplinary divides. *Writing Lab Newsletter, 35*(7-8), 1–5.

Schroeder, C. (2007). Countering SoTL marginalization: A model for integrating SoTL with institutional initiatives. *International Journal for the Scholarship of Teaching and Learning, 1*(1), 15. doi:10.20429/ijsotl.2007.010115

Sheesley, D. F. (2001). Burnout and the academic teaching librarian: An examination of the problem and suggested solutions. *Journal of Academic Librarianship, 27*(6), 447–451. doi:10.1016/S0099-1333(01)00264-6

Shulman, L. S. (2000). From Minsk to Pinsk: Why a Scholarship of Teaching and Learning? *The Journal of Scholarship of Teaching and Learning, 1*(1), 48–52.

Simmons, N. (2016). Synthesizing SoTL institutional initiatives toward national impact. *New Directions for Teaching and Learning, 146*(146), 95–102. doi:10.1002/tl.20192

Simpson, D., Fincher, R. M. E., Hafler, J. P., Irby, D. M., Richards, B. F., Rosenfeld, G. C., & Viggiano, T. R. (2007). Advancing educators and education by defining the components and evidence associated with educational scholarship. *Medical Education, 41*(10), 1002–1009. doi:10.1111/j.1365-2923.2007.02844.x PMID:17822412

Smetkowski, B., Conway, K., & Starrett, D. (2009). SoTL, CASTL, and the CSTL at Southeast Missouri State University: A symbiotic relationship. *Transformative Dialogues, 3*(1), 1–15.

Smith, E. R., Calderwood, P. E., Storms, S. B., Lopez, P. G., & Colwell, R. P. (2016). Institutionalizing faculty mentoring within a Community of Practice model. *To Improve the Academy, 35*(1), 35-71.

Stes, A., & Van Petegem, P. (2011). Instructional development for early career academics: An overview of impact. *Educational Research, 53*(4), 459–474. doi:10.1080/00131881.2011.625156

Stigler, J., & Hiebert, J. (1999). *The teaching gap: Best ideas from the world's teachers for improving education in the classroom.* New York, NY: Free Press.

Taylor, K. L. (2010). Understanding the disciplines within the context of educational development. *New Directions for Teaching and Learning, 122*(122), 59–67. doi:10.1002/tl.398

University of Central Missouri College of Education Faculty. (2018). *College of Education guidelines for promotion/tenure.* Retrieved from https://www.ucmo.edu/offices/general-counsel/university-policy-library/academic-policies/promotion-and-tenure-college-guidelines/coe-promotion-tenure-2018.pdf

University of Western Ontario Faculty Association. (2014). *Faculty collective agreement between the University of Western Ontario and the University of Western Ontario Faculty Association, July 1, 2014 - June 30, 2018.* Retrieved from https://www.uwo.ca/facultyrelations/pdf/collective_agreements/faculty.pdf

Vander Kloet, M., Frake-Mistak, M., McGinn, M. K., Caldecott, M., Aspenlieder, E. D., Beres, J. L., & Gill, A. (2017). Conditions for contingent instructors engaged in the Scholarship of Teaching and Learning. *The Canadian Journal for the Scholarship of Teaching and Learning, 8*(2). doi:10.5206/cjsotl-rcacea.2017.2.9

Vescio, V., Ross, D., & Adams, A. (2008). A review of research on the impact of professional learning communities on teaching practice and student learning. *Teaching and Teacher Education, 24*(1), 80–91. doi:10.1016/j.tate.2007.01.004

Walters, W. H. (2016). Faculty status of librarians at US research universities. *Journal of Academic Librarianship, 42*(2), 161–171. doi:10.1016/j.acalib.2015.11.002

Wardle, E. A., & Mayorga, M. G. (2016). Burnout among the counseling profession: A survey of future professional counselors. *Journal of Educational Psychology, 10*(1), 9–15.

Wenger, E., McDermott, R. A., & Snyder, W. (2002). *Cultivating Communities of Practice: A guide to managing knowledge.* Boston, MA: Harvard Business Press.

Wood, P., & Cajkler, W. (2018). Lesson study: A collaborative approach to scholarship for teaching and learning in higher education. *Journal of Further and Higher Education, 42*(3), 313–326. doi:10.1080/0309877X.2016.1261093

Wright, M. C., Lohe, D. R., & Little, D. (2018). The role of a center for teaching and learning in a de-centered educational world. *Change: The Magazine of Higher Learning, 50*(6), 38–44. doi:10.1080/00 091383.2018.1540826

Wuetherick, B., & Yu, S. (2016). The Canadian teaching commons: The Scholarship of Teaching and Learning in Canadian higher education. *New Directions for Teaching and Learning, 146*(146), 23–30. doi:10.1002/tl.20183

KEY TERMS AND DEFINITIONS

Academic Librarians: Individuals who work in a post-secondary library, often with faculty rank.

Clinical Faculty: Faculty members whose primary responsibility is working with students in a laboratory or patient setting.

Counselors: Individuals who work in a post-secondary medical or psychological setting, often with faculty rank.

Learning Specialists: Individuals who tutor students and teach remedial courses, often with faculty rank.

Macro Level: SoTL work that is conducted at the university level.

Mega Level: SoTL work that is conducted in national or international contexts.

Meso Level: SoTL work that is conducted at the department level.

Micro Level: SoTL work that is conducted at the level of individual faculty.

Non-Standard Faculty: Individuals whose job responsibilities are not traditional faculty duties, but who are included in faculty associations or unions and hold the rank of faculty at a post-secondary institution.

Section 3
Faculty Developers as Partners in SoTL

This section is dedicated to the role of the faculty developer and his or her role in supporting and promoting a culture of SoTL across an institution. Despite the competing commitments that faculty members face, faculty developers are in a role that contributes to teaching excellence, and one way to do this is through SoTL. The first part of this section shares scenarios and case studies which illustrate the nature of these relationships through the perspectives of both faculty members and faculty developers. The section concludes with a chapter discussing research ethics and implications for SoTL with an emphasis on the role of the faculty developer.

Chapter 8
Using SoTL to Foster a Research Approach to Teaching and Learning in Higher Education

Erik Brogt
University of Canterbury, New Zealand

Kerry Shephard
University of Otago, New Zealand

Bernadette Knewstubb
Victoria University of Wellington, New Zealand

Tracy Leigh Rogers
https://orcid.org/0000-0003-1898-9358
University of Otago, New Zealand

ABSTRACT

This chapter discusses how Scholarship of Teaching and Learning (SoTL) can be used to foster a research approach to teaching and learning and how faculty development that supports colleagues to engage in SoTL can support the development of scholarly faculty. Both the process and the product of SoTL are discussed, conceptualised as different levels of SoTL engagement. The role of the faculty developer in such scholarship is discussed, drawing on Pedagogical Content Knowledge as a framework for engagement in SoTL projects. Last, implications for the work of a faculty developer are drawn and future avenues of research in faculty development proposed.

INTRODUCTION

In his influential work, Boyer (1990; 1996) formulated four broad categories of scholarship. The scholarship of discovery is fundamental research; the scholarship of integration involves bringing different areas of knowledge together; the scholarship of application (or engagement) is the practical use of knowledge

DOI: 10.4018/978-1-7998-2212-7.ch008

and expertise working with the wider community, and the Scholarship of Teaching and Learning is the study of the processes of teaching and learning. Each scholarship has six criteria: clear goals, adequate preparation/appropriate procedures, appropriate methods, significant results, effective presentation, and reflective critique. Boyer's concepts have since been extended. Hutchings and Shulman (1999), in particular, emphasised that scholarship in the context of teaching requires that the work be made public; available for peer review and critique according to accepted standards; and able to be reproduced and built on by other scholars. These requirements, in principle, could apply to all scholarly practices.

While most faculty would be quite comfortable with such notions in relation to their disciplinary research, applying the principles to teaching in higher education may not be as obvious, whether in theory or in practice. All four scholarships, however, have strong commonalities where any individual scholarship can be taken as a vantage point and incorporate the other scholarships. Faculty developers[1] operate across all scholarships, like any other scholar, but have a central focus on Scholarship of Teaching and Learning, as it applies to higher education.

The Scholarship of Teaching and Learning (SoTL) has been a cornerstone of faculty development for the last 30 years. However, the conceptualisation and operationalisation of SoTL, and its links to the other areas of scholarship, is likely to be quite different for faculty developers and discipline-based faculty. This chapter argues that promoting SoTL as a tool to systematically investigate teaching practice can also promote the other scholarships, rather than standing in opposition to them. In a SoTL approach to learning and teaching, scholarly teachers' efforts to learn about their teaching through research is one aspect of their scholarship. This approach echoes the way research is employed by faculty to become more scholarly in their discipline. Faculty developers therefore need to highlight the essential similarities between learning to research and learning to teach in higher education. Both are inherently scholarly and research-based practices, or should be, because both are underpinned by a drive to learn something. This chapter explores ways faculty developers can accompany discipline-based colleagues on their SoTL journeys. For the faculty developer, the overall aim of engaging discipline-based colleagues in SoTL is to foster a research approach to questions about teaching and learning, for the benefit of scholars, their students, and their institutions. The chapter concludes by considering the implications for faculty developers and potential future research agendas for faculty development[2].

RESEARCH AND TEACHING IN UNIVERSITIES: FACULTY AS SCHOLARS

Teaching and research are among the core duties of an academic, and are generally equally weighted (in the traditional 40-40-20 model of research-teaching-service). These duties are often conceptualised as separate, and even competing activities or ways of thinking about academic work. The division implies that teaching and research processes and outcomes are so different that being accomplished at one might have no bearing on being accomplished at the other. The separation leads to a hierarchical value or ranking being placed on teaching and research, where research is often depicted as being more important and of higher status than teaching (e.g., Chalmers, 2018).

This hierarchy is evident in the importance placed on research in university rankings or academic hiring and promotion practices at universities. Many faculty members have no formal preparation in teaching before commencing the job (e.g., Walczyk, Ramsey, & Zha, 2007), either in teaching practice or the Scholarship of Teaching and Learning. To assist faculty to develop as teachers, many universities offer workshops and consultations focusing on "how to" teach, rather than "why". The Scholarship of

Teaching and Learning is typically the domain of postgraduate programmes in higher education teaching and learning. Workshops and postgraduate programmes tend to be the domain of faculty developers. Many universities have dedicated faculty developers who have varied roles (Land, 2004; Debowski, 2011; Sutherland, 2018), including support for teaching and SoTL. However, in most universities there is no clear incentive (or mandate) for faculty to engage with teaching development and SoTL (Sabagh & Saroyan, 2014). Nor are there clear strategies for evaluating the quality of teaching beyond student evaluations. Research thus remains the main focus of attention and time commitment, reinforcing the hierarchy.

Over the years, attempts have been made to raise the status and profile of teaching, including an emphasis on making the means for evaluating the quality of teaching resemble those used for research. This has translated into a focus on metrics, accountability, and calls to "professionalise" teaching with qualifications, mentoring, engaging in research on teaching, peer review, competitive funding, disciplinary networks, competitive international pool for positions, performance indicators, codes of ethics, and the like (Probert, 2014; Chalmers, 2018). However, such an approach risks reinforcing the hierarchical distinction between research and teaching, and imposes metrics that are not necessarily valid for assessing teaching practice. Instead, engagement with SoTL can take different forms and levels of depth, and metrics for success need to be aligned to the outcomes of an individual SoTL project as described in the section below (What Constitutes "Success" in SoTL?).

The authors argue that the division between research and teaching is somewhat artificial, as the same academic attitude of rigour and investigation is needed for both. In both research and teaching, to become a proficient and reflective practitioner, key academic activities such as investigation, gathering, analysing and interpreting data, and a willingness to change one's mind in the face of evidence, are critical. However, though the *process* of scholarship is similar, the *products/outcomes* of the scholarships differ. In the case of disciplinary research, the outcomes are more easily measurable and quantifiable than in teaching, through discrete outputs such as presentations or publications in peer-reviewed journals. The authors argue that part of the hierarchy of academic work is not just based on the status of the activity, but also on which data are easiest to collect and quantify.

Faculty Developers as Colleagues and Scholars

SoTL provides faculty developers with a means to both support teaching and bridge the divide between research and teaching. SoTL enables faculty developers to support faculty members' teaching practices through the use of theoretically and empirically-derived research evidence and established good teaching practice. SoTL, as a scholarship, provides evidence-based "good practice" as well as a systematic way to analyse, interpret and understand teaching and learning. SoTL aligns with the evidence-based approaches that faculty already take in their disciplinary research. SoTL discussions can therefore highlight parallels between the different areas of scholarship, such as the requirement to learn and investigate in a systematic way.

SoTL may help faculty to reintegrate different aspects of their academic role, and identify how similar attitudes and processes apply to all areas of scholarship. Faculty may have different levels[3] of engagement in the different areas of scholarship, and the evidence base for success will be different depending on the scholarship and the desired outcome. Regardless, success in one of the areas of scholarship means faculty develop as scholars overall.

To fulfil the three main duties of an academic—research, teaching, and service—faculty should be encouraged to investigate their practices, be they blue skies research in their discipline, applied research in their discipline, teaching practices, or community engagement. To maintain the notion of the academic as the all-rounder, and given the higher levels of expertise in (and thus comfort with) disciplinary research compared with teaching, promoting a research approach to teaching can promote engagement with teaching and teaching development. The different roles of faculty are thus conceived as research-based scholarly behaviour to enable faculty to create internal coherence for their professional identity (Sutherland, 2018) and a logical path forward for the faculty developer.

SoTL AS A VEHICLE FOR BROADER ENGAGEMENT IN SCHOLARSHIP

Whether SoTL is developed as an entity in its own right or, as emphasised in this chapter, as one element of a broader engagement with scholarship, there appears to be no doubt that it has been and continues to be an important vehicle for promoting change in higher education. It will be useful therefore to consider the diverse ways faculty development units, faculty developers, faculty, and academic departments engage with SoTL ideas, principles, and practices. Within the Australasian higher education community, members of the Higher Education Research and Development Society of Australasia (HERDSA) occasionally adopt four descriptors of engagement conceptualised as points on a continuum (discussed below). All four points may to varying degrees adopt Boyer's six standards for scholarship and Hutchings and Shulman's (1999) requirements for SoTL along with the general principle that the work needs to build on what has come before.

The first point on the continuum refers to faculty with an interest in teaching who are looking for new ideas or different ways to teach their courses. These individuals may be described as "consumers of discipline-based educational research". Most of the literature they consume is tied to the discipline and is practice-based, such as *CBE – Life Sciences Education* and *Journal of Accounting Education* among many others. The broad goals, methods, and application of discipline-based educational research have been usefully summarized by the USA's National Research Council (2012), particularly in the context of science and engineering education.

Next, faculty who want to gain a better understanding of teaching in general may be described as "consumers of general higher educational research". The literature they explore is not necessarily discipline-based, but deals more with issues such as curriculum design, assessment, and pedagogy. Faculty in this category are often participants in postgraduate programmes in higher education teaching and learning. Their involvement with SoTL is often via specialist higher education journals such as *Higher Education* and *Studies in Higher Education*, as well as higher education handbooks and textbooks. The degree of overlap with more mainstream educational journals and educational research that focuses on compulsory, school-based education is often limited, marking a division between research-informed higher education practices and research-informed school-based education practices.

Further along the continuum are university teachers who wish to research their own teaching practices for their own edification or as a line of research into their teaching. The literature on which they draw includes discipline-based and general education research, as well as educational research methods. Often the educational research methodology used to support their research would be described by some educational researchers as action research, and the researchers themselves as "action researchers". Some would identify a quality difference between action research and more theoretically situated research (see for example Sutherland & Grant, 2016) but others would insist that action research may be high-quality research albeit research in which the key researcher has a significant personal stake (Brew, 2002). Some higher education research journals specialise in action research, including journals such as *Action Research* and *Educational Action Research.*

The last category includes faculty who research teaching and learning in higher education and who make significant contributions to higher education discourse via disciplinary or general education journals, or books. They may be described as "higher education researchers". They adopt the highest levels of SoTL practices as described by Boyer and others. Although higher education researchers can no doubt also be researchers in other disciplines, in some cases they specialise in the discipline of higher education. Higher education researchers may have specialist research roles, but may also be faculty developers. Research that focuses on the work of faculty developers is highlighted in journals such as *A Journal of Educational Development* and *International Journal for Academic Development.*

These categorisations lead to some current and often intense debates. Faculty developers and disciplinary faculty ask if it is realistic to expect colleagues in the disciplines to operate at the far, most scholarly, end of the continuum. To do so effectively might require an education-focused PhD as well as a discipline-based PhD. It is broadly accepted that in countries that fund individuals, departments, and institutions differentially on the basis of research quality, some forms of educational research by a disciplinary academic is far less valuable than discipline-based research. Sutherland and Grant (2016), for example, emphasise that strict definitions of research in New Zealand's Performance-based Research Funding system do invalidate some forms of educational research involving an individual's own practices. This is based on the extent to which the research can be categorized as original research, evaluation of personal practice, or a scholarly case study of personal practice. Related aspects of this debate are discussed in detail by Sutherland and Grant (2016). Such differentiation may emphasise a fundamental disrespect for the Scholarship of Teaching and Learning, with regard to the scholarship of research.

The authors of this chapter unite in emphasising that in promoting SoTL, the fundamental concept of a scholarly academic as a person who understands the need to be scholarly as a teacher, as a researcher, as a community-engaged academic is also promoted. Overall, scholars research their own practice, but on the way, they also learn to set clear goals, identify and present significant results, invite and respect peer-review, and understand acceptable standards in a particular domain. These are not trivial undertakings. Similarly, the principal goal of SoTL is to help faculty to develop as scholars. SoTL becomes a means to an end; using the same attitudes, language and methods of scholarly research, familiar to discipline-based researchers, to promote a research outlook on teaching and learning at the individual and institution level. At the same time, faculty engagement in SoTL contributes to their development as researchers, and in varying degrees as scholars in Boyer's other scholarships.

Some faculty developers, particularly those with expertise in higher education research and teaching, can help faculty increase the level of rigour in a SoTL project. Experience suggests that many discipline-based faculty who predominantly do work at the lower end of the SoTL continuum (described above) typically know relatively little about educational research design and methodology. However, with help from a research-active faculty developer, they may be able to embrace SoTL at the level required for an international peer-reviewed publication in high impact journals. The faculty developer can bring the necessary experience in research on teaching, can act as a resource, mentor and collaborator in a SoTL project, and on the way can support the development of the academic as a more rounded scholar.

Faculty developers engaging in SoTL collaboration with discipline-based faculty also serve the institution as a whole. Ideally, the authors would argue, faculty developers would like to empower other faculty with the skills and tools for self-initiated, self-led, and self-sustained inquiry into teaching practices, leading to research-informed or research-led changes in practice. As any university would typically only have a small number of dedicated faculty developers on staff, a model of distributed leadership and development in teaching becomes a necessity. Collaborative SoTL projects thus become a way of creating "knowledgeable others" in academic departments and addressing questions about teaching and learning.

COLLABORATIVE SoTL PROJECTS

In the previous section, the different levels at which faculty might choose to engage with SoTL were discussed. Faculty developers through individual developmental consultation, or through individual, departmental, or institutional projects, as well as through more traditional scholarly research projects support such SoTL activities. Determining how a particular activity fits within the range of SoTL activities is vital. A project's level of engagement in SoTL influences the nature of the project, its outcomes (e.g., Stefani & Baume, 2016), the role faculty members and faculty developers play in the project, and what constitutes acceptable evidence of success. Each of these aspects is discussed in detail below, followed by a closer examination of the different levels of engagement in SoTL and the role of the faculty developer in each.

Outcomes

An important distinction in types of SoTL activities is the intended audience (self/other) and intention (applied/investigative) for different projects, as illustrated in Figure 1. Developing in SoTL or in any other scholarly endeavour does not necessitate it being published as long as some aspect of it is effectively presented to others who have an interest in the study. From a faculty development perspective, the attitude of *investigation* is key, more so than an outcome. It is also possible that a finding might be new to the individual academic, or even to their discipline, but does not necessarily contribute anything new to the field of higher education. For example, the well-established practice of "constructive alignment", developed by John Biggs in the 1990s (e.g., Biggs & Tang, 2007) and developed through his work in Hong Kong, is implemented in departments and institutions as a "new" approach every day, in the authors' experience. What might resemble Boyer's scholarship of discovery for one, may be the scholarship of

Figure 1. Different dimensions of SoTL activities

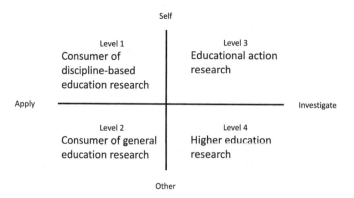

application or integration for another. If the purpose of the project, however, is to promote a research approach to teaching development and to other scholarly activities by the faculty involved, then the most important outcome might be changes in the participants' attitude of *investigation* (O'Byrne et al., 2018).

What Constitutes "Success" in SoTL?

The outcomes discussed above often have associated metrics for success, leading to a series of new questions: Whose success? What does success mean, and for whom? Is the unit of analysis the project, the faculty member, the faculty developer, the nature of the project or the field of enquiry? The evidence base for success is different based on the negotiated outcome of a SoTL project. Faculty developers need to clearly articulate that the outcomes, evidence and potential outputs will differ, and that research metrics (grants, publications) are not necessarily a valid measure of success for the project.

For example, Shephard, Rogers, and Brogt (in press) explored how participating in SoTL research projects affected participants' (conceptions of) teaching. Results suggested that such engagement led to higher levels of reflection on teaching and learning, and an appreciation of tackling questions about teaching and learning with a rigorously academic toolkit, but not did not necessarily involve large changes in teaching practice. So, were those SoTL projects a success? If so, for whom, and who decides? This is an area of potential tension and fragmentation (e.g., Rowland, 2002; Manathunga, 2006), between the different direct and indirect stakeholders in the SoTL project.

The faculty member and faculty developer may interpret success differently. For faculty developers, the input stage (development) of the project and capacity and capability building (e.g., curriculum development) may be important. For the faculty member, success may concern outputs, such as a successful rollout of the curriculum, increased student grades, retention, or pass rates.

The Role of the Faculty Developer in SoTL Collaborations

Faculty developers will play different roles in each SoTL project. This is illustrated in Figure 2, based on the conceptualisation of Pedagogical Content Knowledge (Shulman, 1986; 1987; Brogt & Knewstubb, under review); the combination of (disciplinary) content knowledge and research and of pedagogical knowledge and research to investigate and inform teaching and learning (of the discipline). While a

Figure 2. Content knowledge and pedagogical knowledge as the basis of a SoTL outcome

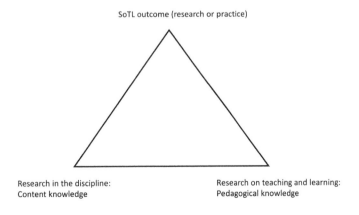

faculty developer or faculty member can take up any position (depending on their background), a common type of collaboration would be where the faculty member contributes knowledge and research of the discipline while the faculty developer brings the knowledge and research of education and SoTL. In collaboration, they work toward a specific SoTL outcome (the apex of the triangle). Based on the outcome, the balance of content knowledge of the discipline or pedagogical knowledge from SoTL or education will vary.

Instigating or being involved in a collaborative SoTL project with discipline-based colleagues can be challenging. Faculty developers need to be aware of the nature of the project, their role in it, and the importance of forging and maintaining a relationship with the faculty member(s). Brogt and Knewstubb (under review) proposed a Theory of Relationship for conceptualising common faculty development scenarios to help faculty developers consciously and deliberately navigate their relationships with faculty members. In the authors' experience, there are two common pitfalls to avoid in SoTL collaborations with faculty members. The first pitfall is the faculty developer misreading the faculty member's agenda and trying to make a SoTL project bigger or smaller than they would like or are comfortable with. This can happen when the driving question of the project is inadequately framed and scoped. For example, a SoTL project question like "how can topic X be taught better" can be addressed at each of the levels in Figure 1. Without a scoping conversation, there is a reasonable probability that the faculty member and faculty developer have different conceptions about the project. The second pitfall is for the faculty developer to try to drive the SoTL agenda. While faculty developers can help shape and inform the agenda based on their expertise in teaching and learning (research), the faculty member needs to have considerable ownership. After all, collaborative SoTL projects are supposed to be done *with*, and not *to* colleagues.

SoTL PROJECTS

The previous section discussed the different levels of SoTL engagement which were illustrated in Figure 1. In this section, the purpose and outcomes, the role of the faculty developer, and possible sources of evidence for success of the project are briefly discussed. In addition, the way in which each level of engagement supports a research approach to teaching and learning is discussed.

Level One: Consumer of Discipline-Based Education Research (Self/Applied)

Purpose and Outcomes

At the first level of engagement with SoTL, the faculty member is often driven by a sense of dissatisfaction (their own, or as expressed by a faculty head, perhaps) with the teaching and learning in their discipline. Their purpose tends to be quite specific and operational, for example to find an interesting assessment of, or an engaging way to teach X. Other times, there may be an overall broad goal, but it may be rather vague, for example to raise student pass rates, or teach their discipline better. In most cases, the SoTL project is seen by the faculty member as constrained to (or even unique to) their discipline, and an issue of pedagogical content knowledge (Shulman, 1986; 1987), and student learning in the discipline, rather than a more generic pedagogical issue. Pedagogical approaches from disciplines that are not related or from more generic education literature may be devalued.

Role of the Faculty Developer

The first role of the faculty developer is to help the faculty member articulate what it is that they seek to learn. It is then incumbent on the faculty developer to act as a pedagogical expert, providing readings, teaching techniques or evaluation tools applicable to the faculty's context. Critical in this case is a faculty developer's awareness of, and sensitivity to the academic culture and (teaching) mores of the discipline and the departmental culture and community (e.g., Mårtensson & Roxå, 2016), so that developmental advice is always within the appropriate context of the discipline. If the faculty member is at a stage where they are not yet ready to engage with the readings, these may need to be paraphrased by the faculty developer. The faculty developer thus acts as a catalyst for action, and an interpreter of educational language. The faculty developer may also act as a "host", politely introducing the academic to others in their discipline or the wider university community who can also assist the faculty member achieve their next goals (in teaching development).

What Constitutes Evidence of Success?

For the faculty member success can be defined in multiple ways, often through an observed change in student actions or behaviour, changes in student outcomes (performance or otherwise), or the student experience. Common lines of evidence would be classroom observations, student assessment data, testimonials, and student evaluations of teaching. In addition, a faculty member may experience changes in their own awareness and approaches to teaching. In the case of some of the authors of this chapter, they encourage the faculty member to keep a structured self-reflective log, usually in line with Brookfield (1995), which can be used for teaching portfolios or academic promotion applications.

For the faculty developer success will be different. Typically, faculty developers hope to see growth and independence in the faculty member with regard to SoTL and teaching practice, which is not always easy to evidence (and quantify). Evidence of success could include a faculty member's ability to independently find research and resources related to teaching and learning in their discipline; articulate/ frame problems and goals in their learning and teaching space; or take up a student-focused approach in the discipline, (e.g., a shift from level one or two to level three as a teacher (Biggs & Tang, 2007)).

How Does It Support a Research Approach to Teaching and Learning?

The practicality of this type of engagement with SoTL often serves as a conduit or catalyst for the faculty member to become more interested/involved in discipline-based SoTL. It can form the start of the academic discourse and literature about teaching and learning in the discipline, which at some point can be generalised to teaching and learning in all disciplines, and the associated literature. A focus on evidence for success can raise awareness of the need for valid and reliable evaluation measures. Moreover, the faculty member may become comfortable with the idea that the question they seek to answer drives the methodology, not the other way around.

Level Two: Consumer of Generalised Education Research (Applied/Other)

Purpose and Outcomes

At this level, the faculty member may wish to develop a more generalised understanding of education research, in order to, for example, draw on generic literature or education literature contextualised in other disciplines. Typically, the purpose is to increase one's pedagogical knowledge, usually with an aim to improve student experience and/or outcomes. This may be driven by the wish to understand a particular pedagogical idea or process, or a more generalised interest in the practice of teaching tertiary students and the associated evidence-bases for success. Examples of projects could include implementation of a flipped classroom in courses, how to draw on students' prior knowledge, or novel ways of using case studies in teaching particular topics. Outcomes at this level might include the ability to articulate one's own questions and interests, or to contribute to the discourse on teaching and learning beyond the individual course level (e.g., at the programme, departmental, or college level).

Role of the Faculty Developer

Many aspects of the faculty developer's role in this second level are similar to those in the first, such as assisting faculty in articulating their issues and goals, and suggesting relevant resources. A large part of the role involves being a resource, a catalyst, a teacher, an interpreter, an evaluator, and a contextualiser. At this level, however, faculty developers may also support faculty in developing their educational discourse; introducing them to education-specific terminology. The faculty developer may also introduce and explain common methodologies used in education research, which may be unfamiliar to faculty. Finally, this is the space most related to concepts of reflective practice and helping faculty develop ways of self-critique.

What Constitutes Evidence for Success?

For the faculty member, the evidence for success will be similar to those stated at the previous level, but typically more generalised (i.e. related to teaching in general, not just teaching of the discipline), and perhaps more critical. Additional lines of evidence would include, for example, newly developed programmes of study, changes in institutional policy and processes, or student outcomes in relation to generic benchmarks such as a graduate profile or governmental educational performance indicators (e.g., employment data, retention, progression and completion numbers). As with the first level, the evidence for this is reasonably readily available and/or quantifiable.

For the faculty developer, evidence for success would again focus on the faculty member's ability to operate independently in SoTL, such as the ability to find and apply more generic educational research to teaching, independently question educational practice, or embed educational concepts on a wider scale (e.g., constructive alignment in the curriculum, addressing diversity in policy and practice).

How Does It Support a Research Approach to Teaching and Learning?

Projects at this level of SoTL engagement are not confined to a single discipline. In comparison with the first level, a faculty member's realisation that educational findings from different disciplines can be generalised across disciplines and, conversely, that educational findings from elsewhere can be applied to their (disciplinary) teaching and learning context can be quite powerful. Engagement with SoTL at this level empowers and equips the faculty member to inform policy within the institution or teaching/pedagogy/curriculum practices at the programme, department or college level. Projects at this level can assist with data/SoTL driven academic decision-making and reducing the number of cases in which an educational wheel is re-invented.

Level Three: Action Research (Self/Investigative)

Purpose and Outcomes

Motivations for action research projects can vary. Often times, there is an intention to publish and add to the literature in discipline-based education research (as in level four below). It can also be a systematic and rigorous way to evaluate a teaching intervention without any intention to publish, but instead to inform the faculty member's own practice at a deeper level than the engagement at level one. Outcomes are often enhanced pedagogical content knowledge (published or not), data to inform further curriculum and teaching (re)development, and improved student outcomes. Ideally, it also leads to changes in teaching practice, though this might not always be the case (Shephard, Rogers, & Brogt, in press). Projects might include measuring the effectiveness of particular teaching or assessment techniques or investigating the student experience in the course or programme.

Role of the Faculty Developer

In supporting action research, faculty developers adopt new roles in line with the shift from application to investigation (see Figure 1). In action research, faculty developers can be mentors, methodologists, ethicists, research assistants, project managers, or teachers. However, in line with the self-focused dimension, faculty developers have a stronger mentorship role - supporting the personal change that may emerge as faculty go through a continuing journey of self-discovery.

One area where the authors have seen discipline-based colleagues needing support is in formulating a research question. Disciplinary research expertise does not always transfer well into the education domain. Faculty developers can probably relate to this, given that most have migrated to faculty development from other disciplines (e.g., Harland & Staniforth, 2008; Green & Little, 2016) and likewise are "non-native speakers" of Education. However, faculty developers have since learned the language and methods of Education and are thus well suited to help faculty navigate educational research and help increase the level of academic rigour in a SoTL action research project.

What Constitutes Evidence for Success?

For faculty, evidence might include specific changes to the curriculum, student evaluations, testimonials, classroom observation reports, research reports, conference or peer-reviewed publications in discipline-specific education outlets, and recommendations for institutional policy change. For the faculty developer, evidence might include the above, but also the (observed or documented) development of the faculty member's ability to design and execute the project and documentation (such as emails or timelines) which illustrate the faculty developer's approach to supporting the faculty member.

How Does It Support a Research Approach to Teaching and Learning?

For a faculty member, it is often interesting to see that questions about teaching and learning can be approached with the same level of academic rigour as discipline-based research questions. Action research has many of the hallmarks of discipline-based research familiar to faculty. While methods and the feel of the research may be unfamiliar and generate some rigorous debate (in the authors' experiences particularly around data sources, validity, analysis and interpretation, and the concept of participant-researchers), the project is still readily recognisable as research.

Level Four: Higher Education Research (Other/Investigative)

Purpose and Outcomes

At the highest level of SoTL engagement, faculty may decide to undertake research into teaching/learning in their own discipline or context for the purposes of dissemination, through publication in a local, national, or international forum. Such research may well employ theoretical perspectives from the philosophical, psychological, or sociological theories, which feed into higher education as a discipline. The purpose of such engagement may be to investigate a theoretical or practical question, which has arisen through their work, or to challenge/further investigate an area, which the faculty member has encountered at earlier levels of SoTL engagement. Projects at this level can be highly varied using the full spectrum of educational research methodologies. Outcomes usually comprise some kind of research output, through a presentation or peer-reviewed research article. This level of SoTL engagement is the basis of the faculty developer's scholarly work and depends on the specific role attributed to them by their institution. SoTL research may constitute the research component of their own 40-40-20 workload model. Thus, it is at this level that the purpose of the faculty member and faculty developer might be seen to be most collegial and aligned.

Role of the Faculty Developer

While both the faculty member and faculty developer will adopt the lens of researcher at this level, the faculty member's disciplinary background may be very different from the social science or philosophical lens of educational research. For this reason, the faculty developer may well adopt a mentorship or even supervisory role, whereby they explain the practical aspects of the research, such as ethics approval, methodologies, and so forth. This may begin as early as helping define appropriate research questions. Beyond this the faculty developer might also act as a *de facto* research assistant or an interdisciplinary partner, drawing on their research skills developed within the higher education discipline). At times, in order to protect potentially vulnerable participants, such as students or identifiable colleagues, the faculty developer may take a more directive or supervisory approach with faculty who have little or no experience of working with human subjects. Regardless of the specific role the faculty developer adopts initially, their end goal and role are to support or to work in partnership with faculty to research and disseminate the products of that research to an open forum. As with the other levels of engagement, it is hoped that the faculty member has engaged with the educational research process in such a way that they would be able to undertake an independent SoTL project in future.

What Constitutes Evidence for Success?

In many ways, evidence for success at this level is the most straightforward, as it echoes the outputs of the scholarships of discovery and integration. For the faculty member, evidence of success is the publication of their scholarship, including the research metrics of citation and readership. However, it would be hoped that more than these metrics, and in common with other forms of scholarship, there would be evidence that the faculty member's research had been adopted by other faculty within and beyond the institution. Such adoption will create a new sense of process beyond the initial theoretical or empirical activities which have led to the publication.

Superficially, evidence of success for the faculty developer is the same as for the faculty member—measurable publication or presentation outputs. This makes sense, given that at this level of engagement the disciplinary focus of education and research come together for both the faculty member and the faculty developer. However, an important difference in the evidence concerns the visibility of the faculty developer's involvement in the SoTL project. The less visible the faculty developer can be in the research project, the greater the faculty member's independence at this level of scholarly engagement. This is not to say that co-authorship of research with the faculty developer is not evidence of successful faculty development. Rather, it is to say that where a faculty member is enabled to undertake and publish research independently, evidence of success is in fact stronger, if less visible.

How Does It Support a Research Approach to Teaching and Learning?

At this level of engagement, teaching, learning and research change their focus. Now, rather than research informing teaching, teaching and learning drive research, in both concrete (practice) and more abstract (theoretical) ways. From the initial level at which faculty members use SoTL to inform their teaching in concrete ways, faculty move through to more abstract ways of thinking about learning and teaching using SoTL as a guiding principle. By this final level what is learned from SoTL is producing new knowledge in line with the scholarship of discovery and emphasising a seamless view of Pedagogical Content Knowledge for the faculty member.

IMPLICATIONS FOR FACULTY DEVELOPERS

This chapter describes how SoTL can be used to foster a research approach to teaching and learning and how faculty development that supports colleagues to engage in SoTL can support the development of scholarly faculty. In essence, this chapter suggests that the substantial objective of faculty development and of faculty developers could be, and perhaps should be, the development of scholars and scholarship rather than, as is often perceived, an exclusive focus on the development of excellent teaching and excellent teachers. The authors argue that the Scholarship of Teaching and Learning has much in common with the scholarships of research, integration and engagement, as all require faculty to research their practices rather than simply to practise them. This commonality suggests that as faculty learn to teach in a scholarly way, they must also learn to research their teaching practices. Learning to teach should be part and parcel of learning to be a scholar, given that many faculty members have roles that include teaching, often in multidisciplinary contexts, a range of community engagement opportunities and obligations, and research. The support processes that exist around faculty members' learning to teach should simultaneously be supporting them to learn to research, to engage with communities and to practice a scholarship in ways that emphasise the diversity and similarity of disciplinary contexts. For faculty developers, SoTL may be a cornerstone, a keystone, or a linchpin in an academic's development, but it needs to be harnessed to help faculty develop as scholars.

This way of thinking about faculty development has implications for the way that institutions, academic departments, and faculty development specialist units are designed and operated and for the way that faculty developers are themselves recruited, developed, supported and valued. These implications are explored in the paragraphs below as a series of research questions, each prefaced by a brief summary of the context surrounding the question.

It is an academic reality that any change programme that incorporates the concept of excellence needs to identify with, and likely embrace, competition. In recent years, higher education has become extraordinarily hierarchical with most universities aware of their current place in international and national league tables and vying with one another to improve their position. A range of quality measures are used to situate institutions in their respective position and most of these depend on various interpretations of the scholarship of each institution's academic caucus. Internationally, we value research outputs, citations and funding, and student opinions of their teachers and of their teaching. Nations use a range of legislative and economic measures to encourage their own institutions to compete for higher rankings (see Fitzpatrick, 2019 for a recent analysis of the nature of and consequences of competitive pursuits of excellence and prestige in higher education). Faculty development units become centre stage in an institution's quest for rank and excellence and nowadays cannot escape some form of neoliberal quantification of value for money.

It is also an academic reality that the way we measure a contribution acts as a driver for many of those involved. For example, measuring the excellence of teaching by highlighting student opinions emphasises student opinion above other measures of teaching quality. How we measure the contribution of faculty development units is currently an important research topic (e.g., Winter et al., 2017). However, we struggle to progress beyond the idea that as faculty developers support the development of good teachers, the performance of these teachers (as measured by the opinions of their students) provides a satisfactory, if indirect, measure of the quality of the work of the faculty developers involved. This chapter, by focussing on scholarship as a product of faculty development, rather than good teaching, introduces a diverse range of scholarly outcomes and outputs that could contribute to these judgments. At present, the work of faculty developers is often measured as the number of hours of workshops facilitated and the number of academic colleagues who attended. To what extent could we, or should we, make use of other metrics such as academic papers on aspects of scholarship written or co-authored or research funds obtained? This argument does suggest that we need to research the consequences of applying varied approaches to judge the quality of faculty development.

A related line of argument suggests that successful faculty development results in developed faculty who no longer need the support of faculty developers as they already present scholarly academic behaviours. As with other academic pursuits, the pursuit of scholarship is likely best seen as a collegiate, team-based activity. As mentioned previously, collaborative SoTL projects become a way of creating "knowledgeable others" in academic departments. These colleagues not only research their own practices, but also collaborate with others in team-based scholarly enquiry. Faculty developers may be involved in these research, development, and evaluative activities of institutional, national, and international importance. The results of these activities might be implemented as local or institutional change, reported locally, or published more widely. How are such enterprises promoted and valued by higher education institutions? What value is placed on the presence of enduring networks of academic colleagues who collaborate to ask scholarly questions about the nature of scholarship itself? Future research could explore the extent to which academic institutions and subject disciplines research their own practices and how these imperatives can be best promoted.

Just as the roles of individual faculty vary, it seems inevitable that individual faculty developers will emphasise different skills and scholarly ambitions. Similarly, it has been understood that the nature of faculty development (with its historical focus on learning to teach) varies between disciplines, in particular between the sciences and humanities (Neuman, 2001). However, by re-conceptualising faculty development as contributing to the pursuit of scholarship, rather than simply the pursuit of excellence in teaching, is it possible to discover that scholarship in different disciplines has more in common than previously imagined? Even so, how will such diversity be managed, developed, and valued? Is there a minimum skill set that will be required and if so, do current faculty developers have this minimum at present? Implicit within the suggestion that scholars research their practice, some minimum level of research skill would seem to be desirable among faculty developers. Is it reasonable to imagine that a faculty developer who is not an accomplished scholar (in the definition of Boyer) could support the development of scholars? Such questions do challenge faculty developers, and these issues are complex, multi-faceted, and undoubtedly mediated by various (academic and institutional) cultural dynamics. Hence, they would constitute a rich ground for research enquiry of a scholarly nature to help inform the debate.

CONCLUSION

In this chapter, the authors explored ways in which faculty developers can support faculty in SoTL projects across four distinct levels of SoTL engagement. Each of these levels supports a scholarly (in the definition of Boyer) approach to teaching and learning. SoTL projects, regardless of the level of SoTL engagement, benefit the faculty member, their students, the faculty developer, and the higher education organisation. For faculty developers as well as higher education institutions, it is critical to have clear outcomes, metrics, and evidence for success defined for projects at the various levels of SoTL engagement. Evaluating faculty development practices associated with SoTL by research-derived metrics such as research grants obtained and peer-reviewed articles published may measure and promote some possible SoTL activity, but including associated scholarly learning and building of organisational social capital about teaching and learning should also be considered as evidence of success.

REFERENCES

Biggs, J. B., & Tang, C. (2007). *Teaching for quality learning at university* (3rd ed.). Maidenhead, UK: McGraw Hill Education & Open University Press.

Boyer, E. L. (1990). *Scholarship reconsidered: Priorities of the professoriate*. Lawrenceville, NJ: Princeton University Press.

Boyer, E. L. (1996). From scholarship reconsidered to scholarship assessed. *Quest, 48*(2), 129–139. doi:10.1080/00336297.1996.10484184

Brew, A. (2002). Research and the faculty developer: A new agenda. *The International Journal for Academic Development, 7*(2), 112–122. doi:10.1080/1360144032000071332

Brogt, E., & Knewstubb, B. (under review). Shifting sands: Conceptualising personal theories of relationship which shape academic development practice.

Brookfield, S. D. (1995). *Becoming a critically reflective teacher.* San Francisco: Jossey Bass.

Chalmers, D. (2018). Why recognising and rewarding excellent teaching in universities matters for students. *4th International Conference on Higher Education Advances.* 10.4995/HEAD18.2018.7981

Debowski, S. (2011). Locating academic development: The first step in evaluation. In L. Stefani (Ed.), *Evaluating the effectiveness of academic development: Principles and practice* (pp. 17–30). New York, NY: Routledge.

Fitzpatrick, E. (2019). For the greater good. *Times Higher Education Supplement, 2403*, 43–45.

Green, D., & Little, D. (2016). Family portrait: A profile of educational developers around the world. *The International Journal for Academic Development, 21*(2), 135–150. doi:10.1080/1360144X.2015.1046875

Harland, T., & Staniforth, D. (2008). A family of strangers: The fragmented nature of academic development. *Teaching in Higher Education, 13*(6), 669–678. doi:10.1080/13562510802452392

Hutchings, P., & Shulman, L. S. (1999). The scholarship of teaching: New elaborations, new developments. *Change: The Magazine of Higher Learning, 31*(5), 10–15. doi:10.1080/00091389909604218

Land, R. (2004). *Educational development: Discourse, identity and practice.* Maidenhead, UK: Society for Research in Higher Education & Open University Press.

Manathunga, C. (2006). Doing educational development ambivalently: Applying post-colonial metaphors to educational development? *The International Journal for Academic Development, 11*(1), 19–29. doi:10.1080/13601440600578771

Mårtensson, K., & Roxå, T. (2016). Working with networks, microcultures and communities. In D. Baume & C. Popovic (Eds.), *Advancing practice in academic development* (pp. 174–187). London: Routledge.

Neumann, R. (2001). Disciplinary differences and university teaching. *Studies in Higher Education, 26*(2), 135–146. doi:10.1080/03075070120052071

O'Byrne, C., McIntyre, G., Townsend, S., Schonthal, B., & Shephard, K. (2018). Can "pooling teaching tips" be more than "pooling teaching tips"? *Tertiary Education and Management, 24*(4), 351–361.

Probert, B. (2014). *Why scholarship matters in higher education.* Australian Government Office for Learning and Teaching.

Rowland, S. (2002). Overcoming fragmentation in professional life: The challenge for academic development. *Higher Education Quarterly, 56*(1), 52–64. doi:10.1111/1468-2273.00202

Sabagh, Z., & Saroyan, A. (2014). Professors' perceived barriers and incentives for teaching improvement. *International Education Research, 2*(3), 18–40. doi:10.12735/ier.v2i3p18

Shephard, K., Rogers, T., & Brogt, E. (in press). Impacts of engaging in research into teaching and learning on academics' conceptions of their development as teachers and on the role of academic developers. *The International Journal for Academic Development*.

Shulman, L. S. (1986). Those who understand: Knowledge growth in teaching. *Educational Researcher*, *15*(2), 4–14. doi:10.3102/0013189X015002004

Shulman, L. S. (1987). Knowledge and teaching: Foundations of the new reform. *Harvard Educational Review*, *57*(1), 1–22. doi:10.17763/haer.57.1.j463w79r56455411

Stefani, L., & Baume, D. (2016). "Is it working?" Outcomes, monitoring and evaluation. In D. Baume & C. Popovic (Eds.), *Advancing practice in academic development*. London: Routledge.

Sutherland, K. A. (2018). Holistic academic development: Is it time to think more broadly about the academic development project. *The International Journal for Academic Development*, *23*(4), 261–273. doi:10.1080/1360144X.2018.1524571

Sutherland, K. A., & Grant, B. (2016). Researching academic development. In C. Popovic & D. Baume (Eds.), *Advancing practice in academic development* (pp. 187–206). London: Routledge.

United States National Research Council. (2012). Discipline-based education research: Understanding and improving learning in undergraduate science and engineering. In S. R. Singer, N. R. Nielsen, & H. A. Schweingruber (Eds.), *Committee on the status, contributions, and future directions of discipline-based education research. Board on Science Education, Division of Behavioral and Social Sciences and Education*. Washington, DC: The National Academies Press.

Walczyk, J. J., Ramsey, L. L., & Zha, P. (2007). Obstacles to instructional innovation according to college science and mathematics faculty. *Journal of Research in Science Teaching*, *44*(1), 85–106. doi:10.1002/tea.20119

Winter, J., Turner, R., Spowart, L., Muneer, R., & Kneale, P. (2017). Evaluating academic development in the higher education sector: Faculty developers' reflections on using a toolkit resource. *Higher Education Research & Development*, *36*(7), 1503–1514. doi:10.1080/07294360.2017.1325351

ENDNOTES

[1] Faculty development in different countries can be called academic development, educational development, or instructional design. For the purposes of this chapter, it is taken to mean educational development in the university sector. In the context of the authors, who are based in New Zealand, academic development carried out by academic developers are the commonly used terms. Academic developers in New Zealand are normally academic staff who do research and teach in the area of higher education development, and who have a clear faculty development support role; working with other academics and the university in general on matters related to teaching and learning. To be consistent with the terminology used in this handbook, we will use the phrase "faculty development" and "faculty developers" instead.

2   While this chapter focuses primarily on faculty development as development of individuals, it is recognised that faculty developers take on broader strategic duties at the programme, department, school, or faculty level as well. While these projects are inherently more complex, the fundamental process that underpins faculty development at the individual level applies to these situations as well.

3   The use of the word "level" denotes a point on a continuum as discussed in the section titles "SoTL as a vehicle for broader engagement in scholarship". It should not be read as a hierarchical position where one "level" is more valued than the other.

Chapter 9
Writing Into the Scholarship of Teaching and Learning:
Approaches to Supporting Faculty to Find Their "Voice"

Kathryn Janet Meldrum
James Cook University, Australia

Kristi Giselsson
James Cook University, Australia

ABSTRACT

The Scholarship of Teaching and Learning (SoTL) has been suggested as an ideal vehicle for engaging faculty with professional development for teaching in higher education. However, previous authors have identified that faculty find writing about SoTL difficult. The aim of this chapter is to support educational developers (EDs) to collaborate with faculty to support writing. Two theoretical frameworks to support collaboration are proposed: the first, the Knowledge Transforming Model of Writing, to assist with the process of writing; the second, an adaptation of Brigugilio's working in the third space framework to support collaboration. The authors utilise both frameworks to reflect on their own SoTL collaboration and subsequently pose questions to support faculty and EDs to do the same. Ultimately, it is proposed that collaboration not only enhances the practices of faculty and EDs but improves what should be an important priority for the wider academy: the learning outcomes of students.

INTRODUCTION

The Scholarship of Teaching and Learning (SoTL) has been suggested as an ideal vehicle for engaging faculty with professional development for teaching in higher education (Amundsen & Wilson, 2012; Fanghanel, 2013). As a vehicle for professional development, SoTL should demonstrate five principles (Felten, 2013); one of which is the need for the findings of any SoTL inquiry to be publicly shared. Public sharing of SoTL findings can take a variety of forms, including writing, and many faculty choose

DOI: 10.4018/978-1-7998-2212-7.ch009

to publish in scholarly journals. However, authors such as Chalmers (2011) and Harland and colleagues (2014) have identified that faculty find writing about SoTL difficult for a number of reasons, principally because it differs from their disciplinary roots. Moreover, faculty are often reluctant to engage with SoTL (Chalmers, 2011; Flavell et al., 2018; Harland, et al., 2014) on the grounds that it is commonly viewed as "a lower form of educational research" (Fanghanel, 2013, p. 67), with disciplinary research being regarded as superior (Flavell, Roberts, Fyfe, & Broughton, 2018). Despite the identification of the multifaceted issues that arise when faculty start to write about SoTL, there is a dearth of scholarly publications related to such challenges. In addition, given the role that educational developers (EDs) play in the professional development of faculty in higher education (Amundsen & Wilson, 2012; Cilliers & Herman, 2010), it is crucial that they are able to understand and incorporate strategies for constructively engaging with faculty to support writing for and about SoTL. Consequently, the aim of this chapter is to support EDs to collaborate with faculty and support writing about SoTL. We explore the opportunities and challenges of such collaboration via reflection on a SoTL project from the perspective of faculty (Kristi Giselsson) and an ED (Kathryn Meldrum).

Two different theoretical frameworks are introduced to support collaboration. The first, the Knowledge Transforming Model of Writing proposed by Bereiter and Scardamalia (as cited in Keys, 1999), provides a framework for supporting both parties in understanding the conceptual, discourse, and rhetorical issues that faculty face as they write about SoTL. The second theoretical framework is an adaption of Briguglio's (2014) third space model. This adaption provides a way to conceptualise how collaboration for writing about SoTL can take place between EDs and faculty. It does this by acknowledging and valuing the professional and contextual characteristics that each brings to a collaboration by posing a series of questions based on the model, used to frame reflections about SoTL by both parties to support establishing a trusting and respectful collaboration.

The chapter begins by providing an overview of the literature that informs educational developers' practice with respect to supporting faculty to develop their SoTL practice through writing. Briguglio's (2014) third space theoretical framework is then proposed to provide a foundation upon which to draw on our own experience in discussing what we brought to the third space in our SoTL writing collaboration. In this section we also discuss the opportunities and challenges that we faced during our collaboration. Finally, the chapter concludes by proposing some strategies to support the collaboration between faculty and EDs as they write for and about SoTL.

BACKGROUND

Educational developers have been described as practitioners who focus on improving learning and teaching in higher education (Amundsen & Wilson, 2012) by working with faculty to support "effective educational practice" (Cilliers & Herman, 2010, p. 254). Green and Little (2016) identified that a sample of EDs in their study came from a range of disciplinary backgrounds, the majority held PhDs, and most work in academic roles. The EDs working in academic roles continued to conduct research as part of their role (Green & Little, 2016). The Scholarship of Teaching and Learning is the research field that is most closely aligned with investigations of teaching and learning practice in higher education (Amundsen & Wilson, 2012). While Green and Little's (2016) investigation did not report the detail of educational developers' work, Amundsen and Wilson (2012) in their conceptual review of work of the field of educational development indicated that practitioners were involved with supporting reflective practice and action and/or inquiry—all of which are fertile fields for SoTL research.

Review of Literature

The Nature of SoTL

The idea of SoTL as a field of research emerged in the 1990s with Boyer's work (Boyer, 1990). Since that time it has grown as a discipline. While it may not be widely accepted (Fanghanel, 2013), it is nevertheless a discipline where new knowledge (Booth & Woollacott, 2018) about teaching and learning in higher education can be shared. Felten (2013) identified five principles of SoTL: 1). Inquiry into scholarly learning; 2). Grounded in context; 3). Methodologically sound; 4). Partnership with students; 5). Public sharing. In addition, Fanghanel (2013) advocated that SoTL should engage with "democratic, dialogic and collaborative inquiry to enable multiple voices" (p. 61) and should be part of educational developers' practice.

SoTL as an Educational Development Practice

As previously mentioned, Amundsen and Wilson's (2012) conceptual review of literature related to educational development identified six clusters of work. First, a skill focus related to the role that EDs play in the development of the specific skills of teaching. Second, a method focus related to supporting faculty to develop different teaching strategies. Third, a reflection focus supporting faculty to develop their conceptualisation(s) of their teaching practice. Fourth, institutional plans for educational development are developed through an institutional focus. Fifth, developing faculty's understanding of discipline-specific pedagogy. Sixth, educational developers' involvement with individuals or groups investigating teaching and learning practice through action research or an inquiry focus. In framing our discussion about writing into and about SoTL we draw on two foci of Amundsen and Wilson's (2012) conceptual framework: educational developers' roles in supporting reflecting on teaching practice and their involvement as collaborators or supporters of action research or inquiry into teaching and learning.

SoTL as Reflective Practice

In faculty development, reflection is seen as instrumental in supporting change in or clarification of teaching practice (McAlpine & Weston, 2002). Amundsen and Wilson (2012) identified that, in the context of educational development, reflection is positioned as learning and educational developers' work as facilitators in this faculty driven process. The importance of reflection in and on faculty teaching practice has been the subject of recent publications (Botham, 2018; McCormack, Vanags, & Prior, 2014; Pelger & Larsson, 2018; Saalman, 2018). Botham (2018) identified that reflection on the development of a submission for a Higher Education Academy (now Advance HE) fellowship; the purpose of which is to highlight exemplary teaching practice against five different areas of activity instrumental in supporting faculty to "go backwards to go forwards" (p. 171). Participants in Botham's (2018) investigation also identified that their engagement with reflection was useful for identifying key principles and/or outcomes of their practice in order to identify "lessons learned" (p. 171). McCormack and her colleagues (2014) discussed the challenges of writing about teaching practice when applying for a national teaching award.

They highlighted that the process of writing was a journey from "unhomliness" (p. 937) to a positive re-construction of their faculty identities. Pegler and Larsson (2018) highlighted that reflective writing to provide evidence in teaching portfolios engaged faculty with reflective practice and that the role of EDs was important in this process because they provided support. Support was seen as important because reflection is a new, different, and challenging genre for many faculty. Saalman (2018) added weight to this argument when she identified that a limitation of many faculty's teaching portfolios, deconstructed as part of her investigation, was their poor reflective practices. Clearly, EDs can play a vital role in encouraging and supporting reflective practice in faculty.

SoTL as Action Research and/or Inquiry

Inquiry into teaching practice was the first SoTL principle identified by Felten (2013) and, as Fanghanel (2013) suggested, a recognised means of investigation. Scholarship of Teaching and Learning inquiry often takes an action research approach. While SoTL inquiry may start as an individual faculty member making sense of their teaching practice or evaluating the impact of innovation, it is rarely a solitary endeavour (Amundsen & Wilson, 2012). Often other faculty colleagues or EDs work with faculty as collaborators. Fanghanel (2013) proposed SoTL as a "sophisticated methodology" (p.60) for faculty development and promoted the collaborative nature of SoTL as practice. Faculty development is often achieved through SoTL because, as Amundsen and Wilson (2012) proposed, both the process and the inquiry itself are learning. In this case, the learning is about teaching practice. Consequently, due to the nature of SoTL, the developmental outcomes may be different for each faculty member (Amundsen & Wilson, 2012). One of the roles that EDs can adopt as collaborators in SoTL is to encourage and support the development of a questioning orientation in faculty. In addition, EDs can support faculty to draw on individual reflection, their existing research skills and knowledge, and to situate their findings by grounding their interpretation(s) in the scholarly literature related to higher education teaching practice (Booth &Woollacott, 2018).

Faculty Attitudes Toward SoTL

Harland and colleagues (2014) identified that SoTL has been a "hard sell" (p. 39). The "hard sell" may be attributed to several related reasons. First, disciplinary research has traditionally been prioritised over SoTL in most universities (Flavell et al., 2018; Harland et al., 2014; McCormack et al., 2014). The Scholarship of Teaching and Learning is not regarded as disciplinary research by most faculty, and there is a general perception that its practice is not valued equally with disciplinary research (Chalmers, 2011; Flavell et al., 2018; Ginns, Kitay, & Prosser, 2010; Harland et al., 2014; McCormack et al., 2014). For example, one participant in Flavell and colleagues' (2018) study referred to SoTL research as "Mickey Mouse" (p.191) and McCormack and colleagues (2014) identified that SoTL was not recognised as "real research" (p. 939). Secondly, and potentially as a consequence of the overarching perceptions and different valuing of SoTL, faculty that engage with it may experience negative responses from their colleagues (Ginns et al., 2010; Roxå, Olsson, & Mårtensson, 2008). Many faculty have also reported that engaging in SoTL has impacted on their status and identity within their institution (Flavell et al., 2018; Roxå et al., 2008). Third, faculty who engage with SoTL identified that they initially encounter difficulties with its theoretical foundations, in particular, because they differ to their disciplinary roots (Chalmers, 2011;

Harland et al., 2014). Finally, when faculty intend to publish the results of their findings, they encounter difficulties writing about SoTL (Harland et al., 2014; McCormack et al., 2014; Pelger & Larsson, 2018).

Public Sharing of SoTL

The public sharing of SoTL is often key to educational developers' work with faculty because of the centrality of writing as one of the key modes of sharing SoTL initiatives and findings. Pelger and Larsson (2018) drew on the findings of number of authors to highlight the impact that writing has on developing teaching practice. They identified that faculty struggle with writing their teaching portfolios and suggested that Keys' (1999) conceptualisation of the transactional nature of "writing to learn" (p. 115) might explain the experience. In writing about teaching practice, many faculty encounter the unfamiliar genre of reflective writing coupled with a realisation that the theoretical underpinnings of SoTL are, for most, different from their own discipline (Chalmers, 2011; Harland et al., 2014; Roxå et al., 2008). In addition, they encounter stylistic differences inherent to the SoTL discipline.

Keys, who discussed the role of writing in science education, drew on Bereiter and Scardamalia's knowledge transforming model of writing (Figure 1) to explain "the challenge of generating content for discourse in written text" (Keys, 1999, p. 120).

Figure 1. Knowledge transforming model of writing adapted from knowledge transforming model of composition by Bereiter and Scardamalia as cited in Keys, 1999, Science Education 83(2), 120. Applications relevant to SoTL made by the authors.

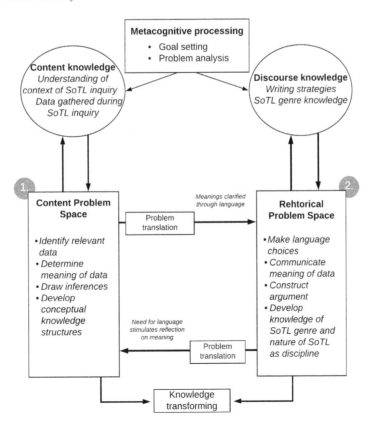

Bereiter and Scardamalia (as cited by Keys, 1999) described two different "spaces" in their model. The "content space where the problems of knowledge and beliefs are considered" (indicated as 1. in Figure 1) (Keys, 1999, p. 120) and the "discourse space" (indicated as 2. in Figure 1) where the writer considers how to express the problems related to the content space. In applying Bereiter and Scardamalia's model to writing for and about SoTL, faculty encounter challenges when making sense of new knowledge from their investigations of teaching practice and its relationship(s) with unfamiliar SoTL theoretical underpinnings in the content space. In the discourse and rhetorical problem space, faculty not only face the challenges of the content space but also of writing in an unfamiliar genre and style. This model is valuable to both faculty and EDs. For faculty, it supports them in understanding that writing for and about SoTL is a different genre, with a distinct conceptual, discourse and rhetorical base. For EDs, it helps them to recognise and understand the challenges faced by faculty and, consequently, how to support them through the content and rhetorical problem spaces.

Despite the issues identified, little is published about the multifaceted challenges that arise when faculty embark on writing about their teaching practice and SoTL research. While recent publications have discussed the difficulty of writing about teaching practice focused on applying for national teaching awards (McCormack et al., 2014) and faculty's capacity to reflect on their practice (Saalman, 2018), there appears to be no published work to date focused on the issues related to writing about SoTL.

"WORKING IN THE THIRD SPACE": A MODEL OF COLLABORATION IN WRITING FOR AND ABOUT SoTL

The working in the third space model of collaboration in writing for and about SoTL draws on Briguglio's (2014) adaptation of Bronstein's (2003) work which focused on collaboration amongst social work and health practitioners. Briguglio (2014) adapted Bronstein's (2003) model to highlight the work of faculty and academic language and literacy specialists to support student learning. In this case, Briguglio's model (Figure 2) has been adapted for the purpose of highlighting the nature of collaboration for SoTL. This adaption provides a way of conceptualising how collaboration for writing about SoTL can take place between EDs and faculty by acknowledging and valuing the professional and contextual characteristics that each bring to a collaboration. In reconfiguring the model for SoTL collaboration, a series of questions based on the model are posed in the Implications for Practice section later in the chapter. Here, we propose that the questions are used to frame reflections about SoTL by both parties to support establishing a trusting and respectful collaboration as they move into the third space.

The third space is where faculty (Space one) and EDs (Space two) meet (Space three)—the intersection of both specialisations. The third space provides opportunities for:

- The creation of new knowledge;
- Further collaboration between faculty and EDs; and
- Reflection by both parties on the process, from a professional and personal perspective.

In addition to notions of collaboration focused on by Briguglio (2014), we also draw on Fanghanel's (2013) conceptualisations of SoTL as "collaborative" (p.60), "democratic", and "dialogic inquiry" (p. 61). The third space theoretical framework provides the foundation upon which we discuss our individual

Figure 2. Working in the third space: A model of collaboration in writing for and about SoTL.
(adapted from Briguglio, 2014)

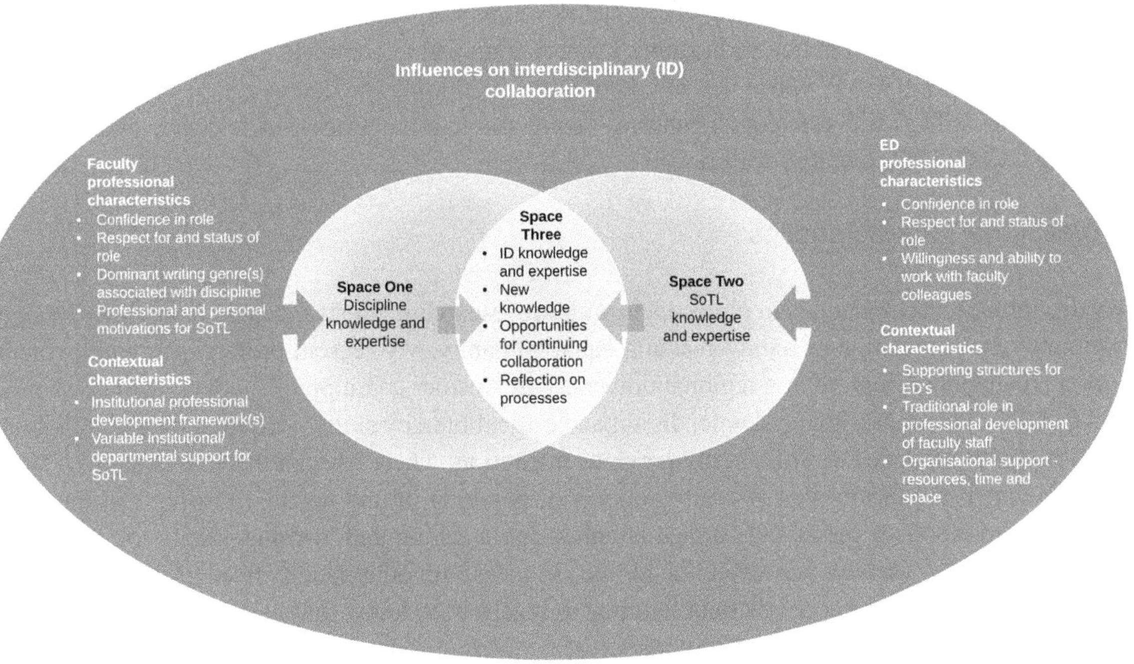

professional and contextual characteristics in addition to the opportunities and challenges that we faced as we came together to collaboratively write for and about SoTL.

COMING TO THE THIRD SPACE: WHAT DO THESE PARTIES BRING?

This section utilises our adaptation of the working in the third space model to discuss our individual professional and contextual characteristics as well as the opportunities and challenges we faced during our collaboration. We acknowledge that our experience is just that—our own—in that the professional and contextual characteristics, as well as the challenges and opportunities that we discuss, may be different to those encountered by other faculty and EDs. Despite the unique experiences that we bring to this chapter, there are generalizable lessons, particularly related to the difficulties that faculty face when engaging with SoTL as research, in general (Chalmers, 2011; Flavell et al., 2018; Harland et al., 2014), and writing, in particular (Harland et al., 2014; McCormack et al., 2014).

Space One: Faculty's Contribution – A Personal Reflection – Kristi Giselsson

In providing a context for my engagement with SoTL and for my collaboration with the ED, Kathryn Meldrum, I will initially discuss some aspects of my professional and contextual characteristics drawn from the working in the third space theoretical model.

Contextual Characteristics

As part of my current institution's professional development framework and my academic role as a full-time lecturer within enabling education, I was encouraged to complete my Graduate Certificate in Academic Practice (GCAP) which was offered fee-free to fulltime staff. Regarding institutional support in relation to SoTL, I was offered a mentor as a guide through the process of rewriting and submitting my final GCAP SoTL research project.

Professional Characteristics

My disciplinary background is in philosophy, with my research interests focusing on highly conceptual explorations of the notion of a universal and equal humanity. My present professional employment is within an enabling program at a regional university in Australia, equipping students with the foundational skills—encompassing academic, digital and critical literacy skills—required to enter university.

I was first introduced to SoTL at my previous institution, where I began the equivalent of a GCAP. Being situated in a faculty that was often openly disparaging of and hostile to SoTL, and then being introduced to practices specifically aimed at enhancing teaching and learning—that took the work of teaching seriously—served as a revelation for me. To meet with other faculty from disparate disciplines and hear stories of their successes (and failures) as teachers, to know that here were people for whom teaching was as important as their disciplinary research, felt, as I described it somewhat embarrassingly emotively at the time, as a "coming home". I then took up employment at my present institute and was fortunately provided with the opportunity to finish the GCAP.

My motivations for taking up these studies again were both professional and personal. I had been teaching as a casual staff member (known in the United States as an adjunct professor) within tertiary education for over eight years and was constantly preoccupied with ways in which to improve my teaching and the learning experiences of my students, but I lacked any structured direction or support in order to do this. At my previous institution, although the first subject of the GCAP was compulsory for commencing staff, it was not usually made available to casual staff, and it was only through the generosity of the leader of the SoTL unit at the time that I was allowed to participate.

Being introduced to the concepts of SoTL had brought a heightened awareness of my teaching methods, and I was eager to learn more. Although my formal student feedback had been consistently positive, I was not confident that my students were actually improving in their critical thinking skills, as I view the ability to think critically as the most significant transferable skill that can be developed in students, regardless of subject content (perhaps due to my background in philosophy). One of the subjects I was now teaching within the enabling program focused specifically on developing critical literacy. As I had been troubled by apparent contradictions within the subject's conceptual framework and its effect on students, I embraced the opportunity provided by the GCAP to conduct a SoTL research project in order to finally test whether my students were indeed improving in their critical thinking skills (or not). After receiving ethics approval, I wrote my final research assessment task for the GCAP based on analysing students' assessment results and their common conceptual and theoretical difficulties within the subject. At the time I was largely unaware that I may have been employing a writing genre that was particular to my own discipline, as writing within philosophy takes on a variety of (highly contested) forms (Peters, 2008). Not having been exposed to the more empirically-based writing characteristic of a number of other disciplines, I happily assumed that everyone wrote as I did. My naiveté was soon to be shattered.

Challenges

To my horror, my assignment was sent back to me as "unsatisfactory". The blow was not just to my pride, although that was considerable. I have a PhD, am a published author within my own discipline, and yet had miserably failed an assessment piece within a field which my former colleagues (when they were polite) regarded as "a lower form of educational research" (Fanghanel, 2013, p. 67). My despair was intricately woven with a feeling of utter helplessness; I had absolutely no idea of what I could have done to improve the paper. I had of course spent a considerable amount of time in creating it: I had read what I thought was quite widely with the SoTL discipline, I had inserted wholly unfamiliar sub-headings such as "Methods" and "Results"—I had even wrestled with recalcitrant percentages. The entire SoTL field now appeared to be wholly opaque and totally incomprehensible. Fortunately, the Subject Coordinator very graciously not only gave me the chance to resubmit, but the opportunity to work with an ED as a mentor in the process of rewriting the paper.

As a consequence, in my first meeting with Kathryn, I was suffused with a sense of shame and mortification—particularly as I was assigned a colleague whom I had (previously) regarded as an equal. Sending her a copy of the paper had been humiliating enough—now we were supposed to actually discuss it. However, at no point did Kathryn ever mention the word "fail", "wrong", "mistake" or "what you should have done was…". To my grateful astonishment, I noticed that Kathryn actually did not say anything negative about my paper at all. On the contrary, she actually complimented me on my writing: something she has kindly and consistently persisted to do throughout our continued collaboration. In short, I was treated with immense tact, compassion and respect. So, the first challenge was definitely the unwelcome feeling of being a complete and utter novice: of discovering that my years of hard-acquired knowledge within my own discipline could not assist me, and that I had to accept defeat…and help.

Kathryn gave me an (unpublished) SoTL paper that she had worked on with another student to read as a model and talked me through an overview of the various sections within it. Kathryn observantly noticed my look of terrorised incomprehension when she attempted to patiently explain the difference between method, methodology, and theoretical frameworks, and deftly drew some diagrams on the back of the paper, tactfully suggesting that it sometimes helped to have a session with a whiteboard. As her simple, clear drawings still made no sense to me, I merely nodded and rearranged my face into what I hoped looked like Enlightened Understanding. After we parted, I compulsively read and reread the model paper, struggling to meet the challenge of applying SoTL's "new theoretical underpinnings" to the content of my own research. I had no idea how to formally interpret the data I had gathered, and simply could not understand why there needed to be so many fiddly…sections—the distinction between methodology and theoretical frameworks proving particularly elusive. I dutifully researched different methodologies and conscientiously inserted extra headings and subheadings, slavishly trying to emulate the model paper. However, despite rearranging my entire paper, I still felt like I was simply faking it; I could simply not grasp why I had to do what I was doing.

Opportunities

And then, finally, a moment of epiphany. After trawling through a number of theoretical frameworks I stumbled across "conceptual framework" (being based, perhaps somewhat obviously, on the analysis of concepts). Not only had I found a theoretical approach that was highly appropriate to my research, in that it illuminated exactly my approach to my analysis of my data, but it also finally made clear to me the approach I had been using in my previous philosophical research (golly, it had a name!). This clarification helped enormously; not just at that moment, but also in that it continued to provide me with an extraordinarily useful framework within which I was able to develop and re-develop the paper at various iterative stages, providing a foundation upon which to focus and refine my argument. I then, with much fear and trembling, sent off the first draft.

In providing feedback, Kathryn was again consideration itself, actually arranging to meet me face to face to talk over her comments, always focusing on positive suggestions in a manner that was never couched as a "should", and always offering encouragement. I had the opportunity to experience again, in Kathryn's gentle and sensitive handling of the situation, both an insight into how some of my own students might feel in the face of failure, and an approach to feedback and mentoring that could constructively and compassionately ameliorate such pain. More drafting and rewriting later, and Kathryn suggested that I could perhaps put my data into a graph in order to make it a bit clearer. After a few moments of Sheer-Fear-of-Excel-Spreadsheet-Terror (What?? Graphs?? Figures?? Statistics??), Kathryn thoughtfully offered to do a whiteboard session to help demonstrate. What followed was awe-inspiring in its simplicity and effectiveness; Kathryn drew two tables on a whiteboard with my data nicely ensconced underneath short, apt headings. I was astounded. My response might seem incomprehensible to researchers well-versed in scientific methods, but as an academic with a background wholly within a graph-free Humanities, I simply had not conceived that information could be conveyed so visually and so succinctly—and all without a single adjective. I joyfully created my tables (so simple!) and inserted my information (so clear!) and discovered, on re-reading the complex and tortured sentences I had previously used to describe my data, yet a further opportunity to admire Kathryn's tact: I could barely make sense of them. I then re-submitted my paper for assessment. It passed. In fact, the marker actually included a list of possible journals I could consider submitting to.

So inspired I was by the whole process that I began another phase of collaboration with Kathryn: preparing the paper for publication. I was initially—but very graciously—rejected by a journal but had the opportunity to refine my argument further in response to the feedback I had received. The process was incredibly enriching, as it helped enormously to clarify my findings. I subsequently submitted the re-written paper to another journal and was offered a chance to re-submit—with one very positive review advising to publish immediately, and the other offering constructive feedback that I felt confident I could respond to. From an inauspicious beginning as an abject SoTL failure, I now had the opportunity to perhaps publish within the field. Moreover, I had the desire to continue SoTL research, as it had ultimately changed the way I approached my teaching practice.

The SoTL project has had a significant impact on my teaching, as reflecting on and examining my practice through the lens of new methodologies brought unexpected insights and unprecedented rigour to my entire approach. Through the SoTL process I was able to gather concrete data by which I could gauge my students' progress, and a framework within which to analysis their achievement. I was able to verify that there were indeed some conceptual weaknesses in the pedagogical framework that was being employed, which I was then able to share with my colleagues and attempt to address. This reflective process is iterative, as I now have a much-heightened awareness of the effects of my teaching practice on student outcomes—and the importance of research in informing this process. So much so, that I have recently approached Kathryn to partner in another SoTL research project: how to best support diverse students within my field. In this new project, Kathryn has introduced me—yet again—to a new approach to gathering and analysing the data we require. However, in contrast to my initial bewildered response to the field of SoTL, I am now unexpectedly excited at the prospect of learning more ways in which to improve my scholarship—and teaching.

Space Two: Educational Developer's Contribution - A Personal Reflection – Kathryn Meldrum

In providing a context for my engagement with SoTL and for my collaboration with faculty, Kristi Giselsson, I want to first discuss some aspects of my professional and contextual characteristics, drawn from the working in the third space theoretical model.

Contextual Characteristics

At present, I am one of two staff formally working in educational development at this institution. Organisational support for our work is variable as both of us also perform other important roles which take precedence over ED work at times. While there is policy and a new framework as supporting structures for EDs, faculty impetus for educational development is low.

Traditionally, the GCAP was the institution's recognised tertiary teaching qualification and one of the primary vehicles for professional development. The GCAP was not mandated by the institution and consequently faculty uptake has been limited to the point where the course has now been discontinued. It comprised four subjects, three of which were core and one elective. The first two core subjects focused on situating the institution in global and national perspectives of higher education as well as curriculum and assessment design. The third subject focused on the use of data to inform teaching and learning in higher education and asked colleagues to design their own SoTL project. The final subject was a choice of electives, one of which was a supported SoTL project utilising the design that faculty proposed in the third core subject. Along with teaching into the core subjects, EDs had been actively collaborating with faculty in this final elective subject. Collaboration was situated around supporting human research ethics applications, data analysis and interpretation, and writing up the project findings for the final assessment task which was examined by a colleague external to the institution. It was in context of this final subject that we began our collaboration.

Professional Characteristics

My disciplinary background is in exercise physiology although I moved to education in the mid-2000s. As a faculty member I was introduced to SoTL while undertaking a tertiary teaching qualification. My own journey writing in and about SoTL was harrowing, although it ended well.

I have been a faculty member at a range of different universities in Australia and the UK before moving into roles that were more akin to that of an ED in 2014. Since moving into ED roles, I have had the pleasure of working with close to 100 faculty members writing into and about SoTL in a variety of different contexts. The different contexts relate to institutions in which faculty have been based and also the type of SoTL writing that they have been engaged with. I have worked with faculty based in Australia, the UK, Asia, and a Pacific Rim country who have been engaged with seeking recognition for their teaching practice through the Higher Education Academy (now Advance HE) Fellowship Scheme and colleagues who have been undertaking professional development opportunities, mostly through post graduate qualifications in academic practice/tertiary teaching.

My underlying philosophy for the ED work that I do draws on the developmental framework proposed by Kenny and her colleagues (2017) and resonates with the principles described by Fanghanel (2004). Although the framework proposed by Kenny and colleagues is relatively recent, (more recent than my work in the ED space) as an educator my philosophical approach has always been very firmly grounded in the principles of social constructivism. In drawing on the fundamental underpinnings of social constructivism, Kenny and colleague's framework "speaks to" me by highlighting "learner-centred and collaborative ways of knowing and being" (p. 1). It is the "collaborative ways of knowing and being" that support my approach to working with faculty on writing for and about SoTL. In addition, having "walked the SoTL road" as faculty, I appreciate the developmental nature of the work and use this knowledge in my approach to supporting SoTL writing.

Challenges

On reflection, my first meeting with Kristi was not like other meetings with colleagues in a SoTL space. My usual engagement with faculty as a mentor for SoTL has been as a collaborator. Some would classify me as a supervisor or advisor (akin to post-graduate research) for a SoTL project, but I have always positioned myself as a collaborator. Being involved with faculty from the outset of a project has enabled me to position myself as such. I have utilised the planning/design phase of a project to discuss the SoTL inquiry as a journey for us as parties to the new knowledge created as a result of it. However, because I was engaged with Kristi "late in the game", I was acutely aware of the situation that brought us together in a new context as mentor and mentee. In addition, that the reason for us being brought together was Kristi's "working towards satisfactory" classification on her final paper.

While Kristi has written about my tact and sensitivity to her situation in her reflection, I would hope that my emotional intelligence would support me to work in this way with anyone. What I want to focus on in this section is the challenge of supporting Kristi to come to understand how to write in a new and different genre because in my experience—for the reasons discussed in the review of literature--Kristi's difficulties were not unusual.

Initial Approach

After reviewing Kristi's submission it was clear to me where she needed support. The first area was in supporting her understanding of SoTL as research and the second in articulating her project findings in the associated language of the discipline. Kristi discussed our initial conversation where I outlined the key points about SoTL as research—the importance of methodology, method and a theoretical framework with which to compare and potentially explain her case study findings. In drawing on the theoretical framework that underpins this chapter (Figure 1): What Kristi brought to the third space was her space one understanding of research as practice from her discipline—philosophy. I brought my space two SoTL knowledge and expertise to share.

In sharing my SoTL knowledge and expertise, one of the strategies that I have consistently used is to provide a model or exemplar paper. Providing a model paper draws on the good practice principles of assessment feedback in higher education. Model papers provide a clear example (Carless, 2015) of what SoTL "looks like" in its final form. When colleagues review a model paper it also supports them to evaluate (McConlogue, 2015) their writing against the work of peers. In this case what I was aiming to achieve by sharing the model paper with Kristi was to provide an illustration of the points that I had been making during our initial discussion in an alternate form for her to consider and reflect upon.

Working Through Writing Drafts

In reviewing Kristi's paper drafts, I was conscious of how she was grappling with her content and discourse knowledge, which Bereiter and Scardamalia identified in their knowledge transforming model of writing. Keys (1999) utilised Bereiter and Scardamalia's model to highlight the role that writing can play in learning about science. Keys identified that writing in the science genre provided an environment in which the writer could be reflective and how this led to an opportunity to produce new knowledge. I argue that colleagues new to SoTL come to learn about it through their writing and have utilised a further adaptation of Bereiter and Scardamalia's model (Figure 1) (cited by Keys, 1999, p. 120) to illustrate how some aspects of Kristi's narrative reflection demonstrate the interactions between the content and rhetorical spaces.

In applying Bereiter and Scardamalia's model to Kristi's writing (see Figure 1), she brought: her understanding of the student experience of her subject's assessment regime—having used this as impetus for her SoTL project; the data that she had gathered during her inquiry (content knowledge); her existing understanding of writing strategies; and her bourgeoning SoTL genre knowledge (discourse knowledge) to her SoTL writing. Initially, as Kristi has reflected in her narrative, the focus on finding an appropriate theoretical framework, in particular, was helpful in assisting her to engage with her findings and focus her argument. The integration of the theoretical framework into her writing supported Kristi to develop in both the content and rhetorical problem spaces. In the content problem space, it assisted her in drawing inferences from her data and developing conceptual knowledge structures. This transferred through the rhetorical problem space in order to communicate the meaning of her data (in relation to the theoretical framework) and to effectively construct her argument. Interestingly, the focus on locating a theoretical framework also gave Kristi the language to describe a research approach that she has used in her own discipline.

As Kristi's writing progressed, I could see how her content and discourse knowledge were developing through the interactions in problem translation between each space. Keys (1999) identified that this is where writers "engage in the knowledge-transforming model" (p. 120) as opposed to knowledge-telling. As an example of how Kristi's discourse knowledge was developing through her writing, she reflected on the impact of the whiteboard session that we had where I illustrated how to use tables to represent her data more clearly. This interaction between us supported her further development in the rhetorical problem space, particularly to communicate the meaning of her data. From my recollection, constructing the tables also helped her to see where there were gaps in the data that she was utilising to build her argument. Kristi came to this realisation when, after I had drawn the tables on the whiteboard, we did not have enough data to fill both tables. Consequentially, the whiteboard session also supported Kristi to further reflect in the content problem space.

Opportunities

In reflecting on the opportunities that this collaboration has provided me as an ED, I want to highlight the reciprocal nature of this work. In navigating and negotiating Kristi's revised SoTL submission, we have collectively deepened our understanding of the nature of SoTL. I raise this point because it is the conversations that we have had collectively negotiating the problems between the content and rhetorical spaces (Figure 1) that have brought a richness to our understanding of the nature of Kristi's inquiry into practice. Her initial "failure" has provided us both with an opportunity to engage more deeply with the issues of curriculum and the student experience of it. In addition, my experience has reaffirmed the importance of the approaches that I take to support faculty. The experience of working with Kristi has been different for me as my role was to remediate her initial paper submission. However, in doing so, I adopted the same approaches that are customary in my practice to support her successful outcome.

Reflecting on Working in the Third Space

In drawing on the working in the third space model (Figure 2), Kristi and I have been able to identify our individual knowledge and expertise. Our collaboration has brought about new knowledge, and we are both hopeful that she will be able to publicly share it in a scholarly publication. For me, this would make the hard work that Kristi has invested in developing her ideas and reflecting on their meaning for her practice a worthwhile venture. As Kristi has highlighted in her narrative, this experience has brought other collaboration opportunities that we are pursuing. First, the opportunity to collaborate on this chapter. Secondly, (so far) another collaborative SoTL inquiry where we are working as partners from the outset. Finally, in reflecting on the processes of engaging in SoTL, I have invested some time in investigating the nature of writing for this discipline and genre. Articulating the difficulty that faculty have in writing about SoTL and utilising a theoretical framework (Figure 1) with which to discuss an example has also provided some solace for Kristi, for which I am thankful.

IMPLICATIONS ON PRACTICE: STRATEGIES FOR NEGOTIATING THE THIRD SPACE

This section is focused on how to support writing for and about SoTL utilising the third space as a framework (Figure 2). It focuses on supporting EDs and faculty to work together effectively by highlighting the importance of understanding the professional and contextual characteristics that each bring to the collaboration. We draw on our experience to pose questions intended to support EDs and faculty to reflect as they prepare for and begin to work with faculty on a SoTL writing project. These questions are not intended to be exhaustive, but to support each party as they reflect on their own situation so that they may be in a better position to engage collaboratively with each other.

Three different sets of questions are posed as strategies for engaging EDs and faculty and preparing them to collaborate. In utilising the proposed strategies, the first set of questions under the heading *Overarching ED questions* probably only needs to be considered by an ED once, on their first ever engagement with faculty in a collaborative SoTL writing project. The second set of questions is posed in Table 1. The questions in Table 1 provide an opportunity for faculty and EDs to reflect on their professional and contextual characteristics. These questions could be provided to both parties in a questionnaire format, but it is not suggested that sharing of individual reflections be mandated as part of the collaboration. They are reflection points only; however, it is suggested that faculty and EDs use the reflections as a basis for sharing their professional stories at the initial meeting. Other questions to consider at the initial meeting are posed under the heading *The initial meeting: Points for discussion.*

Educational Developers Preparing for Initial Engagement With Faculty

The primary consideration should be the context in which EDs and faculty work within an institution. One of the first considerations should be the contextual characteristics of the institution and subsequently the individual departments within it. When considering institutional and/or departmental support for SoTL, sometimes there can be a mismatch between the requirements of the institutional developmental framework(s) and support for faculty to actually engage with SoTL. For example, there may be mandated SoTL-based professional development for early career academics that are part of their probational requirements. While early career academics might be eager to engage with building their knowledge about their teaching practice through SoTL, multiple competing priorities such as high teaching workloads, the pressure to conduct research and publish, and the need to complete a GCAP qualification all take time that departments may not be willing to provide (Flavell et al., 2018). Time-poor faculty may feel pressured by the competing priorities and may not be able to actively embrace their SoTL engagement opportunities. The following overarching questions are designed to support EDs to consider the "big picture" of their work in supporting the professional development of faculty at their institution.

Overarching ED Questions

As previously mentioned, these questions may only need to be considered by an ED once. They may also be useful in supporting new EDs to understand the contextual characteristics of an institution that they have just joined.

1. What is/are the institutional professional development framework(s) that guide your work as an ED?
2. What is/are the underlying institutional philosophical and/or quality assurance principles underpinning the framework?
3. How do the underlying institutional philosophical and/or quality assurance principles impact faculty engagement with SoTL in particular?
4. How does the institution enact the imperative for SoTL?
5. What is/are the hidden agendas for SoTL at an institutional level?
6. What strategies could be employed to proactively support engagement with SoTL?
7. How can you negotiate negativity of faculty when SoTL engagement is mandated? What skills/support might you need to draw on? Where might this support be available?

It is not necessary for EDs to share the responses to these questions at their initial meeting with faculty. However, aspects of how the institution and/or departments value SoTL and/or the associated professional development frameworks may emerge during conversation and these questions provide a platform for preparing for discussions about them.

Faculty and EDs Reflecting on Their Practice: Preparing for the Initial Meeting

In preparing to collaborate, it is suggested that both faculty and EDs review the questions in Table 1. These questions are designed to help both parties to reflect on what professional and contextual characteristics they bring to the collaboration. In reflecting on practice, both parties might also become aware of tension points, such as the departmental milieu for SoTL, which could be discussed at the initial meeting. While responses to the questions in Table 1 will be as individual as the respondents, it is worth both parties taking the time to consider them prior to the initial meeting. Honest reflections will provide a starting point for sharing professional stories at the initial meeting. Sharing professional stories is intended to support building trusting and mutually respectful relationships that are important for collaboration.

The Initial Meeting: Points for Discussion

The reflection questions posed in Table 1 should provide both parties with a focus for their first meeting. It is intended that they will be helpful in the process of engaging faculty and EDs with each other and the SoTL project that they intend to collaborate on. In terms of progressing the collaboration, it is

Table 1. Questions for faculty and educational developers to reflect on prior to their initial meeting

Faculty Reflection Questions		**Educational Developer Reflection Questions**	
Professional characteristics	What reservations do I have regarding SoTL (if any)? What are they founded on?	**Professional characteristics**	What is my confidence level in my role as an ED?
	What areas of my teaching/the curriculum/learning activities would I like to improve/ test/know more about?		What do I bring to the conversation? How can you collaborate with this particular faculty member?
	How do I really know the effect that my teaching/the curriculum/ learning activities have on my students?		What supports my credibility?
	How am I open to the possibility that something about my practice could be improved?		How can I articulate my willingness and ability to work with faculty?
	What am doing that is worth documenting and sharing with other practitioners?		
	What is my disciplinary research and writing background?		
	What is my experience and confidence in my role as faculty?		
Contextual Characteristics	What is my understanding of how this institution supports my engagement with SoTL?	**Contextual Characteristics**	What is my perception of how the faculty member's department engages with SoTL?
	How does my department engage with SoTL?		Do your support structures enable you to engage deeply with collaborating with faculty?
			How is my role defined and does it present me with opportunities to collaborate with colleagues as posited by the working in the third space theoretical framework? (Consider what you might need to advocate for and to whom, to support collaboration)
			What organisational support structures do I have (resources, time and space) that help me to collaborate?

important that what is discussed at the initial meeting provides the foundation. Aside from building a trusting and respectful relationship through sharing professional stories, the terms of the collaboration should also be discussed. The following questions are suggested as a starting point:

1. What do we bring to the conversation? How can we collaborate?
2. How will our collaboration be recognised by the institution and our departments?
3. What material resources do we need?
4. How much time do we have to commit to this collaboration?
5. Do we have the appropriate space (privacy) to engage in this work collaboratively?
6. What is/are the terms of our engagement?
7. What is the process and structure (e.g., How often should we meet? When and where? What are the expectations between meetings? How will we record what needs to be done at and between meetings?)
8. What can we expect from each other?

As previously discussed, while these questions are by no means exhaustive, they provide a foundation to support faculty and EDs to focus on and consider their professional and contextual characteristics before engaging in collaboration.

Reflecting on the Outcomes of Working in the Third Space

While the questions posed above provide an opportunity for faculty and EDs to consider what they bring to the third space prior to and at the commencement of a collaborative opportunity, it may also be worthwhile to reflect on the outcomes of the collaboration. Using the third space features as identified in Figure 2 provides an opportunity to celebrate new knowledge created as a result of the collaboration and to share it as widely as possible within the institutional context. This has the potential to support other colleagues considering SoTL collaborations. This type of approach also has the potential to strengthen institutional and/or departmental perspectives about SoTL, especially if they are not wholly supportive of it (Roxå et al., 2008). As the academy has traditionally prioritised research over teaching, faculty can tend to regard teaching—and subsequently SoTL research—as being of less value (Chalmers, 2011; Flavell et al., 2018; Harland et al., 2014; McCormack et al., 2014). Taking the time to reflect on the process of the collaboration, not only to feedback and feed forward on the approach to the collaboration, but also to support faculty to appreciate the impact of the SoTL project on their teaching practice, is worthwhile. Finally, considering opportunities for continuing collaboration, or at least coming to an understanding about whether this is desirable for both parties, is a worthwhile conversation to have prior to finalising the SoTL engagement.

CONCLUSION

Despite the centrality of writing as a means of sharing the outcomes of SoTL inquiry, surprisingly little has been published about the challenges and opportunities that it presents faculty and the role that EDs play in supporting it. This chapter utilises two different theoretical frameworks: the Knowledge Transforming Model of Writing (Bereiter & Scardamalia cited by Keys, 1999) and an adaptation of the working in the third space theoretical framework (Briguglio, 2014) to discuss opportunities for faculty and EDs to collaborate on a SoTL writing project. We illustrate how the third space model, in particular, provided us with a framework with which to consider our professional and contextual characteristics by discussing the interactions between ourselves as mentor and mentee during our collaboration. This collaboration provided us with a range of challenges and opportunities to reflect on our respective practices as faculty and ED. In relation to faculty, the challenge of reflection on practice, learning new content, and discursive knowledge was rewarded with the opportunity to both substantially improve teaching practice and to engage in further collaborative projects. In relation to an ED, taking the time to understand the perspective of faculty and having empathy for the journey of learning about a new discipline proved invaluable. The time taken in support of faculty, especially in the conversations focused in and on SoTL, were particularly rewarding. We further discussed the implications of the working in the third space framework by posing a range of questions that can help support EDs and faculty when considering the professional and contextual characteristics of their potential collaborations. Finally, we indicated the potential such collaborations have to positively impact more widely on departments and institutions. Ultimately, we suggest that continued collaboration in the third space has the potential to not only enhance the practices of faculty and EDs—to help them to find their "voice"—but to improve what should be an important priority for the wider academy: the learning outcomes of students.

REFERENCES

Amundsen, C., & Wilson, M. (2012). Are we asking the right questions?: A conceptual review of the educational development literature in higher education. *Review of Educational Research, 82*(1), 90–126. doi:10.3102/0034654312438409

Booth, S., & Woollacott, L. C. (2018). On the constitution of SoTL: Its domains and contexts. *Higher Education, 75*(3), 537–551. doi:10.100710734-017-0156-7

Botham, K. A. (2018). The perceived impact on academics' teaching practice of engaging with a higher education institution's CPD scheme. *Innovations in Education and Teaching International, 55*(2), 164–175. doi:10.1080/14703297.2017.1371056

Boyer, E. L. (1990). *Scholarship reconsidered: Priorities of the professoriate.* Lawrenceville, NJ: Princeton University Press.

Briguglio, C. (2014). *Working in the third space: Promoting interdisciplinary collaboration to embed English language development into the disciplines.* Retrieved from http://altf.org/wp-content/uploads/2016/08/Briguglio_C_NTF_report_2014.pdf

Carless, D. (2015). *Excellence in university assessment: Learning from award-winning practice.* London, UK: Routledge. doi:10.4324/9781315740621

Chalmers, D. (2011). Progress and challenges to the recognition and reward of the Scholarship of Teaching in higher education. *Higher Education Research & Development, 30*(1), 25–38. doi:10.1080/07294360.2011.536970

Cilliers, F. J., & Herman, N. (2010). Impact of an educational development programme on teaching practice of academics at a research-intensive university. *The International Journal for Academic Development*, *15*(3), 253–267. doi:10.1080/1360144X.2010.497698

Fanghanel, J. (2004). Capturing dissonance in university teacher education environments. *Studies in Higher Education*, *29*(5), 575–590. doi:10.1080/0307507042000261553

Fanghanel, J. (2013). Going Public with Pedagogical Inquiries: SoTL as a Methodology for Faculty Professional Development. *Teaching and Learning Inquiry: The ISSOTL Journal*, *1*(1), 59–70. doi:10.20343/teachlearninqu.1.1.59

Felten, P. (2013). Principles of Good Practice in SoTL. *Teaching and Learning Inquiry: The ISSOTL Journal*, *1*(1), 121–125. doi:10.20343/teachlearninqu.1.1.121

Flavell, H., Roberts, L., Fyfe, G., & Broughton, M. (2018). Shifting goal posts: The impact of academic workforce reshaping and the introduction of teaching academic roles on the Scholarship of Teaching and Learning. *Australian Educational Researcher*, *45*(2), 179–194. doi:10.100713384-017-0247-6

Ginns, P., Kitay, J., & Prosser, M. (2010). Transfer of academic staff learning in a research-intensive university. *Teaching in Higher Education*, *15*(3), 235–246. doi:10.1080/13562511003740783

Green, D. A., & Little, D. (2016). Family portrait: A profile of educational developers around the world. *The International Journal for Academic Development*, *21*(2), 135–150. doi:10.1080/136014 4X.2015.1046875

Harland, T., Raja Hussain, R. M., & Bakar, A. A. (2014). The Scholarship of Teaching and Learning: Challenges for Malaysian academics. *Teaching in Higher Education*, *19*(1), 38–48. doi:10.1080/1356 2517.2013.827654

Kenny, N., Berenson, C., Chick, N., Johnson, C., Keegan, D., Read, E., & Reid, L. (2017). *A developmental framework for teaching expertise in postsecondary education*. Paper presented at the International Society for the Scholarship of Teaching and Learning (ISSOTL) Conference, Calgary, Alberta, Canada. Retrieved from http://connections.ucalgaryblogs.ca/files/2017/11/CC3_Teaching-Expertise-Framework-Fall-2017.pdf

Keys, C. W. (1999). Revitalizing instruction in scientific genres: Connecting knowledge production with writing to learn in science. *Science Education*, *83*(2), 115–130. doi:10.1002/(SICI)1098-237X(199903)83:2<115::AID-SCE2>3.0.CO;2-Q

McAlpine, L., & Weston, C. (2002). Reflection: Issues related to improving professors' teaching and students' learning. *Instructional Science*, *28*(5), 363–385. doi:10.1023/A:1026583208230

McConlogue, T. (2015). Making judgements: Investigating the process of composing and receiving peer feedback. *Studies in Higher Education*, *40*(9), 1495–1506. doi:10.1080/03075079.2013.868878

McCormack, C., Vanags, T., & Prior, R. (2014). "Things fall apart so they can fall together": Uncovering the hidden side of writing a teaching award application. *Higher Education Research & Development*, *33*(5), 935–948. doi:10.1080/07294360.2014.890569

Pelger, S., & Larsson, M. (2018). Advancement towards the Scholarship of Teaching and Learning through the writing of teaching portfolios. *The International Journal for Academic Development, 23*(3), 179–191. doi:10.1080/1360144X.2018.1435417

Peters, M. A. (2008). Academic Writing, Genres and Philosophy. *Educational Philosophy and Theory, 40*(7), 819–831. doi:10.1111/j.1469-5812.2008.00511.x

Roxå, T., Olsson, T., & Mårtensson, K. (2008). Appropriate Use of Theory in the Scholarship of Teaching and Learning as a Strategy for Institutional Development. *Arts and Humanities in Higher Education, 7*(3), 276–294. doi:10.1177/1474022208094412

Saalman, E. (2018). *How do teachers reflect upon their teaching in teaching portfolios? – Analysis of teachers' portfolios at seminars on how to document your pedagogical qualifications and skills at the chalmers university of technology.* Paper presented at the International Symposium on Project Approaches in Engineering Education, Brasilia, Brazil.

Chapter 10
Using Mid-Semester Assessment Programs (MAPs) as a Catalyst for the Scholarship of Teaching and Learning (SoTL)

Alisa Hutchinson
Wayne State University, USA

Anabel Stoeckle
Wayne State University, USA

ABSTRACT

Mid-Semester Assessment Programs (MAPs) have been successfully utilized as a professional development tool for faculty interested in improving their teaching in the context of higher education by assessing voluntary formative student feedback that guides changes instructors make in the classroom. Faculty centers and educational developers have the unique opportunity to recruit instructors via MAPs who have participated in these programs to promote and support the scholarship of teaching and learning (SoTL) among faculty who already display an innate interest in best teaching practices and are open to advancing their own teaching in order to improve student learning and to propel student success. This chapter provides a guide for educational developers who seek to become active partners for faculty to become interested and engaged in the scholarship of teaching and learning through a unique recruitment mechanism that serves as a natural steppingstone for faculty not having engaged with SoTL yet.

INTRODUCTION

Mid-semester assessment programs (MAPs) are a valuable tool for universities and their instructors to understand and improve teaching and learning. Originally known as small-group instructional diagnosis (Clark & Redmond, 1982), such programs share a core emphasis on gathering formative feedback from students about teaching and learning in classes while there is still time in the semester for individual

DOI: 10.4018/978-1-7998-2212-7.ch010

instructors to make changes. Research indicates that instructors find the process more credible than end-of-the-semester evaluations and more useful for improving teaching and learning when student feedback is acted upon (Blue, Wentzell, & Evans, 2008; Sozer, Zeybekoglu, & Kaya, 2019; Veeck, O'Reilly, MacMillan, & Yu, 2016). Formative feedback collected from mid-semester evaluations also has been shown to improve student perceptions of teaching and learning as well as satisfaction and motivation (Blue et al., 2008; Sozer et al., 2019; Veeck et al., 2016).

Because MAPs are an established formative assessment process in higher education institutions (Diamond, 2004), and as their utility for improving teaching and learning has been documented in the research literature, they offer a unique opportunity to leverage an existing faculty development activity to support the Scholarship of Teaching and Learning (SoTL) by providing action-oriented, evidence-based techniques without the resource demands associated with implementing a brand-new initiative.

The goal of combining MAPs with SoTL is twofold. First and foremost, MAPs can improve teaching practices on campus by assessing classroom practices in the middle of the semester and by providing explicit recommendations that are rooted in student perspectives, that capture classroom dynamics, and that are tailored to individual instructor's needs. The individual consultations and recommendations that occur in the context of MAPs encourage faculty to pause and reflect on their teaching practice and make adjustments based on the educational developers' recommendations. They also have a wider campus impact since MAPs can reach many instructors—and therefore a multitude of students—every semester. Secondly, MAPs can be utilized as a recruiting mechanism for Center for Teaching and Learning's (CTL) educational developers (ED) to recruit faculty to start their own SoTL projects; faculty voluntarily participating in formative assessment tend to be already invested in improving their own teaching practice, care about their students learning, and are open to suggestions and changes that stem from evidence-based teaching practices from SoTL. In short, they are very likely to already have a mindset that shares values with SoTL, even if they haven't been exposed to it as a discipline or a possible research venue for themselves.

This chapter offers a guide for CTLs and EDs on how to position MAPs as a catalyst for structured inquiry into teaching and learning. Educational developers are uniquely positioned to use MAPs to influence both instructors and leaders at various organizational levels to engage in SoTL research around faculty development, curriculum design, and institutional decision-making. The chapter begins with overviews of SoTL and MAPs, before examining the integration of MAPs with the four core practices of SoTL—framing questions, gathering evidence, refining insights, and sharing knowledge publicly (Huber & Hutchings, 2005). This chapter will support educational developers and Centers for Teaching and Learning (CTLs) in (1) extending their role by positioning SoTL as serious and meaningful research work (Huber, 2004) and (2) recruiting and guiding faculty and institutional leaders who may be interested in engaging in SoTL.

Overview of SoTL

While definitions of Scholarship of Teaching and Learning (SoTL) vary in emphasis and perspective (see McKinney, 2004 & 2007, for reviews), they share a common emphasis on engagement in the systematic, reflective study of teaching and learning to generate knowledge that is shared publicly. Many instructors put effort into being effective teachers, and within this group, many may draw on scholarly insights and evidence-based practices to improve their work in the classroom. However, it is only when they approach this work with the mindset and tools of a researcher that their efforts engage with the territory of SoTL—where issues of teaching and learning are rigorously explored and documented.

The broader interpretations of this core definition suggest some degree of ambiguity is a necessary condition, which is not surprising when considering the interdisciplinary nature of the field. Faculty from all ranks, disciplines, and institutional types can contribute to SoTL, yet they come to this endeavor with distinctly different ways of experiencing and understanding what the terms "teaching" and "learning" might mean depending on their own disciplines, research traditions, signature pedagogies, and contexts. What SoTL means to an adjunct English instructor teaching several online sections of an introductory composition class may be quite different than a team of computer science professors who teach a linked sequence of project-based courses in a face-to-face graduate program. The English professor may be primarily concerned about student motivation and wonder if providing video feedback will help engage students more with their revisions. The computer science instructors, on the other hand, may be interested in experimenting with a flipped classroom approach in all of their classes and want to know its effect on student learning. Their students are different, the cognitive demands of their content are different, and their learning goals are different—yet when they engage in SoTL, they are sharing a curiosity about teaching and learning as well as a desire to generate and share meaningful insights about these processes.

SoTL is traditionally associated with either individual instructors or small teams of instructors using their own courses as a context or laboratory for exploring pedagogical practices (Hubball, Pearson, & Clarke, 2013). As an example, three books aimed to serve as guides or overviews of engaging in SoTL (Bishop-Clark & Dietz-Uhler, 2012; Huber, 2004; McKinney, 2007) all frame the process around the idea of an individual faculty member engaging in SoTL work. Hubball et al. (2013) challenge this notion and advocate for SoTL to be inclusive of research at the level of programs, departments, or institutions around questions of curriculum, educational leadership, and program quality. This has been termed Scholarship of Curriculum Practice (SoCP), a specialized practice under the broader SoTL umbrella (Hubball et al., 2013). McKinney (2007) emphasizes that program assessment alone does not qualify as SoTL work, given that it is intended to satisfy internal reporting requirements rather than generate insights that add to academic discourse around teaching and learning. However, SoTL (and its child, SoCP) provide important mechanisms that can elevate assessment work around curriculum and leadership from mere reporting to meaningful research capable of sparking innovation and improvement within and beyond the institution. An example of SoTL at this level could be a law school that wants to introduce low-stakes, formative quizzes in all its first-year law courses, a significant departure from the discipline's tradition of high-stakes final exams as the sole assessment during a semester. Not only might this be important to improving student outcomes and contribute to program-level reporting, it may also have important implications for evolving the signature pedagogy of legal education. Thus, framing this as a SoTL project existing at an organizational level allows for a richer understanding of the relationship between pedagogy and learning while also driving innovation in practice and improvement in student outcomes.

The Center for Teaching and Learning (CTL)—the central hub of activity around teaching and learning—can play an important collaborative role in SoTL, both for individual instructors as well as colleagues at the departmental and institutional level. In particular, campus-wide programming around formative assessment of teaching and learning, such as MAPs, can serve as a jumping off point introducing faculty and leadership to SoTL as well as serve as an important source of data for SoTL projects. In order to illustrate different pathways for incorporating MAPs in SoTL, the three hypothetical SoTL examples (based on our cumulative experiences) presented in this section will be continued in later sections of the chapter. This approach accommodates the inclusion of a range of contextual variables that might be found in higher education in order to explore the MAP-SoTL relationship from different perspectives. Throughout this chapter, the three examples of instructors from English, computer science, and law will be revisited to illustrate potential applications for MAPs and SoTL. The next section provides an overview of MAPs and the typical components included in them.

Overview of MAPs

Mid-semester assessment programs (MAPs), also known as small group instructional diagnosis (SGID) or quick course diagnosis (QCD), are typically implemented to guide faculty through the process of assessing their own teaching practice. MAPs allow instructors to make rapid, small-to-medium changes based on student feedback to improve their teaching in the current semester as well as to cultivate meaningful adjustments to their teaching in upcoming semesters. Moreover, offering a form of formative assessment in the middle of the semester helps to create a culture in which constant reflection and improvement among faculty is encouraged and celebrated by using timely student feedback as a tool to guide the assessment process. Typically, mid-semester assessment programs, commonly offered by a university's CTL, include trained facilitators or EDs who (1) meet with the instructor at the beginning of the process, (2) collect students' formative feedback about what is going well in the course and what could be improved, and (3) analyze the feedback and share their findings with the instructor (Blue et al., 2008; Coffman, 1991; Clark & Redmond, 1982; Sozer et al., 2019). In practice, the details of MAPs implementation may vary, and this section of the chapter will present a summary of different ways MAPs can be structured and enacted. Regardless of the collection method, we see a potential to use student feedback from MAPs beyond their intended use of faculty development to inform SoTL by serving as a unique data collection tool to guide educational developers to promote best teaching practices rooted in student feedback.

Mid-Semester Assessment Programs as a Faculty Development Tool

One way for instructors wanting to improve their teaching is to assess their own end-of-semester evaluations. However, not only do these assessments occur at the end of the semester after a course has been substantially concluded, it might also take quite some time for them to be returned to the instructor and therefore cannot serve as a timely feedback tool to adjust an instructor's teaching. In addition to this problematic element of timing, end-of-semester course evaluations are generally rated low in terms of both student perceptions and effectiveness from the instructor's perspective since they can only use that information for future classes. Furthermore, end-of-semester course evaluations may provide limited qualitative feedback to guide the assessment process depending on the willingness of students to offer written responses to open-ended questions, while quantitative questions (typically in the form of Likert scales), may not adequately align with what students perceive to be important to teaching and learning in the classroom but instead seek to force an institutional framework on students' feedback.

Because of these limitations of course evaluations that occur at the end of the semester and are solely summative in nature, Clark & Redmond (1982) developed the Small Group Instructional Diagnosis (SGID) which allows instructors to gather formative student feedback in the middle of the semester in order to make changes to the course while it is still taking place (Finelli et al., 2011; Snooks et al., 2004). In addition to being considered useful from the instructor's perspective by allowing for "course corrections" during the semester, students feel heard and taken seriously when their feedback is given weight and their motivation increases (Blue et al., 2008).

Core Elements of Mid-Semester Assessment Programs

Formative Midterm-Assessment Programs may vary from institution to institution in terms of some of the details but usually share the following core elements, as discussed in more detail elsewhere (Finelli et al., 2011, Snooks et al., 2014):

1. During a **pre-consultation**, the instructor shares expectations and information with the ED (who will serve as their MAP facilitator) on what is happening in the classroom as well as their teaching style/preferences. In turn, the ED shares an overview of the MAP process with the instructor and answers any questions they might have about what to expect from their MAP

2. The ED **visits the classroom** to collect student feedback (and sometimes to observe the instructor teaching). The details of this portion of MAPs can differ in its execution, including how student feedback is collected and which questions are asked, but usually include the following three components based on both the instructor needs and available resources:

    a. For the student feedback portion, the ED invites students to reflect on open-ended guiding questions designed to prompt thoughts on what is going well in the classroom as well as which aspects of the class need improvement. Three prompts that are commonly used are 1) What do you like about the course? 2) What do you think needs improvement? 3) What suggestions do you have for bringing about these improvements? (Snooks et al., 2004, p. 112). This part is either done by students writing down their thoughts individually or by working in small groups. It is most typical that this feedback is collected anonymously, with no student names attached to the comments; this anonymity encourages students to feel comfortable sharing candid feedback since their comments cannot be traced to them personally.

    b. Some formats include a portion that involves observing the instructor teaching at the beginning of the class and/or videotaping or taking notes. However, oftentimes the teaching observation part isn't included since it requires additional time and staff resources that might not be available at an institution.

    c. Finally, in some MAP processes, the ED invites students to share their feedback with the group and asks the class to come to a consensus on which aspects are the most important to everyone.

3. The ED then thematically **codes the data** gathered during the classroom visit. Again, it is most common for the feedback from a course to be aggregated and anonymous, so the instructor does not know which student made which comment. Once the comments are aggregated, the ED then organizes them into themes to make them more useful for the instructor and to facilitate a meaningful discussion about what is happening in their classroom. The researchers' institution uses the principles of effective instruction described by Chickering and Gamson (1987) as the basis for coding MAP comments into themes. There is no standard convention for theming MAPs, although it is recommended that CTLs decide on a coding or theming approach for their particular MAP process and train their consultants in its use to ensure consistency. While there is an initial time investment in deciding on a coding approach and training EDs to implement it, the burden lessens over time. It should be noted that, at least at the researchers' institution, only one ED themes the

data for a given course, as the purpose of doing so is primarily organizational in nature to make the feedback more comprehensible to the instructor.

4.   The instructor and the ED meet for a **post-MAP consultation** to discuss their students' feedback, recurring themes, and potential changes or strategies to implement both in the short-term and long-term. Again, while there may be variations in MAP processes across institutions, it is most common for MAP feedback to only be shared with the instructor and not other colleagues; the confidentiality of the process helps to ensure its integrity and value. Once the feedback has been given to the instructor, any other sharing or use of it is at their discretion (although ethical considerations and IRB approval would be needed to use it in research, as described in more detail in a subsequent section).

In the next section, some possible variations of the MAP process are outlined; depending on resources, especially the second step of the classroom visit above might be adapted to how much personnel is available, and the observation part and the consensus part might either be abbreviated or left out.

Other Features and Variations of MAPs

While end-of-semester evaluations are oftentimes mandated by universities with results that can be made publicly available (depending on the institution), MAPs are usually both voluntary and confidential. Instructors sign up to participate because they would like to have access to informal and anonymous student feedback that is not shared with department chairs or other administrators and colleagues. If MAPs are positioned as a mandatory activity, it may diminish the value of the process for supporting reflective improvement by undermining the instructor's sense of agency and privacy. The potential for higher rates of participation should be weighed against the potential that experience itself will suffer. Carefully framing the experience as non-punitive, confidential, and aimed at supporting incremental improvement may help alleviate this concern.

MAPs can vary based on the time and resources that are available on campus. Even though the data is primarily qualitative in nature—collected in response to open-ended questions that enable capturing all potential student feedback—it can also have quantitative components. For example, an online-survey with a mix of Likert-scale and open-ended questions might be administered in large-lecture classrooms to provide some external structure to the data given the large number of participants. While some universities have staff within their CTL to facilitate formative assessments with their faculty, other universities might have to eliminate the classroom observation, to omit the activity asking students to come to a classroom consensus, or to self-organize their instructors in order to gather valuable mid-semester student feedback (Snooks et al., 2004). Instead, universities might choose let students work in small groups to respond only to the open-ended questions in order to speed up the process or to administer the survey online (Payette & Brown, 2018; Veeck et al., 2016). In cases where faculty do not have access to the institutionally-provided resources offered by a CTL, they can facilitate the process in abbreviated form themselves, as suggested by Snooks et al. (2004).

MAPs and SoTL

The purpose of using MAPs as formative assessment is to not have to rely on instructors' assumptions about what is going on in their classes but instead to make meaningful changes in course design and planning that are rooted in authentic student feedback. However, in addition to serving as an assessment tool of instructor performance, MAP data can be utilized beyond its initial purpose to inform and further the Scholarship of Teaching and Learning. The following sections will provide an overview of the four defining features of SoTL research: framing questions, gathering evidence, generating insight, and public knowledge sharing. In exploring each, explicit connections will be made between SoTL and MAPs in relation to each defining feature. Three examples will be carried throughout to illustrate different possibilities for SoTL and MAPs at each step.

Ethical Considerations around MAP Data and SoTL

Ethical considerations are a crucial part of all SoTL research endeavors and projects that incorporate MAP feedback are certainly no exception since they will involve collecting and analyzing data from human subjects. Before students' MAP feedback is incorporated in a SoTL project, the researchers must consider both broad ethical issues as well as related practical tasks that may be necessary to secure Institutional Review Board (IRB) approval. This section will first discuss three key ethical concerns discussed in Bishop-Clark and Dietz-Uhler (2012) and McKinney (2007): informed consent, privacy, and protection from harm. Then it will cover implications for IRB review based on these issues as they relate to MAPs.

Informed consent refers to a research participant's right to know about the nature of the study they are joining as well as its potential risks, benefits, consequences, and use of results. Potential subjects must have a clear and complete understanding of the study in order to give them the information they need to make a decision about whether to participate or not. Further, they must be able to make this decision free from any pressure to participate; in other words, declining to take part must not negatively impact their lives in any way (Bishop-Clark & Dietz-Uhler, 2012; McKinney, 2007). In terms of MAP data, this means students must be made aware prior to participating in the MAP process that their feedback may be used in a research study, and they must be given the option to decline to be included in the study, while still being allowed to participate in the MAP if they so desire. In addition, there should be no penalty to them in terms of their progress in the course should they opt out of either aspect. Given the power relationships in the classroom, it will be especially crucial for instructors to reinforce to students that there will not be any repercussions should they choose not to participate. Because the MAP process is typically facilitated by an ED, this adds an additional layer of protection for students because they will share their decision whether to participate with an external representative rather than directly with their instructor. For MAPs that will be included in a research project, the ED should (1) work with the instructor to ensure IRB approval is received prior to the MAP process, (2) gain clarity on the particular IRB requirements regarding assent or consent for that project from the instructor, and (3) incorporate those requirements in their data collection processes when they gather student feedback. It should be noted that the requirements for documenting informed consent may vary by institution from passive assent to more specific requirements for positive consent, so it will be up to the ED and the instructor to ensure this information is clearly communicated and incorporated in the facilitation of the MAP.

Ensuring privacy means that participants' identities should not be linked to research data collected about their perceptions or performance (Bishop-Clark & Dietz-Uhler, 2012; McKinney, 2007). In the case of MAPs, it is typical for student feedback to be anonymous as a standard component of the activity. For example, at the researchers' institution, students handwrite their comments and do not add their names to their comment sheet. The consultant then types up the comments before sharing them with the instructor. It is also emphasized to students during the facilitation of the MAP that their identities will not be linked in any way to their comments, so they should feel confident in being candid in their feedback. Thus, depending on the institution's particular approach to MAPs, privacy is likely already be built into the process. If it is not, students should be made clearly aware of this prior to giving consent or assent to participate.

Protection from harm refers to the obligation to protect participants from any harm that might arise due to the research, be it physical, emotional, or social (Bishop-Clark & Dietz-Uhler, 2012; McKinney, 2007). Students are unlikely to experience physical harm related to SoTL context; it is incumbent upon instructors and EDs to ensure emotional and social harm are minimized as well. For MAPs data, this can be primarily averted by adhering to the needs for informed consent and privacy as noted above. If students are able to freely decide whether to participate, and if their MAP feedback comments are kept anonymous, the likelihood of adverse social or emotional consequences should be minimal. To further protect students, it may be advisable for the ED to hold onto the informed consent documentation until final grades for the semester have been entered as an extra layer of protection against harm, as this will prevent the possibility of even unconscious bias in grading by the instructor based on whether a student participated.

Because IRB requirements may vary by institution, it is difficult to make specific recommendations about preparing IRB submissions that include collecting and analyzing MAP data. At the authors' institution, such submissions would likely qualify for exempt or expedited review, which generally involve a shorter application and review period, and may cover several semesters without needing to gain new approval each semester. It would be beneficial for EDs to have familiarity with IRB requirements at their own institution and even to develop sample language around MAP data collection and analysis to support instructors who plan to incorporate it in their research (and thus, in their IRB submission).

OVERVIEW OF THE FOUR DEFINING FEATURES OF SoTL

Given SoTL's breadth of scope, it can be helpful to have a basic framework to organize the activities associated with engagement in it. Huber & Hutchings (2005) propose four defining features of SoTL: framing questions, gathering evidence, generating insight, and sharing knowledge publicly. These features serve as the structure of the next sections of the chapter and provide a roadmap for understanding how MAPs can integrate with SoTL research.

1. **Framing questions**. This initial step is crucial to the success of a SoTL project. Without an interesting question, the resulting insights may be flat and inconsequential. This section discusses how the MAPs process can be used as a recruiting tool to introduce faculty to SoTL and the types of SoTL questions that can help them translate their innate interest in teaching into actionable research projects.

2. **Gathering evidence**. This section addresses the role of MAPs in capturing formative feedback from students as a source of evidence for SoTL, as well as working with faculty to see MAPs data as credible and significant, to gain facility working with qualitative data, and to identify other types of data to use in conjunction with MAPs feedback.

3. **Generating insight**. Once underway, SoTL projects exist within the dynamic and often messy context of the classroom. This state of flux is both where and how insight emerges, and educational developers involved in MAPs can support faculty by helping them choose a suitable research ap-

proach for this context, by providing an external checkpoint for data collection, and by acting as a supportive sounding board.

4. **Sharing knowledge publicly**. It is through public sharing and review that SoTL endeavors enter into the realm of scholarship. This section will discuss opportunities for public sharing, including a range of opportunities beyond traditional publications, that educational developers can consider in order to support SoTL researchers involved in MAPs.

Defining Feature #1: Framing Questions

Research is only as meaningful as the questions it attempts to ask and answer; thus, as with all research endeavors, question-framing is crucial to the success of SoTL projects. Question-framing, or questioning, is the first of the four defining features of SoTL. Even though the four defining features do not have to occur in a linear manner, asking questions usually constitutes the first important entry point when it comes to turning a faculty member's own teaching into scholarly research projects (Huber & Hutchins 2005).

In this section, we will examine what question framing can entail in the context of formative mid-semester assessments that can inform future SoTL projects among faculty. In order to make the discussion less abstract, one specific example that stems from a common MAP finding will help to frame the discussion on (1) the types of questions that are relevant and meaningful to SoTL; (2) approaches that educational developers can use to introduce question framing for SoTL during consultations, to gauge instructors' interests for SoTL, and to provide feedback on the types of questions that may be fruitful for SoTL research; and (3) introducing question framing at the departmental or institutional level.

MAPs as a Recruitment Tool for Faculty Who Already Have a SoTL Mindset

MAPs consultations are a natural context for introducing individual instructors to SoTL as a field of inquiry and discourse while also helping them identify potential research questions that are relevant to this discourse. Because many faculty members are already engaged in disciplinary research, this prior experience can serve as a bridge to understanding how these skills can be shifted to structure inquiries around teaching and learning. In addition, educational developers can use the broad knowledge they have gained to connect with leadership at the department or institutional level. They can also leverage their professional network to identify potential collaborators for research questions that would benefit from cooperative efforts within or across departments or the institution.

One tenet of question framing within SoTL is that instructors have an innate desire or curiosity to learn more about and understand their students' learning, which in turn will inspire the types of questions that they will be asking. Even though faculty have been trained to ask questions within their field of expertise, they often have not been exposed to the same approach when it comes to their own teaching. Many instructors, especially at typical research institutions, have received little pedagogical background training even though teaching is a crucial component of their job besides research and service: "it is worth remembering that teaching is not, for most academics, an arena in which they have developed (or received training to inculcate) habits and skills of inquiry" (Huber & Hutchings, 2005, p. 23). Faculty who are already actively engaged in SoTL research have an innate curiosity about student learning and teaching; faculty who participate in mid-semester assessments and meet with educational developers to develop strategies for improving learning in their class also are committed to excellence in teaching. Consequently, educational developers who facilitate mid-semester feedback are in the unique position to have access to and reach out to faculty who are already invested in good teaching practices as indicated by their commitment to self-enroll in a MAP. The educational developer can assist faculty to implement evidence-based teaching practices rooted in student feedback; they can likewise support faculty in developing the necessary habits and skills of inquiry necessary to engage with SoTL. MAPs can provide conversational space for faculty to ask questions about what is going on in the classroom, how can it be investigated, and how their question framing can adhere to research standards that they would apply to their research projects in their own field of inquiry.

Types of SoTL Questions That Align With MAPs

Educational developers can either use MAPs as a starting point to recruit instructors who care about teaching and use their existing MAP data as a foundation for question framing or inspire instructors to start asking questions that go beyond the suggestions that were given by students and spark their own ideas. Hutchings (2000) suggests the following overarching taxonomy of questions that are appropriate for the Scholarship of Teaching and Learning in general and also apply to common formative student feedback categories: "what works?" questions, which center around the effectiveness of teaching practices; "what is?" questions, which can either assess prior student learning or describe current pedagogical approaches *without* evaluating them; and "vision of the possible" questions, which imagine taking pedagogical approaches into new territories with the goal to expand the students' learning in new ways. In addition to these three broad questions that can categorize the types of question framing that is possible within SoTL, Hutchings (2000) also suggests a fourth, much broader category of theory building that contribute to SoTL by "formulating new conceptual frameworks" that add to SoTL from a theoretical perspective. These four inquiry questions included in Hutchings' taxonomy can help guide the concrete questions inspired by MAP feedback into more specific, researchable SoTL questions. The next section, MAPs and SoTL in practice, outlines possible questions that faculty might start asking based on their MAP feedback data rooted in examples from three different fields - English, computer science, and law.

MAPS AND SOTL IN PRACTICE

To illustrate how MAPs can guide faculty members through a SoTL research project, the aforementioned three examples—an adjunct English instructor teaching introductory composition courses online, a team of computer science instructors who flipped their classroom, and the law school who introduces a new format of testing—will be used to lay out how an educational developer might approach faculty to start looking at their own teaching with a new research lens and what SoTL questions they could start asking based on their MAP data.

Defining Feature #1: Framing Questions

- A crucial part of the online introductory composition classes in English is that the students stay motivated throughout the semester and implement the instructor's feedback of early drafts in order to successfully finish the final writing project. The first time she taught the class online the previous semester, she noticed that the final papers did not align with what she had envisioned, and students had failed to incorporate her suggestions, and that students had mentioned in her MAP that they felt unprepared for the final paper. An example of a research question she could pursue is:

- ○ *How does providing video feedback on assignments impact the quality of final papers?* (an example of a "what works" question) Moving forward, she could change the way she gives feedback on drafts and start providing video feedback in addition to written comments in one of her two sections of the class while she continues to provide only written feedback in the other section of the class in order to find out what form of feedback works better.

- The computer science team started implementing a flipped classroom structure in all of their introductory classes and want to find out how it affects their students' learning without directly prompting the student on feedback regarding the changed structure. Since the MAP questions are open-ended and focus on the overall learning experience, they want to see if and how students mention the flipped classroom approach. An example of asking questions about their teaching could be:
  - ○ *How do students navigate a flipped classroom experience, and what are common difficulties?* (an example of a "what is" question).

- The law school wants to change how their students are tested in their introductory courses and want to experiment with multiple low-stake assignments throughout the semester instead of having one single high-stakes exam at the end of the semester. Inquiry questions the department might want to pursue are:
  - ○ *What would happen if we changed the way our students are tested? How can we change assessments in a meaningful way that increase student motivation and retention?* (an example of a "vision of the possible" question).

These are only three in-practice examples instructors might start asking inspired by their MAP data on their pathway to SoTL research; however, the questions might change over time or become more clear further along as the project progresses and the instructor begins to gather evidence (defining feature #2) and to generate insight (defining feature #3).

Defining Feature #2: Gathering Evidence

Once faculty members have identified interesting and meaningful questions, the next logical step in the SoTL process is to begin to gather and explore evidence around these questions—the second defining feature of SoTL as outlined by Huber & Hutchings (2005). This section will explore the role of formative feedback from MAPs in evidence gathering for SoTL, and specific challenges that educational developers may encounter when working with faculty to incorporate MAPs into their SoTL project. It also provides examples of how mid-semester feedback can be used as a source of data in SoTL projects in the "MAPs & SoTL in Practice" subsection.

The MAP process can generate rich qualitative feedback directly from students about their perceptions of teaching and learning after several weeks of the course have elapsed. Drawing on the research literature and confirmed by the authors' collective experience with MAP consultations, student comments typically address (in no particular order) organization, communication, learning activities, instructional delivery, course materials, assignments, feedback, clarity, pacing, and relevance of the content (Blue et al., 2008; Sozer et al., 2019). Thus, MAP data will be best suited for questions that benefit from formative perception data relative to these components of the learning experience.

Even when an instructor has identified a question that is compatible with formative data around student perceptions, EDs may need to provide them with further support in understanding how MAPs data can be useful to their SoTL project. Some potential challenges include:

- Recognition of MAP data as being credible and significant
- Expertise in using qualitative data
- Knowledge of research methodologies that incorporate formative data
- Integration of MAP data with other sources of evidence

Credibility and Significance of MAPs Data

Huber & Hutchings (2005) rightfully point out that faculty judgements about the credibility and significance of research evidence may depend on the home discipline and/or research experience of the individual faculty member. Those from disciplines with primarily quantitative research traditions, such as the natural sciences, might come to the process with mindsets that value large sample sizes and objective data. On the other hand, disciplines that utilize qualitative data more frequently, such as the humanities, may already value the types of feedback associated with MAPs. For the social sciences and education, there are research traditions associated with both types of data, as well as mixed methods research that integrates qualitative and quantitative data. It will be the educational developer's challenge to appreciate the unique expertise that the instructor brings to the table from their field and meet faculty where they are in terms of their own research backgrounds. This will allow educational developers to provide meaningful guidance to faculty in understanding how MAPs data may act as an important data source for their project.

Expertise in Using Qualitative Data

One strategy for meeting challenges around credibility and significance may be to support faculty who don't typically use qualitative data to improve their expertise in using this type of evidence. Because MAP data is typically coded by an educational developer prior to sharing it with the instructor as described previously in this chapter, it may be possible for a SoTL project to use data as it was coded by the CTL's educational developer; in these cases, it may be helpful for the educational developer to share the research that guides the MAP coding process for that CTL. In the case of the authors' CTL, we rely on Chickering and Gamson's (1987) principles for good practice in undergraduate instruction as the basis for our coding approach. The pre-MAP consultation could serve as an important opportunity to share the CTL's rationale to data coding and possibly work with the faculty member to develop a coding approach that is customized to their SoTL project when appropriate. Finally, for faculty who may want to use individual approaches to coding their raw student feedback, the educational developer should be prepared to provide references around qualitative data analysis that faculty could use to develop their skills.

Integrating MAP Data With Other Forms of Evidence

It is important to recognize that student feedback collected during MAPs is one source of information that can (and likely should) be integrated with other evidence for most research projects. Thus, educational developers should be prepared to suggest other potential sources of data to faculty. Both McKinney (2007) and Bishop-Clark and Dietz-Uhler (2012) identify a variety of data that could be used in SoTL, including interviews, focus groups, observations, surveys, or interviews; student work (including tests, quizzes, reflective writing, projects or other assignments) is also a potential source of evidence. Obviously, given the range of options, it is not possible to compare MAPs data to them all. However, it will be important for instructors (and their partners in the CTL) to develop a logical strategy for data collection, with a clear rationale for each data source and its relationship to the research questions and other evidence gathered. As the example data sources suggest, it is quite possible that a MAPS-driven SoTL project will involve both qualitative data (at a minimum, the student feedback from the mid-semester assessment) along with quantitative data (i.e., numeric data, perhaps from surveys or assignment grades). As always, the research questions will drive the types of evidence necessary to arrive at meaningful answers. It is quite possible, and perhaps even preferable, to integrate both types of data in order to generate richer findings. Mixed-methods research design is an established approach to integrating qualitative and quantitative data collection, analysis, and integrate with the goal of improving both the scope and detail of research insights (Creswell, 2014; Johnson, Onwuegbuzie, & Turner, 2007).

MAPs and SoTL in Practice

- The adjunct English instructor might feel comfortable working with students' written MAPs feedback, given her academic background, but have less experience collecting and analyzing data in the context of SoTL. The educational developer could support this instructor by explaining how formative MAPs feedback might fit with other sources of evidence, such as summative assessment of student writing before and after feedback, as well as pre- and post-surveys of student attitudes about feedback.

- The computer science instructors are already gathering data around student interaction with online resources for the flipped classroom, but are unsure of the value of MAPs data as a source of credible evidence for their SoTL project. The educational developer's job here is to help these faculty connect formative MAPs data to the quantitative analytics they are already gathering in order to see the value of the relationship. For example, they are collecting data on student interactions with online videos; they could then use MAPs data to learn more about student perceptions that might illuminate that objective behavioral data.

- The law school leadership team already gathers data around first year law courses for program assessment purposes and they want to begin collecting MAPs data to gain more insight into how their assessment approach is experienced by students. At the same time, they are not sure how to incorporate large amounts of qualitative MAPs data into with the objective data they collect already. The educational developer's job in this case is to help the law school team develop strategies for coding and analyzing as well as documenting and integrating the insights they gain from it.

Defining Feature #3: Refining Insights

The first two defining features (framing questions and gathering evidence) were largely concerned with the planning and decision-making aspects of MAPs—SoTL projects—the tasks that must be completed before launching into the messy, shifting, and exciting tumult associated with the actual context and events of learning (Huber & Hutchings, 2005). It is here that many faculty may be confronted with the reality that typical research approaches don't always translate to the classroom—it is difficult if not impossible to exert clear and consistent control over variables, influences, and actions amidst the bustling environment of teaching and learning. Many other faculty members may find themselves in the strange position of being an active participant in an unfolding research project, when they are more used to being a dispassionate observer on the outside looking in. Furthermore, the demands of teaching and discipline-specific research once a semester is underway may end up pushing SoTL projects to the back burner. This section will outline three key ways that educational developers can use MAPs to contribute to successful outcomes for faculty in relation to this aspect of SoTL:

- Identifying research frameworks that incorporate formative data
- Positioning MAPs as an external checkpoint for data collection
- Providing a supportive sounding board for the MAPs—SoTL researcher

Research Frameworks that Incorporate Formative Data

Faculty may also face a knowledge gap around research frameworks that incorporate formative data as a core component of the research process. Again, it will be important for the educational developer to understand the disciplinary research experience that instructors will bring to the MAPs—SoTL experience in order to help them identify how formative data will fit into their methodology strategies. Relevant approaches include action research (Bradbury, 2015) as well as developmental research and formative research (see Wang & Hannafin, 2005, for overviews), as these are all centered around developing knowledge and insight in the context of real-world problem-solving and thus benefit from formative data to improve outcomes.

Design-based research (DBR) emerged in 2003, has become increasingly recognized as a useful framework for research on teaching and learning, and may be particularly well-suited to MAPs—SoTL projects (Anderson & Shattuck, 2012; Design-Based Research Collective [DBRC], 2003; Wang & Hannafin, 2005). It is characterized by being pragmatically linked to real-world contexts; grounded in theory and practice; interactive, iterative and flexible; integrative; and contextual (DBRC, 2003; Wang & Hannafin, 2005, pg. 8). In other words, DBR is a context-bound investigation of a problem through repeated attempts to design a solution to that problem – an approach that may be naturally appealing to many SoTL scholars.

It is driven by and contributes to both theory and practice, while relying on an integrative and eclectic approach to data collection and analysis over iterations of an intervention. Thus, it is well-suited approach for the rich, dynamic, and evolving nature of contextual research on teaching and learning, as well as providing a framework for ensuring resulting insights contribute to both academic discourse and practitioner knowledge. Educational developers may be better positioned to support faculty if they have some understanding of DBR and the other research approaches mentioned and if they are prepared with strategies for introducing them during MAPs consultations for faculty who show interest in conducting MAPs--SoTL projects. (Anderson & Shattuck, 2012; DBRC, 2003; and Wang & Hannafin, 2005, are all good starting points for gaining foundational knowledge of DBR and its potential role in MAPs—SoTL research.)

Positioning MAPs as an External Checkpoint for Data Collection

The goal of this task is simple but essential: the educational developer should highlight that MAPs are an easy way for faculty to lean on an external program to serve as a checkpoint for data collection (and possibly data analysis) for their SoTL process. Because MAPs are typically an institution-wide service provided every semester by a CTL, there is no extra burden on either side to incorporate a MAPs consultation for formative evidence gathering. This may relieve faculty to know that at least one element of data collection is accounted for and will be managed largely by someone else; likewise, for projects that will be using MAPs data as it is coded by the educational developer, a portion of the data analysis will be handled by an outside supporter as well. Having a natural checkpoint such as this may also help instructors revisit other aspects of their MAPs—SoTL research simply by bringing the project into the foreground again.

Providing a Supportive Sounding Board for the MAPs—SoTL Researcher

As mentioned previously, some faculty may be unfamiliar with the active role they will be taking in the research context when they undertake a MAPs—SoTL project. They are not on the outside looking in, but rather in the fray alongside their participants. This presents a unique challenge in that the instructor needs to reflect on and consider their standpoint within the research embedded into the context that they are researching. This can be both challenging and energizing—in either case, it is helpful to have an objective yet supportive ally who can serve as a knowledgeable confident and sounding board as faculty explore these aspects of their MAPs—SoTL research experience. MAPs consultations provide a natural opportunity for educational developers to introduce the possibility of serving as a sounding board for instructors engaged in research; ideally, as a collegial relationship grows, the faculty member may feel comfortable reaching out to the educational developer outside of scheduled MAPs consultations. This underscores the potential value of a trusting and open relationship with faculty, one that is both open to learning yet respectful of boundaries, in order to support their goals around teaching and scholarship.

MAPs and SoTL in Practice

- The adjunct English instructor teaches several sections of introductory writing and also works part-time at another job while searching for a tenure-track position. She is busy and finds it difficult to make time for research activities. The MAPs process offers a built-in, external data collection strategy that will take up no more than a few hours of her time while providing her with rich feedback for her study.
- The computer science instructors are planning to refine their flipped classroom over several semesters, so the ED can work with these instructors to gain an understanding of DBR and its connection to mixed-methods research using formative data.
- The law school leadership team has developed and implemented a coding strategy to help manage formative MAPs feedback from all of their first-year students. However, they ask the educational developer to review their progress and act as an external reviewer for those feedback items that are challenging to code. The ED's expertise in teaching and learning can help keep the research process focused and in alignment with SoTL discourse.

Defining Feature #4: Sharing Knowledge Publicly

The last core practice of SoTL constitutes the sharing of knowledge or "going public" (Huber & Hutchings, 2005; McKinney, 2007), since one goal of the field is to open classroom doors that have previously been closed and not only start the conversation around teaching in higher education but also to share knowledge in a way that enables other faculty to continue with the shared goal to improve the academy. In the context of scholarship that is rooted in MAPs, it can either be propelled by individual instructors or can be initiated on the institutional level (through CTLs, departments, or at the university level). Additionally, since both teaching and research are part of tenure requirements, faculty can turn something they already have to do (teaching) into disciplinary research and contribute to SoTL.

Avenues for sharing knowledge and "going public" with lessons learned can be formal or informal and can range from traditional forms of knowledge sharing such as peer-reviewed publications or conference presentations, to other forms of going public such as departmental brown bags, or podcasts and blogs. As these examples illustrate, possible avenues of knowledge-sharing, even though they can take more creative formats, have at its core to "recognize teaching as serious intellectual work" (Huber, 2004) and share insights gained with people in their field.

In the context of MAPs, one pathway of knowledge sharing that lends itself to a first avenue for new SoTL researchers is their home base: their own campus community. Learning communities and brown bags either within departments or across disciplines are ideal outlets for SoTL knowledge-sharing since they are both aimed at improving teaching practices and at the lively exchange of ideas surrounding pedagogy with colleagues who share the goal of successful student learning at their own institution. Events like this can be facilitated by CTLs or can be faculty-led; they can be recurring events or intermittent; they can take a structured format of a formal presentation or they can be open-ended forums with the goal of generating even more ideas for researchable SoTL projects. Despite the variability of *how* knowledge can be shared, they all have in common that insights gained and lessons learned based on SoTL research will be shared publicly, allowing attendees to ask questions and to learn from SoTL research and to possibly implement strategies into their own teaching, and to also provide valuable feedback to faculty to then improve their SoTL research.

Potential avenues of knowledge-sharing of SoTL work might also be discipline-specific and McKinney (2007) suggests publications, presentations, and web postings as outlets to "go public" that go beyond the campus community and are exposed to a peer review process.

Taken together, the four core elements of SoTL research, framing questions, gathering evidence, refining insights, and finally, public knowledge sharing oftentimes are not linear and a straight-forward process but can also be iterative in nature.

MAPs and SoTL in Practice

Besides sharing their SoTL work internally through departmental or university-wide events, the following outlets could be used to "go public":

- The adjunct English instructor could publish her findings that resulted from incorporating video feedback in her online classes and her analysis of how it affects student's performance in their final papers in a discipline-specific teaching journal.

- The team of computer science instructors could share their key take-aways from switching from traditional lecture-style courses to a flipped-classroom via web postings such as a blog-post, including mistakes made to avoid and other recommendations for instructors who also consider switching to a flipped classroom.
- The law school leadership team could present their lessons learned from making changes to the commonly used assessment structure—changing from one-time high-stakes exams to multiple exams that are low-stakes—at a conference with colleagues from the same field. They could also engage the audience in a discussion about the implications that changing the culture of examination might have for the future of their field.

MOVING FORWARD: STRATEGIES FOR EDUCATIONAL DEVELOPERS AND CENTERS FOR TEACHING AND LEARNING (CTL)

Using MAPs as a stepping stone to reach out to faculty and to actively recruit them for SoTL purposes entails both opportunities and challenges for educational developers and CTLs. Educational developers in teaching CTLs are uniquely positioned to use their role as facilitators of a program that occurs once a semester, the mid-semester assessment program, to not only help an individual instructor to reflect on their teaching practice but to go further and to build bridges between teaching practices in other disciplines and the Scholarship of Teaching and Learning. Educational developers have the unique opportunity to recruit faculty and to mobilize departments who would not have considered conducting research in the realm of teaching and learning. What are some strategies that can be employed to overcome moving forward?

Starting a Mid-Semester Assessment Program

While some universities might already have a mid-semester assessment program in place that allows faculty to gather formative student feedback, other institutions might not offer a program yet that supports this form of faculty teaching development. If you are interested in starting a mid-semester assessment program, either facilitated by the university's CTL or organized by faculty, consider this resource to help you get started:

- Payette, P. R., & Brown, M. K. (2018). Gathering mid-semester feedback: Three variations to improve instruction. *IDEA Paper #67.*

Building Educational Developers' Capacity for SoTL Research

Educational developers might face the challenge to become more explicit about what SoTL actually entails, translate our mission to instructors from other fields that have signature pedagogies, intrigue other professionals to become interested and invested in SoTL by providing them with easily accessible ideas and resources, and finally, to make an impact across disciplines.

Educational developers will also be better prepared to support SoTL research in general by developing research expertise; Creswell (2014) is a good starting point for a broad overview of quantitative, qualitative, and mixed-methods research. Specific to using MAPs data in SoTL, familiarity with action research (Bradbury, 2015) and design-based research (DBRC, 2003; Wang & Hannafin, 2005) might be valuable knowledge as well. Finally, Flick (2013) is a good starting point for developing knowledge of qualitative data coding and analysis.

Besides ensuring that educational developers have the necessary resources and training to assist faculty on their SoTL endeavors, establishing relationships with faculty and researchers to support collaboration and spread the word about MAPs and SoTL is crucial for successful future SoTL projects. CTLs have to be conscious about the time and resources that are necessary for both training educational developers and to collaborate with faculty to recruit and guide them for their SoTL research.

Building the Center for Teaching and Learning's (CTL) Capacity for SoTL Research

In order to be successful in using MAPs to spark and contribute to SoTL projects, CTLs will need to allot time and resources for educational developers to work on developing SoTL expertise as described above. Incorporating programming around SoTL for faculty (learning communities, workshops, institutes, on-demand resources, public sharing opportunities) is another important approach for demonstrating the CTL's commitment to SoTL endeavors.

In order to model the value of SoTL at the organizational level, CTLs can engage in SoTL research specifically around their own MAP program. The authors are currently collaborating with colleagues in institutional research at our university to investigate the impact of participation in MAPs with student and faculty outcomes, as one example. This underscores our next point, to seek partnerships at the departmental and institutional level in order to spread the word about SoTL and its value to their missions around teaching and learning by moving beyond reporting to research.

Finally, advocating for the value of SoTL to hiring, tenure, and promotion decisions is a crucial, yet potentially challenging, component to increasing SoTL capacity in faculty. In the increasingly competitive context of higher education, faculty must be confident that their SoTL work will help them move closer to their professional goals.

REFERENCES

Anderson, T., & Shattuck, J. (2012). Design-based research: A decade of progress in education research? *Educational Researcher, 41*(1), 16–25. doi:10.3102/0013189X11428813

Bishop-Clark, C., & Dietz-Uhler, B. (2012). *Engaging in the Scholarship of Teaching and Learning: A guide to the process, and how to develop a project from start to finish.* Sterling, VA: Stylus Publishing, LLC.

Blue, J., Wentzell, G. W., & Evins, M. J. (2008). What do students want? Small group instructional diagnoses of STEM faculty. *Proceedings of the 2014 Physics Education Research Conference*, 43-46.

Bradbury, H. (Ed.). (2015). *The Sage handbook of action research.* Thousand Oaks, CA: Sage Publications. doi:10.4135/9781473921290

Chickering, A. W., & Gamson, Z. F. (1987). Seven principles for good practice in undergraduate education. *AAHE Bulletin, 3,* 7.

Clark, D., & Redmond, M. (1982). *Small group instructional diagnosis: Final report*. ERIC Document Reproduction Service No. ED217954.

Creswell, J. W. (2014). *Research design: Qualitative, quantitative, and mixed methods approaches*. Thousand Oaks, CA: Sage Publications.

Design-Based Research Collective. (2003). Design-based research: An emerging paradigm for educational inquiry. *Educational Researcher, 32*(1), 5–8. doi:10.3102/0013189X032001005

Diamond, M. R. (2004). The usefulness of structured mid-term feedback as a catalyst for change in higher education classes. *Active Learning in Higher Education, 5*(3), 217–231. doi:10.1177/1469787404046845

Finelli, C. J., Pinder-Grover, T., & Wright, M. C. (2011). Consultations on teaching: Using student feedback for instructional improvement. In C. E. Cook & M. Kaplan (Eds.), *Advancing the culture of teaching on campus: How a teaching center can make a difference* (pp. 65–79). Sterling, VA: Stylus Publishers.

Flick, U. (Ed.). (2013). *The SAGE handbook of qualitative data analysis*. Thousand Oaks, CA: Sage Publications.

Hubball, H., Pearson, M. L., & Clarke, A. (2013). SoTL inquiry in broader curricular and institutional contexts: Theoretical underpinnings and emerging trends. *Teaching & Learning Inquiry, 1*(1), 41–57.

Huber, M. (2004). *Balancing acts: The Scholarship of Teaching and Learning in academic careers*. Washington, DC: American Association for Higher Education and the Carnegie Foundation for the Advancement of Teaching.

Huber, M., & Hutchings, P. (2005). *The advancement of learning: Building the teaching commons*. San Francisco, CA: Jossey-Bass.

Hutchings, P. (2000). Introduction: Approaching the Scholarship of Teaching and Learning. In P. Hutchings (Ed.), *Opening lines: Approaches to the Scholarship of Teaching and Learning* (pp. 1–10). Menlo Park, CA: The Carnegie Foundation for the Advancement of Teaching.

Johnson, R. B., Onwuegbuzie, A. J., & Turner, L. A. (2007). Toward a definition of mixed methods research. *Journal of Mixed Methods Research, 1*(2), 112–133. doi:10.1177/1558689806298224

McKinney, K. (2004). The Scholarship of Teaching and Learning: Past lessons, current challenges, and future visions. *To Improve the Academy, 22*, 3-19.

McKinney, K. (2007). *Enhancing learning through the Scholarship of Teaching and Learning: The challenges and joys of juggling*. San Francisco, CA: Jossey-Bass.

Payette, P. R., & Brown, M. K. (2018). Gathering mid-semester feedback: Three variations to improve instruction. *IDEA Paper #67*.

Snooks, M. K., Neeley, S. E., & Williamson, K. M. (2004), 7: From SGID and GIFT to BBQ: Streamlining midterm student evaluations to improve teaching and learning. *To Improve the Academy, 22*, 110-124.

Sozer, E. M., Zeybekoglu, Z., & Kaya, M. (2019). Using mid-semester course evaluation as a feedback tool for improving learning and teaching in higher education. *Assessment & Evaluation in Higher Education*, 1–14.

Veeck, A., O'Reilly, K., MacMillan, A., & Yu, H. (2016). The use of collaborative midterm student evaluations to provide actionable results. *Journal of Marketing Education*, *38*(3), 157–169. doi:10.1177/0273475315619652

Wang, F., & Hannafin, M. J. (2005). Design-based research and technology-enhanced learning environments. *Educational Technology Research and Development*, *53*(4), 5–23. doi:10.1007/BF02504682

Chapter 11

At the Crossroads of Transformative Learning and SoTL:
The Flipped Classroom in Teacher Education

Rachel C. Plews
iD https://orcid.org/0000-0001-6194-218X
Haute école pédagogique du canton de Vaud, Switzerland

Moira Laffranchini Ngoenha
Haute école pédagogique du canton de Vaud, Switzerland

ABSTRACT

This chapter explores the ongoing collaboration between an educational developer and a faculty member at a university of teacher education in Switzerland as an inquiry into one's teaching practice to improve the implementation of the flipped classroom approach. Through the lens of transformative learning theory, the chapter examines how SoTL can serve as faculty enrichment in addition to an approach for systematic reflection on practice. Special attention is paid to the role of the educational developer as a mentor throughout the inquiry. The chapter concludes with practical strategies for developing a productive SoTL relationship between educational developers and faculty member, as well as visibility across an institution.

INTRODUCTION

The Scholarship of Teaching and Learning (SoTL) is a form of inquiry "in student learning that informs and enhances teaching practice, and therefore improves student learning" (Fanghanel, 2013, p.59). As a form of professional development, SoTL aims to engage faculty members in discussions about their

DOI: 10.4018/978-1-7998-2212-7.ch011

inquiries with the potential to better understand their teaching and student learning in higher education. When thinking about pedagogical innovation, SoTL can be a useful methodology to monitor and evaluate the changes initiated as the process involves cycles of reflection and experimentation. The flipped classroom presents itself as one of these pedagogical innovations as faculty members are challenged to think differently about the time and spaces used for learning to make students more active in their learning, resulting in more profound knowledge (Farmer, 2018). Pedagogical innovations are a catalyst to launch the discussion on SoTL, as these innovations serve to challenge previously held views and assumptions through the literature and research into one's practice.

At the University of Teacher Education of the Canton of Vaud, one of the primary roles of the Center for Teaching Support is to promote and support the Scholarship of Teaching and Learning throughout the institution. The faculty development team is in place to collaborate at different levels - to open the discussions about the significance of inquiry into one's teaching practice, to assist with the development of the inquiry, to accompany the faculty member throughout the inquiry, and to help promote exchange around the inquiry. At the start of the work together, the faculty developer and the faculty member work together to define the objectives of the work together, as well as the roles of each involved, which can evolve as the project does.

This chapter aims to explore a practical example of this collaboration between an educational developer and a faculty member engaging in a SoTL initiative on the flipped classroom approach. The chapter begins with an integrative literature review of three domains – the Scholarship of Teaching and Learning, transformative learning theory, and pedagogical innovation/the flipped classroom. Next, an illustrative example of collaborative SoTL activity is shared from both the perspectives of the educational developer and the faculty member. This example is aligned with the theory of transformative learning. Finally, the chapter concludes with practical recommendations for fostering successful SoTL collaborations.

BACKGROUND

The Scholarship of Teaching and Learning (SoTL)

In his book *Scholarship Reconsidered: Priorities of the Professoriate*, Ernest Boyer (1990) proposed a new paradigm of scholarship, comprised of four key areas – the scholarship of discovery (new scientific knowledge), the scholarship of integration (making connections across disciplines), the scholarship of application (relating theory to practice), and the scholarship of teaching (preparing for the future classroom). This last domain evolved into the Scholarship of Teaching and Learning (SoTL) to address not only teaching practices but also student learning. SoTL, as well as the other forms of scholarship, can be measured by six standards: "clear goals, appropriate procedures, adequate resources, effective communication, significant results, and careful and thoughtful self-critique" (Boyer, 1996, p.135). When engaging in SoTL, the aim is to look back at one's teaching practice and move forward with a change to improve one's practice.

O'Brien (2008) presented SoTL as an "invitation to look closely into pedagogical practice and to engage deeply in evidence-based analysis of how our students learn effectively" (p.1). The overall aim is to deepen student learning, improve teaching, and advance teaching practice through the exploration of what works, or what doesn't work. The four distinct attributes of SoTL activity are a concern for students and their learning; the presence of a deliberate design for how teaching and learning can move forward with these concerns in mind; the systematic implementation, analysis, and evaluation of the design also linking back to the original interest; and contribution to SoTL knowledge and practice (O'Brien, 2008). To begin working on a SoTL activity, O'Brien presented the SoTL Compass with four guiding questions:

1.   What will my students learn, and why is it worth learning?
2.   Who are my students, and how do students learn effectively?
3.   What can I do to support students to learn effectively?
4.   How do I know if my teaching and my students' learning have been effective?

To further develop the practice of SoTL, Bélise, Lison, and Bédard (2016) presented a cycle identifying the phases of a SoTL inquiry. Figure 1 shows these phases beginning with the analysis of one's practice. This phases, combined with the second phase of knowledge acquisition (theoretical and practice-based), permits focus on a particular aspect of teaching and learning, and identification of the changes that will lead to deeper student learning, improved teaching, or advancement in practice (O'Brien, 2008). After the change is planned, it is implemented into the teaching practice. Finally, there are four ways to evaluate the change, which correspond to Boyer's six criteria presented earlier in this section – self-evaluation, peer evaluation, student evaluations of teaching, and external observations from those familiar with the faculty member's work (Boyer, 1996; Bélise, Lison, & Bédard, 2016). The final phase is to share the results of the inquiry. The sharing can be done at different levels—locally, within national networks, and internationally.

Figure 1. Phases of a SoTL inquiry
adapted from Bélise, Lison, & Bédard (2016)

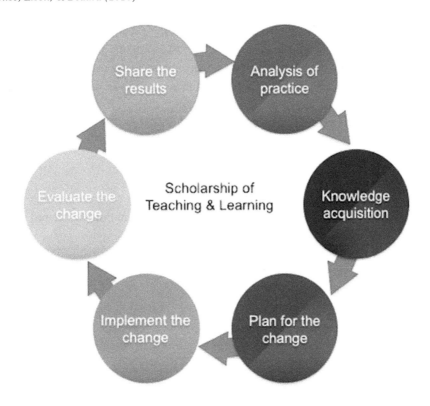

Transformative Learning Theory (TLT)

Transformative learning theory (TLT) is the process by which previously uncritically related assumptions, beliefs, values, and perspectives are questioned and thereby become more open, permeable, and better validated (Cranton, 2000; Mezirow, 2000). The three themes that facilitate transformative learning include the centrality of the personal experience, critical reflection on the experience, and rational discourse as a means of learning. Individuals make meaning of the world through experiences, filtered by their frames of reference, or the web of assumptions and expectations through which they move through their experiences (Mezirow, 1991). When something new or unexpected is encountered, they can choose to either reject the new information or to question their previously-held assumptions.

Central to critical reflection is the recognition that one's previously-held views no longer fit; they are too narrow and limiting (Mezirow, 1991). This is not about suggesting that one's beliefs are right or wrong, but more about being open to new perspectives. Mezirow (1991, 1997) describes three types of reflection: (1) content reflection, or what has occurred, (2) process reflection, or how this happened and how I think this way, and (3) premise reflection, reflecting on the importance of experience. Not all reflection leads to transformative learning, but it is most likely in premise reflection, actively questioning the validity of our assumptions underlying how we see the world.

Discourse is the process of individuals engaging in dialogue to help them make meaning of an experience (Mezirow, 2000; Cranton, 2008). Reflective discourse within the domain of transformative learning has the objective of identifying a common understanding surrounding an interpretation or a belief. Ideal conditions that facilitate discourse include the availability of accurate and complete information, freedom from coercion, openness to alternative points of view, an ability to take an objective standpoint, an awareness of the context of ideas, equitable opportunity to participate in the discourse, and an overall willingness to seek understanding and agreement.

From a more practical perspective, Daloz (2000) viewed the goal of transformative learning as lifelong personal development. The teacher's role is that of a mentor, someone who guides, challenges, encourages, and supports the learner. Daloz presented that discourse is practiced through story-telling, and both the mentor and the learner learn from this mutual story-telling in the areas of adult development, cognitive growth, and intellectual and ethical development.

Transformative learning is presented in the following 10 phases (Mezirow, 2000):

- A disorienting dilemma
- Self-examination
- A critical assessment of one's assumptions
- Recognition that one's discontent and the process of transformation are shared
- Exploration of new roles, relationships, and actions
- Planning a course of action
- Acquiring knowledge and skills for implementing one's plans
- Provisionally trying out new roles
- Building competence and self-confidence in the new roles and relationships
- Reintegration into life with new perspectives

The Flipped Classroom

The driving forces behind pedagogical innovations are two-fold—the overall advancements of technology in society and the consistent and emerging challenges in higher education, including rising costs, accountability, and a push for innovations in research and practice with students at the center (Bishop & Verleger, 2013; Hutchings & Quinney, 2015). The flipped classroom, a popular pedagogical innovation in recent years, represents a shift in thinking about the use of time for teaching and learning. Knowledge transfer, traditionally what takes place during a face-to-face lecture, now occurs before coming to class, with the class time used for activities requiring higher level thinking skills (Hutchings & Quinney, 2015; Farmer, 2018). By replacing the lecture with activities, there is more time for interaction between the teacher and the student, and also among the students themselves (Roehl, Reddy, & Shannon, 2015; Little, 2015; O'Flaherty & Phillips, 2015).

The Flipped Learning Network (2014) describes the flipped classroom as the methods and strategies that the teacher puts in place but flipped learning as an expansion of this concept to increase the involvement of the students. This network presents the four pillars of flipped learning: (1) Flexible environment, (2) Learning culture, (3) Intentional content, and (4) Professional Educator; the acronym FLIP is used for this process. The flexible environment means that students can decide when and where to learn, and educators work on scaffolding the learning and assessment. The learning culture is one that is student-centered, as opposed to teacher-centered. The intentional content refers to the teacher deciding what resources and materials students can use to learn on their own, and subsequently, what resources and activities will be used in class to maximize the time together. Finally, the professional educator refers to the increased demands on the teacher when implementing the flipped classroom, providing ongoing support, continuous assessment, and interaction during the activities. There is the need to be more reflective in one's practice, both in the planning for and delivery of instruction.

While much of the literature focuses on the planning for the flipped classroom, there is also literature that explores teaching delivery when implementing the flipped classroom. Chen et al. (2014) critiqued the original FLIP model due to its focus on content planning, not on active delivery, its perspective from a teacher viewpoint only, and the lack of consideration of learning spaces and platforms, or more specifically the place for digital technologies in the implementation of the flipped classroom. Their work expanded the model by adding three additional pillars, resulting in a FLIPPED model. The original four pillars remained consistent, but the new dimensions were P—progressive networking activities, E—engaging and effective learner experiences, and D—diversified and seamless learning platforms. These additional elements focus on the learner and the space in which the learner works in and out of the classroom.

One of the critical aspects of successful implementation of the flipped classroom is the management of the transitions from out-of-class to in-class activities. Farmer (2018, p. 18) presented an approach to the flipped classroom differentiating the when, who, and how of knowledge transfer and knowledge assimilation. In between these two instructional phases, the teacher must gain an awareness of the student comprehension of the learning material before having them come to class through online activities to assess knowledge acquisition and basic comprehension. The approach showcases each student's work individually on structured tasks outside of the classroom before moving into working collaboratively on structured tasks, discussions, debates, and other activities during class. Students then go back to working on individually structured activity after class, where the focus can be reflective. This approach highlights the progression of the cognitive levels associated with the tasks in and out of class.

Figure 2. Adapted model of mentoring
(Daloz, 1999).

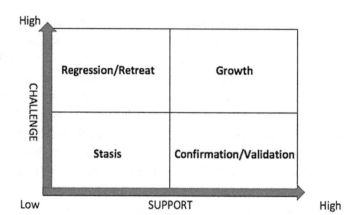

TRANSFORMATIVE LEARNING AND SoTL

The Role of the Educational Developer

During this collaboration, the role of the educational developer was to accompany the faculty member in a SoTL initiative, while also ensuring a cohesive professional development opportunity. Transformative Learning Theory served as the lens to guide this personal, professional development with the focus on reflection and broadening perspectives. The educational developer assumed the role of a mentor as described by Daloz (2000) with the focus on guiding the faculty member through the SoTL activities, challenging ideas and assumptions, supporting the faculty member throughout the process, and being a cheerleader, someone who consistently encourages inquiry and learning, as well as persistence. This idea challenges the paradigm of "the sage on the stage" to a new paradigm of "the guide on the side" (Daloz, 1999). Figure 2 shows the implications of finding the balance between challenge and support when mentoring.

The ideal mentoring relationship has both a high level of support and a high challenge, which leads to growth. If the challenge is too high, and the support levels don't match the needs, there can be a retreat, an abandonment of the task at hand. If both the challenge and support are insufficient, there will be stand-still, a lack of progress. Finally, if the support is high, but the challenge is too low, there will only be a relationship of validation, or confirmation of one's progress. The objective for the educational developer is to maintain the high challenge/high support mentality that will foster growth through the SoTL initiative.

In the posture of *the guide*, the educational developer supports the faculty member through the phases of the SoTL process. This begins with a discussion on what SoTL is and what the different phases might look like during the process. The guide helps to bring structure so that the project can be seen as something realistic to accomplish in a given timeframe and with existing resources. The role is seen as one that contributes to helping the faculty member make decisions that align with the scope of the inquiry.

In the posture of *challenger*, the role is to provoke discussion around existing assumptions and to help identify and consider additional perspectives in one's thinking. If there is little challenge, the depth of the relationship is compromised, as the project or tasks don't move forward and additional perspectives might not be considered.

In the posture of *supporter,* the faculty member is provided with resources and ideas of how to navigate through the different phases of SoTL. This support includes discussion on current practice and the proposed change or intervention, an exchange of relevant literature and experience, the logistics to carry out the plan, check-ins during the implementation of the change, and reflection and discourse to evaluate the change. To complete the cycle, decisions are made on how to share the work. Recognizing and celebrating milestones and achievements along the way represent the posture of the *cheerleader.*

SoTL as a Transformative Learning Opportunity

As previously discussed, an inquiry into one's teaching is often triggered by an event such as student feedback, results of student evaluations, changes in student performance, or other events influencing the teaching and learning environment, including the evaluation of a pedagogical change implemented. This event can result in a disorienting dilemma for the faculty member if these events aren't congru-

Figure 3. Mapping of transformative learning and SoTL

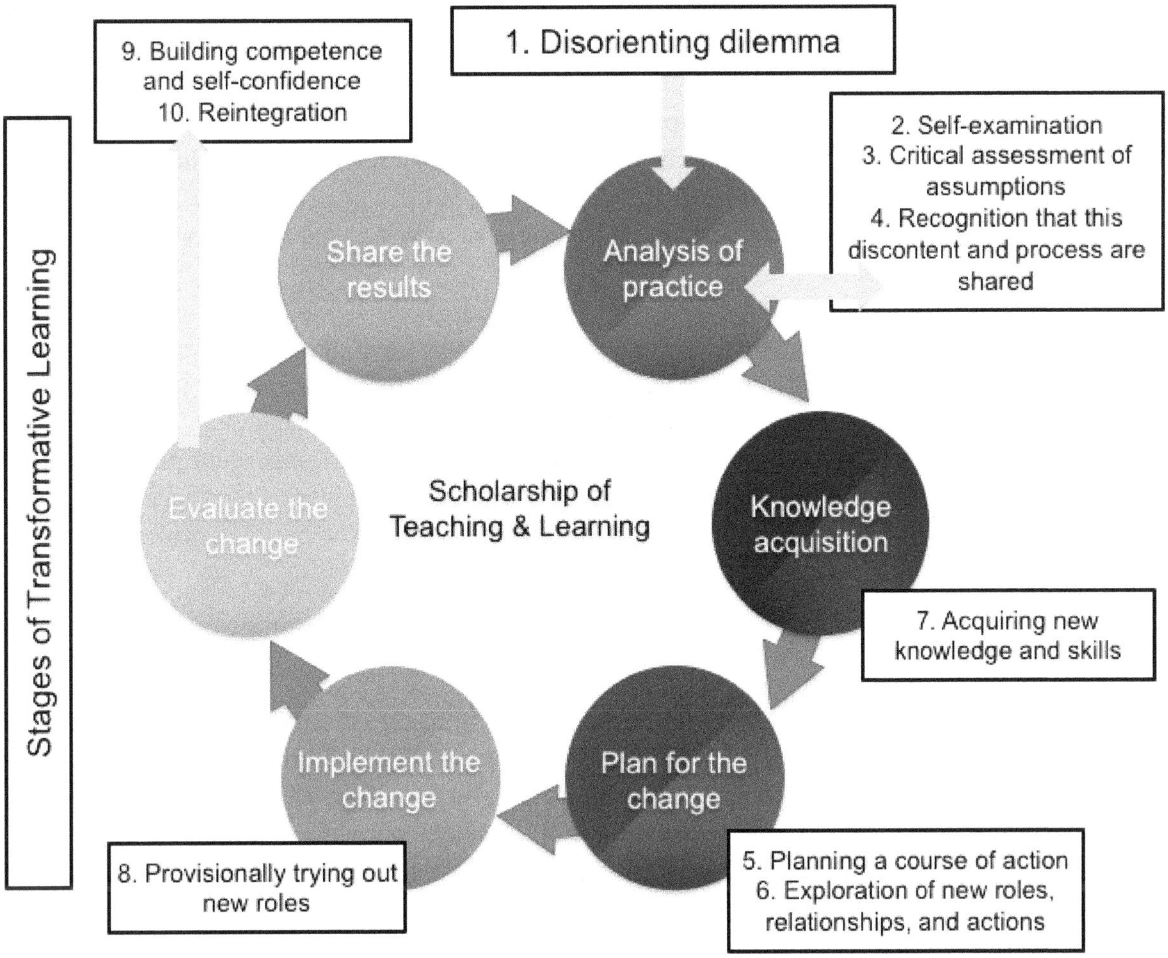

ent with the faculty member's beliefs and assumptions. For example, the literature tells us that active pedagogies result in deeper (improved) learning. However, after implementing the flipped classroom, the faculty member receives negative feedback from the students on the end-of-semester course evaluations. The faculty member has read about the benefits of this type of learning, has attended workshops on strategies and tools to implement this format, and has read many publications to prepare the course, so these negative results come as a surprise, and not knowing exactly where to turn next, the disorienting dilemma presents itself. Figure 3 shows the overlapping of the SoTL process and the transformative learning process commencing with this disorienting dilemma as a trigger to begin the analysis of one's practice. This section continues with an examination of the different phases and learning events that occurred in this SoTL collaboration.

The Disorienting Dilemma

The disorienting dilemma that the faculty member faced in this work resulted from a mismatch in the expectations of the teaching and learning that was to occur with the flipped classroom methodology. After having experienced professional development workshops and having read the literature about this innovative format, the faculty member believed that this type of active pedagogy was better for learning. The students could work before class for the "knowledge transfer" phase of learning and then come to class and actively participate to assimilate the knowledge and continue to make meaning of their learning. The disorienting dilemma presented with the following complexities:

- Lack of student preparation for the flipped class sessions
- A decrease in scores on the end-of-semester evaluations, along with various comments criticizing the method
- Students self-reported that they learned a lot during the semester and the performance (grades) was similar to prior semesters

The problem was therefore summarized in the form of a statement questioning teaching practice: *There are clear benefits for student learning using the flipped classroom, but maybe I should just listen to the feedback and go back to a more traditional way of teaching.*

Although this chapter is not being written from the student experience, it is also quite possible that the students themselves were also facing a disorienting dilemma when encountering the flipped classroom, many for the first time. This is a consideration for the faculty member who can then explore the notion of transformative learning for the students as well as for him or herself.

The Analysis of Practice

After independent reflection on her own, the faculty member initiated a discussion with the educational developer. After a description of the course and its structure, the reflection was stimulated using Mezirow's (1991) three types of reflection—content, process, and premise reflection. This move towards a reflective discourse between the two parties fostered some of the phases of transformative learning—mainly self-examination, critical assessment of one's assumptions, and the recognition that this is not an isolated dilemma; others face similar challenges.

During the *content reflection*, the faculty member was encouraged to think about "What happened here?" This involved the self-examination of her role as the teacher and then a discussion on what occurred in the teaching and learning environment. This took the form of a description of the overall course syllabus and then quickly moved to the topic of the flipped classroom. The faculty member summarized the events as follows:

- The flipped classroom was implemented for a total of three class sessions, where the students were expected to read an article before coming to class and then engage in a discussion with other students using the Jigsaw discussion method. The students signed up to put themselves in groups for the semester.
- The coordination of the Jigsaw discussion method was a challenge because while the groups had been formed, there were often group members missing or some who had not done the work outside of class.
- There was scaffolding provided in the form of semi-structured questions for the student discussions, and the faculty member circulated in the room during this time to provide on-going feedback.
- After these three sessions, there were then three sessions of working time where the students had to construct a project based on their work during the flipped sessions. This project was not graded and was only submitted to the faculty member at the end of the course before the final exam.
- The faculty member was not pleased with the end-of-semester evaluations as there were critical comments from the students about this format. However, student performance remained similar to previous semesters.

After this content reflection, it was clear to the faculty developer that there were additional layers of complexity. This discussion was not only about what happened with the flipped classroom but also with other teaching strategies and the organization of the course.

During the *process reflection*, the main question came to "How did I come to think this way?" In this stage, the faculty member recounted her knowledge of the flipped classroom, her discussion with other faculty members who also had worked in this way, and her general view that active learning was better for the students: If they engage with the material instead of being passive participants, this can result in deeper learning. The students often commented that they wanted to be passive and have the expert teacher transmit the knowledge to them. As educators, we work towards models of deeper learning, but should we treat from what we know and succumb to student preferences? During this time, the educational developer had to provoke the discussion to center around knowledge of the flipped classroom, putting this into practice, and the significance of sharing "why" with the students right from the start.

During the *premise reflection* phase, the discussion moved to "Why is this important?" In this stage, we began to co-construct the meaning behind the different reflections, leading to possible pathways to encourage students that they can learn better with active pedagogies; even though their perceptions might not be positive at the start, being open to new perspectives on teaching and learning is even more important for future teachers and their development. The why also helps us to determine how to more effectively begin the semester when incorporating a pedagogical innovation so that that previous ways of thinking for the students can be overcome from the start.

Knowledge Acquisition

There is a significant body of literature on the flipped classroom and pedagogical innovation. Putting it into practice can be somewhat more complicated. Therefore, in addition to continued reading and discussion on the flipped classroom, for which a working literature review is constructed, the educational developer presented the Community of Inquiry Model (COI) (Garrison, 1999) as a complementary model when thinking about the flipped classroom. Rooted in the social constructivist paradigm (Vygotsky, 1978), the framework presents the educational experience as a blend of three elements—cognitive presence, teaching presence, and social presence, all impacted by the communication medium used for teaching and learning. Cognitive presence, considered the most essential element, indicates how the participants in a community of inquiry make meaning of their learning. Social presence is how the participants project their characteristics, needs, and interests, which has a direct influence on cognitive presence and on affective learning outcomes if present. The third element, teaching presence, consists of the design of the educational experience and then the facilitation of the experience.

In addition to the COI model, there was also discussion and resource sharing around the subject of design principles. Design principles are a practical source for implementing the flipped classroom. The Center for Teaching & Learning at Vanderbilt University (Brame, 2013) provides four design principles for the flipped classroom including exposing students to course content prior to class, providing an incentive for students to prepare for class, providing a mechanism to assess student understanding (before or at the start of class), and providing in-class activities that focus on higher level cognitive activities. Kim et al. (2014) conducted a research study of three different scenarios of the flipped classroom at the University of Southern California around the design and implementation of the flipped classroom using the Revised Community of Inquiry (RCOI) Framework, and the Teaching Orientation Survey, a scale designed to rate the design and implementation of the different activities experienced in a flipped classroom. Nine design principles, addressing the critical areas of the RCOI framework emerged from this study, the first three of which were adapted from Brame's work. These principles are as follows:

1. Provide an opportunity for students to gain exposure before class
2. Provide an incentive for students to prepare before class (additional activities, comments for launching discussion)
3. Provide a mechanism to assess student understanding (formative assessment)
4. Provide clear connections between in-class and out-of-class activities
5. Provide clearly defined and well-structured guidance
6. Provide enough time for students to carry out the assignments (time to apply the knowledge, information, and skills acquired online)
7. Provide facilitation for building a learning community (facilitation and guidance for student collaboration)
8. Provide prompt/adaptive feedback on individual or group work
9. Provide technologies familiar and easy to access (p. 43-46)

One potential limitation of these principles was that they were designed in the context of classrooms with 50 students, so additional resources and support mechanisms might need to be in place for larger classes (Kim et al., 2014).

Planning for the Change

After the analysis of practice and knowledge acquisition, the educational developer worked with the faculty member on course organization and support using some of the design principles. A decision was taken to make incremental additions to support the flipped classroom methodology. To address principle one, on the first day of class, students were asked to contribute to a Padlet (an application embedded into the course Moodle site for easy access) which asked them to respond to two prompts, the first about their prior experience with the flipped classroom and the second about their perceptions for this specific semester. This activity was completed after an overview of the essential elements of the flipped classroom, and why this active pedagogy was selected by the faculty member.

The design principles two and three specify the creation of an incentive for students to complete the work, as well as some type of formative assessment to check for comprehension. The decision was made to do this in a "lite" manner by having students respond to prompts about their selected reading before coming to class. The questions were posed on Padlet, which allowed the students to post anonymously and also respond to other's comments. This ultimately lead to them self-organizing when in class with potential discussion points already identified. This also served as a way to check on student comprehension through their participation and sharing online. While the anonymous nature of the activity did not permit the tracking of individual students, it helped provide a snapshot of the overall group.

Also, the following other changes were made:

- The group work (resulting from the flipped sessions) would now be evaluated, and students would receive a grade for this work
- The choices for the articles for the themes were streamlined to align more closely with the learning objectives for the course
- The jigsaw method for face-to-face activities was adapted to have a more flexible structure with the groups being formed on the day of class to avoid absent students. Those students who were present worked together without an impact on the group process due to the absence of their colleagues.

Implementing the Change

The implementation of the changes to facilitate the flipped classroom methodology also mirrored the dimensions of the COI framework and the design principles. At the start of the semester, the flipped classroom was explained to the students to better prepare them for this type of learning. They were also allowed to share their personal experiences with flipped learning on a Padlet, to better familiarize themselves with the exercises that would come later in the semester. This initial exercise aligned with design principle nine and the exercises were integrated into Moodle, a system that the students were already comfortable in navigating.

The faculty member then moved through the course syllabus. When it came time to the three class sessions that would use the flipped classroom methodology, the students were reminded of how they should proceed with selecting a reading on one of the topics identified, read and take notes, and then contribute to the Padlet before coming to class. This helped to address design principle four. When the students arrived, they were given a worksheet to scaffold their discussions, along with the reminder to review the notes on the Padlet to incorporate some of the individual ideas into the collective discussion. This worksheet, in addition to the question, prompts on the Padlet addressed design principle five by providing structure and guidance. The faculty member focused on circulating to work with the different groups throughout the session, focusing on the clarification of concepts and provoking the application of theory to practice. This ongoing presence and feedback provided reassurance and support for the students while they continued to work with their peers, corresponding to design principle eight. At the end of each session, there was time dedicated to a debriefing and sharing so that the various groups could be exposed to further ideas and discussions. This step helped to synthesize the knowledge gained from both the in-class and out-of-class activities and served to help facilitate a broader learning community.

Evaluating the Change

The evaluation phase of this SoTL inquiry was two-fold as the inquiry was also explored from a personal development standpoint. First, the initial student perceptions of the flipped classroom were compared with the end-of-the-semester perceptions using their qualitative comments from the Padlet activities. The comments were extracted and analyzed using InVivo into three broad categories of experience with the flipped classroom, general perceptions of the flipped classroom, and the perspective the response was delivered in (student voice compared to teacher's voice).

In terms of prior experience, 45% (12) of the student Padlet comments specified that the student had never been in a class that used this type of pedagogy, and they were not familiar with the term. Two of the students had prior experience at HEP, and two of the students had prior experience at another institution. Three students had some knowledge of what the approach entails, but they had not experienced it themselves as a learner. One student had done some research work on active learning methods, which included some study of the flipped classroom.

When asked about their perceptions of the flipped classroom (after being given an article and a description by the faculty member), many students admitted uncertainty about the effectiveness of their learning in this way. They also commented on the potential quality of the course suffering, as well as their personal learning preferences not aligning with this approach. There were ten comments reflecting enthusiasm as this was a new way for them to learn. While most of the students responded from the perspective of their own learning in a flipped classroom approach, some of them responded from the perspective of themselves being in the role of the teacher and how they could see the benefits for their own students.

At the end of the semester, the students were asked to respond to more specific questions. The first question was, *"From the perspective of being a student, what are the limits associated with learning with the flipped classroom?"* The students cited the limits to be group dynamics and participation, readiness for autonomous learning, and the need for assurance of learning from the instructor. Some students commented that they were not expecting this type of active learning at university and that they wanted to be passive in the classroom—these comments aligned with the previous year's student evaluations of teaching concerning the comments on this approach.

The second question was, *"From the perspective of being a student, what are the strengths associated with this approach?"* The students cited deeper learning (due to having to explain content to other students), discussions and exchange over different ideas, and the chance to self-assess throughout the sessions. There was an overall consensus that they learned more through the exchange in a group as opposed to just reading by oneself at home.

Finally, the students were asked, *"How have your perceptions of this approach changed since the start of the semester?"* Unfortunately, here, the students did not show much evolution from their initial perceptions relating to the effectiveness of their learning with this pedagogy. They reinforced the idea that relying on their classmates was not consistent as not everyone had the same commitment to the course or the learning. However, there were comments corresponding to the perspective that as a future teacher, they could see potential benefits for their students.

The second part of the evaluation phase stems from the faculty member's perspective in her professional development. This involved the ongoing discourse between the faculty member and the educational developer throughout the implementation. These discussions facilitated the emergence of the dimensions of transformative learning. These ideas are shared in more detail in the subsequent individual reflections.

Sharing the Results

In this exploratory inquiry between a faculty member and an educational developer, there are different aspects to be shared. First, there are the results of the SoTL inquiry on the flipped classroom and student learning. The initial aim is to share this work at an academic conference in Switzerland focused on technology in teaching and learning, under the specific sub-theme of the flipped classroom. The researchers also intend to continue the study into the next academic year with a more specific inquiry related to the COI model and the design principles to have more detailed data for analysis. By sharing these initial results, as well as the details of the collaborative learning process, one aim is to encourage the exchange on this pedagogy among multiple faculty members to develop a model for the flipped classroom specific to universities of teacher education.

There are very few research articles on the flipped classroom specific to Switzerland. In a Web of Science search (July 2019) with the keywords "flipped classroom" and "Switzerland" there were three results with themes related to the flipped classroom, but not of a study of its implementation in practice. When using the keywords "blended learning" and "Switzerland," there were five results, two of which were directly related to classroom practices. Whether it be at the institutional, local, national, or international level, if this study continues over time, there will be additional opportunities for sharing at various levels.

Reflections from the Educational Developer

When working with a faculty member on a SoTL initiative, my work revolves around the idea of enrichment—faculty members are not producers, but they are creators (Stabile & Ritchie, 2013). A SoTL project involves creation—in the form of a change in the teaching and learning environment—something that the faculty member believes will improve his or her teaching and student learning. This extends the idea of other work that is done in faculty development, but it shows more of a commitment to a collaborative professional development relationship, one of learning together. From this perspective, I was able to make the connections between a SoTL inquiry and transformative learning, leading to an experience of enrichment.

The disorienting dilemma can be a delicate area to approach. One exposes a level of vulnerability when disclosing a challenge in his or her professional practice. However, others may often be facing a similar problem; in fact, we realized that this disorienting dilemma with the flipped classroom was one that we might often encounter—a misalignment of expectations in the teaching and learning environment. When the educational developer can take a disorienting dilemma and co-create an inquiry to help resolve this dilemma, the discussion moves from one of vulnerability and *"what went wrong?"* to *"how can we make a change that will improve our practice?"*

My role as the educational developer was rooted in the four roles described earlier in this chapter—guide, challenger, supporter, and cheerleader. When discussing the idea of conducting an inquiry into one's teaching practice to help gain evidence to inform future decisions, it is important to take the time to reflect on our assumptions about teaching and learning. In their book *Engaging the Six Cultures of the Academy*, Bergquist and Pawlak (2008, p. 98) discussed assumptions of the formulation of teaching and learning strategies in the following ways:

- Using replicating personal experience (doing what my favorite teacher did)
- Through intuition (what feels right)
- Through hard-earned experience (doing what I have found to be effective as I have a lot of experience)
- Through appeasement (doing what the students want or will tolerate)
- By nihilistic retreat (doing whatever gets me through the class)

The process of SoTL helps us to move away from the assumptions that many of us possess to help us justify what we do with evidence from our practice. Reflective practice and discourse allow us to challenge these ideas that we may have held for a while, supporting the trial of "new roles" in practice.

From my perspective, I look at SoTL as an investment—both personally and professionally. In collaboration, all stakeholders need to find personal value in this investment. Different faculty members will value the different roles taken on in various manors, and it is up to the educational developer to align with what is valued most (or to demonstrate the value in all of these roles!). For some, it can be the role of the *guide* who gets you from point A to point B with a well-defined project. For others, the value is in the role of a *challenger* who can introduce new ideas and ways of thinking to provoke existing points of view and habits of mind. The value in the role of a supporter is that you are not alone in this work, and if things do not go as planned, there is always another way. Finally, everyone loves a *cheerleader*, someone who is there to help motivate you, encourage you, and celebrate the progress in your professional development.

Reflections From the Faculty Member

There are many reasons why I decided to investigate and experiment with an innovative pedagogical approach in the broad sense, adopting the flipped classroom approach with jigsaw sessions and documenting the process of these change through SoTL. Certainly, the most plausible and immediate explanation lies in the desire to improve student learning. This explanation, although significant, removes the question of the quality of teaching, which is transformed into the acceptance of the change of method to increase student performance, as seen in the results of the final evaluations and student grades. Indeed, measurable outcomes are certainly an indicator of the degree of learning and possibly of the quality of teaching; however, these two elements are not necessarily linked and interdependent. It is quite possible that the teaching provided by the faculty member may be recognized as quality (by other parameters such as the perception or pleasure of the students in taking this course, or its relevance, the "good talk" of the faculty member), but that it does not lead to deep learning or the desired learning in quantity or depth. (For example, evaluation results show that students have a good understanding of the theme, but they cannot describe all the issues or make connections with professional skills.) The type of evaluation also plays a role in the results obtained and therefore influences this quality indicator through the grades. These questions are at the heart of the search for innovation in the classroom.

My motivations were also more personal, related to the satisfaction of teaching or transmitting content, seeing students "sticking" to the subject, "entering" into the subject taught, and embracing it to the same degree as I do. It is also important for me to establish contact with students (resulting from the experience of teaching in large groups), to be able to see them progress in their learning, and to accompany them in their quest for understanding.

However, the search for solutions in terms of learning and personal satisfaction is not easy to find and even less easy to implement. The faculty member may feel lacking in means, time, critical distance, and resources to reflect on his or her teaching and the changes to be made. Teaching at the higher level can be a solitary task from which it is difficult to find a knowledgeable and available "critical friend" to discuss in-depth one's practice, the organization of the course, and the teaching methods or to interpret students' reactions, requests, or even criticism. Moreover, considering changes, especially when they are radical or significant, is not always easy in a context characterized by overwork and subsequent lack of time. The change is also destabilizing, both for the faculty member and for students who are led to experiment with a new method of learning as adults and almost at the end of their study "career". Moreover, in the case of the flipped class described in this chapter, the students have arrived at Master level via "conventional" or "classic" learning: Why should they change now?

Faced with these different levels of questioning and their complexity, the presence of the educational developer is fundamental. First of all, this individual takes on the role of the role of an active, interested, professional, and neutral listener. She or he supports the faculty member in the maze of questions, and especially in the search for appropriate solutions and their possible implementation. It is a real energy catalyst, a real support. Many pedagogical innovations would not have taken place without this professional support.

Finally, the implementation of an analysis of pedagogical practices through SoTL brings an evidence-based approach to the changes made by introducing a dimension of distance and objectification of the action. The data collected and analyzed in collaboration with the educational developer are essential elements for feedback from the faculty member but also necessary for the presentation and acceptance of pedagogical innovations by students.

SOLUTIONS AND RECOMMENDATIONS

Through this SoTL inquiry and the subsequent reflections of the educational developer and the faculty member, some recommendations were drafted in order to establish and maintain these types of collaborations. While every working relationship is different, these suggestions provide an overall starting point to not only embark on a SoTL initiative, but to ensure that it progresses to the point of sharing the results of the inquiry.

Define the Nature of the Work Together

Acai et al. (2017) define a SoTL partnership as a "relationship in which all participants engage in a process that is intended to investigate curricular or pedagogical issues" (p.2). According to their work, there are four factors impacting this relationship—motivation to participate, challenges, power, and definitions of success.

- **Motivation to Participate***:* On a surface level, this might not appear to be an issue at a university of teacher education, but there still exists the tension between this type of research and discipline-based research that faculty members at all higher education institutions face. The educational developer can help motivate SoTL research by communicating the value of SoTL for a faculty member's personal teaching development. Faculty members can continue with their research agendas in their discipline while complementing and supporting their teaching activities through SoTL.
- **Challenges:** Common challenges arising in SoTL partnerships can be the navigation of traditional roles, the balance of guidance and self-direction, and time to build meaningful relationships (Acai et al., 2017). There can also be challenges assumed from working relationships before the SoTL activity.
- **Power:** Consider the potential implications of power imbalance. Are those working on the SoTL activity at an equivalent level within the hierarchy of the organization, or it possible that the dynamics might be skewed?
- **Definitions of Success***:* What is the intended level of the inquiry? What are the indicators and definitions of success? One faculty member might have the intention of publishing a scientific article, while others might wish to take progressive steps beginning with a simple sharing of the SoTL findings in a discussion with peers. There can be a progression over time, for example starting the relationship with a pilot project that over time becomes a more extensive inquiry, but this is something to discuss early in the process to avoid a discrepancy in expectations related to a successful initiative.

Develop a Project That is Personally Meaningful to the Faculty Member

To foster commitment from faculty members in terms of their learning, it is important to move beyond the traditional notions of training (compliance) and development (deficiency) to the paradigm of faculty enrichment (Stabile & Ritchie, 2013). This paradigm includes the ideas of an individual's core mission (why do I teach), an individual's professional identity as a teacher, one's beliefs and attitudes related to education, and reflective practice (moving from thoughts to action) (Stabile & Ritchie, 2013).

A SoTL inquiry can be viewed as a faculty enrichment opportunity as it is often a project that is deeply personal. In this aspect, it is important to select an area of the faculty member's teaching that is not only important to the improvement of practice and student learning, but an area that is of interest to the faculty member so that the work can potentially continue after the initial inquiry. In the example discussed in this chapter, the flipped classroom approach was at the center of the inquiry. Over the past few years, this approach has been seen often in the literature and continues to be a theme developed in many faculty training programs under the umbrella of active learning and learner-centered education practices.

Educational developers can help faculty members uncover a disorienting dilemma in their practice, which then serves as a starting point for a SoTL inquiry. This dilemma can be found through individual consultations on a teaching topic, from student evaluations of teaching, from peer observations of teaching, from workshops or other interactive training formats, or from any activity that prompts reflection at an individual or collective level. By combining the lenses of SoTL and transformative learning theory, the faculty member has the potential to learn not only about his teaching, but also the possibility to emerge from the inquiry with broader perspectives in the field.

Encourage a Larger Community for SoTL Across the Institution

The last phase of a SoTL inquiry is "going public," (Felton, 2013), or quite simply sharing the inquiry and results with others. Those engaged in SoTL have to disseminate the results of their inquiry, opening it up to peer review and discussion. This can take place in many forms with varying layers of complexity. Below you will find some examples of how SoTL can be shared in a local institutional context and beyond:

- **Inside the Institution**: Presentation and discussion with discipline-based colleagues, presentation and discussion with students, 'blog or similar piece in a campus newsletter or website feature, participation in faculty development programming.
- **Beyond the Institution**: national conferences (discipline or SoTL based), international conferences, academic journals and scientific publications, contributions to edited books, presentations to academic and professional associations. (While SoTL work can extend to international scientific journals, it is important to remember that studies requiring extensive empirical evidence are more aligned with the work of a discipline-based pedagogical researcher.)

In addition to "going public" with SoTL and encouraging colleagues to discuss the ongoing work, the appropriate institutional supports should be in place to recognize and reward SoTL activities in order to ensure the sustainability of and appreciation for the continued work. Hubball and Clarke (2010) identified three major areas for this support: (1) within recognition and rewards systems for promotion and tenure, (2) with dedicated professional development support for SoTL work, and (3) with accommodations for workload and professional roles to make the time and space for SoTL. Other chapters in this publication address these areas of support in more detail.

FUTURE RESEARCH DIRECTIONS

This collaboration involved an inquiry into the flipped classroom approach during one academic semester, with the overall objective to improve teaching and student learning. The authors can imagine the continuation of this inquiry to include additional technological dimensions that will help to facilitate the learning in the personal space. Further research can include work with other faculty members who are also engaged in pedagogical innovations to study the impact of such innovations on teaching across a module or across a program.

CONCLUSION

Whether SoTL is classroom-oriented with an emphasis on an individual's context or theory-hypothesis driven with an emphasis on producing new knowledge (Felton, 2013), a SoTL inquiry can take place with faculty members who have different levels of interest based upon context, future development goals, and enrichment opportunities. It is intended to be inclusive towards faculty of all levels and disciplines, and with the focus on practice, it is accessible for both discipline-based researchers and teaching-focused faculty alike. By exploring SoTL from the transformative learning lens, we see that a disorienting dilemma can serve as a catalyst to launch an inquiry into one's teaching, and that the evidence obtained from this inquiry can help shape new perspectives and teaching in one's own teaching practice, within disciplines and departments, and across an institution.

REFERENCES

Acai, A., Akesson, B., Allen, M., Chen, V., Mathany, C., McCollum, B., & Verwoord, R. E. (2017). Success in student-faculty/staff SoTL partnerships: Motivations, challenges, power, and definitions. *The Canadian Journal for the Scholarship of Teaching and Learning, 8*(2), n2. doi:10.5206/cjsotl-rcacea.2017.2.8

Bergquist, W. H., & Pawlak, K. (2008). *Engaging the six cultures of the academy: Revised and expanded edition of the four cultures of the academy.* San Francisco, CA: John Wiley & Sons.

Bishop, J. L., & Verleger, M. A. (2013, June). The flipped classroom: A survey of the research. *ASEE National Conference Proceedings, 30*(9), 1-18.

Boyer, E. L. (1990). *Scholarship reconsidered: Priorities of the professoriate.* Lawrenceville, NJ: Princeton University Press.

Boyer, E. L. (1996). From scholarship reconsidered to scholarship assessed. *Quest, 48*(2), 129–139. doi:10.1080/00336297.1996.10484184

Brame, C. J. (2013). *Flipping the classroom.* Retrieved from http://cft.vanderbilt.edu/guides-sub-pages/flipping-the-classroom/

Chen, Y., Wang, Y., & Chen, N. S. (2014). Is FLIP enough? Or should we use the FLIPPED model instead? *Computers & Education, 79*, 16–27. doi:10.1016/j.compedu.2014.07.004

Cranton, P. (2000). Individual differences and transformative learning. In J. Mezirow & ... (Eds.), *Learning as transformation: Critical perspectives on theory in progress* (pp. 181–204). San Francisco, CA: Jossey-Bass.

Daloz, L. (1999). *Mentor: Guiding the journey of adult learners.* San Francisco, CA: Jossey-Bass.

Daloz, L. (2000). Transformative learning for the common good. In J. Mezirow & ... (Eds.), *Learning as transformation: Critical perspectives on theory in progress* (pp. 103–123). San Francisco, CA: Jossey-Bass.

Fanghanel, J. (2013). Going public with pedagogical inquiries: SoTL as a methodology for faculty professional development. *Teaching & Learning Inquiry, 1*(1), 59–70. doi:10.20343/teachlearninqu.1.1.59

Farmer, R. (2018). The what, the how, and the why of the flipped classroom. *Innovative Practice in Higher Education, 3*(2), 14–31.

Felton, P. (2013). Principles of good practice in SoTL. *Teaching and Learning Inquiry: The ISSOTL Journal, 1*(1), 121–125. doi:10.20343/teachlearninqu.1.1.121

Flipped Learning Network (FLN). (2014). *The four pillars of F-L-I-P*. Retrieved from https://flippedlearning.org/definition-of-flipped-learning/

Garrison, D. R., Anderson, T., & Archer, W. (1999). Critical inquiry in a text-based environment: Computer conferencing in higher education. *The Internet and Higher Education, 2*(2-3), 87–105. doi:10.1016/S1096-7516(00)00016-6

Hubball, H., & Clarke, A. (2010). Diverse methodological approaches and considerations for SoTL in higher education. *The Canadian Journal for the Scholarship of Teaching and Learning, 1*(1), 1–11. doi:10.5206/cjsotl-rcacea.2010.1.2

Hutchings, M., & Quinney, A. (2015). The flipped classroom, disruptive pedagogies, enabling technologies, and wicked problems: Responding to" The bomb in the basement". *Electronic Journal of E-Learning, 13*(2), 106-119.

Kim, M. K., Kim, S. M., Khera, O., & Getman, J. (2014). The experience of three flipped classrooms in an urban university: An exploration of design principles. *The Internet and Higher Education, 22*, 37–50. doi:10.1016/j.iheduc.2014.04.003

Little, C. (2015). The flipped classroom in further education: Literature review and case study. *Research in Post-Compulsory Education, 20*(3), 265–279. doi:10.1080/13596748.2015.1063260

Mezirow, J. (2003). Transformative learning as discourse. *Journal of Transformative Education, 1*(1), 58–63. doi:10.1177/1541344603252172

O'Flaherty, J., & Phillips, C. (2015). The use of flipped classrooms in higher education: A scoping review. *The Internet and Higher Education, 25*, 85–95. doi:10.1016/j.iheduc.2015.02.002

Roehl, A., Reddy, S. L., & Shannon, G. J. (2013). The flipped classroom: An opportunity to engage millennial students through active learning strategies. *Journal of Family and Consumer Sciences, 105*(2), 44–49. doi:10.14307/JFCS105.2.12

Schwartz, B. M., & Haynie, A. (2013). Faculty development centers and the role of SoTL. *New Directions for Teaching and Learning, 2013*(133), 101–111. doi:10.1002/tl.20079

Stabile, C., & Ritchie, W. F. (2013). Clarifying the differences between training, development, and enrichment: The role of institutional belief constructs in creating the purpose of faculty learning initiatives. *New Directions for Teaching and Learning, 2013*(133), 71–84. doi:10.1002/tl.20047

ADDITIONAL READING

Bélisle, M., Lison, C., & Bédard, D. (2016). Accompagner le Scholarship of Teaching and Learning. In A. Daele & E. Sylvestre (Eds.), *Le conseil pédagogique dans l'enseignement supérieur: cadres de références, outils d'analyse et de développement*. Bruxelles: De Boeck.

Hubball, H., Clarke, A., & Poole, G. (2010). Ten-year reflections on mentoring SoTL research in a research-intensive university. *The International Journal for Academic Development, 15*(2), 117–129. doi:10.1080/13601441003737758

KEY TERMS AND DEFINITIONS

Flipped Classroom: A pedagogical approach focused on student-centered learning where students engage in knowledge-transfer activities outside of the classroom, and then actively integrate and assimilate their learning collectively inside the classroom.

Jigsaw Classroom: Term used by Aronson (1978) to explain a method of teaching and learning where small groups of students work together on one aspect of a topic, and then teach it to the rest of the group, who have studied different aspects of the same topic.

SoTL: The Scholarship of Teaching and Learning; an inquiry into one's own teaching practice to improve one's teaching. Transformative Learning: "Learning that transforms problematic frames of reference—sets of fixed assumptions and expectations (habits of mind, meaning perspectives, mindsets)—to make them more inclusive, discriminating, open, reflective, and emotionally able to change" (Mezirow, 2003, p. 58).

Chapter 12
The Role of Educational Developer in Supporting Research Ethics in SoTL

Lisa Margaret Fedoruk
University of Calgary, Canada

Kiara Mikita
University of Calgary, Canada

ABSTRACT

This chapter stems from popular misconceptions demonstrated by educators who lack familiarity with the significance and necessity of honoring ethical guidelines and practices when conducting SoTL research. The authors articulate the value of incorporating ethical principles and practices in research design and provide educational developers with much needed critical information about ethical considerations when conducting SoTL research. An overview of the purpose and functions of review ethics boards is included, along with common scenarios involving ethical dilemmas educators may encounter when embarking on a SoTL research study. Reflective questions to contemplate and strategies about how ethical practices can and should be embedded into SoTL research planning and design are explained. A framework and applicable resource are provided so that educational developers may guide and support instructor/ researchers through safe and ethical SoTL inquires.

INTRODUCTION

This chapter is dedicated to the exploration of ethics in the Scholarship of Teaching and Learning (SoTL) research. The authors explain the importance of ethics when undertaking SoTL projects and processes of obtaining ethics approval through global research ethics boards. They provide tangible and practical examples from the field that contain applicable strategies about how ethical practices can be embedded into SoTL research and describe the role of educational developers in guiding and supporting best practices

DOI: 10.4018/978-1-7998-2212-7.ch012

in this area. Finally, ethical considerations and questions to contemplate when planning and designing a SoTL study are offered through a tangible tool for readers to use as a guide for future SoTL projects.

Within a Canadian context, SoTL involves research aimed at improving student learning and/or teaching practices in higher education. It is informed by carrying out relevant research, conducted by disciplinary experts who gather and analyze relevant evidence (or data) from learners. As scholarship, the outcomes are then shared broadly to contribute to knowledge and practices to teaching and learning (McKinney, 2006; Miller-Young & Yeo, 2015). Because SoTL inquiry largely comprises research that involves human participants, those interested and involved in conducting SoTL research have a responsibility to act ethically and obtain clearance from their respective institutional ethics review boards (e.g., Research Ethics Boards/REBs in Canada, Institutional Review Boards/IRBs in the USA, Human Research Ethics Committees/HRECs in Australia, Research Ethics Committees/RECs in the United Kingdom.) For academics interested in studying their teaching and/or student learning, it is imperative that they critically consider the ethical implications of their SoTL investigations to mitigate potential harm to participants.

In Canada, it is necessary to adhere to core principles of respect for persons, concern for welfare, and justice by way of treating participants fairly and equally, as mandated by the Tri-Council Policy Statement, titled Ethical Conduct for Research Involving Humans, 2nd edition (TCPS2) (Government of Canada, 2019). The TCPS2 is a national document that governs ethics in all research involving human participants in Canada taking place in learning institutions eligible for funding.[1] Similarly, in the USA, IRBs stipulate that respect for persons, beneficence, and justice (the Belmont principles) are three core principles that must be adhered to when conducting research involving human participants. Institutional review boards in the USA hold the responsibility to oversee research proposals from an ethics perspective. In the United Kingdom the National Research Ethics Service was established to maintain the UK-wide framework for ethical review of research involving human participants (Vadeboncoeur, Townsend, Foster, & Sheehan, 2016). However, each institution creates their own approaches, requirements and responses of RECs. Lastly, in Australia, HRECs review research proposals that involve human participants via the National Statement on Ethical Conduct in Human Research (2007). This national document sets out the requirements for a HREC's assembly in a higher educational institution, its operation and membership.

Drawing upon the aforementioned examples of global ethics review boards, one can conclude that ethical considerations are embodied through various higher educational committees and boards with the common purpose of negating harm to human participants in research. It is imperative that all researchers consult their institution's ethics review board for context-specific requirements when embarking on a SoTL research study.

RESEARCH ETHICS REVIEW

The duty of researchers to have respect and concern for the welfare of their participants and uphold justice (Government of Canada, 2019) stems from historical incidents in which participants unnecessarily suffered for the purposes of research. One example stems from unethical and inhumane medical procedures performed on concentration camp victims without their consent during World War II in various Nazi-occupied European countries. This mistreatment resulted in physical and mental disabilities, deformities, impairments, and deaths. From an international perspective, the Belmont Report, the Helsinki Declaration, the Nuremberg Code, and Canada's initial TCPS document are examples of policies created to protect participants primarily in health care/biomedical studies. Research ethics practices have evolved such that it has arguably become part of common understanding and practice that high-risk research in which participants' physical or psychological well-being may be compromised will require institutional ethics board certification. However, when risk of harm is or appears low, it remains uncertain whether ethics certification is required. Sometimes risk may appear non-existent, for example, because of blind spots with respect to power differentials. This grey zone—often emerging in SoTL research—is precisely what warrants this chapter.

More recently, non-medical interdisciplinary fields of inquiry have postulated that there is a need to recognize and acknowledge the risks involving participant well-being on issues such as conflicts of interest and power relationships (e.g., instructor power over students might make them feel unduly influenced, coerced, or compelled to participate); consent processes (e.g., ensure students are fully informed, participate voluntarily, and know their rights); fairness and equity in research participation (e.g., respecting the vulnerability of individuals/groups and implementing inclusivity and fairness); and privacy and confidentiality (e.g., protecting participant identities and safeguarding data.) Thus, most higher education institutions globally are responsible for implementing one or more REBs to review research proposals to mitigate or negate risk. In Canada, if a researcher or institution of higher learning lacks compliance with the TCPS2, consequences may entail suspension of research funding with ineligibility to apply for future grants (Stockley & Balkwill, 2013).

Application of ethical considerations to SoTL inquiry requires researchers to ask themselves difficult questions in an attempt to mitigate unfamiliar dilemmas. This is most common when research is conducted in classrooms and when researchers finds themselves occupying dual roles of instructor and researcher. With proper planning and consideration, the instructor/researcher can address relevant issues that have important implications for the ethical review process. Therefore, it is imperative that people engaged in SoTL research have a sound understanding of how to apply ethical practices to their research design and work and are knowledgeable about the processes in which it will be evaluated by their institution's REB. This often means becoming familiar with local/regional ethical practices and policies and the institution's ethical requirements; ethical practices common to a particular discipline or type of research (e.g., SoTL); and/or popular misconceptions surrounding research ethics.

The importance for researchers to familiarize themselves with their institution's REB policies and protocols stems from the fact that global, cross-cultural review boards may have differing research ethics requirements (Morris, 2015; Edwards et al., 2012; Hearnshaw, 2004; Goodyear-Smith, Lobb, Davies, Nachson, & Seelau, 2002). These differences in requirements may impact when one should seek REB approval or not. When in doubt and prior to conducting any research, it is best to seek the advice of the institution's REB and/or submit a proposal about the intended inquiry. In certain cases, the REB may indicate that a study is exempt from a full review (very minimal to no risks exist.) In countries like Canada, the USA, the UK and Australia, REB members often consist of interdisciplinary faculty, student(s), community member(s), expert(s) on research ethics, and those with proficiency in the areas of research supported by the institution. The REB will assess key aspects surrounding issues such as privacy, confidentiality, conflicts of interest, consent, and how potential risks will be handled. More specifically, "REB members assigned to each proposal evaluate the nature of risks to the participant, how the researcher proposes to minimize or manage [the] risks, and whether the benefits of the research (to the participants, to society) justify those risks" (Stockley & Balkwill, 2013, p. 4). Ultimately, the REB is responsible for evaluating ethical standing for affiliates' research.

DUAL ROLES: WHY ETHICAL CONSIDERATIONS ARE IMPORTANT IN SOTL

Significantly, SoTL researchers and students using a participatory research model occupy dual roles: the roles of instructors/researchers and students/participants. In other words, often within the context of SoTL research, a single role and relationship becomes two: instructors are no longer just responsible for facilitating student learning, but also serve as researchers responsible for the oversight of research participants. Likewise, students are no longer just learners but also become research participants.

A general rule of thumb in SoTL work is that the instructor/researcher is always an instructor first, and this role should be privileged over that of the researcher (Hutchings, 2003; MacLean & Poole, 2010). When in doubt, research priorities and outcomes should be considered second to student learning. This is to ensure that the learning that students attend post-secondary institutions for is not sidelined or compromised by their instructors' research interests. Instructor/researchers should therefore be mindful of these dual roles through research design and execution. Four areas of ethical consideration are high-lighted in order to help instructor/researchers achieve the related principles of ethical practice. Instructor/researchers should be mindful of the following areas:

- Conflicts of interest and power relationships, in order to mitigate unduly influencing or coercing student participation and/or exacerbating the power imbalances between them.
- Consent processes, in order to ensure that students' decisions to participate in the research (or not) are informed and voluntary.
- Fairness and equity in research participate, in order to be inclusive, fair, and equitable when selecting participants.
- Privacy and confidentiality, in order to protect participants' information and the integrity of the research project.

Notably, most instructors demonstrate care for students and student learning, and a clear orientation toward ethical practice (understood broadly as moral principles that direct a person's conduct or behavior). However, a commonly held misconception entails that only research involving glaringly risky practices require ethics certification. Instructor/researchers sometimes feel offended when it is recommended that they seek ethics approval, as though this implies that not having sought approval means they have been acting unethically. This is often not at all the case. Instead, disregarding an ethics review can be more a product of researchers' blind spots than an absence of ethical orientation. This research is not unethical per se, yet it might not be conducted in accordance with institutional research ethics practices. It is precisely within this ostensive grey zone of research – one that demonstrates an orientation to ethics but without institutional ethics approval – where SoTL work can find itself precariously suspended. Importantly, the process of incorporating ethical considerations into the research design helps avoid the trappings of blind spots.

In the sections that follow, the aforementioned areas of ethical consideration are described through ethical dilemmas (scenarios) and practical strategies. Though not directly representative of any specific persons, these representations reflect an amalgam of common scenarios that the authors, as educational developers, have observed when engaged in SoTL consultations. Of note, many parallels exist between ethical considerations, and some of the same strategies can be implemented to negate risks found in multiple scenarios such as privacy and confidentiality. The following scenarios and strategies can serve as powerful reflective and reflexive tools useful to educational developers to guide SoTL researchers in conducting ethically certified learning and teaching studies. In addition, at the end of each ethical area for consideration, the authors have included suggestions on how educational developers can advise instructor/researchers through processes of ethical research design and implementation.

CONFLICTS OF INTEREST AND POWER RELATIONSHIPS

Being mindful of conflicts of interest and power relationships requires that instructors remain cognizant of dual roles and remain sensitive to the inherent power differentials between instructors and students. It is in the context of this power difference that students might feel obligated to participate in a study that, for any number of reasons, they would rather not. Accordingly, at every step of research design and execution, instructors should do all they can to keep from making students feel unduly influenced, coerced, or compelled to participate. On a practical level, this involves ensuring that every aspect of the study—from when students are notified and provided with information about it, through to dissemination of results—has been designed in such a way that students are able to freely choose to participate. Designing the study requires attending to blind spots, anticipating and then modifying aspects of the study where students might feel pressured to participate. Instructors could invite former, trusted students to discuss and review the research study material with them, to help alleviate any lingering blind spots (importantly, instructors should only consult with former students whose grades, courses, or evaluation they no longer have a role in determining, to keep from replicating the very problem they are trying to avoid). Students might be invited to answer the following questions: "Are there ways in which participating in this research—or not—might be something that students feel like they had to do? If so, why? How might this be altered?"

I have a wonderful relationship with my students and consistently great teaching evaluations. I'm also really transparent about always wanting to do better as an instructor. So, I know my students are willing to help me better facilitate their learning by participating in my research study. (Pietro)

Pietro's comment reflects just these sorts of blind spots. While Pietro's aims are laudable—always wanting to improve as an instructor—he cannot assume that all students will want to participate in his study. Pietro's students might indeed have great relationships with him, evaluate him highly, and want him to continue to improve as an instructor; however, his students still might not want to participate in the study. Students will have myriad reasons for choosing to participate, or not, and they must be extended the information and opportunity to make a fully informed decision. Designing a study that is mindful of this helps mitigate assumptions about students' interest in participating and helps researchers prepare safeguards for students to ensure that their participation is voluntary and informed.

Use of a Third Party

A third party is a person who does not have perceived authority or power over participants and can act as an intermediary between instructors and students. Only this person will know which students are research participants, and students will be informed of this intermediary role before deciding whether to participate. Under the direction of the instructor/researcher, a third party might do any of the following:

- Introduce/present the study to students/potential participants.
- Collect and store consent forms.
- Field participants' questions.
- De-identify and then direct students'/participants' questions to the instructor/researcher and relay responses back to them.
- Provide students/participants with updates and/or ongoing information about the study.
- Conduct interviews and/or lead focus groups with students/participants.

Collecting Data at the End of Term

Collecting data via surveys, interviews, and/or focus groups could be done at the end of the term, after final grades have been submitted to the registrar and released to students, and after the appeal deadline has passed. Doing so this way creates space for students to feel as though participating in their instructor's research will not hamper their current course outcomes.

Analyzing Student Work After Identifying Information Is Removed

Analysis of data with identifying information removed (de-identified), can be done separately from or in conjunction with the previous strategy (collecting data at end of term.) In such cases, the data might consist of student work or feedback collected throughout the term as part of regular course activities, for example, and/or might include data generated specifically for the purposes of the research (e.g., surveys, interviews, and/or focus groups about some aspect of research interest). In any case, conflicts of interest and power differentials can be seen to be mitigated by these efforts.

Studying Other Students

The students/participants in a study, over which instructors have no direct authority or power, represent another way to work toward limiting the conflicts of interest or impacts of power that they might experience in SoTL studies. In such cases, instructors may wish to exchange sites (where instructor/researchers conduct studies in each other's classes, for example) or examine a research question in a course or class that is not their own.

Advising Pietro

Pietro's assumptions about his relationship with his students and desire to better facilitate their learning might be correct; however, his dual role as instructor and researcher means that Pietro must do what he can to mitigate conflicts of interests and power differences. Moving forward, Pietro might design his study involving a third party, collect data at the end of the term, and/or analyze the data once identifying student information has been removed. Pietro might hire a teaching assistant (TA) from another department, for example, to assist with the study. The third party/TA could be the person who, while Pietro is elsewhere on campus, introduces Pietro's students to the study, takes up questions for Pietro to answer, collects and stores consent forms, oversees the administration of further research instruments after the term is complete, and de-identifies the data for analysis. All of this information would be communicated to students/prospective research participants as part of their introduction to the study. The students can then make informed decisions about whether to participate in Pietro's research.

CONSENT PROCESSES

Attending to dual roles and the power differentials between instructors and students also requires developing clear consent processes. Students' participation in research should always be fully informed and voluntary, and students should know their rights when deciding whether to participate in research. In practice, this requires that students are provided with as much information as possible about their participation in the research and that students freely choose to participate (as opposed to feeling influenced, coerced, or compelled such as in Pietro's case). It is also important that students are aware of their obligations as participants and the processes involved in participating and withdrawing from portions or all of the research. Any and all consequences associated with participating, choosing not to participate, and/or participating and then choosing to withdraw should be clearly articulated. All of this information should be made available, in writing, to students. Instructors who choose to consult with former, trusted students to help them avoid blind spots, might invite said students to review the informed consent form/ material, and respond to the following questions: "What else would you want to know before making a decision about participating in this research?" and "In what ways might students feel compelled to participate or compromised in their ability to withdraw from the study without consequence?"

In my research project, I'll just use the feedback that my students have given me throughout the course, and the feedback I've given them. I'll also use their improved grades to speak to the changes I've made to demonstrate how I've grown in my teaching. I won't use any students' names, so their identities will be protected. (Taysha)

Although this scenario crosses multiple ethical areas (consent and confidentiality), Taysha's comment addresses some of the nuances of students' consent to participate in research, assuming her students will want to participate. Taysha describes using de-identified student feedback and grades as metrics in her research but does not speak about asking her students for their consent to do so. Taysha is demonstrating consideration for students' confidentiality by not identifying whose feedback and grades she will refer to, but she has not articulated this process to her students, nor what the parameters of confidentiality are. The potential problem associated with Taysha's use of student data become more visible if Taysha's class consists of a small number of students (e.g., 10), in a niche study area, or at a rural college. While some or all of Taysha's students might not mind that this makes them more vulnerable to being identified in her research, they have not been given the opportunity to decide this and to adjudicate their level of comfort with this risk for themselves. A study designed to allow students to make these fully informed decisions for themselves allows for voluntary, informed participation in the research.

Describe and Discuss the Research Before Seeking Consent

Students should be made aware of the purpose, benefits, risks, and consequences of the research before asking for their consent. Written consent materials should include clear and transparent descriptions of the project (even if this has already been shared with students in some other, non-written way). Ensure that participants are made aware of whom they might direct questions to about the study, before, during, and after it is complete. Whenever possible, a brief explanation of the research could be included on the course syllabus. For example, the syllabus could state, "Please be advised that within this course you will have the opportunity to volunteer as a research participant in a study that examines reading comprehension of second year, undergraduate students, as they progress through Language and Literature 201. Details will be provided at the commencement of the course." Additionally, if using data collection tools such as focus groups as part of the design, it may be advisable to articulate why focus group data are preferable over interview data and that focus group members will be advised about this confidentiality caveat. Likewise, in cases in which video or audio data will be recorded, it may be advisable to speak to why this data collection method is preferable over others (e.g., in terms of the research design). Instructors should establish that consenting students are given the opportunity to choose, on the consent form, whether or not they are consenting to their video presence viewed by the research team and shared during research dissemination.

Clarifying There Are No Repercussions for Refusal or Withdrawal

Instructors should clearly communicate to students—and guarantee—that there are no repercussions for their refusal to consent. Furthermore, instructors should be explicit in terms of letting students know that there are no favors or costs to those who do or do not participate in the research.

Keeping Consent Processes – and Participation – Confidential

Whenever possible, the use of web-based survey tools that allow for anonymous participation are risk averse because anonymous online participation can eliminate identifiers and peer pressure and create space for those who do not wish to participate to privately decline. If paper consent forms are circulated in a classroom setting, instructors should ensure that all students turn in a form to avoid identifying non-participants. Instructors should make sure that students are able to freely and privately choose or refuse to participate, or to withdraw from participation within a reasonable timeframe. Finally, instructors should confirm that withdrawal processes are simple (e.g., sending an email request to a third party), and they are clear about what will happen to their data after students have withdrawn (e.g., that wherever possible it will be extracted and destroyed).

Keeping Incentives – If Used – to a Minimum

Instructors should make sure that incentives are minimal enough to avoid undue influence (e.g., a $25 bookstore gift card or entry into a drawing for a $50 gift card). If the incentive includes a small, incremental increase to their grades (e.g., 1% to 5%), instructors must establish that non-participants will be afforded the same opportunity to achieve the same incentive through an alternative option that is equivalent in time and effort. Lastly, instructors must articulate clear timelines about opting in and out of participation in the study are made clear.

Advising Taysha

Taysha's dual role as instructor/researcher (much the same as Pietro's) requires that she provide clearly communicated information about the purpose, benefits, risks, and consequences of her research and then seek students' informed consent before using their data. In cases in which consent is retrospectively sought, it might be advisable for her to consult with her REB in terms of what is ethically reasonable and feasible, all things considered. If, on the other hand, Taysha is in the planning stages of conducting research using student feedback and grades, she could indicate as much in her course outline, and ensure that her students are made aware of what participation in the research entails. She will need to verify that this is done in written form. If she has chosen to incorporate incentives, she must keep these minimal and, where possible, make available via alternative routes to non-participating students. Taysha should invite participation in a manner that preserves (in confidence) who opts in or out of the study as well as those who later choose to withdraw.

FAIRNESS AND EQUITY IN RESEARCH PARTICIPATION

It is essential that instructors are mindful of fairness and equity in their SoTL studies. Doing so requires that instructors carefully attend to the assumptions that inform their research, participation criteria, access to participation, and an equitable distribution of research benefits. These efforts are to ensure that the research demonstrates inclusivity, fairness, and equity by respecting the vulnerability of individuals and groups and by ensuring accessible research results.

On a practical level, being inclusive means ensuring that barriers to participation (e.g., in terms of ability, language, access, and so forth) are minimized or eradicated, that inclusion and exclusion rationale and criteria are justifiable and articulated, and that assumptions about participant capacity have not been made. Similarly, being fair and equitable in SoTL work means ensuring that research benefits are equitably distributed among research groups and that research results are accessible to all those involved. Prospective participants should be informed of potential benefits arising from participation in the research, of relevant contingencies and modifications that might occur in the event that some participants are disproportionately dis/advantaged by participation in the study, and of how research results will be made available to them.

It's important to me to demonstrate that students who have historically been disadvantaged by conventional post-secondary teaching and learning practices can thrive when afforded the appropriate opportunities. I'm going to provide these students with an alternative lesson stream so that they can similarly succeed and study the process. (Luc)

Luc's statement indicates that he wants to create equitable learning opportunities between historically advantaged and disadvantaged students. How Luc determines inclusion and exclusion criteria as well as the conditions of the opportunities he generates will be of paramount importance. For example, how will Luc identify and determine "historical disadvantage," and how does he plan to attempt to generate equitable "appropriate opportunities"? Luc's consultation of appropriate resources (e.g., about culture, equity, diversity, inclusion) including, but not limited to skilled colleagues and relevant literature will be crucial to ensure that Luc does not, inadvertently, reproduce some of the problems he seeks to respond to.

Use of Intermediaries

If participation in the study may be affected by language barriers, instructors should involve intermediaries competent in both languages to assist with communication between the instructor/researcher (or third party) and participants.

Articulation of Inclusion/Exclusion Criteria

If the study excludes particular groups, instructors should explain how this exclusion is relevant to the specific research project. For example, in course outlines, instructors could state, "Because this research is focused on women's experiences of power relationships, and because our work is anchored in gender theory, only students who identify as female will be recruited for this study."

Identify Assumptions

Instructors should invite colleagues and/or former students to help identify assumptions about in/excluded participants to ensure that criteria do not suffer from blind spots. For example, it would be erroneous to assume that students with physical disabilities should be excluded from a study that uses physical activity games to assess comprehension of biomechanics principles.

Monitoring Disparity and Contingency Planning

If comparison groups are being used, the impact of an intervention should be closely monitored to verify that one group does not experience significantly greater benefits or challenges than the other group. The instructor/researcher is responsible for determining whether the discrepancy between groups becomes unethical and deciding when contingencies and/or modifications to a study may be required. For example, if an instructor is teaching two sections of a course, one involving a "flipped classroom" model that becomes significantly more advantageous for the participants in that section, the instructor may decide to flip both sections to mitigate an unethical disparity between the two groups.

Making Results Accessible to Participants

Instructors should ensure that study results are made available to participants, whether in print or electronically, and that all participants are aware of how to access these materials. In general, research results should be made available to participants in culturally appropriate and meaningful formats, such as in reports done in plain language in addition to academic reporting. Instructors can invite participants to provide contact information (e.g., email addresses) to allow for them to be reached with dissemination outcomes (e.g., written summaries, publications) that may be produced in the future.

Advising Luc

Luc's aim of creating (more) equitable learning opportunities among diverse students is important. His dual role as instructor/researcher means that how he goes about this can significantly impact the learning and research experiences of his students/participants. As a result, Luc must make sure that the way he approaches teaching and learning and his research project is inclusive, fair, and equitable, that he respects the vulnerability of those he seeks to work with, and that the results are accessible to those who choose to participate. As he plans his study, Luc should do what he can to identify and address any assumptions that might inform his work, clearly articulate participant criteria, involve relevant intermediaries, engage in contingency planning, and monitor for sizeable disparity between research groups. He should also guarantee that participants are aware of possible research benefits and how to access research results.

PRIVACY AND CONFIDENTIALITY

Privacy and confidentiality are ethical areas for consideration in all of the aforementioned scenarios. This again demonstrates the interconnection between multiple ethical considerations in most situations that instructors/researcher must contend with when engaging in SoTL inquiry. Instructor/researchers should secure the integrity of the research project by protecting participant confidentiality and participant identities, and safeguarding data. On a practical level, this means that instructors/researchers are careful with all aspects of research data, from participant information through to the data participants generate, and are mindful of how this data is examined and shared. Doing so requires clear communication and agreements between research team members about confidentiality issues, data protection logistics, and how data will be analyzed and disseminated. Equally, secondary use of data should be undertaken with caution and respect for participant confidentiality and while protecting participant identities. Researchers should also be ethically mindful when contacting former students and/or using institutionally generated student email addresses.

I have no preference at all about whether students participate in my research or not. I will ensure that those who don't will engage in equivalent learning activities and exercises as those who do to ensure equity in outcomes. (Somita)

Somita notes that she has no preference whether students participate, and that she will provide equivalent learning opportunities for participants and non-participants alike. How Somita sees out these plans will be crucial in terms of confirming that students' identities as participants will be protected and confidential. For example, if learning activities and exercises are clearly demarcated for "participants" and "non-participants," it will become clear among students (and likely to Somita herself) who among them is in each group. Participant identities are therefore no longer protected and, as a result, the study may be compromised (i.e., participants may feel compelled to participate, given their visibility, and therefore may not feel that their consent is freely given). Somita will therefore need to be mindful, moving forward, to see/plan out her study in a way that takes these considerations into account.

Clarity About Confidentiality Within Research Teams and With Participants

Instructors should ensure that confidentiality obligations are discussed with research teams and with participants during the informed consent process. Research team members should sign appropriate confidentiality agreements (when relevant.) They should agree not to share identifying information about participants or in disseminated data, agree not to share information with outside people or groups without the expressed and informed consent of participants, and agree to inform participants of confidentiality breaches and how they have been addressed.

Engaging in Practices to Protect Student Identities

Whenever possible, student data should be de-identified, whether by the instructor/researcher or by a third party. Likewise, if it does not compromise research objectives, small group data should be presented in aggregate form absent identifying information. If the aims of the research cannot be achieved by aggregating data in small group studies, and/or if the identifiability of participants is a significant risk that students/participants might experience as a result of participating, participants should be informed of this during the consent process.

Engaging in Practices to Safeguard Data

Measures taken to safeguard data for the full life cycle of said data (from collection, use, dissemination, retention, and/or disposal) should be articulated in the informed consent process. It is recommended that encryption software and/or password protected digital documents, folders, and/or systems be used to protect participant information and data, and that all hardcopies of such material are kept under lock and key. A list of all people with access to confidential information should be kept and routinely updated. When appropriate, all confidential material should be destroyed upon completion of the study (e.g., by reformatting/wiping digital storage and shredding hard copied material).

Being Judicious About Use of Secondary Data

Secondary data consists of information originally collected for other purposes but studied for different reasons in teaching and learning research. This data might include student work, information obtained for program evaluation, student records, or other identifiable materials collected for educational or administrative purposes. Reasons to engage in secondary use of data include avoiding duplication of data already collected, confirming or critiquing conclusions yielded, comparing changes in a sample over time, applying new hypotheses testing, and/or confirming the authenticity of data. Privacy and consent considerations arise whenever secondary data could reasonably be linked to specific people and when it is possible that those people could be identified through data linkage or in disseminated work (TCPS2, Chapter 5, Section D).

Researchers might therefore consider whether identifiable information is necessary to their research; the use of identifiable information absent consent is likely to affect the welfare of those who may be identified; they can take appropriate measures to protect individuals' privacy and safeguard identifiable information; researchers can comply with the identifiable parties' previously expressed preferences; it is possible to seek the consent of the identifiable individuals; and/or the researchers have obtained any other necessary permissions to engage in secondary use of data. Finally, researchers might nonetheless seek REB consultation and/or approval to use data in this secondary fashion.

Being Ethically Mindful of Use of Student Contact Information

If instructors/researchers wish to recruit former students as participants in their research studies, it may be advantageous to involve a third party to recruit these students. Use of a third party is good practice in cases where former students might nevertheless want to enroll in a future course of the instructor, to serve on a graduate student or advisory committee, to seek reference letters, and so forth.

If researchers wish to contact students using institutionally generated email addresses, they should be mindful of general overuse of email and inbox flooding. One example is to indicate to potential participants upon initial contact that only one email will be sent via the recruitment process with a timeline for response. Researchers should contemplate how the benefits of contacting students this way outweigh the drawbacks that may be associated with doing so, who will be contacting students, and the nature of the contact person's relationship with them.

Advising Somita

Somita's interest in ensuring equity between participants and non-participants in her study is clear in her statement that equivalent learning activities and exercises will be made available to both groups. Importantly, in terms of protecting student identities, this will require that Somita designs a study in which engagement in these activities and exercises will not identify which students are and are not participating in the study, or, if it does, that participants are informed of this and have consented to this probability.

Somita, like the other researchers described at the outset of this section, will have to ensure that confidentiality is maintained around participant information and generated data, and that she engages in practices to safeguard this data, such as confidentiality agreements among team members, password protected and/or encrypted software, and hardcopies that are maintained under lock and key. Likewise, should Somita or her colleagues involve the use of secondary data, they should be ethically mindful about how to go about it, having considered, for example, whether the identifiability of participants is a risk worth taking and/or if it is possible still to secure participant consent. If this research involves contacting former students or use of institutionally available contact information, Somita and her colleagues should do so either via use of a third party and/or after reflection about who might be best to contact students and why.

FRAMEWORK TO CONSIDER WHEN DESIGNING ETHICAL SOTL RESEARCH

It is important for anyone embarking on a SoTL research project to understand why and how to apply ethical constructs throughout the research design process. Without practicing ethical mindedness throughout the study design, being confronted with a list of ethics considerations just prior to embarking upon the research can be experienced as punitive and result in "delays in ethics review, frustration on the part of researchers, and resentment towards REBs and their role within the research process" (Stockley & Balkwill, 2013, p. 4). Educational developers can foster a culture of research ethics through awareness and application of ethical principles in research design. The ensuing framework, which has been adapted from Faller and Norman (2015, p. 3), and Fedoruk (2017, p. 16), can also be implemented by educational developers to guide researcher/instructors through reflective questions at the onset of a SoTL research project. This framework is an applicable tool to manage ethical issues at the design stage

Table 1. Framework for planning/designing ethical SoTL research

Purpose, Participation, Consent
• What is the question or problem under investigation? Why is it important to investigate? • Whose consent is required? • Are there ways in which participating in this research—or not—might be something that students feel like they had to do? If so, why? How might this be altered? • Will students feel obligated to participate or compromised in their ability to withdraw at any time without consequence? • What power relationships need to be considered by potential participants involved in the study? • Are there issues of gender, race, culture, or status difference that need to be taken into account? • Are there any individuals or groups that this research might directly or indirectly exclude? • Could a third-party help with the consent to mitigate power differentials?
Methods
• What methods will be implemented in the inquiry, and what type of data will be gathered? • Are data collection methods biased against any groups? • Are there adequate safeguards to protect participants' information and data? • When will data collection activities occur (e.g., during class time, at the end of the course/term, after the appeals deadline)? • Will students be involved in gathering data? • Could a third-party help in gathering data?
Analysis
• What type of analysis will be used? • Is the analysis technique sufficiently transparent? • Who will be involved in analyzing data (e.g., self, students, a third-party)? • If students are involved in analysis, how will participants' privacy and confidentiality of the data be protected (e.g., use of codes, pseudonyms, anonymization at time of transcription)?
Results and Dissemination
• Who will see the results and products of the study? • How can the results of the study can be accessible to all participants? • What negative or embarrassing data might emerge from the findings, and who might be harmed by it? • How can contributions to the study by various participants (including colleagues and students) be acknowledged and/or cited, while maintaining appropriate confidentiality?

*For a downloadable copy of this framework as a table with room for notes and resources, please see: https://taylorinstitute.ucalgary.ca/ resources/ethics-scholarship-teaching-and-learning

that can strengthen research proposals and promote ethical mindedness through the entire study and can help mitigate delays and/or frustrations.

In addition to guiding researchers/instructors in designing ethical SoTL projects, educational developers also have the opportunity to build collaborative relationships with their institute's REB, resulting in a cohesive and productive review process for all involved. Promotion, outreach, and education in collaboration with REB members and administrative staff can also serve as ongoing support mechanisms for those requiring guidance.

CONCLUSION

Within this chapter, the authors highlighted the importance, significance, and necessity of honoring and implementing ethical guidelines and practices when conducting SoTL research. One of the important roles of educational developers is to provide guidance and support to faculty, students and staff by way of ensuring the value of incorporating ethical principles and practices in research design. This chapter has provided information about the processes and requirements of REBs, along with the importance of understanding how to protect participants from unnecessary suffering for the purposes of research. In an attempt to dispel misconceptions about the research ethics process, the authors have offered applicable strategies about how ethical practices can and should be incorporated into SoTL research planning/design and have supplied a framework to consider at the outset of a SoTL study.

REFERENCES

Australian Government. National Health and Medical Research Council. (2007). *National statement on ethical conduct in human research*. Retrieved from https://www.nhmrc.gov.au/about-us/publications/ national-statement-ethical-conduct-human-research-2007-updated-2018#toc__2102

De Vries, R., DeBruin, D. A., & Goodgame, A. (2004). Ethics review of social, behavioral, and economic research: Where should we go from here? *Ethics & Behavior, 14*(4), 351–368. doi:10.120715327019eb1404_6 PMID:16625729

DuBois, J. M. (2004). Is compliance a professional virtue of researchers? Reflections on promoting the responsible conduct of research. *Ethics & Behavior, 14*(4), 383–395. doi:10.120715327019eb1404_8 PMID:16625734

Edwards, N., Viehbeck, S., Hämäläinen, R. M., Rus, D., Skovgaard, T., van de Goor, I., ... Aro, A. R. (2012). Challenges of ethical clearance in international health policy and social sciences research: Experiences and recommendations from a multi-country research programme. *Public Health Reviews, 34*(1), 1–18. doi:10.1007/BF03391663 PMID:26236074

Eisen, A., & Berry, R. M. (2002). The absent professor: Why we don't teach research ethics and what to do about it. *The American Journal of Bioethics, 2*(4), 38–49. doi:10.1162/152651602320957556 PMID:12762924

Faller, S. E., & Norman, C. (2015). *Ethics & the IRB review process: A guide for SoTL researchers at UC*. Retrieved from: https://www.uc.edu/content/dam/uc/cetl/docs/IRB%20for%20SoTL.pdf

Fedoruk, L. (2017). *Ethics in the Scholarship of Teaching and Learning: Key principles and strategies for ethical practice. Taylor Institute for Teaching and Learning Guide Series*. Calgary, AB: Taylor Institute for Teaching and Learning at the University of Calgary. Retrieved from www.ucalgary.ca/ taylorinstitute/guides

Goodyear-Smith, F., Lobb, B., Davies, G., Nachson, I., & Seelau, S. M. (2002). International variation in ethics committee requirements: Comparisons across five Westernised nations. *BMC Medical Ethics, 3*(1), 1–8. doi:10.1186/1472-6939-3-2 PMID:11964190

Government of Canada, Canadian Institutes of Health Research, Natural Sciences and Engineering Research Council of Canada, and Social Sciences and Humanities Research Council. (2014). *Tri-council policy statement: Ethical conduct for research involving humans*. Retrieved from http://www.pre.ethics. gc.ca/eng/policy-politique/initiatives/tcps2-eptc2/Default/

Hearnshaw, H. (2004). Comparison of requirements of research ethics committees in 11 European countries for a non-invasive interventional study. *BMJ (Clinical Research Ed.)*, *328*(7432), 140–141. doi:10.1136/bmj.328.7432.140 PMID:14726341

Hutchings, P. (2003). Competing goods: Ethical issues in the Scholarship of Teaching and Learning. *Change: The Magazine of Higher Learning*, *35*(5), 26–33. doi:10.1080/00091380309604116

McKinney, K. (2006). Attitudinal and structural factors contributing to challenges in the work of the Scholarship of Teaching and Learning. *New Directions for Institutional Research*, *2006*(129), 37–50. doi:10.1002/ir.170

Miller-Young, J., & Yeo, M. (2015). Conceptualizing and communicating SoTL: A framework for the field. *Teaching & Learning Inquiry*, *3*(2), 37–53. doi:10.20343/teachlearninqu.3.2.37

Morris, N. (2015). Providing ethical guidance for collaborative research in developing countries. *Research Ethics Review*, *11*(4), 211–235. doi:10.1177/1747016115586759 PMID:26640509

Stockley, D., & Balkwill, L. L. (2013). Raising awareness of research ethics in SoTL: The role of educational developers. *The Canadian Journal for the Scholarship of Teaching and Learning*, *4*(1), 7. doi:10.5206/cjsotl-rcacea.2013.1.7

Vadeboncoeur, C., Townsend, N., Foster, C., & Sheehan, M. (2016). Variation in university research ethics review: Reflections following an inter-university study in England. *Research Ethics Review*, *12*(4), 217–233. doi:10.1177/1747016116652650

Vallance, R. J. (2005). Research ethics: Reforming postgraduate formation. *Issues in Educational Research*, *15*(2), 193–205.

ENDNOTE

[1]   Made up of three federal research agencies (Canadian Institutes of Health Research /CIHR; Natural Sciences and Engineering Research Council/NSERC; and Social Sciences and Humanities Research Council/SSHRC,) this tri-council is responsible "for policy development, evolution and interpretation, as well as public outreach and education" (Stockley & Balkwill, 2013, p. 3).

Section 4
SoTL in Action: Case Studies From the Field

In this section, examples of SoTL inquiries across diverse contexts and disciplines are presented. The aim is to showcase individual work in the field that represents strong practical examples of SoTL. While these studies are rooted in different literature and take on different methodological approaches, they all have the common goal of improving student learning.

Chapter 13
Practicing What We Teach:
Using SoTL to Challenge Preservice Teachers' Assumptions With the Reading/Writing Workshop Model

Michelle L. Amos
https://orcid.org/0000-0001-7177-0916
University of Central Missouri, USA

Morgan Ely
University of Central Missouri, USA

ABSTRACT

Using the SoTL framework provides students with an accessible, relevant model of professional and critical reflection on practice. Explicit participation in this research can benefit students with scaffolded practice applying reflection to instruction. Guiding students in examining assumptions around literacy supports meaningful integration of these skills in instructional design. This transformation of students' frames of reference requires meaningful reflection and a challenge to their current beliefs about disciplinary literacy. This study uses Reading/Writing Workshop format to individualize instruction, engage students in self-directed learning, and facilitate differentiation and formative assessment. This redesigned course used experiential learning and a social constructivist model to build collaboration and real-world communication skills. Transformation is supported through structured reflection. Thus, a data collection instrument was adapted from Brookfield's Critical Incident Questionnaire to guide students with specific, practiced, and meaningful reflection.

INTRODUCTION

There is an established significant need for literacy education instruction for preservice teachers in the United States, especially for those preparing to serve students in the middle grades across all content areas. As noted by Fang and Wei (2010), "adolescents need support when interacting with the dense,

DOI: 10.4018/978-1-7998-2212-7.ch013

complex texts in secondary content areas" (p. 262). Graham, Kerkoff, and Spires (2017) similarly advocate all teachers to support students' reading and writing within the structures of their disciplines. These academic demands are prominent in the Common Core State Standards (CCSS) that have been adopted across the majority of states within the United States of America (US) in which "students are expected to develop and demonstrate the sophisticated and distinct skills applied by real historians and scientists" (Duhaylongsod, Snow, Selman, & Donovan, 2015, p. 588). Solis, Miciak, Vaughn, and Fletcher (2014) similarly note that for low-level adolescent readers, focused instruction using content area texts to build prior knowledge should be implemented in both middle and high school.

Teachers whose undergraduate education has prepared them to teach social studies, science, math, or English/language arts (ELA) have a great deal of knowledge they can share with students about how to make sense of and use information from the various sources prevalent in their subject areas (Schoenbach, Greenleaf, & Murphy, 2012). Unfortunately, our observations echo these findings as we have seen that many of our preservice teachers majoring in math, science, and social studies content areas lack awareness of this existent knowledge, skill to effectively communicate these strategies to their future students, and confidence in their own identities as readers and writers. Schoenbach et al. (2012) note this as a national problem with almost half of first year students underprepared for college-level literacy tasks. Duhaylongsod et al. (2015) reinforce this in their work with social studies teachers and their students, finding "many students do not have access to teachers with the deep understanding that facilitates the successful implementation of disciplinary literacy curricula in history" (p. 589).

In Missouri, teacher preparation programs require eight credit hours of introduction to literacy coursework for all preservice middle grades teachers, regardless of content area specialization. Determining the most effective way to prepare these teachers to serve middle-grade learners in their future classrooms is the focus of this action research. As professors of literacy education, we sought to reconfigure a required course to activate students' existent disciplinary literacy knowledge as they plan lessons in an interdisciplinary team to integrate literacy strategies within their content area and develop both competence and confidence as readers and writers. To do this, we used the reading and writing workshop framework, discussions around disciplinary literacy professional development texts, and a New Literacy Studies conception of the threshold concept of literacy.

For our purposes, literacy is the socially and culturally situated interaction or transaction (Rosenblatt, 1960) between the reader and the text. Texts include traditional forms of novels and textbooks as well as discipline-specific formats, the arts, numeracy, digital literacies, and speaking, listening and viewing. This broad definition of literacy and texts builds on the work of Gee (2001), Street (2005) and others, and is distinctly different from the limited idea of "English class" that most of our students bring with them. Challenging these assumptions within our class is a key element of the course design, and one of our overarching goals is to refine students' understanding of the threshold concept of literacy, defined by Meyer and Land (2005) as "a conceptual gateway" that may lead to "a transformed internal view of subject matter, subject landscape, or even world view" (p. 373).

Using a Scholarship of Teaching and Learning (SoTL) framework of ongoing, systematic examination of practice with feedback and refinement, this study spans three semesters of instruction, transitioning a traditional literacy education course into a reading/writing workshop format similar to that used in the local schools. In keeping with the work of Felten (2013), to further the advancement of good practices in the classroom, we have incorporated the elements of design suggested to implement SoTL in our classroom. As such, this inquiry was focused on student learning, grounded in context, methodologically sound, and conducted in partnership with students; details on each of these elements is included in the chapter that follows. This work has previously been publicly disseminated at conferences focused on both Transformative Learning (2017) and Middle Grades Education (2018).

Feedback from initial student participants was collected using an adapted Critical Incident Questionnaire (Brookfield, 1986) and used to shape changes for the iterations of the course that followed. Analysis of feedback revealed that the academic demands of this structure challenged preservice teachers' assumptions about literacy in the middle grades classroom and impacted their preparedness and self-efficacy in supporting the needs of their future students across the content areas.

LITERATUE REVIEW—THE CONTEXT FOR OUR WORK

Literacy Needs and Middle School Students

According to the National Center for Education Statistics (2018), there exists a decline in students' writing performance as they advance into secondary grades. In the US, the middle school concept was widely adopted in the 1970s (Rockoff & Lockwood, 2010). Instead of expecting students to transition from the elementary school with a small class size and single primary classroom instruction to the relative anonymity and shifting schedule of the junior high school environment, the middle school focuses on the specific needs of students typically in grades six to eight (ages 11-14). While these schools are typically larger than the elementary school, students are divided into "teams" on each grade level. Each grade level team has a teacher in each content area who shares responsibility for roughly 150 students. Curriculum planning, data sharing, and behavioral interventions are shared across all teachers to allow for coordinated efforts toward student achievement. This seeks to mediate what Rockoff and Lockwood (2010) the "pronounced influence" that cohort size has on student academic success during these grades (p. 74). Our University program focuses on the specific needs of early adolescents, and our preservice teachers are certified to teach grades five to nine, though most seek placement within a middle school setting.

According to the National Center for Education Statistics (2018), there exists a decline in students' writing performance as they advance into secondary grades. In fact, according to McKenna, Conradi, Lawrence, Jang, and Meyer (2012) over a quarter of middle and high school students in the United States have lacked the skills needed to succeed consistently since the National Assessment of Educational Progress (NAEP) was put into use more than 40 years ago. Based on recent NAEP data, Schoenbach et al. (2012) note that "two-thirds of US high school students are unable to read and comprehend complex academic materials, think critically about texts, synthesize information from multiple sources, or communicate clearly what they have learned" (p. 3). These concerns are not limited to the US; McKenna et al. additionally cite findings from the Program for International Student Assessment showing that in 2009, all 65 countries in the Organization for Economic Co-operation and Development "faced sizable proportions of students functioning below the baseline level of proficiency" (p. 283). They additionally note that the issue of proficiency becomes more complex as students move into disciplinary texts in adolescence.

The reasons for this decline are complex, including the compartmentalization of curriculum in the middle school and the limits of time spend on each subject (Fang & Wei, 2010). The standard number of minutes spent in each content area, based on state mandates for contact hours per credit earned, is 40-50 minutes per day, a significant drop from the ninety-minute allocation for in-school reading recommended at the elementary school level (Sanacore & Palumbo, 2010). One remedy for this is the integration of both content area literacy and disciplinary literacy instruction in all classes, detailed later. According to Sanacore and Palumbo (2010), "from these subject-based topics (content-area studies), students can gain important insights about interdisciplinary concepts that can be applied to art, music, science, mathematics, and other curricular areas" (p. 181). One barrier to this is that content area teachers may lack training to provide this instruction. As Fang and Wei (2010) note in their study with middle school teachers, "science teachers…lacked substantive backgrounds in science reading and held fragmented beliefs about the cognitive and metacognitive reading skills needed to learn effectively from science texts" (p. 265).

Likewise, according to the NAEP (2007), reading scores have stagnated, and these scores are particularly concerning for students with disabilities. Because of these deficiencies, the Common Core State Standards (CCSS), adopted in the US, include cross-disciplinary literacy standards in each content area in the middle grades to prepare students for participation in the workforce. This inclusion is "predicated on the idea that content area teachers will use their expertise to teach, guide, and engage students in the reading, writing, speaking, and language relevant to the respective discipline" (Council of Chief State School Officers and National Governors Association, 2010).

In addition to low achievement level, attitudes toward reading shift in the middle grades. From 1984 to 2012, the percentage of fourth grade students who reported reading for fun almost every day stayed the same at 53%; in contrast, eighth grade student responses to the same NAEP survey item started lower, at 35% in 1984, and fell to 27% in 2012 (Musu-Gilette, 2015). McKenna et al. (2012) also found that attitudes generally worsen over age and over time:

Examinations of responses to the item 'Reading is a favorite activity' from 2002 to 2007 reveal a startling trend. Across those years, between 33% and 40% of fourth graders characterized it as 'a lot like me'. In those same years, however, only 10-14% of eighth-grade students strongly agreed with the statement. In fact, 66-68% of eighth graders either disagreed or strongly disagreed with it. (p. 287)

Likewise, Rockoff and Lockwood (2010) observe that "for the last two decades, education researchers and developmental psychologists have been documenting changes in attitudes and motivation as children enter adolescence, changes that some hypothesize are exacerbated by middle school curricula and practices" (p. 69). As with the findings of lower reading achievement among middle schoolers, the shift in attitudes toward reading are also found internationally. McKenna et al. (2012) note "PISA findings have revealed that the percentage of 15-year-old students who said that read for pleasure every day fell, on average, from 69% in 2000 to 64% in 2009 across OECD countries (OECD, 2010)" (p. 287).

Literacy Needs and Preservice Teachers

Despite this established need, engaging future math and science teachers in literacy coursework necessitates creating an understanding of relevance within their future classrooms. Counihan and Silcox (2014) report on an interdisciplinary project launched at a rural community middle school after the authors realized that students were not transferring skills learned in writing classes to compositions assigned in the math curriculum. In their work, they note that National Council of the Teachers of Mathematics Process Standards ask middle school students "to communicate their mathematical thinking coherently and clearly to peers, teachers, and others" (p. 34). Martin (2015) similarly notes, writing in math "provides opportunities for students to demonstrate mathematical understanding and construct arguments" (p. 302).

Preparation for preservice teachers to work with literacy is additionally relevant in content areas with specific writing formats, such as science, as it can support student understanding of the identities, activities, and patterns of thinking within the field (Pytash, 2013). Fang and Wei (2010) note the lack of effective strategies for middle school students faced with the need to explore and understand challenging science texts. Their research concludes:

with the reconceptualization of science literacy as involving not only knowledge of the scientific processes and content (i.e. the derived sense), but also the ability to read and reason with texts (i.e., the fundamental sense), it is encouraging that even a modest amount of reading infusion made a significant difference in the students' science literacy. (p. 270)

While the terms are used interchangeably in common parlance, there is a difference between content area literacy and disciplinary literacy. Put briefly, content area literacy is the use of general reading strategies when approaching texts written in different content areas while disciplinary literacy involves a content-area specific approach. As explained by Graham, Kerkoff, and Spires (2017), "Disciplinary literacy is different from its counterpart—content area literacy—in that disciplinary literacy emphasizes thinking and understanding like an "insider" or an expert in the disciplinary field" (p. 64). Hynd-Shanahan (2013) notes that disciplinary literacy does not ask every teacher should be a teacher of reading; instead "disciplinary literacy is a way to emphasize and embrace the different demands a text places on readers and writers in the various disciplines" (p. 93). Finally, Cardullo and Zygouris-Coe (2012) propose that disciplinary literacy "is the core of understanding the disciplines" (p. 64).

While this "insider" role empowers content-area teachers to draw on their content-area knowledge and approach in relating literacy strategy instruction to their classrooms, the approach is held in tension with the collaborative nature of the middle school concept. As noted by Graham, Kerkoff, and Spires (2017), "Disciplinary literacy has been slow to be recognized by middle grades researchers; perhaps because, on the surface, disciplinary literacy seems contrary to the interdisciplinary nature of middle grades curriculum" (p. 64). In our context, and especially in the culminating One Book, One School project, the preservice teachers involved in this study are engaged in introducing their major area content and disciplinary literacy while working in concert with an interdisciplinary group on a shared focal text.

Literacy Needs Addressed: Our Inquiry into Student Learning

To address these needs, we transitioned the Application of Content Area Literacy for Middle Level Learners course to a Reading Workshop and Writing Workshop format for presenting course content to our students. Our course design reflects the values and structures presented by Schoenbach et al. (2012) as the Reading Apprenticeship Framework. This is a specific iteration of a socio-culturally based Cognitive Apprenticeship "in which mental activities characteristic of certain kinds of cognitive tasks—such as computation, written composition, interpreting texts, and the like—are internalized and appropriated by learners through social supports of various kinds" (p. 22). This was well-suited to our goal of increasing both competence and confidence through action and reflection as it is structured as a "collaborative inquiry into reading and thinking processes" (Schonebach et al., 2012, p. 13).

Among the dimensions addressed by Schonebach et al. (2012), our course focused on the Personal Dimensions of developing reader identity, developing metacognition, developing reader fluency and stamina, and developing reader confidence and range: the Cognitive Dimensions of monitoring comprehension, breaking it down, and setting reading purposes and adjusting reading processes; the Knowledge-Building Dimensions of surfacing, building, and refining schema, building knowledge of texts, building knowledge of language (which we linked to the threshold concept of New Literacy Studies), and building knowledge of disciplinary discourse and practice; and the Social Dimensions of creating safety, sharing text talk, and noticing and appropriating others' ways of reading (p. 25).

The workshop model that we employed has a number of foundational thinkers, including Murray (1989), Atwell (1991), and Graves (1994); it has been more recently adapted into the Reading and Writing Project by Calkins (1994) and adopted widely, especially in the northeastern United States. The model is student-centered and student-directed and focused on individual pacing, goals, and conferences. In reading, students select books at their level and interest, often in an assigned genre or in a small group. Books are discussed and reflected on in journals. Reading strategies are introduced, often using a shared mentor text, with strategies then applied to individual (or small-group) readings. In writing, the process of writing is emphasized, with time spent on brainstorming, multiple drafts, revising, conferencing, and publication. Again, the work is often an assigned genre or format with the focal topic selected by the student. Conferencing with peers and with the teacher provide formative feedback and allow for students to progress at different rates through the process. In both models, the emphasis is on students spending time in the act of reading or writing, on the interdependence of reading and writing, and on the process in developing skills to progress toward excellence in each.

The workshop is commonly used in elementary and middle grades as a way to individualize instruction, engage students in self-directed learning, and facilitate differentiation and formative assessment (Teague, Anfara, Wilson, Gaines, & Beavers, 2012). In addition to general use in the elementary classrooms, recent research has explored the use of the writing workshop model in science and math content areas, providing opportunities for additional instruction in content area, application of learning, and information about student understanding. However, as Wendt (2013), notes, "the typical math or science teacher, for example, may lack the support and training necessary to fully implement the teaching of literacy" (p. 40).

Given the potential value of this teaching model, it is important to instruct preservice middle school teachers about the workshop model. Experiential learning has been established as an "ideal framework for delivering middle grades curriculum" (Kleine & McBryar, 2009, p. 29). Pytash (2013) specifically notes, "preservice teachers need to write and to experience the instructional approaches they might use in their future classrooms" as many preservice teachers assume that their own students will arrive with knowledge of content area writing which research has demonstrated they often lack (p. 808). Addressing the varied needs and experiences of both preservice teachers and their future students is another reason it is imperative to incorporate this experiential learning into literacy education courses.

In addition to the value of experiential learning, the workshop presentation employs a social constructivist model which is increasingly prized in classrooms at all levels as teachers seek to build collaboration and other real-world communication skills. Based on the work of Vygotsky, this model encourages the social mediation of learning. According to Schoenbach et al. (2012), in discussing the impact of this approach on the Reading Apprenticeship Framework, a collaborative and discussion-based approach to knowledge exploration "both supports learners and challenges them to grow" (p. 21). As cited in Martin (2015), Beck and Kosnik (2006), note "the act of writing may appear to be an isolated activity for an individual; however, the social environment and interactions of the writer are instrumental to his or her ability to construct meaning" (p. 304). As stated by Schoenbach et al., "very little authentic discussion takes place in typical classrooms, yet for all students…talking with others is a powerful way to work out one's ideas and articulate them" (p. 23).

Another consideration in this research is supporting teacher candidates as they move from reflection-on-action to reflection-in-action (Schön, 1983). This evolution in thinking can be supported by the use of structured reflection both on course content and on individual learning and application. Throughout the undergraduate coursework, preservice teachers are required to submit formal reflections on their experiences observing and teaching in local schools. After the course under study, while students are in their final internship placement, they are responsible for a Teacher Work Sample that includes a detailed and analytical reflection. We expect students to systematically reflect on their experiences and identify areas for professional and personal growth. To support this habit, the data collection instrument in this study is adapted from Brookfield's Critical Incident Questionnaire (1986) to increase student focus on specific, practiced, and meaningful reflection.

This critical self-evaluation fits well within the progression of stages used in Transformative Learning Theory (Mezirow, 2006). Put briefly, this theory posits that when faced with a disorienting dilemma that challenges assumptions about the nature of the world, a learner can modify existing habits of mind through exploring new roles with others and reintegrating with newly refined perspective. As noted by Felten et al. (2013), this lens is well-suited for work with adult learners. "Educators are increasingly recognizing that engaging students actively in shaping their learning experience can be transformative for both students and faculty" (p. 63). Graham, Kerkoff, and Spires (2017) note that introducing students "to the different habits of mind associated with the different disciplines" (p. 78) is a key consideration in the academic preparation of preservice teachers.

Creating opportunities for students to challenge existing beliefs around the nature of reading and writing and the value of interdisciplinary literacy is an embedded goal of this course. Providing a supportive environment for our students to explore their identities as teachers and as readers and writers is another key consideration in the course redesign. In our courses, the deliberate creation of what has been labeled a "holding space" (Drago-Severson, 2009) or a "liminal space" (Meyer & Land, 2005) is central. We both work to build relationships with students in each of our classes—we teach them that interpersonal relationships are key to interacting positively with middle school learners, and we consciously seek to model that within our own interactions.

Empowering Students through Research Partnership

Engaging with our students as co-inquirers similarly invites them to engage in the habits of critical reflection and collaboration that are necessary in their future careers. It is notable that this shift in the power dynamic requires new roles for both students and researchers, which can be uncomfortable as roles are redefined:

A more equal faculty-student relationship is unfamiliar territory and its novelty and ambiguity often lead both parties to at least initial discomfort and uncertainty. Persistence in this liminal space, however, offers the possibility of challenging and disrupting established norms, promoting integration and inclusion rather than marginalization and exclusion of student voice...Bringing multiple perspectives to bear on inquiry into teaching and learning practice can cause students and faculty to encounter dissonant, contested, and troublesome knowledge, provoking them to question their assumptions. Such deeper questioning may lead to crossing thresholds of understanding, which allow fundamentally new ways of thinking that cannot be undone. (Meyer, Land, & Bailie, 2010, as cited in Felten, 2013)

We feel that pushing through this discomfort is worthwhile for us and for our students as it provides both a model of reflective practice and the tools to engage their own future students. As noted by Werder and Otis (2010), "This metacognitive orientation enhances both student learning and faculty teaching" (p. 65).

METHODOLOGY

Our Goals

The course targeted in this study, Application of Content Area Literacy for Middle Level Learners (EDFL3240), is designed to help prepare middle level teachers to address language, literacy, and literature within disciplinary instruction, focusing on promoting basic and higher-order literacy within the content areas along with longer-range goals of promoting progress toward reading maturity. More than focusing on helping students with "learning to read," this course emphasizes the knowledge, skills, and dispositions teachers need for helping students with "reading to learn" and also "writing to learn." It does so in the context of promoting reading, writing, thinking, speaking, and literature as integral parts of specific subject instruction. (Course syllabus, 2018)

A student learning outcome is the actual event or activity a student will perform in order to reach the objective of the lesson. Objectives are hard to measure, where outcomes produce actual evidence of completion. Our preservice teachers demonstrated their understanding of the objective by creating the "One Book, One School" (OBOS) project. This project allows the students to show their complete understanding of the learning objective.

Student learning objectives (SLOs) were our primary consideration during the restructuring of the course:

1. Demonstrate understanding of the foundations of reading research and instruction and related foundations of teaching and learning through reflections, discussions, and instructional planning.
2. Demonstrate understanding of, and design curriculum. using methods to help students improve their effectiveness in pre-reading, reading, and post-reading, including using writing as a thinking tool.
3. Demonstrate understanding of, and design curriculum, using methods for improving vocabulary acquisition.
4. Demonstrate understanding of, and design curriculum, using elements of higher-order literacy, including close reading and using writing as a thinking tool.
5. Demonstrate understanding of, and design curriculum, promoting interdisciplinary reading, writing, thinking, speaking, and use of literature and trade books.
6. Develop discipline-specific applications of reading methods.
7. Create content area literacy instruction for students in diverse and exceptional populations, including culturally responsive pedagogy and differentiated instruction.

Creative Thinking and (Service) Learning

As the College of Education strives to create an atmosphere of reflective practitioners, the University of Central Missouri continues to grow in service learning. This allows preservice teachers to interact with students ranging in various levels of experience. In situations such as this, the acts of service can be found while the pre-service teachers are working toward a greater good for the community by embracing students on all levels.

Application of Content Area Literacy to the Middle Level Learner and Introduction to the Language, Literacy, and Literature in the Middle Level Classroom courses are the courses that we manipulated into a design that would better serve the students earning a degree in education from the University of Central Missouri. These courses focus on implementing culturally responsive reading and writing programs in the middle school classroom.

We, the researchers, quickly realized how difficult it was for students to master all of the student learning outcome expectations in these two courses. We understood the importance of focusing on reading and writing separately, even though both topics were covered in each course. We decided to split the course into two sections; one for writing and one for reading. Once this design was accepted into the college, the students were assigned to only one of the sections with the expectation they would take part in activities from both focus areas. To begin, we had what we referred to as "home classes". The corresponding instructor was in charge of those students. However, the students would receive instruction from both teachers. Each instructor focused on either reading or writing practice. The students switched classes each week in order to receive more specialized instruction from the corresponding instructor. This rotation continued for the duration of the semester. Although students enrolled in only one course, they were given instruction in two sections.

Throughout the course, students were assigned several "self-guided" assignments. They were given a topic and a goal, but the path they took to reach that goal, was up to them to determine. Before the assignments or projects began, the students aided in the creation of rubrics for each assignment. We decided, as a class what the focus of the assignment should be, and what the main points for grading would be upon completion. As students moved closer to their goal, if rubrics and scoring guides needed to be updated, we made that decision together as a class. By doing this, the students understood the importance of having their own students give input into their rubrics, scoring guides and assignments.

During the first iteration, we collaborated to set up the two offered sections (n=13, n=17) as a reading/writing workshop on a "block" schedule. Each professor taught four sessions of workshop, with one professor focused on developing content for reading and the other on writing, with the students alternating each week with their "home team". As we had both interacted with all of the students in the first semester of coursework, they were familiar with each of us, as we seek to interact with students through field observations, journaling, and other interactions in the first semester together. Though they had registered for a course with their "home team" teacher, they were almost universally open to the new design (only one student noted displeasure with interacting with both professors in reflections).

The course structure used a common reading text, *The Giver* (Lowry, 1993), which we explored using literature circles, reader response journals, and writing workshops which focused on narrative, informed opinion, and persuasive pieces integrating instruction on the six traits of writing. The course culminated in four-week plan for a One Book, One School (OBOS) curriculum unit focused on student-selected trade books, completed in interdisciplinary teams, and shared in presentations (assignment available as Appendix A). We used *Creating Literacy Instruction for Middle-Level Learners* (Gunning, 2015), also used in the previous course, as the primary text during this semester. Additional sessions were taught collaboratively with the full group (n=30), and students participated in four weeks of field placement in the middle of the semester. We intended to emulate the structure that students would encounter in middle schools while demonstrating ways in which reading and writing could connect to content area instruction. For each week the pre-service teachers observed in the field classrooms, they were required to write a reflection focused on specific questions. These questions are designed to help them critically analyze what is occurred in the middle school classroom, and how it might be similar to what their own classroom will be like one day.

While we consistently strive to model critical self-reflection and encourage open dialogue, we also sought to solicit focused and anonymous input from students. As noted previously, the co-inquiry model empowers students to contribute directly to the design and implementation of curriculum. Likewise, using a simple reflective framework—designed for students to provide formative or summative feedback, but also useful for self-reflection—provided our students with an additional tool for use in their future classrooms. As is key in SoTL work, collaboration with students in pursuit of improved outcomes was a transparent and ongoing element of this undertaking. In this way, we worked to model both critical reflection and response to formative feedback in planning instruction. For this, we asked all students in the initial course offering to respond to the following items, adapted from the Critical Incident Questionnaire by Brookfield (2005):

1. At what moment in the course did you feel most engaged with what was happening?
2. At what moment in the course did you feel most distanced from what was happening?
3. What action that anyone (teacher or student) took in the course did you find most affirming and helpful?
4. What action that anyone (teacher or student) took in the course did you find most puzzling or confusing?
5. What about the course surprised you the most? (This could be something about your own reactions to what went on, or something that someone did, or anything else that occurs to you.)

In response to student feedback, and as a necessity due to lower enrollment, the next iteration of the course was a combined class structure (n=22) that included both reading workshop and writing workshop in each week's instruction. We also implemented a seminar in lieu of field experience and adopted ancillary texts focused specifically on content area literacies. Student feedback for the structure presented in each iteration of the course is shared in the results section to follow. The original intent was to gather information about curriculum for future revision; however, these questionnaire items also revealed other themes relevant to the shifting of student assumptions about literacy which will also be discussed later. We considered feedback from student reflections such as these—both at midterm and end of semester—alongside formal assessment results in a reflection-to-intervention cycle to determine improvements in subsequent terms.

During the first two offerings of the course, detailed herein, data was formally collected three times. At the end of the first semester, we solicited student feedback using the CIQ as detailed previously. This same measure was used in the second course at midterm and at the end of the term. Quotes used in the sections that follow are drawn from these measures. Additionally, we considered relevant student feedback from end-of-course evaluations. Informal observations and casual dialogue with students was likewise drawn from in collaborative discussions. In the third, most recent, iteration of the course, informal feedback was solicited from students throughout the semester for the explicit purpose of course improvement in future terms, though this data was not codified for research purposes.

To examine the data, we initially met at the end of the first semester to review student feedback and plan changes for the second term. Though the course has been limited to one section in the semesters that followed, we have continued this collaborative reflection each term in service to meeting students' needs. In each meeting, all responses are read by each researcher. Next, we note positive, neutral, and negative comments. Notably, there were few comments that were neutral, in part due to the CIQ framework, and likely also because students were familiar with the respect and responsiveness afforded to their input. From these general categories, we sought out themes within each area which are detailed using quotes from student responses below. Our initial results clustered around the topics of course structure and transformative shifts around assumptions about our threshold concept of literacy. We have continued to use those two clusters in analysis during following semesters, with subtopics as noted below.

SIGNIFICANT FINDINGS

Course Structure—Responding to Student Concerns

During the first semester of the new course, the curriculum format received mixed reviews. Among the positive aspects of the course, students specifically noted the usefulness of peer and self-assessment in writing as "It forced me to relook at my paper to see what I could improve on, too." In contrast, others noted that having to write a draft on demand for immediate feedback was stressful. Another noted that "A lot of students in our class really hate writing and seriously struggled with this workshop. This confused me because I feel like we were given plenty of tools to help make the process smooth." While still another noted in response to the questionnaire item about what was confusing, "None. This was really well-constructed. If anything, I wish we could have spent more time on it." Finally, one student commented "It was actually super-duper fun. I'd love to do something similar." Although not particularly specific, this final comment was heartening as it represented that at least some of the students were highly engaged throughout.

However, some students were frustrated by the structure, which was deemed "terrible" by one respondent. Another stated that they were confused by "how one week we focused on writing, the next week on reading, and how we switched focuses each week." A third echoed the disjointed nature of the courses, stating "I wish there was a stronger connection between reading and writing workshops"

Additionally, although one student stated that they "actually liked the One Book, One School project and correlation from literacy to content area, another repeated critique of the initial structure that the connection between ELA and content area literacy was not universally apparent. One student complained that "writing has nothing to do with my major. This class is pointless for those of us who aren't ELA majors." Another stated "the connection of actually doing this is in my classroom was hard to connect/visualize. It would be difficult to recreate in my own class later."

Based on these initial results, and in response to decreased enrollment, we made significant changes. Specifically, the single course section included both reading and writing in each class session, previewed topics before on-demand writing, revised writing assignments to provide additional peer feedback in addition to peer and self-assessment, and replaced the field experience with a seminar and ancillary text study focused on literacy in the content areas. Content-area text options for the seminar are provided in Appendix B.

The second iteration of the course included significant feedback which reflected the curriculum changes. One student noted that they were surprised that they "didn't like writing as much as I thought," and others noted frustration with lack of peer feedback before the peer assessment of the final draft. Still, these changes were generally well-received. One student stated "I enjoy writing and spend a lot of my spare time writing for fun, so this has been a very pleasant experience. If anything, this class has increased my productivity with writing and given me new ways to think when writing. Also, I am not complaining as much about the editing process as I used to. I used to fall in the camp of 'I wrote it right the first time' and despised editing. I'm learning." They praised the use of student-created rubrics, which were created in groups following introduction of each new writing piece, because "it helped with starting the paper" and "we felt like we were a part of the grading process." As to the reading components, students stated that they "felt engaged in Literature Circles when I had a role to do" and "learn best in groups and being able to speak."

Students in the second iteration also indicated an increase in perceived relevance of ELA in connection to other content areas. One student noted, "the thing that surprised me the most is the amount of literacy content that I have been able to relate to both my ELA and math content areas." Another stated, "You can use literacy in every class period, whether that be math, science, or art." These responses validated the decision to replace the field experience with reflective seminars and content-area literacy text study. Further support for this change came from a GroupMe application-based text conversation shared with the professor, in which one student stated, "Yes! Reuse this book!' while another added, "this book was a lot less dry than our actual textbook." Students also noted the value of the reflective seminars focused on examining teacher beliefs crafting a philosophy statement, for example stating they were surprised by "the opportunity to objectively look at how our experience tied into our personality as an educator."

In the third iteration of the course, students have not noted the same concerns over the "disconnect". While not a response to student request, the core textbook used in both literacy courses was replaced with readings more targeted to course objectives and student needs. Each set of articles and web resources balances general content about literacy with specialized content related to interdisciplinary literacy. As such, students had a set of resources tailored to their future content area instruction as well as the needed resources for planning the final project. The reliance on the use of online materials organized in the course management system required ongoing online interaction with the course. This need to navigate was likely made more acceptable as it saved them having to invest in a textbook. They did note in course evaluations that the inclusion of a "homework slide" in materials online helped them to stay focused. While this had been a part of previous iterations, students spent more time online in the course management system this term, which likely raised their awareness of this feature.

Additionally, the common novel was changed to *Unwind* (Schusterman, 2007). As with *The Giver* and *Code Orange*, the author is a popular writer for teens and the content allows for multiple challenging conversations around topics that are contemporary debates. Students were both engaged with and excited to discuss the text. In deciding on books for the OBOS project, many students sought out books with similar dystopian themes. Additionally, students continued to note the usefulness of the content-area focused reading, as evidenced by their preparation and participation in group discussions surrounding the texts.

Based on gathered feedback, course reviews, and the data collected for this study, we changed a few components in the most recent iteration of the writing workshop. To better integrate collaboration, online peer feedback using google forms within the course management system was implemented between class sessions, with students bringing a revised draft to class on their computers to participate in peer and self-assessment before submitting a final draft electronically. A guest speaker from the library addressed issues of media bias and search techniques to support student engagement with the library databases as many of these students have not previously had to write research papers. In the seminar discussions around teaching philosophy, students were required to bring in the philosophy statement developed in an earlier course to explicitly examine how their assumptions have shifted during their time in the program. They then developed these beliefs into an extensive Philosophy of Education piece, which many chose to develop into a cover letter in an extended session was offered on in response to their concerns. Of note, all students stayed beyond their scheduled time to participate.

Educational Philosophy—Transformation of Student Assumptions

Addressing SLOs as noted on the syllabus was the primary requirement in restructuring the course. Thus, the new design needed to ensure that preservice teachers mastered the course content and made connections between literacy instruction and the needs of their future students. Beyond this, we wanted to craft a course that would challenge and engage these preservice teachers, leading to active learning within an environment that supported this learning and exploration. It is important to note that the course discussed here is the second in a sequence of required literacy education introduction courses. As such, students' strengths, weaknesses, learning styles, and personalities were well-known. Additionally, 26 of the 30 students were majoring in math, science, or social studies tracks within the middle grades program; only four of the students were English/Language Arts (ELA) middle grades majors.

This overarching goal of challenging assumptions to support student growth in preparation for their future careers informs all course planning throughout the department. Student responses to three of the questionnaire items revealed information about student perceptions of the ability of this course to meet that goal.

Responses to item three, *what action that anyone (teacher or student) took in the course did you find most affirming and helpful,* included comments about the suitability of the classroom for exploration of ideas and assumptions. As defined by Drago-Severson (2012), a holding space for growth is a setting in which a learner is supported in genuine engagement around the difficult work of self-examination and refining of beliefs and frames of reference. Meyer and Land (2005) refer to this as a liminal space, where students can transition from one state of understanding or knowing—one set of assumptions—to a new, more refined understanding through the shift in habits of thinking around a threshold concept. Primary among these supports were professor availability and feedback, with one respondent stating the professor "was so helpful and would communicate with us exactly what was needed." Feedback on writing was also viewed as a positive element of relationship-building, as was the use of student work as exemplars, a technique frequently used in middle grades writing workshop classes. One student noted "When Dr. A asked to use my work for her PowerPoint, I felt like I was doing something right with my writing and it made me feel good."

Student reactions to item four, *what action that anyone (teacher or student) took in the course did you did most puzzling or confusing,* offered information about challenges to assumptions, the disorienting dilemma that can initiate the examination of existing beliefs and students' reactions to these. These clustered around the different benefits of collaborative learning and a discussion-based curriculum. One student noted, "Working with groups about *The Giver* was when I was most engaged. Giving each other feedback helped me and other classmates." Another noted that within the literature circles, "requiring/

facilitating class discussion helped me understand the content better." Students also noted that working with informed opinion pieces that required research on two sides of a contemporary issue in education required them to move beyond the comfort of current frames of reference. One stated they were surprised by how they were "able to write from both sides of a story" while another said that they found it affirming when "people disagree with viewpoints so everyone gets a variety of answers", suggesting that the classroom environment allowed students to both challenge assumptions and support safe exploration of other ways of thinking.

Given the cultivation of a holding space and deliberate introduction of opportunities for a disorienting dilemma, we sought evidence of resulting perspective transformation. Question five, *what about the course surprised you the most,* included answers that revealed changing assumptions about literacy, education, and student identities as readers and writers. A few content area majors noted "how easy it was to adapt learning activities for literacy into math" and other subjects and expressed surprise at "being able to somehow find a connection to content areas for the book" (OBOS project). Students shifted their perspectives about writing in general, noting surprise at "the amount of work that it takes to have a decent writing piece." While one student was surprised by "how much I really don't like writing", most others responded positively with comments such as surprise about "how much I like writing if I enjoy the assignment" and "how much I did not dread turning in my papers." As to reading, students noted surprise that they liked "*The Giver* that much. I don't really like reading, but it made me explore reading" while another stated, "I actually read the book assigned and enjoyed it! The only books/novels I read this semester were for this class."

Taken together, these responses suggest that shifting course organization has increased both reported transformation of assumptions and some shift in the perception of literacy relevance in content areas. As noted previously, we believe that this understanding of literacy as including a broad range of texts and of being shaped both socially and by disciplinary traditions is a key element in our students' future implementation of disciplinary literacy instruction in their future classrooms. Given these initial findings, the second iteration to the course increased deliberate emphasis on the role of literacy across the disciplines and on increasing the sharing of ideas through peer editing and structured seminar discussions including reflection on educator beliefs. Overall, respondents seemed to welcome and respond to these changes. Specifically, student feedback noted how the peer relationships in the shared holding space contributed to learning. One stated, "I was surprised how comfortable yet distinguished the ideas and conversations were." Another noted, "When we were in our Science group, it was affirming when other students would listen to my idea and then elaborate upon it. We were building great ideas!"

The combination of peer support and discussion-based interactions was also raised in comments about the exposure to diverse perspectives and opportunity to explore other habits of mind. One student stated, "we get to share ideas and see how other people in our content think as well as across content to other subjects' and another added "I'm surprised by the different views some have when posed with a topic." The importance of discussion and peer engagement was echoed in comments about the course structure, as well, with one student noting that "Literature Circles helped me extend my understanding and possibly change my viewpoint" and another stating "one of the more surprising things is how much more we get to share our ideas with classmates in seminar."

As before, successful support of transformational learning is evidenced when students report a change in their assumptions or their frames of reference. Here, these refined beliefs included both reflections on the connection of literacy across content areas and students' own identity as readers and writers. Interdisciplinary connections were expressed frequently, including the discovery that "you can use literacy in every class period, whether that be math, science, or art." As in the previous semester, students noted surprise about their own skills. One ELA major noted "I learned that I still have a few things to work on" while other students noted "It surprised me how much I loved the writing. I remembered that I loved writing as a kid and should do it more." Finally, students noted the usefulness of the curriculum in building their own skills, stating "I actually grew as a writer! I expected to get a little better, but I grew more than I thought I would."

In the third iteration of the course, a significant change was introducing an in-depth reflective analysis of their teaching philosophy in lieu of a persuasive letter. In crafting their Philosophy of Education statements, students were asked to identify a core belief in each of six areas, determine a source for this belief—experiential, observational, or academic—and state how that belief will be upheld in their own classrooms. Student discussion on these topics had to be curtailed by time constraints and was continued in other shared classes, a sign of genuine student engagement in this exploration. In comparing these new in-depth, examined works with their earlier, simplistic explanations of their philosophy of education completed before beginning coursework in their major, many students noted that they were surprised by the depth of thinking they had done "below the surface" of their classes and the impact that this reflection on ideas and experiences would have in their future classrooms.

Considered as a whole, the transformative learning evidenced in student responses across the courses considered here suggest that this structure, focused on student engagement with the work of reading and writing, modeled on the active learning common in middle grades classrooms and supported with constructive feedback from instructors and peers offers an opportunity for learning more and learning more deeply while fully addressing the SLOs as required for this course.

DISCUSSION AND IMPLICATIONS FOR PRACTICE

Based on the student responses shared above, the course revision met the primary goals of increasing student engagement and skill in reading and writing, inspiring them to value interdisciplinary literacy, and preparing them to integrate literacy into different content areas. The success of this curricular change both encourages ongoing refinement and supports the need for explicit and systematic inquiry into the student experience and focused reflection on findings. This thoughtful, collaborative activity serves a dual role: improved instruction for students and professional development for instructors.

Implications for Preservice Curriculum

Beyond the specifics of this course, there are multiple implications for other preservice teacher programs. These include strategies for engagement, support for risk-taking and transformational learning, and preparing students for the unique challenges of teaching in a middle school using common core literacy standards.

One of the key successes of this course lay in the students actually doing what we expect them to be able to teach. Our iteration of the Reading Apprenticeship Model addresses this need directly. As noted by Schonbach et al. (2012), "Researchers working in a social-cognitive tradition have described a variety of cognitive apprenticeships, in which mental activities characteristic of certain kinds of cognitive tasks—such as computation, written composition, interpreting texts, and the like—are internalized and appropriated by learners through social supports of various kinds" (p. 22). They entered the class with varied levels of familiarity with the reading and writing workshops, and the more-experienced students were able to take the lead in their groups in literature circles; in most cases, this "expert" was a student who was not an ELA content-area major, allowing these students an opportunity to take a leadership role. Many of the comments included notes about both how difficult the work of reading and writing is and how much students were surprised that they enjoyed the work. Their engagement and enjoyment were directly related to the course structure; telling students about a curriculum structure falls far short of the learning involved in them actively participating in the curriculum. One of the concerns as this curriculum launched was whether a learning structure typically used in elementary and middle schools would be too simplistic for adults to engage with; however, as in writing circles for professional authors, these students were willing to participate wholeheartedly in exploring a new learning experience. This success is echoed in the use of SOTL research—engaging with students as co-investigators, soliciting ongoing feedback, and modeling the important work of reflection and analysis of curricular changes similarly includes students in the meaning-making of research.

In part, this format seemed to be successful as it also included explicit connections between the students' content area specialization and literacy, highlighted in class discussions. These students didn't mind reading if they saw it as useful, and selecting texts and topics that related to their future careers as content-area middle school teachers ensured that they were invested in the materials. Further, selecting a common text for literature study that had ready connections to science and math encouraged those students to have an immediate purpose for reading. The selection of writing prompts that linked personal experience and interests encouraged students to work to best communicate their ideas. The importance of choice is not limited to middle-grade learners—when possible, allowing this choice in the college classroom seems to have a similar positive impact on student success. The importance of this was repeatedly mentioned in student comments about the hard work that they were willing to undertake in the writing process due to their personal investment in the topic.

Much of the course, from literature circles to seminar sessions to peer conferencing, is focused on discussion-based learning, including structures introduced by Brookfield (2005). Students in the middle grades program learn that whoever is talking the most is learning the most; at the same time, these students did not see talking as working. Their responses also noted how impressed they were with the depth of their academic conversations and how much they felt valued in these discussions. Use of literature circle roles emphasized the need to prepare for a discussion—both as a learner and as a teacher. Peer conferencing formats provided scaffolds for conversations around writing. Perhaps most importantly, many students who readily stated that they were "not writers" were able to use conferencing to have meaningful conversations around writing; focusing on different traits for each piece also limited the perceived risk in these discussions. Varied feedback was another important element in the course. Asking students for feedback—on their learning, their thinking, and on the course itself—increased engagement as students knew that their voices were being carefully considered. Written feedback on final pieces provided evaluative information beyond the rubric while feedback in the reader response journals allowed for more casual conversation around the book. Peer feedback in conferences and in assessments sparked discussion about meaning, structure, and voice in addition to a shared investment in the final papers. Including examples of current and past students' work, anonymously and with permission, also incorporated student voices and celebrated work effort. These successes both served as reinforcement of the foundational theory behind the workshop format and as a model for supporting similar dialogue in their future classrooms.

The collected feedback was instrumental in creating a holding space to support both content area learning required by the course curriculum and the transformational learning that support students in becoming teachers. Asking students to take risks—in reading, writing, and thinking—requires creating an environment in which they are the center of decision-making, where they are heard and valued, and where their work and insights are celebrated. In crafting a course that will prepare students for teaching and planning in a middle school setting and creating a setting for student growth, the creation of a supportive space may not be a conscious decision, but in retrospect, it is a necessary component. These students will be graduating within a year and joining a faculty that will likely include interdisciplinary planning. The challenge of this planning can and should start before students are in their workplace. Based on the pride expressed in and quality of the One Book, One School project presentations, students' ready engagement in undertaking this complex challenge demonstrates their readiness for similar collaborative interdisciplinary challenges in their future workplaces.

Implications for Practice

Beyond the refinement of the curriculum informed by students' feedback and reinforced by informal conversation and observation, there were multiple changes to the researchers' practice in response to this SOTL research undertaking.

Throughout the three iterations of the course, our regular meetings to examine student feedback and to collaboratively plan class sessions in response to the feedback were an invariably valuable commitment of finite time available on campus. While the total time commitment was less than ten hours over the course of the semester, these focused conversations were reminiscent of the common planning time implemented in K-12 institutions. Although enrollment has not allowed for multiple sections or this or other classes within the program, continuing dialogues about shared students and drawing from other professors' ideas and experiences provides an opportunity for growth and professional development.

The CIQ as a simple method for collecting anonymous feedback was useful in gathering candid commentary in-the-moment. In addition to midterm and end-of-course feedback, this tool can be used after any new activity or topic, or even at the end of each week's classes to check student understanding and engagement. Students were receptive to changes after the midterm CIQ analysis when these modifications were explicitly linked to the comments received.

Modeling action research by engaging in this work with students reinforces the need for critical reflection on practice. Perhaps more importantly, it demonstrates that improving teaching practice is a lifelong, serious pursuit. Committing to openly examining what works, collaborating with students to meet their needs, and discussing the reflection-to-instruction framework both frequently and candidly shows students that their success is key and that teaching is both challenging and thoughtful work. We aspire that the students in these classes will carry forward this commitment to collaborative improvement to their own future classrooms.

NEXT STEPS

One of the primary impacts of our ongoing SoTL work with this class is the opportunity to consistently reflect on our teaching practice to refine both this course and other classes within this program.

By consistently soliciting input from students toward improving their learning experience for this work, we have learned that the program coursework does not include instruction in creating a cover letter or resume, two formal documents required for their internship applications. As such, we are collaborating with the career services office to include this as an extension of the philosophy of education paper. An additional change implemented this year was to include student choice in the selection of the common trade novel.

Meeting regularly to coordinate our efforts has also offered us the opportunity to introduce SoTL work to other professors in our program with the goal of improving student preparation. One of the topics currently under investigation is the impact of the workshop model on students' perception of their readiness to incorporate literacy components in their own classrooms, which we intend to measure using Likert-scale measures at the start and end of the term. While the SLOs for the course are currently used as items on a reflective exam to determine student mastery of these objectives, we also plan to implement a pre-course use of these same items to determine students' existing knowledge at the start of the term to determine growth.

In addition to transforming student perspectives, our SoTL work together has transformed our own practice. Given the need for literacy education—for preservice teachers and for the middle school students in their classrooms—we are certain to continue to reflect on and actively refine our instruction to meet this need.

REFERENCES

Atwell, N. (1991). *In the middle: Writing, reading, and learning with adolescents*. Portsmouth, NH: Heinemann Educational Books.

Beck, C., & Kosnik, C. (2006). *Innovations in teacher education: A social constructivist approach*. Albany, NY: State University of New York Press.

Brookfield, S. (1986). *Understanding and facilitating adult learning: A comprehensive analysis of principles and effective practices*. San Francisco, CA: Jossey-Bass.

Brookfield, S. (2005). *Discussion as a way of teaching: Tools and techniques for democratic classrooms*. San Francisco, CA: Jossey-Bass.

Calkins, L. (1994). The art of teaching writing (New ed.). Portsmouth, NH: Heinemann.

Cardullo, V., & Zygouris-Coe, V. (2013). *Eighth-grade students reading nonfiction literature on the IPAD: An exploratory case study* (ProQuest Dissertations Publishing). Retrieved from http://search.proquest.com/docview/1500850648/

Cooney, C. (2005). *Code orange*. New York, NY: Laurel-Leaf.

Council of Chief State School Officers (CCSSO) and the National Governors Association (NGA). (2010). *Common core state standards for English language arts & literacy in history/social studies, science, and technical subjects*. Retrieved from http://www.corestandards.org/assets/CCSSI_ELA%20Standards.pdf

Counihan, E., & Silcox, A. (2014). Internal rhyme, isosceles triangles, and iMovie: A middle school collaboration to integrate English and geometry. *English Journal, 103*(3), 34–40. PMID:25286485

Drago-Severson, E. (2009). *Leading adult learning: Supporting adult development in our schools.* Thousand Oaks, CA: Corwin Press.

Drago-Severson, E. (2012). *Helping educators grow: Practices and strategies for leadership development.* Cambridge, MA: Harvard Education Press.

Duhaylongsod, L., Snow, C. E., Selman, R. L., & Donovan, M. S. (2015). Toward disciplinary literacy: Dilemmas and challenges in designing history curriculum to support middle school students. *Harvard Educational Review*, *85*(4), 587–608. doi:10.17763/0017-8055.85.4.587

Fang, Z., & Wei, Y. (2010). Improving middle school students' science literacy through reading infusion. *The Journal of Educational Research*, *103*(4), 262–273. doi:10.1080/00220670903383051

Felten, P. (2013). Principles of good practice in SoTL. *Teaching and Learning Inquiry: The ISSOTL Journal.*, *1*(1), 121–125. doi:10.20343/teachlearninqu.1.1.121

Felten, P., Bragg, J., Bumbry, M., Hill, J., Hornsby, K., Pratt, M., & Weller, S. (2013). A call for expanding inclusive student engagement in SoTL. *Teaching & Learning Inquiry: The ISSOTL Journal*, *1*(2), 63–74. doi:10.20343/teachlearninqu.1.2.63

Gee, J. (2001). Reading as situated language: A sociocognitive perspective. *Journal of Adolescent & Adult Literacy*, *44*(8), 714–725. doi:10.1598/JAAL.44.8.3

Graham, A., Kerkhoff, S., & Spires, H. (2017). Disciplinary literacy in the middle school: Exploring pedagogical tensions. *Middle Grades Research Journal*, *11*(1), 63–83.

Graves, D. H. (1994). *A fresh look at writing.* Portsmouth, NH: Heinemann.

Gunning, T. G. (2015). *Creating literacy instruction for middle-level learners* (2nd ed.). Boston, MA: Pearson Learning Solutions.

Hynd-Shanahan, C. (2013). What does it take? The challenge of disciplinary literacy. *Journal of Adolescent & Adult Literacy*, *57*(2), 93–98. doi:10.1002/JAAL.226

Kleine, K., & McBryar, L. (2009). Preservice teachers experience middle grades curriculum. *Middle School Journal*, *40*(3), 28–36. doi:10.1080/00940771.2009.11495584

Lowry, L. (1993). *The giver.* Boston, MA: Houghton Mifflin.

Martin, C. L. (2015). Writing as a tool to demonstrate mathematical understanding. *School Science and Mathematics*, *115*(6), 302–313. doi:10.1111sm.12131

McKenna, M. C., Conradi, K., Lawrence, C., Jang, B. G., & Meyer, J. P. (2012). Reading attitudes of middle school students: Results of a U.S. survey. *Reading Research Quarterly*, *47*(3), 283–306. doi:10.1002/rrq.021

Meyer, J. H. F., & Land, R. (2005). Threshold concepts and troublesome knowledge (2): Epistemological considerations and a conceptual framework for teaching and learning. *Higher Education*, *49*(3), 373–388. doi:10.100710734-004-6779-5

Mezirow, J. D. (2006). *Learning as transformation: Critical perspectives on a theory in progress*. San Francisco, CA: Jossey-Bass.

Murray, D. M. (1989). *Expecting the unexpected: Teaching myself--and others--to read and write*. Portsmouth, NH: Boynton/Cook.

Musu-Gillette, L. (2015). *Reading for fun: Using NAEP data to explore student attitudes*. Retrieved October 1, 2019, from https://nces.ed.gov/blogs/nces/post/reading-for-fun-using-naep-data-to-explore-student-attitudes

National Center for Educational Statistics (Ed.). (2018, September 17). *Student groups and trends reports*. Retrieved October 1, 2019, from https://nces.ed.gov/nationsreportcard/groups_trends/

National Governors Association Center for Best Practices & Council of Chief State School Officers. (2010). *Common core state standards initiative*. Retrieved December 23, 2010 from http://www.corestandards.org/the-standards/english-language-arts-standards

Pytash, K. (2013). Secondary preservice teachers' development of teaching scientific writing. *The Association for Science Teacher Education.*, *24*(5), 793–810. doi:10.100710972-013-9338-z

Rockoff, J., & Lockwood, B. (2010). How and why middle schools harm student achievement. *Education Next*, (Fall): 68–77.

Rosenblatt, L. (1960). Literature: The reader's role. *English Journal*, *49*(5), 304. doi:10.2307/810700

Sanacore, J., & Palumbo, A. (2010). Middle school students need more opportunities to read across the curriculum. *The Clearing House: A Journal of Educational Strategies, Issues and Ideas*, *83*(5), 180–185. doi:10.1080/00098650903583735

Schoenbach, R., Greenleaf, C., & Murphy, L. (2012). *Reading for understanding : How reading apprenticeship improves disciplinary learning in secondary and college classrooms*. San Francisco, CA: Jossey-Bass, A Wiley Imprint.

Schön, D. (1987). *Educating the reflective practitioner: Toward a new design for teaching and learning in the professions* (1st ed.). San Francisco, CA: Jossey-Bass.

Shusterman, N. (2007). *Unwind*. New York: Simon & Schuster Books for Young Readers.

Solis, M., Miciak, J., Vaughn, S., & Fletcher, J. M. (2014). Why intensive interventions matter: Longitudinal studies of adolescents with reading disabilities and poor reading comprehension. *Learning Disability Quarterly*, *37*(4), 218–229. doi:10.1177/0731948714528806 PMID:25378799

Street, B. V. (2005). Recent applications of new literacy studies in educational contexts. *Research in the Teaching of English*, *39*(4), 417–423. Retrieved from https://login.cyrano.ucmo.edu/login?url=https://search-proquest-com.cyrano.ucmo.edu/docview/215345525?accountid=6143

Teague, G., Anfara, V. Jr, Wilson, N., Gaines, C., & Beavers, J. (2012). Instructional practices in the middle grades. *NASSP Bulletin*, *96*(3), 203–227. doi:10.1177/0192636512458451

Wendt, J. (2013). Combating the crisis in adolescent literacy: Exploring literacy in the secondary classroom. *American Secondary Education*, *41*(2), 38–48.

Werder, C., & Otis, M. M. (2010). *Engaging student voices in the study of teaching and learning*. Sterling, VA: Stylus.

APPENDIX 1

One Book, One School

Objective: Your team will develop a Literacy Program to be implemented into a middle school setting. This will be considered a "One Book, One School" program. Your team will build a cross-curricular unit based on a young-adult novel to be carried out across all content areas in a school.

Groups: Each group will consist of 3-5 people of different content areas. We have divided the content areas based on the students in this class. You will have the chance to build your own groups based upon that need.

Books: Your group will determine a grade level you are focused on teaching. After deciding on a grade-level, you must choose a young adult fiction novel that features an **ethical dilemma**.

Requirements:

1. Start with the text reading level, which should be between 6-8 grade, to start. If there are integrated supports for readers, such as in-class reading with think-alouds, you may go up a grade. If you want to have students primarily read independently at home as homework, you may want to go down a grade level.

2. Over Spring Break, read your book. It is important for you to take notes during the reading. Make sure to mark the sections you feel you could connect to your content area. This will make it easier to go back and build your lessons.

3. Develop a calendar of a minimum of 8 days and a maximum of 15 days, depending on the length of your book. Include which content area will focus on the book one each day. For Example: At my previous school, we had each content area + one elective take a weekday during the program to help with student focus and teacher planning (for example, Math was on Mondays). (15 points, group)

   It may be helpful to work backwards from the section that spoke to you and design the calendar to ensure that reading day matches with your content area. Also, decide on at least one school-based support to students who may struggle with the text so that they are not left to their own devices at home to grapple with the reading.

4. Design a lesson plan within your content area. It must have a content area objective, SLOs, a formative assessment that can be used to guide instruction during the class, integrated technology, and differentiation for an ELL, a student with ADHD/Dyslexia, and a gifted student. (IEPs for each will be provided with a case study description).

   You can either plan to have students pre-read the content as homework (include some note-taking guide/review of salient content), or you can have them read a portion as homework (specify what part) and spend up to 15 minutes in class with follow-up and some read-aloud variation. (60 points, individually graded)

5. As a group, develop a Summative Assessment Menu (see handout)

   Each group member will be responsible for creating a two-sentence activity description in each menu section. For ONE of the activities, develop an explanation of the strategy used, a detailed rubric, specific mastery objectives, and an exemplar of outstanding work. Unlike the lesson plan, these may be closer to your content area. They should be connected to the book in some way, but you need not specify ELA standards. (40 points, individually graded)

6. Other components that must be included in your presentation:

    a. A letter home to parents to discuss what you are doing with the "One Book, One School" project. (15 points, group)

    b. A plan for an intervention program (School-wide and classroom-wide) for students who are struggling to complete the required work. (10 points, group)

    c. A plan for implementing technology into the unit. Explain what you are using and how you plan to implement it into the OBOS program. (10 points, group)

    d. At least one content area must complete a webquest for the students to complete during the unit. (15 points, group)

    e. Professional development opportunity/training description for teachers who will be implementing OBOS. (10 points, group)

    f. Field trip proposal for capstone activity. Explanation of how it links to the unit. Estimate of cost per student/chaperone for admission. (15 points, group)

7. Peer and Self-Assessment (60 points, individual)

8. Presentation (50 points, group)

Total points earned based on group effort: 140
Total points earned based on individual effort: 160

APPENDIX 2

Content Area Supplemental Text Options

ELA

Wilhelm, J. (2016). *You gotta BE the book*. New York, NY: Teachers College Press.

Math

Hoffer, W. (2016). *Developing literate mathematicians: A guide for integrating language and literacy instruction into secondary mathematics*. Reston, VA: NCTM.

Science

Elliott, L., Jackson, K., & Salter, I. (2016). *Composing science: A facilitator's guide to writing in the science classroom*. New York, NY: Teachers College Press.

Social Studies

Windburg, S., Martin, D., & Monte-Sano, C. (2012). *Reading like a historian: Teaching literacy in middle and high school history classrooms.* New York, NY: Teachers College Press.

Chapter 14
Scholarly Rigor:
Focusing Reflection Through Engaging in an Academic Dialogue

Rob Hallis

 https://orcid.org/0000-0002-5852-9404

University of Central Missouri, USA

ABSTRACT

The Scholarship of Teaching and Learning nurtures an academic discussion of best instructional practices. This case study examines the role domain knowledge plays in determining extent to which students can effectively analyze an opinion piece from a major news organization, locate a relevant source to support their view of the issue, and reflect on the quality of their work. The goal of analyzing an opinion piece is twofold: it fosters critical thinking in analyzing the strength of an argument and it promotes information management skills in locating and incorporating relevant sources in a real-world scenario. Students, however, exhibited difficulties in accurately completing the assignment and usually overestimated their expertise. This chapter traces how each step in the process of making this study public clarifies the issues encountered. The focus here, however, centers on the context within which the study was formulated, those issues that contributed to framing the research question, and how the context of inquiry served to deepen insights in interpreting the results.

INTRODUCTION

The classroom is more than the space within which students learn and teachers teach. Whether online or face-to-face, this space is where the mind of the student and that of the teacher meet with the goal of learning: mastering the content of a discipline, acquiring a skill, or reflecting on a practice. "The increased interest of students, governments, accrediting agencies, industry, and the mass media in the performance, responsiveness and accountability of higher education since the late 1980s is a global phenomenon" (Welsh & Metcalf, 2003, p. 33). A number of metrics assess the extent to which educational objectives are clearly stated and met in the classroom, in the program, and at the university level (Shulman, 1988;

DOI: 10.4018/978-1-7998-2212-7.ch014

Lin, 2016), and faculty continue to explore their teaching effectiveness in the classroom as well as in their graduate preparation (Keig & Waggoner, 1994; Chism & Chism, 2007; Mallon, Hays, Bradley, Huisman, & Belanger, 2019). Research developed through the Scholarship of Teaching and Learning (SoTL) provides a "way of grounding our scholarly teaching within theories of learning both established and developing" (Mallon et al., 2019, p. ix). Although librarians use SoTL to improve instructional practices, few have published in the area (McNiff & Hays, 2017, p. 370). This chapter seeks to address this gap.

Faculty must choose appropriate techniques and methods to package course material in a manner that meaningfully engages the student and addresses curricular demands. SoTL supports these activities through transforming teaching problems into research questions (Bass, 1999) and answering these questions through a framework that provides perspective for accessing new pedagogies, technologies, and methods for effectively nurturing student learning. In short, faculty must become self-reflective teachers, familiar with pedagogical tools and skills, aware of the instructional task at hand, and self-aware enough to select the proper tool for the task.

Clearly, faculty assess students on a regular basis through a variety of assignments. A reflective practitioner will return to these artifacts when revising an assignment or changing the sequence of course content. Scanning students' work, however, may only provide anecdotal evidence as outliers may overshadow equally weighing everyone's work. While a cursory examination of students' work may lead to ideas about improving one's teaching, scholarly investigation provides a more rigorous scaffold within which to critically evaluate classroom techniques. This chapter provides a case study that evaluates the role that domain knowledge plays when students need to identify the key ideas in an opinion piece and locate additional information to support the student's point of view on the issue. The focus of this chapter, however, is twofold: an investigation into revealing barriers that students experience when analyzing an opinion piece, and exploring the professional development involved in constructing that research. Following a brief literature review, I will discuss the context within which this study originated, issues that framed the question, the process of gathering and analyzing students' work, and the broader significance of this study for librarianship in particular and teaching in general.

LITERATURE REVIEW

For nearly 30 years, the SoTL provided a source for research-based investigations into a wide range of issues educators encounter in the classroom. Schulman (1988) categorized these inquiries into five dimensions: problems, investigations, methods, settings, and purposes. He predicted a fundamental shift in the importance of evidence based inquiry into classroom effectiveness:

I believe that by 2005 there will be a fundamental recognition at colleges and universities in the United States that good teaching requires serious investigation into teaching and learning. I believe we will begin to see a fundamental reconception of our shared understanding of good teaching. Ultimately, investigative work into teaching and learning will not be an intriguing aside, or an add-on, but an essential facet of good teaching built into the expected repertoire of scholarly practice. (Shulman, 1988, p. 105)

His predictions are fulfilled in the heightened emphasis on professional development opportunities through campus teaching and learning programs for faculty; the emphasis on learning outcomes at the course, program, and university level; and the growing number of SoTL publications.

In *Opening Lines: Approaches to the Scholarship of Teaching and Learning,* Hutchings (2000) presents case studies from eight different authors; each summarizes an investigation into student performance in their classroom. The research question that forms the heart of these scholarly investigations organically grows from the recognition that students are not mastering content. Universally, these authors realized students were experiencing difficulties and used their background to focus a question and interpret results, while incorporating the 4 Cs: critical thinking, communication, collaboration, and creativity (National Education Association, 2018).

Critical thinking involves intentionally discussing the method of analysis, evaluation, and self-reflection. Through gradated practice and timely feedback on an activity, critical thinking can improve a skill through purposefully considering how to apply that skill to particular situations (Van Gelder, 2005). Communication involves the effective exchange of information through a variety of media as well as effectively listening in diverse environments (National Education Association, 2018, p. 14). Collaboration requires an inclusive environment to nurture the process of learning. When collaboration occurs in research, students gain a deeper connection with the process as well as the informational content (Weller, Domarkaite, lam, & Metta, 2013, p. 1). Creativity engages students in an opportunity to explore various solutions without "getting it wrong". It provides students an opportunity to bridge theory and practice (Bennett, 2011, p. 1). Although creativity is generally regarded as an important element of successful learning, and "while many instructors agree that their institutions have a responsibility to develop students' creative capacities, creativity is less frequently named as an official learning outcome… it highlights a specific gap that needs to be addressed" (Marquis & Henderson, 2015, p. 159). Within this context, library instruction poses some unique challenges.

Librarians teach habits of mind through instructing students in information literacy (Mallon et al., 2019). Faculty often invite librarians for a single session about finding and evaluating appropriate information for an assignment. The faculty member, however, creates and grades the assignment, so librarians may not see the extent to which their instruction was reflected in student work. Traditionally, students need to find several scholarly articles and integrate them in an essay. As pedagogies embraced Problem-Based Inquiry, students have greater latitude in selecting a topic, which requires a more nuanced approach to locating appropriate material. They may investigate a current event, which requires locating a valid primary source and integrating related scholarly sources; students need to develop adequate background knowledge to understand the topic. They may investigate a literary work, which requires scholarly interpretations of that work. They may write a persuasive essay, which could include magazine articles as well as scholarly sources. Thus, students need to develop a wide range of skills, break old habits, and perhaps cultivate background knowledge to complete an assignment.

PRELUDE TO A STUDY

Hutchings (2000) notes the studies gathered for *Opening Lines: Approaches to the Scholarship of Teaching and Learning* focused on methods which included techniques such as ethnographic interviews, focus groups, classroom observations, portfolios, and surveys. She briefly mentions the value of exploring the context within which contributors began their investigation of the classroom experience (p. 2). Exploring the mind-set of these authors is especially valuable, as it reveals the perspectives from which research questions developed as well as the way the results are interpreted. The eight case studies are from faculty in different disciplines who sought to address a variety of issues in the learning experience while employing a range of methods. Despite this variation, there are several common fundamental traits. Faculty were aware of a gap between student expectations and performance before they began their formal investigation. They considered the performance issues of their students over a period of time, reviewed relevant literature for options, often tried several different techniques along the way, and each were actively engaged in assessing teaching effectiveness through professional activities before they began the published study.

For example, Duffy, a professor of psychology at Middlesex Community College, published on service learning and received awards for excellence in teaching and service learning initiatives. Her chapter described the work she did to help her students develop a deeper appreciation of the complexity of abnormal psychology. Service learning provided a "real-world" learning experience for her class. Moreover, introducing the concept of resiliency helped students overcome the feeling of being overwhelmed by the intractable problems often encountered in studying abnormal psychology (Duffy, 2000).

A professor of chemistry at the University of Notre Dame, Jacobs, moved beyond the laboratory to develop appropriate supplemental material to improve student success in his chemistry class. In his chapter, he described the difficulties that some students experienced with general chemistry. They had not learned how to work through a process or work with material at the level of detail needed for this class. He used SAT math scores to identify at risk students. These students were then eligible to attend an alternative section of this class and given supplemental experiences such as working in pairs on conceptually based questions, and participating in additional cooperative learning activities within the class. Longitudinal data show approximately forty percent more students were successful because of the methods used in these alternative sections (Jacobs, 2000).

During my twenty-five years as a librarian, the sources, search tools, and even the role of librarians have changed significantly. Throughout these changes, however, fundamental constants remain. Librarians can serve as a mentor in deciphering an assignment (Badke, 2014b). They can also untangle the complications behind the enticing simplicity of Google searching (Badke, 2014a). Nevertheless, the past decade has marked a dramatic shift from orienting students to where things are on a shelf to developing their skills for searching and evaluating information using a variety of search tools and techniques. Now one needs to "spend less time demonstrating the features of library databases and do more to help students navigate the self-indexing nature of scholarly texts" (Fister, 2015, p. 95). Key elements in this shift involve developing a greater awareness of techniques and methods as well as appropriate times to use them. "In SoTL research, the classroom becomes a site of inquiry where teaching and assessment practices and approaches are often both the methods and the object of study in terms of how well they facilitate student learning" (Mcniff & Hays, 2017, p. 367).

Search engines may now be easier to navigate, and eresources may be more convenient to access, but students continue to experience difficulties locating and evaluating appropriate information for academic purposes. 84% of the students surveyed reported difficulties just getting started, and many reported difficulties when asked to narrow a topic, construct an effective search, select sources from the list of results, or evaluate the validity of a source (Head & Eisenberg, 2010, p. 25). Leckie (1996) concluded that students were desperately seeking citations. Twenty years later, students have the same struggle (Rose-Wiles & Hofmann, 2013). "Whether they were conducting research for a college course or for personal reasons, nearly all of the students in our sample had developed an information-seeking strategy reliant on a small set of common information sources—close at hand, tried, and true" (Head & Eisenberg, 2010, p. 3). Nevertheless, these students believe they are more proficient in finding material than their skills demonstrate. Within this context, SoTL becomes an indispensable resource to bridge this gap through evaluating alternate pedagogies for teaching and for gaining an insight into students' learning behavior.

As a librarian, faculty asked me to provide instruction on the use of library resources to complete their assignments. I have researched developments in pedagogy, student learning, technology, and methods for best practices in familiarizing students with the sources available in a modern library. As a result, these instructional encounters have changed over the years to better engage students and focus instruction on completing a specific assignment rather leading a general orientation to the library. Students now need to integrate relevant information within problem-based assignments, distinguish relevant databases from a dizzying array of options, and incorporate a broader scope of relevant informational sources. Rather than roaming the stacks for print sources, library instruction now focuses on using online search tools to locate sources and requires sophisticated means of evaluating sources based on relevance, accuracy, and appropriateness to the topic.

Guided notes provide a vehicle for students to take notes on the process of identifying appropriate library resources for the specific requirements of the assignment. This sheet evolved over the years to incorporate ideas and techniques from a number of sources. Scholarly literature, professional development workshops and collaboratively working with colleagues improved the activity-sheet as well as the classroom environment within which the students work. In turn, I share my observations of innovative classroom activities at professional conferences at the state, regional, and national level. Through this journey, the structure of the activity sheet evolved. The current version of the activity-sheet serves to guide students as they focus on their individual topic for the assignment and specifically link the assignment to sources available through the library. These guided notes provide a scaffolded process for finding and evaluating information. In the classroom, Appreciative Inquiry (AI) serves to acknowledge searching expertise students have in this activity and to collaboratively develop a plan to build on these skills to meet the requirements of the current assignment. I use the principles of Self-Regulated-Learning (SRL) because students need to develop proficiency with a variety of tools and techniques, to reinforce the ability to select an appropriate tool and method to evaluate sources for their assignment.

The activity sheet serves to structure the process students should use when searching for information, identifying the best tool for locating these sources, and evaluating the validity and relevance of the sources they select in relation to the assignment at hand. [Appendix 1] For the students and instructors, guided notes provide a framework for the procedure to locate and evaluate appropriate sources for their assignment. For the librarian, it serves as a way to practically link the instruction and library resources to the student's assignment. For the researcher, it provides a formative assessment of the student's thought process as they begin work on an assignment.

The basic mechanics of searching [Discovery] is developed by building more sophisticated skills in describing and evaluating sources for use in academic work. The questions need to be more focused. The key words need to be more descriptive, and manipulating a database needs to develop to include filtering the results [Dream]. The worksheet provides a framework for structuring the exercise [Design], and working through the exercise steps the student through the various stages of locating and evaluating material for the essay [Deliver]. (Hallis, 2018, p. 122)

SRL refers to developing a student's ability to guide their own learning. They develop a competence with necessary skills and tools, an understanding of the assignment, and an ability to reflectively select the most appropriate way to complete the task at hand (Zimmerman & Martinez-Pons, 1990). Preparing students to locate appropriate material for their paper requires strategic knowledge, which includes an understanding the functionality and content of various databases, criteria for vetting a variety of sources, and the conventions used to citing material in an academic conversation. Knowledge about the task refers to the requirements of the assignment, and self-knowledge refers to the ability to select the most appropriate strategic knowledge to complete the assignment (Zimmerman & Kitsantas, 2007). SRL is not deliberate practice; whereas deliberate practice involves optimizing specific tasks through repetitive practice, SRL involves thoughtfully selecting appropriate tools and techniques through self-reflection. Students are aware of the functionality and differences among a variety of databases as well as the formats of informational sources. They use appropriate methods to evaluate the sources they select, and they are able to incorporate these sources in their assignment. Finally, students are able to use the assigned method of citation to document the sources they select.

Librarians are aware of the different search tools, the different types of information, and how to integrate these sources into an assignment. They are familiar with the traits of reliable information in a variety of formats and can share how to apply various methods of evaluation. Finally, they are aware of the various techniques used to cite material. As a result, librarians become self-regulated teachers: they are aware of a number of techniques and methods for finding and evaluating information, aware of the various techniques for evaluating sources, and familiar with the requirements for citing sources used in various disciplines. As experts, they are expected to select appropriate tools to address the requirements for a particular assignment and mentor this process within an instructional session.

Students generally first encounter an assignment that specifically makes use of library resources in a second semester English composition course, which includes an assignment that requires students to write an extended essay using a variety of sources to support their ideas. Specific assignments from the various sections of the class range from analyzing a work of fiction to addressing current events. Students needed to incorporate several sources in their essay, many of which must be scholarly in nature. An instructional session with a librarian traces the process students should follow: stating and focusing a research interest through posing an initial question and two to three related questions; deriving descriptive terms from those questions; and using those terms to execute a search in a discovery tool. Students then select appropriate sources from the list of results and incorporate them in the essay. My instruction used guided notes to frame critical stages within the search process as well as to facilitate classroom discussion; students completed the guided notes as part of their writing assignment.

During these classes, I found that students would frequently follow the process and participate in the discussions. Their essays, however, exhibited a poor choice of sources, which showed used unproductive means for locating sources and did not vet the quality of this material. Consequently, I began a longitudinal study from 2012-2018 to determine why students did not adopt the methods modeled in the instructional session. Over the years, I have had access to over 900 papers produced in 50 sections of these classes with a variety of faculty.

The majority of students successfully met the prescribed requirements for the assignment. They selected and cited the required number of sources and the necessary number of scholarly sources. Examining the activity sheets, however, revealed that students had not developed a focused question, frequently used search terms that were too broad or unrelated to their topic, were not able to evaluate credible sources for the assignment, and were unable to link the source to their essay. Their guided notes revealed that students frequently resorted to patch writing, where quotes were clumsily inserted various places in the essay. Furthermore, the quality of the sources raised concerns with their method of locating and evaluating material. Closely examining four aspects from two submissions provides an insight into the challenges that students' experience.

Table 1 contrasts four aspects of two submissions. The examples contrast proficient work with inexperienced work. The first section deals with the question the student wants to investigate. The stronger submission provided more precise words to describe the topic and subsequent questions further clarified that issue. These questions identified a particular type of energy source, and this issue was further clarified geographically and in terms of safety. The weaker submission vaguely referred to an issue, a terrorist attack. The subsequent questions did not serve to clarify this vaguely stated issue. In the next step, students were to derive key words from their questions to describe the type of information they needed. The stronger submission, having more focused questions, used words that more accurately described the needed information. The weaker submission, with vague questions, selected vague key words.

The next step in the research process asked students to select a relevant source for background information and a related scholarly source that addresses their questions from the list of results. They evaluated the validity of a source using a CRAAP test (Blakeslee, 2004). This method of analysis asks one to evaluate several aspects of a source to see if it is Current, Relevant, Accurate, Authorative, and examines the author's Purpose. The table compares how two students considered the authority of a background source and a scholarly source. The stronger submission considered the reputation of the publication, and the author's credentials. The weaker submission misses the mark, referring rather to how well the author wrote or how much work must have been used to produce the article.

In the next planning step, students explain how well the sources answers the questions they raised. The stronger submission identifies how each source provided an answer to how Japan uses hydrogen fuel cells, while the weaker submission only speaks in generalities of how the sources will contribute to completing the assignment. In their self-evaluation, however, both students showed confidence in finding materials. The stronger submission, however, discussed how well the student accomplished specific tasks, while the weaker submission generally discussed the student's aspirations in vague terms.

It is quite common to overestimate one's ability. Kruger and Dunning (1999) found that people often overestimate their skills in areas where they have the least expertise. Such illusory superiority is evident in self-assessments of their competence. This illusory superiority, however, poses an additional challenge for library instruction, especially in the compressed time-frame of a single class period. Students see little need to improve their skills because they believe they are already competent. Apathy may pose an additional challenge to developing new skills. The challenge of engaging students has been studied by Nilson and Zimmerman (2013). In describing how to create a Self-Reflective Learner, she summarizes an apparent apathy on the part of the student that undermines efforts to engage them in the following way: "Specifically, these students take little or no responsibility for their own learning, blaming their shortcomings in achievement on their "ineffective" instruction and the "too advanced" (p. 20).

FRAMING THE QUESTION

Investigating how students work with an opinion piece organically grew from years of working to improve student learning in library instruction described above. Following instructional session in English classes, professors anecdotally reported that essays were better and that students generally used more appropriate sources. Analyzing the activity-sheet and essay in conjunction with in-class interviews revealed that 4-5 students in each section of 20-25 were able to locate, evaluate, and incorporate appropriate sources

Table 1. Comparison of Students activity-sheet[1]

High-Achieving	Low Achieving
Questions -What are hydrogen fuel cells? -Why does japan want to switch to them? -Are hydrogen fuel cells safe? Key Words -Japan/ hydrogen fuel / power / vehicles	**Questions:** -Who caused the terrorist attack? -Where did the terrorists come from? -How recent are the attacks? Key Words -Attacks / recent / where / who
Authority: -Background Source The article was publicized in Bloomberg which delivers business and markets news, data, analysis, and video to the world: featuring stories from Businessweek and Bloomberg News. -Scholarly Source Book authors are from the department of mechanical Science and Engineering at the Tokyo institute of Technology.	**Authority:** -Background Source Shows how well the author wrote -Scholarly Source Shows that he put in a lot of work
Tying sources together: The first source gave me information on what Japan has done and is doing in order to make hydrogen fuel power sources a reality, and the second gave me information on why Japan is shifting to a hydrogen powered society.	**Tying sources together:** Tying sources will help write my paper by helping me explain what is going on
Self Evaluation: +I think I was able to pick very strong reliable sources to back my research +All of the sources I chose gave facts to support my research from reliable source + The library search tool made it a lot easier to find the information I needed. +All of my sources were either current or within the past few years + I believe I was able to take what I needed from each source and easily integrate it into my paper.	**Self Evaluation:** + I feel positive about this area + Assignments are good +Words are great to be used in the paper +I feel that it is very accurate +I feel I did well on it.

before instruction. Another 4-5 students clung to habits that were only somewhat successful following instruction. Consequently, instruction benefitted approximately 10-12 students in each section. A simple rubric measured the extent to which the essay followed the requirements for information found on the professors' guidelines; this only confirmed that most students merely listed the number of sources and used correct citation format. A qualitative examination of weaker submissions, however, revealed the thought process behind these mistakes.

Through evaluating the quality of the sources they select, students reveal the justification for their selection and the extent to which a source was appropriate for their essay. A qualitative analysis of these responses determined that parroting acceptable catch phrases as "peer-reviewed" and "appears in an academic journal" may obscure the fact that students fail to consider whether a source relates to the issues discussed in their essay, critically evaluating the authors' credentials, or considering if a bibliography was present. Most articles in a library's database are academic in nature, but students may not select one relevant to their topic. Furthermore, students frequently used "Peer Reviewed" as a criterion for considering a source to be scholarly, even when the publication had no author listed and no bibliography present. On the other hand, students who evaluated the source in relation to their essay demonstrated a deeper understanding of the evaluation process, and convincingly linked the source within their essay. Supporting students in developing more effective analysis was the impetus for this work. This work served to focus a research question on the link between domain knowledge, information management skills, and self-reflection.

The current study investigates the extent to which domain knowledge has an effect on an analysis of an opinion piece. An opinion piece provides unique challenges to college students. On one level, students are quite familiar with the idea of using "scholarly sources" for their academic assignments. A scholarly author generally has a doctoral degree and works at an institution of higher learning. The author meticulously cites sources and tries to avoid bias through critically addressing an extensive literature in the review. These articles undergo peer review and appear in scholarly journals. Having this framework of expectations, students experience difficulty when called upon to analyze an opinion piece. The authors of these opinion pieces generally do not have scholarly credentials. They refer to sources rather than formally cite them, and there is no bibliography listed. In addition, the piece is biased, as the author wants to persuade readers to adopt a particular solution to an issue. In addition, students may lack domain knowledge to sufficiently understand the issue. Domain knowledge refers to the factual and conceptual knowledge and the ways individuals structure this information (Grossman, 1990). "[I]t is believed that increased background information is positively correlated with increased reading comprehension" (Tracey & Morrow, 2012, p. 31).

The assignment requires students analyze a brief opinion piece in an information management class. The purpose for analyzing an opinion piece is twofold. Through the assignment, students develop critical thinking skills by evaluating the strength of the argument used in the article. They then turn to information management skills to locate and vet additional information to support their view of the issue. To complete the assignment, students need to locate the main point and supporting facts in the article; evaluate the quality of the sources the author used; and successfully locate one reliable source that supports their view of the issue. Students also need technical skills in using the course management system, Blackboard, as well as familiarity with accessing and manipulating a PDF file. They need to have some domain expertise to understand the issue discussed and any jargon the author may use. They also need information management skills to locate a relevant and reliable source from a library database to support their view, evaluate that source, and justify the selection.

Their work revealed that the majority of students were having problems on several levels. Like the authors in *Opening Lines*, I was aware of a gap between my expectations and the analysis my students submitted. The current study is my most recent inquiry in how to effectively close the gap. This work is built on the experience gained through analyzing the assignments described above. During this time, I explored a number of different techniques before settling on AI and SRL. My research focus was to investigate the extent to which students' understanding of content influences their ability to locate and evaluate information.

GATHERING EVIDENCE

I used the activity sheet from this assignment as an artifact for analysis through collecting the assignment in a classroom environment. The analysis, however, went beyond investigating the degree to which students successfully completed the assignment or the grade they received. I was interested in the extent to which their familiarity with the issue raised in the opinion piece affected their analysis of the article, how they discussed the strength of the argument used by the author, and how they evaluated the source they selected to support their opinion. The student's domain knowledge became evident through com-

Table 2. Analysis of Friedman's Opinion Piece

High-Achieving	Low-Achieving
Describe the main point of the article, and three facts used to support his opinion: Main Point: Jihadist zeal will require multiple revolutions to stem by Arab-Muslum and West world to shd their ambivalence Fact 1: U.S. presidents never confront Saudi Arabia about radicalism because of the oil addition Fact II: Arab journalist wrote that "protests against the recent terrorist attacks in France should have been held in their Muslim capitals rather than in Paris because, in this case, it is Muslims who are involved in the crisis and stand accused" Fact III: It is important for Muslim communities to disown the Paris crime and Islamic extremism.	**Describe the main point of the article, and three facts used to support his opinion:** Main Point: How there are contradictions and mixed feelings about the jihadist. It is hard to overcome this because Fact 1: On how Europe countries are to accept their new Muslim immigrants and their values. Fact II: How the Muslim community does not have religious authority. This allows for one too many different versions of being Muslim. Fact III: How even the U.S. is unsure about all of this but are more concern about their oil addictions. Not only that but President Obama was not at the Giant Anti-terrorism march.

paring their responses across several areas of their guided notes. Students needed to identify the author and consider his expertise on the first part of the activity-sheet. [Appendix 1] They then described what sources they used to find unfamiliar terms. Taken as a whole, the answers reveal the extent to which students confabulate across unfamiliar concepts when evaluating the strength of the argument used in the article, when asking unrelated questions about the article, and when searching for additional information about issues discussed in the article.

In the article used, "Ambivalence will not overcome extremism," Friedman (2015) detailed why he believes that efforts to thwart Jihadist attacks have not been effective. He concludes that ongoing efforts need to come from the Arab-Muslim world, and the West needs to hold regimes in the region account-

Table 3. Analyzing the Strength of the Argument

High-Achieving	Low-Achieving
Measure the strength/weakness of this article using the strength of argument using the Quality of Argument Chart: **Were multiple sources of evidence used?** -Arab journalists, University of Cairo statistics, George Froeidman, geopolitical reporter. **What kinds of evidence were they?** -Quotes on their opinion that backs up the authors point, and evidence that proves his point statistically. **Does the author cite the sources he used?** -Does not contain full citations but states names and their positions to use their words. **In what ways does the author acknowledge other points of view?** -By stating hat others think about Muslim communities integrating in America. **What indicates the author didn't "cherry pick" the facts used in the article?** -He provided a full quote from an Arab journalist and completes every thought.	**Measure the strength/weakness of this article using the strength of argument using the Quality of Argument Chart:** **Were multiple sources of evidence used?** -Yes **What kinds of evidence were they?** -He quoted from a respected journalist **Does the author cite the sources he used?** -Yes, he credits the information by providing the journalist name, Abdul Rahman Al-Rashed **In what ways does the author acknowledge other points of view?** **When he quoted from the journalist, he did get his point of view on this subject matter.** -Thought only one person's thought was provided so it would still be his point of view of things. **What indicates the author didn't "cherry pick" the facts used in the article?** -Seems like the information provided were cherry picked to help prove this point.

Table 4. Formulating the Question and Deriving Key Words

High-Achieving	Low-Achieving
Two Questions 1. What are jihadist beliefs? 2. How many Islamic extreme groups exist?	**Two Questions** 1. Why is Obama missing the march such a bad thing? 2. What other heads of country were at the march?
Key Words Jihadist, Beliefs, Facts Number of responses ____12,992_____ total, ____970____Magazine, ___2,450____ Journal ___2,248___ Book	**Key Words** Obama anti-terrorism march Paris Number of responses _1145_ total, _10_Magazine, _60_ Journal ___676___ Book

able in despite our dependence on Mideast oil. He refers to several specific current events and quotes a respected Arab journalist in support of his conclusion.

The study examined assignments from eight course sections across two years. From nearly 200 submissions, two assignments provide contrasting outliers of the students' work. In Table 2, the first section analyzes the intent of Friedman's article. The stronger submission identified the main point as well as the facts used to support his conclusion. Although identifying supporting facts, the weaker submission misses the main point of the article.

In Table 3, students evaluate the strength of the article through considering the number and credibility of the sources used and evidence of bias. The stronger submission identifies several sources Friedman used and how this information is used in the article. The student further acknowledges that an extended quote from a different journalist provided an additional point of view. The weaker submission says multiple sources were used but only refers to one source of evidence, overlooking the additional evidence provided by Friedman.

The next section focuses on information management skills, specifically asking students to formulate a question and select descriptive words from that question to use as keywords for a search. Students next evaluate sources they select by discussing the extent to which a source is current, relevant, accurate, and authorative, and the purpose behind publishing that source. They are then asked to specifically link the selected sources to the questions they wanted to answer and ultimately back to Friedman's article.

In Table 4, students use the information from the opinion piece to formulate a question they would like to investigate. The stronger submission identifies two questions that relate to the issues Friedman raised and selects key words that describe this type of information. The number of results located through the library's discovery tool indicate that there were prospective results in each type of format. The weaker submission focused on one event Friedman discussed, Obama's visit to Paris following a terrorist attack. The student failed, however, to include this event in the discussion of the strength of Friedman's argument. Furthermore, focusing a search on such a recent event meant that it is unlikely that books or scholarly articles would be relevant to the question, even though they may appear in the list of results.

In Table 5, students explain why they would use a particular source in to support their view of the issue(s) raised by Friedman. The stronger submission specifically refers to a central issue in both Friedman's article and the questions the students wants to answer. The weaker submission vaguely refers to the source as foundational to the topic.

Table 5. Justification for Selecting a Source

High-Achieving	Low-Achieving
I would use this resource as it provides quality information about the struggle of the Islamic civil wars.	I would use this resource because this plays as a foundation to the topic at hand

Students explain how the selected sources support their view of the issue(s) Friedman raises in Table 6. The stronger submission identifies how each source ties into issues in both Friedman's article and the questions the students wants to answer. The weaker submission appears to closely link sources to the issue raised until one realizes that the sources the student selected were written before Obama actually visited Paris.

Finally, students reflect on their performance at the end of the activity-sheet. Table 7 compares these students' self-assessment. The stronger submission left this section blank. The weaker submission concluded that they excelled in all areas of the activity-sheet.

LESSONS LEARNED

SoTL provides a means for exploring classroom effectiveness outside the traditional tribal associations of academia (Becher & Trowler, 1989). Investigating pedagogy from a discipline-specific perspective provides a diversity that enriches the SoTL literature. Kuhn (1962) revealed that people outside a discipline are often responsible for revolutionary thoughts because they were not indoctrinated into a discipline. Wiggins and McTighe (2005) called the discrepancy between faculty expectations and student performance an "Expert Blindspot". Such shortsightedness may also exist between the tribal associations of faculty within a discipline and the interdisciplinary requirements for evaluating teaching of that discipline. Taking a reflective step back from the content to examine how to effectively present it provides a necessary space within which to examine the classroom. Consequently, SoTL provides a perspective to add to our instructional toolbox and contribute our discoveries.

Publishing one's work clearly adds to the rigor of the question, the literature review, and the framework for drawing conclusions. These activities naturally develop from a scholarly frame of mind about

Table 6. Tying Information Together

High-Achieving	Low-Achieving
My book source talked about the impact of terrorism on the US government, like how we are less likely to trust them after 9/11 and hiw it is much harder for them to convince the United States popularion to "just trust them" after they let an attack like that happen on United States soil My journal article talks more about the impact on the communities terrorism surrounds in the Middle East, more specifically people in Israel. They compared two communities but they found in both that subjects who were unstable (like those who lost loved ones or were divorced or widowed) were more likely to geel the effects of terrorism than those who weren't (like those who are married and who did not lose a loved one to terrorist acts).	These sources answer why former President Obama not being at the Paris march was such a big deal which was because he stated that France was the oldest ally to America yet it did not seem important enough for he himself to be present and make a speech there, as well as giving the estimate of 40 other figureheads of other nations present at the march in Paris. [Note both sources were written before the attack and the other sources were not relevant to the student's question.]

Table 7. Self-Assessment

High-Achieving	Low-Achieving
Blank	All +

teaching and exploring methods to close the gap between student performance and professor expectations. The background for this work included previous studies, pedagogical outlooks and years of working to align student performance with my expectations for their success. Clearly, peer review helps to raise the bar of participation and engaging in the academic conversation through "going public." Developing a methodological approach to teaching, however, forms a foundation to all SoTL studies.

Students in an Information Management class analyzed an opinion piece three times during the course of the semester. The study compared these assignments to see the extent to which familiarity with the issue had an effect on the success of the search for additional information. Domain knowledge plays an important role in analyzing the piece and selecting additional information to address the issue. This was evident in how students analyzed the issues raised in the article, in the questions they asked, in evaluating the sources they chose to substantiate their view, and in how they explicitly tied the source to the article through the question they asked.

In later submissions, students demonstrated an improvement in developing a familiarity with the issues as well as recognizing the structure of an opinion piece. Each opinion piece discussed a different issue, so students were not able to build on previous familiarity with an issue in later assignments. Approximately 20% of the students passed the first iteration of this assignment. By the third assignment, approximately 70% of the students accurately identified the main point of an opinion article as well as the facts used to support that view.

Although the study demonstrated that student performance improved, I sought to understand the challenges students experienced. This became clear when comparing their answers across different sections of the activity-sheet. Viewing the data from this perspective illustrated that domain knowledge, the deeper understanding of the issues discussed in such an article, is adequate when they can analyze the article, ask relevant questions, appropriately search for related information, and explicitly tie the source to the article. Without this background, students may not be able to select relevant articles to support their view of an issue raised in an opinion piece. Consequently, the depth of their familiarity with the issue becomes evident when they are asked to investigate the issue more deeply and tie additional information to the issue discussed.

Clearly this investigation merged two behaviors that need to be considered separately; accurately evaluating how well one does through self-reflection, and convincing students to take the time to acquire adequate domain knowledge about a topic in order to complete an assignment. Future work needs to be done to identify how to improve one's ability to accurately evaluate competence as well as the value of taking time to contextualize an assignment. The current study demonstrated that a clearer picture of a student's ability emerged only when analyzing responses across a number of specific tasks. The next step in evaluating a successful strategy for instructing students in an analysis of an opinion piece would provide more clearly defined metrics for evaluating their competence throughout the process instead of merely having a single point of reflection at the end of the exercise. In addition, providing opportunities for peer evaluation may bridge the gap between perceived performance and actual performance.

Although there remains a sharp divide between what students' say they do and what they actually do, creating an awareness of this bias may provide an effective comping mechanism for compensating for it.

REFERENCES

Badke, W. (2014a). The convenience factor in information seeking. *Online Searcher*, *38*(6), 68–70.

Badke, W. (2014b). Those baffling assignments. *Online Searcher*, *38*(3), 71–73.

Bartsch, R. A. (2013). Designing SoTL studies-part I: Validity. *New Directions for Teaching and Learning*, *136*(136), 17–33. doi:10.1002/tl.20073

Bass, R. (1999). The scholarship of teaching: What's the problem? *Inventio: Creative Thinking about. Learning and Teaching*, *1*(1), 1–10.

Becher, T., & Trowler, P. (1989). *Academic tribes and territories—Intellectual enquiry and the cultures of disciplines*. Buckingham, UK: Society for Research into Higher Education/Open University Press.

Bennett, D. (2011). *A pedagogy of uncertainty: The role of creativity and innovation in enhancing student engagement*. Centre for Research and Graduate Studies-Humanities. Retrieved from url: https://espace.curtin.edu.au/bitstream/handle/20.500.11937/21731/167368_167368.pdf?sequence=2&isAllowed=y

Blakeslee, S. (2004). The CRAAP test. *LOEX Quarterly*, *31*(3), 6–7.

Blankstein, M., & Wolff-Eisenberg, C. (2019, April 12). *Ithaka S+R US faculty survey 2018*. Retrieved August 1, 2019, from doi:10.18665r.311199

Chism, N., & Chism, G. (2007). *Peer review of teaching: A sourcebook* (2nd ed.). Bolton, MA: Anker Pub. Co.

Duffy, D. K. (2000). Resilient students, resilient communities. In P. Hutchings (Ed.), *Opening lines: Approaches to the Scholarship of Teaching and Learning* (pp. 23–30). Menlo Park, CA: Carnegie Publications.

Fister, B. (2015). The social life of knowledge: Faculty epistemologies. In T. A. Swanson & H. Jagman (Eds.), *Not just where to click: Teaching students how to think about information* (pp. 87–104). Chicago, IL: Association of College and Research Libraries.

Friedman, T. (2015). Ambivalence will not overcome extremism. *Kansas City Star*, *1/16*(15), 17A.

Grossman, P. M. (1990). *The making of a teacher: Teacher knowledge and teacher education*. New York, NY: Teachers College Press.

Hallis, R. (2018). Promoting self-regulated learning in the first-year writing classroom. In G. Veach (Ed.), Teaching information literacy and writing studies: Volume 1, first year composition courses (pp. 111-126). West Lafayette, IN: Purdue University Press.

Head, A. J., & Eisenberg, M. B. (2010). *Truth be told: How college students evaluate and use information in the digital age*. Seattle, WA: University of Washington Information School, Project Information Literacy. Retrieved from http://www.projectinfolit.org/uploads/2/7/5/4/27541717/pil_fall2010_survey_fullreport1.pdf

Hutchings, P. (2000). *Opening lines: Approaches to the Scholarship of Teaching and Learning*. Menlo Park, CA: Carnegie Publications.

Jacobs, D. (2000). A chemical mixture of methods. In P. Hutchings (Ed.), *Opening lines: approaches to the Scholarship of Teaching and Learning* (pp. 63–71). Menlo Park, CA: Carnegie Publications.

Keig, L., & Waggoner, M. (1994). *Collaborative peer review: The role of faculty in improving college teaching*. Washington, DC: Graduate School of Education and Human Development, George Washington University.

Kruger, J., & Dunning, D. (1999). Unskilled and unaware of it: How difficulties in recognizing one's own incompetence lead to inflated self-assessments. *Journal of Personality and Social Psychology*, *77*(6), 1121–1134. doi:10.1037/0022-3514.77.6.1121 PMID:10626367

Kuhn, T. S. (1962). *The structure of scientific revolutions*. Chicago, IL: University of Chicago Press.

Leckie, G. J. (1996). Desperately seeking citations: Uncovering faculty assumptions about the undergraduate research. *Journal of Academic Librarianship*, *22*(3), 201–208. doi:10.1016/S0099-1333(96)90059-2

Lin, Y. P. (2016). The purpose and value of higher education: An economic perspective. *International Journal of Economics and Accounting*, *7*(1), 66–73. doi:10.1504/IJEA.2016.076755

Mallon, M., Hays, L., Bradley, C., Huisman, R., & Belanger, J. (2019). The grounded instruction librarian: Participating in the Scholarship of Teaching and Learning. Chicago, IL: Association of College and Research Libraries, a division of the American Library Association.

Marquis, E., & Henderson, J. (2015). Teaching creativity across disciplines at Ontario universities. *Canadian Journal of Higher Education*, *45*(1), 148–166. Retrieved from http://search.proquest.com/docview/1680769339/

Mcniff, L., & Hays, L. (2017). SoTL in the LIS classroom: Helping future academic librarians become more engaged teachers. *Communications in Information Literacy*, *11*(2), 366–377. doi:10.15760/comminfolit.2017.11.2.8

National Education Association. (2018). *Preparing 21st century students for a global society*. Retrieved from National Education Association Web: http://www.nea.org/assets/docs/A-Guide-to-Four-Cs.pdf

Nilson, L. B., & Zimmerman, B. J. (2013). *Creating self-regulated learners*. Sterling, VA: Stylus Publishing.

O'Brien, M. (2008). Navigating the SoTL landscape: A compass, map and some tools for getting started. *International Journal for the Scholarship of Teaching and Learning*, *2*(2), 1–20. doi:10.20429/ijsotl.2008.020215

Rose-Wiles, L. M., & Hofmann, M. A. (2013). Still desperately seeking citations: Undergraduate research in the age of web-scale discovery. *Journal of Library Administration*, *53*(2-3), 147–166. doi:10.1080/01930826.2013.853493

Schulman, L. S. (1988). *American educational research in education*. Washington, DC: American Educational Research Association.

Schulman, S. (2012). Argumentation step-by-step: Learning critical thinking through deliberate practice. *Teaching Philosophy*, *35*(1), 41–62. doi:10.5840/teachphil20123514

Srivastva, S., & Cooperrider, D. (1990). *Appreciative management and leadership: The power of positive thought and action in organizations*. San Francisco, CA: Jossey-Bass.

Tracey, D., & Morrow, L. (2012). *Lenses on reading: An introduction to theories and models* (2nd ed.). New York, NY: The Guilford Press.

Van Gelder, T. (2005). Teaching critical thinking: Some lessons from cognitive science. *College Teaching*, *53*(1), 41–48. doi:10.3200/CTCH.53.1.41-48

Weller, S., Domarkaite, G., Lam, J., & Metta, L. (2013). Student-faculty co-inquiry into student reading: Recognizing SoTL as pedagogic practice. *International Journal for the Scholarship of Teaching and Learning*, *7*(2), 1–16. doi:10.20429/ijsotl.2013.070209

Welsh, J., & Metcalf, J. (2003). Cultivating faculty support for institutional effectiveness activities: Benchmarking best practices. *Assessment & Evaluation in Higher Education*, *28*(1), 33–45. doi:10.1080/02602930301682

Wiggins, G., & McTighe, J. (2005). *Understanding by design* (2nd ed.). Alexandra, VA: ASCD.

Wolff, C., Rod, A. B., & Schonfeld, R. C. (2016, April 4). *Ithaka S+R US faculty survey 2015*. Retrieved from http://www.sr.ithaka.org /publications/ithaka-sr-us-faculty-survey-2015/

Zimmerman, B., & Martinez-Pons, M. (1990). Student differences in self-regulated learning: Relating grade, sex, and giftedness to self-efficacy and strategy use. *Journal of Educational Psychology*, *82*(1), 51–59. doi:10.1037/0022-0663.82.1.51

Zimmerman, B. J., & Kitsantas, A. (2007). A writer's discipline: The development of self-regulatory skill. In Studies in writing, Volume 19, writing and motivation (pp. 51-69). Oxford, UK: Elsevier.

ENDNOTE

Tables contain an exact transcription from students' activity sheets.

APPENDIX 1

Guided Notes Sheet

1. Who is the author of the article, and what indicates you can trust him?
2. Identify the source you used to look up unfamiliar words:
3. Describe the main point of the article, and three facts used to support his opinion:
   a. Main Point:
      i. Fact 1:
      ii. Fact II:
      iii. Fact III:
4. Measure the strength/weakness of this article using the strength of argument using the Quality of Argument Chart:
   a. Were multiple sources of evidence used?
   b. What kinds of evidence were they?
   c. Does the author cite the sources he used?
   d. In what ways does the author acknowledge other points of view?
   e. What indicates the author didn't "cherry pick" the facts used in the article?
5. Please use the CRAAP rubric and evaluate this article (Table 8).

Table 8.

Subscores for each element [0-3]	
Currency Score: _____	
Relevance Score: _____	
Authority Score: _____	
Accuracy Score: _____	
Purpose Score: _____	
Total Score: _____	Would you use this resource? Why?

What two questions would you like to answer that the opinion piece did not?

1.
2.

    Searching for information to answer one of your questions using Central Search
    Which 3-4 Key Words associated with your question would be useful for a search in Central Search?
    Write the Number of responses:

_____ Total, _____ Magazine, _____ Journal, _____ Book

    What type of information do you need to locate to answer the question you expressed above??

[Remember, **Current Information** is in newspapers. **Background Information** is in books or general interest magazines, and **Specialized Information** is in scholarly journals or trade magazines.]

My background information came from:

[APA Citation]

The CRAAP score for this source was ___. Why would you use this for your topic?

An unconnected source that came up in this search was:

[APA Citation]

The CRAAP score for this source was ___. Why would you use this for your topic?

Carefully evaluate information from either source above using the criteria discussed in class for one source (Table 9).

Table 9.

Subscores for each element	Please use a strong argument statement to support the score you assigned to one of the sources.
Currency Score: _____	
Relevance Score: _____	
Authority Score: _____	
Accuracy Score: _____	
Purpose Score: _____	
Total Score: _____	**Would you use this resource? Why?**

My scholarly information came from:

[APA Citation]

The CRAAP score was ___. Why would you use this for your topic?

An unrelated source in my search:

[APA Citation]

The CRAAP score was ___. Why would you not use this for your topic?

Carefully evaluate Information from either source above using the criteria discussed in class for one source (Table 10).

Table 10.

Subscores for each element	Please use a strong argument statement to support the score you assigned to one of the sources.
Currency Score: _____	
Relevance Score: _____	
Authority Score: _____	
Accuracy Score: _____	
Purpose Score: _____	
Total Score: _____	**Would you use this resource? Why?**

Tying Your Information Together

Please explain how each of the sources you choose contributed to the answer(s) you sought (Table 11).

Table 11.

My Grading Criteria		
Feature	+/√/-	Comment
Identifying Info		
Search Strategy		
Evaluating Info		
Integrating Info		

Chapter 15
Developing an Online Simulation to Teach Enzyme Kinetics to Undergraduate Biochemistry Students:
An Academic and Educational Designer Perspective

Maurizio Costabile

iD https://orcid.org/0000-0002-2162-6497

University of South Australia, Australia

Hayley Timms

University of South Australia, Australia

ABSTRACT

One approach used in teaching scientific principles is laboratory practical classes. However, it can be challenging to teach concepts prior to their introduction in lectures. Academic teaching staff that wish to use alternative approaches to bridge this gap and, in turn, enhance student learning, often require help from their local Educational Developers (EDs). This chapter outlines the process of identifying a problem and then developing, implementing, and evaluating an online interactive simulation to teach enzyme kinetics to undergraduate students at the University of South Australia (UniSA). The challenges faced by the academic and ED in developing the simulation are covered. By the end of the chapter, the reader (academic or ED) will have a better appreciation of the challenges faced in developing a new teaching approach as well as the strategies that can be used to address these challenges.

DOI: 10.4018/978-1-7998-2212-7.ch015

INTRODUCTION

Experimental sciences, by their nature, are grounded in a laboratory setting. As a result, academics devote much time instructing undergraduate science students in laboratory-based learning. Typical tasks include teaching students how to use standard laboratory equipment, which is then used to demonstrate fundamental concepts of the respective discipline. Such teaching is aligned with the delivery of course content through didactic lectures and tutorials. However, due to timetabling constraints and large class sizes, it is not uncommon for some students to undertake a laboratory practical without yet having been taught the underlying principles. This was the case for second-year undergraduate Biochemistry students at the University of South Australia (UniSA). The practical Enzyme Kinetics was delivered several weeks before the lecture content due to the rotation system of laboratory practicals and the logical order in which lecture topics are delivered. As a result, some students found the practical challenging, and based on their performance in the written practical report, they did not sufficiently learn all the key concepts. Additionally, it was observed that this practical was found to be intrinsically demanding for students, even with assistance from lecture material and laboratory technicians.

To address these two issues, the authors sought an alternative approach, not constrained by laboratory availability or lecture timetabling. With digital technologies now an integral part of university teaching, it was logical to explore the creation of an online resource that would enable, extend and even enhance student learning (Henderson et al., 2017). After several discussions over the best way to achieve this, the authors developed an online interactive simulation that would provide students with the required background information about enzyme kinetics and deliver additional support for the written practical report. The simulation was purposely designed to take the students through the exact steps they would perform in the laboratory class, assisting with data manipulation, calculations, and providing a quiz section for a self-guided review of their understanding. As Horton (2012) explains, in a true simulation, the learner decides and acts and can practice multiple times. Using a web-based resource allowed students to review the content multiple times to absorb and understand concepts. Thus, students had unlimited opportunities to use the simulation both before and after the practical session. Being able to access the simulation anytime gave the students the opportunity to feel empowered and in control of their learning (Smith, 2008).

This chapter describes and discusses this innovation in relation to the Scholarship of Teaching and Learning (SoTL), from the perspective of the academic and the educational designer (ED). The academic has taught Biochemistry at UniSA for 21 years. His doctoral training was in the fields of cell biology and biochemistry, specializing in Immunology. His teaching has evolved through a combination of carefully observing learning issues and implementing and assessing alternative strategies. In response to disappointing student performance in the Enzyme Kinetics practical, he sought another approach to teaching (Costabile, 2014). The ED has been an educational designer for 12 years with particular expertise in online simulations. She was instrumental in the creation of a fictitious simulated city called Horizon that has been a key teaching platform in the Nursing and Midwifery programs for the last five years. She has also built online modules covering topics from Social Media to Aboriginal Cultural Insights and Understanding, which are currently used by students University-wide. The ED has also been a part-time teaching academic for several years, teaching *Children's Literature* and *Global Experience: Professional Development*, which has given her insight into the practical applications of the principles of flexible and empowering pedagogy in an online environment.

BACKGROUND

Biochemistry is "the branch of science concerned with the chemical and physicochemical processes and substances that occur within living organisms" (Oxford Dictionary, 2019). Given the crucial role of biochemistry in understanding fundamental cell biology, it is a core course in undergraduate science programs. However, Biochemistry is also known to be a difficult course for undergraduate students to learn (Wood, 2010). Part of this difficulty arises because the teaching of underlying principles routinely occurs through complex laboratory practical exercises. At UniSA, due to timetabling and laboratory space limitations, three multicomponent practical sessions are undertaken by students. Based on academic-student interactions and written report grades, the enzyme kinetics practical was routinely found to be challenging by students. Enzymes are the workhorse of the cell; how an enzyme is studied in the laboratory and is regulated under varying cellular conditions is the basis of enzyme kinetics. Thus, it is critical that students have a good understanding of how enzymes work and how their activity can vary, such as following administration of medications.

As mentioned previously, this practical has been challenging for students since many undertake the session prior to the fundamental concepts being delivered in lectures. Students also struggle with the mathematical manipulations required to generate data and, in turn, interpreting the changes in enzyme activity illustrated by the data. To address these challenges, the authors sought an approach where the students could have access to the background information prior to the practical session and have the necessary support to analyse and interpret the data generated in class. The authors chose to pilot an online interactive simulation in an effort to enhance student performance (Varghese et al., 2012).

The simulation was developed in a staged manner, with a background section providing key details on enzyme properties at a depth sufficient for the students to complete the practical. To make the online-to-laboratory transition as seamless as possible, the simulation component was a replica of the exact steps to be undertaken in the laboratory session. This approach allowed the student to dedicate more time thinking about the processes and concepts being demonstrated, rather than the mechanical steps being performed. Once the data was generated, substantial guidance, feedback and examples were provided with the necessary mathematical operations and calculations. Finally, a formative multiple-choice quiz section was included where the students could test their understanding of the material.

THE SCHOLARSHIP OF TEACHING AND LEARNING

The development of the simulation did not begin as a Scholarship of Teaching and Learning (SoTL) project but evolved into one over several years. The academic has a laboratory background with no formal training in SoTL, but he was aware that with rapidly evolving technology and a civic culture of involvement and creativity, the twenty-first-century academic faces increased challenges and opportunities for academic scholarship (Hyman et al., 2002). Because of this, the academic realised that creating the simulation was not only an opportunity to help students but to improve upon his scholarly teaching and use this as a professional development opportunity to advance his e-learning skills. Boyer's Model of Scholarship (Boyer, 1990) provides a framework for higher education providers to consider scholarship using four themes: discovery, integration, application, and teaching. Collectively, these themes illustrate the importance of distilling and integrating knowledge into teaching through curriculum and teaching practices (TEQSA, 2017). The journey in developing the simulation, implementing, analysing and disseminating the new teaching approach has led to a deep interest in educational research, and the academic has now transitioned to a teaching-focussed role.

Shulman (2011) states that teachers should design their courses courageously and experiment with their teaching creativity. Creating the simulation gave rise to the academic reviewing his teaching practices and the support resources being provided to students. Shulman (2011) also says that once innovations have been implemented, teachers have an ethical and professional obligation to study their efficacy along with their intended and unintended consequences. Therefore, the academic evaluated the simulation; after the feedback was studied, he made changes, re-evaluated, and disseminated his findings to his peers at multiple levels. At the school level, the academic showcased the simulation to colleagues, demonstrating how a historical problem could be improved and have a measurable impact. After receiving positive feedback from students who wanted simulation resources available for other courses, the academic suggested to his colleagues that similar simulations be built in other courses in the same program year level. This suggestion met with some resistance, with staff feedback including that "they could not see how simulations could be applied to their course" and that "they already had additional resources available"—even if in some cases these resources were not used in their teaching. Others were not prepared to take the time to learn the skills necessary to create the simulations – even though the academic and the ED offered to assist them with the process. However, the academic's interest did not wane! The impact of the simulation has been acknowledged at the University level with an award for Outstanding Contributions to Digital Learning as well as internationally with an Online Learning Consortium citation. These acknowledgements encouraged him to continue to create further simulations and investigate their educational impact.

The academic has also presented his findings at both local and international conferences. He was invited to present and give a workshop on the role of simulations in biochemistry teaching at ConBio in Japan in 2017. Attendees were asked three short questions to gauge the issues faced in their laboratory-based teaching. The majority of respondents indicated that their most significant problem was students attending laboratory practicals un-prepared, closely followed with a poor understanding of concepts. To address these challenges, the most common approach was online instruction and reinforcing to students that they come prepared. Perhaps not surprisingly, most indicated these strategies had not been successful. Thus poor student performance in laboratory classes is a broad issue faced by many academics. The simulation the authors developed and its benefits to student learning, therefore, have even greater potential as a general teaching aid.

Even though he met with some resistance from colleagues over the simulation, the academic's SoTL journey continued, and he was instrumental in creating a Scholarship Excellence Network (SCENE) within the Division of Health Sciences at UniSA. The SCENE program began early 2019 and is a mentoring scheme that seeks to create a sustainable structure and utilise the knowledge and skills of successful candidates who have demonstrated excellence in teaching to systematically identify and support staff at scale. Those mentored, in turn, become mentors themselves, providing sustainability and growth over time.

As for the ED, having been a part-time teaching academic has given her insight into the teaching and learning needs of academics. Her SoTL journey has focused on e-learning with a particular interest in sustainability by providing staff with ongoing professional development, advice, and real-world examples surrounding best teaching and learning practices in an online environment. She assists academics in reviewing their teaching practices then assists with implementing those new strategies. Boyer's (1990) framework was expanded upon by Rice (1992) by incorporating the addition of *learning*. With regard to the interpretation of *learning* in SoTL, Harland, Hussain, and Bakar (2014, p. 40) state, "It has never been clear whether or not the addition of "learning" was about the academics' own learning or the learning opportunities provided for students". The ED has to understand both the teaching side (academic) and the learning side (student) to support and best advise her colleagues.

The ED has also been instrumental in creating and piloting a fictitious online simulated city called Horizon City. The city simulated a "real" city by providing patients with homes, background information about them and their families, their patient data, current health problems, and the skills a student would need to learn in order to provide proper patient care. The simulation was first piloted with a single, second-year undergraduate course and grew from there. After obtaining student feedback and disseminating the success of the simulation to her peers, the simulation has grown to include more patients in the city and is now an integral part of both the Midwifery and Nursing undergraduate programs at UniSA.

Due to a lack of resources surrounding social media etiquette within UniSA, the ED was approached by the Academic Dean of the Division of Health Sciences to become involved in the creation and pilot of a Social Media online module. With assistance from several colleagues (Nayia Cominos, Rosanne Crouch, and Richard McInnes), the social media module was researched, created, and piloted in a health science course. After the pilot, student evaluation was sought and minor changes were made. The module and student feedback were then disseminated at several divisional and school/faculty meetings before being opened University-wide. Over fourteen programs now use the module to teach students the "do's and don'ts" of social media usage. The ED, along with her colleagues, presented their findings on the Social Media module at the 2018 Australian and New Zealand Association for Health Professional Educators (ANZAHPE) conference, where the paper was well-received. A second module, concentrating on using social media to build a professional profile is currently in the creation phase. Because of this expertise in online simulation, the ED had no reservations in agreeing to upskill and assist the academic with the creation and implementation of the Enzyme Kinetics simulation.

THE SIMULATION

The *Cambridge Dictionary* describes simulation as "a model of a real activity, created for training purposes or to solve a problem" (Cambridge Online Dictionary, 2019). Since students struggling with the laboratory practical were a historical problem, creating an online simulation of the steps and processes used in the practical seemed a logical way to address the educational deficiency. Clark and Mayer (2011) indicate that there are two types of simulations: operational and conceptual. Operational simulations teach procedural skills, while conceptual simulations focus on concepts and strategic knowledge. The simulation the authors created was a mix of both types, as it included conceptual information on enzymes along with the procedural skills necessary to complete the practical.

A Historical Education Problem

Biochemistry at UniSA is a compulsory second-year undergraduate course taken by a diverse student cohort. Students are enrolled in Laboratory Medicine, Medical Science, Nutrition and Food Science, Pharmaceutical Science, Health Science, and Human Movement programs. Consequently, there is broad diversity in their background knowledge of chemistry and biology as well as University entrance scores. Due to limitations in the availability of suitable laboratory space, as well as access to sufficient pieces of laboratory equipment, Biochemistry practicals are scheduled to run either in the morning or afternoon on the same day. A maximum of 30 students can be accommodated in each class, so a total of 60 students can be taught in one day. The Enzyme Kinetics practical is first performed in week four, while the lecture content is not delivered until week seven. It was noted that even after the lectures had been presented, students still found it difficult to complete the practical and understand the concepts being demonstrated. With the move towards digital learning globally as well as at UniSA, the authors decided to pilot an online interactive simulation as a tool to enhance student performance (Varghese et al., 2012).

Identifying the Appropriate Software

Having decided to pilot an online simulation, the first challenge was to determine the best software to develop the learning resource. At the time of this initiative (2013), the University of New South Wales had introduced a platform for developing interactive online learning modules (SmartSparrow™). This platform was run in-house but was too expensive for our limited budget. The distance between the developer and the authors was also seen as a hurdle in the effective communication of our learning needs. There was also the matter of edits or changes to the module that could only be made by the external provider, which would result in significant delays and added cost. Due to these constraints, an alternative form of software that could be purchased, developed and edited within UniSA was required. After much discussion and viewing of examples of different resources and software available, Articulate Storyline (http://www.articulate.com) was selected. This software was chosen for several reasons: it was flexible, allowing the academic to generate his teaching vision; it was sufficiently simple to use, which suited the academic's skill level, yet had enough features that more complex elements and interactions could be added to future simulations. Furthermore, it was sustainable in that the academic could update the module as needed, and more importantly, the simulation resource generated would meet the students' needs (Horton, 2012).

Storyline is built with an interface similar to Microsoft PowerPoint™, simplifying the learning process for new users. There is also an extensive online user community, with freely available examples and templates. Also, the ED had significant expertise with Storyline and could provide "at elbow" support and training to develop the academic's skill level. As mentioned previously, cost was also a significant consideration in software purchase choice. The academic negotiated with the university to fund the purchase of an individual user software license. The ED assisted with negotiations by providing the university with pricing, a comparison of software and legitimate reasons to purchase a single license (instead of institutional licence), for the academic. The university agreed, and the software was then purchased (approximately $1000 AUD) and downloaded from the Articulate website to the academic's computer.

Software Challenges

The ease of use, moderate cost, and online and local support were key factors in choosing Storyline to generate the simulation. The software proved to be easy to use, with the academic readily learning the basics. However, the availability of an ED who was expert in the software and able to provide support for its more advanced features proved invaluable. The ED had to be as committed to the simulation project as the academic as she knew the time needed to master the Storyline software and create a complex resource would be lengthy (approximately 40-50 hours). Therefore, it should be noted that the generation of the simulation required a substantial investment of time from *both* the academic and the ED. The academic had to learn the software and its capabilities, then apply those new skills to the simulation to recreate the laboratory practical. The ED provided support to the academic at every step, from conception through to the delivery of the simulation, as well as after implementation to improve the resource following student feedback. The ED assisted the academic with determining the required functionality for each section and individual page of the simulation, organised copyrighted images and created the overall "look" of the simulation.

Since the simulation was deployed through the UniSA Learning Management System (LMS), Moodle, a plethora of possible browsers could be used to access the simulation. These included Microsoft Explorer, Edge, Firefox, Chrome, and Safari, which can be used with Microsoft Windows or the Apple Operating System. During the testing phase, we quickly realised that software incompatibilities existed and, as a result, had to specify which browsers were compatible with the simulation. This was due to Storyline using Flash-based software when the simulation is published. In some cases, students had to download the compatible browser or use a University-based computer due to issues with the loading and progression of the simulation. The authors also had to ensure that the software could be used on a range of devices (such as Windows laptop, iPad, MacBook, Smartphone) to provide equity across the cohort.

Translating a Face-to-Face Practical into an Online Simulation

The next challenge was how to translate the physical practical onto an online environment that would faithfully deliver the key learning outcomes, cover all necessary material, and engage the students. The learning outcomes associated with the practical were as follows:

By the end of the practical, students will be able to:

1. Understand the chemical reaction catalysed by alkaline phosphatase.
2. Understand how enzyme kinetics are studied in a Biochemistry laboratory.
3. Understand the concepts of maximal velocity (Vmax) and substrate concentration equal to half of Vmax (Km).
4. Be able to plot all data generated in the practical correctly.
5. Be able to interpret a Lineweaver-Burk plot.
6. Be able to calculate changes in Km and Vmax in the presence and absence of inorganic phosphate.
7. Be able to explain why and how Km, but not Vmax changes when inorganic phosphate is added.

One of the challenges faced by the ED was understanding the historical problem from a student perspective and then assessing the best way to support students in their learning (Gustafson & Branch, 1997). This meant the ED had to go through the practical steps, review the background information on enzyme kinetics, and understand the subsequent information garnered for the written report. The ED also had to consider what the academic wanted to achieve by creating an online simulation versus their then-current technical ability. Conversely, the academic had to articulate what skills needed to be developed for the students to be successful in the practical. However, the academic had limited previous experience with simulations and online resource development software (Roblyer & Edwards, 2000; LeBlanc, 2013).

The ED incorporated a structured approach in the development of the simulation, including storyboarding and identifying any other elements (including images, videos, or graphs) that needed to be incorporated. Storyboarding was a vital part of the creation process as it allowed both the academic and the ED to envisage each step of the module and identify what would be required of the learner, such as reading or calculating on each individual page. Designing an effective online simulation meant ensur-

Figure 1. The laboratory notebook design of the simulation

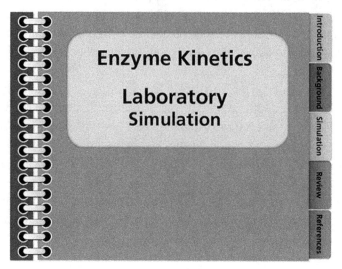

ing the simulation had student learning as its focus and met the student's learning needs and outcomes for the practical (Rossett, 2002). What started as a simple, linear simulation proved to be quite complex when broken down into the individual steps. However, this part of the planning did provide both the ED and the academic with a better understanding of the laboratory practical and what was expected from a student perspective.

Design Process

In keeping with the laboratory theme, the authors chose to mimic a spiral laboratory notebook when designing the student interface (Figure 1). Tabs were added to the right-hand side to make accessing individual sections quick and easy. This way, the student could choose which section they required. For example, students who had not yet received the lectures could select the background tab to learn the fundamentals of the practical. Of course, this section could also be used by those students who wanted to refresh their understanding.

Similarly, after the laboratory session, the students could go directly to the simulation section and gain the assistance required to analyse and interpret the data generated in class. By purposely using this approach, the simulation provided the opportunity for students to be in control of their learning as well as the pace at which they wanted to learn (Smith, 2008). The simulation includes a main character who resembles a female laboratory technician. She leads the student through the simulation providing hints, tips, and feedback along the way. This approach mimics how the practicals are taught in the laboratory as students can ask for assistance from teaching staff (Figure 2).

Given that the academic knew that some students in the cohort would have little or no background information before the practical, a detailed background section on enzymes and how their kinetics are studied was the obvious starting point for the simulation. This section needed to provide sufficient yet relevant information for students to be able to gain an understanding of the basic concepts before the practical session. The next section was the simulation itself. The authors purposely made this part interactive, requiring the student to enter calculated results to progress further into the simulation (Figure

Figure 2. Results page where a calculated value must be entered to progress in the simulation.

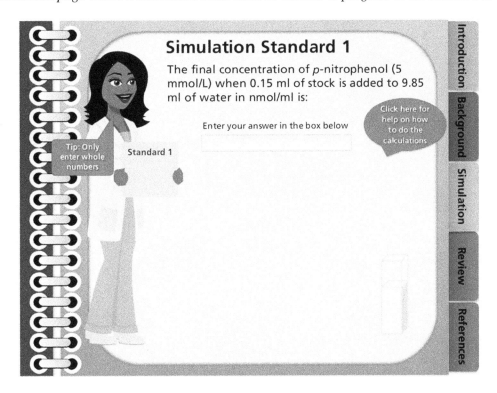

2). If they entered incorrect values, instant feedback was provided. Making errors is an integral part of the learning process, and feedback is essential if students are to learn from their mistakes (Biggs & Tang, 2011).

The authors were also mindful that some students may not have the confidence or required mathematical skills to undertake the calculations. As a result, the simulation included two slides that explained alternate ways of calculating the required answer. These alternate approaches were used to complement the different ways in which students learn (both textual and visual) and to facilitate the understanding of fundamental mathematical calculations (Paivio, 1986) (Figure 3).

Once the data had been entered, students were required to graph their data and calculate key parameters. These are graphs that the students are likely to have never encountered before; hence, interactive assistance was provided with both the plotting as well as the interpretation of the graphed data (Figure 4). The two boxes are "hotspot" regions where key definitions and additional information is provided to the student.

After completing all the steps in the simulation, the students could test their understanding of the material via ten multiple choice questions (MCQs) (Figure 5). Importantly, this section was completely formative, giving the students the freedom to choose whether they wanted to make use of this section or not. If they chose to answer the questions, they were provided with immediate feedback allowing them to monitor their own learning (Ally, 2008).

University resources are often created in a stepwise manner. A student must complete one task to move onto the next. This ensures that all students are provided with the same opportunities for learning at the same time. However, students do not all have the same level of knowledge, nor do they work at

Figure 3. Slide explaining the steps required to calculate the concentration of a reagent.

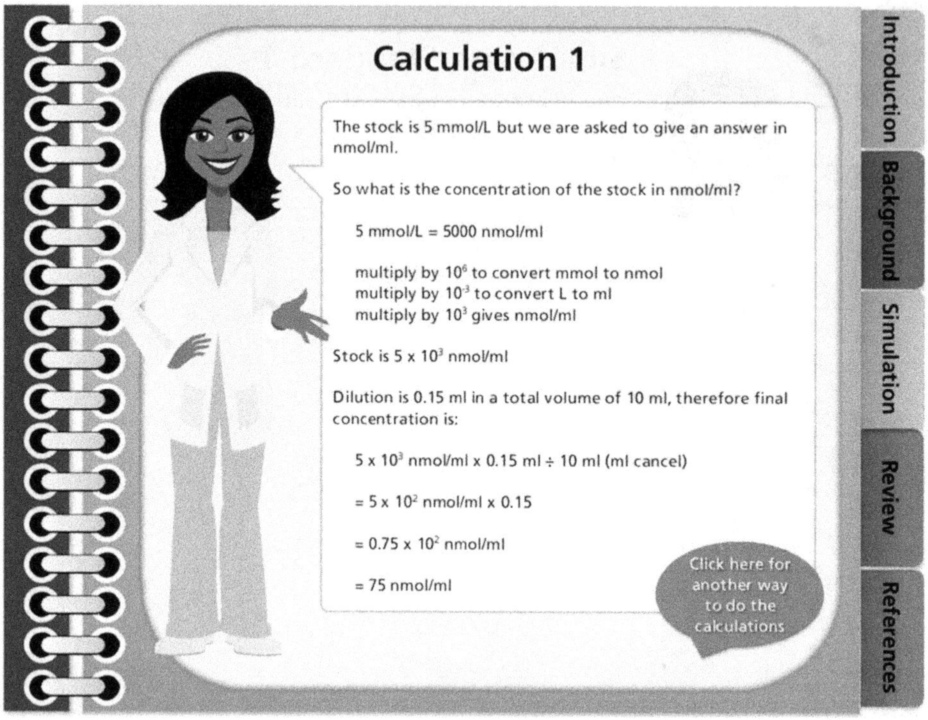

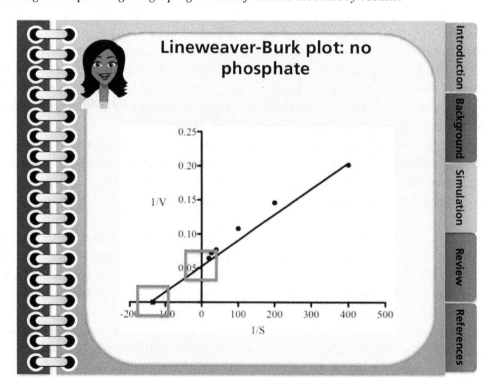

Calculation 1
The stock is 5 mmol/L but we are asked to give an answer in nmol/ml.
So what is the concentration of the stock in nmol/ml?
5 mmol/L = 5000 nmol/ml
multiply by 10^6 to convert mmol to nmol
multiply by 10^{-3} to convert L to ml
multiply by 10^3 gives nmol/ml
Stock is 5 x 10^3 nmol/ml
Dilution is 0.15 ml in a total volume of 10 ml, therefore final concentration is:
5 x 10^3 nmol/ml x 0.15 ml ÷ 10 ml (ml cancel)
= 5 x 10^2 nmol/ml x 0.15
= 0.75 x 10^2 nmol/ml
= 75 nmol/ml
Click here for another way to do the calculations
Introduction
Background
Simulation
Review
References

Figure 4. Diagram explaining the graph generated from the laboratory results.

Lineweaver-Burk plot: no phosphate
0.25
0.20
1/V
0.15
0.10
100
200
300
400
500
0
1/S
Introduction
Background
Simulation
Review
References

Figure 5. Sample multiple-choice question.

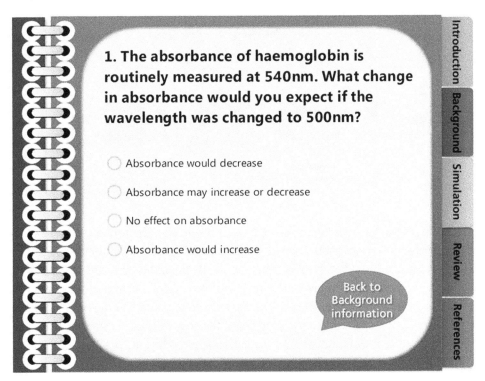

the same pace, which can limit some student's progression. Thus, a teaching approach should provide students with structure so they do not get lost, but not at the price of inhibiting students who learn more quickly. The difference between what a learner can do without help and what they can do with help is referred to as the Zone of Proximal Development (Vygotsky, 1980). The interactive simulation allowed for both of these aspects to be addressed as students could choose which section(s) to attempt and also choose their own pace when using the simulation (Smith, 2008).

The academic and the ED also did not want the simulation to be a learning hurdle for students, as this would lead to dissatisfaction and a reduction in use (Chang & Chang, 2012). As a result, a great deal of time was spent thinking about keeping the interactions simple, providing instructions on how to navigate each slide, as well as thorough testing of the module before its implementation. The students were encouraged to use the simulation as many times as necessary to assist with their understanding of the practical. This is where the ED's experience came in to play.

Having built other online simulations and modules for student learning, the ED knew that student learning styles play an important role in e-learning. As we know, students have different preferred ways of learning, some through images, some through text, while others prefer experimentation or examples (Truong, 2016). The ED incorporated visual, aural, textual, verbal, and logical styles to the simulation to accommodate different learning styles.

As discussed, the ED has knowledge concerning learning styles but also needed to bring an instructional design focus to the simulation. To mimic the tasks in the laboratory, the ED chose a "Design Coached Task Simulation" or "Coach-me" activity, which guides the learner in performing a simulated task (Horton, 2012). Coach-me simulations guide learners through tasks by getting them to complete

Figure 6. The architecture of coach-me activities
(Horton, 2012).

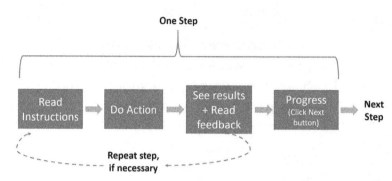

the actions rather than watch them be performed. As a result, they require a different combination or sequence of experiences in comparison to a demonstration. A Coach-me simulation begins with instructions or background information before the learner performs the necessary step or task, which is before results or feedback. One of the fundamental design principles of the coached simulation is that a student should never fail or be unable to complete the simulation due to a lack of information, or succeed without thinking (Horton, 2012). Learners who completed the step or task incorrectly were provided with corrective feedback before they could attempt the action again (Horton, 2012).

Online simulations tend to have elements of gamification such as scoring, specific goals, reward-driven tasks, and unpredictability. Games also guide players through a mastery process while engaging in difficult tasks (Koster, 2004). However, as the authors wanted to simulate a laboratory practical and background theories and practices, not all gamification elements fit. As mentioned previously, the simulation appears similar to a laboratory notebook, with a central character (the laboratory technician) that students can identify with and learn to trust. The character provides hints and tips to assist students and guides them through the simulation. The goal is to complete the simulation, including the MCQs before attempting the practical. The reward is not a badge or points but adding to a students' knowledge base on enzyme kinetics; knowledge they will need to be successful in future courses. Using an interactive online simulation instead of a text-based set of instructions for the practical means that the simulation is more engaging and interactive and not as static as other forms of learning. Designing a relevant but also interesting and engaging activity assists students to develop more complex knowledge bases and efficient automatic behaviours (Boettcher & Conrad, 2010).

Implementation in Class

Before the introduction of the simulation in 2014, students were first given an overview of the rationale behind the development of the simulation at lectures, tutorials, and via email. All students were encouraged to complete the simulation after the lecture content as an aid to learning and in preparation for a mid-semester quiz and for the end of semester examination. Students were advised that the simulation may take up to thirty minutes to complete if they completed all sections. The academic then determined the best time to implement the simulation for student success. The academic tested giving access either before the practical or limiting it to only being available after the practical session. Not surprisingly, student feedback overwhelmingly indicated that having access to the simulation BEFORE the practical was the best option. As a result, since 2015, the simulation has been made available at the beginning of the semester and remains open until the end of the examination period.

At the end of each semester, the LMS is accessed, and student usage data relating to the simulation is collected. This data included which student(s) had accessed the simulation, when they had accessed the simulation, how long they accessed the simulation, how often they accessed the simulation, and their responses to the MCQs. Of these measures, the time used by each student accessing the simulation was the least reliable, as students consistently failed to log out of the system, thus providing an inaccurate measure of their usage.

RESULTS

The simulation was developed as a new pedagogical model that aimed to further engage students in their education and was devised to address historical key issues. The simulation was seen as a novel and interactive learning approach by students, as opposed to the generally passive approach associated with lectures. Students were given a post-simulation questionnaire to gauge their responses to the new approach and to see where the simulation could be improved. Any new SoTL approach should be evaluated and the data used not only to improve student learning but also add to the scholarship of teaching (Hyman et al., 2002). The resulting data gathered are mainly qualitative, but the academic also reviewed quantitative data (usage and student grades) as part of the simulation's effectiveness. Ethical clearance for this study was obtained by the UniSA Human Ethics Committee (#32625).

Impact on Student Academic Performance

The impact of implementing the enzyme kinetics simulation on student performance over 2014-2017 was quantitatively measured by comparing student performance in the formal practical report. This data was compared to the 2011-2013 cohorts. Scores for the written practical report were compared to scores prior to the simulation and were analysed using GraphPad Prism (v8.0). As shown in Table 1, there was a significant increase in mean score following the introduction of the simulation compared to previous cohorts. It was possible that these variances may have been due to differences between cohorts. However, when data between years were compared, no differences in either the median or interquartile range between cohorts was observed, indicating similar performance by the differing groups. Importantly, since its introduction, there are significantly fewer students in the lower 25th percentile compared to the previous cohorts. As a result, the variances in student performance are likely to be due to the impact of the new educational approach.

The data demonstrate that the simulation specifically impacted the weaker performing students who previously may have failed the written practical report due to their lack of understanding of central concepts. It is also clear that the introduction of the enzyme kinetics simulation was both consistent and reproducible, with similar improvements in student results in future cohorts (Table 1). Academics importantly focus on all students, but weaker students require greater assistance to grasp fundamental concepts fully, and they, in turn, require greater support. It is clear from this intervention that it has been successfully and consistently applied in this course. Based on the results from 2014 and 2015, the academic was successful in obtaining further university funding to develop additional interactive simulations to enhance student teaching and learning of undergraduate Biochemistry and Immunology.

Table 1. Student scores for the enzyme kinetics practical report** comparing 2011-2013 cohorts (no simulation) to 2014-2017 cohorts (with simulation) Students t-test * p < 0.05. ** The practical report was graded with a maximum score of 10.

Parameter	2011-13	2014	2015	2016	2017
Student number	302	120	124	126	128
Min Score	4.5	5.5	6.3	6	5.5
Median Score	8	8.4	8.2	8.1	8
Max score	9	9.5	9	9.5	9
Mean score	7.708	8.1*	7.995*	8.1*	7.83*
Standard error	0.051	0.075	0.063	0.07	0.06

Since 2015, data showing the effect of the simulation has also been included in the practical manual as an encouragement to the students to use the resource as part of their learning.

Student Evaluation

To ensure that the students' needs were met, the academic and ED analysed student feedback, which led to the modification of the resource for future cohorts (Kane-Gill, 2013). More information on the individual steps was added, as was a voice over or audio of the laboratory technician's instructions. Shulman (2011) says that students should be treated more like partners or collaborators in any pedagogical enterprise rather than being treated as human subjects or testers. Therefore, the authors took great care to provide students with a voice so they could provide constructive feedback on the simulation and be part of the modification process.

Themes

In 2014, at completion of the simulation, students were asked, *"What were the best aspects of this simulation?"* The written comments were collected, and the most common themes were identified from their feedback. The data obtained (n=30) were analysed by thematic analysis and is summarised into the four main themes below.

Engagement

In a 2017 survey of 1658 undergraduate students exploring their digital learning experiences by Henderson et al., one of the key themes was "seeing information in different ways". Over the last decade, the ED has come to understand that students need and want more interactive learning opportunities, and that static learning, (e.g. text-based information or lectures) can often be unappealing, which in turn means reduced student participation. A critical aspect of the development of the simulation was that it had to display information in a new way so that students could engage with the new approach more easily than with historical methods of lecture material and a practical book. The simulation also needed to allow every student to actively take control of their learning as well as the pace at which they learn. Both aspects were appreciated by the students, as evidenced by the following feedback:

Do it (the simulation) in your own time and from home.

It (the simulation) was much more engaging and less time consuming than looking through notes and a textbook.

The sim provided the information in a new way which helps understanding.

I referred to the sim numerous times to help with my understanding of the practical results and feel I wouldn't have been able to do my write up without it. (Student comments)

To achieve this new approach to learning, the role of the ED should not be underestimated, as they provided the skills and knowledge of how best to construct and visually present the material that was learner-centred, engaging, and interactive.

Prior Preparation

As mentioned previously, due to scheduling, the academic was forced to run practical sessions before covering the didactic material in lectures. That means some students are at a disadvantage and in turn, have a steep learning curve with the practical exercise. The inclusion of the background section in the simulation provided the necessary information concerning enzyme kinetics, which was required for the successful completion of the practical exercise. Being able to access the simulation in preparation for the laboratory practical was highlighted as being a positive aspect of the simulation:

Explained a topic that has not yet been covered in lectures before the practical class on that topic.

Being able to run through the practical before actually attending is really helpful and will save a lot of time and calculation errors during the practical itself. (Student comments)

Calculations

Over his biochemistry teaching career, the academic has noted that many students struggle with laboratory-based mathematics, and this was especially true for the enzyme kinetics practical. An inability to truly appreciate the function of each calculation significantly affects the ability of the student to understand what the data is demonstrating and, in turn, the whole concept of the practical. In the simulation, the authors purposely provided two divergent ways of performing sample calculations. These alternate approaches were chosen to cater to the varying learning styles of students. One explanation was a step-by-step approach, explaining each stage of the calculation, while the other was more succinct, combining the same operations. The benefits of this assistance are seen in the comments below:

The explanation of calculations before attending the wet lab session provided a clearer understanding of the calculations and concepts before commencing the practical.

It (the simulation) included a lot of background information and revision that is useful for the practical, especially mathematical equations. (Student comments)

As with the simulation itself, the academic has been careful only to include the mathematics that is required for the practicals. There is always the temptation to include more, since "more is better"; however, this leaves the possibility of students questioning why information is included when it is not needed for any of the practical classes. Anecdotal evidence suggests that this has been successful as far fewer questions have been asked about the fundamental calculations for all practicals since the simulations introduction in 2014. If a mathematics question has been asked about the practical, the enquiring students admit to not having accessed the simulation before the class.

Revision

The provision of information is important in a simulation; however, an opportunity for the students to test their knowledge as they are progressing and to receive immediate feedback is critical for their learning (Ally, 2008). As a result, the simulation also included a formative, MCQ section, where students could test their understanding of the underlying concepts and receive immediate and appropriate feedback. The simulation was also used by students to reinforce the main concepts of enzyme kinetics for the end of semester exam.

I liked the quiz at the end which tested what I had just learnt and helped reinforce points.

Explanation at every step and the chance to attempt as many times as required. (Student comments)

Two years later, in 2016, the feedback themes were similar. When the new cohort of students were asked, *"What were the best aspects of this simulation?"*, 32% of respondents indicated that the fundamental math theory was the best aspect, 26% that multiple-choice questions were the best aspect, with 19% considering the background information to be the best aspect of the simulation.

Additional Feedback

Apart from these four specific themes, another recurring theme was the overall use of simulations as a teaching aid. There were many requests for additional simulations for all the Biochemistry practical classes as well as having them developed for other courses.

I really think this supported my learning and it should be used for all practicals, not just enzyme kinetics.

It's (the simulation) very helpful, and I really hope it will be expanded to other subjects. (Student comments)

These comments have been seen each year consistently amongst different cohorts of students. As a result, individual simulations have been developed for each of the Biochemistry practicals. The other two practicals include:
Laboratory techniques:

- Pipette accuracy
- Reagent preparation and incompatibility
- Amino acid solubility

- Beer-Lambert law

Protein determination:

- Biuret method
- Folin-Ciocalteau method
- A280 method

The academic also sought feedback from fellow teaching staff who piloted a simulation as part of their teaching on lung physiology. The following comment was received from the Course Coordinator following its implementation:

Student marks were better for sections where there had been underpinning tutorial questions, which included the simulation. (Dr. Parkinson-Lawrence)

Finally, there is a sense of personal satisfaction and motivation when students appreciate the effort that has been placed on trying to improve a teaching approach:

Job well done! (Student comment)

Limitations and Considerations to This Approach

As with any new teaching intervention, there are always some constraints that may not be obvious before embarking on a new approach. In terms of developing a simulation, there needs to be a clear desire, motivation, and sufficient time to initiate and pursue the development of simulation(s) by the relevant teaching staff. Storyline was chosen as the software, and this is but one of many choices available in the marketplace. No matter how simple (and in turn limited) they may be, all software has a learning period for the user to become familiar with their correct use. The other alternative is that the academic acts solely as the subject matter expert and uses the expertise of the ED to develop the simulation as required. If that option is chosen, there is still an obvious cost associated with this as the academic will still need to gather materials and liaise with the ED throughout the creation, implementation, and evaluation of the simulation. Creating the resources this way can be problematic as the academic is then reliant on the ED to edit or update the simulation.

Which brings us to sustainability. If the teaching academic creates the simulation, then they can also do any revisions or edits needed. They can also create further resources for teaching without relying on a third party (the ED). Even so, teaching support is needed at the institutional level either through the provision of funding, teaching relief, or access to in-house educational design experts. If an academic does not have access to an in-house ED then they need to be aware of the time expectations. It took a considerable time for the authors to create, test, implement, evaluate, and subsequently update the simulation. Embarking on what seemed to be a simple resource creation took many hours of work (over forty hours) for both the academic and the ED. However, learning the software could be seen as a professional development opportunity and there is a large community of Storyline users to assist—you are not alone! Assistance is available via the Storyline website along with templates, instructional videos, hints and tips, and forums.

Education of the students in using the simulation(s) is also another consideration. Clear, direct instructions both on the LMS and built into the simulation are needed to ensure that students know how to access as well as use the simulation to its full benefit. However, if multiple simulations are used consistently within or across courses, then the students become familiar with the approach required, and the learning curve diminishes.

If you build it, they will come! This is not necessarily the case. The potential of digital technologies to enhance student learning has been well established with benefits including equity, efficiency and personalised learning processes (Henderson et al., 2017). However, for any educational initiative to have an impact on student learning, the students must engage with the resource being provided. Students with higher levels of self-directed learning and those who are motivated to do something out of curiosity and enjoyment are more successful in online settings (Kebritchi et al., 2017). Not all students made use of the simulation either before or even after the practical. These students may be high achievers and already have a good understanding of the material, or conversely, they may be weak students who have not engaged with the material and thought it not useful or worth their time. Indeed, the data collected from the LMS did demonstrate that a subset of students opened the simulation and then rapidly (within 10 sec) closed it, never making use of it again.

It should be pointed out that once a simulation is generated, it can be readily modified and used in another setting if a similar approach is being used. This, in turn, allows for a reduction in the time required to generate a new version of the simulation in another course. For example, the academic has generated a mathematics simulation for the Biochemistry students, which, after slight modification is now being used to teach 1st-year students in pharmacy and laboratory medicine with success. These simulations can be used across borders as long as the technology is compatible (SCORM compliant) and the language factor is taken into account (English).

In terms of suitability, there is no limit to what can be delivered, but in some cases, some lateral thought is required. As with any endeavour, there needs to be a desire and motivation from all parties to generate a successful product.

FUTURE RESEARCH DIRECTIONS

Given the success of the Enzyme Kinetics simulation, the academic has continued to develop further interactive simulations for teaching both practical and complex lecture-based content in Biochemistry and Immunology. As a recently transitioned, teaching-focused academic, he has disseminated the impact of this practice at the school, University-wide, and at national and international conferences. The ED has been able to use the findings and experience to promote the use of simulation and engaging online activities to other university staff. She has created a series of online resources for bacteria identification that mimics microscope findings for students studying Nutrition. Several staff have also gone on to create their own dynamic online resources, replacing "static" paper-based resources. The simulations now used University wide are a working example of Boyer's themes in action by building new knowledge, interpreting that knowledge across disciplines, aiding individuals and professions in solving problems, and connecting scholarship with practice (Boyer, 1990).

The development of the Enzyme Kinetics simulation has led to the building of a culture of innovation within the academics' School of Pharmacy and Medical Sciences. There has been an uptake of interactive simulations by other staff within the school as engaging teaching aids. It has also provided the academic with an opportunity to mentor colleagues in this approach and create the Scholarship Excellence Network (SCENE).

CONCLUSION

This chapter has focused on the interplay between an academic and an ED in the development of an interactive Biochemistry simulation. This interaction can lead to the development of new skills for both parties as well as the development of learning resources which have the potential to greatly benefit student performance. This, in turn, led to a laboratory-focussed academic to review his teaching practice using a SoTL based approach (Hyman et al., 2002).

It is essential that academic staff wishing to develop computer-based simulations using Articulate Storyline are aware of the time required in both learning the software as well as developing and troubleshooting the resources produced. The importance of the ED in this process should not be underestimated by the academic, as they have valuable expertise and can enhance the learning process for both parties. Higher education institutions need to provide professional development for teachers, training for students, and technical support to assist with online content development (Kebritchi et al., 2017). The authors suggest that the interaction between the academic and ED can lead to fruitful outputs benefiting all parties involved, as well as the development of teaching material that can beneficially impact student success and add to the development of SoTL-based activities.

ACKNOWLEDGMENT

All authors have no financial interests, direct or indirect (dual commitment) that might affect the conduct or reporting of this work.

The authors would like to thank Rita Costabile for proofreading and testing of the simulation and Professors Allan Evans and Esther May for funding support. They would also like to thank Nayia Cominos and David Birbeck for critical feedback.

REFERENCES

Ally, M. (2008). *Foundations of educational theory for online learning. The theory and practice of online learning* (2nd ed.). Athabasca, Alberta: Athabasca University Press.

Biochemistry. (2019). Retrieved from https://en.oxforddictionaries.com/definition/biochemistry

Boettcher, J., & Conrad, R. (2010). *The online teaching survival guide*. San Francisco, CA: Jossey Bass.

Boyer, E. L. (1990). *Scholarship reconsidered: Priorities of the professoriate*. Princeton, NJ: The Carnegie Foundation for the Advancement of Teaching.

Chang, I.-Y., & Chang, W.-Y. (2012). The effect of student learning motivation on learning satisfaction. *International Journal of Organizational Innovation*, *4*(3), 281–305.

Chien, T.-K. (2007). Using the learning satisfaction improving model to enhance the teaching quality. *Quality Assurance in Education, 15*(2), 192–214. doi:10.1108/09684880710748947

Clark, R. C., & Mayer, R. E. (2011). *E-learning and science of instruction* (3rd ed.). San Francisco, CA: Pfeiffer. doi:10.1002/9781118255971

Clark, R. C., Nguyen, F., & Sweller, J. (2006). *Efficiency in learning: Evidence-based guidelines to manage cognitive load.* San Francisco, CA: Pfeiffer.

Costabile, M. (2014, September). *Assessment of an e-Learning simulation for the teaching of enzyme kinetics. Changing Horizons: Local Learning for Global Impact.* Paper presented at the HERGA conference, Adelaide, Australia.

Gustafson, K. L., & Branch, R. M. (1997). Revisioning models of instructional development. *Educational Technology Research and Development, 45*(3), 73–89. doi:10.1007/BF02299731

Harland, T., Hussain, R. M. R., & Bakar, A. A. (2014). The Scholarship of Teaching and Learning: Challenges for Malaysian academics. *Teaching in Higher Education, 19*(1), 38–48. doi:10.1080/1356 2517.2013.827654

Henderson, M., Selvyn, N., & Aston, R. (2017). What works and why? Student perceptions of useful digital technology in university teaching and learning. *Studies in Higher Education, 42*(8), 1567–1579. doi:10.1080/03075079.2015.1007946

Horton, W. K. (2012). *E-Learning by Design* (2nd ed.). San Francisco, CA: Pfieffer.

Hyman, D., Gurgevich, E., Alter, T., Ayers, J., Cash, E., Fahnline, D., ... Wright, H. (2002). Beyond Boyer: The UniSCOPE model of scholarship for the 21st century. *Journal of Higher Education Outreach & Engagement, 7*(1-2), 41–65.

Kane-Gill, S. L., Williams, E. A., Smithburger, P. L., & Seybert, A. L. (2013). Tips for developing an integrated online and simulation course based on six years of experience. *Pharmacy, 1*(1), 34–42. doi:10.3390/pharmacy1010034

Kebritchi, M., Lipschuetz, A., & Santiague, L. (2017). Issues and challenges for teaching successful online courses in higher education: A literature review. *Journal of Educational Technology Systems, 46*(1), 4–29. doi:10.1177/0047239516661713

Koster, R. (2004). *A theory of fun.* New York, NY: Paraglyph Press.

LeBlanc, E. J. (2013). Designing interactive eLearning for your students. In R. McBride & M. Searson (Eds.), *Proceedings of Society for Information Technology & Teacher Education International Conference 2013* (p. 684). Chesapeake, VA: Association for the Advancement of Computing in Education.

Paivio, A. (1986). *Mental representations: A dual coding approach.* Oxford, UK: Oxford University Press.

Pollock, E., Chandler, P., & Sweller, J. (2002). Assimilating complex information. *Learning and Instruction*, *12*(1), 61–86. doi:10.1016/S0959-4752(01)00016-0

Rice, R. E. (1992). Towards a broader conception of scholarship: The American context. In T. Whiston & R. Geiger (Eds.), *Research and higher education: The United Kingdom and the United States* (pp. 117–129). Buckingham, UK: SRE and Open University Press.

Roblyer, M. D., & Edwards, J. (2000). *Integrating educational technology into teaching* (2nd ed.). Saddle River, NJ: Prentice Hall.

Rossett, A. (2002). Waking in the night and thinking about e-learning. In A. Rossett (Ed.), *The ASTD e-learning handbook* (pp. 3–18). New York, NY: McGraw-Hill.

Simulation. (2019). Retrieved from https://dictionary.cambridge.org/dictionary/english/simulation

Smith, R. (2008). *Conquering the content*. San Francisco, CA: Jossey Bass.

Sullivan, G. M., & Artino, A. R. Jr. (2013). Analyzing and interpreting data from Likert-type scales. *Journal of Graduate Medical Education*, *5*(4), 541–542. doi:10.4300/JGME-5-4-18 PMID:24454995

TEQSA Guidance Note Scholarship. (2017). (Version 2.3). Retrieved from https://www.teqsa.gov.au/sites/g/files/net2046/f/guidance-note-scholarship-v2-3.docx?v=1508129079

Truong, H. (2016). Integrating learning styles and adaptive e-learning system: Current developments, problems, and opportunities. *Computers in Human Behaviour, 55*(B), 1185-1193.

Varghese, J., Faith, M., & Jacob, M. (2012). Impact of e-resources on learning in biochemistry: First-year medical students' perceptions. *BMC Medical Education*, *12*(1), 21–30. doi:10.1186/1472-6920-12-21 PMID:22510159

Vygotsky, L. S. (1980). *Mind in society: Development of higher psychological processes*. Harvard, MA: Harvard University Press. doi:10.2307/j.ctvjf9vz4

Wood, E. J. (1990). Biochemistry is a difficult subject for both student and teacher. *Biochemical Education*, *18*(4), 170–172. doi:10.1016/0307-4412(90)90123-6

ADDITIONAL READING

Dixson, M. (2010). Creating effective student engagement in online courses: What do students find engaging? *The Journal of Scholarship of Teaching and Learning*, *10*(2), 1–13.

Lee, J., & Hammer, J. (2011). Gamification in education: What, how, why bother? *Academic Exchange Quarterly*, *15*(2), 1–5.

Light, G., Cox, R., & Calkins, S. (2010). *Learning and teaching in higher education* (2nd ed.). Thousand Oaks, CA: Sage Publications Ltd.

Manburg, J., Moore, R., Griffin, D., & Seperson, M. (2017). Building reflective practice through an online diversity simulation in an undergraduate teacher education program. *Contemporary Issues in Technology & Teacher Education, 17*(1), 128–153.

Miller, A. (2016). Benchmarking learner education using online business simulation. *International Journal of Cyber Society and Education, 9*(1), 17–33. doi:10.7903/ijcse.1418

Chapter 16
Insights Into an Interdisciplinary Project on Critical Reflection in Nursing:
Using SFL and LCT to Enhance SoTL Research and Practice

Namala Lakshmi Tilakaratna

National University of Singapore, Singapore

Mark Brooke

(iD) https://orcid.org/0000-0002-3071-6806

National University of Singapore, Singapore

Laetitia Monbec

National University of Singapore, Singapore

Siew Tiang Lau

National University of Singapore, Singapore

Vivien Xi Wu

National University of Singapore, Singapore

Yah Shih Chan

National University of Singapore, Singapore

ABSTRACT

The chapter provides a description of the first stage of an SoTL project consisting of an interdisciplinary research collaboration between nursing disciplinary experts from the Alice Lee Centre for Nursing Studies (ALCNS) and academic literacy experts from the Centre for English Language Communication (CELC) at the National University of Singapore (NUS). This stage includes the creation of appropriate lesson material for teaching critical reflection drawing on Focus Group Discussions (FGDs) with nurs-

DOI: 10.4018/978-1-7998-2212-7.ch016

ing lecturers and the use of 'model' reflective writing texts from high-scoring students in past cohorts analysed using Systemic Functional linguistic frameworks such as genre pedagogy, appraisal, The Legitimation Code Theory tool of semantic waves. The intervention was designed to improve the highly valued skill of 'critical reflection' in nursing undergraduate clinical modules drawing on the use of rigorous theoretical frameworks that make visible salient linguistics resources and knowledge practices drawing on SFL and LCT.

INTRODUCTION

This chapter provides a description of the first stage of a SoTL project titled *Reflecting in Undergraduate Nursing: An Interdisciplinary Approach to Embedding Critical Reflection in Undergraduate Nursing Practice*. The project is an interdisciplinary research collaboration between nursing disciplinary experts from the Alice Lee Centre for Nursing Studies (ALCNS) and academic literacy experts from the Centre for English Language Communication (CELC) at the National University of Singapore (NUS) that is supported by a Teaching Enhancement Grant from the university's Centre for Development of Teaching and Learning.

In order to address the SoTL objective to show "how learning is made possible" (Trigwell et al., 2000) through reflection, the project aims to move beyond purely disciplinary understandings of teaching and learning to incorporating a "cross-disciplinary" (Kreber, 2013) description of how nursing students reflect on clinical practice in a manner that is valued by their subject lecturers. The cross-disciplinary collaboration was achieved by drawing on the insight of nursing lecturers in a FGD and the expertise of academic literacy experts through the analysis of student assignments for linguistic features and knowledge practices.

The two FGDs with nursing lecturers aimed to understand critical reflection in the discipline of nursing from the perspective of disciplinary experts. Questions were designed to uncover why nursing staff chose critical reflection as a type of assessment, what they thought the value of such reflections was for undergraduate nursing students, and finally, to understand what counts as "deep" reflection in the discipline. The FGDs were complemented by the analysis of the reflective writing texts from students. The text analysis addresses Shulman's (2005) call for a "comparative study of signature pedagogies across professions" in order to "offer alternative approaches for improving professional education that might not otherwise be considered" (p. 58). To enhance the understanding of critical reflection in nursing clinical practice, texts were analysed through the use of rigorous theoretical frameworks of Genre (Martin & Rose, 2008) and Appraisal (Martin & White, 2005) (Systemic Functional Linguistic theory - SFL) to make visible salient linguistics resources in texts and semantic waves (Maton, 2014; Szenes, Tilakaratna, & Maton, 2015), and to make visible knowledge practices (Legitimation Code Theory - LCT) relevant to nursing reflective practice. SFL and LCT frameworks were employed to uncover deep critical reflection in undergraduate nursing because these two theoretical fields operate "side by side as analytical frameworks providing complementary analyses that are then integrated" (Maton & Doran, 2017, p. 613). The frameworks draw on the academic literacy experts' knowledge of linguistics and knowledge practices and the analysis aims to provide nursing disciplinary experts an "alternative approach" to understanding critical reflection in nursing clinical practice.

The results from the first stage of the project are intended to inform an intervention to improve the highly valued skill of "critical reflection" in nursing undergraduate clinical modules.

Table 1. Phases of the SoTL project "Reflecting in undergraduate nursing: An interdisciplinary approach to embedding critical reflection in undergraduate nursing practice"

Project Phase	Activity	Activity Period	Month/Year
Phase 1 – Pre-intervention Student text analysis FGDs, and rubric development	Collection of student assignments and FGDs with lecturers	3 months	July - September 2018
	Analysis of student assignments and rubric development, training of lecturers, and feedback session on rubric	6 months	September – March 2019
Phase 2 – teaching intervention	Creation of online material for flipped classroom content	5 months	March – August 2019
	Intervention stage – delivery of online materials	18 months	August 2019 – December 2020
Phase 3 – Post-intervention Evaluation of project – student assignment analysis, analysis of FGDs with lecturers	Post-intervention data gathering	12 months	December 2019 - January 2021
	Post-intervention evaluation of data	9 months	August 2020- Mar 2021
	Final changes to the lesson material based on post-intervention results	6 months	Jan -Jun 2021

A more detailed description of the phases of the ongoing project is outlined in Table 1.

In sharing the results from the first stage of the project, this chapter aims to address one of the concerns in SoTL literature: for disciplinary research to be made transparent for public scrutiny to show how learning is made possible (Trigwell et al., 2000). We begin our article with a brief exploration of how reflective practice in nursing is valued in the context of professional nursing and how it is conceptualised from a disciplinary perspective. This is followed by an introduction to the SFL and LCT frameworks used in this study and a description of the two data sets comprising the focus group discussions and critical reflection assignments. The remainder of the chapter will focus on explaining how the detailed thematic analysis of the focus group discussions and coding of the linguistic resources and knowledge practices employed by undergraduate nursing students has led to more nuanced and detailed description of critical reflection in clinical nursing practice. We conclude by discussing how the data collection and analysis in Phase 1 of the project has facilitated the creation of appropriate lesson material for teaching critical reflection so that nursing undergraduate students will be able to draw valuable learning from their experiences and emerge as critically reflective practitioners in preparation for future clinical nursing practice.

Reflective Practice in Undergraduate Nursing

Supportive clinical learning environments and effective coaching by clinical educators are well-documented to have positively influenced student learning outcomes during clinical attachments (Tanda & Denham, 2009). Additionally, nurses in the clinical setting and nursing educators are aware that the clinical environment within which nursing education occurs is dynamic and encompasses complex variables. This means that students do not always have positive experiences in the clinical setting (O'Mara et al., 2013). Additionally, the authors acknowledge that educators can facilitate students' capacities in reflection and generate ideas for coping and transforming future situations (O'Mara *et al,* 2013). Reflection is now regarded as an essential capacity and core to self-regulation and learning (Mann, 2016).

Figure 1. Adapted from Gibb's (1988) Reflective Cycle

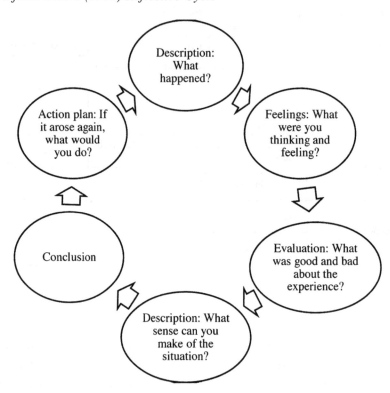

Needless to say, nursing educators need to be developed first in order to adequately support the development of students' reflection skills. According to Dekker-Groen (2013), there is a growing consensus that effective professional development of academic teachers should include the following core features: content, active learning, coherence, duration, and collective participation (Desimone, 2009; Garet et al., 2001; Penuel et al., 2007). "Content" refers to knowledge about what the students should learn from their reflection and knowledge about the teaching activities required to support students' learning from their clinical experiences. Moreover, providing feedback on students' reflection by the academic teacher or clinical facilitator is identified as one of the key strategies used to facilitate meaningful reflection. Therefore, the goal is for students to eventually develop critical thinking and social awareness in the process of thinking about and interpreting situations, events, experiences, and emotions that have occurred.

Recent research on critical reflection in the ALCNS Bachelor of Nursing programme identified that students write reflections that are predominantly descriptive in nature despite the use of frameworks such as Gibb's (1998) "Reflective Cycle" as a model for the process of reflection (Wu et al., 2016a; Wu et al., 2015). Gibbs' (1988) Reflective Cycle, a well-known framework in this field (see studies from Burns et al., 2000; Husebø et al., 2015; and Reid, 1993; Wu et al., 2015; and Wu et al., 2016), is used as a model to guide critical reflections and includes six stages: *Description* of the experience; *Feelings* about it; *Evaluation* (positive and negative) of the experience; *Analysis* to develop understanding of it; *Conclusion*, describing learning and how the event might have been differently managed; and *Action plan*, telling how a different approach might be taken in the future if this problem emerges again. This last criterion implies that practitioners experience a transformation in their practice. Figure 1 provides a visual representation of this model.

The first stage of the project attempts to address the lack of depth in undergraduate critical reflection at the ALCNS by asking the following research questions:

What constitutes "deep reflection" in clinical nursing practice?

How can we make "deep reflection" explicit and visible in creating effective pedagogic interventions? How can we identify the impact and outcome of teaching "deep reflection" through measuring student learning?

To address these questions, academic literacy experts drew on selected analytical frameworks from Systemic Functional Linguistics (SFL) and Legitimation Code Theory (LCT). In the section below, we begin by introducing the theoretical frameworks used in this project, starting with a description of SFL and the two analytical frameworks of *Genre* and *Appraisal* that were used to explore how critical reflection in undergraduate nursing is structured and how the personal subjective engagement with evaluative meaning is enabled through the use of a range of resources as revealed through the analysis of high-scoring texts. This is followed by an introduction to LCT analytical tool of *Semantics* with a focus om semantic gravity, which is used to account for how students move between the concrete particulars of the specific incident encountered in their reflections and nursing theories, the practices and procedures that they draw on to interpret this particular incident. In addition to the introduction to the analytical frameworks which demonstrate how academic literacy experts can unpack disciplinary meanings in texts, insights into critical reflection in undergraduate nursing are discussed with reference to extracts from the nursing Focus Group Discussions. The 'Results and Discussion' section below will discuss the preliminary findings from applying SFL/LCT analyses to a corpus of student texts. Extracts from high-scoring texts are produced to demonstrate how students deploy linguistic resources and knowledge practices to demonstrate their capacity for "deep reflection" in undergraduate nursing.

Theoretical Frameworks and Analytical Findings

This section introduces the three analytical frameworks used to explore how students write critical reflection texts in the discipline of nursing. The section begins with an overview of Systemic Functional Linguistics and introduces Genre theory and Appraisal. The section then introduces Legitimation Code Theory and the tool of semantic waves.

A Theory of Language: Systemic Functional Linguistics (SFL)

SFL theory is a theory of language developed by Michael Halliday and extended by a range of scholars (Halliday & Matthiessen, 2014; Martin, 1992; Martin & White, 2003) and is particularly interesting because of its conceptualization of language (and other semiotic systems) as context-dependent systems of choices. Decades of research have generated detailed descriptions of linguistic, or meaning-making, resources specific to various disciplinary discourse domains. Briefly, SFL allows for a systematic description of language at multi levels, from broad context (genre), whole text systems and paragraphs (Discourse Semantics) to sentence level (Lexicogrammar). Secondly, SFL describes language as performing three broad functions concurrently: engaging a range of linguistic resources to discuss the topic, to communicate meanings related to social relations between interactants, including evaluative meanings, and to produce a text that develops cohesively. Academic discourse deploys these meanings differently according to disciplinary contexts, specific assignments, and stages of these assignments. These insights from SFL, therefore, allow for a systematic description of different patterns of language from whole texts to sentences and in various specific contexts. This represents a significant shift from a more traditional approach to language which tends to prioritize sentence level issues and grammatical accuracy rather than a focus on the way language is used to create expected meanings. SFL has been used in a wide range of higher educational SoTL research (Dreyfus et al., 2016; Coffin & Donohue, 2014) as well as specific rubric development work (Jones, 2011; Szenes, 2011; Dreyfus et al., 2016).

In this study, SFL enabled us to reveal the language patterns recurrent in high scoring critical reflection assignments and to compare them with low and mid-scoring assignments. These findings were then used to make the patterns visible to the nursing lecturers and to students through a range of academic literacy materials and rubrics.

The Structure of Critical Reflection: Genre Theory

In Systemic Functional Linguistics, the term *genre* refers to unfolding text which follows stages and recognizable patterns which social actors deploy to achieve a certain goal (Martin & Rose, 2008). Genre is defined as a "staged, goal-oriented social process" (Martin & Rose, 2007, p.8). Martin and Rose (2007), among others, have classified common elemental genres according to social purposes. These elemental genres are classified into three broad social purpose categories: engaging, informing, and

Figure 2. Knowledge genres in the school
(Rose & Martin, 2014, p.276)

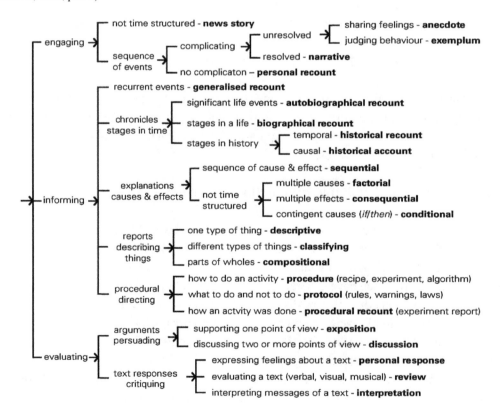

evaluating (Rose & Martin, 2012, p.128). The figure below shows the complete School genres taxonomy which includes narratives, different types of explanation genres, procedures, classifying, descriptive and compositional reports, expositions, discussions, and more. Each genre is then described for its typical structural elements, or stages, which can be obligatory or optional. These stages tend to occur in a specific, expected order in the text to serve a specific purpose and achieve the goal of the text. The typical resources deployed in each stage at various levels of language (whole texts/Discourse Semantics, and sentence level/Lexicogrammar) can then be described.

SFL researchers have mapped genres for several school subjects, such as English and Literature (Christie & Macken-Horarik, 2007; Rothery & Stenglin, 1997), History (Coffin, 2006; Schleppegrell, 2004); Geography (Wignell, Martin, & Eggins, 1989) and Science (Halliday & Martin, 1993; Lemke, 1990). In higher educational settings, these elemental genres often combine into extended texts, or macro genres, which combine several elemental genres in various logical relations to achieve a social purpose (Dreyfus et al., 2016; Martin & Rose, 2008). For example, Dreyfus et al. (2016) describe the undergraduate Biology lab report as a macro-genre because it contains several elemental science genres such as descriptions and classifications, as well as analytical exposition and explanations. Nesi & Gardner (2012) compiled and analysed the BAWE corpus, a collection of postgraduate and undergraduate student assignments in a range of disciplines from universities in the UK to map the types of writing requirements and to highlight commonalities and differences across assignment types and disciplines. The authors classified assignments according to their social purpose into 13 genre families which bridge discipline boundaries: *Essay, Methodological Recount, Critique, Explanation, Case Study, Exercise, Design Specification, Proposal, Narrative Recount, Research Report, Problem Question, Empathy Writing,* and *Literature Survey*.

The critical reflections written by health students in the BAWE corpus are classified in the Narrative Recount family. The social purpose of assignments in the Narrative Recounts is to "demonstrate knowledge of the field of study, critical thinking and the ability to apply appropriate methods of enquiry" (Nesi & Gardner, 2012, p. 214). The social purpose of these types of assignments is also to demonstrate or develop awareness of motives and/or behaviours (Nesi & Gardner, 2012, p. 42) and to evaluate one's (or others') behaviours and actions, involving an affective dimension. This affective dimension, as Nesi and Gardner (2012) explain, can be challenging for students when relating, for example, to an admission of mistake or weakness. In the BAWE corpus, reflection assignments aim to show that the student can reflect and evaluate elements of knowledge or behaviours and use academic reading or experimental data to support this evaluation. The student then explains how this experience is likely to alter their future practice. Nesi and Gardner (2012) show that, in their corpus, 25% of the occurrences of the word *insight* are in the Narrative Recount genre family.

Szenes et al. (2015) have described the following stages for similar reflection assignments in Social Work, which we draw on.

- Introduction—where the student discusses the importance of reflection
- Critical Incident—in which the student describes a problematic event which triggered the reflection
- Excavation—where the student unpacks the critical incident, explains it, rationalizes, or evaluates her actions
- Transformation—in which the student discusses the lesson learned, and the need to change in the future
- Coda—which sees the student reconnecting the importance of critical reflection

Drawing on this theoretical framework, genre patterns in the high, low and mid critical reflection assignments were analysed. The focus group data then showed the generic patterns which were particularly valued by lecturers. We asked the following questions:

- What kind of genre is the reflection assignment in Nursing?
- What is the generic structure?
- Which stages are obligatory, and which stages are not?
- What weighting do the stages have in the different low-mid-high scripts?

The findings are discussed in the section on 'Results and Discussion' below.

Emotion and Opinion in Critical Reflection: The Appraisal Framework from Systemic Functional Linguistics

Appraisal is used in this project to make visible evaluative meaning and its targets or sources, as well as how an accumulation of these resources can create an "evaluative key" (Hood, 2006, p. 38) of positive or negative values built up over the course of a high-scoring critical reflection assignment.

The appraisal framework developed by Martin and White (2005) consists of three interacting domains of Attitude, Graduation, and Engagement. Attitude, shown in Figure 3 below, consists of emotions (Affect), judgments of behaviour (Judgment) and evaluation of things (Appreciation). Graduation is a resource for grading evaluation through amplifying feelings or blurring categories (Martin & White, 2005, p. 35). Finally, Engagement deals with the source of Attitude and how it is managed within text.

In more common sense terms, we can distinguish between regions of Attitude as types of emotion and opinion. "Emotion" refers to attitudinal assessments that are indicated through descriptions of "emotional reactions" or "states of human subjects" while "opinion" refers to "positive or negative assessments" (White, 2004). Bednarek (2009) draws on this distinction to classify Affect as types of emotion, while Judgement and Appreciation are classified as forms of opinion. Emotions as realised by resources of Affect expressed as positive or negative feelings such as happiness/unhappiness, security/insecurity, and satisfaction/dissatisfaction (e.g., *I feel nervous about bathing the patient*). Emotions are often triggered by something; in the case of reflective writing in nursing, this is the specific incident or situation that students are engaged in (e.g., assisted bathing of patients). In addition, the person who feels the Affect, or the "Emoter" in the case of the nursing reflections, is predominantly the student but can also extend to the patient.

Figure 3. The domain of attitude
(adapted from Martin & White, 2005, p. 35)

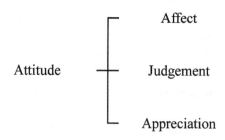

The second type of evaluative meaning that is prevalent in reflective writing is Judgements of behaviour. Judgements can be subdivided into types of "social esteem" that are concerned with normality (how un/usual someone is), capacity (how capable they are), and tenacity (how resolute they are) (e.g., *The clinical instructor helped me to bathe the patient*). The second type is "social sanction", which is associated with values that underpin "civic duty and religious observances" (Martin & White, 2005, p. 52). It includes two types: veracity (how truthful someone is) and propriety (how ethical someone is). Judgements typically involve a Target towards whom the judgement is directed (e.g., I *should have covered the patient while they were changing their clothes*).

Tilakaratna and Szenes (2017; 2019) have drawn on Appraisal to show how students engage with emotions and opinions in reflective writing in fields such as business and social work in the context of an Australian university. Their research has revealed that students in these disciplines focus on negative emotions and negative opinions, which are triggered by their insecurity regarding the incident that they chose to reflect on. In addition, their research has found a high level of negative self-judgement across the texts. The extension of this research to the context of NUS, in the exploration of subjects such as Public Communication, English for Academic Purposes, and Engineering by Tilakaratna, Brooke, and Monbec (2019) has revealed that students in Asian contexts focus on both negative incidents and negative self-judgement as well as *positive* self-judgement in relation to their transformation over the course of their studies. Particularly significant is the role that mentors play in the development of professional behavior.

Below, the tool of semantic gravity in Legitimation Code Theory is introduced. Semantics explores how students move between the concrete particulars of an incident that triggered reflection and relate this to principles, procedures, and theories relevant to clinical nursing practice.

Abstraction and Concreteness in Critical Reflection: Semantic Gravity from Legitimation Code Theory

Legitimation Code Theory (LCT) is a framework for analysing principles of practice in educational fields to reveal the "rules of the game". LCT seeks to make these codes visible so that they may be taught and learned to lead to academic achievement. semantics gravity from LCT explores the DNA of knowledge and the codes that may enable knowledge-building. Semantic gravity (SG+/-) is defined by Maton (2013) as:

The degree to which meaning relates to its context, whether that is social or symbolic. Semantic gravity may be relatively stronger (+) or weaker (–) along a continuum of strengths. The stronger the semantic gravity (SG+), the more closely meaning is related to its context; the weaker the gravity (SG–), the less dependent meaning is on its context. (p. 65)

Semantic gravity conceptualizes the degree to which meanings relate to context. A continuum is used to map how these meanings may move from stronger to weaker or from weaker to stronger context-dependency. To exemplify, Maton (2013) describes how the name for a specific plant in Biology or a specific event in History are knowledge structures that are specific and therefore embody stronger semantic gravity. In contrast, a species of plant or theory to explain historical events such as historical causation embody weaker semantic gravity as these are meanings that are more generic and transferable across contexts. If the knowledge structure is transferable across contexts, and can be used to analyse different

Figure 4. Illustrative profiles and semantic ranges
(adapted from Maton, 2013, p. 13)

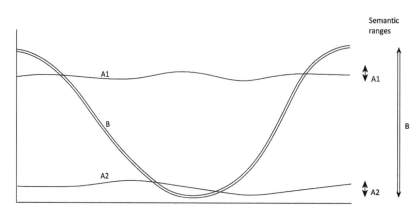

phenomena, it can represent the accumulation of knowledge or knowledge building. The shifts from SG-to SG+ or SG+ to SG- produce semantic gravity waves. These waves are presented below as profile B:

Analysts can record this process of gravity waving on a graph as above and construct a visual representation or semantic gravity profile indicating semantic gravity ranges. In addition to waves, flatlines can be recorded as profiles with very limited range (refer to A1 and A2 in Figure 1) to represent consistently abstract or concrete knowledge structures. Additionally, "down escalators" (Figure 2) or steep slopes downwards with meanings starting in abstraction but then shifting quickly to concrete meanings, can be depicted. Similarly, "up-escalators" can be mapped if meanings shift from the concrete to the very abstract. For both the "down escalators" and "up-escalators", meanings are not being connected across contexts. This represents "segmented learning" rather than "cumulative learning" (Maton, 2013).

Szenes, Tilakaratna, and Maton (2015) present how valued critical reflection assignments from Social Work and Business Faculty students during practicum experiences produced complex semantic gravity profiles shifting between meanings on the semantic gravity continuum. The following is provided as a highly-scored reflection:

In my incident, the emerging themes that I believe warrant further investigation relate to professional practice, namely the issue of boundaries, gender, and power. The irony of my distinction only becomes clear now. While I expect to be able to put on a professional "mask", consisting of the professional skills and knowledge of social work practice when working with clients, I expect clients like Jared to "bare all", to reveal to me their personal problems, issues, and insecurities. Sommers-Flanagan and Sommers-Flanagan (2007) refer to this concept as "one-way intimacies" (Sommers-Flanagan & Sommers-Flanagan, 2007, p. 163), and as a necessary component of helping relationships. (pp. 580-581)

In this example, there is an interplay between knowledge structures that are both abstract and concrete. The subjects of gender and power represent weaker semantic gravity as these are abstract terms with multiple meanings. Information relating to personal experience through a short narrative represents relatively stronger semantic gravity. The writer refers to a specific individual, a very context-dependent knowledge structure. The reflection then moves back to more generalized meanings with the notion of "one-way intimacies" accompanied with an academic source (Sommers-Flanagan & Sommers-Flanagan,

2007, p. 163). Again, this is less context-dependent as it is an analytical tool for viewing human relations across contexts and thus a more general meaning is realised. It is possible for another reflector to apply the same analytical tool to another related or different context or use another tool for the same context, and so on. To sum up, it can be observed that as it shifts along the semantic gravity continuum, the valued discourse is creating semantic gravity waves. In this project, the authors sought to uncover whether similar profiles were present and valued in the same way and to uncover the types of subject matter that were discussed along the continuum.

Description of the Data

For the first phase of the project, two types of data were collected: student reflective writing assignments from the cohort of undergraduate nurses undertaking clinical practice units and Focus Group Discussions involving the nursing lecturers. These two data sets are described in greater detail below.

Critical Reflection Assignments for Clinical Nursing Practice

Critical reflection forms an important component of clinical practice experiences that are at the core of the Alice Lee Centre for Nursing Studies (ALCNS) Bachelor of Science (BSc) (Nursing) programme, which has incorporated core concepts of health, person, environment, and nursing. At ALCNS, clinical practice enables students to develop clinical skills and professional competency through a structured programme that includes on-campus clinical laboratory learning and simulation experiences and is followed by end of semester clinical attachments in various Healthcare Institutes for a period of two to nine weeks. The primary aims of the BSc (Nursing) programmes are to prepare graduate nurses to be reflective, safe, competent, and caring nursing practitioners who exercise informed clinical judgement in the delivery of evidence-based care that will improve patient outcomes. To enable nursing students to emerge as critical thinkers capable of fulfilling the role of a self-reflective nursing practitioner, NUS nursing educators designed individual critical reflection writing tasks to reveal how students engage and learn from difficult clinical experiences. The tasks are assessed in a module and the specific assessment criteria for critical reflection in the unit *Fundamentals of Nursing* are described below.

Description of the Module (Fundamentals of Nursing)

The Fundamentals of Nursing is the first nursing module undertaken by the undergraduate during their first year of study. The module focuses on the development of foundation knowledge and skills for the provision of nursing care to patients in a variety of health care settings. The focus is on enabling the patient and the nurse to confidently and competently assess, plan, implement, and evaluate care around the fundamental care needs.

To improve the realism for learning, a new initiative to allow the year one students to have hands-on clinical experience during their first semester was implemented. This arrangement was made in 2018 for the first-year students to integrate the theory to practice, through applying what they have learnt on the real patients in hospital during the semester. This programme was added with the emphasis on bridging the theory-practice gap in collaboration with a tertiary hospital in Singapore. The programme allowed the first year students to have six hours in learning about person-centred care and various clinical procedures in simulated clinical wards, and apply what they had learnt for four hours at the hospital. They

Table 2. Marking criteria for reflection assignment

Reflection Assignment Procedure/ Activity performed: _____

(1) Gibb's Reflective Model
    • Description of the encounter, experience, or any problem that arose during the clinical visitation
    • Feelings and Reflection: Identify your assumptions, values, beliefs, emotions, and motives based on your experience
    • Evaluation of the performance and experience. Analysis of the deeper meanings from a different perspective (including feedback from tutor/peer). Research using academic references or literature (minimum of 5). Synthesise and integrate the information to complement a broader discussion.
       • Conclude and integrate how the experience informs nursing practice. Plan of action for future encounters.
         - Focus on knowledge issues
         - Links and comparisons between one's performance and standard procedure
         - Shows relevance and sophisticated understanding

(2) Knower's perspective
    • Displays independent learning
    • Self- awareness with different perspectives
    • Uses varied appropriate examples

(3) Analysis of knowledge issues
    • Shows insight and depth of topic
    • Main points well-justified
    • Arguments and counter-arguments are justified

(4) Organisation of ideas
    • Well-structured with key ideas explained
    • Factual accuracy
    • APA (6th ed.) reference guide

then returned to the on-campus clinical laboratory for another four hours of skills training, followed by a second hospital field visit to provide care for the patients, working alongside the ward nurses and clinical instructors.

At the hospital, two to five students shadowed a registered or enrolled nurse and assisted in providing fundamental care under supervision. The students communicated with the patients, and participated in many aspects of patient care, such as assisting in bathing, feeding of patients and taking care of patient's hygiene needs. They also conducted assessment such as taking vital signs, assessing the patients' skin condition, and assisting in wound care. The sessions included 270 students and ran over eight weekends.

Assessment, Rubrics, and Student Cohort: Frameworks Used

After eight hours of clinical experience, the students were required to write a reflection journal on what they had learnt from the patient care experience and how they could do better in the future. Reflective learning is a process in which students learn about themselves and make sense of the deep learning experience (Kolb, 1984). Schon (1983) defined reflective practice as having the capability to reflect in action while doing, and after an action has been performed. In order to enable this process, Kolb (1984) created a cyclical model, which involves critical evaluation of learners on their learning. Adapting and extending on Kolb's model to include personal and subjective feelings, Gibbs' Reflective Cycle, used by the nursing lecturers to teach reflective practice, starts with a description of the critical incident, examining feelings about the incident and evaluating the experience. This is followed by an analysis of the situation, reviewing potential actions to improve the situation, and finally, identifying areas in which students require further development.

Reflective learning is critical in building capacity to restructure and reframe knowledge, and it develops the students as independent learners. The marking criteria is shown in Table 2.

Focus Group Discussions (FGD)

The rationale for the FGDs was to enable nursing faculty and education/ literacy experts to meet together and produce data to make visible what is valued as successful critical reflection in the nursing faculty. This was done to provide a platform for nurses to discuss their ideas from their own experiences, but also included a response to student nurse reflective journal samples supplied by the faculty prior to the meeting. Two sessions of FGDs lasting for about one hour each time were conducted. Each session comprised five or six different participants from the faculty. Thus, data from over 10 nursing faculty members were collected. These sessions were digitally recorded. They were then transcribed by a third-party research assistant, before being verified by one of the co-investigators. The two transcripts amounted to approximately 15,000 words in total. The content from the two focus groups was then coded thematically to reflect the values and concerns of the nursing lecturers. Before each focus group, education/ literacy experts asked members to reflect on questions about the importance of critical reflection and their opinions about the critical reflection assignment (see Appendix). After this stage, a set of three sample assignments (high, medium, and low-scoring papers marked by nursing tutors) were discussed. Nursing faculty discussed what they valued in the high scoring paper and what could be improved in the other two. Again, these student assignments were shared with nursing lecturers before the meeting to allow them time to prepare what they wanted to share.

A number of topics were observed from the data collected. These topics were labelled and then relationships between them created to form categories. These categories were making the most of learning situations; ability to reflect critically by thinking back and forward effectively for personal growth; developing professionalism; making the most of nursing knowledge; maintaining physical and psychological balance; ability to communicate effectively.

RESULTS AND DISCUSSION

Below we discuss the key theoretical frameworks used in this study namely Genre (Martin &. Rose, 2008), Appraisal (Martin & White, 2005), and Semantics (Maton, 2014). We begin each section with key extracts from the focus group discussions where nursing lecturers identify aspects of critical reflection that are particularly challenging for students. We then highlight the findings from the Nvivo analysis which demonstrates how high-scoring students show their capacity to produce certain patterns of language and knowledge practices that constitute "deep reflection" in nursing clinical practice.

Genre – Structures of Reflective Texts – Obligatory and Optional Staging

During the focus group discussion, the nursing lecturers highlighted the key purpose of the reflection and the type of structure they expected and valued. For them, the assignment aims to cultivate a life-long habit of reflecting on practice; while in the shorter term, it provides the assessors with a window into the learning and thinking processes of the students. The nursing students' critical reflections analyzed here clearly belong to the narrative recount genre family, more specifically narratives of personal experi-

Table 3. Stages in nursing critical reflection

Stages	Purpose	Key Linguistic Features
Introduction	General orientation of the Placement. The student may explain the importance of reflection in nursing. Orientation to the text (focus of the entity/procedure being reflected upon).	Factual description (place/time/length) Thesis statement type of sentence: use of will
Orientation	Description of the specific setting: the ward, the patient, the precise procedure.	Narrative/past simple and past continuous/ circumstantial
Critical Incident	Event that triggers the reflection is described.	Narrative/Past simple; evaluation
Excavation	Unpacking/analysis of the event; Making the thinking process visible; Link to relevant literature to explain/ hypothesize/rationalise	Shift to defining, thinking Present simple Citations
Transformation	Statement of alteration in the student's understanding. The student may explain how the experience will inform future nursing practice.	Modality Should or Will to indicate recommended future action
(Coda)	Emphasizing the role/importance of CR in nursing practice	General statement: present simple, definition of the role of a nurse.

ence. The reflections recount a temporal series of events, often describing the steps of a procedure the nursing student completed on a patient. The post-event recount allows the student to review and reflect on skills deployed during the procedure and to demonstrate to the nursing lecturer the way the activity has impacted the student. In our data set, the self-evaluation dimension described in Nesi & Gardner is also clearly present (discussed below).

The nursing lecturers also allude to text structure which they value, and to certain stages through which they expect the student to develop their texts. These comments are provided below as the generic stages are described.

The high-scoring scripts consistently presented the following 6 stages:

Introduction ^ Orientation ^ Critical Incident ^ Excavation ^ Transformation ^(Coda)[1]

Table 3 shows the stages, their purposes, and the key linguistic features.

In the Introduction, successful writers succinctly state the placement location (Hospital, Ward) and then focus on the text itself, making a short statement on the value of reflection, and indicating what the text will specifically discuss:

I was placed in Hospital x. (3_133)

Hence, I will be focusing my / reflection on the assisted bath and assessment skills performed with reference to various aspects of the Entrustable Professional Activities (EPA) guideline. (3_133)

The Orientation discusses the specific and precise setting of the critical incident:

One particular patient I would like to focus on is..., who had a history of...; he felt...

The Critical Incident describes the moment when the nursing student experience was "jolted" by an error made, which can be highlighted by the patient, or the senior nurse, or by the student himself. The incident could also take the form of a confusing event, where the student's assumptions may, for example, be challenged. Beyond the factual description, the writer gives access to their inner thoughts as the critical incident unfolds, as shown in these two examples from the data:

I felt incompetent as I was unable to understand what emotion Mr. Tan was conveying (8_228)

My intention was simply to help, but later on I realised that I had unintentionally deprived him of opportunities for self-care (6-200)

Due to the space constraint in the cubicle, I was unable to assess Mdm X's back thoroughly for any broken skin. At one point, I even caused slight discomfort to Mdm X while attempting to clean between her right toes (3-133)

In the FGD, nursing lecturers specified that they expect the critical event to be short and to simply highlight the problematic issue which will then be developed through the next stage.

The excavation stage is the key element of the task, according to the nursing lecturers, and takes the largest amount of text in the high-scoring scripts. This stage provides, according to a nursing lecturer, access to the thinking process of the student, as nicely expressed in this lecturer's statement: "I like to read [reflection assignments] about things I couldn't see. The thinking process is what I like to read in a reflection." The student below shows the thinking process which led to her evaluating her skills as still needing to develop. While doing this, she thoughtfully acknowledged the challenges inherent to handling bathing of an elderly patient and shows the assessor that she is aware of the professional guidelines:

I felt that the negative experiences arose from my lack of knowledge in caring for a patient with limb fractures. For instance, because of my poor preparation, I often found myself thinking of what the next steps are. Yet I had to maintain a certain level of confidence so that Mdm X could entrust me in bathing her. Furthermore, the fear of causing more pain to her resulted in compromising the quality of care delivered. For instance, certain body parts such as her right foot and toes might not be thoroughly cleansed since I did not want to add pressure to them. However, according to the Core Competencies of Registered Nurse guidelines by the Singapore Nursing Board, it is the responsibility of a nurse to utilise her professional judgement and evidence-based knowledge to consistently and continuously deliver a holistic quality of care to the patients (Singapore Nursing Board, 2018). Hence it is important for us to use our critical thinking skills and ethical reasonings based on the Code for Nurses and Midwives to provide beneficence to the patients and advocate for their best interests (Singapore Nursing Board, 2018). After all, personal hygiene including bathing should not be neglected as it can help to reduce hospital-acquired infections. (Becker' s Clinical Leadership & Infection Control, 2106) (3_133)

In the FGD, the lecturers signal this stage as the most challenging for students in Year 1 and comment that many students *miss the opportunity for reflection* by simply stating a feeling or an observation, without going beyond the descriptive.

A lecturer explains:

...as the reader, I am interested to know why you were shy. [...]. Are there previous experiences which have triggered me to be so shy when I face similar episodes? [...]So to me, that is description. A lot of people can describe feelings but to examine why you feel this way is another level of reflection, which she has not demonstrate in this assignment.

The transformation, while often brief, tends to summarise the learning this experience has led to, and reaffirm the impact on the student nurse, and their future practice:

Hence some of future action plans I would consider that may help in minimising such resistance are: to administer analgesia prior to a bath if required, explain the procedure to the patient so that he/she can anticipate any impending discomfort, encourage patient to voice out his/her concerns and understand more about the patient's injury prior to the bath so I can be more organised and systematic to know the specific precautions to take on. In addition, I can also consider bed sponging as an alternative method if the patient strongly refuses assisted shower. (Lynn, 201 1) (3_133)

The Coda then lifts the discussion back to general nursing knowledge and to the benefit of critical reflection on professional nursing practice:

This attachment, albeit short, has given me a valuable insight to go beyond being a "robot nurse" who only performs the tasks but to be a critical thinker so that each patient's specific needs could be met. (3_133)

The stages in the high scoring reflections were characterized as follows:

Introductions were concise and factual. The Orientations were clearly focused on the one event or nursing skill reflected upon in the following text. The Critical Incidents are described concisely, precisely, and used as a springboard for the excavation to start. The Excavations are the longest stage of the text. The descriptions are concise, but the analysis, explanations, and conjectures are detailed and consistently linked with content of the module (literature, or expert knower). The link with the literature is genuine, and it is clearly relevant to the precise critical incident described. The Transformation stage was short in even the best scripts but precisely referred to an impact on future practice. Finally the Coda relates back to the benefit of Critical Thinking for general nursing practice, and is often omitted, even in the best scripts.

The section below explores how evaluative meaning is distributed across the three main stages of the critical reflection: Critical Incident, Excavation, and Transformation.

Emotions and Opinion in Nursing Reflective Texts

Emotions and evaluations are an important component of successful critical reflections. Research on critical reflection writing notes that reflective writing is concerned with "unsettling individual assumptions" and involves a certain amount discomfort or unease in order to motivate learning (Fook & Gardner, 2007, p. 16). Discomfort or unease with a particular "critical incident" or situation that students encounter often manifest in the assignment in the discussion of "emotions" (Passila & Vince, 2016, p. 48) or "personal and emotional concerns" (Crème, 2008, p. 60). Notably, many of the emotions discussed are predominantly negative in nature with students focussing on what went wrong or how they were emotionally affected by the difficult situation they faced (see, for instance, Tilakaratna & Szenes, 2017; 2019).

In the context of NUS nursing, the use of the Gibb's framework explicitly foregrounds the use of emotion and evaluation in critical reflection assignments. Following the initial description phase of the reflective cycle in which students describe a particularly difficult or problematic incident that triggers the reflection, Gibb's framework proposes that students engage with their feelings (e.g., "what were you thinking and feeling?") and evaluate their experiences ("what was good and bad about the experience?"). In the FGDs, nursing staff indicated that "engaging with feelings" was a "very important" part of the reflective writing. They noted that:

If students did not digest or release their feelings, they may be stuck at that stage. We have to talk about the physical and psychological balance. If we didn't take care of the psychological part, it would not be balanced and this would impact his/her future. If you talk about simulation and they have strong feelings about it, it is important to talk about it before they discuss other aspects objectively.

Importantly, nursing staff thus noted the need to engage with the psychological in order to move from the "subjective" to the "objective" aspects of nursing including engagement with the specific nursing procedures (such as assisted bathing) that form part of their clinical practice sessions as well as the nursing theories that support students' learning of these particular procedures. It was also highlighted that the inability to move past emotionally difficult situations in clinical nursing practice would make it "difficult for [for students[to objectively reflect on what has happened if it has affected them emotionally... [t]here should be a good balance between the mind and heart part so students can adequately reflect and move from there to the next step." Therefore, the engagement with emotions is considered an important step to objectively discussing the critical incident or difficult situation that students face in clinical practice and to evaluating their own and others' behavior in the Critical Incident stage.

As emotions and opinions are primarily discussed in the Critical Incident, Excavation, and Transformation stages of the text, examples of how evaluation is deployed in these stages is explored in greater detail below.

Emotions are primarily discussed in the Critical Incident stage of the reflective texts to describe the event that triggers the reflection. Students typically use resources of negative affect to share their own feelings of insecurity (e.g., *anxious, concerns*) triggered by the patient's condition or by the student's lack of experience/abilities. In addition, students use neutral affect "surprise" to indicate "unsettling of assumptions" (e.g., I was *surprised* to learn that…).

While emotions typically refer to how the students feel in the clinical practice situation, they draw on resources of judgement to evaluate their own behaviour and the behaviour of significant others in the text such as Clinical Instructors, who are responsible for guiding and supporting them during their clinical placements. Notably, when referring to their own behaviour, students use resources of negative judgement to evaluate their lack of capacity (e.g., *that I could only assist Mdm X from the front*) in relation to the clinical procedure. Alternatively, they choose to positively evaluate the role of a Clinical Instructor (e.g., *my CI was patient, [she was] guiding me*) as a catalyst for positive behaviour (e.g., *[she] helped me to stay more organised and focused*).

In the Excavation stage, where the students unpack and analyse the specific incident that triggers reflection, the student may explain how a negative or difficult critical incident can have positive learning

Figure 5. Semantic gravity profile of a high-scoring (56/60) critical reflection paper

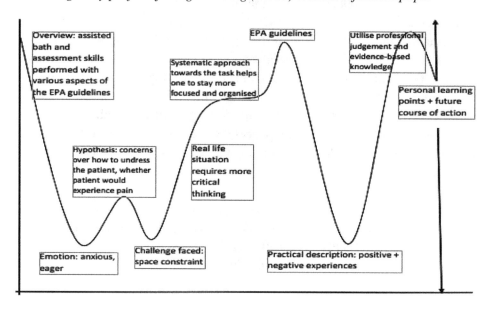

outcomes (e.g., *The whole experience was relatively positive*).The student may link this to their positive capacity (e.g., *I had managed to adhere closely to some parts of the guidelines of EPA 1-5; I also noticed and highlighted to Cl*) or their negative capacity (e.g. *I was unable to assess Mdm X's back*). In addition, they may choose to delve deeper into their lack of capacity (e.g. *I felt that the negative experiences arose from my lack of knowledge*)

In the final stage of Transformation students produce statements of alteration in their understanding and explain how the experience will inform future nursing practice. Students use resources of modality (e.g., can, may, should, would) throughout the transformation—this shows a shift from past actions and analysis of these actions in the present to transformative behaviour in the future. The focus for nursing students is on expressing in the form of capacity with future orientation (e.g., *I can be more organised and systematic*).

In the highest-ranking scripts, the Transformation was present although often quite succinct, possibly showing that nursing students in their very first placement struggle to project themselves in the future as fully-fledged nurses. This is acknowledged by the nursing lecturers who describe how much the skill of reflection is acquired through time, and how difficult it can be for some nursing students to take the habit to question, probe, evaluate (excavation) and to apply, predict, and project (Transformation).

Semantics in Nursing Reflective Texts

Using semantic gravity to analyse the nursing experts' data as well as the critical reflections produced by nursing students helped to provide findings on practices that are valued. An example of a semantic gravity profile of a high-scoring (56/60) critical reflection paper is discussed below in Figure 5.

From the profile above, it is evident that the student-nurse shifts from the abstract theoretical to the concrete specific several times. At the weakest semantic gravity level (SG-) during the Introduction and Orientation stages, there is an overview of the Entrustable Professional Activities (EPA) paradigm. This is referred to as it relates to an experience during practicum. The nurse states that this was her "first experience in an assisted shower during the attachment" and how "prior to this attachment, [she] did not realise that a seemingly simple shower could involve so many nursing practices." She then discusses the critical event of an assisted bathing and how she felt while she undressed a patient. Thus, she applied general, context-independent principles of practice to a specific experience. After that, she presents how she considers this event from a more abstract, generalised viewpoint (SG-), hypothesising how it might be done to reduce anxiety for her and patients based on her reflections after the event during the excavation stage. She then returns to discuss more of the challenges faced during the event (SG+) (e.g., a lack of space in the hospital bathroom). This then leads to a discussion on the importance of critical thinking in difficult situations (SG-) and continues to generalisations about how it is important to be able to approach tasks of this nature systematically (SG-). The student states:

I felt that the negative experiences arose from my lack of knowledge in caring for a patient with limb fractures. For instance, because of my poor preparation, I often found myself thinking of what the next steps are.

The discourse leads back to the point that having EPA guidelines give a student nurse a set of codes constructed through experience and in tandem with scientific knowledge. Having these guidelines is very important as a student nurse cannot predict all of the problems that might arise. With the guidelines, however, predictions are more easily facilitated (SG-). The student emphasises the importance of "critical thinking skills and ethical reasonings based on the Code for Nurses and Midwives to provide beneficence to the patients and advocate for their best interests". She also refers to important academic sources from the nursing faculty and references authors in her reflection on general principles of practice (SG-). This subject-matter is part of the Transformation stage and the learning that has occurred. She concludes:

This attachment, albeit short, has given me a valuable insight to go beyond being a "robot nurse" who only performs the tasks but to be a critical thinker so that each patient's specific needs could be met.

As she refers to her own learning here and not nurses in general, to conclude the critical reflection, it represents stronger semantic gravity (SG+) than the previous content about the "Code for nurses and midwives", which is a generalised abstract knowledge structure (SG-) referring to no individual person, what might be termed an "every-nurse" or "every-midwife". Therefore, this is a slight shift towards SG+. However, it is weaker in semantic gravity than the description of the event or hypothesising about how she might act in the same circumstance as it is a generalisable knowledge structure for a range of tasks (SG-). It therefore acts as subject-matter summing up the student's transformation. This reference to the benefit of critical thinking also acts as part of the Coda, helping to end the reflection with subject matter towards SG-.

One common feature of high scoring critical reflection papers is this complex interplay between levels of abstraction. Students who demonstrate an ability to move from the experiential (SG+) to a more generalised personal theoretical (still applying "I", but in a context-independent nature such as "in the future, I would do … if the same situation arose …") tends to be less evident in lower scoring papers. Additionally, effective critical reflectors draw on abstract theoretical knowledge from faculty (SG-) and the clinical instructors (SG-) to view an event from a more theoretical position (SG-). This is done by appropriately applying general principles of practice in nursing (SG-) to the event in order to judge and evaluate it. In contrast, low-achieving reflections seem to be too descriptive (SG+) and lack appropriate analysis of the event. This produces contextually-dependent rather than independent learning in the reflections. Therefore, rather than constructing semantic gravity waves, low achievers tend to produce SG+ flatlines.

CONCLUSION

This chapter has described the first stage of a large cross-disciplinary research project involving the coding and description of valued features of nursing undergraduate critical reflection assignments drawing on selected tools from Systemic Functional Linguistics and Legitimation Code Theory. As Hutchings and Huber (2008, p. 238) note, the place of theory, particularly education theory, in SoTL research has been widely debated. They note that as SoTL practitioners in the field come from a wide range of disciplines, and that engaging with theoretical frameworks that are outside these disciplines leads to a number of challenges in terms of appropriate application and depth. Despite this, Hutchings and Huber conclude that theory can play "enlightening purposes" in SoTL by "becoming a kind of boundary object that brings scholars with similar interests together, creating a shared lexicon, providing direction for further research, and unifying diverse efforts to explain a complex phenomenon" (p. 238). In drawing on the disciplinary knowledge of nursing lecturers through FGDs, academic literacy experts were able to understand what constitutes valued reflection in nursing clinical practice. This insight was used to identify relevant analytical frameworks from two complex theoretical frameworks of SFL and LCT. The selected frameworks included Genre analysis, Appraisal analysis and semantic gravity wave profiles, which were used to deconstruct student nurses' critical reflections and reveal what counts as "deep" reflection and reveals the following insights into nursing critical reflection.

The uncovering of genre staging and structure enables a valued but often challenging skill like critical reflection to be explicitly taught to students as an unfolding process. Genre analysis of high-scoring texts revealed a consistently recognizable genre structure produced by high scoring students consisting of six stages: Introduction, Orientation, Critical Reflection, Excavation, Transformation, and Coda. As nursing educators pointed out in the FGDs, enabling students to internalize and make reflective practice intuitive is an end-goal of explicitly teaching reflections to students and asking them to engage in reflective practice throughout their clinical placements. Providing students with structure and language features that emerge within the different stages allows students to organize the complex evaluative meanings and disciplinary theoretical understandings that arise in clinical practice situations and to analyse these situations in order to improve future practice.

The application of the second framework of Attitude to the student data revealed that successful students showed engagement with negative emotions and negative self-judgement. In addition, they positively evaluated the role of their clinical instructors and showed a capacity for transformation within the event itself in terms of improved future practice. Revealing explicitly the kinds of evaluative meanings deployed by students across the different stages of reflection will enable nursing educators to show students how to engage with the personal and subjective in an academic context. As the FGD revealed, moving past the emotional and cathartic in reflections allows students to engage with their growing professional identities and professionalism as they move away from, as one of the students phrased it in their critical reflection, a "robot nurse" towards becoming self-reflective nursing practitioners.

Drawing on Legitimation Code Theory's semantic gravity, which describes the DNA of knowledge, provides a platform for the content of a text to be analysed in great depth, no matter the discipline. Thus, a semantic gravity profile is a representation of meanings across a text and how these relate to each other. Providing an analysis of this sort acts as a sound overview of these meanings Additionally, a semantic gravity profile is a sound visualization of the content of a text presenting its different meanings. This strategy was clearly appreciated by the nursing faculty evidenced in meetings when the literacy experts presented findings from their analyses of the student nurse texts.

These results of the linguistic and knowledge practices analyses were shared with nursing lecturers in a session where academic literacy experts showed the FGD responses, the Gibb's framework, and the corresponding frameworks and results from the data that show what constitutes deep reflection. This sharing session enabled literacy experts to unpack theoretical frameworks so that particularly complex educational theory concepts were made relevant to disciplinary experts providing a "shared lexicon" (Hutchings and Huber, 2008, p. 238) that enabled the team to explain and discuss the complex phenomenon of reflection in clinical nursing practice.

The next stage of the project will involve the use of these results to create a rubric that draws on the genre structure and its overlap with stages of Gibb's reflective cycle as the basis for an effective scaffold for students and lecturers to view what is valued for successful reflective writing in the discipline, and how to approach the task of producing a valued critical reflection response. This chapter showed how the use of complex SFL and LCT frameworks can be unpacked by academic literacy experts to help to make visible the *practices* of academic writing, in this case, critical reflection writing, based on *evidence* of sound and valued texts in the disciplines. From this collaboration, it is clear that these theoretical approaches can be used by experts in education and literacy working with disciplinary experts in fields where practicum is essential. It has proven to be easily accessible to a wider community of disciplinary staff.

The project also clearly demonstrated the value of interdisciplinary collaboration in SoTL where nursing educators were able to provide disciplinary insights into the process of how undergraduate nursing students development their identities as professional nurses. Meanwhile, academic literacy experts were able to explicitly reveal these meanings in examples of successful high scoring students through the use of highly valued theoretical frameworks. The collaboration has demonstrated that the use of theoretically valued and explicit frameworks can make visible what disciplinary experts know to be intuitively valued in their disciplines. In addition, it has facilitated a deeper understanding of how knowledge is construed in reflective practice in the discipline of nursing and in nursing care. For SoTL research, which has been critiqued for not engaging with education theory (Hutchings & Huber, 2008), cross-disciplinary collaborations have the potential to provide an opportunity for disciplinary and education experts to draw on each other's knowledge to enable deeper understanding of disciplinary practice; provide "alternative approaches" to understanding a discipline (Shulman, 2005, p. 58); provide a shared "lexicon" for the analysis and discussion of research and finally, an opportunity to create "larger and more effective communities of practice" (Hutchings & Huber, 2008, p. 238).

REFERENCES

AACN. (2008). *The essentials of baccalaureate education for professional nursing practice.* Retrieved from http://www.aacn.nche.edu/publications/baccalaureate-essentials

Christie, F., & Macken-Horarik, M. (2007). Verticality in subject English. In F. Christie & J. R. Martin (Eds.), *Language, knowledge, and pedagogy*. London: Continuum.

Coffin, C. (2006). *Historical discourse*. London: Continuum.

Coffin, C., & Donohue, J. (2014). A language as social semiotic-based approach to teaching and learning in higher education (Language Learning Monograph Series). Chichester, UK: Wiley-Blackwell.

Dekker-Groen, A. M., van der Schaaf, M. F., & Stokking, K. M. (2011). Teacher competences required for developing reflection skills of nursing students. *Journal of Advanced Nursing*, *67*(7), 1568–1579. doi:10.1111/j.1365-2648.2010.05591.x PMID:21332576

Desimone, L. M. (2009). Improving impact studies of teachers' professional development: Towards better conceptualizations and measures. *Educational Researcher*, *38*(3), 181–199. doi:10.3102/0013189X08331140

Dreyfus, S. J., Humphrey, S., Mahboob, A., & Martin, J. R. (2016). *Genre pedagogy in higher education: The SLATE project*. Basingstoke, UK: Palgrave Macmillan. doi:10.1007/978-1-137-31000-2

Fook, J., Collington, V., Ross, R., Ruch, G., & West, L. (2016). *Researching critical reflection: Multidisciplinary perspectives*. London: Routledge.

Garet, M. S., Porter, A., Desimone, L., Birman, B. F., & Suk Yoon, K. (2001). What makes professional development effective? Results from a national sample of teachers. *American Educational Research Journal*, *38*(4), 915–945. doi:10.3102/00028312038004915

Gibbs, G. (1988). *Learning by doing: A guide to teaching and learning methods*. Oxford, UK: Further Education Unit. Oxford Polytechnic.

Halliday, M. A. K., & Martin, J. R. (1993). *Writing science*. London: The Falmer Press.

Halliday, M. A. K., & Matthiessen, C. M. I. M. (2014). *Introduction to functional grammar* (4th ed.). Abingdon, UK: Routledge. doi:10.4324/9780203783771

Hutchings, P., & Huber, M. T. (2008). Placing theory in the Scholarship of Teaching and Learning. *Arts and Humanities in Higher Education*, *7*(3), 229–244. doi:10.1177/1474022208094409

Jones, J. (2011). Using MASUS to assess writing outcomes: A case study of different pathways. *English language entry pathways: Innovations, outcomes and future directions*.

Kolb, D. A. (1984). *Experiential learning: Experience as the source of learning and development*. Englewood Cliffs, NJ: Prentice-Hall.

Kreber, C. (2013). The transformative potential of the Scholarship of Teaching. *Teaching and Learning Inquiry: The ISSOTL Journal*, *1*(1), 5–18. doi:10.20343/teachlearninqu.1.1.5

Lemke, J. L. (1990). *Talking science: Language, learning and values*. Norwood, NJ: Ablex.

Mann, K. V. (2016). Reflection's role in learning: Increasing engagement and deepening participation. *Perspectives on Medical Education*, *5*(5), 259–261. doi:10.100740037-016-0296-y PMID:27638389

Martin, J. R. (1992). *English text*. Amsterdam: John Benjamins Publishing Company. doi:10.1075/z.59

Martin, J. R., & Rose, D. (2007). *Working with discourse: Meaning beyond the clause* (2nd ed.). London: Bloomsbury.

Martin, J. R., & Rose, D. (2008). *Genres relations: Mapping culture*. London: Equinox.

Martin, J. R., & White, P. R. (2005). *The language of evaluation*. Basingstoke, UK: Palgrave Macmillan. doi:10.1057/9780230511910

Maton, K. (2013). Making semantic waves: A key to cumulative knowledge-building. *Linguistics and Education*, *24*(1), 8–22. doi:10.1016/j.linged.2012.11.005

Maton, K., & Doran, Y. J. (2017). SFL and code theory. In T. Bartlett & G. O'Grady (Eds.), *The Routledge systemic functional linguistic handbook*. London: Routledge.

Nesi, H., & Gardner, S. (2012). *Genres across the disciplines: Student writing in higher education*. Cambridge, UK: Cambridge University Press.

O'Mara, L., McDonald, J., Gillespie, M., Brown, H., & Miles, L. (2014). Challenging clinical learning environments: Experiences of undergraduate nursing students. *Nurse Education in Practice*, *14*(2), 208–213. doi:10.1016/j.nepr.2013.08.012 PMID:24063792

Penuel, W. R., Fishman, B. J., Yamaguchi, R., & Gallagher, L. P. (2007). What makes professional development effective? Strategies that foster curriculum implementation. *American Educational Research Journal*, *44*(4), 921–958. doi:10.3102/0002831207308221

Peters, K., McInnes, S. & Halcomb, E. (2015). Nursing students' experiences of clinical placement in community settings: A qualitative study. *Collegian, 22*(2), 175-181.

Rose, D., & Martin, J. R. (2012). *Learning to write, reading to learn: Genre knowledge and pedagogy in the Sydney School*. London: Equinox.

Rose, D., & Martin, J. R. (2014). Intervening in contexts of schooling. In J. Flowerdew (Ed.), *Discourse in context* (pp. 273–300). London: Bloomsbury.

Rothery, J., & Stenglin, M. (1997). Entertaining and instructing: Exploring experience through story. In F. Christie & J. R. Martin (Eds.), *Genre and institutions: Social practices in the workplace and school* (pp. 231–263). London: Cassell.

Schleppegrell, M. J. (2004). *The language of schooling: A functional linguistics perspective*. Mahwah, NJ: Lawrence Erlbaum Associates. doi:10.4324/9781410610317

Schon, D. (1983). *The reflective practitioner: How professionals think in action*. New York, NY: Basic Books.

Shulman, S. (2005, Summer). Signature pedagogies in the professions. *Daedalus*, *134*(3), 52–59. doi:10.1162/0011526054622015

Szenes, E. (2011). *Unpublished 3x3 model for Business in the Global Environment course*. University of Sydney.

Szenes, E., Tilakaratna, N., & Maton, K. (2015). The knowledge practices of critical thinking. In M. Davies & R. Barnett (Eds.), *The Palgrave handbook of critical thinking in higher education* (pp. 573–591). New York, NY: Palgrave Macmillan. doi:10.1057/9781137378057_34

Tanda, R., & Denham, S. A. (2009). Clinical instruction and student outcomes. *Teaching and Learning in Nursing, 4*(4), 139–147. doi:10.1016/j.teln.2009.01.002

Tilakaratna, N., & Szenes, E. (2017). The linguistic construction of critical "self-reflection" in social work and business. In P. Chapell & J. Knox (Eds.), *Transforming Contexts: Papers from the 44th International Systemic Functional Congress*. Academic Press.

Tilakaratna, N., & Szenes, E. (2019). (Un)critical reflection: Uncovering hidden. In C. Winberg, S. McKenna, & K. Wilmot (Eds.), *Building knowledge in higher education: Enhancing teaching and learning with legitimation code theory*. London: Routledge.

Trigwell, K., Martin, E., Benjamin, J., & Prosser, M. (2000). Scholarship of teaching: A model. *Higher Education Research & Development, 19*(2), 155–168. doi:10.1080/072943600445628

Wignell, P., Martin, J. R., & Eggins, S. (1989). The discourse of geography : Ordering and explaining the experiential world. *Linguistics and Education, 1*(4), 359–391. doi:10.1016/S0898-5898(89)80007-5

Wu, X. V., Enskär, K., Heng, G. N. D., Pua, L. H., & Wang, W. (2016a). The perspectives of preceptors regarding clinical assessment for undergraduate nursing students. *International Nursing Review, 63*(3), 473–481. doi:10.1111/inr.12272 PMID:27100137

Wu, X. V., Enskär, K., Pua, L. H., Heng, D. G. N., & Wang, W. (2016b). Development and psychometric testing of Holistic Clinical Assessment Tool (HCAT) for undergraduate nursing students. *BMC Medical Education, 16*(1), 1–9. doi:10.118612909-016-0768-0 PMID:27658587

Wu, X. V., Wang, W., Pua, L. H., Heng, D. G., & Enskar, K. (2015). Undergraduate nursing students' perspectives on clinical assessment at transition to practice. *Contemporary Nurse, 51*(2-3), 272–285. doi:10.1080/10376178.2016.1163232 PMID:26956057

ENDNOTE

According to conventions in SFL theory, the sign ^ indicates 'is followed by'; brackets indicate the stage is optional.

APPENDIX

Focus Group Questions

1. How do you define "critical reflection" in nursing?
2. Do you think that there is a difference between "reflection" and "critical reflection"?
3. Do you believe that teaching critical reflection as a skill is important?
4. Do you set some form of assessment for critical reflection assignments in your discipline?
5. Do you use any frameworks for teaching critical reflection (e.g., Gibbs, 1998)?
6. Do you find that these frameworks are useful for teaching student reflection?
7. How important is theoretical knowledge for reflections (e.g., literature on effective patient care or hygiene?) What purpose does theoretical knowledge play in understanding critical incidents during practicum?
8. How important is critical reflection for the construction of the nurse's "identity"?
9. How important is the application of learning from a critical incident for future practice?

Chapter 17

A Case Study in the Application of Transformative Learning Theory:
The Redesign of an Online Course in Order to Achieve Deep Learning

Jenna Kammer
https://orcid.org/0000-0002-4739-767X
University of Central Missouri, USA

ABSTRACT

Transformative learning can be used as a strategy for measuring teacher effectiveness in online courses. By measuring the transformations that occur within their courses, instructors can understand more about the activities and experiences that are the most impactful for students. In addition, instructors can create opportunities for transformation by designing learning experiences that encourage students to critically self-reflect. This chapter presents an exploratory study that examined instructor and student perceptions of transformation in an online school library graduate program. The data was used to redesign one unit in a course on reference and information services to create opportunities for students to experience transformation with the content.

INTRODUCTION

Transformative learning is a powerful learning theory that explains the steps adults undertake as they develop new perspectives and assumptions about their understanding of the world (Mezirow, 1981). In online graduate programs, transformative learning can be a particularly relevant strategy for guiding adult graduate students through the process of learning new things about a field of study, which may also involve reshaping current ideologies. It is particularly common for major learning experiences like

DOI: 10.4018/978-1-7998-2212-7.ch017

study abroad or internships to serve as transformative learning experiences, but can learning activities within online classes have the same impact?

This chapter is a case study of one library science professor's experience to learn more about how online students experienced perspective transformation in their graduate program. This case study was conducted as a means of faculty development and is grounded in the Scholarship of Teaching and Learning (SoTL), where a professor seeks evidence of teaching and learning to improve effectiveness. In particular, this case examines the learning activities in an online program to understand more about how online students are impacted so that improvements can be made to a specific course. The goals of this chapter are to: (1) Present transformative learning theory as a method for evaluating the effectiveness of teaching and learning (2) Share a process for other faculty to use to design transformative experiences in their online courses.

DISCIPLINARY PERSPECTIVE

This case study takes place in a library science graduate program at a state university. This program is a professional program that prepares teachers to become school librarians (see "teacher" definition). Preparation to become a school librarian involves learning curriculum that connects the role of the school librarian with state standards in librarianship and content areas, and national standards for school librarianship (American Library Association, n.d).

The job of the school librarian has changed significantly over the years. Wine (2016) explained that school librarians have experienced radical change and adapted their role to developments in society related to accessing and using information in print and digital formats. Many teachers still imagine that the school librarian serves as the gatekeeper for the school's books and a promoter of reading (Gavigan & Lance, 2015). In addition to these responsibilities, the school librarian may also be a teacher and leader of inquiry, technology and information. Many studies have shown a correlation between school library programs and student achievement (for example, see Lance and Kachel, 2018, who discuss the different types of studies that explore the connection between the school library and student achievement). Misconceptions about the value and importance of the school library can be problematic for securing funding, staffing them with certified librarians, or simply making use of the library as a resource within the school community.

With the introduction of new National School Library Standards in 2018 by the American Association of School Librarians (AASL), it became even more clear that a good school librarian must design a school library program that serves as a center for learning within the entire school. However, many new graduate students come to library science programs with little experience in libraries and preconceived ideas of what librarians do (Cherry et al., 2011). In school librarianship in particular, professional standards have evolved that require school library candidates to adopt an inclusive, innovative, globally connected, and technology-infused practice of librarianship. School librarians are leaders in their schools who protect intellectual freedom and ensure equitable access to information (Wine, 2016). This is very different from the "keeper of the books" image that many associate with school librarians (p. 208). Budd (1995) historically described these misconceptions as related to a positivistic tendency within the field of library science: The practice of collecting, organizing, and retrieving information resources is construed as process-driven, rather than understood as an epistemological approach to librarianship that is more reflective of the people using the systems.

Because graduate students in library science may enter a program with existing notions about the role of a school librarian, the professor must work to introduce the principles, ethics, and theories of librarianship that are foundational to the field. Dall'Alba (2009) recognized that students entering professional programs are expected to go through a period of transformation as they learn about professional "ways of being" (p. 44). Professors must ensure they support and develop graduate students through this transformation into a new profession. In this chapter, transformative learning is examined as one way that professors can evaluate their own teaching practice in a field where changing perceptions is essential. Educators of school librarians seek to provide learning experiences for adult learners to prepare them for the realities of being a school librarian while also teaching them to be reflective practitioners. How can an educator know that the learning activities they consider to be transformative, are truly transformative for the student? This chapter presents a process of examining transformative learning as a means of understanding more about the impact of learning activities on perspective transformation in school librarian graduate education.

THEORETICAL PERSPECTIVE

Transformative Learning

Transformative learning is rooted in transformation theory, a theory of socialization that explains how adults break down existing thought processes to create new interpretations (Mezirow, 1991). Mezirow (2009) described transformative learning as "learning that transforms problematic frames of reference to make them more inclusive, discriminating, reflective, open, and emotionally able to change" (p. 22). Proponents of transformative learning argue that one must engage in critical reflection in order to begin the process of changing one's initial assumptions. In particular, when one reflects on a viewpoint that is different from their own, they may start to experience a change as part of the learning experience (King, 2005). It is through self-reflection and critique of one's experiences, followed by action to make changes, that transformation can occur.

A truly transformative experience requires that students move from pre-existing beliefs and ways of thinking to better and improved habits of mind (i.e. new ways of thinking) (Mezirow, 2000). Transformative learning theory in adult learning is based on constructivist assumptions which suggest that careful learning design has the potential to shift ideologies so that students are able to reshape and reimagine what they know to be true about a phenomenon (Mezirow, 1994). Specifically, Mezirow (1994, p. 224) stated that there are four ways to learn, all of which include a shift in perspective and beliefs: (1) By refining or elaborating our meaning schemes, (2) Learning new meaning schemes, (3) Transforming meaning schemes, and (4) Transforming meaning perspectives.

Transformative learning can be used as an instructional practice when a professor designs learning experiences that allow students to insert new practices into existing ones (Nohl, 2015). Nohl conducted biographical narrative interviews with 80 people from various social groups over a period of about 10 years. Nohl's findings indicate that transformation may happen silently (i.e. the participant does not realize they are undergoing a transformation), and he proposed that transformative learning does not need to start with a "disorienting dilemma" but instead can happen when a new practice is added to old habits. This process cannot be understood until the participant has had ample time to reflect on how an experience might have impacted one's practice. This finding challenges the notion of Mezirow's model in that transformative learning may not happen during the learning experience, but instead may happen after the learning experience is over.

At one time, transformative learning was one of the most widely researched topics in adult education (Taylor, 1997; King, 2000). Critical views of transformative learning have suggested that research was traditionally limited to specific social groups. For example, the first study on transformative learning examined the experiences of women who were reentering college after taking time off to raise families (Mezirow, 1981). Taylor (1997) suggested that Mezirow's model of transformative learning was not representative of all populations and instead had limited application to women returning to school after taking time off. In addition, transformative learning is said to occur after a "disorienting dilemma". The problem is that not all "disorienting dilemmas" are the same for all people, nor will everyone have a transformative experience, or shift their perspective, after experiencing one. After an extensive literature review of transformative learning, Taylor (1997) found that there may actually be four factors that affect holistic transformation in adult education that are unrelated to Mezirow's steps: affective learning, nonconscious learning, relationships, and the collective unconscious. These factors indicate that adults have unique experiences that are related to other aspects of their life, including relationships with other students and the relationships in their personal life. In addition, adults are not isolated from the experiences of society and may be shaped by media, news, and other professionals that are not part of a graduate program.

In this study, the model of transformative learning used includes four dimensions: the disorienting dilemma, continuous engagement in critical reflection, rational discourse, and synthesis of different perspectives and deliberation in decision-making (Mezirow, 2000; King, 2009). This model is relevant to designing transformative learning opportunities within a course or curriculum (King, 2009). Through this cycle, adult learners alternate between reflection and taking action to create social change. Many authors have made various recommendations for professors to create learning activities that support learners as they enter different stages of transformation (Kasl & Elias, 2000; Leibler, 2000; Taylor, 2000; Cercone, 2008; Ryman et al., 2009; King, 2009; Nohl, 2015; King, 2018) (see Table 1).

Transformation in Online Learning

Online learning has been recognized as an educational platform that is especially practical for adult online learners (Allen & Seaman, 2007). Online learning provides adults with the flexibility they need to work or raise a family while simultaneously pursuing additional qualifications. Palloff and Pratt (2001) presented many studies indicating online learning was as effective as traditional classroom learning. Soffer and Nachmias (2018) found that online learning can be even more successful than classroom learning for some learners because students spend more time with course content and were more familiar with course structure. Related to the study in this chapter, Cercone (2008) suggested that transformative learning is one of several adult learning theories that are particularly effective to use in online courses. This is because online courses often include opportunities for critical reflection, activities that foster autonomous thinking, and self-directed learning.

In online courses, professors design learning activities that replace what might happen in a face-to-face classroom. Instead of synchronous, verbal group discussions, discussions in an online class will often be text-based and asynchronous. The online environment can create challenges for professors who are learning the best way to teach their content in an online environment. Kebritchi, Lipschuetz, and Saniague (2017) conducted a meta-analysis that found that changing one's teaching style to suit the online

Table 1. The dimensions of transformative learning and corresponding learning activities

Dimension	Description	Learning Activity/Recommendations
Disorienting Dilemma	An experience that creates discomfort and starts the process of questioning assumptions	• Identify the habits of mind students already have (Kasl & Elias, 2000) • Provide authentic learning experiences that allow for disorienting dilemmas to arise (Nohl, 2015) • Allow for interaction between students with different backgrounds to learn more about each other's experiences (Kasl & Elias, 2000) • Consider various ethical dilemmas that allow students to negotiate their own interpretations (Leiber, 2000)
Critical Reflection	The process of evaluating assumptions and new content	• Incorporate self-evaluation (Taylor, 2000) • Allow students to self-identify their level of knowledge (King, 2018) • Provide students with multiple resources that encourage different viewpoints (Cercone, 2008)
Rational Discourse	Engaging with others on the evaluation of assumptions	• Create opportunities for students to discuss with others in peer learning groups, either synchronously or asynchronously (Cercone, 2008) • Allow students to share their expertise with each other or to take various leadership roles (Ryman et al, 2009) • Establish expectations for effective, professional discourse, including instructor support through the process (King, 2009)
Decision-Making	Choosing to make changes or move forward with new assumptions	• What next? Ask students to consider their future actions

environment was one factor that made online teaching challenging. Developing meaningful content was also a perceived challenge for professors who taught online. However, online learning also provides new opportunities for each student to participate frequently (for example, many online graduate classes require weekly posts to the discussion board), and professors can then learn more about each student. Cranton (2010) explained that online courses offer a unique environment that is well-suited for transformative learning in that the discussion remains accessible, all students participate, discussions are often reflective, and students work with others that they may not necessarily meet in person. Students enter the class with prior knowledge or preconceived ideas about the content, but they are also able to share and learn from others living in different places or working in different types of schools. For example, one student may work in a rural school with no funding for technology, while another may work in the most highly funded public school in the state. The question is, how can an online professor know that students are growing and developing new perceptions beyond those with which they started?

When teaching online, it can be challenging to know whether deep learning is happening and what learning activities are the most meaningful for students. Online professors can gather clues from students about their meaningful learning experiences through discourse or interactions; however, they cannot truly know about each student's transformation unless a targeted effort is used to understand more about how students are changing perspectives through a course. Meyers (2008) explained that the discussion board is an excellent tool for investigating transformation in online courses. But the discussion board itself does not invoke transformative learning. It requires the design of critically reflective discussion questions, coupled with the student's intent to take advantage of the learning opportunity, for transformative learning to occur. Professors can examine the discourse in the discussion board for evidence of critical reflection, or even transformation.

Applying adult learning theories to online education is important for the success of these students. Cercone (2008) compared several adult learning theories, including transformative learning, with andragogy and explained that it is essential to design online courses for adult learners that include a combination of learning theories to maintain motivation, engagement, and achievement for online learners. In particular, transformative learning provides a structure for reflecting and connecting content with one's personal life, which is part of andragogy. Cercone suggested that without the application of learning theory to an online course, adult learners are not approached as a whole person. These theories can support development of the emotions, feelings, and attitudes of adult learners in addition to developing their cognitive abilities and knowledge.

Professors strive to learn more about the effectiveness of their instruction (McKinney, 2004). King (2009) recommends transformative learning as one way to evaluate educational practice because it can identify how and where "significant learning" (a term used by Dee Fink (2003) to describe instruction that is meaningful to students inside and outside of the classroom) is happening within an educational experience. Boyer et al. (2006) used critical discourse analysis to examine a series of reflective writings within an online course in educational leadership to determine how transformative learning was happening. Using a coding rubric that included Mezirow's (2000) four phases of transformative learning, researchers examined the reflection for evidence of transformation. They found that these students (who were all new to online learning) experienced transformation by simply being in the online class, learning new technology and processing content with others. The disorienting dilemmas (the first phase of the transformative learning model) experienced by the students were unique for each student. Researchers were able to determine the level of transformation by examining the narratives for expressive use of language and specific reference to situations that were new or unfamiliar.

Transformative learning has also been used as a framework for evaluating the Scholarship of Teaching and learning (SoTL). In one example, King (2018) described how his institution created an initiative called The Student Transformative Learning Record (STLR) to ensure transformation in their undergraduate curriculum. The STLR program provided badges for students whose assessments indicated learning at different levels (exposure, integration, and transformation) of the learning cycle within different tenets (discipline knowledge, global and cultural competencies, health and wellness, leadership, research, creativity and scholarly activity, and service learning and engagement). The findings from this program indicated that online courses were particularly effective for reflection as student evidence of learning was easier to track over time. In addition, journaling in online courses was found to be particularly effective for measuring how students showed competency at the different levels of learning.

The Online Professor's Role in Transformative Learning

It is common that library science graduate students in study abroad or internship courses will experience some sort of transformation in the type of learning experience that is designed to expose students to other cultures and ways of life (Namaste, 2017). However, having a transformative experience within the traditional online course is less natural, and learning experiences must be designed by the professor to encourage transformation. To develop effective online courses, professors must seek to understand more about the online student experience and the kinds of activities that foster deeper learning experiences. The challenge is further exacerbated by the fact that many online professors often feel disconnected from students and may be unsure of their own teaching effectiveness in the online environment (Kebritchi et al., 2017). While many studies have looked at the Scholarship of Teaching and Learning in online education

(Gorsky & Blau, 2009; Palloff & Pratt, 2001; Allen & Seaman, 2013), few have examined the role of transformational learning as a strategy for reflecting on the impact of course design on student learning.

Professors should regularly examine their teaching to understand more about its effectiveness (McKinney, 2004). The Scholarship of Teaching and Learning (SoTL) suggests that professors look beyond content to understand more about the impact that their teaching is having on their students learning. Kreber (2013) explained that professors have a responsibility to examine their teaching for transformation so that they can provide a more authentic learning experience for students. While experiences like study abroad and internships can certainly provoke reflection and transformation, professors of graduate students in professional programs must also examine how well their teaching helps students to develop new ways of connecting the course content with their practice. This is where transformative learning comes into play: By examining student work for evidence of transformative learning, professors can understand more about the impact of their teaching on their students. Cranton (2011) specifically looked at SoTL through the lens of transformative learning and explained that working to improve teaching practice can make instruction more effective, and have transformative effects for the professors themselves.

In addition to designing opportunities for transformation, Boyer et al. (2006) found that social constructionism is also critical. Specifically, the professor's behavior is a factor in the success of transformational learning in online courses. Professors should promote collegial interaction and a safe secure environment for students to have open discussions. Students should understand etiquette expectations. Ryman et al. (2009) also found that professors must create an environment of mutual trust to encourage community building before transformation can occur. Specifically, Ryman et al. explained that there are specific factors which must be present in the learning environment before transformation can happen including, social presence, authentic learning, interdependency, critical discourse, and opportunities for leadership. Each of these factors work together to create a learning community that encourages students to build relationships, share new meaning, and create new knowledge.

There is general agreement that professors can create opportunities for transformation within their online classes (Boyer et al., 2006; Meyers, 2008; Ryman et al., 2009; Kurtz & Sponder, 2010; Henderson, 2010; King, 2018). However, specific social strategies support this kind of learning more than others. To encourage transformation in online courses, Meyers (2008) recommends that profesors: (a) create a safe and inviting environment; (b) encourage students to think about their experiences, beliefs, and biases; (c) use teaching strategies that promote student engagement and participation; (d) pose real-world problems, and (e) help students implement action-oriented solutions (p. 220). Even though hooks (1994) speaks of learning in general, her work is relevant to transformative learning in collaborative environments (such as participating in an online discussion board). hooks explained how learners must feel empowered when they are learning. Empowerment comes from teaching with concern for the students' sense of well-being: Paying attention to emotions and feelings are a critical part of fostering a love of learning. This can be applied to studying the transformative experiences of students in a course: Without paying attention to feelings, emotions and struggles, the professor is less likely to recognize transformation or act as a guide through the process.

Professors may also try to understand more about a student's current habits and then systematically integrate new frames of reference. Nohl's (2015) work indicated that transformation can occur when these habits are changed. Kasl and Elias (2000) explained how they increased students understanding of race and privilege. In their class, small groups were created to allow for intimate discussions. The small groups collaborated to establish an initial frame of reference at the beginning of the program. Later in the course, the professors introduced a new frame of reference to gradually help students to understand more about race and cultural diversity. Particularly for a topic like diversity, purposefully introducing new ideas allowed students to transform more gradually within a process that has been carefully constructed by the professors. Specifically, students were able to identify triggering conversations that both were significant in encouraging reflection and lead to re-evaluating individual and group context of race and culture.

With careful planning, learning activities can be integrated into a course that provides opportunities for critical reflection. King's (2009) work demonstrated how professors can create learning activities which can facilitate transformative learning. Specifically, she conducted an in-depth literature review to determine five sub-categories of learning activities that could have a profound effect on transformation: critical thinking assignments (like essays, journals, readings, deep thought and reflection), class discussions (group projects, discussion about a specific topic), student self-assessments (self-evaluation of one's work in the course), discovery of one's voice (being able to articulate concerns), and miscellaneous activities (class activities, projects, practicum). King's work also recognizes that personal experiences outside the classroom, and outside of the control of the professor, can have a profound effect on transformation, such as having a baby, getting a new job, or a death in the family. King also recognized that support from teachers, advisors, other students, or mentors in the field can also be precipitous in leading to transformative experiences.

THE CASE IN THIS STUDY

Transformative learning is a particularly useful concept to consider for online teaching (Cercone, 2008). Even if not familiar with the theory, many professors will recognize a student's transformation through student conversations, reflections, or comments made about their learning experiences. Anecdotal evidence from students can give a professor an idea about transformation in students on an individual basis. There are also strategies that can be used to examine transformation on a larger scale to understand more about the experiences of students within the full program. As learned from the literature, transformation can be unique for each student with some students not being aware it is happening. Transformation may not be immediate and may take place over time, only to be realized later through reflection.

The author of this case study used transformative learning as a guide for exploring her own practice of teaching and learning in an online graduate program. This practice is grounded in the Scholarship of Teaching and Learning which suggests that understanding more about what works (and what does not) in teaching is critical for improving higher education (McKinney, 2012). After two years as a new professor, it became clear that to develop as a professor, it was necessary to examine the student experience more deeply to understand which learning activities were truly impacting students. The following description presents the process and results of this exploration by sharing student and professor's perceptions of transformation within one graduate program to help understand ways to design more impactful learning activities. The interest in this study was spurred by a webinar related to instructional design for online classes for the Association of Library and Information Science Education, where the discussion indicated that other online professors were interested in understanding more about transformative learning as a strategy in online classes (Kammer & Zhou, 2018). It was originally posited that only significant learning experiences like study abroad or internships could provide a transformative experience. However, King's (2009) work indicated that transformation can happen gradually through smaller learning experiences. This study asked professors and students in a school library program to think about their coursework in order to understand which activities were foundational in shifting perspectives about the field of school librarianship.

Institutional Context

The program in this study enrolls approximately 100 graduate students and is fully online. The majority of students are from within the state, but the online nature of the program also attracts national and international candidates. The program is not cohort-based, though there has been a cohort at one point in the program's history. Students complete 24 hours of coursework related to Library and Information Sciences (LIS), three hours of practicum, where they work within a school library and with students directly, and a research project at the end of the program consisting of action research or a well-developed literature review. Another important aspect of this program is that it is a professional program: the program prepares practicing teachers to be effective school librarians based on established standards for initial school librarian preparation (ALA/AASL, 2010).

This graduate program for library and information services is a program in a midwestern state university. In this program, current k-12 teachers take graduate level coursework to become certified as a school librarian, or simply to learn more about the practice of school librarianship. In this state, k-12 teachers can become certified as school librarians by testing in to the position (even if they do not have graduate level coursework). However, many teachers will move into school librarian positions and find that they need coursework in LIS to understand more about the role of the school librarian. Subjects like cataloging, collection development, collaborating, and information resources are often challenging for school librarians to learn without LIS coursework.

One of the tenure requirements at this institution is to show evidence of effective teaching. "Effective teaching" can be interpreted in many ways. Many professors will use averages of course evaluations or other student achievement to show effectiveness. Because there is room for interpretation in how to demonstrate "effective teaching," there is a great deal of freedom for faculty to explore their own teaching practice in unique ways. This study was designed to examine effectiveness to find areas of improvement. It uses survey and interview data to inform faculty development by looking at the student-reported areas of transformative learning. That made it possible to determine (1) What worked in other courses, and (2) What gaps in transformation existed. This discussion does not intend to present the findings of this small study. Instead, it presents the process of examining one's teaching for transformative learning and using those findings to develop as a professor and to make subsequent changes to courses.

Looking for Evidence of Transformation

How can a professor know which elements of teaching are the most effective to encourage students to open their minds to new ways of thinking and actively question their existing assumptions? It seemed most appropriate to simply ask them: Perhaps the students themselves can explain which content in the LIS program was most transformative for them. King's (2009) work on transformative learning was significant in that she provided a method for uncovering an answer to this question. This work analyzed the activities within a classroom that contribute to perspective transformation. King had already conducted research on which learning activities were the most conducive to transformation with an adult classroom. In addition, she had already created a validated survey (the Learning Activities Survey) that examined the contribution of specific learning activities towards perspective transformation.

Professor Perspectives

The study began by asking other professors in the program about which activities they felt were transformative in their classes and why they felt that way. Professors were asked to share their experiences with transformative learning by completing a Google form. No identifying information was collected. Often, professors in a program may be unaware of the learning activities in other classes, let alone which activities are most valued by the students. The feedback from this survey informed the learning activities listed for King's (2009) Learning Activities Survey. For example, one professor listed that using video chat for discussions was transformative, so that learning activity was added to the list of learning activities in the student survey. Based on the responses from professors, the culminating list of learning activities included:

- Assigned readings
- Attending a conference or professional development workshop
- Class assignment/project
- Deep, concentrated thought
- Field experience (i.e. visiting a library)
- Group project
- Internship
- Meeting as a class (online in Skype, Zoom or in person)
- Practicum
- Talking with a librarian (formal or informal interview)
- Writing an essay
- Writing/journaling
- Writing a self-evaluation
- None

Results of this query indicated that each professor had at least one assignment in each class that they felt was transformative for students. They explained that completing independent research projects, learning from other students, creating practical activities which can be applied to the real world, and writing discussion board responses that show progression of learning throughout the semester were considered to be potentially transformative in their courses.

Because this study was conducted to inform teaching, the author reflected on the same questions asked of the professors in relation to her own courses. She felt the most transformative activities were the ones that gave students an opportunity to do the work of a school librarian, such as analyzing a list of resources that had been pulled from the library management system for gaps in content and currency. However, the author thought that students may actually choose a different activity as transformative such as a visit to a local public library. This was very similar to the other professors as they each had a learning activity they personally felt was transformative, and a different activity they said was transformative for their students. This was particularly interesting because student data later indicated that the activities professors felt were transformative were similar to the activities that most impacted students as well.

In addition, professors were asked how they know that their learning activities were transformative. Their responses indicated that they knew the activity was transformative because of comments that the students had made about the assignments, including statements that indicated the activity was their

Figure 1. Student responses to the question, "Which activities were the most transformative for you?"

favorite part of the class, or that it had a significant impact on them. This is important because it is data that can be collected while teaching: When students comment on an activity being meaningful, it may be leading to a transformative experience for them. Two professors also described how the discussion board was a significant place for uncovering transformation. One said, "While I think of my bigger assignments as transformative, I do think that students also learn quite well and change their ideas significantly based on the feedback they receive from other students and myself via the discussion board. Just having a structured place to have these conversations about librarianship is vital." Boyer et al. (2006) made similar claims in their work related to finding evidence of transformation through the reflection that happens in the discussion board. The discussion board can be a reflective opportunity for students (with a discussion prompt that leads to critical reflection), and it is a collaborative space where students can interact and test out new ideas.

Student Perspectives

The next phase of the study was to deliver the student survey to current students and alumni. The survey was based on King's (2009) Learning Activities Survey and was distributed through the LIS program's Facebook group which includes current and past students. The survey showed that it was viewed 166 times and received 33 responses (a 20% response rate). There are 217 members in this Facebook group, though not all are active. Even though alumni may have taken a different curriculum than what is offered in the program now, they still were able to reflect on the learning experiences that were memorable to them. Also, Nohl (2015) stated that transformative learning may not be immediate and happens over time. What a current student sees as transformative now may differ once they complete their degree and have a full-time job in a school library. Students were asked to select the learning activities that they experienced in the program then identify the ones that were most transformative for them from the list. The results indicated that "class assignments," "assigned readings," and "talking to a librarian," were the most transformative for students (see Figure 1). "Writing an essay" was the only response to receive 0 responses.

In addition, students were asked to elaborate on their responses using open-ended responses. These responses were coded to determine into which type of learning theory they might fall (experiential learning, collaborative learning, etc.). The open-ended responses showed some differences from the learning activities that were selected. In the open-ended comments, one person indicated that essays were actually transformative, though no one had selected "writing an essay" as being a transformative experience in the multiple-choice question. The other results indicated that students felt that the most transformative learning activities were related to developing small projects in courses that could actually be used in the school library with real students. Another common answer was that experiencing the school library first-hand through a practicum, interview, or observation experience was transformative. Few described their experiences talking with a librarian in the open-ended responses, even though that was a common selection in the multiple-choice section. It was concluded that experiential learning activities were indeed the most transformative for the most students. It was also concluded that transformation was different for each student, and even the same student may experience it differently in different activities. The main takeaway from the student survey was that students were transforming throughout the variety of learning activities in the program.

Another interesting finding in the student data was that students indicated they were most transformed by thinking about philosophical issues in school libraries that they had not considered before. For example, several students addressed that they had new perspectives on privacy and the role of the library, or that they had a new perspective on assigning reading levels to books. These are ethical issues that are addressed in school library curriculum. One conclusion drawn from this data was that there were some areas clearly identified by students as being transformative, while other areas of the curriculum that were not addressed (for example, information literacy) may need more attention in the program curriculum.

DISCUSSION

Gathering data from students and professors about transformation in their program was the first step in understanding more about the power of the learning activities offered in the program. Before starting this research, it was expected that students would say the practicum course (where they work in a school library for over 80 hours in one semester) was the most transformative course in the program. It seemed natural that experiencing a school library with a certified school librarian could really transform one's perceptions about school libraries, particularly if they did not have prior experience in libraries. It was unexpected that the students themselves would indicate that the coursework, including readings and projects, were actually transformative as well. Students indicated that they were hopeful about trying the coursework that they created in an actual library with students. In addition, it was surprising how many students indicated that they experienced a philosophical shift in perspective by learning more about the school library profession.

The goal of this project was to determine which learning activities were the most transformative and to use that information to better design online courses. The students indicated there were a few learning activities that were selected more frequently than others that are worth considering when designing for transformative learning. In addition to class projects and assigned readings, students also felt that talking to librarians and visiting a library were transformative. Perhaps these activities could be more fully integrated into coursework for school librarians or applied in different strategies (library observations, interviews with librarians, authentic scenarios).

In addition, each professor felt that they had specific learning activities that were transformative. Each activity mentioned by the professors was also mentioned by the students. Without interviews, it is hard to understand the relevance of this, but it can be assumed that professors can pick up on cues within their courses that indicate how transformative an activity or a learning experience is. Professors indicated that phrases such as "I never thought of this before" were very telling when understanding the impact of an assignment. Professors also indicated that they already look for evidence of learning by examining student's progress in thinking throughout the semester as disclosed on the discussion board. The main takeaway from this is that professors may already be providing learning activities with the potential to transform or to measure transformation. Perhaps including additional aspects of Mezirow's (2009) model, like critical reflection, could make that existing learning activity more valuable to students. At a minimum, professors should consider providing opportunities for students to express their thoughts and feelings through reflective activities. These reflective activities can help guide professors to understand more about the impact of the assignment.

REDESIGN TO FOSTER TRANSFORMATIVE LEARNING

After learning more about the student's experiences of transformation in the program, the examination of learning activities and reflective opportunities at the course level began. The process included using the data from the professor and student surveys to consider the best way to redesign a course so that transformation could be encouraged and measured. The course used in this example is called Reference Sources and Services. Students learn about information resources and how to create library services that support library users as they seek information. Students enter this class with prior knowledge related to finding their own information, often relying on Google's top three results for information. This class was selected to redesign for transformative learning because learning activities from this course were not listed as transformative by participants (students did not reference experiences from this class as one of their transformative experiences in the program). In addition, the content requires a paradigm shift as students learn to think past what they already know about searching for information.

The central question of this redesign was to understand more about the process of integrating transformative learning experiences within an online, asynchronous course. A course like this does not include a study abroad opportunity or a practicum activity. It is online, with asynchronous class discussions, a textbook, and weekly instructional modules prepared by the professor. There are four assessments in the class, including one key assessment used for program evaluation. To incorporate a transformative experience, one unit was selected. The process for introducing opportunities to measure transformation included the following steps (see Figure 2):

First, the goal for transformation was established. In this class, the goal for transformation was related to one specific unit in the course. The goal was for students to critically consider additional search strategies and resources for solving an information problem.

Second, opportunities for critical reflection were created at three checkpoints in the class (beginning, middle, and end). To understand the search strategy and resources that students consulted, it was important to create checkpoints at the beginning, middle, and end of the unit. These checkpoints asked students to reflect on how they use an information search strategy and where they think they can improve.

Third, learning activities were designed to encourage self-reflection and to encourage new habits. A specific learning activity was adopted at this stage that would allow students to critically consider all resources available to them, as well as to determine the ones most appropriate for problem-solving. Using the Mezirow strategy of the disorienting dilemma, three cases were developed to encourage the use of progressively advanced resources and search techniques. The cases asked students to consider a typical information request in a school library and to articulate which resources and search strategies

Figure 2. The process of redesigning for transformation in a unit on Information Resources in a course on Information Resources and Services.

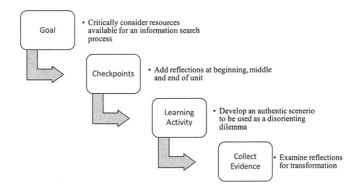

they would recommend for solving these problems. It was determined that the learning activities in this step could be exchanged for other activities based on the success of the activity. For example, instead of a disorienting dilemma, students could interview a librarian to understand more about how they solve information problems.

Fourth, evidence of transformation can be evaluated at each checkpoint. In the last step, a tool must be selected that allows the professor to best observe the transformation of learning between the checkpoints. In this class, the blog tool was selected as it compiled the reflections into one area for grading. For example, the student makes posts one at-a-time, but the professor can view them compiled in one window. Discourse analysis was used to review the posts for keywords that indicated transformation. In the final reflection, students were asked, "How has your awareness of resources and strategies changed after completing this unit?" This prompt allowed students to self-reflect specifically on any changes in their experience.

Reflections on the Redesign

After conducting this unit once, students seemed to increase their awareness of resources throughout the three checkpoints. Their responses to the scenarios showed increased depth of knowledge and a discourse analysis indicated that some students were indeed using resources they would not have considered before. One student explained, "I never would have tried this resource if it were not for this assignment." However, the transformation was not apparent in all students with all cases, so the redesign will continue by adjusting the cases to be more specific and useful. For example, one case was interpreted in several ways, causing confusion and misinterpretation. In the future, cases will be vetted with other colleagues before being used with students.

Proper selection of a tool to collect critical reflections was also essential. The tool should be one that allows for reflections to be aggregated through the semester so that students and professors can easily review the posts collectively. For this class, the professor chose the blog tool within the learning management system. First, this tool is already present in the course, so additional login or training is not required. Second, this tool allows for repeated posts, collected within a single topic so that they can be reviewed by the professor individually, or collectively at the end of the course. In addition, the blog tool allows students to review and comment on each other's posts, thus creating the opportunity for considering another's point of view and interacting with the learning community.

After the first implementation of the redesign, the professor was able to analyze the reflections for evidence of transformation. Students were not assessed on whether they indicated that they had a transformation; however, the professor was able to utilize the reflections for teaching effectiveness to determine if the content was meaningful to students. Specifically, the reflections demonstrated activities and projects that were most impactful to students, misconceptions from teaching materials, and student-perceived learning development over the duration of the course.

When reviewing the reflections, it was important to use discourse analysis to look for key terms that indicate transformation. King (2009) indicated that phrases like "I see things differently now" or "I have had such a radical change in my view of issues" (p. 4) are key for identifying perspective changes. Professors can read reflections looking for these phrases to get an idea as to what changes are happening with students. In this redesign, the reflections also indicated which activities were more significant than others. One result of the reflections is that an assignment was removed and replaced with one that took students deeper into one of the learning concepts that they indicated wanting further knowledge.

Though a faculty member conducted this study for her own development, faculty developers can also learn from these findings. In particular, it may be useful for faculty developers to consider transformation when providing training for faculty who are teaching online. The transformative learning theory model serves as a framework for individual units or entire courses. Or, faculty developers can simply ask faculty to reflect on where they feel that their students are transforming, or how they can improve the course design so that opportunities to engage in reflection and analysis are more available. Finally, faculty developers may also wish to consider the "disorienting dilemma" as a strategy for creating more engaging online courses.

FUTURE RESEARCH DIRECTIONS

Transformative learning is often studied after a transformation has taken place. There is less literature that discusses instructional design for online learning that can lead to transformation. For the Scholarship of Teaching and Learning, this can be problematic in that less is known about designing for transformation. This study indicated that surveys of professors and students are only the first step in learning about what is transformational in online courses. However, they can provide guidance for determining gaps in content areas and the most effective learning activities. Future studies might include using discourse analysis within a course to understand more about transformation happening in reflections and discussions. In addition, a longitudinal study that includes interviews with students at the beginning and end of the program may be able to better identify how they have changed perspectives as the program has progressed. Finally, studying the impact of specific instructional design strategies on transformative learning may be particularly beneficial to the literature on transformative learning and the Scholarship of Teaching and Learning.

CONCLUSION

When professors are purposeful about including transformative learning opportunities in their courses, deeper learning can occur. The study in this chapter indicated that students are eager to reflect and reconsider assumptions as they learn new material that can prepare them to work in a school library. However, the findings in this study also indicate that transformation is unique for each student and may occur with different learning activities and at different times. The professor can create reflective opportunities for students to examine their learning with a view to understanding more about their own perspective transformations. Measuring transformation is not easy for professors, but strategies like discourse analysis can be used to understand more about transformations that might be happening within a course or unit. Transformative learning should also be considered to be a longitudinal process. Students may not realize they are experiencing transformations until the learning activity is complete, or they have actually had an additional life experience that they can connect with the activity. One suggestion may be for graduate programs to consider evaluating the unique transformation of each student at the beginning, middle, and end of the graduate program; this will help ensure that students are making progress and developing new habits of mind and understanding of the field.

ACKNOWLEDGMENT

This research received no specific grant from any funding agency in the public, commercial, or not-for-profit sectors.

REFERENCES

ALA/AASL. (2010). *ALA/AASL standards for initial preparation of school librarians*. Retrieved from http://www.ala.org/aasl/sites/ala.org.aasl/files/content/aasleducation/schoollibrary/2010_standards_with_rubrics.pdf

Allen, I. E., & Seaman, J. (2007). *Making the grade: Online education in the United States*. Sloan Consortium.

American Association of School Librarians (AASL). (2018). *National school library standards for learners, school librarians, and school libraries*. Chicago, IL: ALA Editions.

Boyer, N. R., Maher, P. A., & Kirkman, S. (2006). Transformative learning in online settings: The use of self-direction, metacognition, and collaborative learning. *Journal of Transformative Education*, *4*(4), 335–361. doi:10.1177/1541344606295318

Budd, J. (1995). An epistemological foundation for library and information science. *The Library Quarterly*, *65*(3), 295–318. doi:10.1086/602799

Cercone, K. (2008). Characteristics of adult learners with implications for online learning design. *Association for the Advancement of Computing in Education Journal*, *16*(2), 137–159.

Cherry, J. M., Duff, W. M., Singh, N., & Freund, L. (2011). Student perceptions of the information professions and their master's program in information studies. *Library & Information Science Research, 33*(2), 120–131. doi:10.1016/j.lisr.2010.09.004

Cranton, P. (2010). Transformative learning in an online environment. *International Journal of Adult Vocational Education and Technology, 1*, 1–9.

Cranton, P. (2011). A transformative perspective on the Scholarship of Teaching and Learning. *Higher Education Research & Development, 30*(1), 75–86. doi:10.1080/07294360.2011.536974

Dall'Alba, G. (2009). Learning professional ways of being: Ambiguities of becoming. *Educational Philosophy and Theory, 41*(1), 34–45. doi:10.1111/j.1469-5812.2008.00475.x

Fink, L. D. (2013). *Creating significant learning experiences: An integrated approach to designing college courses*. Hoboken, NJ: John Wiley & Sons.

Gavigan, K., & Lance, K. C. (2015). Everybody's teacher: Administrators' and teachers' perceptions of school librarians. Findings from the South Carolina Association of School Librarians impact study. *Teacher Librarian, 43*(1), 8.

Gorsky, P., & Blau, I. (2009). Online teaching effectiveness: A tale of two instructors. *The International Review of Research in Open and Distributed Learning, 10*(3). doi:10.19173/irrodl.v10i3.712

Helyer, R. (2015). Learning through reflection: The critical role of reflection in work-based learning. *Journal of Work-Applied Management, 7*(1), 15–27. doi:10.1108/JWAM-10-2015-003

Henderson, J. (2010). *An exploration of transformative learning in the online environment*. Paper presented at 26th Annual Conference on Distance Teaching and Learning, Madison, WI.

hooks, b. (1994). *Teaching to transgress*. Routledge.

Kammer, J., & Zhou, G. (2018). *Foundations of instructional design for online courses*. Retrieved from https://ali.memberclicks.net/alise-xchange-october-2018

Kasl, E., & Elias, D. (2000). Creating new habits of mind in small groups. In *Learning as Transformation: Critical Perspectives on a Theory in Progress* (pp. 229–252). San Francisco, CA: Jossey-Bass.

Kebritchi, M., Lipschuetz, A., & Santiague, L. (2017). Issues and challenges for teaching successful online courses in higher education: A literature review. *Journal of Educational Technology Systems, 46*(1), 4–29. doi:10.1177/0047239516661713

King, J. (2018). Transformative learning in online college courses: Process and evidence. *International Journal on Innovations in Online Education, 2*(2). doi:10.1615/IntJInnovOnlineEdu.2018028557

King, K. (2009). *Handbook of the evolving research of transformative learning*. Charlotte, NC: Information Age Publishing.

Kreber, C. (2013). The transformative potential of the scholarship of teaching. *Teaching & Learning Inquiry, 1*(1), 5–18. doi:10.20343/teachlearninqu.1.1.5

Kurtz, G., & Sponder, B. (2010). SoTL in online education: Strategies and practices for using new media for teaching and learning online. *International Journal for the Scholarship of Teaching and Learning*, *4*(1). doi:10.20429/ijsotl.2010.040101

Lance, K. C., & Kachel, D. E. (2018). Why school librarians matter: What years of research tell us. *Phi Delta Kappan*, *99*(7), 15–20. doi:10.1177/0031721718767854

Leibler, R. (2000). Stimulating cognitive and ethical development. In K. Taylor, C. Marienau, & M. Fiddler (Eds.), *Developing adult learners: Strategies for teachers and trainers* (pp. 217–220). San Francisco, CA: Jossey-Bass.

McKinney, K. (2004). The Scholarship of Teaching and Learning: Past lessons, current challenges, and future visions. *To Improve the Academy, 22*(1), 3-19.

McKinney, K. (2012). Making a difference: Application of SoTL to enhance learning. *The Journal of Scholarship of Teaching and Learning*, *12*(1), 1–7.

Meyers, S. A. (2008). Using transformative pedagogy when teaching online. *College Teaching*, *56*(4), 219–224. doi:10.3200/CTCH.56.4.219-224

Mezirow, J. (1981). A critical theory of adult learning and education. *Adult Education*, *32*(1), 3–24. doi:10.1177/074171368103200101

Mezirow, J. (1991). Transformation theory and cultural context: A reply to Clark and Wilson. *Adult Education Quarterly*, *41*(3), 188–192. doi:10.1177/0001848191041003004

Mezirow, J. (1994). Understanding transformation theory. *Adult Education Quarterly*, *44*(4), 222–232. doi:10.1177/074171369404400403

Mezirow, J. (2000). *Learning as transformation: Critical perspectives on a theory in progress*. San Francisco, CA: Jossey-Bass.

Mezirow, J. (2009). Transformative learning theory. In J. Mezirow & E. W. Taylor (Eds.), *Transformative Learning in Practice: Insights from Community* (pp. 18–33). San Francisco, CA: Jossey-Bass.

Namaste, N. B. (2017). Designing and evaluating students' transformative learning. *The Canadian Journal for the Scholarship of Teaching and Learning*, *8*(3), 3. doi:10.5206/cjsotl-rcacea.2017.3.5

Nohl, A. M. (2015). Typical phases of transformative learning: A practice-based model. *Adult Education Quarterly*, *65*(1), 35–49. doi:10.1177/0741713614558582

Palloff, R. M., & Pratt, K. (2001). *Lessons for the cyberspace classroom: The realities of online teaching*. San Francisco, CA: Jossey-Bass.

Ryman, S. E., Burrell, L., Hardham, G., Richardson, B., & Ross, J. (2009). Creating and sustaining online learning communities: Designing for transformative learning. *International Journal of Pedagogies and Learning*, *5*(3), 32–45. doi:10.5172/ijpl.5.3.32

Soffer, T., & Nachmias, R. (2018). Effectiveness of learning in online academic courses compared with face-to-face courses in higher education. *Journal of Computer Assisted Learning*, *34*(5), 534–543. doi:10.1111/jcal.12258

Taylor, E. W. (1997). Building upon the theoretical debate: A critical review of the empirical studies of Mezirow's transformative learning theory. *Adult Education Quarterly, 48*(1), 34–59. doi:10.1177/074171369704800104

Taylor, K. (2000). Teaching with developmental intentions. In *Learning as Transformation: Critical Perspectives on a Theory in Progress* (pp. 229–252). San Francisco, CA: Jossey-Bass.

The American Library Association ALA. (n.d.). *Library education and licensing*. Retrieved from http://www.ala.org/aasl/about/ed/recruit/license

Wine, L. D. (2016). School librarians as technology leaders: An evolution in practice. *Journal of Education for Library and Information Science, 57*(2), 207–220. doi:10.3138/jelis.57.2.207

ADDITIONAL READING

Cranton, P. (1994). *Understanding and promoting transformative learning: A Guide for Educators of Adults*. San Francisco, CA: Jossey-Bass.

Gagné, R. M., & Driscoll, M. P. (1988). *Essentials of learning for instruction*. Englewood Cliffs, NJ: Prentice-Hall.

McKinney, K. (Ed.). (2013). *The Scholarship of Teaching and Learning in and across disciplines*. Bloomington, IN: Indiana University Press.

Smith, P. L., & Ragan, T. J. (2004). *Instructional design*. Danvers, MA: John Wiley & Sons.

KEY TERMS AND DEFINITIONS

Learning Activity: An instructional activity designed to encourage learning of content in a course.
Online Learning: Learning in a fully online, digital environment.
Professor: A faculty member teaching in higher education.
School Librarianship: Librarians working within a K-12 school community.
Teacher: An elementary or secondary teacher teaching in public or private school.
Transformative Learning: Changing one's assumptions by transforming perspective or worldview.

Chapter 18
Enabling Scholarship of Teaching and Learning Activities Across a Curriculum Design Framework:
A Lever for Faculty Engagement

Deanna Meth
https://orcid.org/0000-0002-8749-3164
Queensland University of Technology, Australia

Holly R. Russell
https://orcid.org/0000-0001-8676-9272
Queensland University of Technology, Australia

Rachel Fitzgerald
https://orcid.org/0000-0003-2905-6895
Queensland University of Technology, Australia

Henk Huijser
https://orcid.org/0000-0001-9699-4940
Queensland University of Technology, Australia

ABSTRACT

This chapter outlines the multiple ways in which Scholarship of Teaching and Learning (SoTL) activities might be activated and/or realized through the processes of curriculum and learning design of a degree program. Key dual enablers for these activities are an underpinning curriculum framework, bringing a series of defined developmental steps each underpinned by SoTL, and the Curriculum Design Studio construct as a vehicle for collaborative ways of working between staff, including academics and curriculum designers and students. Drawing on evidence from the practices of four curriculum designers, examples are presented across a wide range of disciplinary areas. In many instances, SoTL not only

DOI: 10.4018/978-1-7998-2212-7.ch018

brings an evidence base to the work, but also the potential for research outputs, thus becoming a useful lever for academic staff to engage in ongoing curriculum design discussions and evidence-informed practice. Such activities serve to mitigate against acknowledged challenges faced by academics such as lack of adequate time for such activities and the pressure to produce research outputs.

INTRODUCTION

The Scholarship of Teaching and Learning (SoTL) is a cornerstone of learning development in higher education worldwide because it has a focus on evidence to inform practice. This is a deceptively simple idea, but to abide by its principles in an effective manner is not as simple as it sounds. As the authors will argue in this chapter, evidence-informed practice requires both structured and multifaceted approaches to curriculum design where SoTL is consistently woven through the fabric of design at all stages and ultimately built within implementation and teaching delivery. In this conceptualization of SoTL, the emphasis is on evidence for effective practice, and this comes in different forms:

- Evidence that informs initial ideas around curriculum design and renewal, including evaluation data from previous iterations or data around specific student cohorts.
- Evidence that suggested educational approaches have been shown to work in other contexts, thus providing a basis on which to build.
- Building evidence streams into the design itself, in the form of identified measures of success, which can then be used in an ongoing basis for evaluation.
- Using collected data/evidence to disseminate success (and points of learning) to the broader academic community.

In this chapter, the aim is to outline a structured process around curriculum design and renewal that has been initiated in the Learning and Teaching Unit at the Queensland University of Technology (QUT), Australia, and the role of SoTL in that process. This process is based on a framework for curriculum design called the Future-Focused Curriculum Framework (FFCF), which is an iterative model with the intent to enable meaningful change to the design of programs, placing learners at the center of their learning. The chapter is written from the standpoint of four curriculum designers who work collaboratively with academics on program development within a Curriculum Design Studio setting, a space conducive to collaborative development, with disciplinary-focused support.

The chapter proceeds to outline and demonstrate how this framework embraces and exploits the full potential of SoTL in all its different forms across the framework, fulfilling Felten's (2013) principles of good practice: inquiry focused on student learning, grounded in context, methodologically sound, conducted in partnership with students, and appropriately public (p. 122). Each step of the framework intentionally builds on and/or aims to grow the scholarly evidence base, thus yielding multiple benefits to not only the quality of the program under development, but also academics' own practice and research profiles, whilst enabling cross-institutional research collaborations with curriculum designers and others. Discussion of how this plays out in practice is enriched through a range of discipline-based examples spanning Science, Education, Design, Law and Urban Development. As part of this work, a discussion around challenges in engaging faculty staff and the role of SoTL as a lever in such engagement is incorporated as an important element before concluding the chapter by presenting a summary of transferable learning points and opportunities identified across the chapter.

A Future-Focused Curriculum Framework

The Queensland University of Technology (QUT) FFCF is designed to support program leaders and curriculum designers in their quest to design authentic, future-focused, programmatic design. It aims to balance national higher education accreditation expectations with an institutional strategic vision to address specific agendas to offer authentic, real-world curricula (Kelder & Carr, 2017). This framework affords the means to overcome issues with inconsistent approaches to curriculum design. The theoretical lens for this framework is the design of authentic curriculum (Herrington & Herrington, 2006; Lengyel et al., 2019). The authors see authentic curriculum as problem-based and focused on real-world issues. It can be argued that one cannot design truly authentic learning (Petraglia, 1998); however, authenticity in our view is about providing, as much as possible, a realistic and authentic context in relation to real-world experience. Also underpinning the FFCF is the concept of identifying what the students are expected to achieve across a whole program (Biggs & Tang, 2011; Lattuca & Stark, 2009). The future-focused element is essential in this conceptualization, as it directs the focus towards future expectations and trends, both in the labor market and in a broader sense (EGFSN, 2016). It also draws heavily on available evidence to make such predictions in an informed manner, including SoTL-based evidence.

The FFCF builds upon Lattuca and Stark's (2009) eight elements that inform the development of a future-focused framework to provide an opportunity for program managers to identify critical factors to optimize student learning including "purpose, content, sequence, learners, instructional process, instructional materials, evaluation, and adjustment" (p. 5). The QUT FFCF guides program teams through five key stages: *Visualize, Create, Transform, Realize,* and *Review and Refine,* and for each, SoTL forms an integral element, albeit in different guises. The *Review and Refine* stage, in particular, has a clear link to quality assurance processes (O'Neill & Palmer, 2004); however, SoTL provides the impetus for engagement on the part of academics, or what is referred to in this chapter as a lever.

Stage 1, *Visualize,* focuses on the sociocultural context, including external and internal influences. Daily (2011) suggests this is a key theme to deliver uniqueness of the offering for an institution and its cultural characteristics. To visualize future-focused needs necessarily requires scanning the horizon to future-proof the offering (Lattuca & Stark, 2009), which resonates with blue sky thinking (Wrigley, Bucolo, & Straker, 2016). In other words, how do we expect the world to change in the short, medium, and long term, and/or how do we want the world to change? And how does that feed into the (re-)design of a specific program? Therefore, developmental activities at this stage encompass stakeholder partnering, internal and external research, external referencing, and strategic prioritization, including reviews by the relevant formal institutional committees for new, postgraduate, and higher risk programs as appropriate.

During this stage, evidence and data collection, including primary data collection, may involve market research and demographics around likely future cohorts, comparisons with programs offered at other institutions, expectations of employers around specific disciplines, and future labor market predictions. These kinds of data not only inform decisions around *what* will be designed but also *how* it will be designed and *for whom,* thus returning to Felten's (2013) key principle that the inquiry focuses on students and their learning (p. 122). This in turn informs, for example, the choice of teaching approaches, technologies used, authentic assessment design, and so on, based on what existing SoTL shows about such approaches. Ultimately, such data can be incorporated in scholarly output at a later stage, after implementation and evaluation.

The *Create* stage (Stage 2) represents what Lattuca and Stark (2009) call the academic plan (p. 4). This stage also reflects what Laiken (2006) suggests is core to transformative learning and the basis of a learning organization – it enables a shared vision of the program and consensus on the key features. The *Create* stage allows the program team to align values, goals, and actions, which in turn will inform the day to day practice upon implementation (Laiken, 2006, p. 21). In creating a distinctive learning profile, this stage is informed by data collected during Stage 1, and involves graduate profiles, developing program learning outcomes, and the prototyping of a "real-world learning" journey. This notion is QUT's underpinning strategic mission, itself rooted in sector-wide scholarly evidence related to experiential and contextual curricula and learning. It involves internal and external stakeholder reviews, including work with external professional accrediting bodies, which forms another set of underpinning evidence.

Stage 3, *Transform* the program of learning, includes the design and mapping of the program structure, authentic assessment and learning design, identifying blended learning modes, and program/unit outlines and design. This stage involves further review points and ultimately, endorsement at discipline, faculty and institutional levels. Again, existing SoTL is part of the evidence base that informs the *Transform* stage, particularly as key pedagogies best suited to teaching the future-focused knowledge and skills are investigated. Here, a thorough investigation of the existing SoTL becomes key to identifying the appropriate learning and teaching approaches that will ensure the successful delivery of the real-world learning experiences that are integral to the program design.

Stage 4, *Realize* the learning design, involves detailed assessment design, detailed learning plans, resource curation and/or creation and support for learning, and a review of learning designs. It is at this stage that evaluation design becomes a crucial element. In other words, what will the measures of success be, how will that data be collected, and by whom? These data can then be used to both inform reviews and revisions, as well as scholarly outputs (providing ethical approval has been sought) around the learning and teaching design and implementation, either at the program level or at the program/unit level.

Most critically, the final stage, *Review and Refine*, collates evidence gathered on the implementation of the units/modules and/or whole of program, using key learning points to "refine" subsequent iterations of teaching and learning, i.e. SoTL-led and informed. Such data thus become the backbone of potential SoTL outputs and dissemination across the institution and wider sector.

The Curriculum Design Studio Construct

While faculties own the curriculum design processes, particularly on an administrative level, at QUT, centrally positioned "curriculum design studios" (CDS), which are aligned to specific disciplinary areas, provide dedicated developmental support to the faculties. These "studios" are made up of faculty-linked teams that include curriculum designers, learning designers, and educational technologists, and ideally these teams work closely with faculty academics through all the stages of the FFCF. These "studios" thus provide a space where the university's strategic directions and the faculties' aims and objectives can be brought together in curriculum design activities. This agile model is such that program development teams, comprising curriculum designers, learning designers, faculty academics, and very often students, might work together as and when needed. Program teams are also able to draw on specialized expertise in areas such as student support, employability skills, work-integrated learning, and library and scholarship skills as and when required.

The CDS is arguably a liminal space for sustainable partnerships (Fitzgerald, Huijser, Meth, & Neilan, 2019) where academics have an opportunity to engage with curriculum design outside of their usual office contexts. This has educational benefits, and a shared language is often co-constructed within such learning communities, which has the potential to be highly beneficial in the program design process.

Mårtensson, Roxå, and Stensaker (2014) note that educational paradigms set within micro cultures, such as the CDS, bring in-built traditions and ways of approaching ongoing discussions related to learning and teaching. This does not simply happen; it is a process that involves building trust and developing shared visions and goals that are of mutual benefit. While this is a process that needs to be carefully managed, it does not depend on leadership in the traditional sense (Crawford, Dawkins, Martin, & Lewis, 2019), but rather on distributed leadership through collaboration, as in a Community of Practice (Wenger, McDermott, & Snyder, 2002).

According to Trigwell (2012), good practice involves going public, and while the model we propose is discipline-specific, those working in curriculum design studios (academics and non-academics) openly share ideas and frameworks across faculties, as well as with the wider academic community through scholarly outputs. This process creates the potential for interdisciplinary collaborations and projects across faculties, or at least across disciplines (Power & Handley, 2019). Partly because of its potential outputs, and partly because of its focus on scholarly evidence, SoTL can be an important "glue" or lever in whether the CDS is successful.

Sensitivity to Local Contexts

As a deliberate construct developed by institutional leadership, the CDS settings allow for relationships and Communities of Practice to develop (Wenger et al., 2002), which in turn allows for evidence-based practice in a localized context. This process aligns closely to Felten's (2013) suggestion that good practice in SoTL must be grounded in a local context. With the combination of a curriculum framework underpinned by SoTL and the design studio model for enacting and enabling this work, SoTL activities are seen playing out across a range of disciplines in a variety of ways. These are not always without their challenges, and sensitivity to local context is critical to engagement: involvement and buy-in to curriculum development and design as well as SoTL. Therefore, an awareness of disciplinary-specific policies and practices in the areas of learning, teaching, and also research must be sustained.

The chapter now moves to outline practical discipline-specific examples of SoTL activities being undertaken across the FFCF stages and enabled through the design studio construct. Activities have been clustered to sustain and endorse Felten's (2013) principles of good practice in SoTL.

REALISING SCHOLARSHIP OF TEACHING AND LEARNING ACTIVITIES ACROSS THE FRAMEWORK: IN-BUILT AGILITY

The Scholarship of Teaching and Learning is integral to each stage of the FFCF. A key feature of the framework is that it informs the development of real-world learning that is focused on the future of work. Real-world learning underpinnings are in themselves identified and developed through examination of the existing literature on learning and teaching in specific contexts and the linkages between learning and work (Herrington & Herrington, 2006). The dual aim of engaging faculty in the curriculum design studio work and ensuring program design and renewal follow a scholarly approach to creating real-world, future-focused learning opportunities and assessment, requires in-built agility. The Curriculum Design Studios aim to foster an open and critical inquiry approach to program design and renewal by framing research questions and intentionally designing in SoTL opportunities from the outset.

Designing in SoTL Opportunities from the Outset

In the initial ideation of a new program or a program transformation, questions are formed to identify how the program can prepare students for the future of work in their industry and what design features and key pedagogies will address the future-focused needs. The FFCF provides the designers and academics, working in partnership through the CDS, a guide to assist program teams with identifying opportunities for Scholarship of Teaching and Learning at the outset. When academics commit to the large body of work that is necessary to ensure a scholarly approach to program design, there is incentive for them in knowing that the work will have a scholarly underpinning and may also produce research outputs (Fanghanel, Pritchard, Potter, & Wisker, 2016). Practically, this occurs in various ways and to different degrees across faculties. A particular challenge identified in a previous program renewal process was that program teams often began the process without having identified specific research questions in advance, and evaluation and scholarship of curriculum and learning and teaching in a program was often disparate and occurred in isolation from the whole of program context. The following examples provide insight into how various faculties, with the support of the FFCF and CDS, have attempted to frame their SoTL goals.

Urban Development

Initial discussions with the program team during the reaccreditation of the Bachelor of Urban Development Honors degree revealed that while there was general interest from academic staff to engage in Scholarship of Teaching and Learning, and while pockets of work were being done in this area, there was an appetite for creating a cohesive plan to conduct research on the innovations that were proposed in the degree, namely the introduction of human-centered design and design thinking frameworks for teaching problem-solving and collaboration. Additionally, the newly accredited program introduced problem-based learning in core units throughout the degree, culminating in a work-integrated, applied research project in the Capstone unit. The research questions that emerged centered around whether design thinking and problem-based learning are effective for building problem-solving and collaboration skills in Urban Development students.

Because the CDS work collaboratively across faculties, they were able to link the academics teaching design thinking for the first time in the Urban Development degree to those teaching in the Law and Design schools, both to share ideas for learning activities and assessment and to expand the research project to investigate and compare how design thinking enhances problem-solving and collaboration skills across disciplines. Beginning with a large-scale ethics application to conduct interdisciplinary research in this area enabled the program teams to hone in on the specific research questions they wanted to investigate, which then informed the evaluation plan for the *Review and Refine* stage of the program design, and created a clear picture of how the faculty could engage in SoTL throughout the process.

Law

At the outset of the redesign of the Bachelor of Laws (Honors) degree, the program team understood that they would need to address the technological disruption to the legal industry. Recent reports and press coverage had been decrying the oversaturation of law graduates in a declining legal profession (Karmel & Carroll, 2016). While the faculty had plenty of experiential evidence to draw on to support this future-focused theme, and other law schools in Australia were beginning to dabble in this area, there was a sparsity of literature focused on law curriculum and learning and teaching approaches that prepare students with the critical thinking and people skills necessary to distinguish them in a technologically-disrupted industry (Canick, 2014; Bentley & Squelch, 2014). Coupled with the decision to focus on embedding knowledge of how the legal industry might respond to technological disruption, and of critical thinking and people skills, the program team worked with the Curriculum Design Studio to design and develop a new minor in Law, Technology, and Innovation as a differentiating feature of the degree. The program team recognized the opportunity to further distinguish the law faculty through the development of a strategy for evaluating the innovative approaches to teaching and learning adopted by the units in the minor and producing research outputs to contribute to the emerging scholarship in this space.

Design

The new Bachelor of Design degree at QUT has been developed with future-focused priorities, bringing to the fore transdisciplinary design education, digital and international learning innovations, and new opportunities for double degrees with disciplines such as Business, Law, and Engineering. Prior to the new program going live in February 2019, a collaboration between the Curriculum Designer, Head of School, and Academic Program Director for the degree led to the development of a large-scale ethics application for research into the program, its curriculum content and delivery, and importantly, the impact on student and staff learning and development. This will serve to enable qualitative and quantitative scholarly research into the new degree in an ongoing way over a five year period. Defined as a nested suite of research projects, this gives scope for academics to follow their particular areas of interest and undertake detailed research on areas they have been tasked with teaching, often linking to their own ongoing disciplinary research. In addition to bringing a solid evidence base for evaluation of the new program, this piece of work is seen as an overarching enabler in promoting and endorsing ongoing SoTL activity in the School. To date, three individual research projects are underway in this area.

Scholarly Grounding and Approaches from Stage 1, *Visualize*

In the initial *Visualize* phase, scholarship occurs through environmental scans, research into the changing disciplinary context of a program, and competitor analyses. The purpose of this phase of the curriculum design is to craft the narrative of the distinguishing features of a program. Increasingly, SoTL features heavily in this phase as we consider innovations in learning theory and pedagogy in higher education in general as well as within specific disciplines.

For instance, in the curriculum transformation for the Bachelor of Laws (Honors) degree, a focus of the initial ideation sessions was on the possibility of offering a fully online law degree. A result of the interrogation of the literature as well as conversations with external accreditation bodies informed the decision to retain a face-to-face component of the degree but adopt a hybrid model where students have the option to study externally as online students or internally through an intentionally blended approach (Bennett, 2014).

Another example of how program teams engage with SoTL in the *Visualize* phase of the framework was the exploration of different frameworks for teaching problem-solving within a Bachelor of Urban Development Honors Degree as introduced briefly above. When analyzing the internal program data and discussing the degree with students and alumni through focus groups, the program team identified a gap in the development of problem-solving skills in the current version of the program. This, coupled with feedback from industry partners that prioritized innovative thinking and collaboration, led the program team to research innovative approaches to teaching problem-solving skills and collaboration, and ultimately to selecting design thinking as a methodology for building these skills. As a result, design thinking was embedded throughout the degree. The program team also identified that while design thinking has been researched widely in higher education (Koh, Chai, Wong, & Hong, 2015), there was limited literature on design thinking within an urban development degree. The unit coordinators of the design thinking units within the degree were interested in engaging in Scholarship of Teaching and Learning to inform future iterations of the program as well as address this gap and contribute to the body of knowledge.

In scoping the nature of the new Bachelor of Design degree during the *Visualize* phase, a rich evidence base was drawn upon to ensure adherence to future-focused needs. Research was undertaken through focus groups with design industry experts and students, where views on desirable graduate qualities such as connectivity to other disciplines, industry, and communities, the ability to work across disciplines, and entrepreneurial mindsets were elicited. Developmental discussions also drew on a timely, large-scale research publication from their national body, the Design Institute of Australia (Robertson, 2013), which detailed the shifting focus of design disciplines and rapid growth in multimedia, web, and technology design fields of employment. Additionally, market demand research for such shifts in curricular focus was endorsed through reports from national and international employment agencies. These data were coupled with peer-reviewed, published research previously undertaken by academics in the School on aspects of design education in areas such as student collaboration (Crowther, Scott, & Allen, 2016) and interdisciplinary field trips (Scott, Jerome, & Thomson, 2001), to design an education the School believes is necessary to meet changing needs in the labor market, thereby future-proofing students' skills.

The "future focus" of the FFCF is very important and in some cases can lead to considerable dilemmas, especially for disciplines that are going through a paradigm shift in terms of their practice. Sometimes this is fueled by technological change. For example, in the Biology discipline, and more specifically in genetics and genome research, large data sets are increasingly important and central to the types of research that are undertaken (Chang et al., 2015; Loh, Kichaev, Gazal, Schoech, & Price, 2018). The collection of large data sets requires large and very expensive equipment, which has made the more traditional idea of the "lone researcher" going about their data collection an increasingly outdated image. If the equipment is too expensive for a university to acquire and/or to gain access to, this raises the question of how to design a future-focused curriculum that is fit for purpose and would adequately prepare students for life after their studies. The cost and relevance issues potentially relate to other sciences as well, for example physics and medical science, and ways to address them may be developed, for example in the form of simulations. However, the point here is that the FFCF allows us to focus on dilemmas such as these that arise, based on the available evidence, and then to find the best ways to address them. In other words, it creates a safeguard against programs continuing to be offered that are no longer relevant or fit for purpose.

Partnerships with Students to Enrich Evidence-based Approaches

Felten (2013) suggests that "good practice requires that inquiry into learning be conducted in partnership with students" (p. 123). In our experience with FFCF, partnership with students raises the Scholarship of Teaching and Learning through critical discussion, reflection, and engagement with the program team.

Education

In the Faculty of Education, student partners engaged with the program team across the curriculum. The faculty recruited students as curriculum design partners through a targeted recruitment across current cohorts, recognizing the importance of the student voice as part of curriculum design. The CDS curriculum designer engaged in the recruitment process with faculty partners and together ensured that students represented different cohort years, different majors (Early Childhood, Primary, and Secondary) and different grade profiles. The partner students brought differing critical perspectives to the design and implementation stage and were engaged in curriculum design both in their own major and beyond; for example, during the *Create* stage, student partners engaged in discussion and contribution with program coordinators to create a shared vision (Laiken, 2006) which subsequently translated into graduate profile and program learning outcomes for all undergraduate students. This exercise allowed students to critically question the theoretical frameworks that underpin the design of teaching education (e.g., the theory practice nexus that underpins teacher education) (Korthagen & Kessels, 1999).

Evaluation of the curriculum design process highlighted that student input at the *Transform* and *Realize* stages was highly valued. Seeing the requirements, particularly for assessment from a critical student viewpoint and from differing grade perspectives, helped academic staff to design more authentic assessment and rationales for learning activities in relation to professional activities and the teaching research nexus (Korthagan & Kessels, 1999). By engaging in active conversations with student partners about requirements and relevance of learning activities, academic staff began to value the logic of constructive alignment (Biggs & Tang, 2011) connecting learning outcomes, assessment, and learning activities in more clear and unambiguous language and design. Feedback from students demonstrated how the curriculum became more relevant to them, and they were able to share this understanding with peers. Tinto (2015) suggests that curriculum relevance and quality contribute to improved retention, one of the underpinning requirements for this redesign of the program, as an added advantage to this work. In this example, engaging students in partnered learning opportunities was a valuable SoTL experience for all involved (Fitzgerald et al., 2019).

Science

The students-as-partners initiative has played out somewhat differently in the Faculty of Science and Engineering, being directly related to the *Realize* stage of the FFCF only. In other words, the *Visualize, Create,* and *Transform* stages had already occurred at the time the Curriculum Design Studio team became involved. The particular program we were assigned to work on had already been accredited. Furthermore, out of the accreditation process, a list of priorities for improvement had been identified. Key themes amongst those priorities were Work-Integrated Learning (WIL), authentic assessment, and employability skills. It was therefore decided to recruit a team of student partners related to each of the majors in the Science program: Physics, Chemistry, Biology, Environmental Science, and Earth Science. Five students were recruited in a similar way as had happened elsewhere in the university (Shaw, Rueckert, Smith, Tredinnick, & Lee, 2017). The selection was a workshop-based recruitment process where student partners were not interviewed separately, but rather asked to work with the curriculum and learning designers and faculty academics to work on focused tasks, which mirrored what they eventually were expected to do as part of the partnership process.

The students-as-partners project focused on employability skills across the science degree, and five students were ultimately brought into the Curriculum Design Studio to collaborate on approaches to improve the integration of employability skills across the different Science majors (Suleman, 2018). These five students were all high-performing students, and they were all either in the second or third year of their degrees. SoTL was a key element in the process from the very start on a number of levels. Firstly, the validity of the students-as-partners process itself was based on growing evidence in the higher education sector about the value that students can bring to curriculum design (Matthews, Dwyer, Hine, & Turner, 2018). Secondly, SoTL informed the evidence that the students found in their conceptualizations of employability skills and how to approach this across the curriculum. The partnership operated like a Community of Practice (Wenger et al., 2002) and included faculty academics at various points. The students performed primary and secondary research and sector-wide comparisons, and they subsequently developed a research-based report with recommendations on how to embed employability skills across the curriculum more consistently, and how to communicate this to students in a more effective manner. The report was then presented in an open forum to the whole faculty, and the follow up actions are currently still being implemented.

Thus, the students-as-partners process can stimulate new insights, and it potentially has mutual benefits. However, the process can present challenges as well, as it can be time consuming and there are issues of sustainability of partnerships in the longer term (Ntem & Cook-Sather, 2018). The important point here, however, is that the process is both informed by and informs SoTL-based approaches to curriculum design, which is an attractive proposition for all parties involved: students, curriculum and learning designers, and faculty academics. The partnership has been at its most productive when SoTL has directly informed the discussions around the most appropriate ways of embedding employability skills across the curriculum.

Law

The Law faculty's approach to student partnerships in program design and development involved the creation of a law student council for curriculum and learning design at the outset of the program transformation for the Bachelor of Laws (Honors) degree. The selection of students was informed through partnerships with the equity committee, Indigenous student support officers, and the institution's Student Success Group to ensure an equitable representation of the entire student cohort. The student council consists of twelve students ranging from first-year to fourth-year students. The student council was oriented to the process of curriculum design, including the internal and external requirements for accreditation and the FFCF. Select students engaged in literature review projects to inform the development of the degree context in the *Visualize* phase of the FFCF. One student conducted a literature review on how technology is disrupting the legal profession and participated in a working party to embed legal futures and disruptive technology throughout the core degree. Another student, from the Indigenous Australian community, conducted an interrogation of the current curriculum with a specific focus on Indigenous Australian knowledges and perspectives. She then produced an evidence-based report on how other law degrees have embedded indigenous knowledges and perspectives in their degrees and made recommendations for how Law could approach this in their curriculum transformation.

In the *Create* phase, the program team partnered with student council members to create learner profiles reflective of the diverse cohort of learners in the law degree. The learner profiles were then vetted with the wider student population through student surveys and focus groups. The student council also participated in workshops to define the new graduate profile and program learning outcomes and provided feedback on the learner journeys. The *Transform* phase of the FFCF involved the student council in workshops to map the progression of skills throughout the degree and to create an assessment blueprint that identified which assessments in which units introduced, developed and advanced the key skills as defined by the program learning outcomes. The students provided feedback on the design of the Capstone unit as well as the new first year core units within the degree. As part of the *Realize* phase, the law student council partnered with learning designers to provide feedback and test the learner experience for the new online unit sites.

Design

In the School of Design, as part of the *Realize* phase of curriculum design, student partners were employed to do research and bring an evidence base to the development of a model for a graduate professional portfolio. This component of the degree is integral to bringing necessary industry and sector-wide relevance with a future focus. Students worked in partnership with staff across seven design disciplines to understand the drivers for and needs of graduate portfolios. This included drawing on literature in this area and gathering evidence from industry contacts, academic staff, and their student peers. Beyond the model as a product for use, capturing the collaboration between academics, the curriculum designer and students, learnings from this research are being written up as scholarly outputs for sector-wide dissemination, introducing new data to an area with which most universities are currently grappling (Chaudhuri & Cabau, 2017).

Going Public: Research Levers and SoTL Outputs

A central element to the FFCF is the *Review and Refine* stage, which is incidentally also the stage where the importance of SoTL is at its most pronounced. *Review and Refine* should not be seen as something that happens after all the other stages are completed in a linear manner. Instead, it is important to consider reviewing and refining at every stage of the process, including *Visualize*. In this way, SoTL can inform every step of the design and create potential scholarly outputs in the process (Fanghanel et al., 2016). An added bonus is that the latter are attractive to most academics, so scholarly approaches and outcomes can serve as a lever for academics to become more engaged in scholarly approaches to learning and teaching. The CDS model works well in this respect as curriculum and learning designers can take the lead on SoTL-based projects, as they have the expertise and networks to do so, while for many discipline-based academics, SoTL is a relatively new pathway to publication. The argument here is that integrating SoTL in the curriculum design process has the potential to stimulate deeper engagement from all involved and thus effecting more scholarly and evidence-based approaches to curriculum design.

One example in the Faculty of Science and Engineering involved a unit that had been singled out for innovation; the academic approached the CDS and wanted to redesign the unit in order to make it more relevant to contemporary work-based environments. The main complicating factor was that the unit had a highly diverse cohort of students from different majors in the degree. Thus, the first step was to do thorough research on current work environments as well as potential future trends of those work environments (Jorre de St Jorre & Oliver, 2018). This informed the initial discussions around learning outcomes. Based on this initial evidence and a resulting set of learning outcomes, the academic, and the curriculum and learning designers then set out to explore potential learning and teaching approaches, including assessment, which would be able to deliver the outcomes. One of the key elements of the unit was the use of data. In previous iterations, students had been provided with a clean set of data, and they had been told what to do with those data. However, that did not address the increasing importance of graduates having to address complicated problems, including collecting data and cleaning it themselves. Thus, the decision was made to develop an app that would allow students to collect data themselves through working in groups in a problem-based approach (Kek & Huijser, 2017).

From the beginning, there were considerable risks involved in this approach, especially for the academic, related to workload implications and student responses to this new approach. In other words, what if the academic struggled to facilitate the problem-based approach? What if the students responded badly to what they were asked to do? What if things went wrong with the technology? In the first instance, all of these risks turned into reality. However, the fact that the process was based on SoTL from the beginning helped to work through the initial challenges. Ultimately, the unit was successful, and the students had a rewarding and engaging learning experience. Because the design was evidence-based, we were confident that the approach was the right one, but we also expected initial challenges. However, we ensured that these challenges were addressed in an agile manner, and we incorporated a rigorous evaluation strategy from the beginning. Ultimately, students noted that they felt extremely challenged, particularly by having to clean large data sets, but they loved the fact that the work was relevant, current, and approximated what they would be expected to do in a work context upon graduation. Some even changed their major as a result because they could now see an employment pathway. The unit has just run for the second time, and based on the feedback gathered, the results have been outstanding, with all the initial challenges overcome. A collaborative paper was subsequently submitted that discusses this process, which was a partnership between the academic and the curriculum and learning designers. The data that informed the paper was based on evaluation data gathered throughout the process. Ethics approval had been gained early on to facilitate this process. Overall, this SoTL-informed practice ensured that the academic became engaged and stayed the course through the challenging initial parts, and it has transformed his practice ever since. The CDS construct allows us to replicate this model many times over.

SUMMARIZING AND TRANSFERRING LEARNINGS

In drawing the chapter together, Table 1 summarizes the practical examples outlined above to provide a transferable set of SoTL-linked activities that may be undertaken across the area of curriculum design. In keeping with the grounding of the chapter, activities are situated within the principles of SoTL as outlined by Felten (2013, p. 122).

Issues and Challenges

Going public (Felten, 2013) and sharing conversations is not necessarily straightforward. There are many challenges engaging participants in this process. One example of this came from one participating faculty member, who was unwilling to support research data collection during an evaluation process. They expressed discomfort with sharing their lived experience and were only willing to participate in focus groups for the purpose of reviewing and improving faculty practice but were unwilling for any specific comments to be "on the record". This was disappointing, as the survey and two focus groups had produced outcomes rich in evidence of impact worth sharing.

Table 1. Summary of opportunities to embed SoTL at various stages of curriculum design, grounded in Felten's (2013) principles of good practice in SoTL

Principle (Felten, 2013)	Activities and Structures Rooted in or Enabling of SoTL
Inquiry focused on student learning	Future-focused curriculum framework.
Grounded in context	Collaborative teams grounded in faculty, disciplinary program, and external body contexts—catered for within Curriculum Design Studio construct.
Methodologically sound	Future-focused curriculum framework, itself a methodologically sound approach, underpins the core design of programs. Using this model also enables program teams engaged in design to consider theoretical evidence to underpin learning and teaching approaches.
Conducted in partnership with students	Students as curriculum design partners. Students improving integration of employability skills across a program. Creating a Student Council for curriculum and learning design across the program. Students as researchers for portfolio models.
Appropriately public	Designing in a longitudinal program of research as a new program is delivered, including large-scale ethics considerations. Staff and staff-student collaborations for SoTL research outputs from curriculum implementation, review, and refinement.

There are a number of such lessons learned about engagement with the FFCF and program design more broadly that would be highly valuable to a wider community; however, it is evident that curriculum design is a highly personal experience for the academics involved, and they are sometimes unwilling to share their experiences and reflections.

Another key challenge and potential risk is the often rigid and structurally-embedded divide between "research" and "learning and teaching" (Parkin, 2017, p. 21). This plays out in multiple ways, including time and recognition for learning and teaching activities and the relative value of SoTL research outputs as opposed to disciplinary ones. The risk here is that SoTL may be considered of lesser value than disciplinary research, and potentially perceived to undermine faculty research agendas. There is often a blurring of boundaries between day-to-day, necessary and institutionally in-built program evaluation, reflections on educational and academic practice in an ongoing scholarly way, Scholarship of Teaching and Learning, and higher education research. Whilst part of the same spectrum of activities (Ashwin et al., 2015, p. 341), the extent to which such activities might be undertaken is often limited by barriers cited above. What is clear, however, is the value to be gained from engaging in SoTL activities, and Ashwin et al. (2015), note the links between SoTL activities and academic promotion and teaching fellowship awards.

The authors recognize that this model may pose a challenge to institutions who may not have the resources or structures to support a CDS model. In institutions where a CDS construct might not exist, the key to ensuring the embedding of SoTL approaches across course design would be to ensure that faculty learning and teaching managers are able to align a set of activities similar to those identified in the table above with their own course design processes. This would include an acknowledgement of the need to source individuals with the necessary skills sets to carry out such SoTL-led work.

While we have outlined an ideal framework and setting in this chapter providing a base from which SoTL activities might best be enabled, and included a suite of practical case study examples of how it has already worked successfully, we have also highlighted a range of risks that could potentially derail this approach. Whilst such risks will not come as a surprise to any higher education institution, surfacing and retaining an awareness of them has, in the authors' experiences, aided in more carefully negotiated and better designed work. This includes sustaining an ongoing awareness of localized policies and practices and an appreciation of attitudes towards SoTL as opposed to disciplinary research.

The chapter has evidenced that SoTL offers a potential to break through some of these obstacles, or at least blur some of the entrenched lines of perception and can thus function not only as a lever for enhancing faculty engagement and whole-of-program development, but also open up alternative (and in some cases parallel) pathways for academic career advancement.

FUTURE RESEARCH DIRECTIONS

Given this is offered as a "carrot" to draw academics more deeply into learning and teaching activities, future studies should seek to focus on the impact of embedded SoTL activities on disciplinary academics, as individuals: their identity, development, and recognition. Additionally, the collective endeavors, inputs of and impacts on academic schools or departments as a whole would be another obvious angle of research at the case institution.

CONCLUSION

Overall, the Future-Focused Curriculum Framework, in combination with the Curriculum Design Studio construct, allow for a holistic approach to curriculum design and implementation within a learning ecology where SoTL is a crucial underpinning element to the process. SoTL is noted as a stimulant for, and form of professional development of, academic staff. The evidence that is collected through the various stages of the framework, in particular during the *Realize* and *Review and Refine* stages, can be used to develop collaborative publications between faculty academics themselves, and curriculum designers and faculty academics. In addition, it can be used by faculty academics for promotion, learning and teaching fellowship applications, and individual and collaborative teaching awards. The SoTL-based data thus constitute a crucial lever for engagement in the form of an incentive for potential career development of academic staff (Fanghanel et al., 2015). Additionally, through the process, teaching approaches and students' learning experiences are enhanced.

ACKNOWLEDGMENT

The authors would like to acknowledge the leadership of Associate Professor Judith Smith and her work with Dr. Fiona Lombard in establishing and defining the Future Focused Curriculum Framework and pilots of Curriculum Design Studio ways of working at QUT, upon which this chapter builds.

REFERENCES

Ashwin, P., Boud, D., Coate, K., Hallett, F., Keane, E., & Krause, K. (2015). *Reflective teaching in higher education*. London, UK: Bloomsbury Academic.

Bennett, S. C. (2014). Distance learning in law. *Seton Hall Legislative Journal, 38*(1), 1–15.

Bentley, D., & Squelch, J. (2014). Employer perspectives on essential knowledge, skills and attributes for law graduates to work in a global context. *Legal Education Review, 24*(1), 93–114.

Biggs, J., & Tang, C. (2011). *Teaching for quality learning at university* (4th ed.). Maidenhead, UK: McGraw-Hill Education.

Canick, S. (2014). Infusing technology skills into the law curriculum. *Capital University Law Review, 42*(3), 663–708.

Chang, C., Chow, C., Tellier, L., Vattikuti, S., Purcell, S., & Lee, J. (2015). Second-generation PLINK: Rising to the challenge of larger and richer datasets. *GigaScience, 4*(7). doi:10.118613742-015-0047-8 PMID:25722852

Chaudhuri, T., & Cabau, B. (Eds.). (2017). *E-Portfolios in higher education: A multidisciplinary approach*. Singapore: Springer. doi:10.1007/978-981-10-3803-7

Crawford, J., Dawkins, S., Martin, A., & Lewis, G. (2019). Putting the leader back into authentic leadership: Reconceptualising and rethinking leaders. *Australian Journal of Management*. doi:10.1177/0312896219836460

Crowther, P., Scott, A., & Allen, T. (2016). Perceptions of collaboration amongst novice design students. In R. Tucker (Ed.), *Collaboration and Student Engagement in Design Education* (pp. 126–144). IGI Global.

Daily, E. (2011). Enhancing learning, teaching, assessment and curriculum in higher education: Theory, cases, practices. Teaching Theology and Religion, 14(3), 295–297. doi:10.1111/j.1467-9647.2011.00728.x

Expert Group on Future Skills Needs (Ireland) (EGFSN). (2016). *Guidance for higher education providers on current and future skills needs of enterprise: Springboard+ 2016 including ICT skills conversion*. Retrieved from http://hdl.voced.edu.au/10707/400180

Fanghanel, J., McGowan, S., Parker, P., Mcconnell, C., Potter, J., Locke, W., & Healey, M. (2015). *Literature review. Defining and supporting the Scholarship of Teaching and Learning (SoTL): a sector-wide study*. York, UK: Higher Education Academy.

Fanghanel, J., Pritchard, J., Potter, J., & Wisker, G. (2016). *Defining and supporting the Scholarship of Teaching and Learning (SoTL): A sector-wide study*. York, UK: Higher Education Academy. Retrieved from https://repository.uwl.ac.uk/id/eprint/2066/1/literature_review.pdf

Felten, P. (2013). Principles of good practice in SoTL. *Teaching and Learning Inquiry: The ISSOTL Journal, 1*(1), 121–125. doi:10.20343/teachlearninqu.1.1.121

Fitzgerald, F., Huijser, H., Meth, D., & Neilan, K. (2019). Student-staff partnerships in academic development: The course design studio as a model for sustainable course-wide impact. *The International Journal for Academic Development*, 1–13. doi:10.1080/1360144X.2019.1631170

Herrington, A., & Herrington, J. (2006). What is an authentic learning environment? In T. Herrington & J. Herrington (Eds.), *Authentic learning environments in higher education* (pp. 1–14). Hershey, PA: IGI Global. doi:10.4018/978-1-59140-594-8.ch001

Jorre de St Jorre, T., & Oliver, B. (2018). Want students to engage? Contextualise graduate learning outcomes and assess for employability. *Higher Education Research & Development, 37*(1), 44–57. doi :10.1080/07294360.2017.1339183

Karmel, T., & Carroll, D. (2016). *Has the graduate job market been swamped?* NILS working paper series No. 228/2016. Adelaide, Australia: National Institute of Labour Studies.

Kek, M. Y. C. A., & Huijser, H. (2017). *Problem-based learning into the future: Imagining an agile PBL ecology for learning.* Singapore: Springer. doi:10.1007/978-981-10-2454-2

Kelder, J., & Carr, A. (2017). Embedding evaluation and scholarship into curriculum and teaching: The curriculum evaluation framework. In A. Horshed, P. Bartholomew, J. Branch & C. Nygaard (Eds.), New innovations in teaching and learning in higher education (pp. 430-451). Upper Farringdon: Libri Publishing.

Koh, J. H. L., Chai, C. S., Wong, B., & Hong, H. Y. (2015). *Design thinking for education: Conceptions and applications in teaching and learning.* Singapore: Springer.

Korthagen, F. A. J., & Kessels, J. P. A. M. (1999). Linking theory and practice: Changing the pedagogy of teacher education. *Educational Researcher, 28*(4), 4–17. doi:10.3102/0013189X028004004

Laiken, M. (2006). Authentic graduate education for personal and workplace transformation. In T. Herrington & J. Herrington (Eds.), *Authentic learning environments in higher education* (pp. 15–33). Hershey, PA: IGI Global. doi:10.4018/978-1-59140-594-8.ch002

Lattuca, L., & Stark, J. (2009). *Shaping the college curriculum academic plans in context* (2nd ed.). San Francisco, CA: Jossey-Bass.

Lengyel, A., Szöke, S., Kovács, S., Dénes Dávid, L., Bácsné Bába, E., & Müller, A. (2019). Assessing the essential pre-conditions of an authentic sustainability curriculum. *International Journal of Sustainability in Higher Education, 20*(2), 309–340. doi:10.1108/IJSHE-09-2018-0150

Loh, P., Kichaev, G., Gazal, S., Schoech, A., & Price, A. (2018). Mixed-model association for biobank-scale datasets. *Nature Genetics, 50*(7), 906–908. doi:10.103841588-018-0144-6 PMID:29892013

Mårtensson, K., Roxå, T., & Stensaker, B. (2014). From quality assurance to quality practices: An investigation of strong microcultures in teaching and learning. *Studies in Higher Education, 39*(4), 534–545. doi:10.1080/03075079.2012.709493

Matthews, K. E., Dwyer, A., Hine, L., & Turner, J. (2018). Conceptions of students as partners. *Higher Education, 76*(6), 957–971. doi:10.100710734-018-0257-y

Ntem, A., & Cook-Sather, A. (2018). Resistances and resiliencies in pedagogical partnership: Student partners' perspectives. *International Journal for Students as Partners, 2*(1). doi:10.15173/ijsap.v2i1.3372

O'Neill, M. A., & Palmer, A. (2004). Importance-performance analysis: A useful tool for directing continuous quality improvement in higher education. *Quality Assurance in Education, 12*(1), 39–52. doi:10.1108/09684880410517423

Parkin, D. (2017). *Leading learning and teaching in higher education: The key guide to designing and delivering courses.* Abingdon, UK: Routledge.

Petraglia, J. (1998). *Reality by design: The rhetoric and technology of authenticity in education.* Mahwah, NJ: Lawrence Erlbaum Associates. doi:10.4324/9781410601254

Power, E. J., & Handley, J. (2019). A best-practice model for integrating interdisciplinarity into the higher education student experience. *Studies in Higher Education, 44*(3), 554–570. doi:10.1080/0307 5079.2017.1389876

Robertson, D. (2013). *Australian Design 2013: Issues and concerns in the Design professions.* Melbourne, Australia: Design Institute of Australia PN034 (Issue B). Retrieved July 17, 2019 from https://www.design.org.au/documents/item/127

Scott, A., Jerome, K., & Thomson, S. (2001) Orientating Design Education: Implementing an orientation field trip as an introduction to design education. In V. Popovic, T. Kim, (Eds.), *Proceedings ICSID Educational Seminar 2001*, (pp. 62-68). Seongnam City, South Korea: Academic Press.

Shaw, N., Rueckert, C., Smith, J., Tredinnick, J., & Lee, M. (2017). Students as partners in the real world: A whole-institution approach, a whole of institution case study. *International Journal for Students as Partners, 1*(1). doi:10.15173/ijsap.v1i1.3079

Suleman, F. (2018). The employability skills of higher education graduates: Insights into conceptual frameworks and methodological options. *Higher Education, 76*(2), 263–278. doi:10.100710734-017-0207-0

Tinto, V. (2015). Through the eyes of students. *Journal of College Student Retention, 19*(3), 254–269. doi:10.1177/1521025115621917

Trigwell, K. (2012). Scholarship of Teaching and Learning. In L. Hunt & D. Chalmers (Eds.), *University teaching in focus: A learning-centred approach* (pp. 253 267). London, UK: Routledge. doi:10.4324/9780203079690-15

Wenger, E., McDermott, R., & Snyder, W. (2002). *Cultivating Communities of Practice.* Boston, MA: Harvard Business School Press.

Wrigley, C., Bucolo, S., & Straker, K. (2016). Designing new business models: Blue sky thinking and testing. *The Journal of Business Strategy, 37*(5), 22–31. doi:10.1108/JBS-04-2015-0041

ADDITIONAL READING

Arthur, L. (2016). Communities of Practice in higher education: Professional learning in an academic career. *The International Journal for Academic Development, 21*(3), 230–241. doi:10.1080/136014 4X.2015.1127813

Assiter, A. (2017). *Transferable skills in higher education.* London: Routledge. doi:10.4324/9781315041605

Bovill, C., Cook-Sather, A., Felten, P., Millard, L., & Moore-Cherry, N. (2016). Addressing potential challenges in co-creating learning and teaching: Overcoming resistance, navigating institutional norms and ensuring inclusivity in student–staff partnerships. *Higher Education, 71*(2), 195–208. doi:10.100710734-015-9896-4

Bronnimann, J., West, D., Huijser, H., & Heath, D. (2018). Applying learning analytics to the Scholarship of Teaching and Learning. *Innovative Higher Education, 43*(5), 353–367. doi:10.100710755-018-9431-5

Bryan, C., & Clegg, K. (Eds.). (2019). *Innovative Assessment in Higher Education: A Handbook for Academic Practitioners*. London: Routledge. doi:10.4324/9780429506857

Driscoll, A., & Sandmann, L. R. (2016). From maverick to mainstream: The scholarship of engagement. *Journal of Higher Education Outreach & Engagement, 20*(1), 83–94.

Healey, M., Flint, A., & Harrington, K. (2016). Students as partners: Reflections on a conceptual model. *Teaching & Learning Inquiry, 4*(2), 1–13. doi:10.20343/teachlearninqu.4.2.3

Mercer-Mapstone, L., Dvorakova, S. L., Matthews, K. E., Abbot, S., Cheng, B., Felten, P., & Swaim, K. (2017). A systematic literature review of students as partners in higher education. *International Journal for Students as Partners, 1*(1). doi:10.15173/ijsap.v1i1.3119

Norton, L. (2018). *Action research in teaching and learning: A practical guide to conducting pedagogical research in universities*. London: Routledge. doi:10.4324/9781315147581

KEY TERMS AND DEFINITIONS

Communities of Practice: Groups of individuals linked by their shared concerns or interests who work together collectively to solve such concerns and further develop knowledge and/or practice in that area.

Curriculum Design Framework: A framework which denotes a series of stages by which to undertake the process of curriculum design.

Curriculum Designer: A curriculum designer works collaboratively with academics and academic support staff to design curriculum through all stages and enable the approval and implementation of curriculum. Depending on national and institutional contexts, "curriculum designer" may have considerable overlaps with the terms "educational developer" and/or "academic developer."

Faculty: A term denoting an organizational and management structure in the university which brings together Schools/disciplines into a cognate group, for example, the Creative Industries Faculty comprises the Schools of Design, Creative Practice, and Communication. In the North American context, it is used to denote teaching staff working higher education institutions.

Future-Focused Curriculum: A curriculum which places a strong emphasis on skills, knowledge and competencies predicted by the labor market and wider research to be those of future individual, societal and industry needs.

Program: As in course of study, or chosen degree, sometimes written as programme (UK spelling).

Students-as-Partners: Describes the increasingly recommended practice of collaborative course development between students and staff. This may occur on a range of scales and for varying durations.

Section 5
Addressing the Challenges and Assessing the Impact of SoTL

This final section of the book discusses common challenges faced by faculty and faculty developers with SoTL before moving into a chapter highlighting an example of the impact of SoTL on both professional development and educational quality improvement. Chapter 19 looks at the challenges encountered when implementing a SoTL program as an ongoing faculty development initiative. The final chapter presents one practice example, which could provide a basis for discussion focused more on the impact of SoTL to combat the potential barriers or challenges often encountered.

Chapter 19
Overcoming Challenges to Impactful SoTL

Sherry Fukuzawa
(iD) https://orcid.org/0000-0001-6858-9358
University of Toronto, Mississauga, Canada

Dianne Ashbourne
University of Toronto, Mississauga, Canada

Fiona Rawle
University of Toronto, Mississauga, Canada

ABSTRACT

In order for teaching and learning to improve throughout an institution, the Scholarship of Teaching and Learning (SoTL) must be valued within institutional culture and contribute to the scholarly identity of researchers. This chapter emphasizes some of the challenges for SoTL researchers, whether educational developers or faculty members, to consider as they begin their foray into educational research. SoTL challenges are divided into four inter-related themes: (1) scholarly identity, (2) institutional challenges, (3) accessing and searching the SoTL literature, and (4) conducting SoTL research (SoTL research design, methodology, funding and time commitments, and ethical considerations). The chapter includes a series of opportunities and resources to help SoTL researchers reframe these challenges into opportunities for their institutions.

INTRODUCTION

The Scholarship of Teaching and Learning (SoTL) is an evolving discipline that focuses on purposeful and reflective inquiry into post-secondary instruction and student learning (Boyer, 1990). Despite the existence of differing definitions of SoTL (Hutchings, 2008; McKinney, 2007; Felten, 2013), it is broadly accepted to have a foundation built upon reflective scholarly practice that extends beyond scholarly teaching to include critical inquiry of teaching and learning. In addition, SoTL is seen as a core part of

DOI: 10.4018/978-1-7998-2212-7.ch019

academic identity (Manarin & Abrahamson, 2016; Simmons et al., 2013), and is a crucial component of faculty development (Fanghanel, 2013). SoTL is critically important to improving teaching practice, meeting student learning outcomes, and enhancing the student learning experience and overall learning landscape. However, despite the wide recognition of the value and importance of SoTL, persistent challenges exist to impactful SoTL work.

To further explore potential challenges and barriers to SoTL work, we conducted a scoping literature review of scholarly peer-reviewed journals. From this review, we identified multiple challenges that aligned to four main themes: (1) Scholarly Identity; (2) Institutional Challenges; (3) Accessing and Searching the SoTL Literature; and (4) Conducting SoTL Research. The category of "Institutional Challenges" was further categorized into three themed-levels, including macro-level challenges such as institutional policies; meso-level challenges including departments and teaching and learning centers (TLCs); and micro-level challenges such as faculty considerations or precarious instructors. The category of "Conducting SoTL Research" was further categorized into: SoTL Research Design, Methodology, Funding, Time Commitments, and Ethical Considerations. In addition to these challenges, the review also revealed strategies that can be used to overcome some of the barriers presented. It is important to note that scholarly identity was found to be a recurring theme that weaves throughout all the other identified themes. It will thus be discussed alongside all the themes as a persistent challenge to SoTL practice.

SCHOLARLY IDENTITY

Scholarly identity is commonly defined by academic disciplinary scholarship that is valued in the Academy through the ideals of academic freedom and peer-reviewed research outcomes (Bennett et al., 2016; Fanghanel, 2012). Simmons and colleagues (2013) have argued that SoTL is considered a core part of scholarly identity. However, we have found compelling arguments in the literature that SoTL work exists in a liminal space and working in such a space poses a unique set of challenges to scholarly identity (Fanghanel, 2012; Mathany, Clow, & Aspenlieder, 2017). Professional identify in Academia can be marked along disciplinary lines through different ways of thinking (Becher & Trowler, 2001), and recognition is primarily based on disciplinary scholarship, with disciplinary expertise acting as the barometer for hiring, promotion, and tenure. Research in SoTL involves risk-taking outside of this established, and administratively reinforced, professional identity (Mathany et al., 2017). This risk increases the lower an individual sits in the institutional hierarchy. For example, precarious instructors (e.g., graduate students and contingent/adjunct instructors) take the greatest risks and often have the least institutional support to engage in SoTL, even though they are often responsible for large proportions of teaching loads (Simmons et al., 2013). In addition, it can be difficult for faculty to identify SoTL research norms since it is a relatively new field and often outside of the discipline they were trained in (Billot, Rowland, Carnell, Amundsen, & Evans, 2017; Simmons & Taylor, 2019). It is not hard to imagine the challenge of undertaking a research project that is outside of your established scope of practice and not necessarily recognized by your disciplinary colleagues. In order to confidently traverse this liminal space, disciplinary scholars need support, recognition, and guidance to engage meaningfully with SoTL practice and conduct SoTL research (Bennett et al., 2016; Simmons, 2011).

Table 1. Scholarly identity: Summary of challenges and strategies

Challenges	Strategies	Resources
Tensions of expanding on one's disciplinary identity; working in a liminal space; self-doubt. SoTL work being outside of the researcher's discipline. Difficulty aligning and associating with SoTL colleagues. Lack of recognition and support from the institution and disciplinary colleagues, for SoTL work; marginalized identity.	Identifying the need for creativity; Multi-disciplinary, multi-expertise communities for new emerging identities Sustained engagement and professional development programs aimed at increasing confidence working in a new field and fostering connections between colleagues. Positioning of educational developers and appointment of teaching stream faculty may encourage greater institutional value of SoTL projects.	Key References: Fanghanel (2012) Lee & Boud (2003) Lea & Stierer (2011) Miller-Young, et al., (2018) Simmons et al., (2013) Case Study: Bennett et al., (2016)

Strategies for Overcoming Barriers in Developing a SoTL Scholarly Identity

As with many of the challenges noted in this chapter, working in this liminal space can be reframed as an opportunity. Little and Green (2012) suggest that working in a liminal space can have positive outcomes, including fostering creative possibilities. The multi-disciplinary nature of SoTL provides an opportunity to develop a new collaborative "hybrid" scholarly identity that includes a diversity of expertise (e.g. case study in Bennett et al., 2016) built on the foundation of peer learning (Lea & Stierer, 2011; Lee & Boud, 2003). Professional development programs for increasing SoTL expertise are commonly referred to in the literature as both an opportunity to increase participants' confidence in themselves as SoTL researchers and, more generally, as an opportunity to help establish a SoTL identity (Billot et al., 2017; Mathany et al., 2017; Simmons et al., 2013). For educational developers, having an understanding of the challenges facing novice SoTL researchers presents an opportunity to more successfully guide them, noting however that their success relies largely on their understanding of the complexity of these challenges. Educational developers, due to their unique positioning within an institution, can help break down disciplinary barriers and help researchers find common ground (Mathany et al., 2017). The relatively new category of "teaching stream" faculty, which has been adopted at several institutions, may help to embed SoTL research within disciplines and encourage the institutional value of cross-disciplinary SoTL projects.

CHALLENGES TO SOTL WITHIN THE INSTITUTION

Broadening the definition of SoTL has fostered a growing and increasingly diverse body of pedagogical scholarship (Huber & Hutchings 2005; Mathany et al., 2017; Prosser, 2008). This positive SoTL impact coincides with the rising emphasis on evidence-based teaching and learning across post-secondary institutions. The hierarchical structure of post-secondary institutions means that institutional policies must recognize and prioritize SoTL research for it to be adopted across the institution. Unfortunately, a misalignment of expectations amongst institutional hierarchical levels from micro (instructors), meso (department and faculty), and macro (institution) results in inherently-linked challenges across each of these levels that primarily permeate from the macro-level downwards (Buch, 2008; Shreeve, 2011; Wuetherick & Yu, 2016). Of note, instructors, in the micro-level, face different challenges based on

Figure 1. Hierarchical levels affecting institutional SoTL practice
(Figure adapted from Fukuzawa et al., (2017) and Williams et al., (2013).)
The Institutional challenges to SoTL Research are based on interrelated considerations from differing priorities by macro-level institutional policies and the unique challenges faced by meso-level middle management versus micro-level instructors that we have divided into two sub-levels based on their status within the institution (i.e., permanent faculty or precarious instructors).

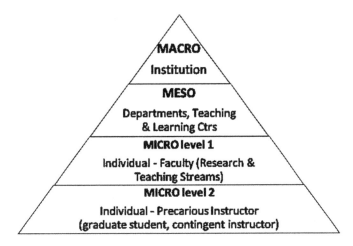

their status within the Academy. For example, instructors without permanent status (e.g., contingent instructors and graduate student instructors) have the greatest challenges to SoTL practice due to their limited access to Institutional support systems from the meso- and macro- levels (Fukuzawa, Vander Kloet, Frake-Mistak, Caldelott, & Cassidy, 2017; Kezar & Sam, 2013; for case studies refer to Vander Kloet, Mistak, McGinn, Caldecott, Aspenlieder, Beres, Fukuzawa, Cassidy, & Gill, 2017).

Macro-Level Challenges: Institutional Policies

Macro-level policies dictate the overall goals and values within an institution, and the institutional academic plan provides support and structure for pedagogical practices at all other levels (Lock, Kim, Koh, & Wilcox, 2018). Indeed, academic plans often prioritize "excellence in teaching" or "teaching expertise"; however, scholarly teaching goes beyond student opinion surveys, peer evaluations, and discipline-specific teaching tips (Dewer, 2008). Evidence-based teaching requires SoTL to produce long-term qualitative and quantitative improvements in both the teaching landscape and student learning that extend beyond the researcher's own courses (Biggs & Tang, 2011). SoTL is grounded in research in effective methods of assessment, program design, and instructional methodology (Dewer, 2008). These long term SoTL projects require dedicated macro-level institutional funding streams for meso-level department resources in educational development and broad institutional recognition of merit for micro-level instructors who are engaged in SoTL work (Asmar, 2004; Major & Palmer, 2006; Martensson, Roxa, & Olsson, 2011). However, it has been shown that macro-level institutional recognition and award systems do not equate SoTL with disciplinary research (Buch, 2008; Wuetherick & Yu, 2016). In a typical promotion process for a tenure stream faculty member, research and teaching are evaluated separately, with disciplinary research accounted for in the research portfolio and SoTL research as part of the teaching assessment (Wuetherick & Yu, 2016). Additionally, teaching is often assessed primarily through peer and student evaluations and performance appraisals, while SoTL research is not usually required. Importantly, SoTL is frequently considered to be an "extra" skill as opposed to a "core" skill, in the academic portfolio, especially when involving inter- and cross-disciplinary projects (Dewar, 2008; Simmons & Marquis, 2017). This means that pedagogical research holds significantly less weight in promotion decisions at many institutions. In this way, macro-level institutional policies around teaching can potentially marginalize pedagogical innovation and research. In fact, instructors may be hesitant to engage in SoTL because they may not be recognized for their efforts in "institutional accountability" measures (Chalmers, 2011; Kenny & Evers, 2010; Lock et al., 2018; Weston & McAlpine, 2001).

A prevailing institutional culture that devalues SoTL in relation to other scholarly activities means that improving the resources for SoTL activities may not be enough to encourage widespread SoTL research across an institution (Simmons & Marquis, 2017). Boshier (2009) suggests that post-secondary institutions operate on a business model that emphasizes deliverables and quantitative outputs. Best practices and promotion are determined by academic outputs such as publications in high impact journals that attract external funding opportunities and elevate the prestige of the institution as a whole (Boshier, 2009). Importantly, this socioeconomic paradigm doesn't easily align with the long-term investment in SoTL that is needed before institution-wide advances in student learning can be assessed (Boshier, 2009; Lock et al., 2013). Macro-level administration must have a long-term vision for evidence-based pedagogy and demonstrate leadership through funding streams and promotional criteria (Dewer, 2008; Wuetherick & Yu, 2016). Myatt, Gannaway, Chia, Fraser, and McDonald (2018) point to a gap in the literature on institutional best practices to develop SoTL research capacity.

Meso-Level Challenges: Disciplinary Limitations

Program development in post-secondary institutions operates largely under the direction of independent disciplinary units led by Deans and Departmental Chairs (Healey, Bradford, Roberts & Knight, 2013). This meso-level acts as a "conduit" for information between the macro- and the micro-levels and therefore is critical in the alignment of micro-level SoTL activities with macro-level support (Williams et al., 2013). Since discipline-specific departments are at the center of curricular programming, they may also influence SoTL priorities at the macro-level (Roy, Borin, & Kustra, 2007). However, Wuetherick, and Yu (2016, p. 27) found that faculty perception of departmental support for SoTL projects varied greatly, and departmental culture led to colleagues viewing SoTL research as "problematic". However, a disconnect exists, as Miller-Young, Yeo, & Manarin, (2018, p. 3) note that STEM related disciplines often de-value SoTL research as "subjective," while scholars in the humanities find that SoTL lacks "reflexivity", and educational fields are uneasy with of the interdisciplinary focus of many SoTL projects.

Of note, departments often cannot properly assess the validity of SoTL research because it is outside of their disciplinary scope, resulting in departments being seen as unsupportive to micro-level instructors who engage in SoTL (Kelly, Nesbit, & Oliver, 2012; Marquis et al., 2017). Disciplinary affiliation forms the primary scholarly identity for academic departments and this is disseminated to micro-level instructors (Miller-Young et al., 2018; Zibrowski, Weston, & Goldszmidt, 2008), and departmental conformity emphasizes disciplinary research as the foundation of professional identity (Healey et al., 2013).

For micro-level instructors to engage in SoTL, they also need to be well supported by meso-level educational development mechanisms outside their departments. Meso-level leadership in teaching and learning centers can contribute pedagogical expertise to guide and moderate interdisciplinary discussions involving SoTL (Kelly et al., 2012; Miller-Young & Yeo, 2015; Miller-Young et al., 2018; Strober,

2011). Highly productive SoTL must translate directly into improved teaching and learning outcomes to move out of the margins at research-intensive institutions (Asarta et al., 2018).

Meso-Level Challenges: Teaching & Learning Centers

Meso-level disciplinary challenges to SoTL research are primarily dealt with by Teaching and Learning Centers (TLCs) (Forgie, Yonge, & Luth, 2018). Educational developers are the logical pedagogical connection between disciplines to encourage and support SoTL research projects. This meso-level leadership provides a number of diverse roles in support of teaching and learning in the Academy. Forgie et al. (2018) surveyed fourteen TLCs across Canada and found that all directors indicated that their scope of practice is determined by macro-level administrative policies. In order to properly encourage and support SoTL projects, TLCs need macro-level funding and support (Gray & Shandle, 2009). However, macro-level funding often prioritizes disciplinary research over teaching (including SoTL projects) (Asarta et al., 2018). The resulting budgetary constraints on TLCs limits the time and resources they can afford to spend supporting individual long-term SoTL projects (Forgie et al., 2018). This lack of funding is occurring in an environment where TLCs are currently expanding their scope of practice (e.g. individual consultations, workshops, Communities of Practice, funding awards, cultural competencies) (Forgie et al., 2018). In order to maximize their influence on teaching and learning in the institution, most TLCs rely on websites and online sources to disseminate SoTL resources and access to SoTL workshops and Communities of Practice. King (2004) found that only 1/3 of faculty access information on TLC websites. This lack of visibility undermines the credibility of the TLC as an essential part of the SoTL process (Forgie et al., 2018). Metrics on TLCs are often based on workshop participations and evaluations (King, 2004). TLCs at the meso-level need to demonstrate a correlation between SoTL projects and improvements in student learning in order to secure macro-level policies and funding that prioritize SoTL research (Charbonneau, 2009; Poole, Taylor, & Thompson, 2007; Woodhouse & Force, 2010). Importantly, TLCs must be a central driver of change in macro-level priorities around teaching and learning to enrich a culture that values pedagogical research (Marquis et al., 2017).

Micro-Level 1: Faculty Considerations

Even though macro-level policies of promotion and merit have direct consequences on the pedagogical practice of instructors at the micro-level, faculty perceptions of scholarship often include SoTL research (Asarta et al., 2018; Boshier, 2009; Buch, 2008; Kenny & Evers, 2010). Micro-level instructors frequently express a professional interest and motivation to improve their teaching but are held back by their obligation to compete with other disciplinary scholars in their department (Mathany et al., 2017; Zibrowski et al., 2008). There is a prevailing misconception that SoTL research "is less rigorous, easier to perform, and easier to get published than disciplinary research, and therefore, serious researchers with high-quality research skills will not spend their time and effort in this area" (Asarta et al., 2018, p. 736). Also, SoTL research is outside of their professional training, and involves an element of risk-taking (Kelly et al., 2012). These macro- and meso-level restrictions may impede innovative teaching practices and act as a deterrent to SoTL engagement (Lock et al., 2018).

Of note, teaching stream faculty are often encouraged to engage in SoTL (Mathany et al., 2017). However, teaching stream faculty are evaluated and promoted based on their "established" teaching practice excellence. SoTL can be risk-taking for them because they may perceive it as highlighting ongoing teaching challenges and even failures. SoTL often involves a discussion of teaching challenges that can be misinterpreted as evidence of a failed instructor (Breunig, 2017). This in turn may be viewed negatively at the meso-level for vulnerable untenured faculty who do not want to advertise their mistakes (Cotton, Miller, & Kneale, 2018; Johnsen, Pacht, van Slyck, & Tsao, 2009).

Another challenge is the fact that pedagogical research is usually outside the expertise of most faculty members, even many teaching-focused faculty come from diverse disciplines and do not have direct training in SoTL methodology (Kelly et al., 2012). Faculty that transition from discipline training into SoTL research will need intensive support, especially from the Departmental or TLC meso-level (Marquis et al., 2017; Mengal, 2016). Their SoTL research projects must be recognized and promoted at the macro-level to ensure that SoTL is a valued part of the scholarly identity. As Kelly and colleagues (2012) explain, this support needs to address training in SoTL methodologies, but it must also go beyond methodological approaches to include discussions of the influence of narrative, and appreciation of time for impactful SoTL work.

Micro-Level 2: Precarious Instructors

Graduate Students

There is limited pedagogical training, assessment, or documented value placed on SoTL in graduate programs (Kenny & Evers, 2010). Graduate students must compete within their own disciplines and do not have the time, incentives, or the knowledge to take on research in any other field (Mathany et al., 2017). Credited mentorships and collaborations may play an important role in introducing the key principles of SoTL to early career academics, and the infusion of SoTL through an institution may have its greatest chance in this new generation of researchers (Mathany et al., 2017; Trepanier, 2017). There must be a direct connection between SoTL output and improved learning measurables (such as number of graduates and employability) for SoTL to become important to all institutional stakeholders (Asarta et al., 2018).

Contingent Instructors

Contingent instructors are responsible for a significant amount of the teaching load at post-secondary institutions (Dobbie & Robinson, 2008; Field, Jones, Stephenson, & Khoyetsyan, 2014). However, they are presented with significant challenges when engaging in SoTL. Their precarious position in the Academy means that they often do not have access to macro- or meso-level support systems or funding (Dobbins, 2011; Kezar & Sam, 2013; Gehrke & Kezar, 2015). The precarious nature of their contract makes long term planning and execution of a SoTL project difficult (Brownlee, 2015; Schuetz, 2002). Also, contingent faculty commonly feel isolated and inferior to permanent faculty and they are often considered to be "below average" researchers by their meso-level disciplines because they do not have permanent academic status (Austen, 2011; Dobbins, 2011; Schuetz, 2002; Vander Kloet et al., 2017).

Strategies for Overcoming Institutional Challenges to SoTL

The Society of Teaching and Learning in Higher Education promotes SoTL as integral to a "national strategy to protect and enhance the quality of teaching and learning in higher education" (Woodhouse & Force, 2010, p. 1). Mega-level inter-institutional connections amongst meso-level TLCs have invigorated the SoTL movement (Poole et al., 2007; Wuetherick & Yu, 2016). Conceptual spaces such as "teaching commons" provide communities for educators to converse and share pedagogical innovations across national and international lines (Huber & Hutchings, 2008), and there is a growing call to recognize SoTL as a core component of institutional research (Shreeve, 2011). Hutchings, Huber, and Ciccone (2011) suggest that the SoTL movement operating outside of a particular institution is more inclusive and "consistent with the movement's language: this is scholarly work, not a bureaucratic requirement" (p.10).

Within institutions, interwoven relationships between micro-, meso-, and macro- levels are a way to overcome the tension between institutional levels. Williams et al. (2013) suggest that these relationships can be composed of social networks or Communities of Practice composed of members from all institutional levels. These semi-structured groups cultivate communication and sharing of expertise so that SoTL has a primary role in academic culture (see Hubball, Clarke, & Poole, 2010; Martensson et al., 2011). For example, collaborations across disciplines and between faculty and educational developers can overcome barriers by combining knowledge of the pedagogical literature with practical teaching challenges (McKinney & Jarvis, 2009). Collaborations such as this also allow for time and resource efficiencies in SoTL projects (Kelley, 2008). Of note, however, macro-level administrators must be engaged in these networks to have a cultural impact that is felt throughout the institution (Roxa & Martensson, 2009). Myatt et al., (2018, p. 148) recently created a conceptual framework to examine institutional macro-level SoTL capacity building. This flexible framework is based on Healey's (2014) inventory of strategies to promote SoTL engagement, and Hamilton's (2014) "structured typology of SoTL support activities". The framework is a starting point for institutions to examine their current SoTL support systems and to develop institutional definitions and policies for different levels and contexts.

Meso-level TLC's can begin the process of institutional SoTL development by creating networks of SoTL programs that provide pedagogical support and a sense of community for micro-level instructors interested in SoTL research (Kezar, Gallants, & Lester, 2011; Marquis et al., 2017). These networks may also involve micro-level precarious faculty (Fukuzawa et al., 2017). Once these networks demonstrate

Table 2. Institutional challenges and opportunities

Challenges	Strategies	Resources
Institutional policies for promotion criteria. Funding streams and recognition for SoTL practice at all levels in the institution. Valued risk-taking to go outside of disciplinary expertise (scholarly identity).	Mega-level inter-institutional networks. Communities of Practice involving all institutional levels. TLCs are in a central Institutional position to provide SoTL guidance.	Key References: Hamilton (2014) Healey (2014) McKinney (2007) Williams et al., (2013) Institutional Conceptual Framework: Myatt et al., (2018) The Carnegie Foundation for the Advancement of Teaching http://www.carnegiefoundation.org International Society for the Scholarship of Teaching and Learning http://www.issotl.org Case Study on UBC's SoTL Leadership Faculty Certificate Program: Hubball et al., (2010) Faculty Case Study: Mengal (2016 Case studies of challenges for precarious instructors: (Vander Kloet et al., 2017)

results in teaching and learning, meso-level managers can take the evidence to the macro-level administration to initiate institutional participation in SoTL projects (Williams et al., 2013). This alignment of macro-level initiatives will foster sustainable change in institutional culture (Poole et al., 2007).

ACCESSING AND SEARCHING THE SOTL LITERATURE

As with all research, a literature review is a necessary first step. With SoTL research, it can be an especially difficult initial hurdle for novice researchers unfamiliar with the field. New SoTL researchers often experience frustration and a crisis of confidence when confronted with new terms, methodology, and conventions (Weller, 2011; Marquis et al., 2017). Specialist terminology and jargon used in SoTL work can pose a major barrier to comprehension for novice researchers (Weller, 2011; Green, 2009). Even when researchers develop familiarity with the terminology, the SoTL literature can be quite difficult to search. As we experienced firsthand while writing this chapter, the SoTL literature is not networked particularly well and is missing the search connections typical in many other fields. Inconsistent search terms also pose a problem, even for experienced SoTL researchers. A particularly apt metaphor for the state of SoTL literature is offered by Weimer (2006), who describes it as "a house cobbled together by many different occupants, all working together without blueprints and very little money" (p. 51).

Challenges with SoTL Dissemination

The dissemination of pedagogical research occurs through diverse outlets that can be confusing for novice SoTL researchers. Dewer (2008, p.18) points to the importance of understanding the distinction between "good teaching", "scholarly teaching", and the "Scholarship of Teaching and Learning". According to Dewer (2008), good teaching is determined by successful student learning. In contrast, scholarly teaching is informed by disciplinary research with pedagogical methods and assessment. SoTL contributes to scholarly teaching and extends beyond the practice of a singular classroom or discipline. Of course all three concepts are not mutually exclusive, but this distinction is important when it comes to researching SoTL literature. Discipline-specific pedagogical journals are common and often highlight pedagogical research within a discipline and provide teaching guidelines or "tips". Teaching tips are usually based on student evaluations of a particular teaching technique, while discipline specific pedagogy involves the methods, theory, and empirical research that are unique to a particular field (Dewar, 2008). It can be confusing to access and understand the literature because most research projects do not fall into a single category (Dewar, 2008). If someone is interested in engaging in SoTL they may stick to the familiar resources in their discipline and miss out on the larger pedagogical methods published in teaching and learning journals (Green, 2009). Additionally, a significant percentage of SoTL work is only available through conference proceedings and institutional websites (Chick, 2018). Notably, finding a starting point when conducting a literature review is made more difficult by the lack of a widely agreed-upon cannon of literature. Not only do these difficulties affect researchers at the beginning of their work, researchers also experience difficulty and confusion associated with choosing an appropriate vehicle for disseminating their work. Finding appropriate and valued outlets for disseminating SoTL work can present a major challenge and ultimately this choice can influence the way their work is perceived by their institution and other stakeholders (Billot et al., 2017; Witman & Richlin, 2007). Another barrier to dissemination is that teaching-stream faculty and precarious instructors often do not have available funds to pay for open-access publisher options, further limiting the scope of journals to submit their work. High impact disciplinary journals that are valued for academic promotional criteria often do not prioritize SoTL research submissions, thus further perpetuating the misconception that SoTL research is less academically rigorous (Asarta et al., 2018; Chick 2013). The diversity of teaching and learning journals makes it difficult for meso- and macro-levels to determine an impact factor that is relevant for promotion and merit. In Buch's (2008) sample of 31 tenure-track faculty, more than 40% published in teaching and learning journals, however less than half considered this to be part of their scholarly work. Marcketti & Freeman (2016) noted an increase in SoTL grants at Iowa State University after SoTL was acknowledged in the "faculty handbook, position descriptions, and professional responsibility statements" (p. 26). However, the SoTL grants did not translate into an increase in SoTL publications. This suggested that SoTL grants were acquired to improve curricular teaching, but the barrier to publications outside of research disciplines remained. The authors recommended that meso-level resources at Teaching and Learning Centers should prioritize fostering pedagogical grants into peer-reviewed SoTL outputs. However, they recognize that a cultural shift in departments and institutions from policy recognition toward collegial acceptance and value must take place (Marcketti & Freeman, 2016; Ciccone, Huber, Hutchings, & Cambridge, 2009).

Strategies for Engaging with the SoTL Literature

Mentorship programs that lead novice SoTL researchers through a program aimed at supporting them as they learn about the field can be an effective method of reducing these initial frustrations and helping establish confidence (Billot et al., 2017; Mathany et al., 2017; Simmons et al., 2013). Collaborations across disciplines and between faculty and educational developers can overcome this barrier by combining knowledge of the pedagogical literature with practical teaching challenges (McKinney & Jarvis, 2009). Reference lists, bibliographies, and SoTL library guides can be less overwhelming places to start for those new to the field. Many universities have started to establish SoTL library guides (LibGuides) to combat the problem of fragmented SoTL search results. For example, the University of Toronto SoTL LibGuide can be found at https://guides.library.utoronto.ca/SOTL_journals_databases.

CONDUCTING SOTL RESEARCH

SoTL Research Design and Methodology

SoTL research questions can be investigated using a wide variety of methodological approaches from experimental design to self-study to grounded theory to phenomenology (Hubball & Clarke, 2010). That said, there is a definite dominance of social science research methodology within the SoTL literature. Many journals signal the dominance of the social sciences within SoTL by favouring work characterized as "data-driven" and requiring APA formatting for citations (Bloch-Schulman, Conkling, Linkon, Manarin, & Perkins, 2016; Potter & Wuetherick, 2015). For scholars outside of the social sciences, this can cause epistemological discomfort and methodological alienation (Billot et al., 2017; Chick, 2014; Hubball & Clarke, 2010; Miller-Young et al., 2018; Simmons et al., 2013). STEM scholars commonly express discomfort with the subjectivity and qualitative nature of SoTL research, while humanities

Table 3. Accessing and searching the SoTL literature: Challenges and strategies

Challenges	Strategies	Resources
Frustration and crisis of confidence when confronted with new terms, methodology, and conventions. Literature is not well-networked and is missing connections typical of other fields. Confusion around distinguishing features of "good teaching", "scholarly teaching", and "Scholarship of Teaching and Learning". Tendency to stick within disciplinary literature and miss broader pedagogical work. No widely agreed upon canon of literature. Lack of funds to pay for open-access publisher options to disseminate work.	Mentorship programs. Reference lists, bibliographies, and SoTL library guides provide a starting point and help combat the problem of fragmented search results. Collaboration with educational developers.	Key Reference: Chick et al., (2014) McKinney (2007) University of Toronto SoTL LibGuide: https://guides.library.utoronto.ca/SOTL_journals_databases University of Calgary Resource on SoTL Searching: https://library.ucalgary.ca/c.php?g=455466&p=4029348 Grant Goals: Preparing the Literature Review. https://library.ucalgary.ca/c.php?g=455466&p=4156864 SoTL Research Guide. Vanderbilt University Center for Teaching: http://my.vanderbilt.edu/sotl

scholars express discomfort with the lack of reflexivity and positioning of SoTL within the empirical realm (Huber & Hutchings, 2008; Miller-Young, et al., 2018; Potter & Wuetherick, 2015).

The intellectual diversity of SoTL can lead to disagreement over the legitimacy of work and what constitutes methodological rigor (Bloch-Schulman et al., 2016; McKinney, 2012; Trigwell, Martin, Benjamin, & Prosser, 2000). While there is no accepted "best approach" for conducting SoTL research, there are better approaches for addressing particular questions, though this is often not recognized by novice SoTL researchers who tend to select methodological approaches that are common within their disciplinary field (Hubball & Clarke, 2010). As noted above, selecting the best research approach often means that researchers need to work with unfamiliar methodologies that fall outside their disciplinary training, and this may act to undermine their established scholarly identity (Healey, 2008; Kenny & Evers, 2010).

Funding and Time for SoTL Work

Due to the complex diversity of teaching and learning practice, proper SoTL methodological approaches often involve longitudinal studies or a mixed method approaches. These types of methods require more resources and time than researchers have at their disposal due to the relatively small number of SoTL grants available. There are significantly fewer research grants for SoTL work than for disciplinary research. This is true for both institutional and external grants. In preparation for this chapter, we did a review of institutional grant listings, and divided them into "Supporting SoTL" and "Excluding SoTL" categories. Consistently there were more grant offerings and higher grant values in the "Excluding SoTL" category. Of note, several institutions did not even offer grants in support of SoTL work, whereas others only recently added granting programs for SoTL. Despite this gap, more SoTL funding opportunities are regularly being developed; however, they do not yet meet the documented need for this type of funding. Of note, securing funding is the first step of support for a well-researched SoTL project, however the time commitment is another significant challenge (Goldszmidt, Zimbrowski, & Weston, 2008; McKinney, 2007; Zimbrowski et al., 2008). When macro- and meso-levels undervalue SoTL research, the time taken by micro-level instructors to engage in SoTL projects is an extra add-on to their research portfolios (Zimbrowski et al., 2008). This is complicated by the fact that rigorous SoTL research often requires a long-term commitment to achieve quantitative results. Funding and time-release for SoTL research must go hand in hand for quality SoTL work to be properly disseminated and used to promote enhanced teaching and learning throughout the Academy (Kenny & Evers, 2010).

Ethical Considerations in SoTL Work

Underlying all choices related to methodology and research design are judgements about ethical research. Hutchings (2003) urges SoTL researchers to consider "who benefits and who is at risk when the complex dynamics of teaching and learning are documented and publicly represented" (p. 28). SoTL research often requires instructors to take on the dual role of instructor-researcher, which if not considered and managed carefully can result in a number of ethical complications. The instructor as researcher can create a power imbalance with students as participants and affect a student's consent to participate in the study. Specifically, this power differential may cause students to feel uncomfortable declining to participate in their instructor's pedagogical research. Students may worry that instructors will value their work differently or be ostracized from their peers if they do not participate. It is essential that students understand that they will not incur social penalties for choosing not to participate in a study (MacLean & Poole, 2010). When students enroll in a course, their goal is to gain knowledge, skills, or credentials. SoTL researchers must be diligent in ensuring that research goals do not overshadow students' primary purpose of participating in the course. This includes ensuring that students are not losing time from their regular course hours to participate in a SoTL project. Activities like completing surveys, listening to a study recruitment pitch, and completing informed consent paperwork all take time away from regular course activities.

As Hutchings (2003) suggests, there is some disagreement as to whether the classroom is a private privileged space, or a public community space. Certain pedagogical models (i.e. community-based learning or collaborative learning) and technology have moved classrooms into the public domain and changed expectations about the privacy of student work. Protecting students' confidentiality is of the utmost importance in SoTL research. This becomes especially important if the study involves accessing student-participants' academic data.

When selecting appropriate methodology, an added ethical complication involves the selection of research designs. An excellent example is the use of control groups when instructors have good reason to believe that the intervention being tested on the treatment group may lead to better outcomes for students. Additionally, researchers with certain disciplinary backgrounds (e.g. psychology) may be more familiar working with human subjects than researchers from other disciplines (e.g. mathematics).

SoTL research sometimes blurs the lines between quality assurance work and traditional scholarly inquiry making it unclear when approval from a research ethics board is required (Healey et al., 2013). Misunderstandings about the need to pursue ethics approval is common among novice SoTL researchers. Seemingly similar activities such as action research, program evaluation, and quality assurance muddy the waters, leading to confusion among researchers as to whether an ethical review is required (Linder, Elek, & Calderon, 2014; Stockley & Balkwill, 2013). Researchers often see an ethics review as a barrier to their research. Macro-level unfamiliarity with SoTL research methods can make the process of determining the need to pursue ethics approval even more convoluted. In Canada, the Tri-Council Policy statement advises that when data collection activities move past a basic assessment of in-course class activities with the aim of producing more generalizable findings, research should be reviewed by an ethics board (TCPS, 1998, p. 11).

Strategies for Overcoming Barriers to SoTL Research

Critical consideration and careful management of the ethical implications of SoTL inquiry not only mitigate potential harm to research participants, but also create an opportunity for researchers to reflect upon their own identities and the values that guide their work. Thankfully, there are a number of excellent resources to help SoTL researchers navigate the ethical complexities inherent in the work. MacLean and Poole (2010) wrote an introduction to ethical considerations for novice SoTL researchers, including a helpful list of four key considerations. There are also several excellent ethics guides for SoTL researchers that present questions for researchers to consider (e.g., Ethics in the Scholarship of Teaching and Learning from the *Taylor Institute for Teaching and Learning Guide Series*). Many of these guides display acute awareness of the diverse disciplinary backgrounds of SoTL researchers and make a concerted effort not to privilege certain epistemological positions. An excellent example is the Ethical SoTL Matrix offered by Healey et al., (2013), which aims to provide researchers from different disciplinary backgrounds the opportunity to reflect on SoTL.

Furthermore, positioning students as collaborators and co-investigators in a research study instead of subjects presents an opportunity to address ethical dilemmas stemming from the power discrepancy between instructor-researcher and student-participant (Burman & Kleinsasser, 2004; Hutchings, 2003; MacLean & Poole, 2010). In addition to the ethical benefits, students as co-investigators can reflect

Table 4. Conducting SoTL research: Challenges and strategies

Challenges	Strategies	Resources
There are limited funding opportunities for SoTL research. Undervalued SoTL research means that the time commitment is not recognized or awarded. SoTL projects often require a long-term commitment to a project. Dominance of social sciences research methods. Intellectual diversity of SoTL work leads to disagreement over methodological rigor. Tendency to select methods based on disciplinary familiarity rather than appropriateness for research question. Relatively small number of grants available to support SoTL research.	Institution-dependent grants exist at the department, faculty, and institutional level. External grants are being developed to include SoTL funding. There should be time-release for SoTL research. Opportunity for researchers to reflect upon their own identities and the values that guide their work. Positioning students as collaborators and co-investigators. Professional development programming (i.e., SoTL fellowship program). SoTL conceptualized as open and inclusive of a wide variety of work.	Key References: Acai et al. (2017) MacLean & Poole (2010) Miller-Young et al. (2018) Stockley & Balkwill (2013) Facilitating organizational change in higher education: Kezar (2001) Ethical SoTL Matrix: Healey et al. (2013) Fedoruk (2017) Table 2 (p. 16) in the Ethics in the Scholarship of Teaching and Learning: Key principles and strategies for ethical practice from the *Taylor Institute for Teaching and Learning Guide Series* www.ucalgary.ca/taylorinstitute/guides Funding for SoTL Research from the *Centre for Teaching Support & Innovation at the University of Toronto.* https://teaching.utoronto.ca/wp-content/uploads/2018/08/SoTL-TipSheet_Funding-for-SoTL-Research.pdf Fenton & Szala-Meneok (2010). Research on Teaching and Learning Guidebook. http://cll.mcmaster.ca/resources/pdf/redo_guidebook.pdf

more purposefully about their role in their education (Felten et al., 2013). Acai et al. (2017) suggest a set of questions aimed at improving instructor-student partnerships.

Professional development programming provides an opportunity to address challenges related to research design, methodology, and ethics. In particular, programming with sustained engagement and intensive support, such as a SoTL fellowship or mentorship program, can make great strides toward familiarizing novice SoTL researchers with new methodologies. Conceptualizing SoTL research using Huber and Hutchings' (2005) well-known "big tent" philosophy, in short that the field should be open and inclusive of a wide variety of work, may reduce the intimidation many new researchers feel. Conversations with colleagues can also help to identify ethical blind spots in study design. Stockley and Balkwill (2013) highlight the opportunities that educational developers have to highlight research ethics at the research design phase and to emphasize the potential practical consequences of not pursuing ethics review. They also suggest that educational developers work collaboratively with Research Ethics Board members to develop outreach and education to proactively address common issues and questions.

CONCLUSION

In sum, the challenges to impactful SoTL work span multiple levels within and beyond the Institution, and threaded throughout the landscape of these levels is the core issue of scholarly identity. Opportunities and efforts to overcome these challenges need to come from all institutional levels identified in this chapter. Specifically, to empower faculty to conduct effective SoTL work, instructors need to have this work valued in annual performance reviews and tenure file decisions. Additionally, SoTL practitioners need access to both institutional and external SoTL grants and support and feedback in preparing these grants. The key to overcoming several challenges identified here is a shift in perception on the value of SoTL: In order for SoTL to be pursued more rigorously and thoroughly it needs to be explicitly valued by the academic institutions and members that comprise the scholarly community.

REFERENCES

Acai, A., Akesson, B., Allen, M., Chen, V., Mathany, C., McCollum, B., & Verwoord, R. (2017). Success in student-faculty/staff SoTL partnerships: Motivations, challenges, power, and definitions. *The Canadian Journal for the Scholarship of Teaching and Learning, 8*(2), 1–20. doi:10.5206/cjsotl-rcacea.2017.2.8

Asarta, C. J., Bento, R., Fornaciari, C. J., Lund Dean, K., Arbaugh, J. B., & Hwang, A. (2018). The Scholarship of Teaching and Learning: Changing the dominant narrative about (and in) research institutions. *Journal of Management Education, 42*(6), 731–748. doi:10.1177/1052562918777271

Asmar, C. (2004). Innovations in scholarship at a student-centered research university: An Australian example. *Innovative Higher Education, 29*(1), 49–65. doi:10.1023/B:IHIE.0000035366.71782.d8

Austen, V. (2011). "Haven't we heard this all before?" Contingent faculty and unchanging times. *English Studies in Canada, 37*(1), 13–16. doi:10.1353/esc.2011.0005

Becher, T., & Trowler, P. (2001). *Academic tribes and territories: Intellectual enquiry and the cultures of disciplines* (2nd ed.). Buckingham, UK: Open University Press/SRHE.

Bennett, R., Hobson, J., Jones, A., Martin-Lynch, P., Scutt, C., Strehlow, K., & Veitch, S. (2016). Being chimera: A monstrous identity for SoTL academics. *Higher Education Research & Development, 35*(2), 217–228. doi:10.1080/07294360.2015.1087473

Biggs, J., & Tang, C. (2011). Train-the-trainers: Implementing outcomes-based teaching and learning in Malaysian higher education. *Malaysian Journal of Learning and Instruction, 8*, 1–19.

Billot, J., Rowland, S., Carnell, B., Amundsen, C., & Evans, T. (2017). How experienced SoTL researchers develop the credibility of their work. *Teaching & Learning Inquiry, 5*(1). doi:10.20343/teachlearninqu.5.1.8

Bloch-Schulman, S., Conkling, S., Linkon, S. L., Manarin, K., & Perkins, K. (2016). Asking bigger questions: An invitation to further conversation. *Teaching & Learning Inquiry, 4*(1). doi:10.20343/teachlearninqu.4.1.12

Boshier, R. (2009). Why is the Scholarship of Teaching and Learning such a hard sell? *Higher Education Research & Development, 28*(1), 1–15. doi:10.1080/07294360802444321

Boyer, E. L. (1990). Scholarship reconsidered: Priorities of the professoriate. *Carnegie Foundation for the Advancement of Teaching.* Retrieved from https://eric.ed.gov/?id=ED326149

Breunig, M. (2017). Experientially learning and teaching in a student-directed classroom. *Journal of Experiential Education, 40*(3), 1–18. doi:10.1177/1053825917690870

Brownlee, J. (2015). Contract faculty in Canada: Using access to information requests to uncover hidden academics in Canadian universities. *Higher Education, 70*(5), 787–805. doi:10.100710734-015-9867-9

Buch, K. (2008). Faculty perceptions of SoTL at a research institution: A preliminary study. *Teaching of Psychology, 35*(4), 297–300. doi:10.1080/00986280802377149

Burman, M. E., & Kleinsasser, A. (2004). Ethical guidelines for use of student work: Moving from teaching's invisibility to inquiry's visibility in the Scholarship of Teaching and Learning. *The Journal of General Education, 53*(1), 59–79. doi:10.1353/jge.2004.0018

Chalmers, D. (2011). Progress and challenges to the recognition and reward of the Scholarship of Teaching in higher education. *Higher Education Research & Development, 30*(1), 25–38. doi:10.1080/0729 4360.2011.536970

Charbonneau, L. (2009). Congress '09- Scholarship of Teaching and Learning is not good enough. *University Affairs.* Retrieved from: www.universityaffairs.ca/margin-nbotes/tag/gary-poole

Chick, N. (2013). *Scholarship of Teaching and Learning guide.* Vanderbilt University Center for Teaching. Retrieved from http://my.vanderbilt.edu/sotl

Chick, N. (2014). "Methodologically sound" under the "big tent": An ongoing conversation. *International Journal for the Scholarship of Teaching and Learning, 8*(2), 3.

Chick, N., Cornell-Swanson, L., Lazarides, K., & Meyers, R. (2014). Reconciling apples & oranges: A constructivist SoTL writing program. *International Journal for the Scholarship of Teaching and Learning, 8*(2), 13. doi:10.20429/ijsotl.2014.080213

Chick, N. L. (Ed.). (2018). *SoTL in Action.* Sterling, VA: Stylus Publishing.

Ciccone, A., Huber, M. T., Hutchings, P., & Cambridge, B. (2009). *Exploring impact: A survey of participants in the CASTL Institutional leadership and affiliates program.* The Carnegie Foundation for the Advancement of Teaching.

Cotton, D., Miller, W., & Kneale, P. (2018). The Cinderella of academia: Is higher education pedagogic research undervalued in UK research assessment? *Studies in Higher Education, 43*(9), 1625–1636. doi :10.1080/03075079.2016.1276549

Dewar, J. M. (2008). An apology for the Scholarship of Teaching and Learning. *InSight: A Journal of Scholarly Teaching, 3,* 17-22. Retrieved from: https://files.eric.ed.gov/fulltext/EJ888405.pdf

Dobbie, D., & Robinson, I. (2008). Reorganizing higher education in the United States and Canada: The erosion of tenure and the unionization of contingent faculty. *Labor Studies Journal, 33*(2), 117–140. doi:10.1177/0160449X07301241

Dobbins, K. (2011). Personal reflections: Reflections on SoTL by a casual lecturer: Personal benefits, long-term challenges. *International Journal for the Scholarship of Teaching and Learning, 5*(2), 6. doi:10.20429/ijsotl.2011.050224

Fanghanel, J. (2012). *Being an academic.* Abingdon, UK: Routledge.

Fanghanel, J. (2013). Going public with pedagogical inquiries: SoTL as a methodology for faculty professional development. *Teaching and Learning Inquiry: The ISSOTL Journal, 1*(1), 59–70. doi:10.20343/ teachlearninqu.1.1.59

Fedoruk, L. (2017). *Ethics in the Scholarship of Teaching and Learning: Key principles and strategies for ethical practice. Taylor Institute for Teaching and Learning Guide Series.* Calgary, AB: Taylor Institute for Teaching and Learning at the University of Calgary. Retrieved from www.ucalgary.ca/ taylorinstitute/guides

Felten, P. (2013). Principles of good practice in SoTL. Teaching & learning inquiry. *The ISSOTL Journal, 1*(1), 121–125. doi:10.2979/teachlearninqu.1.1.121

Felten, P., Bagg, J., Bumbry, M., Hill, J., Hornsby, K., Pratt, M., & Weller, S. (2013). A call for expanding inclusive student engagement in SoTL. *Teaching & Learning Inquiry: The ISSOTL Journal, 1*(2), 63–74. doi:10.20343/teachlearninqu.1.2.63

Fenton, N., & Szala-Meneok, K. (2011). *Research on teaching and learning guidebook.* McMaster University Center for Leadership in Learning. Retrieved from http://cll.mcmaster.ca/resources/pdf/ redo_guidebook.pdf

Field, C., Jones, G., Stephenson, G., & Khoyestsyan, A. (2014). *The "Other" university teacher: Non-full-time instructors at Ontario universities.* Toronto: Higher Educational Quality Council of Ontario. Retrieved from http://heqco.ca/en-CA/Research%20Publications/Pages/Summary.aspx?link=145

Forgie, S. E., Yonge, O., & Luth, R. (2018). Centres for teaching and learning across Canada: What's Going On? *The Canadian Journal for the Scholarship of Teaching and Learning, 9*(1). doi:10.5206/ cjsotl-rcacea.2018.1.9

Fukuzawa, S., Vander Kloet, M., Frake-Mistak, M., Caldecott, M., & Cassidy, A. (2017, October). *SoTL aspirations: Multi-disciplinary writing groups as an entrance into the practice of SoTL for contingent instructors*. Poster presentation at the International Society for the Scholarship of Teaching and Learning, Calgary, Alberta.

Gehrke, S., & Kezar, A. (2015). Supporting non-tenure-track faculty at 4-year colleges and universities: A national study of dean's values and decisions. *Educational Policy*, *29*(6), 926–960. doi:10.1177/0895904814531651

Goldszmidt, M., Zimbrowski, E., & Weston, W. (2008). Education scholarship: It's not just a question of "degree". *Medical Teacher*, *30*(1), 34–39. doi:10.1080/01421590701754136 PMID:18278649

Gray, T., & Shandle, S. (2009). Launching or revitalizing a teaching center: Principles and portraits of practice. *Journal of Faculty Development*, *23*(2), 5–12.

Green, D. (2009). New academics' perceptions of the language of teaching and learning: Identifying and overcoming linguistic barriers. *The International Journal for Academic Development*, *14*(1), 33–45. doi:10.1080/13601440802659254

Hamilton, D. (2014). Building a culture of pedagogical enquiry: Institutional support strategies for developing the Scholarship of Teaching and Learning. *Advances in Scholarship of Teaching and Learning*, *1*(1). Retrieved from https://tlc.unisim.edu.sg/research/AdvSoTL/pdf/doug_hamliltion. Pdf

Healey, M. (2008). On discipline-based approaches to SoTL. *The International Commons, 3*(1), 2-3. Retrieved from http://www.issotl.org/newsletter.html

Healey, M. (2014). *Strategies to support staff/faculty engagement in pedagogic research (PedR) & Scholarship of Teaching and Learning (SoTL)*. Retrieved from https://www. mickhealey.co.uk/?wpdmdl=1312

Healey, M., Bradford, M., Roberts, C., & Knight, Y. (2013). Collaborative discipline-based curriculum change: Applying change academy processes at department level. *The International Journal for Academic Development*, *18*(1), 31–44. doi:10.1080/1360144X.2011.628394

Hubball, H., & Clarke, A. (2010). Diverse methodological approaches and considerations for SOTL in higher education. *The Canadian Journal for the Scholarship of Teaching and Learning*, *1*(1). doi:10.5206/cjsotl-rcacea.2010.1.2

Hubball, H., Clarke, A., & Poole, G. (2010). Ten-year reflections on mentoring SoTL in a research-intensive university. *The International Journal for Academic Development*, *15*(2), 117–129. doi:10.1080/13601441003737758

Huber, M. T., & Hutchings, P. (2005). *The advancement of learning: Building the learning commons*. San Francisco, CA: Jossey-Bass.

Huber, M. T., & Hutchings, P. (2008). Editorial: The Scholarship of Teaching and Learning in the humanities: The place—and problem—of theory. *Arts and Humanities in Higher Education, 7*(3), 227–228. doi:10.1177/1474022208094408

Hutchings, P. (2003). Competing goods: Ethical issues in the Scholarship of Teaching and Learning. *Change: The Magazine of Higher Learning*, *35*(5), 26–33. doi:10.1080/00091380309604116

Hutchings, P., Huber, M., & Ciccone, A. (2011). Feature essays: Getting there: An integrative vision of the Scholarship of Teaching and Learning. *International Journal for the Scholarship of Scholarship of Teaching and Learning, 5*(1), 31. doi:10.20429/ijsotl.2011.050131

Johnsen, H., Pacht, M., van Slyck, P., & Tsao, T. (2009). The messy teaching conversation: Toward a model of collegial reflection, exchange, and scholarship on classroom problems. *Teaching English in the Two-Year College, 37*(2), 119–136.

Kelley, B. (2008). Trading zones: Building connections to past research in the Scholarship of Teaching and Learning. *INSight: A Journal of Scholarly Teaching, 3,* 10-16.

Kelly, N., Nesbit, S., & Oliver, C. (2012). A Difficult Journey: Transitioning from STEM to SoTL. *International Journal for the Scholarship of Teaching and Learning, 6*(1). doi:10.20429/ijsotl.2012.060118

Kenny, N., & Evers, F. (2010). Responding to the challenging dilemma of faculty engagement in research on teaching and learning and disciplinary research. *Collected Essays on Learning and Teaching, 3,* 21–26. doi:10.22329/celt.v3i0.3234

Kezar, A. (2001). *Understanding and facilitating organizational change in higher education in the 21st century.* San Francisco, CA: Jossey-Bass.

Kezar, A., Gallants, T., & Lester, J. (2011). Everyday people making a difference on college campuses: The tempered grassroots leadership tactics of faculty and staff. *Studies in Higher Education, 73,* 435–460. doi:10.1353/jhe.2002.0038

Kezar, A., & Sam, C. (2013). Institutionalizing equitable policies and practices for contingent faculty. *The Journal of Higher Education, 84*(1), 56–87. doi:10.1353/jhe.2013.0002

King, H. (2004). Continuing professional development in higher education: What do academics do? *Educational Developments, 5*(4), 1–5.

Lea, M. R., & Stierer, B. (2011). Changing academic identities in changing academic workplaces: Learning from academics' everyday professional writing practices. *Teaching in Higher Education, 16*(6), 605–616. doi:10.1080/13562517.2011.560380

Lee, A., & Boud, D. (2003). Writing groups, change, and academic identity: Research development as local practice. *Studies in Higher Education, 28*(2), 187–200. doi:10.1080/0307507032000058109

Linder, K. E., Elek, E. D., & Calderon, L. (2014). SoTL and the Institutional Review Board: Considerations before navigating the application process for classroom research in higher education. *The Journal of Scholarship of Teaching and Learning, 14*(2), 1–14. doi:10.14434/josotl.v14i2.4217

Little, D., & Green, D. A. (2012). Betwixt and between: Academic developers in the margins. *The International Journal for Academic Development, 17*(3), 203–215. doi:10.1080/1360144X.2012.700895

Lock, J., Kim, B., Koh, K., & Wilcox, G. (2018). Navigating the tensions of innovative assessment and pedagogy in higher education. *The Canadian Journal for the Scholarship of Teaching and Learning, 9*(1), 1–20. doi:10.5206/cjsotl-rcacea.2018.1.8

MacLean, M., & Poole, G. (2010). An introduction to ethical considerations for novices to research in teaching and learning in Canada. *The Canadian Journal for the Scholarship of Teaching and Learning, 1*(2). doi:10.5206/cjsotl-rcacea.2010.2.7

Major, C., & Palmer, B. (2006). Reshaping teaching and learning: The transformation of faculty pedagogical content knowledge. *Higher Education: The International Journal of Higher Education Research, 51*(4), 619–647. doi:10.100710734-004-1391-2

Manarin, K., & Abrahamson, E. (2016). Troublesome knowledge of SoTL. *International Journal for the Scholarship of Teaching and Learning, 10*(2), 1–6. doi:10.20429/ijsotl.2016.100202

Marcketti, S., & Freeman, S. (2016). SoTL evidence on promotion and tenure vitas at a research university. *The Journal of Scholarship of Teaching and Learning, 16*(5), 19–31. doi:10.14434//josotl.v16i5.21152

Marquis, E., Holmes, T., Apostolou, K., Centea, D., Cockcroft, R., Knorr, K., ... Karamanis, T. (2017). SoTL Research Fellows: Collaborative pathfinding through uncertain terrain. *The Canadian Journal for the Scholarship of Teaching and Learning, 8*(3), 1–19. doi:10.5206/cjsotl-rcacea.2017.3.9

Martensson, K., Roxa, T., & Olsson, T. (2011). Developing a quality culture through the Scholarship of Teaching and Learning. Higher Education Research & Development. *Journal of Higher Education Research and Development Society of Australasia, 30*(1), 51–62. doi:10.1080/07294360.2011.536972

Mathany, C., Clow, K. M., & Aspenlieder, E. D. (2017). Exploring the role of the Scholarship of Teaching and Learning in the context of the professional identities of faculty, graduate students, and staff in higher education. *The Canadian Journal for the Scholarship of Teaching and Learning, 8*(3). doi:10.5206/cjsotl-rcacea.2017.3.10

McKinney, K. (2007). *Enhancing learning through the scholarship of teaching and learning: The challenges and joys of juggling.* Anker Publishing Co.

McKinney, K. (2012). Increasing the impact of SoTL: Two sometimes neglected opportunities. *International Journal for the Scholarship of Teaching and Learning, 6*(1). doi:10.20429/ijsotl.2012.060103

McKinney, K., & Jarvis, P. (2009). Beyond lines on the CV: Faculty applications of their Scholarship of Teaching and Learning research. *International Journal for the Scholarship of Teaching and Learning, 3*(1). doi:10.20429/ijsotl.2009.030107

Mengel, T. (2016). The Scholarship of Teaching and Learning (SoTL) at Renaissance College (University of New Brunswick): A case study of SoTL at the faculty level. *New Directions for Teaching and Learning, 2016*(146), 39–45. doi:10.1002/tl.20185

Miller-Young, J., & Yeo, M. (2015). Conceptualizing and communicating SoTL: A framework for the field. *Teaching & Learning Inquiry, 3*(2), 37–53. doi:10.20343/teachlearninqu.3.2.37

Miller-Young, J., Yeo, M., & Manarin, K. (2018). Challenges to disciplinary knowing and identity: Experiences of scholars in a SoTL development program. *International Journal for the Scholarship of Teaching and Learning, 1*(3), 1–6. doi:10.20429/ijsotl.2018.120103

Myatt, P., Gannaway, D., Chia, I., Fraser, K., & McDonald, J. (2018). Reflecting on institutional support for SoTL engagement: Developing a conceptual framework. *The International Journal for Academic Development, 23*(2), 147–160. doi:10.1080/1360144X.2017.1346511

Poole, G., Taylor, L., & Thompson, J. (2007). Using the Scholarship of Teaching and Learning at disciplinary, national, and institutional levels to strategically improve quality of post-secondary education. *International Journal for the Scholarship of Teaching and Learning, 1*(2), 3. doi:10.20429/ijsotl.2007.010203

Potter, M. K., & Wuetherick, B. (2015). Who is represented in the teaching commons?: SoTL through the lenses of arts and humanities. *The Canadian Journal for the Scholarship of Teaching and Learning, 6*(2), 2. doi:10.5206/cjsotl-rcacea.2015.2.2

Prosser, M. (2008). The Scholarship of Teaching and Learning: What is it? A Personal View. *International Journal for the Scholarship of Teaching and Learning, 2*(2). doi:10.20429/ijsotl.2008.020202

Roxa, T., & Martensson, K. (2009). Significant conversations and significant networks—Exploring the backstage of the teaching arena. *Studies in Higher Education, 34*(5), 547–559. doi:10.1080/03075070802597200

Roy, D., Borin, P., & Kustra, E. (2007). Assisting curriculum change through departmental initiatives. *New Directions for Teaching and Learning, 112*(112), 21–32. doi:10.1002/tl.295

Schuetz, P. (2002). Instructional practices of part-time and full-time faculty. *New Directions for Community Colleges, 118*(118), 39–46. doi:10.1002/cc.62

Shreeve, A. (2011). Joining the dots: The Scholarship of Teaching as part of institutional research. *Higher Education Research & Development, 30*(1), 63–74. doi:10.1080/07294360.2011.536973

Simmons, N. (2011). Mapping a mirage: Documenting the Scholarship of Teaching and Learning. *Collected Essays on Learning and Teaching, 1*, 2. doi:10.22329/celt.v1i0.3170

Simmons, N., Abrahamson, E., Deshler, J. M., Kinsington-Miller, B., Manarin, K., Moron-Garcia, S., ... Renc-Roe, J. (2013). Conflicts and configurations in a liminal space: SoTL scholars' identity development. *Teaching & Learning Inquiry, 1*(2), 9–21. doi:10.20343/teachlearninqu.1.2.9

Simmons, N., & Marquis, E. (2017). Defining the Scholarship of Teaching and Learning. *The Canadian Journal for the Scholarship of Teaching and Learning, 8*(2), 1–5. doi:10.5206/cjsotl-rcacea.2017.2.2

Simmons, N., & Taylor, K. L. (2019). Leadership for the Scholarship of Teaching and Learning: Understanding bridges and gaps in practice. *The Canadian Journal for the Scholarship of Teaching and Learning, 10*(1). doi:10.5206/cjsotl-rcacea.2019.1.7995

Stockley, D., & Balkwill, L. (2013). Raising awareness of research ethics in SoTL: The role of educational developers. *The Canadian Journal for the Scholarship of Teaching and Learning, 4*(1). doi:10.5206/cjsotl-rcacea.2013.1.7

Strober, M. (2011). *Interdisciplinary conversations: Challenging habits of thought*. Stanford, CA: Stanford University Press.

Trepanier, L. (2017). SoTL as a subfield for political science graduate programs. *Journal of Political Science Education, 13*(2), 138–151. doi:10.1080/15512169.2016.1227264

Tri-council, P. S. (1998). *Ethical conduct for research involving humans/Medical Research Council of Canada, Natural Sciences and Engineering Research Council of Canada, Social Sciences and Humanities Research Council of Canada.* Ottawa: Medical Research Council of Canada. Retrieved from http://science-catalogue.canada.ca/record=2649284~S6

Trigwell, K., Martin, E., Benjamin, J., & Prosser, M. (2000). Scholarship of teaching: A model. *Higher Education Research & Development, 19*(2), 155–168. doi:10.1080/072943600445628

Vander Kloet, M., Mistak, M., McGinn, M., Caldecott, M., Aspenlieder, E., Beres, J., ... Gill, A. (2017). Conditions of contingent instructors engaged in the Scholarship of Teaching and Learning. *The Canadian Journal for the Scholarship of Teaching and Learning, 8*(2), 2. doi:10.5206/cjsotl-rcacea.2017.2.9

Weimer, M. (2006). *Enhancing scholarly work on teaching and learning: Professional literature that makes a difference.* San Francisco, CA: Jossey-Bass.

Weller, S. (2011). New lecturers' accounts of reading higher education research. *Studies in Continuing Education, 33*(1), 93–106. doi:10.1080/0158037X.2010.516744

Weston, C. B., & McAlpine, L. (2001). Making explicit the development toward the scholarship of teaching. *New Directions for Teaching and Learning, 86*(86), 89–97. doi:10.1002/tl.19

Williams, A., Verwood, R., Beery, T., Dalton, H., McKinnon, J., Strickland, K., ... Poole, G. (2013). The power of social networks: A model for weaving the Scholarship of Teaching and Learning into institutional culture. *Teaching & Learning Inquiry, 1*(2), 49–62. doi:10.20343/teachlearninqu.1.2.49

Witman, P. D., & Richlin, L. (2007). The status of the Scholarship of Teaching and Learning in the discipline. *International Journal for the Scholarship of Teaching and Learning, 1*(1), 14. doi:10.20429/ijsotl.2007.010114

Woodhouse, R. A., & Force, K. (2010). Educational development websites: What do they tell us about how Canadian centres support the Scholarship of Teaching and Learning? *The Canadian Journal for the Scholarship of Teaching and Learning, 1*(1). doi:10.5206/cjsotl-rcacea.2010.1.4

Wuethrick, B., & Yu, S. (2016). The Canadian teaching commons: The Scholarship of Teaching and Learning in Canadian higher education. *New Directions for Teaching and Learning, 2016*(146), 23–30. doi:10.1002/tl.20183

Zibrowski, E., Weston, W., & Golszmidt, M. (2008). I don't have time: Issues of fragmentation, prioritization, and motivation for education scholarship among medical faculty. *Medical Education, 42*(9), 872–878. doi:10.1111/j.1365-2923.2008.03145.x PMID:18715484

KEY TERMS AND DEFINITIONS

Contingent Instructors: Instructors in post-secondary institutions that do not have permanent status.
Institutional Accountability Measures: Criteria for promotion in post-secondary institutions.
Institutional Culture: The collective values in a post-secondary institution that sets the priorities for macro, meso, and micro levels.

Liminal Space: The fluid, transitional location from which many scholars navigate SoTL research.

Mega-Level SoTL Networks: Inter-institutional networks that engage in a national and international dialogue on SoTL.

Reflexivity: The inter-relationship between variables so that a clear bi-directional cause and effect cannot be determined.

Scholarly Identity: The meaning researchers attach to the roles and tasks they perform. Often strongly tied to disciplinary identity but can be redefined depending on the context in which one is working.

Chapter 20

Exploring the Impact of SoTL on Day-to-Day Learning and Teaching:
A Conceptual Framework for Professional Development and Quality Improvement

Andrea Rose Carr
https://orcid.org/0000-0001-8201-7890
University of Tasmania, Australia

Jo-Anne Kelder
https://orcid.org/0000-0002-8618-0537
University of Tasmania, Australia

Joseph Crawford
https://orcid.org/0000-0002-2191-6216
University of Tasmania, Australia

ABSTRACT

The Curriculum Evaluation Research (CER) Framework was developed as a response to increasing scrutiny and expectations of the higher education sector, including legislated standards for curriculum and professional teachers that explicitly require a systematic and comprehensive approach to evaluating curriculum. The CER Framework is designed to facilitate a scholarly environment to drive and assure the quality of a curriculum and the capabilities of its teaching team. It stems from a synthesis of teacher as action researcher (TAAR), quality improvement (QI), quality assurance (QA), and the Scholarship of Teaching and Learning (SoTL) applied to the curriculum as it is designed, taught, and revised. In this chapter, the implementation of the CER Framework to the University College is reviewed and evaluated. The University College is an organisational unit comprises approximately 600 students and 80 staff. This chapter includes a reflection on the barriers and enablers of implementing the CER Framework.

DOI: 10.4018/978-1-7998-2212-7.ch020

INTRODUCTION

Globally, universities are facing scrutiny in relation to the quality of educational services they provide and outcomes for students. The higher education sector presents a radically evolving education market characterised by competition, efficiency dividends, and transformation towards mass education (Leathwood & Phillips, 2000). In the United Kingdom, a National Committee of Inquiry into Higher Education (The Dearing Report: NCIHE, 1997) articulated a 20-year vision for a learning society underpinned by teaching, scholarship, and research. In Australia, the Department of Education, Employment, and Workplace Relations commissioned a similar review (Bradley et al., 2008) into higher education, which articulated sector-wide limitations related to assurance of quality in learning and teaching practice.

Beyond the challenge of assurance of quality is the need to demonstrate continuous development of academic staff capabilities in learning and teaching. For example, the OECD (2008) recognised and praised the New Zealand higher education staff professional development strategy that enabled effective responses to increasing diversity via larger international enrolments. In a UK study ($n = 2,649$ staff), Knight et al. (2008) highlight that professional development capability, including teaching and learning skill, is of growing concern within the higher education setting.

This chapter presents a case study of one response to Australian regulatory requirements for scholarship and expectations that institutions and their teaching staff demonstrate continuous improvement of curriculum (here referring to a program of study leading to an award, for example a Diploma of Business Studies, Bachelor of Music, Master of Information Systems). Specifically, the *Higher Education Standards Framework* (HES Framework) 2015, includes standards specifically referring to scholarship, supported by a *Guidance Note: Scholarship* (TEQSA, 2018) to articulate requirements for an institution to support and resource a "scholarly environment" and for all teaching staff to be actively engaged in scholarship related to the curriculum.

We begin with an overview of the Australian higher education sector within which we situate this case study. We articulate two themes: *curriculum evaluation* and *professional development of higher education teachers*. We then introduce the Curriculum Evaluation Research (CER) Framework, adopted by a number of teaching teams within the higher education sector across Australia. This has enabled a holistic approach to the wide range of institutional issues in relation to quality of teaching and learning. Curriculum evaluation is presented from three quality orientations: Quality Improvement (QI), Quality Assurance (QA) and Scholarship of Teaching and Learning (SoTL)—a formulation underpinning the CER Framework from its inception (Kelder & Carr, 2016). Conceptually, the CER Framework provides a way to organize for the integration and alignment of scholarship, quality improvement and quality assurance with professional development. Professional development of teachers in the higher education sector is presented in the context of viewing Teachers As Action Researchers (TAAR: Laurillard, 2008), specifically addressing professional development opportunities for staff identified as part of the implementation of the CER Framework. By providing a way of synthesizing the two themes, the CER Framework can be used to facilitate a collaborative, teaching team-based practice of iterative cycles of activity, guided by three orientations to quality over the life cycle of a curriculum and highlighting opportunities for informal and formal professional development.

We examine the CER Framework as a way to integrate SoTL into the day-to-day learning and teaching activities, including professional development. Next, we discuss the key learnings with a focus on how universities can use scholarship to simultaneously engage staff in curriculum evaluation and ongoing professional development that compasses quality improvement and assurance. We ask three questions within the context of a case study of an organisational unit of the University of Tasmania, the University College:

1.   How effectively has the CER framework been implemented, and what were the implementation enablers and inhibitors?
2.   What types of natural data are available for QI, QA, and SoTL analysis from day-to-day curriculum delivery with the CER framework?
3.   How can the CER framework be used to simultaneously facilitate professional development for scholarship *and* establish curriculum evaluation (continuous cycles of action research to improve curriculum and teaching)?

CONTEXT

Australian Higher Education

The landscape in Australia has evolved substantially to respond to market pressures and constantly evolving current and future student needs. In the Australian higher education context, the Tertiary Education Quality and Standards Authority (TEQSA) was established with a federal government mandate and responsibility for ensuring quality assurance in Australian higher education through the *Tertiary Education Quality and Standards Agency Act 2011* (TEQSA, 2017). The *Higher Education Standards Framework* (HES Framework) *2015* is the legislative instrument that prescribes standards for higher education institutions (HEIs). TEQSA monitors self-accrediting higher education providers (both universities and private higher education providers) for their compliance and progress towards the standards highlighted in the HES Framework.

The HES Framework includes a minimum standard for higher education institutions in assuring continuous evaluation that informs ongoing curriculum design, development, and delivery. The HES Framework mandates a planned approach to regularly and comprehensively review curriculum; its focus is whole-of-curriculum, referred to as the *course* (program of tertiary study leading to an award diploma or degree). Guidance on the regulator's expectations are set out in the *TEQSA Guidance Note: Scholarship*, including,

that all academic staff are active in scholarship that informs their teaching ... [and] ... teaching staff:

• are engaged in scholarship (which may include research) that is directly relevant to informing both the content and methods of their teaching

• keep up to date with developments in the field of education or discipline in which they teach

• have an informed and advanced understanding of the field and/or how it is taught, learned and applied in practice. (TEQSA, 2018, p. 3)

During an HEI audit cycle, TEQSA will look for evidence of a "scholarly environment" and "culture as the context in which curriculum is designed, delivered, revised and assured", across the institution and by individual teachers. Scholarship is mandated by the HES Framework as a method of improving professional practice from academics through either individual-level activities (e.g., personal professional development) or whole-of-institution activities (e.g., policy frameworks and staff development) (TEQSA, 2018).

A culture of continuing scholarship is a fundamental characteristic of higher education. Failure to undertake scholarship, both by individual staff and across a provider's fields of education, has a number of predictable and unacceptable consequences. (TEQSA 2018, p.4)

Scholarship is inextricably linked to quality. TEQSA's aim is to assure that, overall, teachers employed by higher education providers are active in scholarship and able to demonstrate they have both disciplinary and pedagogical knowledge that is current and relevant, underpinned by evaluation and reflection, to produce contemporary and effective curricula. Applied to both institutions and individual teachers, the requirement for scholarship can be viewed as an opportunity to structure curriculum-related activities to provide all members of a teaching team with a cohesive approach to scholarship.

Curriculum Evaluation

The United Kingdom has "two consistent approaches" to curriculum evaluation (Leathwood & Phillips, 2000, p. 315): quality assurance (QA) and teacher as action researcher (TAAR: Kember, 2000; McNiff & Whitehead, 2012). More broadly, there are also two other forms of curriculum evaluation that occur: quality improvement (QI) and Scholarship of Teaching and Learning (SoTL). QA is supported by activities such as course monitoring, peer review, benchmarking, and routine solicited student feedback; it enables cross-institutional benchmarking to assess performance (Coates, 2006; Westernheijden et al., 2007). TAAR originates in the school sector and is supported by reflective pedagogical practice, pursuing a research agenda, and applying improvement at the classroom level (Laurillard, 2008). QI, in the UK context referred to as Quality Enhancement (QE), is the ability to continuously improve on existing performance, using existing performance as a baseline with which to improve on (Newton, 1997). SoTL is underpinned by three broad rationales: professionalism, pragmatism, and policy (Shulman, 2001). Key to curriculum evaluation is pragmatism, that is engaging in activities to ensure that learning and teaching practice is improving.

Each of these models (TAAR, QI, QA, SoTL) have their benefits. For example, the QA provides accessible systems to evaluate key indicators such as cost per student and completion rates (Johnes & Taylor, 1990). It enables and informs responses to issues as they emerge, and uses a quality improvement framework to identify best practice for responding to challenges. The TAAR model's strength is its contextualisation within environments unconstrained by universality but focused on situational and temporal quality improvements in the classroom (Looi Chng & Coombs, 2004). Teachers with a TAAR mindset focus on interrogating the boundaries between the known and unknown (Rath, 2002). QI adopts many of the foundations of TAAR, with a focus on incremental improvement in courses and units by evaluating existing practice and experimenting with new practice.

Contrast these with the broader agenda of SoTL, where the goal is to develop new knowledge on better teaching and learning pedagogies and practice. Categorised in his seminal work by Boyer (1990), SoTL has four forms: teaching, integration, application of knowledge, and discovery. Teaching quality initiatives in the 1990s in Australia primarily emphasised institution-level outcomes, with low regard for teaching quality improvement compared to disciplinary research performance (Chalmers, 2010). However, throughout the almost two decades of the new millennium, the tone changed towards recognition of teaching performance and, subsequently, the ability to demonstrate learning and teaching quality (Chalmers, 2007). Similar conversations emerged in the UK (Gosling, 2004) and informed a global SoTL movement focused on curriculum innovation, evaluation, and improvement.

While prompting useful practices and offering methods for the assurance of quality, the models neglect key areas of curriculum evaluation. QA focuses on broad sweeping course- and institution-level improvement that fails to consider the unique contexts that exist in certain environments. TAAR is highly contextual, strengthened by its ability to enable teacher self-development and continuous improvement through evaluation of unit- and class-level change, but lacks the broad overview. QI is similar in its contextual and incremental focus, also lacking broader scope. SoTL – scholarship grounded in the curriculum and its teachers – is integrally connected to the teacher's motivation and capability, and typically practiced by a minority of academics, rarely by teaching teams.

The global SoTL movement has raised the status of scholarship within HEIs (for example, in the University of Tasmania, via institutional grants and awards programs and demonstrated leadership and impact within learning and teaching as a requirement for promotion). Significantly, in the Australian context, the HES Framework, overseen by the regulatory body TEQSA, has explicitly named and mandated scholarship in the standards and explained the implications for HEIs and their accreditation status. However the barriers to effectively embedding scholarship into teaching practices of teaching teams are significant and HEIs are yet to achieve the scholarly environment that encompasses all teachers and all curriculum.

Professional Development for Curriculum Evaluation

Professional development of academics is an underdeveloped field of inquiry in higher education. Growing interest is emerging in the interplay between professional development, technology, pedagogy, and cognitive content (Rienties et al., 2013). Professional development for academics often takes the form of research-based quality improvement to curriculum, developing the skills of the academic at the same time. The goals of professional development can include enhancing student learning, enhancing participation, curriculum innovation, responding to the changing nature of work, and enabling efficiency and effectiveness through flexibility (Edwards & Nicoll, 2006). Professional development occurs in a range of activities and contexts, including individual critical reflection, peer review, and education training.

A key goal of professional development is to enable academics to develop themselves and continuously improve their teaching. Many make the case for professionalisation (e.g. Gornitzka & Larsen, 2004; Lueddeke, 2003) and note the political tensions and anxiety accompanying this proposition (Lee & McWilliam, 2009). The rationale for professionalisation stems from the assumption that initial training during a PhD may be temporarily sufficient but not adequate in the longer term in complex contemporary academies (Boud & Brew, 2013). A key enabler of professional development in the Australian higher education context is set out in the TEQSA Standards and *Guidance Note: Scholarship*, that mandates all higher education providers undertake and support activity and continuing teacher development (TEQSA, 2018).

The practice of professional development is facilitated within the CER Framework, with impact on quality *because* it is done in the context of collaboration by a teaching team focused on their common curriculum. A course-wide and course-long research plan, aligned to an evaluation plan, can be used to identify scholarship capabilities. Alongside this, a scholarly environment and routine analysis of curriculum and teaching data will be,

... informed by current ideas for teaching the subject/discipline, such as improved pedagogies, learning processes, curricula, academic policies, and learning materials by and trained in advanced practices ... [and] ... exploring, testing, practising, and communicating understanding of what practices are most effective in the context of the discipline (pedagogical content knowledge). (TEQSA, 2018, p. 8)

CURRICULUM EVALUATION RESEARCH (CER) FRAMEWORK

Theory

The CER Framework (Kelder & Carr, 2017) takes three decision-making orientations (QI, QA, and SoTL) and synthesises these into one cohesive framework for a teaching team to implement evidence-based innovation and continuous improvement of their curriculum design and delivery. The CER Framework is a conceptual approach to finding and exploiting the intersections between different models for curriculum evaluation that compasses scholarship and transcends the limitations of independently applying a single model. The Framework focuses on enhancing student learning through activating the teaching team to understand themselves and their role in curriculum evaluation through the lens of *Teachers As Action Researchers* (TAAR). Teaching teams collectively plan, do, and review action research cycles, applied to the whole course curriculum, such that QI, QA and SoTL activities are integrated and aligned, linked and leveraged.

This is a shift from siloed activity (e.g. individual academics incrementally changing their units for quality improvement; external staff appointed to report course standards via external benchmarking and internal monitoring for quality assurance) *to* the whole of a teaching team engaged in SoTL research

Table 1. Process and objectives of curriculum evaluation models

Evaluation	Process and Objective
CER Framework	Synthesis of the SoTL, QA, QI, and TAAR models: a strategic enabler of planned, routine data collection and analysis to inform decision making on curriculum and teaching, through teaching teams focused on three orientations to quality (QI, QA, and SoTL).
Scholarship of Teaching and Learning (SoTL)	A planned and implemented research program to drive curriculum and teaching quality, using ethics-approved procedures for data collection and analysis with peer-reviewed dissemination of findings.
Quality assurance (QA)	A planned and implemented evaluation program to demonstrate level of quality. Reporting key course and institutional outcomes using measurement against required metrics and cross-institution benchmarking against standards.
Quality improvement (QI)	Continuous, incremental quality improvement processes applied to curriculum at the micro-level (unit), with reference to meso-level (course). Focus is evaluation of problems identified and addressed; opportunities to innovate curriculum; outcomes inform next iteration of improvement.
Teacher as Action Researcher (TAAR)	Continuous, incremental quality improvement of curriculum (micro- and meso- level), with potential to report against standards (QA) and also for broader impact (SoTL). Active and targeted professional development to enhance skills and knowledge relevant to curriculum.

that is relevant to the discipline/field being taught by the curriculum and linked to advances in practice (TEQSA, 2018).

The value of this approach (particularly in the Australian context) is the ability to go beyond government and sector minimums of course level quality assurance to enable teaching teams to plan collaborative effort at micro-level (e.g. unit of a course curriculum), meso-level (e.g. whole of course curriculum), and macro-level (e.g. cross-institutional) to foster relevance, currency, efficiency, and innovation of their curriculum. And thus, is an answer to Bateman's (2019) "compliance rock and quality hard place" argument.

Underpinning the CER Framework is recognition that each curriculum has a lifecycle and that there are different orientations towards measuring outcomes, impact, and effectiveness of curricula through the duration of design and delivery (Phillips et al., 2012). The lifecycle of curriculum is characterised by design, delivery and review for renewal or transformation. Within the Australian context, the HES Framework expects that any curriculum being delivered must have an ongoing and planned evaluation cycle. In new curricula, data is collected and analysed for QI. When the curriculum is mature, the focus turns to QA (e.g., external reporting against standards with defined metrics). When a curriculum lifecycle has reached maturity (no major changes needed), attention can be turned to considering its impact on student learning and student outcomes and disseminating findings (SoTL).

In the development of the CER Framework, we considered how one framework could be adaptable and responsive enough to be able to collect data for a course curriculum that is useful and relevant at different stages of its lifecycle. That is, data collected should be usable beyond QI and QA purposes to include ethically-approved analysis that can be disseminated via peer-reviewed publication of findings (SoTL). This highlights the concept of leveraging the outcomes of routine QI activities into QA and SOTL activities and outcomes. A design-based approach to curriculum evaluation and research can simplify the data collection and analysis required, by ensuring alignment of educational research questions with questions asked by external accreditation agents and questions asked by a teachers of their units and the course as a whole.

Practice

The CER Framework identifies the connected nature of QI, QA, and SoTL through their iterative cycles of quality activities. Just as QI and QA cycles are governed by an evaluation plan (e.g., schedule of annual reports against defined metrics, peer review of assessment for designated units, and benchmarking against similar curriculum), so the SoTL cycle is governed by a research plan (which underpins the ethics application).

The cyclic nature of QI, QA, and SOTL activities means it is possible (and efficient) to align the evaluation plan with the research plan. The coordination of three differently-oriented quality activities can link and leverage the outputs of each. This can be especially effective in the context of a teaching team working as a Community of Practice and focused on quality enhancement of a course. Individual teaching team members can prioritise different orientations in relation to their teaching and curriculum, but overall the team effort will be coordinated to ensure all three kinds of quality activities are supported (see Figure 1).

A collective understanding that the same data (natural data) is collected once, but available for three objectives can be used to decide each teaching team member's participation levels and scope, with higher levels of participation encouraged as staff members are motivated and develop their capabilities.

Figure 1. CER framework as axCycle of quality activities driven by TAAR
(Acuna & Kelder 2019)

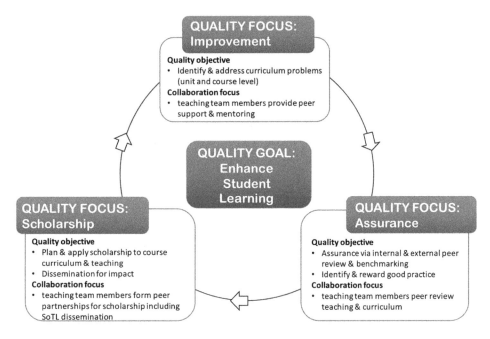

- All teaching team members will engage with routinely with QI activities.
- Some (more senior) members will be responsible for QA activities (scheduled activities in evaluation plan).
- Some (e.g., Course Coordinator, Ethics Chief Investigator) will lead SoTL activities (scheduled activities in research plan) and build a scholarly culture where teachers are motivated and supported to develop their capabilities in scholarship, including participating in data analysis and writing activities.

TAAR is critical to successful practice and the ability of a teaching team to embed the CER Framework and adopt the essential activities into their routine teaching practice and relationships is facilitated by key supporting resources (Figure 2). Two types of resources are normally readily accessible to the teaching team: 1) infrastructure provided by any higher education institution: governance instruments (e.g., research management and curriculum evaluation policies) and 2) the online learning management system (LMS).

The CER Framework was first implemented in a fully online course in the University of Tasmania's Faculty of Health. The program of scholarship was integral to the development and evaluation of the course, producing 20 scholarly outputs in two years. Subsequently, this initiative has garnered much interest with a range of invited presentations and workshops being conducted nationally (e.g., HECQ Forum, University of Melbourne, Swinburne University of Technology, University of South Australia, William Angliss Institute) and institutionally (e.g., Research Week Workshops, Faculty of Education). In 2018 the researchers were invited to work with the Western Australian Network for Dissemination (WAND) group of five universities to advise on, and implement curriculum evaluation and research (see website https://www.wand.edu.au/2018-wand-sotl-project). In 2019, the Australian Council of Deans

Figure 2. CER framework essentials
(adapted from Kelder et al., 2017)

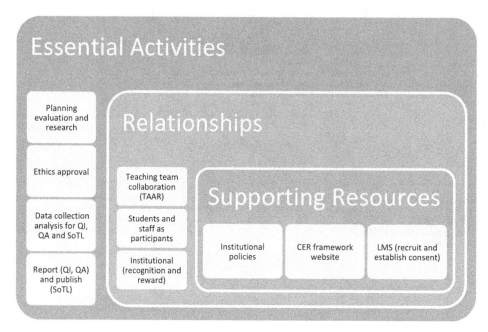

of Science awarded a joint fellowship to adapt the CER framework for STEM disciplines in Australian higher education institutions. The CER Framework and associated activity has been presented at national and international conferences and has produced and informed 14 scholarly outputs.

Enabling Resources

The authors have developed a suite of resources specifically to support the adoption and implementation of the CER Framework (see http://www.utas.edu.au/college/cer-framework). These resources have been developed and used in the context of teaching team activities and relationships with each other and their students (see Figure 2).

The centerpiece resource is an example ethics application to approve course-wide and course-life evaluation and research. This example ethics application includes procedures on how the institution's LMS is used to establish participant consent for their natural data (data generated naturally during curriculum delivery and assessment of learning) to be used for research purposes. Recognition and professional development of teaching teams is a key enabler of using the resources successfully.

The example ethics application is designed to establish ethical approval for a teaching team to establish a routine data collection regime for an entire course and the duration of its delivery. It provides a rich longitudinal data set to address a range of questions under the QI, QA, SoTL, and/or TAAR orientations and to publish findings. These include:

- identifying antecedents of student learning outcomes to inform quality improvement and assurance decisions,
- creating baseline data for key quality assurance metrics,

- enabling measurement of incremental changes in metrics of quality, student knowledge, skills, and capabilities over time,
- measuring course design and delivery effectiveness, and
- measuring the changes in student outcomes across courses and time.

An ethics application based on the life cycle of a course (typically 5 to 7 years) provides a foundation for planned curriculum evaluation that can be strategically leveraged for scholarship, including dissemination by publication. The protocols for data management protects all stakeholders and ensures scholarship is relevant to improving and assuring the curriculum. The example ethics application has been used as a basis for several applications to the University of Tasmania Social Sciences Human Research Ethics Committee (SSHREC), including an application by the University College for all their courses to be covered under a single application.

Applications for research into a course for its duration need to address individual institutional requisites. We recommend our practice of proactively engaging in early conversations with the Chair of the SSHREC to ensure coverage of all key areas given the scale and scope of the research plan. Our SSHREC had a significant focus on documenting a step-by-step procedure with ethical considerations at each step.

The learning management system (LMS) used in our institution is branded My Learning Online (MyLO) and plays a key role in the implementation of SoTL under the CER Framework. A "one stop shop" to connect with participants of research (students, staff, key stakeholders), it also provides a space to gather consent from participants, engage with students as partners in research/scholarship, and communicate research outcomes.

Teaching Teams

Teaching teams are groups of academics that typically operate within the same course, discipline, or (as for the University College) cross-disciplinary curricula. In the context of CER, a teaching team typically begins with a group of academics (and relevant professional/administrative staff) that are working within a course. A course-level research and evaluation plan must be developed that provides high-level guidance for the team (Carr et al., 2014). A broad strategic level of leadership (e.g., shared or distributed leadership: Pearce & Conger, 2002; Spillane, 2005), needs to be underpinned by a genuine focus on developing authentic leader behaviors including awareness, sincerity, balanced processing, a positive moral perspective, and informal influence (see Crawford et al., 2019).

Recognition of the fluidity of leaders and followers within a teaching team is important, insofar as an individual leader on one evaluation project may be a follower in another evaluation project (Crawford et al., 2018). In addition to project leaders and project team members, the membership of the group should also be fluid (like a Community of Practice: Johnson, 2001). Membership of the TAAR team may be initially restricted to those involved in a course or unit of study but may expand temporarily to enable expert advice on specific pedagogies and methodologies. The aim of a a team is to enable improved quality and teaching through development of teachers and curriculum innovation.

In establishing a TAAR team, one should consider its purpose, enable a physical or virtual place to situate, define codes of conduct, and specify roles (including subgroup establishment) (Palloff & Pratt, 1999). TAAR teams enable learning and development of members within a social and physical context of real-world problems through a constructivist lens (Squire & Johnson, 2000; Wenger, 2010). Enabling followers (and team members) within the team to exhibit positive organisational engagement is critical

Figure 3. Establishing a TAAR-CER teaching team

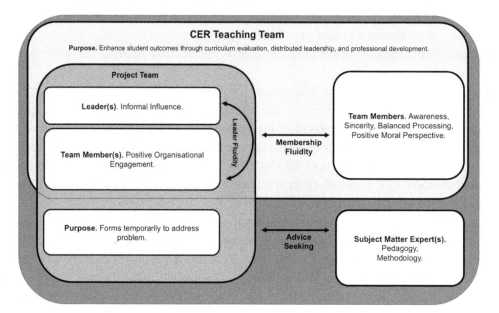

to ensuring followers contribute actively and authentically to the team and its outcomes (Crawford et al., 2018). See Figure 3.

Ethics protocols can be developed in advance of a series of TAAR-style tasks with the opportunity to embed peer review; use benchmark data from previous TAAR programs; establish a supportive teaching team to enable effective evaluation; and include the support of a Data Manager when there is a need for re-identifiable data that can be cross-matched, rather than anonymous aggregated data. Likewise, incremental changes made through a professional development-focused project within the CER Framework can enable future practice improvements, future longitudinal studies, and demonstrable evidence of quality improvement.

The CER Framework is intended to provide a scholarly environment that facilitates building staff capability and embedding practices to both assure quality and measure the impact of curriculum for student learning. The CER Framework, under the title *"Everyday Scholarship Engaging Every Teacher"* was named a finalist in the 2019 Australasian Academic Development Good Practice Awards, based on various implementations across seven years.

In 2013-2014, the CER Framework was developed in the context of a multi-disciplinary team including academic teaching staff from the fields of education, neuroscience, nursing, speech pathology and psychology, clinicians, student advisors, and professional staff members. In the initial semesters of course delivery, curriculum development occurred in a "just in time" space. A collegial system of team-based peer review was established to ensure constructively aligned curricula both within and across units. It proved to be an efficient, inclusive and opportunistic approach to integrate processes for quality assurance and improvement with ongoing curricula development. This course-wide framework was an adaptation of the Peer Assisted Teaching Scheme (PATS: Carbone, 2014). The original mentor-mentee approach, which aimed to reinvigorate and remediate underperforming courses and units, was reframed as a whole-of-team, collaborative mentoring initiative for quality assurance and improvement of curricula. This collegial, collaborative approach supported the professional growth of staff that, in turn, resulted in positive student learning experiences for students. The course received multiple institutional and national awards.

CASE STUDY AND METHODOLOGY

This chapter adopts a case study methodology (e.g., Houghton et al., 2013) to explore the integration of the CER Framework into the University College context, including the resources that best enabled such integration. This case study will explore the role that the CER Framework plays in establishing opportunities for scholarly output through a planned approach to SoTL. During the process of day-to-day curriculum delivery, there is a wealth of natural data available for carefully considered reflection and scholarly output. Natural data is the data generated by students during their studies and by staff in the process of developing and delivering curricula and assessing student learning (e.g., assessment tasks, feedback, peer review: Kelder et al., 2017).

University College

University College is a teaching-intensive academic unit of the University of Tasmania, offering sub-bachelor qualifications that are industry-informed and employability-focused. They also function as a progressive pathway to University of Tasmania bachelor degrees offered across the University. University College offers a range of innovative and flexible preparation programs of study which cater to students who often believe higher education is out of their reach. These programs provide accredited qualifications, with specific skills and knowledge designed to connect graduates into employment in local Tasmanian industries. While many University College academic staff have master and doctoral-level qualifications, others are industry experts, bringing real-world expertise to the classroom. University College is committed to employing teaching staff who have strong personal links and extensive practical experience of employment within the industry sector targeted by a course program (and the focus of the specific units (subjects) they teach). In recognition that people offered teaching-focused positions on the basis of strong industry knowledge and skills will rarely have training or qualifications in higher education delivery, a team of curriculum designers, online pedagogues, educational developers, and technicians are employed to provide pedagogical and design support in curriculum design and delivery to all teaching-focused staff.

University College's practice-based pedagogy draws upon an outcome-based education model and is informed by purposefully designed work-integrated and experiential learning approaches (e.g., Jackson, 2015; Kolb & Kolb, 2005). The model of experiential education focusses on two core components, "the experience" and "the practice". It exposes students to key practitioner elements informed by academic principles and industry knowledge; underpins strong theoretical and practice-based knowledge; and delivers opportunities for students to develop a range of skills and employment capabilities.

The process for implementation of the CER Framework began with adapting the foundational support resources developed as an outcome of a prior implementation of the CER Framework: institutional policies on research and curriculum management, development of course-wide and course-long ethics application, and setting up an online place on the institutional learning management system (LMS) for student and staff recruitment and consent to participate in the research.

Table 2. Policies informing curriculum evaluation design

Policy	Content Relevant to Evaluation	Evaluation Type
Course management	Design, redesign, performance monitoring, management representing a typical QA approach based on key metrics.	QA
Course advisory	Provision of external and internal expertise for monitoring and evaluating a course's currency and future readiness.	QA
Course review	Mandating a formal annual course review process using collected data and available data (e.g., student evaluations, Australia-wide graduate surveys).	QA
Student evaluation survey	Procedure for collection and use of an institutionally mandated student evaluation survey for every unit of study delivered.	QA, QI
Learning and teaching evaluation	Documenting a variety of formative and summative evaluation options with a focus on continuous improvement at the staff-level.	TAAR, QI
Quality management	Establishes a framework for continuous improvement leveraging OADRI (Objectives, Approach, Deployment, Results, and Improvement).	QA, QI
Curriculum Reviews	Procedure for conducting any level of review (unit; course).	QA, QI
Surveys	Conducted for internal quality assurance (with students and/or staff).	QA, QI
Data management	Ownership, collection, management, and storage of research data	No reference to SoTL research data.
Research ethics	Identifies ethical requirements of research.	
Responsible conduct of research	Identifies responsible conduct components of the Australian National Code.	

Policies and Procedures

The CER Framework was designed to enable compliance with institutional policies and procedures on research and curriculum management as well as those designed for learning and teaching quality assurance. The multiplicity of policies and procedures identified (see Table 2) was a significant challenge for a coherent and integrated approach to curriculum evaluation and Teachers as Action Researchers (TAAR) undertaking scholarship.

TEQSA (2018) provides guidance for scholarship, noting that it can be characterised as individual activity (e.g. teacher as action researcher) or whole of institution (e.g. quality assurance and quality improvement). According to TEQSA (2018), a successful culture of scholarship is an integral support mechanism for learning and teaching, and includes: a) currency of ideas and issues, b) informing current teaching practice (e.g., pedagogy, activities, policies, and curriculum), c) engagement in evaluation and reflection of teaching and learning for improvement, d) communication across scholars in relevant fields, e) fostering student learning and, f) exploring, implementing, and communicating the most effective learning and teaching practice in specific discipline contexts.

In summary, the sheer number and associated workload generated by institutional policies and procedures make it difficult for teaching staff to have a integrated and coherent approach to curriculum evaluation. The CER Framework is deliberately designed to guide planning for curriculum evaluation that integrates meeting requirements with meaningful activities that inform curriculum and teaching practice.

Learning Management System (LMS)

The University of Tasmania uses a proprietary LMS, branded MyLO, that provides students a single entry to their course workload via an individual list of links to their enrolled units of study. These units of study each have their own nested webpage within the platform that includes unit information, learning activities (often organised by weeks or modules), assessment information, discussion boards, and the ability to submit assignments and ask questions. Outside of enrolled course-based units, students are often automatically enrolled in a suite of non-award units designed to support their learning (e.g., Getting Started in MyLO, Academic Integrity, Work Health and Safety, ResumePLUS, Academic and Study Skills Development, etc.). The University College used the MyLO functionality to develop a non-award, all-year instance on the LMS that extends beyond the time-limited boundaries of units and courses. It is named the University College *Research Room*. All students in the University College and all staff are given access to the *Research Room* using the enrolment function. The purpose of the *Research Room* is to:

- provide information about the process of participation (information sheet),
- invite participation and enable consent changes (online form),
- provide ongoing updates on the research via interim deidentified whole-of-course College reports, and
- enable future research project invitations to be added within the *Research Room* navigation.

The ability to communicate with students through the *Research Room* is an important enabler of the implementation of the CER Framework and scholarship activity. However, another key enabler is to engage students as participants and to build relationships and communication channels that foster a sense of partnership. Continuing communication, via email, in class, and within online unit offerings, outlining the research project and regular updates to students to either provide their consent to participate or remove their consent ensures the ethical implementation of the project.

Natural Data

Natural data is data which is generated by staff and students during the design, development and delivery of curriculum. The CER Framework's ability to collect and store data is only limited by what an institution's ethics committee will approve. Within the University College context, approved data includes all student submissions for assessment, student demographic, outcomes and satisfaction data, teacher, unit, and course data. There are also different levels of analysis (micro, meso, and macro) approved (Walls et al., 2018). These include, for example, individual, dyad, groups/teams, units of study, cohorts, courses, and institution-wide.

The role of analysis in "big data" analytics applications applied to learning and teaching is the ability to understand the individual student outcomes and interactions with different factors. The role of such big data is to facilitate an evidence-based approach to higher education reform activities and enable learning and teaching improvements (Siemens & Long, 2011). Within the CER Framework, we offer some suggestions for potentially useful data to be collected from each unit that can be analysed to inform improvement and validation of curriculum that achieves goals for students' experiences and outcomes of learning.

Table 3. Units of analysis and data sets

Unit of Analysis	Examples of Data
Students	Demographic, capability and behavioral assessments, grades, enrolment pathway, and ratings of teacher, units, and course.
Teachers	Delivery methods, preparation types, demographic, capability and behavioral assessments (survey, peer review), and critical reflections.
Units of study	Institutional survey evaluations, enrolment numbers, methods of assessment, intended learning outcomes, attrition, failure rates, grade averages, trends.
Assessments	Submission, assessment documents, grades, teacher feedback, and whether the student reviewed the feedback.
Courses	Attrition, turnover, aggregated grades, aggregated student and staff evaluations, employment, and future salaries.

Ethics

Of the three foundational resources that support the implementation of the CER Framework, developing the example ethics application for the scope and scale of data to be collected was complex. The *Australian National Statement for Ethical Conduct of Research 2007* (updated May 2015) was consulted as the governing Code for Ethics in Australian research. For the implementation of the CER Framework, the researchers used the example ethics application resource for course curriculum (developed from prior implementations of the CER Framework) as the basis for our application to cover all courses in University College. We sought to define the planned procedure and carefully consider the implication of each component. Our approved ethics application sets out the research plan, the aims of the project, selection and recruitment of participants, monitoring and management of data, reporting compliance, and a suite of information sheets, consent documentation, and other attachments. The final version of the ethics application has been formatted as an example that can serve as a basis for researchers to apply the CER Framework to their institutions (particularly within the Australian context).

Our institution's ethics committee required statements of ethical commitments and procedures about data management, conflicts of interest, and coercion risks. Data management was complicated by the need to be able to deidentify data at the end of each teaching period and be able to match with existing data within a dataset. For example, a student participating in study period 1 would have their natural data added to the database in a deidentified manner. At the end of study period 2 (assuming a student has not withdrawn consent), the data is collected, matched, deidentified, and incorporated into the database.

During this process, it is necessary to ensure that the evaluation and research team (which includes some staff or students with data) could not identify student and staff participants. An individual with no teaching responsibility is formally allocated the role of Data Manager to ensure this process is fulfilled effectively and confidentially. Conflicts of interest and coercion could exist in scenarios where the Head of School has direct access to identifiable evaluation data that could highlight grounds for performance review or worse. Likewise, conflicts of interest could occur where a lecturer can identify their students (particularly those who gave negative feedback, reviews, etc.), or where a student felt they had to participate because of their lecturer's involvement. In fact, these were not difficult obstacles to overcome and should not present a serious barrier to implementing an effective method of evaluating curriculum through research that is overseen at the level of Institution, College/Faculty, School or Discipline.

Teaching Team

The University College teaching teams (as TAAR teams) for each course are still forming and formulating action research projects. For example, one team is currently evaluating the ability of survey tools to measure behavioral change across short terms (10 weeks); seeking to enable effective quality assurance through assuring that intended learning outcomes with a behavioral focus are being achieved; and enabling quality improvement by considering how such evidence can inform better practice. Within 12 months, University College TAAR teaching teams presented on five projects at the University of Tasmania's peer-reviewed *Teaching Matters* conference in 2019. Topics included: Assessment for Learning, Blended and Flipped Curriculum Approaches, Portfolios of Practice and, Leadership. Team members more experienced in scholarship have presented at national and international higher education conferences (e.g., HERDSA 2018 and 2019, WACE 2019).

The key challenge with establishing a teaching team to undertake evaluation and research is to empower all members to feel capable of presenting an idea for an innovation or new evaluation area for further inquiry. Fluid team membership enables positive outcomes for allowing individuals with temporally busy loads (e.g., busy during parts of terms and semesters) to withdraw or not participate from a project but reengage with or propose a future project. It also allows individuals to participate in activities that support their professional development.

DISCUSSION

Thus far, we have articulated a framework and connected it to both curriculum evaluation for quality and professional development for staff. A cohesive and fluid evaluation and research team enabled a highly effective process for both professional development and curriculum evaluation and research. The key underpinning of the CER Framework is the ability to respond to a wide range of TAAR, QI, QA, and SoTL needs within the one setting. The next section summarizes the enablers and barriers identified during the various implementations, while highlighting the natural data that can be collected and the kinds of questions that can be addressed.

Enablers

The key enablers included top management team support, teaching team support, and institutional analysis (situational awareness).

The first enabler of the CER Framework in University College was top management team support. This is not surprising given that strategic change that has support of the senior members of the organisation tend to be better resources and more carefully considered (Wiersema & Bantel, 1992). Early engagement and endorsement from the leaders of University College empowered the evaluation and research team to address policy and administrative barriers with relative ease. In our situation, we used a previous case study of the successful implementation of the CER Framework within a different context as a proof of concept (see Canty et al., 2014).

The second enabler was teaching team support. Top-down support for change enables resourcing, and fast resolutions for strategic and administrative challenges are key foundations to successful change. Bottom-up support for change enables implementation and operationalisation of the CER Framework. In

University College, early conversations with a small group of highly engaged academics and the formation of a first teaching team was a solution to allow for a proof of concept within the specific context. After such implementation, conversations organically occurred and were enabled by the informal influence of the project leaders, the positive organisational engagement of the project team members, and the authenticity of the team more broadly. By speaking openly and empowering employee voice, change can be more successful, and resistance can be better responded to (Bryant, 2006).

The third enabler was situational awareness of the institutional context. The CER Framework operates within the policies and parameters of the University College, but also the University of Tasmania. The policy platform and strategic documents of the University had to be understood to ensure any changes complied with requirements. Some decisions were altered by sections of policy. In addition, the higher education legislative frameworks at a national level were also considered. An understanding of what the University would likely be assessed for in future years by the Government quality accrediting body enabled tailoring of the Framework for future benefit. Thinking strategically about what *will* be needed is equally as critical as thinking about what *is* needed.

Barriers

The key barriers included: ethical standards, managing datasets, and analysis. There are significant barriers to ensure mandated ethical standards are met in the context of a course-wide and course-long research plan underpinned by a CER Framework. Micro-level TAAR and QI research on single units of study comprising a award course can be aggregated and matched into one large, longitudinal dataset and analysed to answer a range of research questions directed towards informing curriculum quality. The resources that support implementing the CER Framework include addressing barriers to data collection, for example to what extent data can be gathered and matched, drawing from students, teachers, units, and courses. Privacy and confidentiality are key to assuring that participants will not be negatively affected by participating. Examples of solutions to ethical challenges include the use of a Data Manager with no teaching responsibility to ensure complete anonymity of matched data. To assure that students and/or teachers do not feel coercion to participate, students and/or staff can consent or remove consent at any time anonymously online.

The second barrier is managing (very large) datasets. A single unit of study usually involves a unit coordinator, lecturer(s), tutor(s), marker(s), student(s), and administrative staff. Thus it is difficult to collect all possible data associated with a unit. Obtaining extended consent from every individual is not probable. This means that datasets are incomplete, and advanced protocols are required for valid analysis. For example, if students' participation rate is 60%, the student data could suffer from non-response bias (Fosnacht et al., 2017). In research comparing four survey implementations, it was found that higher education student respondents were more likely to be female, socially engaged, and investigative in personality (Porter & Whitcomb, 2005). In contrast, participants were less likely to be receiving financial support and enterprising in personality than those who did not participate. While larger response rates are positive, we recognise not every student will participate.

The CER Framework involves all teaching team staff as participant researchers, with direct opportunity to exclude data identifiable to them. The collegial and collaborative culture means that the issue of non-participation in the research by teaching staff is uncommon. In any case, student participation without teacher participation does not prevent student data being analyzed.

The third barrier is analysis. The volume of data can be overwhelming for a teaching team seeking to identify data relevant to analysis for their research questions. One approach to the challenge of data analysis is to look at the data with one of two lenses: grounded theory/inductive (Conrad, 1982) and hypothetico-deductive (Summers, 1982). The first is exploring what emerges, as it emerges. Grounded theory involves the construction of knowledge through exploration. In this case, as new data comes into the database, the TAAR teaching teams can explore the stories that emerge and tag concepts that may form into an explanation of what is occurring and why (Eich, 2008). The second uses the traditional scientific method to theorize a falsifiable hypothesis and using the data collected, new data, or a combination to test the truth of the hypothesis (Tonidandel et al., 2018). Both alternatives offer useful methods for considering and exploring the dataset that will emerge over time.

Professional Development for Scholarship

The CER Framework facilitates professional development of members of a teaching team through peer engagement and reflection. Attendance to most conferences typically enables improved disciplinary knowledge, learning about the latest trends in a field of inquiry (Raj Adhikari, 2010). Institutional awareness can act as an enabler if it means a teaching team can access resources to engage in scholarly activity. A teaching team, by working together to use data collected to assess current practice and trial new practice, enables more than innovations in teaching. It stimulates and enhances the development of those teaching team members.

Underlying reflective practice is the ability to gain deeper self-awareness about the impact and foundations of their performance (Walkington, 2005). This practice stems from being both an actor (i.e., a teacher) and third-party critic (i.e., a researcher) looking at their own teaching practice for improvement (Osterman & Kottkamp, 2004). The process of theorizing ways to improve teaching, examining data collected, reflecting, and scrutinizing results with the extant literature enables development of self and development of learning practice. The CER Framework offers a unique and consolidated approach for this process to be supported by colleagues. It enables the development over time of a "scholarly environment" for curriculum design and delivery that is articulated in the *TEQSA Guidance Note: Scholarship* (TEQSA, 2018).

Setting a Scholarly Evaluation and Research Agenda

Setting a scholarly evalution and research agenda within a Higher Education environment is both rewarding and challenging. Rewarding in that teachers can actively undertake research that underpins the quality of their curriculum and also having the ability to share their practice and outcomes. Challenging in that SoTL is, in many instances, not recognised as a valid, worthy activity. The *TEQSA Guidance Note: Scholarship* (TEQSA, 2018) is an important document that we expect will have strong corrective influence in the event Australian HEIs find their accreditation status is negatively affected by failure to demonstrate the expected environment for scholarship.

While the CER Framework enables staff to engage in scholarly work, the outcomes are predicated on the commitment of the teaching team leader (e.g. Course Coordinator). The leader's role is to foster collegial and collaborative work that allows teachers to evidence the impact of their teaching and their curriculum, assure and improve the quality of their curriculum, and produce outputs that disseminate new knowledge and practice. In the busyness of academic teaching life, an engaged leader providing some degree of individualised attention to team members is necessary to enable the furthest extension of quality activity (SoTL) to measure or report the impact of their teaching.

A challenge is that scholarship by TAAR teaching teams requires resourcing: Workload models need to include time for research into curriculum, and a data manager is needed to manage the big data sets that accumulate to maintain participant confidentiality. An effective scholarly environment also implies time and resources for peer review of teaching, professional development activities, data analysis, and writing grant applications or papers for publication. The CER Framework can be used to identify and plan for these activities, but managers need to allocate the resources.

FUTURE RESEARCH

Building Rigorous Theory and Measurement

The CER Framework is under constant development, adaptation, and improvement with each implementation. To develop a theory of curriculum evaluation, further exploration is planned. That is, to specify key concepts in relation to the literature and where are the boundary conditions for such a theory (Suddaby, 2010). Best practice for theory means specifying elements of interest, explaining the relationships between elements, justifying the assumptions of the theory, identifying clear definitions for each element, and identifying semantic relationships with external constructs (Crawford & Kelder, 2019). In practice, this means considering each of the elements of curriculum evaluation, including, but not limited to QI, QA, TAAR, and SOTL. For curriculum evaluation, there is conceptual ambiguity about the overlap between each of these elements. If a teacher engages in an activity which improves their unit using action research (i.e. using TAAR to evaluate and improve curriculum), is this not also like the role of QI? Understanding the distinct parts is critical to an enabler of genuine curriculum evaluation and improvement. We encourage scholars to take up the quest to accurately define each of the elements, independently and together, and determine how they can be distinguished.

The benefit of a concise theory of curriculum evaluation and its elements, is enabling a quantitative assessment that may enable measurement of organisational, team, or individual baselines. A tool of this nature should be able to identify and assess the individual elements, as well as such elements in aggregate, given that curriculum evaluation is likely a formative first-order, reflective second-order construct (Diamantopoulos et al., 2008; Edwards, 2001). Such a practice could enable a higher education institution to sense-test their current engagement with curriculum evaluation, on both a conceptual and practical level. Conceptually, an organisation can identify how they perform in curriculum evaluation against other organisations and identify strengths and deficiencies in current methodological approaches. Practically, an organisation can use such a tool to assure quality of their curriculum evaluation process (e.g., benchmarking with other organisations) as well as identify opportunities to improve the quality of their processes (e.g., correcting deficient areas and promoting the positive areas).

A Nomological Network

The current literature in higher education, and education more broadly, has not emphasised the antecedents and outcomes of curriculum evaluation (i.e., the nomological network of curriculum evaluation). Future research should begin this pursuit, including attention to elements such as governmental regulatory pressures (e.g., HESF in Australia), promotion aspiration, collegial culture, accreditation challenges, workload barriers, organisational culture, the nature of employment among others. Some of these concepts, while non-exhaustive, are identified as antecedents to one or more element of curriculum evaluation. For example, promotion aspiration is linked to engagement of SoTL (Haigh et al., 2011), but how does this relate to engagement with QI or QA? Identifying predictive relationships with external factors outside of the curriculum evaluation model is critical, and this will form as policy enablers and inhibitors to creating environments conducive to proactive improvement and evaluation of curriculum.

CONCLUSION

This chapter presented the CER Framework as a way for institutions and individual teachers to respond to regulatory and stakeholder expectations for quality assured curriculum and teaching, underpinned by and developed within a scholarly environment. Just as higher education institutions are required to demonstrate a systematic and comprehensive approach to evaluating curriculum is in place, so they must have evidence of facilitiating and resourcing. In the Australian context, the import of the criteria in the HES Framework is made explicit in the TEQSA Guidance Note: Scholarship:

The effect of these criteria is to require the creation of an institutional climate of scholarship ... The intent of these criteria is that, as a minimum, all teaching and learning in higher education is built on a foundation of advanced knowledge and inquiry, that all academic staff are active in scholarship that informs their teaching. (TEQSA, 2018, p. 3)

The CER Framework is designed to facilitate a scholarly environment that will drive and assure the quality of a curriculum and the capabilities of its teaching team. We claim that the constructs of *teacher as action researcher*, routinely engaging with three cycles of quality activities (focused on quality improvement, quality assurance, and Scholarship of Teaching and Learning) can be effectively applied to the curriculum over its life cycle (as it is designed, taught, and revised). In this chapter, we reviewed the implementation of the CER Framework within the University College to enable rigorous curriculum evaluation with scholarship.

The goal of implementing the CER framework across curriculum delivered by University College is to capitalise on the teaching-focused nature of the University College model for education attainment. This model has demonstrated its scalability in enhancing SoTL practices across a College. Three key enablers of top management team support, teaching team support, and institutional analysis were described along with implementation barriers, including ethical standards, managing datasets, and analysis. Further reflection on the enablers and barriers included advice on potentially fruitful sources of natural data for analysis and stimulating professional of teachers, developing their capabilities to routinely collaborate within a paradigm of action researcher.

The researchers argue that there are many opportunities—and challenges—to setting a scholarly research agenda within a higher education setting. However, scholarship must be valued, nurtured, resourced, and recognised. The CER Framework is grounded in practice. The researchers will continue to develop and share resources to support the implementation of an open source CER Framework. The next development is to scope the nature of quality in curriculum, learning, and teaching and to develop a measure of the impact and effectiveness of the CER Framework in enabling scholarship focused on curriculum quality and student learning.

REFERENCES

Acuna, T., & Kelder, J. A. (2019). ACDS Fellowship—Distributed leadership to embed scholarship in STEM teaching teams. In *Science and Maths TL News. July 2019*. Australian Council of Deans of Science Teaching and Learning Centre. Available: http://www.acds-tlcc.edu.au/publications/

Australian National Statement for Ethical Conduct of Research. (2007). Online Resource: https://www.nhmrc.gov.au/book/nationalstatement-ethical-conduct-human-research

Bateman, D. (2019). Unis between a compliance rock and a quality hard place. *Campus Morning Mail*. Available: http://campusmorningmail.com.au/news/between-a-compliance-rock-and-a-quality-hard-place/

Boud, D., & Brew, A. (2013). Reconceptualising academic work as professional practice: Implications for academic development. *The International Journal for Academic Development*, *18*(3), 208–221. doi:10.1080/1360144X.2012.671771

Boyer, E. (1990). *Scholarship reconsidered: Priorities of the professoriate*. San Francisco, CA: Jossey-Bass.

Bryant, M. (2006). Talking about change: Understanding employee responses through qualitative research. *Management Decision*, *44*(2), 246–258. doi:10.1108/00251740610650229

Canty, A., Burke, K., Carr, A., Ceperkovic, H., Elliott, K., Goldberg, L., & Minstrell, M. (2014). Online learning and aspirations in the Bachelor of Dementia Care degree. Aspirations Matter 2014, Launceston, Australia.

Carbone, A. (2014). A peer-assisted teaching scheme to improve units with critically low student satisfaction: Opportunities and challenges. *Higher Education Research & Development*, *33*(3), 425–439. doi:10.1080/07294360.2013.841644

Carr, A., Kelder, J.-A., & Sondermeyer, J. (2014). An evidence-based approach to the design of a learning program: Evaluating preliminary data sets. *International Journal of Learning, Teaching, and Educational Research*, *7*(1), 201–216.

Chalmers, D. (2007). *A review of Australian and international quality systems and indicators of learning and teaching (version 1.2)*. Melbourne, Australia: The Carrick Institute for Learning and Teaching in Higher Education.

Chalmers, D. (2011). Progress and challenges to the recognition and reward of the scholarship of teaching in higher education. *Higher Education Research & Development*, *30*(1), 25–38. doi:10.1080/07294360.2011.536970

Coates, H. (2005). The value of student engagement for higher education quality assurance. *Quality in Higher Education*, *11*(1), 25–36. doi:10.1080/13538320500074915

Conrad, C. (1982). Grounded theory: An alternative approach to research in higher education. *The Review of Higher Education, 5*(4), 239–249. doi:10.1353/rhe.1982.0010

Crawford, J., Dawkins, S., Martin, A., & Lewis, G. (2018). Conceptualising authentic followers and developing a future research agenda. In *Authentic Leadership and Followership* (pp. 271–293). Cham: Palgrave Macmillan. doi:10.1007/978-3-319-65307-5_11

Crawford, J., Dawkins, S., Martin, A., & Lewis, G. (2019). Putting the leader back into authentic leadership: Reconceptualising and rethinking leaders. *Australian Journal of Management*; Advanced Online Publication. doi:10.1177/0312896219836460

Crawford, J., & Kelder, J.-A. (2019). Do we measure leadership effectively? Articulating and evaluating scale development psychometrics for best practice. *The Leadership Quarterly, 30*(1), 133–144. doi:10.1016/j.leaqua.2018.07.001

Diamantopoulos, A., Riefler, P., & Roth, K. (2008). Advancing formative measurement models. *Journal of Business Research, 61*(12), 1203–1218. doi:10.1016/j.jbusres.2008.01.009

Ebert-May, D., Derting, T., Hodder, J., Momsen, J., Long, T., & Jardeleza, S. (2011). What we say is not what we do: Effective evaluation of faculty professional development programs. *Bioscience, 61*(7), 550–558. doi:10.1525/bio.2011.61.7.9

Edwards, J. (2001). Multidimensional constructs in organizational behavior research: An integrative analytical framework. *Organizational Research Methods, 4*(2), 144–192. doi:10.1177/109442810142004

Edwards, R., & Nicoll, K. (2006). Expertise, competence and reflection in the rhetoric of professional development. *British Educational Research Journal, 32*(1), 115–131. doi:10.1080/01411920500402052

Eich, D. (2008). A grounded theory of high-quality leadership programs: Perspectives from student leadership development programs in higher education. *Journal of Leadership & Organizational Studies, 15*(2), 176–187. doi:10.1177/1548051808324099

Fosnacht, K., Sarraf, S., Howe, E., & Peck, L. (2017). How important are high response rates for college surveys? *Review of Higher Education, 40*(2), 245–265. doi:10.1353/rhe.2017.0003

Gornitzka, Å., & Larsen, I. (2004). Towards professionalisation? Restructuring of administrative work force in universities. *Higher Education, 47*(4), 455–471. doi:10.1023/B:HIGH.0000020870.06667.f1

Gosling, D. (2004). The impact of a national policy to enhance teaching quality and the status, England, the United Kingdom. *Quality Assurance in Education, 12*(3), 136–149. doi:10.1108/09684880410548762

Haigh, N., Gossman, P., & Jiao, X. (2011). Undertaking an institutional "stock-take" of SoTL: New Zealand university case studies. *Higher Education Research & Development, 30*(1), 9–23. doi:10.108 0/07294360.2011.536969

Houghton, C., Casey, D., Shaw, D., & Murphy, K. (2013). Rigour in qualitative case-study research. *Nurse Researcher, 20*(4), 12–17. doi:10.7748/nr2013.03.20.4.12.e326 PMID:23520707

Jackson, D. (2015). Employability skill development in work-integrated learning: Barriers and best practice. *Studies in Higher Education, 40*(2), 350–367. doi:10.1080/03075079.2013.842221

Johnes, J., & Taylor, T. (1990). *Performance Indicators in Higher Education.* Buckingham, UK: SRHE and the Open University Press.

Johnson, C. (2001). A survey of current research on online Communities of Practice. *The Internet and Higher Education, 4*(1), 45–60. doi:10.1016/S1096-7516(01)00047-1

Kelder, J.-A., & Carr, A. (2016). *Embedding evaluation and research into curriculum design and delivery—workshop.* Paper presented at the 39th Annual Conference of the Higher Education Research and Development Society of Australasia (HERDSA), Freemantle, Australia.

Kelder, J.-A., & Carr, A. (2017). Embedding evaluation and scholarship into curriculum and teaching: The curriculum evaluation research framework. In A. Horsted, P. Bartholomew, J. Branch, & C. Nygaard (Eds.), *New Innovations in Teaching and Learning in Higher Education 2017* (pp. 430–451). Faringdon, UK: Libri Publishing.

Kelder, J.-A., Carr, A., & Walls, J. (2017). *Evidence-based transformation of curriculum: A research and evaluation framework.* Paper presented at the 40th Annual Conference of the Higher Education Research and Development Society of Australasia (HERDSA), Sydney, Australia.

Kember, D. (2000). *Action learning, action research: Improving the quality of teaching and learning.* Abingdon, UK: Routledge. doi:10.4324/9780203016343

Knight, P., Tait, J., & Yorke, M. (2006). The professional learning of teachers in higher education. *Studies in Higher Education, 31*(03), 319–339. doi:10.1080/03075070600680786

Kolb, A., & Kolb, D. (2005). Learning styles and learning spaces: Enhancing experiential learning in higher education. *Academy of Management Learning & Education, 4*(2), 193–212. doi:10.5465/amle.2005.17268566

Laurillard, D. (2008). The teacher as action researcher: Using technology to capture pedagogic form. *Studies in Higher Education, 33*(2), 139–154. doi:10.1080/03075070801915908

Leathwood, C., & Phillips, D. (2000). Developing curriculum evaluation research in higher education: Process, politics and practicalities. *Higher Education, 40*(3), 313–330. doi:10.1023/A:1004183527173

Lee, A., & McWilliam, E. (2008). What game are we in? Living with academic development. *The International Journal for Academic Development, 13*(1), 67–77. doi:10.1080/13601440701860284

Lee Looi Chng, V., & Coombs, S. (2004). Applying self-organised learning to develop critical thinkers for learning organisations: A conversational action research project. *Educational Action Research, 12*(3), 363–386. doi:10.1080/09650790400200256

Lueddeke, G. (2003). Professionalising teaching practice in higher education: A study of disciplinary variation and "teaching-scholarship". *Studies in Higher Education, 28*(2), 213–228. doi:10.1080/0307507032000058082

McNiff, J., & Whitehead, J. (2012). *Action research for teachers: A practical guide.* London, UK: David Fulton Publishers. doi:10.4324/9780203462393

NCIHE. (1997). *Higher education in the learning society: Main report ("The Dearing Report")*. London, UK: Her Majesty's Stationary Office.

Newton, J. (1997). Opportunities for partnership in quality improvement: Responding to the challenge of teaching quality assessment in Wales. *Quality in Higher Education, 3*(1), 37–50. doi:10.1080/1353832960030105

Organisation for Economic Co-operation and Development (OECD). (2008). Tertiary education for the knowledge society: Vol. 1. *Special features: Governance, funding*. Paris, France: OECD.

Organisation for Economic Co-operation and Development (OECD). (2008). Tertiary education for the knowledge society: Vol. 2. *Special features: Equity, innovation, labour market, internationalisation*. Paris, France: OECD.

Osterman, K., & Kottkamp, R. (2004). *Reflective practice for educators: Professional development to improve student learning*. Thousand Oaks, CA: Corwin Press.

Palloff, R., & Pratt, K. (1999). *Building learning communities in cyberspace: Effective strategies for the online classroom*. San Francisco, CA: Jossey-Bass.

Pearce, C., & Conger, J. (2002). *Shared leadership: Reframing the hows and whys of leadership*. Thousand Oaks, CA: SAGE Publications.

Phillips, R., McNaught, G., & Kennedy, C. (2012). *Evaluating e-learning: Guiding research and practice*. New York, NY: Routledge. doi:10.4324/9780203813362

Porter, S., & Whitcomb, M. (2005). Non-response in student surveys: The role of demographics, engagement, and personality. *Research in Higher Education, 46*(2), 127–152. doi:10.100711162-004-1597-2

Raj Adhikari, D. (2010). Knowledge management in academic institutions. *International Journal of Educational Management, 24*(2), 94–104. doi:10.1108/09513541011020918

Rath, A. (2002). Action research as border crossing: Stories from the classroom. In N. Lyons & V. La-Boskey (Eds.), *Narrative inquiry in practice: Advancing the knowledge of teaching* (pp. 146–160). New York, NY: Columbia College Press.

Rice, R. (1992). Towards a broader conception of scholarship: The American context. In T. Whiston & R. Geiger (Eds.), *Research and higher education: The United Kingdom and the United States* (pp. 117–129). Buckingham, UK: SRE and Open University Press.

Rienties, B., Brouwer, N., & Lygo-Baker, S. (2013). The effects of online professional development on higher education teachers' beliefs and intentions towards learning facilitation and technology. *Teaching and Teacher Education, 29*(1), 122–131. doi:10.1016/j.tate.2012.09.002

Shulman, L. (2001). From Minsk to Pinsk: Why a Scholarship of Teaching and Learning? *The Journal of Scholarship of Teaching and Learning, 1*(1), 48–53.

Siemens, G., & Long, P. (2011). Penetrating the fog: Analytics in learning and education. *EDUCAUSE Review, 46*(5), 30–32.

Spillane, J. (2005, June). Distributed leadership. *The Educational Forum, 69*(2), 143–150. doi:10.1080/00131720508984678

Squire, K., & Johnson, C. (2000). Supporting distributed Communities of Practice with interactive television. *Educational Technology Research and Development, 48*(1), 23–43. doi:10.1007/BF02313484

Suddaby, R. (2010). Editor's comments: Construct clarity in theories of management and organization. *Academy of Management Review, 35*(3), 346–357.

Summers, M. (1982). Philosophy of science in the science teacher education curriculum. *European Journal of Science Education, 4*(1), 19–27. doi:10.1080/0140528820040104

TEQSA. (2017). *Higher Education Standards Framework (Threshold Standards) 2015—TEQSA Contextual Overview Version 1.1*. Canberra, Australia: Tertiary Education Quality and Standards Agency.

TEQSA. (2018). *Guidance Note: Scholarship (Version 2.5_2, 12 December 2018)*. Canberra, Australia: Tertiary Education Quality and Standards Agency.

Tonidandel, S., King, E., & Cortina, J. (2018). Big data methods: Leveraging modern data analytic techniques to build organizational science. *Organizational Research Methods, 21*(3), 525–547. doi:10.1177/1094428116677299

Walkington, J. (2005). Becoming a teacher: Encouraging development of teacher identity through reflective practice. *Asia-Pacific Journal of Teacher Education, 33*(1), 53–64. doi:10.1080/1359866052000341124

Walls, J., Carr, A., Kelder, J.-A., & Ennever, E. (2018). Engaging in the "course efficiency" discussion: National drivers and local responses. *Journal of Further and Higher Education*; Advanced Online Publication.

Wenger, E. (2010). Communities of Practice and social learning systems: The career of a concept. In C. Blackmore (Ed.), *Social learning systems and Communities of Practice* (pp. 179–198). London, UK: Springer. doi:10.1007/978-1-84996-133-2_11

Westerheijden, D., Stensaker, B., & Rosa, M. (2007). *Quality assurance in higher education: Trends in regulation, translation and transformation* (Vol. 20). Berlin, Germany: Springer Science & Business Media. doi:10.1007/978-1-4020-6012-0

Wiersema, M., & Bantel, K. (1992). Top management team demography and corporate strategic change. *Academy of Management Journal, 35*(1), 91–121.

Compilation of References

AACN. (2008). *The essentials of baccalaureate education for professional nursing practice*. Retrieved from http://www.aacn.nche.edu/publications/baccalaureate-essentials

Acai, A., Akesson, B., Allen, M., Chen, V., Mathany, C., McCollum, B., & Verwoord, R. E. M. (2017). Conceptualizations of success in student-faculty/staff SoTL partnerships: Motivations, challenges, power, and definitions. *The Canadian Journal for the Scholarship of Teaching and Learning*, 8(2), 1–15. doi:10.5206/cjsotl-rcacea.2017.2.8

Acuna, T., & Kelder, J. A. (2019). ACDS Fellowship—Distributed leadership to embed scholarship in STEM teaching teams. In *Science and Maths TL News. July 2019*. Australian Council of Deans of Science Teaching and Learning Centre. Available: http://www.acds-tlcc.edu.au/publications/

ALA/AASL. (2010). *ALA/AASL standards for initial preparation of school librarians*. Retrieved from http://www.ala.org/aasl/sites/ala.org.aasl/files/content/aasleducation/schoollibrary/2010_standards_with_rubrics.pdf

Albers, C. (2008). Improving pedagogy through action learning and Scholarship of Teaching and Learning. *Teaching Sociology*, 36(1), 79–86. doi:10.1177/0092055X0803600110

Allen, I. E., & Seaman, J. (2007). *Making the grade: Online education in the United States*. Sloan Consortium.

Ally, M. (2008). *Foundations of educational theory for online learning. The theory and practice of online learning* (2nd ed.). Athabasca, Alberta: Athabasca University Press.

American Association of School Librarians (AASL). (2018). *National school library standards for learners, school librarians, and school libraries*. Chicago, IL: ALA Editions.

Amundsen, C., & Wilson, M. (2012). Are we asking the right questions?: A conceptual review of the educational development literature in higher education. *Review of Educational Research*, 82(1), 90–126. doi:10.3102/0034654312438409

Anderson, T., & Shattuck, J. (2012). Design-based research: A decade of progress in education research? *Educational Researcher*, 41(1), 16–25. doi:10.3102/0013189X11428813

Antelope Valley College Federation of Teachers. (2017). *Collective bargaining agreement between Antelope Valley Community College District and Antelope Valley College Federation of Teachers, July 1, 2015 - June 30, 2018*. Retrieved from https://www.avc.edu/sites/default/files/administration/hr/certcontract/Certificated%20Agreement%2C%207-1-15%20-%206-30-18%20%282%29.pdf

Asarta, C. J., Bento, R., Fornaciari, C. J., Lund Dean, K., Arbaugh, J. B., & Hwang, A. (2018). The Scholarship of Teaching and Learning: Changing the dominant narrative about (and in) research institutions. *Journal of Management Education*, 42(6), 731–748. doi:10.1177/1052562918777271

Ash, S. L., & Clayton, P. H. (2004). The articulated learning: An approach to guided reflection and assessment. *Innovative Higher Education*, *29*(2), 137–154. doi:10.1023/B:IHIE.0000048795.84634.4a

Ashwin, P., & Boud, D. (2015). *Reflective teaching in higher education*. London: Bloomsburg Academic.

Ashwin, P., & Trigwell, K. (2004). Investigating staff and educational development. In D. Baume & P. Kahn (Eds.), *Enhancing staff and educational development* (pp. 117–131). London: Routledge. doi:10.4324/9780203416228_chapter_7

Asmar, C. (2004). Innovations in scholarship at a student-centered research university: An Australian example. *Innovative Higher Education*, *29*(1), 49–65. doi:10.1023/B:IHIE.0000035366.71782.d8

Atkinson, M. P. (2014). Context matters for teaching and SoTL: Economic constraints, contingent faculty, and technology. *International Journal for the Scholarship of Teaching and Learning*, *8*(2). doi:10.20429/ijsotl.2014.080202

Atwell, N. (1991). *In the middle: Writing, reading, and learning with adolescents*. Portsmouth, NH: Heinemann Educational Books.

Austen, V. (2011). "Haven't we heard this all before?" Contingent faculty and unchanging times. *English Studies in Canada*, *37*(1), 13–16. doi:10.1353/esc.2011.0005

Australian Government. National Health and Medical Research Council. (2007). *National statement on ethical conduct in human research*. Retrieved from https://www.nhmrc.gov.au/about-us/publications/national-statement-ethical-conduct-human-research-2007-updated-2018#toc__2102

Australian National Statement for Ethical Conduct of Research. (2007). Online Resource: https://www.nhmrc.gov.au/book/nationalstatement-ethical-conduct-human-research

Badke, W. (2014a). The convenience factor in information seeking. *Online Searcher*, *38*(6), 68–70.

Badke, W. (2014b). Those baffling assignments. *Online Searcher*, *38*(3), 71–73.

Bamber, V. (2008). Evaluating lecturer development programmes: Received wisdom or self-knowledge? *The International Journal for Academic Development*, *13*(2), 107–116. doi:10.1080/13601440802076541

Barr, R. B. & Tagg, J. (1995). From teaching to learning: A new paradigm for undergraduate education. *Change: The Magazine of Higher Learning, 27*(6), 12-26.

Barrio Minton, C. A., Wachter Morris, C. A., & Yaites, L. D. (2014). Pedagogy in counselor education: A 10-year content analysis of journals. *Counselor Education and Supervision*, *53*(3), 162–177. doi:10.1002/j.1556-6978.2014.00055.x

Bartsch, R. A. (2013). Designing SoTL studies-part I: Validity. *New Directions for Teaching and Learning*, *136*(136), 17–33. doi:10.1002/tl.20073

Baskerville, D., & Goldblatt, H. (2009). Learning to be a critical friend: From professional indifference through challenge to unguarded conversations. *Cambridge Journal of Education*, *39*(2), 205–221. doi:10.1080/03057640902902260

Bass, R. (1999). The scholarship of teaching: What's the problem? *Inventio, 1*(1).

Bass, R. (1999). The scholarship of teaching: What's the problem? *Inventio: Creative Thinking about. Learning and Teaching*, *1*(1), 1–10.

Bass, R., & Linkon, S. L. (2008). On the evidence of theory: Close reading as a disciplinary model for writing about teaching and learning. *Arts and Humanities in Higher Education*, *7*(3), 245–261. doi:10.1177/1474022208094410

Bateman, D. (2019). Unis between a compliance rock and a quality hard place. *Campus Morning Mail.* Available: http://campusmorningmail.com.au/news/between-a-compliance-rock-and-a-quality-hard-place/

Bath, D., & Smith, C. (2004). Academic developers: An academic tribe claiming their territory in higher education. *The International Journal for Academic Development*, 9(1), 9–27. doi:10.1080/1360144042000296035

Beaudoin, B. (2012). Creating community: From individual reflection to SoTL transformation. *International Journal for the Scholarship of Teaching and Learning*, 6(1), 1–10. doi:10.20429/ijsotl.2012.060117

Becher, T., & Trowler, P. (1989). *Academic tribes and territories—Intellectual enquiry and the cultures of disciplines.* Buckingham, UK: Society for Research into Higher Education/Open University Press.

Becher, T., & Trowler, P. (2001). *Academic tribes and territories: Intellectual enquiry and the cultures of disciplines* (2nd ed.). Buckingham, UK: Open University Press/SRHE.

Beck, C., & Kosnik, C. (2006). *Innovations in teacher education: A social constructivist approach.* Albany, NY: State University of New York Press.

Benade, L. (2015). Teachers' critical reflective practice in the context of twenty-first century learning. *Open Review of Educational Research*, 2(1), 42–54. doi:10.1080/23265507.2014.998159

Bennett, D. (2011). *A pedagogy of uncertainty: The role of creativity and innovation in enhancing student engagement.* Centre for Research and Graduate Studies-Humanities. Retrieved from url: https://espace.curtin.edu.au/bitstream/handle/20.500.11937/21731/167368_167368.pdf?sequence=2&isAllowed=y

Bennett, R., Hobson, J., Jones, A., Martin-Lynch, P., Scutt, C., Strehlow, K., & Veitch, S. (2016). Being chimaera: A monstrous identity for SoTL academics. *Higher Education Research & Development*, 35(2), 217–228. doi:10.1080/07294360.2015.1087473

Bennett, S. C. (2014). Distance learning in law. *Seton Hall Legislative Journal*, 38(1), 1–15.

Bentley, D., & Squelch, J. (2014). Employer perspectives on essential knowledge, skills and attributes for law graduates to work in a global context. *Legal Education Review*, 24(1), 93–114.

Bergh, A., & Fink, G. (2009). Higher education, elite institutions, and inequality. *European Economic Review*, 53(3), 376–384. doi:10.1016/j.euroecorev.2008.06.002

Bergquist, W. H., & Pawlak, K. (2008). *Engaging the six cultures of the academy: Revised and expanded edition of the four cultures of the academy.* San Francisco, CA: John Wiley & Sons.

Biggs, J. B., & Tang, C. (2007). *Teaching for quality learning at university* (3rd ed.). Maidenhead, UK: McGraw Hill Education & Open University Press.

Biggs, J., & Tang, C. (2011). Train-the-trainers: Implementing outcomes-based teaching and learning in Malaysian higher education. *Malaysian Journal of Learning and Instruction*, 8, 1–19.

Billot, J., Rowland, S., Carnell, B., Amundsen, C., & Evans, T. (2017). How experienced SoTL researchers develop the credibility of their work. *Teaching & Learning Inquiry*, 5(1). doi:10.20343/teachlearninqu.5.1.8

Biochemistry. (2019). Retrieved from https://en.oxforddictionaries.com/definition/biochemistry

Bishop, J. L., & Verleger, M. A. (2013, June). The flipped classroom: A survey of the research. *ASEE National Conference Proceedings*, 30(9), 1-18.

Bishop-Clark, C., & Dietz-Uhler, B. (2012). *Engaging in the Scholarship of Teaching and Learning: A guide to the process, and how to develop a project from start to finish.* Sterling, VA: Stylus Publishing, LLC.

Blackmore, P. (2016a) Why research trumps teaching and what can be done about it. In P. Blackmore, R. Blackwell & M. Edmondson (Eds.), *Tackling wicked issues: Prestige, employment outcomes, and the Teaching Excellence Framework*. HEPI Occasional Paper 14. Retrieved from http://www.hepi.ac.uk/wp-content/uploads/2016/09/Hepi_TTWI-Web.pdf

Blackmore, P. (2016b). *Prestige in academic life: Excellence and exclusion*. London: Routledge.

Blackmore, P., & Kandiko, C. (2012). *Strategic curriculum change in universities: Global trends*. London: Routledge / SRHE. doi:10.4324/9780203111628

Black, S., & Allen, J. D. (2019). Part 9: Planning instruction. *The Reference Librarian*, *60*(2), 93–108. doi:10.1080/02763877.2019.1571469

Blakeslee, S. (2004). The CRAAP test. *LOEX Quarterly*, *31*(3), 6–7.

Blankstein, M., & Wolff-Eisenberg, C. (2019, April 12). *Ithaka S+R US faculty survey 2018*. Retrieved August 1, 2019, from doi:10.18665r.311199

Bloch-Schulman, S., Conkling, S., Linkon, S. L., Manarin, K., & Perkins, K. (2016). Asking bigger questions: An invitation to further conversation. *Teaching & Learning Inquiry*, *4*(1). doi:10.20343/teachlearninqu.4.1.12

Blue, J., Wentzell, G. W., & Evins, M. J. (2008). What do students want? Small group instructional diagnoses of STEM faculty. *Proceedings of the 2014 Physics Education Research Conference*, 43-46.

Boettcher, J., & Conrad, R. (2010). *The online teaching survival guide*. San Francisco, CA: Jossey Bass.

Bond, N. (2015). Developing a faculty learning community for non-tenure track professors. *International Journal of Higher Education*, *4*(4), 1–12. doi:10.5430/ijhe.v4n4p1

Booth, S., & Woollacott, L. C. (2018). On the constitution of SoTL: Its domains and contexts. *Higher Education*, *75*(3), 537–551. doi:10.100710734-017-0156-7

Bortolini, K. (2018, November 29). SoTL: The party that no one really wants to go to. *University Affairs*. Retrieved from https://www.universityaffairs.ca/opinion/in-my-opinion/sotl-the-party-that-no-one-really-wants-to-go-to/

Boshier, R. (2009). Why is the Scholarship of Teaching and Learning such a hard sell? *Higher Education Research & Development*, *28*(1), 1–15. doi:10.1080/07294360802444321

Botham, K. A. (2018). The perceived impact on academics' teaching practice of engaging with a higher education institution's CPD scheme. *Innovations in Education and Teaching International*, *55*(2), 164–175. doi:10.1080/14703297.2017.1371056

Boud, D., & Brew, A. (2013). Reconceptualising academic work as professional practice: Implications for academic development. *The International Journal for Academic Development*, *18*(3), 208–221. doi:10.1080/1360144X.2012.671771

Bovill, C., Bulley, C. J., & Moss, K. (2011). Engaging and empowering first-year students through curriculum design: Perspectives from the literature. *Teaching in Higher Education*, *16*(2), 197–209. doi:10.1080/13562517.2010.515024

Bowles-Terry, M., & Donovan, C. (2016). Serving notice on the one-shot: Changing roles for instruction librarians. *The International Information & Library Review*, *48*(2), 137–142. doi:10.1080/10572317.2016.1176457

Boyer, E. L. (1990). Scholarship reconsidered: Priorities of the professoriate. *Carnegie Foundation for the Advancement of Teaching*. Retrieved from https://eric.ed.gov/?id=ED326149

Boyer, E. (1990). *Scholarship reconsidered: Priorities of the professoriate*. Princeton, NJ: Carnegie Foundation for the Advancement of Teaching.

Boyer, E. L. (1996). From scholarship reconsidered to scholarship assessed. *Quest, 48*(2), 129–139. doi:10.1080/0033 6297.1996.10484184

Boyer, N. R., Maher, P. A., & Kirkman, S. (2006). Transformative learning in online settings: The use of self-direction, meta-cognition, and collaborative learning. *Journal of Transformative Education, 4*(4), 335–361. doi:10.1177/1541344606295318

Bradbury, H. (Ed.). (2015). *The Sage handbook of action research.* Thousand Oaks, CA: Sage Publications. doi:10.4135/9781473921290

Bradley, C. (2009). The Scholarship of Teaching and Learning: Opportunities for librarians. *College & Research Libraries News, 70*(5), 276–278. doi:10.5860/crln.70.5.8181

Brame, C. J. (2013). *Flipping the classroom.* Retrieved from http://cft.vanderbilt.edu/guides-sub-pages/flipping-the-classroom/

Breunig, M. (2017). Experientially learning and teaching in a student-directed classroom. *Journal of Experiential Education, 40*(3), 1–18. doi:10.1177/1053825917690870

Brew, A. (2002). Research and the faculty developer: A new agenda. *The International Journal for Academic Development, 7*(2), 112–122. doi:10.1080/1360144032000071332

Briguglio, C. (2014). *Working in the third space: Promoting interdisciplinary collaboration to embed English language development into the disciplines.* Retrieved from http://altf.org/wp-content/uploads/2016/08/Briguglio_C_NTF_report_2014.pdf

Brogt, E., & Knewstubb, B. (under review). Shifting sands: Conceptualising personal theories of relationship which shape academic development practice.

Brookfield, S. (1986). *Understanding and facilitating adult learning: A comprehensive analysis of principles and effective practices.* San Francisco, CA: Jossey-Bass.

Brookfield, S. (2005). *Discussion as a way of teaching: Tools and techniques for democratic classrooms.* San Francisco, CA: Jossey-Bass.

Brookfield, S. D. (1995). *Becoming a critically reflective teacher.* San Francisco: Jossey Bass.

Brownlee, J. (2015). Contract faculty in Canada: Using access to information requests to uncover hidden academics in Canadian universities. *Higher Education, 70*(5), 787–805. doi:10.100710734-015-9867-9

Bryan, J. E., Asher, D., & Karshmer, E. D. (2018). Assessing librarians' teaching of one-shot sessions: A new model for evaluating instructional performance. *College & Undergraduate Libraries, 25*(4), 350–371. doi:10.1080/10691316 .2018.1527268

Bryant, M. (2006). Talking about change: Understanding employee responses through qualitative research. *Management Decision, 44*(2), 246–258. doi:10.1108/00251740610650229

Buch, K. (2008). Faculty perceptions of SoTL at a research institution: A preliminary study. *Teaching of Psychology, 35*(4), 297–300. doi:10.1080/00986280802377149

Budd, J. (1995). An epistemological foundation for library and information science. *The Library Quarterly, 65*(3), 295–318. doi:10.1086/602799

Buffalo State College. (2003). *Supplemental directory of policy statements (DOPS) policy on scholarship encompassing applied research and the scholarship of teaching.* Retrieved July 10, 2019, from http://bscintra.buffalostate.edu/dops/policysect6/060405.pdf

Bunnell, S. L., & Bernstein, D. J. (2012). Overcoming some threshold concepts in scholarly teaching. *Journal of Faculty Development, 23*(3), 14–18.

Burman, M. E., & Kleinsasser, A. (2004). Ethical guidelines for use of student work: Moving from teaching's invisibility to inquiry's visibility in the Scholarship of Teaching and Learning. *The Journal of General Education, 53*(1), 59–79. doi:10.1353/jge.2004.0018

Calkins, L. (1994). The art of teaching writing (New ed.). Portsmouth, NH: Heinemann.

Cambridge, B. L. (2001). Fostering the Scholarship of Teaching and Learning: Communities of Practice. In D. Lieberman & C. Wehlburg (Eds.), *To Improve the Academy* (pp. 3–16). Bolton, MA: Anker. doi:10.1002/j.2334-4822.2001.tb00521.x

Cambridge, B. L. (Ed.). (2004). *Campus progress: Supporting the Scholarship of Teaching and Learning.* Washington, DC: American Association for Higher Education.

Canick, S. (2014). Infusing technology skills into the law curriculum. *Capital University Law Review, 42*(3), 663–708.

Canty, A., Burke, K., Carr, A., Ceperkovic, H., Elliott, K., Goldberg, L., & Minstrell, M. (2014). Online learning and aspirations in the Bachelor of Dementia Care degree. Aspirations Matter 2014, Launceston, Australia.

Carbone, A. (2014). A peer-assisted teaching scheme to improve units with critically low student satisfaction: Opportunities and challenges. *Higher Education Research & Development, 33*(3), 425–439. doi:10.1080/07294360.2013.841644

Cardullo, V., & Zygouris-Coe, V. (2013). *Eighth-grade students reading nonfiction literature on the IPAD: An exploratory case study* (ProQuest Dissertations Publishing). Retrieved from http://search.proquest.com/docview/1500850648/

Carless, D. (2015). *Excellence in university assessment: Learning from award-winning practice.* London, UK: Routledge. doi:10.4324/9781315740621

Carnegie Foundation for the Advancement of Teaching. (n.d.). *Foundation history.* Retrieved from http://www.carnegie-foundation.org/about-us/foundation-history

Carr, A., Kelder, J.-A., & Sondermeyer, J. (2014). An evidence-based approach to the design of a learning program: Evaluating preliminary data sets. *International Journal of Learning, Teaching, and Educational Research, 7*(1), 201–216.

Cerbin, W., & Kopp, B. (2006). Lesson study as a model for building pedagogical knowledge and improving teaching. *International Journal on Teaching and Learning in Higher Education, 18*(3), 250–257.

Cercone, K. (2008). Characteristics of adult learners with implications for online learning design. *Association for the Advancement of Computing in Education Journal, 16*(2), 137–159.

Chalmers, D. (2007). *A review of Australian and international quality systems and indicators of learning and teaching (version 1.2).* Melbourne, Australia: The Carrick Institute for Learning and Teaching in Higher Education.

Chalmers, D. (2011). Progress and challenges to the recognition and reward of the Scholarship of Teaching in higher education. *Higher Education Research & Development, 30*(1), 25–38. doi:10.1080/07294360.2011.536970

Chalmers, D. (2018). Why recognising and rewarding excellent teaching in universities matters for students. *4th International Conference on Higher Education Advances.* 10.4995/HEAD18.2018.7981

Chang, C., Chow, C., Tellier, L., Vattikuti, S., Purcell, S., & Lee, J. (2015). Second-generation PLINK: Rising to the challenge of larger and richer datasets. *GigaScience, 4*(7). doi:10.118613742-015-0047-8 PMID:25722852

Chang, I.-Y., & Chang, W.-Y. (2012). The effect of student learning motivation on learning satisfaction. *International Journal of Organizational Innovation, 4*(3), 281–305.

Charbonneau, L. (2009). Congress '09- Scholarship of Teaching and Learning is not good enough. *University Affairs*. Retrieved from: www.universityaffairs.ca/margin-nbotes/tag/gary-poole

Chaudhuri, T., & Cabau, B. (Eds.). (2017). *E-Portfolios in higher education: A multidisciplinary approach*. Singapore: Springer. doi:10.1007/978-981-10-3803-7

Chen, Y., Wang, Y., & Chen, N. S. (2014). Is FLIP enough? Or should we use the FLIPPED model instead? *Computers & Education*, *79*, 16–27. doi:10.1016/j.compedu.2014.07.004

Cherry, J. M., Duff, W. M., Singh, N., & Freund, L. (2011). Student perceptions of the information professions and their master's program in information studies. *Library & Information Science Research*, *33*(2), 120–131. doi:10.1016/j.lisr.2010.09.004

Chick, N. (2013). *Scholarship of Teaching and Learning guide*. Vanderbilt University Center for Teaching. Retrieved from http://my.vanderbilt.edu/sotl

Chick, N. (2019). *SoTL as public scholarship*. Keynote address at the annual meeting of the International Society for the Scholarship of Teaching and Learning, Atlanta, GA.

Chickering, A. W., & Gamson, Z. F. (1987). Seven principles for good practice in undergraduate education. *AAHE Bulletin*, *3*, 7.

Chick, N. (2014). "Methodologically sound" under the "big tent": An ongoing conversation. *International Journal for the Scholarship of Teaching and Learning*, *8*(2), 3.

Chick, N. L. (2014). 'Methodologically sound' under the 'big tent': An ongoing conversation. *International Journal for the Scholarship of Teaching and Learning*, *8*(2). doi:10.20429/ijsotl.2014.080201

Chick, N. L. (Ed.). (2018). *SoTL in Action*. Sterling, VA: Stylus Publishing.

Chick, N. L. (Ed.). (2018). *SoTL in action: Illuminating critical moments of practice*. Sterling, VA: Stylus.

Chick, N., Cornell-Swanson, L., Lazarides, K., & Meyers, R. (2014). Reconciling apples & oranges: A constructivist SoTL writing program. *International Journal for the Scholarship of Teaching and Learning*, *8*(2), 13. doi:10.20429/ijsotl.2014.080213

Chick, N., & Poole, G. (2018). Editors' introduction: In defense of microscopes. *Teaching & Learning Inquiry*, *6*(1), 1–2. doi:10.20343/teachlearninqu.6.1.1

Chien, T.-K. (2007). Using the learning satisfaction improving model to enhance the teaching quality. *Quality Assurance in Education*, *15*(2), 192–214. doi:10.1108/09684880710748947

Chism, N., & Chism, G. (2007). *Peer review of teaching: A sourcebook* (2nd ed.). Bolton, MA: Anker Pub. Co.

Chng, H. H., & Looker, P. (2013). On the margins of SoTL discourse: An Asian perspective. *Teaching & Learning Inquiry*, *1*(1), 131–145. doi:10.20343/teachlearninqu.1.1.131

Christiano, A., & Neimand, A. (2017). Stop raising awareness already. *Stanford Social Innovation Review*, 33–41. Retrieved from https://ssir.org/articles/entry/stop_raising_awareness_already

Christie, F., & Macken-Horarik, M. (2007). Verticality in subject English. In F. Christie & J. R. Martin (Eds.), *Language, knowledge, and pedagogy*. London: Continuum.

Ciccone, A., Huber, M. T., Hutchings, P., & Cambridge, B. (2009). *Exploring impact: A survey of participants in the CASTL Institutional leadership and affiliates program*. The Carnegie Foundation for the Advancement of Teaching.

Cilliers, F. J., & Herman, N. (2010). Impact of an educational development programme on teaching practice of academics at a research-intensive university. *The International Journal for Academic Development, 15*(3), 253–267. doi:10.1080/1360144X.2010.497698

Clark, D., & Redmond, M. (1982). *Small group instructional diagnosis: Final report.* ERIC Document Reproduction Service No. ED217954.

Clark, R. C., & Mayer, R. E. (2011). *E-learning and science of instruction* (3rd ed.). San Francisco, CA: Pfeiffer. doi:10.1002/9781118255971

Clark, R. C., Nguyen, F., & Sweller, J. (2006). *Efficiency in learning: Evidence-based guidelines to manage cognitive load.* San Francisco, CA: Pfeiffer.

Coates, H. (2005). The value of student engagement for higher education quality assurance. *Quality in Higher Education, 11*(1), 25–36. doi:10.1080/13538320500074915

Coffin, C., & Donohue, J. (2014). A language as social semiotic-based approach to teaching and learning in higher education (Language Learning Monograph Series). Chichester, UK: Wiley-Blackwell.

Coffin, C. (2006). *Historical discourse.* London: Continuum.

Competition & Markets Authority. (2015). *Undergraduate students: Your consumer rights.* Retrieved from: https://assets.publishing.service.gov.uk/government/uploads/system/uploads/attachment_data/file/411288/Students_consumer_rights_60ss.pdf

Conrad, C. (1982). Grounded theory: An alternative approach to research in higher education. *The Review of Higher Education, 5*(4), 239–249. doi:10.1353/rhe.1982.0010

Conservative Party. (2015). *Strong leadership. A clear economic plan. A brighter, more secure future.* Retrieved from https://www.conservatives.com/manifesto2015

Cook-Sather, A., Bovill, C., & Felten, P. (2014). *Engaging students as partners in learning and teaching.* San Francisco, CA: Jossey-Bass.

Cook-Sather, A., Bovill, C., & Felten, P. (2014). *Engaging students as partners in learning and teaching: A guide for faculty.* San Francisco, CA: Jossey-Bass.

Cooney, C. (2005). *Code orange.* New York, NY: Laurel-Leaf.

Costabile, M. (2014, September). *Assessment of an e-Learning simulation for the teaching of enzyme kinetics. Changing Horizons: Local Learning for Global Impact.* Paper presented at the HERGA conference, Adelaide, Australia.

Cotton, D., Miller, W., & Kneale, P. (2018). The Cinderella of academia: Is higher education pedagogic research undervalued in UK research assessment? *Studies in Higher Education, 43*(9), 1625–1636. doi:10.1080/03075079.2016.1276549

Council of Chief State School Officers (CCSSO) and the National Governors Association (NGA). (2010). *Common core state standards for English language arts & literacy in history/social studies, science, and technical subjects.* Retrieved from http://www.corestandards.org/assets/CCSSI_ELA%20Standards.pdf

Counihan, E., & Silcox, A. (2014). Internal rhyme, isosceles triangles, and iMovie: A middle school collaboration to integrate English and geometry. *English Journal, 103*(3), 34–40. PMID:25286485

Cox, C. (2019). Becoming part of the course: Using Blackboard to extend one-shot library instruction. *College & Research Libraries News, 63*(1), 11–39. doi:10.5860/crln.63.1.11

Cox, M. D. (2004). Introduction to faculty learning communities. *New Directions for Teaching and Learning, 97*, 5–23. doi:10.1002/tl.129

Cox, M. D. (2013). The impact of Communities of Practice in support of early-career academics. *The International Journal for Academic Development, 18*(1), 18–30. doi:10.1080/1360144X.2011.599600

Cranton, P. (2000). Individual differences and transformative learning. In J. Mezirow & ... (Eds.), *Learning as transformation: Critical perspectives on theory in progress* (pp. 181–204). San Francisco, CA: Jossey-Bass.

Cranton, P. (2010). Transformative learning in an online environment. *International Journal of Adult Vocational Education and Technology, 1*, 1–9.

Cranton, P. (2011). A transformative perspective on the Scholarship of Teaching and Learning. *Higher Education Research & Development, 30*(1), 75–86. doi:10.1080/07294360.2011.536974

Crawford, J., Dawkins, S., Martin, A., & Lewis, G. (2018). Conceptualising authentic followers and developing a future research agenda. In *Authentic Leadership and Followership* (pp. 271–293). Cham: Palgrave Macmillan. doi:10.1007/978-3-319-65307-5_11

Crawford, J., Dawkins, S., Martin, A., & Lewis, G. (2019). Putting the leader back into authentic leadership: Reconceptualising and rethinking leaders. *Australian Journal of Management.* doi:10.1177/0312896219836460

Crawford, J., & Kelder, J.-A. (2019). Do we measure leadership effectively? Articulating and evaluating scale development psychometrics for best practice. *The Leadership Quarterly, 30*(1), 133–144. doi:10.1016/j.leaqua.2018.07.001

Creswell, J. W. (2014). *Research design: Qualitative, quantitative, and mixed methods approaches.* Thousand Oaks, CA: Sage Publications.

Crowther, P., Scott, A., & Allen, T. (2016). Perceptions of collaboration amongst novice design students. In R. Tucker (Ed.), *Collaboration and Student Engagement in Design Education* (pp. 126–144). IGI Global.

Cruz, L., Cunningham, K., Smentkowski, B., & Steiner, H. (2019). The SoTL scaffold: Supporting evidence-based teaching practice in educational development. *To Improve the Academy, 38*(1).

D'Andrea, V. (2006). Exploring the methodological issues related to pedagogical inquiry in Higher Education. *New Directions for Teaching and Learning, 107*, 89–98. doi:10.1002/tl.247

Daily, E. (2011). Enhancing learning, teaching, assessment and curriculum in higher education: Theory, cases, practices. Teaching Theology and Religion, 14(3), 295–297. doi:10.1111/j.1467-9647.2011.00728.x

Dalhousie Faculty Association. (2018). *A collective agreement between the Board of Governors of Dalhousie University and the Dalhousie Faculty Association, 2017 - 2020.* Retrieved from https://cdn.dal.ca/content/dam/dalhousie/pdf/dept/hr/Academic-Staff-Relations/DFA-2017-20-Collective-Agreement.pdf

Dall'Alba, G. (2009). Learning professional ways of being: Ambiguities of becoming. *Educational Philosophy and Theory, 41*(1), 34–45. doi:10.1111/j.1469-5812.2008.00475.x

Daloz, L. (1999). *Mentor: Guiding the journey of adult learners.* San Francisco, CA: Jossey-Bass.

Daloz, L. (2000). Transformative learning for the common good. In J. Mezirow & ... (Eds.), *Learning as transformation: Critical perspectives on theory in progress* (pp. 103–123). San Francisco, CA: Jossey-Bass.

Danielson, M. A. (2012). SoTL as a generative heuristic methodology for building learning communities. *International Journal for the Scholarship of Teaching and Learning, 6*(2). doi:10.20429/ijsotl.2012.060204 de la Croix, A., & Veen, M. (2018). The reflective zombie: Problematizing the conceptual framework of reflection in medical education. *Perspectives on Medical Education, 7*(6), 394–400. https://doi.org. doi:10.100740037-018-0479-9 PMID:30353284

De Vries, R., DeBruin, D. A., & Goodgame, A. (2004). Ethics review of social, behavioral, and economic research: Where should we go from here? *Ethics & Behavior, 14*(4), 351–368. doi:10.120715327019eb1404_6 PMID:16625729

Debowski, S. (2011). Locating academic development: The first step in evaluation. In L. Stefani (Ed.), *Evaluating the effectiveness of academic development: Principles and practice* (pp. 17–30). New York, NY: Routledge.

Dekker-Groen, A. M., van der Schaaf, M. F., & Stokking, K. M. (2011). Teacher competences required for developing reflection skills of nursing students. *Journal of Advanced Nursing, 67*(7), 1568–1579. doi:10.1111/j.1365-2648.2010.05591.x PMID:21332576

DeLathouwer, E., Roy, W., Martin, A., & Liska, J. (2012). Multidisciplinary collaboration through learning communities: Navigating anxiety. *Collected Essays on Learning and Teaching, 5,* 27–32. doi:10.22329/celt.v5i0.3443

Design-Based Research Collective. (2003). Design-based research: An emerging paradigm for educational inquiry. *Educational Researcher, 32*(1), 5–8. doi:10.3102/0013189X032001005

Desimone, L. M. (2009). Improving impact studies of teachers' professional development: Towards better conceptualizations and measures. *Educational Researcher, 38*(3), 181–199. doi:10.3102/0013189X08331140

Dewar, J. M. (2008). An apology for the Scholarship of Teaching and Learning. *InSight: A Journal of Scholarly Teaching, 3,* 17-22. Retrieved from: https://files.eric.ed.gov/fulltext/EJ888405.pdf

Dewar, J., & Bennett, C. (2010). Situating SoTL within the disciplines: Mathematics in the United States as a case study. *International Journal for the Scholarship of Teaching and Learning, 4*(1). doi:10.20429/ijsotl.2010.040114

Dewey, J. (1933). *How we think.* Buffalo, N.Y.: Prometheus Books.

Dewey, J. (1938). *Experience and education.* New York, NY: Collier Books, Macmillan.

Diamantopoulos, A., Riefler, P., & Roth, K. (2008). Advancing formative measurement models. *Journal of Business Research, 61*(12), 1203–1218. doi:10.1016/j.jbusres.2008.01.009

Diamond, M. R. (2004). The usefulness of structured mid-term feedback as a catalyst for change in higher education classes. *Active Learning in Higher Education, 5*(3), 217–231. doi:10.1177/1469787404046845

Dick, D. D. (2006). Options and possibility: Scholarship in the SIAST nursing division--An example of advancing scholarship in the polytechnic environment. *The College Quarterly, 9*(3).

Dobbie, D., & Robinson, I. (2008). Reorganizing higher education in the United States and Canada: The erosion of tenure and the unionization of contingent faculty. *Labor Studies Journal, 33*(2), 117–140. doi:10.1177/0160449X07301241

Dobbins, K. (2008). Enhancing the Scholarship of Teaching and Learning: A study of factors identified as promoting and hindering the scholarly activities of academics in one faculty. *International Journal for the Scholarship of Teaching and Learning, 2*(2). doi:10.20429/ijsotl.2008.020217

Dobbins, K. (2011). Personal reflections: Reflections on SoTL by a casual lecturer: Personal benefits, long-term challenges. *International Journal for the Scholarship of Teaching and Learning, 5*(2), 6. doi:10.20429/ijsotl.2011.050224

Draeger, J., & Scharff, L. (2019). Catalyzing the exchange and application of SoTL beyond the classroom: An analysis of two types of community spaces. In J. C. Friberg & K. McKinney (Eds.), *Applying SoTL beyond the individual classroom.* Bloomington, IN: Indiana University Press. doi:10.2307/j.ctvpb3w0t.10

Drago-Severson, E. (2009). *Leading adult learning: Supporting adult development in our schools*. Thousand Oaks, CA: Corwin Press.

Drago-Severson, E. (2012). *Helping educators grow: Practices and strategies for leadership development*. Cambridge, MA: Harvard Education Press.

Dreyfus, S. J., Humphrey, S., Mahboob, A., & Martin, J. R. (2016). *Genre pedagogy in higher education: The SLATE project*. Basingstoke, UK: Palgrave Macmillan. doi:10.1007/978-1-137-31000-2

Driscoll, L. G., Parkes, K. A., Tilley-Lubbs, G. A., Brill, J. M., & Bannister, V. R. P. (2009). Navigating the lonely sea: Peer mentoring and collaboration among aspiring women scholars. *Mentoring & Tutoring*, *17*(1), 5–21. doi:10.1080/13611260802699532

DuBois, J. M. (2004). Is compliance a professional virtue of researchers? Reflections on promoting the responsible conduct of research. *Ethics & Behavior*, *14*(4), 383–395. doi:10.120715327019eb1404_8 PMID:16625734

Duffy, D. K. (2000). Resilient students, resilient communities. In P. Hutchings (Ed.), *Opening lines: Approaches to the Scholarship of Teaching and Learning* (pp. 23–30). Menlo Park, CA: Carnegie Publications.

Duhaylongsod, L., Snow, C. E., Selman, R. L., & Donovan, M. S. (2015). Toward disciplinary literacy: Dilemmas and challenges in designing history curriculum to support middle school students. *Harvard Educational Review*, *85*(4), 587–608. doi:10.17763/0017-8055.85.4.587

Ebert-May, D., Derting, T., Hodder, J., Momsen, J., Long, T., & Jardeleza, S. (2011). What we say is not what we do: Effective evaluation of faculty professional development programs. *Bioscience*, *61*(7), 550–558. doi:10.1525/bio.2011.61.7.9

Edwards, J. (2001). Multidimensional constructs in organizational behavior research: An integrative analytical framework. *Organizational Research Methods*, *4*(2), 144–192. doi:10.1177/109442810142004

Edwards, N., Viehbeck, S., Hämäläinen, R. M., Rus, D., Skovgaard, T., van de Goor, I., ... Aro, A. R. (2012). Challenges of ethical clearance in international health policy and social sciences research: Experiences and recommendations from a multi-country research programme. *Public Health Reviews*, *34*(1), 1–18. doi:10.1007/BF03391663 PMID:26236074

Edwards, R., & Nicoll, K. (2006). Expertise, competence and reflection in the rhetoric of professional development. *British Educational Research Journal*, *32*(1), 115–131. doi:10.1080/01411920500402052

Eich, D. (2008). A grounded theory of high-quality leadership programs: Perspectives from student leadership development programs in higher education. *Journal of Leadership & Organizational Studies*, *15*(2), 176–187. doi:10.1177/1548051808324099

Eisen, A., & Berry, R. M. (2002). The absent professor: Why we don't teach research ethics and what to do about it. *The American Journal of Bioethics*, *2*(4), 38–49. doi:10.1162/152651602320957556 PMID:12762924

Elen, J., Lindblom-Ylanne, S., & Clement, M. (2007). Faculty development in research-intensive universities: The role of academics' conceptions on the relationship between research and teaching. *The International Journal for Academic Development*, *12*(2), 123–139. doi:10.1080/13601440701604948

Expert Group on Future Skills Needs (Ireland) (EGFSN). (2016). *Guidance for higher education providers on current and future skills needs of enterprise: Springboard+ 2016 including ICT skills conversion*. Retrieved from http://hdl.voced.edu.au/10707/400180

Faculty Association of Grant MacEwan University. (2017). *Collective agreement between the Board of Governors of Grant MacEwan University and the Faculty Association of Grant MacEwan University, July 1, 2017 - June 30, 2019*. Retrieved from https://www.macewanfa.ca/public/download/documents/42611

Faculty Association of the University of British Columbia. (2017). *Collective agreement between the University of British Columbia and the Faculty Association of the University of British Columbia, July 1, 2016 - June 30, 2019*. Retrieved from https://www.facultyassociation.ubc.ca/assets/media/Faculty-CA-2016-to-2019_V_6July2018.pdf

Faller, S. E., & Norman, C. (2015). *Ethics & the IRB review process: A guide for SoTL researchers at UC*. Retrieved from: https://www.uc.edu/content/dam/uc/cetl/docs/IRB%20for%20SoTL.pdf

Fanghanel, J., Prichard, J., Potter, J., & Wisker, G. (2016). *Defining and supporting the Scholarship of Teaching and Learning (SoTL): A sector-wide study. Executive summary*. Retrieved from: https://www.heacademy.ac.uk/knowledge-hub/defining-and-supporting-scholarship-teaching-and-learning-sotl-sector-wide-study

Fanghanel, J. (2004). Capturing dissonance in university teacher education environments. *Studies in Higher Education*, *29*(5), 575–590. doi:10.1080/0307507042000261553

Fanghanel, J. (2012). *Being an academic*. Abingdon, UK: Routledge.

Fanghanel, J. (2013). Going public with pedagogical inquiries: SoTL as a methodology for faculty professional development. *Teaching & Learning Inquiry*, *1*(1), 59–70. doi:10.20343/teachlearninqu.1.1.59

Fanghanel, J., McGowan, S., Parker, P., Mcconnell, C., Potter, J., Locke, W., & Healey, M. (2015). *Literature review. Defining and supporting the Scholarship of Teaching and Learning (SoTL): a sector-wide study*. York, UK: Higher Education Academy.

Fanghanel, J., McGowan, S., Parker, P., McConnell, C., Potter, J., Locke, W., & Healey, M. (2015). *Literature review. In Defining and supporting the Scholarship of Teaching and Learning (SoTL): A sector-wide study*. York, UK: Higher Education Academy.

Fanghanel, J., Pritchard, J., Potter, J., & Wisker, G. (2016). *Defining and supporting the Scholarship of Teaching and Learning (SoTL): A sector-wide study*. York, UK: Higher Education Academy. Retrieved from https://repository.uwl.ac.uk/id/eprint/2066/1/literature_review.pdf

Fang, Z., & Wei, Y. (2010). Improving middle school students' science literacy through reading infusion. *The Journal of Educational Research*, *103*(4), 262–273. doi:10.1080/00220670903383051

Farmer, R. (2018). The what, the how, and the why of the flipped classroom. *Innovative Practice in Higher Education*, *3*(2), 14–31.

Fedoruk, L. (2017). *Ethics in the Scholarship of Teaching and Learning: Key principles and strategies for ethical practice. Taylor Institute for Teaching and Learning Guide Series*. Calgary, AB: Taylor Institute for Teaching and Learning at the University of Calgary. Retrieved from www.ucalgary.ca/taylorinstitute/guides

Felten, P., & Chick, N. (2018). Is SoTL a signature pedagogy of educational development? *To Improve the Academy*, *37*(1), 4-16. doi:10.002/tia2.20077

Felten, P., Kalish, A., Pingree, A., & Plank, K. M. (2007). Toward a Scholarship of Teaching and Learning in educational development. *To Improve the Academy: A Journal of Educational Development, 25*(1), 93-108.

Felten, P. (2013). Principles of good practice in SoTL. *Teaching & Learning Inquiry*, *1*(1), 121–125. doi:10.20343/teachlearninqu.1.1.121

Felten, P. (2013). Principles of good practice in SoTL. Teaching & learning inquiry. *The ISSOTL Journal*, *1*(1), 121–125. doi:10.2979/teachlearninqu.1.1.121

Felten, P., Abbot, S., Kirkwood, J., Long, A., Lubicz-Nawrocka, T., Mercer-Mapstone, L., & Verwoord, R. (2019). Reimagining the place of students in academic development. *The International Journal for Academic Development, 24*(2), 192–203. doi:10.1080/1360144X.2019.1594235

Felten, P., Bagg, J., Bumbry, M., Hill, J., Hornsby, K., Pratt, M., & Weller, S. (2013). A call for expanding inclusive student engagement in SoTL. *Teaching & Learning Inquiry, 1*(2), 63–74. doi:10.20343/teachlearninqu.1.2.63

Felten, P., Moore, J. L., & Peeples, T. (2019). Multi-institutional SoTL: A case study of practices and outcomes. In J. C. Friberg & K. McKinney (Eds.), *Applying SoTL beyond the individual classroom*. Bloomington, IN: Indiana University Press. doi:10.2307/j.ctvpb3w0t.11

Fenton, N., & Szala-Meneok, K. (2011). *Research on teaching and learning guidebook*. McMaster University Center for Leadership in Learning. Retrieved from http://cll.mcmaster.ca/resources/pdf/redo_guidebook.pdf

Field, C., Jones, G., Stephenson, G., & Khoyestsyan, A. (2014). *The "Other" university teacher: Non-full-time instructors at Ontario universities*. Toronto: Higher Educational Quality Council of Ontario. Retrieved from http://heqco.ca/en-CA/Research%20Publications/Pages/Summary.aspx?link=145

Fields, J., Kenny, N. A., & Mueller, R. A. (2019). Conceptualizing educational leadership in an academic development program. *The International Journal for Academic Development, 24*(3), 218–231. doi:10.1080/1360144X.2019.1570211

Finelli, C. J., Pinder-Grover, T., & Wright, M. C. (2011). Consultations on teaching: Using student feedback for instructional improvement. In C. E. Cook & M. Kaplan (Eds.), *Advancing the culture of teaching on campus: How a teaching center can make a difference* (pp. 65–79). Sterling, VA: Stylus Publishers.

Fink, L. D. (2013). *Creating significant learning experiences: An integrated approach to designing college courses*. Hoboken, NJ: John Wiley & Sons.

Fister, B. (2015). The social life of knowledge: Faculty epistemologies. In T. A. Swanson & H. Jagman (Eds.), *Not just where to click: Teaching students how to think about information* (pp. 87–104). Chicago, IL: Association of College and Research Libraries.

Fitzgerald, F., Huijser, H., Meth, D., & Neilan, K. (2019). Student-staff partnerships in academic development: The course design studio as a model for sustainable course-wide impact. *The International Journal for Academic Development*, 1–13. doi:10.1080/1360144X.2019.1631170

Fitzpatrick, E. (2019). For the greater good. *Times Higher Education Supplement, 2403*, 43–45.

Flavell, H., Roberts, L., Fyfe, G., & Broughton, M. (2018). Shifting goal posts: The impact of academic workforce reshaping and the introduction of teaching academic roles on the Scholarship of Teaching and Learning. *Australian Educational Researcher, 45*(2), 179–194. doi:10.100713384-017-0247-6

Flick, U. (Ed.). (2013). *The SAGE handbook of qualitative data analysis*. Thousand Oaks, CA: Sage Publications.

Flipped Learning Network (FLN). (2014). *The four pillars of F-L-I-P*. Retrieved from https://flippedlearning.org/definition-of-flipped-learning/

Fook, J., Collington, V., Ross, R., Ruch, G., & West, L. (2016). *Researching critical reflection: Multidisciplinary perspectives*. London: Routledge.

Ford, C., & Peaslee, D. (2018, February 26). A community college perspective on creating a SoTL scholars program [web log post]. Retrieved from https://illinoisstateuniversitysotl.wordpress.com/2018/02/26/a-community-college-perspective-on-creating-a-sotl-scholars-program/

Forgie, S. E., Yonge, O., & Luth, R. (2018). Centres for teaching and learning across Canada: What's Going On? *The Canadian Journal for the Scholarship of Teaching and Learning, 9*(1). doi:10.5206/cjsotl-rcacea.2018.1.9

Fosnacht, K., Sarraf, S., Howe, E., & Peck, L. (2017). How important are high response rates for college surveys? *Review of Higher Education, 40*(2), 245–265. doi:10.1353/rhe.2017.0003

Foulger, T. (2005). Innovating professional development standards: A shift to utilize Communities of Practice. *Essays in Education, 14*(1), Article 1. Retrieved from https://openriver.winona.edu/eie/vol14/iss1/1

Friberg, J. (2016, July 25). Knowing who we are [web log post]. Retrieved from https://illinoisstateuniversitysotl.wordpress.com/2016/07/25/knowing-who-we-are/

Friberg, J. C., & McKinney, K. (Eds.). (2019). *Applying SoTL beyond the individual classroom.* Bloomington, IN: Indiana University Press.

Friedman, T. (2015). Ambivalence will not overcome extremism. *Kansas City Star, 1/16*(15), 17A.

Fukuzawa, S., Vander Kloet, M., Frake-Mistak, M., Caldecott, M., & Cassidy, A. (2017, October). *SoTL aspirations: Multi-disciplinary writing groups as an entrance into the practice of SoTL for contingent instructors.* Poster presentation at the International Society for the Scholarship of Teaching and Learning, Calgary, Alberta.

Gannon-Leary, P., & Fontainha, E. (2007). Communities of Practice and virtual learning communities: Benefits, barriers and success factors. *eLearning Papers, 5*, 20-29.

Garet, M. S., Porter, A., Desimone, L., Birman, B. F., & Suk Yoon, K. (2001). What makes professional development effective? Results from a national sample of teachers. *American Educational Research Journal, 38*(4), 915–945. doi:10.3102/00028312038004915

Garrison, D. R., Anderson, T., & Archer, W. (1999). Critical inquiry in a text-based environment: Computer conferencing in higher education. *The Internet and Higher Education, 2*(2-3), 87–105. doi:10.1016/S1096-7516(00)00016-6

Gavigan, K., & Lance, K. C. (2015). Everybody's teacher: Administrators' and teachers' perceptions of school librarians. Findings from the South Carolina Association of School Librarians impact study. *Teacher Librarian, 43*(1), 8.

Gee, J. (2001). Reading as situated language: A sociocognitive perspective. *Journal of Adolescent & Adult Literacy, 44*(8), 714–725. doi:10.1598/JAAL.44.8.3

Geertsema, J. (2016). Academic development, SoTL, and educational research. *The International Journal for Academic Development, 21*(2), 122–134. doi:10.1080/1360144X.2016.1175144

Gehrke, S., & Kezar, A. (2015). Supporting non-tenure-track faculty at 4-year colleges and universities: A national study of dean's values and decisions. *Educational Policy, 29*(6), 926–960. doi:10.1177/0895904814531651

Gershan, M. (2013). *How to use questioning in the classroom: The complete guide.* Germany: Amazon Distribution.

Gibbs, G. (1988). *Learning by doing: A guide to teaching and learning methods.* Oxford, UK: Further Education Unit. Oxford Polytechnic.

Gibbs, G. (2013). Reflections on the changing nature of educational development. *The International Journal for Academic Development, 18*(1), 4–14. doi:10.1080/1360144X.2013.751691

Gilpin, L. (2011). Scholarship of Teaching and Learning trades. *International Journal for the Scholarship of Teaching and Learning, 5*(2). doi:10.20429/ijsotl.2011.050204

www.igi-global.com

Publisher of Peer-Reviewed, Timely, and
Innovative Academic Research Since 1988

IGI Global's Transformative Open Access (OA) Model:
How to Turn Your University Library's Database Acquisitions Into a Source of OA Funding

In response to the OA movement and well in advance of Plan S, IGI Global, early last year, unveiled their OA Fee Waiver (Offset Model) Initiative.

Under this initiative, librarians who invest in IGI Global's InfoSci-Books (5,300+ reference books) and/or InfoSci-Journals (185+ scholarly journals) databases will be able to subsidize their patron's OA article processing charges (APC) when their work is submitted and accepted (after the peer review process) into an IGI Global journal.*

How Does it Work?

1. When a library subscribes or perpetually purchases IGI Global's InfoSci-Databases including InfoSci-Books (5,300+ e-books), InfoSci-Journals (185+ e-journals), and/or their discipline/subject-focused subsets, IGI Global will match the library's investment with a fund of equal value to go toward subsidizing the OA article processing charges (APCs) for their patrons.

   Researchers: Be sure to recommend the InfoSci-Books and InfoSci-Journals to take advantage of this initiative.

2. When a student, faculty, or staff member submits a paper and it is accepted (following the peer review) into one of IGI Global's 185+ scholarly journals, the author will have the option to have their paper published under a traditional publishing model or as OA.

3. When the author chooses to have their paper published under OA, IGI Global will notify them of the OA Fee Waiver (Offset Model) Initiative. If the author decides they would like to take advantage of this initiative, IGI Global will deduct the US$ 1,500 APC from the created fund.

4. This fund will be offered on an annual basis and will renew as the subscription is renewed for each year thereafter. IGI Global will manage the fund and award the APC waivers unless the librarian has a preference as to how the funds should be managed.

Hear From the Experts on This Initiative:

"I'm very happy to have been able to make one of my recent research contributions, 'Visualizing the Social Media Conversations of a National Information Technology Professional Association' featured in the *International Journal of Human Capital and Information Technology Professionals*, freely available along with having access to the valuable resources found within IGI Global's InfoSci-Journals database."

– Prof. Stuart Palmer,
Deakin University, Australia

For More Information, Visit: www.igi-global.com/publish/contributor-resources/open-access or contact IGI Global's Database Team at eresources@igi-global.com.

Gilpin, L., & Liston, D. (2009). Transformative education in the Scholarship of Teaching and Learning: An analysis of SoTL literature. *International Journal for the Scholarship of Teaching and Learning, 3*(2). doi:10.20429/ijsotl.2009.030211

Ginns, P., Kitay, J., & Prosser, M. (2010). Transfer of academic staff learning in a research-intensive university. *Teaching in Higher Education, 15*(3), 235–246. doi:10.1080/13562511003740783

Ginsberg, S. M., & Bernstein, J. L. (2011, January). Growing the Scholarship of Teaching and Learning through institutional culture change. *The Journal of Scholarship of Teaching and Learning, 11*(1), 1–12.

Glassick, C. E., Huber, M. T., & Maeroff, G. I. (1997). *Scholarship assessed: Evaluation of the professoriate.* San Francisco, CA: Jossey-Bass.

Goldszmidt, M., Zimbrowski, E., & Weston, W. (2008). Education scholarship: It's not just a question of "degree". *Medical Teacher, 30*(1), 34–39. doi:10.1080/01421590701754136 PMID:18278649

Goodyear-Smith, F., Lobb, B., Davies, G., Nachson, I., & Seelau, S. M. (2002). International variation in ethics committee requirements: Comparisons across five Westernised nations. *BMC Medical Ethics, 3*(1), 1–8. doi:10.1186/1472-6939-3-2 PMID:11964190

Gornitzka, Å., & Larsen, I. (2004). Towards professionalisation? Restructuring of administrative work force in universities. *Higher Education, 47*(4), 455–471. doi:10.1023/B:HIGH.0000020870.06667.f1

Gorsky, P., & Blau, I. (2009). Online teaching effectiveness: A tale of two instructors. *The International Review of Research in Open and Distributed Learning, 10*(3). doi:10.19173/irrodl.v10i3.712

Gosling, D. (2004). The impact of a national policy to enhance teaching quality and the status, England, the United Kingdom. *Quality Assurance in Education, 12*(3), 136–149. doi:10.1108/09684880410548762

Government of Canada, Canadian Institutes of Health Research, Natural Sciences and Engineering Research Council of Canada, and Social Sciences and Humanities Research Council. (2014). *Tri-council policy statement: Ethical conduct for research involving humans.* Retrieved from http://www.pre.ethics.gc.ca/eng/policy-politique/initiatives/tcps2-eptc2/Default/

Government, H. M. (2017). *Higher Education and Research Act.* Retrieved from http://www.legislation.gov.uk/ukpga/2017/29/contents/enacted

Graduate Outcomes. (2019). *About the survey.* Retrieved from: https://www.graduateoutcomes.ac.uk/about-survey

Graham, A., Kerkhoff, S., & Spires, H. (2017). Disciplinary literacy in the middle school: Exploring pedagogical tensions. *Middle Grades Research Journal, 11*(1), 63–83.

Grant, S., & Hurd, F. (2010). Incorporating critical pedagogy into the Scholarship of Teaching and Learning: Making the journey alongside our students. *International Journal for the Scholarship of Teaching and Learning, 4*(2). doi:10.20429/ijsotl.2010.040220

Graves, D. H. (1994). *A fresh look at writing.* Portsmouth, NH: Heinemann.

Gray, T., & Shandle, S. (2009). Launching or revitalizing a teaching center: Principles and portraits of practice. *Journal of Faculty Development, 23*(2), 5–12.

Green, D. (2009). New academics' perceptions of the language of teaching and learning: Identifying and overcoming linguistic barriers. *The International Journal for Academic Development, 14*(1), 33–45. doi:10.1080/13601440802659254

Green, D., & Little, D. (2016). Family portrait: A profile of educational developers around the world. *The International Journal for Academic Development, 21*(2), 135–150. doi:10.1080/1360144X.2015.1046875

Grigsby, R. K., & Thorndyke, L. (2011). Perspective: Recognizing and rewarding clinical scholarship. *Academic Medicine*, *86*(1), 127–131. doi:10.1097/ACM.0b013e3181ffae5e PMID:21099387

Grossman, P. M. (1990). *The making of a teacher: Teacher knowledge and teacher education*. New York, NY: Teachers College Press.

Gubbins, P. O. (2014). The Scholarship of Teaching and Learning: An opportunity for clinical faculty members in academic pharmacy and other health professions to develop a program of scholarship. *International Journal for the Scholarship of Teaching and Learning*, *8*(1). doi:10.20429/ijsotl.2014.080103

Gunning, T. G. (2015). *Creating literacy instruction for middle-level learners* (2nd ed.). Boston, MA: Pearson Learning Solutions.

Gurung, R. A. R. (2014). Getting foxy: Invoking different magesteria in the Scholarship of Teaching and Learning. *Teaching & Learning Inquiry*, *2*(2), 109–114. doi:10.20343/teachlearninqu.2.2.109

Gurung, R. A. R., & Schwartz, B. M. (2010). Riding the third wave of SoTL. *International Journal for the Scholarship of Teaching and Learning*, *4*(2). doi:10.20429/ijsotl.2010.040205

Gustafson, K. L., & Branch, R. M. (1997). Revisioning models of instructional development. *Educational Technology Research and Development*, *45*(3), 73–89. doi:10.1007/BF02299731

Haigh, N. J. (2012). Sustaining and spreading the positive outcomes of SoTL projects: Issues, insights, and strategies. *The International Journal for Academic Development*, *17*(1), 19–31. doi:10.1080/1360144X.2011.586462

Haigh, N., Gossman, P., & Jiao, X. (2011). Undertaking an institutional "stock-take" of SoTL: New Zealand university case studies. *Higher Education Research & Development*, *30*(1), 9–23. doi:10.1080/07294360.2011.536969

Haley, K., Wiessner, C., & Robinson, E. E. (2009). Encountering new information and perspectives: Constructing knowledge in conference contexts. *Journal of Continuing Higher Education*, *57*(2), 72–82. doi:10.1080/07377360902964384

Halliday, M. A. K., & Martin, J. R. (1993). *Writing science*. London: The Falmer Press.

Halliday, M. A. K., & Matthiessen, C. M. I. M. (2014). *Introduction to functional grammar* (4th ed.). Abingdon, UK: Routledge. doi:10.4324/9780203783771

Hallis, R. (2018). Promoting self-regulated learning in the first-year writing classroom. In G. Veach (Ed.), Teaching information literacy and writing studies: Volume 1, first year composition courses (pp. 111-126). West Lafayette, IN: Purdue University Press.

Hamilton, D. (2014). Building a culture of pedagogical enquiry: Institutional support strategies for developing the Scholarship of Teaching and Learning. *Advances in Scholarship of Teaching and Learning, 1*(1). Retrieved from https://tlc.unisim.edu.sg/research/AdvSoTL/pdf/doug_hamliltion. Pdf

Hammond, J. S. (1976). *Learning by the case method*. Harvard Business School. Case 9-376-241. Retrieved from http://projects.iq.harvard.edu/files/sdpfellowship/files/hbs_casemethod_overview.pdf

Handler, K., & Hays, L. (2019). Librarians as faculty developers: Leading educational development initiatives. *College & Research Libraries News*, *80*(4), 220–235. doi:10.5860/crln.80.4.220

Harland, T., Raja Hussain, R. M., & Bakar, A. A. (2014). The Scholarship of Teaching and Learning: Challenges for Malaysian academics. *Teaching in Higher Education*, *19*(1), 38–48. doi:10.1080/13562517.2013.827654

Harland, T., & Staniforth, D. (2008). A family of strangers: The fragmented nature of academic development. *Teaching in Higher Education*, *13*(6), 669–678. doi:10.1080/13562510802452392

Harris, J., Podis, L. A., Podis, J. A. M., Rafoth, B., Inman, J. A., Sewell, D. N., ... Grimm, N. M. (2001). Reaffirming, reflecting, reforming: Writing center scholarship comes of age. *College English*, *63*(5), 662–668. doi:10.2307/379050

Harris, M. (1995). Talking in the middle: Why writers need writing tutors. *College English*, *57*(1), 27–42. doi:10.2307/378348

Harvey, M., Coulson, D., Mackaway, J., & Winchester-Seeto, T. (2010). Aligning reflection in the cooperative education curriculum. *Asia Pacific Journal of Cooperative Education*, *11*(3), 137–152. Retrieved from https://pdfs.semanticscholar.org/04f4/b126ef8af981e73f765118a2e036fe55c74b.pdf

Hays, L., & Studebaker, B. (2019). Academic instruction librarians' teacher identity development through participation in the Scholarship of Teaching and Learning. *International Journal for the Scholarship of Teaching and Learning*, *13*(2), 4. doi:10.20429/ijsotl.2019.130204

Head, A. J., & Eisenberg, M. B. (2010). *Truth be told: How college students evaluate and use information in the digital age.* Seattle, WA: University of Washington Information School, Project Information Literacy. Retrieved from http://www.projectinfolit.org/uploads/2/7/5/4/27541717/pil_fall2010_survey_fullreport1.pdf

Healey, M. (2008). On discipline-based approaches to SoTL. *The International Commons*, *3*(1), 2-3. Retrieved from http://www.issotl.org/newsletter.html

Healey, M. (2014). *Strategies to support staff/faculty engagement in pedagogic research (PedR) & Scholarship of Teaching and Learning (SoTL).* Retrieved from https://www. mickhealey.co.uk/?wpdmdl=1312

Healey, M., Flint, A., & Harrington, K. (2014). *Engagement through partnership: Students as partners in learning and teaching in higher education.* York, UK: HEA. Retrieved from https://www.heacademy.ac.uk/knowledge-hub/engagement-through-partnership-students-partners-learning-and-teaching-higher

Healey, M. (2000). Developing the scholarship of teaching in higher education: A discipline-based approach. *Higher Education Research & Development*, *19*(2), 169–189. doi:10.1080/072943600445637

Healey, M. (2003). The scholarship of teaching: Issues around an evolving concept. *Journal on Excellence in College Teaching*, *14*(2/3), 5–26.

Healey, M., Bradford, M., Roberts, C., & Knight, Y. (2013). Collaborative discipline-based curriculum change: Applying change academy processes at department level. *The International Journal for Academic Development*, *18*(1), 31–44. doi:10.1080/1360144X.2011.628394

Healey, M., Flint, A., & Harrington, K. (2014). *Engagement through partnership: Students as partners in learning and teaching in higher education.* York, UK: Higher Education Academy. Retrieved from https://www.heacademy.ac.uk/engagement-through-partnership-students-partners-learning-and-teaching-higher-education

Hearnshaw, H. (2004). Comparison of requirements of research ethics committees in 11 European countries for a non-invasive interventional study. *BMJ (Clinical Research Ed.)*, *328*(7432), 140–141. doi:10.1136/bmj.328.7432.140 PMID:14726341

Hebert, C. (2015). Knowing and/or experiencing: A critical examination of the reflective models of John Dewey and Donald Schön. *Reflective Practice*, *16*(3), 361–371. doi:10.1080/14623943.2015.1023281

Heinrich, K. T., & Oberleitner, M. G. (2012). How a faculty group's peer mentoring of each other's scholarship can enhance retention and recruitment. *Journal of Professional Nursing*, *28*(1), 5–12. doi:10.1016/j.profnurs.2011.06.002 PMID:22261599

Helyer, R. (2015). Learning through reflection: The critical role of reflection in work-based learning. *Journal of Work-Applied Management*, *7*(1), 15–27. doi:10.1108/JWAM-10-2015-003

Henderson, J. (2010). *An exploration of transformative learning in the online environment.* Paper presented at 26th Annual Conference on Distance Teaching and Learning, Madison, WI.

Henderson, M., Selvyn, N., & Aston, R. (2017). What works and why? Student perceptions of useful digital technology in university teaching and learning. *Studies in Higher Education, 42*(8), 1567–1579. doi:10.1080/03075079.2015.1007946

Henrich, K. J., & Attebury, R. (2010). Communities of practice at an academic library: A new approach to mentoring at the University of Idaho. *Journal of Academic Librarianship, 36*(2), 158–165. doi:10.1016/j.acalib.2010.01.007

Herrington, A., & Herrington, J. (2006). What is an authentic learning environment? In T. Herrington & J. Herrington (Eds.), *Authentic learning environments in higher education* (pp. 1–14). Hershey, PA: IGI Global. doi:10.4018/978-1-59140-594-8.ch001

Hibbert, P., Sillince, J., Diefenbach, T., & Cunliffe, A. L. (2014). Relationally reflexive practice: A generative approach to theory development in qualitative research. *Organizational Research Methods, 17*(3), 278–298. doi:10.1177/1094428114524829

Hockings, C. (2005). Removing barriers? A study of the conditions affecting teaching innovation. *Teaching in Higher Education, 10*(3), 313–326. doi:10.1080/13562510500122149

Hoessler, C., Britnell, J., & Stockley, D. (2010). Assessing the impact of educational development through the lens of the Scholarship of Teaching and Learning. *New Directions for Teaching and Learning, 122*(122), 81–89. doi:10.1002/tl.400

Holland, B. (2005, July). Scholarship and mission in the 21st century university: The role of engagement. In *Proceedings of the Australian Universities Quality Forum* (pp. 11-17). Academic Press.

hooks, b. (1994). *Teaching to transgress.* Routledge.

Horton, W. K. (2012). *E-Learning by Design* (2nd ed.). San Francisco, CA: Pfieffer.

Houghton, C., Casey, D., Shaw, D., & Murphy, K. (2013). Rigour in qualitative case-study research. *Nurse Researcher, 20*(4), 12–17. doi:10.7748/nr2013.03.20.4.12.e326 PMID:23520707

Houtman, E. (2010). "Trying to figure it out": Academic librarians talk about learning to teach. *Library and Information Research, 34*(107), 18–40. doi:10.29173/lirg246

Hubball, H. T., & Pearson, M. (2010). Grappling with the complexity of undergraduate degree program reform: Critical barriers and emergent strategies. *Transformative Dialogues: Teaching & Learning Journal, 3*(3). Retrieved from http://kwantlen.ca/TD/TD.3.3/TD.3.3_Hubball&Pearson_Undergraduate_Degree_Program_Reform.pdf

Hubball, H. T., & Burt, H. (2004). An integrated approach to developing and implementing learning-centred curricula. *The International Journal for Academic Development, 9*(1), 51–65. doi:10.1080/1360144042000296053

Hubball, H. T., & Clarke, A. (2010). Diverse methodological approaches and considerations for SoTL in higher education. *The Canadian Journal for the Scholarship of Teaching and Learning, 1*(1). doi:10.5206/cjsotl-rcacea.2010.1.2

Hubball, H. T., Clarke, A. C., Webb, A. S., & Johnson, B. (2015). Developing institutional leadership for the Scholarship of Teaching and Learning: Lessons learned with senior educational leaders in multi-national research-intensive university contexts. *International Journal of University Teaching and Faculty Development, 4*(4). Retrieved from https://www.novapublishers.com/catalog/product_info.php?products_id=53411

Hubball, H. T., & Gold, N. (2007). The scholarship of curriculum practice and undergraduate program reform: Integrating theory into practice. *New Directions for Teaching and Learning, 112*(112), 5–14. doi:10.1002/tl.293

Hubball, H. T., Lamberson, M., & Kindler, A. (2012). Strategic restructuring of a centre for teaching and learning in a research-intensive university: Institutional engagement in scholarly approaches to curriculum renewal and pedagogical practices. *International Journal for University Teaching and Faculty Development, 3*(2), 95–110.

Hubball, H. T., Pearson, M., & Clarke, A. (2013). SoTL inquiry in broader curricula and institutional contexts: Theoretical underpinnings and emerging trends. Invited peer-reviewed essay for inaugural issue. *International Journal for Inquiry in Teaching and Learning, 1*(1), 41–57. doi:10.1353/iss.2013.0009

Hubball, H., Clarke, A., & Poole, G. (2010). Ten-year reflections on mentoring SoTL in a research-intensive university. *The International Journal for Academic Development, 15*(2), 117–129. doi:10.1080/13601441003737758

Hubball, H., Pearson, M. L., & Clarke, A. (2013). SoTL inquiry in broader curricular and institutional contexts: Theoretical underpinnings and emerging trends. *Teaching & Learning Inquiry, 1*(1), 41–57.

Huber, M. T., & Hutchings, P. (2006). Building the teaching commons. *Change: The Magazine of Higher Learning, 38*(3), 24-31. Doi:10.3200/CHNG.38.3.24-31

Huber, M. (2004). *Balancing acts: The Scholarship of Teaching and Learning in academic careers.* Washington, DC: American Association for Higher Education and the Carnegie Foundation for the Advancement of Teaching.

Huber, M. T. (2009). Teaching travels: Reflections on the social life of classroom inquiry and innovation. *International Journal for the Scholarship of Teaching and Learning, 3*(2), 2. doi:10.20429/ijsotl.2009.030202

Huber, M. T. (2010). Editorial: CASTL has concluded. Long live the Scholarship of Teaching and Learning. *Arts and Humanities in Higher Education, 9*(1), 5–8. doi:10.1177/1474022209357660

Huber, M. T., & Hutchings, P. (2005). *The advancement of learning: Building the learning commons.* San Francisco, CA: Jossey-Bass.

Huber, M. T., & Hutchings, P. (2005). *The advancement of learning: Building the teaching commons.* San Francisco, CA: Jossey-Bass.

Huber, M. T., & Hutchings, P. (2008). Editorial: The Scholarship of Teaching and Learning in the humanities: The place—and problem—of theory. *Arts and Humanities in Higher Education, 7*(3), 227–228. doi:10.1177/1474022208094408

Huber, M. T., & Morreale, S. P. (2002). Situating the Scholarship of Teaching and Learning. In M. T. Huber & S. P. Morreale (Eds.), *Disciplinary styles in the scholarship of teaching: Exploring common ground* (pp. 1–24). Washington, DC: American Association for Higher Education and the Carnegie Foundation for the Advancement of Teaching.

Hum, G., Amundsen, C., & Emmioglu, E. (2015). Evaluating a teaching development grants program: Our framework, process, initial findings, and reflections. *Studies in Educational Evaluation, 46*, 29–38. doi:10.1016/j.stueduc.2015.02.004

Husbands, C. (2017). Foreword: Ten TEF Lessons. In *Going for gold: Lessons from the TEF provider submissions.* Higher Education Policy Institute Report 99. Retrieved from: https://www.hepi.ac.uk/wp-content/uploads/2017/10/FINAL-HEPI-Going-for-Gold-Report-99-04_10_17-Screen.pdf

Hutchings, M., & Quinney, A. (2015). The flipped classroom, disruptive pedagogies, enabling technologies, and wicked problems: Responding to" The bomb in the basement". *Electronic Journal of E-Learning, 13*(2), 106-119.

Hutchings, P. (2000). Approaching the Scholarship of Teaching and Learning. In P. Hutchings (Ed.), *Opening lines: Approaches to the Scholarship of Teaching and Learning.* Retrieved from http://www.carnegiefoundation.org/elibrary/approaching-scholarship-teaching-and-learning

Hutchings, P., & Shulman, L. (1999). The Scholarship of Teaching: New elaborations, new developments. *Change: The Magazine of Higher Learning, 31*(5), 10-15. Doi:10.1080/00091389909604218

Hutchings, P. (2000). Introduction: Approaching the Scholarship of Teaching and Learning. In P. Hutchings (Ed.), *Opening lines: Approaches to the Scholarship of Teaching and Learning* (pp. 1–10). Menlo Park, CA: The Carnegie Foundation for the Advancement of Teaching.

Hutchings, P. (2000). *Opening lines: Approaches to the Scholarship of Teaching and Learning.* Menlo Park, CA: Carnegie Publications.

Hutchings, P. (2003). Competing goods: Ethical issues in the Scholarship of Teaching and Learning. *Change: The Magazine of Higher Learning, 35*(5), 26–33. doi:10.1080/00091380309604116

Hutchings, P. (2007). Theory: The elephant in the Scholarship of Teaching and Learning room. *International Journal for the Scholarship of Teaching and Learning, 1*(1). doi:10.20429/ijsotl.2007.010102

Hutchings, P., Borin, P., Keesing-Styles, L., Martin, L., Michael, R., Scharff, L., ... Ismail, A. (2013). The Scholarship of Teaching and Learning in an age of accountability: Building bridges. *Teaching & Learning Inquiry, 1*(2), 35–47. doi:10.20343/teachlearninqu.1.2.35

Hutchings, P., & Huber, M. T. (2008). Placing theory in the Scholarship of Teaching and Learning. *Arts and Humanities in Higher Education, 7*(3), 229–244. doi:10.1177/1474022208094409

Hutchings, P., Huber, M. T., & Ciccone, A. (2011). *The Scholarship of Teaching and Learning reconsidered: Institutional integration and impact.* San Francisco, CA: Jossey-Bass.

Hutchings, P., Huber, M., & Ciccone, A. (2011). Feature essays: Getting there: An integrative vision of the Scholarship of Teaching and Learning. *International Journal for the Scholarship of Scholarship of Teaching and Learning, 5*(1), 31. doi:10.20429/ijsotl.2011.050131

Hyman, D., Gurgevich, E., Alter, T., Ayers, J., Cash, E., Fahnline, D., ... Wright, H. (2002). Beyond Boyer: The UniSCOPE model of scholarship for the 21st century. *Journal of Higher Education Outreach & Engagement, 7*(1-2), 41–65.

Hynd-Shanahan, C. (2013). What does it take? The challenge of disciplinary literacy. *Journal of Adolescent & Adult Literacy, 57*(2), 93–98. doi:10.1002/JAAL.226

Institute for Apprenticeships. (2018). *Academic professional standard.* Retrieved from: https://www.instituteforapprenticeships.org/apprenticeship-standards/academic-professional/

Jackson, D. (2015). Employability skill development in work-integrated learning: Barriers and best practice. *Studies in Higher Education, 40*(2), 350–367. doi:10.1080/03075079.2013.842221

Jacobs, D. (2000). A chemical mixture of methods. In P. Hutchings (Ed.), *Opening lines: approaches to the Scholarship of Teaching and Learning* (pp. 63–71). Menlo Park, CA: Carnegie Publications.

Jacobs, L. (2013). Academic status for Canadian academic librarians: A brief history. In J. Dekker & M. Kandiuk (Eds.), *In solidarity: Academic librarians labour activism and union participation in Canada* (pp. 9–37). Sacramento, CA: Library Juice Press.

Jenkins, A., & Healey, M. (2015). International perspectives on strategies to support faculty who teach students via research and inquiry. *Council on Undergraduate Research Quarterly, 35*(3), 31–37. Retrieved from https://www.cur.org/download.aspx?id=3147

Johnes, J., & Taylor, T. (1990). *Performance Indicators in Higher Education.* Buckingham, UK: SRHE and the Open University Press.

Johnsen, H., Pacht, M., van Slyck, P., & Tsao, T. (2009). The messy teaching conversation: Toward a model of collegial reflection, exchange, and scholarship on classroom problems. *Teaching English in the Two-Year College, 37*(2), 119–136.

Johnson, C. (2001). A survey of current research on online Communities of Practice. *The Internet and Higher Education, 4*(1), 45–60. doi:10.1016/S1096-7516(01)00047-1

Johnson, R. B., Onwuegbuzie, A. J., & Turner, L. A. (2007). Toward a definition of mixed methods research. *Journal of Mixed Methods Research, 1*(2), 112–133. doi:10.1177/1558689806298224

Jones, J. (2011). Using MASUS to assess writing outcomes: A case study of different pathways. *English language entry pathways: Innovations, outcomes and future directions.*

Jorre de St Jorre, T., & Oliver, B. (2018). Want students to engage? Contextualise graduate learning outcomes and assess for employability. *Higher Education Research & Development, 37*(1), 44–57. doi:10.1080/07294360.2017.1339183

Julien, H., Gross, M., & Latham, D. (2018). Survey of information literacy instructional practices in U.S. academic libraries. *College & Research Libraries, 79*(2), 179–199. doi:10.5860/crl.79.2.179

Kammer, J., & Zhou, G. (2018). *Foundations of instructional design for online courses.* Retrieved from https://ali.memberclicks.net/alise-xchange-october-2018

Kane-Gill, S. L., Williams, E. A., Smithburger, P. L., & Seybert, A. L. (2013). Tips for developing an integrated online and simulation course based on six years of experience. *Pharmacy, 1*(1), 34–42. doi:10.3390/pharmacy1010034

Kanuka, H. (2011). Keeping the scholarship in the Scholarship of Teaching and Learning. *International Journal for the Scholarship of Teaching and Learning, 5*(1). doi:10.20429/ijsotl.2011.050103

Karabenick, S. A., & Conley, A. (2011). *Teacher motivation for professional development.* Retrieved from http://hub.mspnet.org/media/data/Teacher_PDM.pdf?media_000000007652.pdf

Karmel, T., & Carroll, D. (2016). *Has the graduate job market been swamped?* NILS working paper series No. 228/2016. Adelaide, Australia: National Institute of Labour Studies.

Kasl, E., & Elias, D. (2000). Creating new habits of mind in small groups. In *Learning as Transformation: Critical Perspectives on a Theory in Progress* (pp. 229–252). San Francisco, CA: Jossey-Bass.

Kebritchi, M., Lipschuetz, A., & Santiague, L. (2017). Issues and challenges for teaching successful online courses in higher education: A literature review. *Journal of Educational Technology Systems, 46*(1), 4–29. doi:10.1177/0047239516661713

Keig, L., & Waggoner, M. (1994). *Collaborative peer review: The role of faculty in improving college teaching.* Washington, DC: Graduate School of Education and Human Development, George Washington University.

Kek, M. Y. C. A., & Huijser, H. (2017). *Problem-based learning into the future: Imagining an agile PBL ecology for learning.* Singapore: Springer. doi:10.1007/978-981-10-2454-2

Kelder, J., & Carr, A. (2017). Embedding evaluation and scholarship into curriculum and teaching: The curriculum evaluation framework. In A. Horshed, P. Bartholomew, J. Branch & C. Nygaard (Eds.), New innovations in teaching and learning in higher education (pp. 430-451). Upper Farringdon: Libri Publishing.

Kelder, J.-A., & Carr, A. (2016). *Embedding evaluation and research into curriculum design and delivery—workshop.* Paper presented at the 39th Annual Conference of the Higher Education Research and Development Society of Australasia (HERDSA), Freemantle, Australia.

Kelder, J.-A., Carr, A., & Walls, J. (2017). *Evidence-based transformation of curriculum: A research and evaluation framework.* Paper presented at the 40th Annual Conference of the Higher Education Research and Development Society of Australasia (HERDSA), Sydney, Australia.

Kelder, J.-A., & Carr, A. (2017). Embedding evaluation and scholarship into curriculum and teaching: The curriculum evaluation research framework. In A. Horsted, P. Bartholomew, J. Branch, & C. Nygaard (Eds.), *New Innovations in Teaching and Learning in Higher Education 2017* (pp. 430–451). Faringdon, UK: Libri Publishing.

Kelley, B. (2008). Trading zones: Building connections to past research in the Scholarship of Teaching and Learning. *INSight: A Journal of Scholarly Teaching, 3,* 10-16.

Kelly, N., Nesbit, S., & Oliver, C. (2012). A Difficult Journey: Transitioning from STEM to SoTL. *International Journal for the Scholarship of Teaching and Learning, 6*(1). doi:10.20429/ijsotl.2012.060118

Kember, D. (2000). *Action learning, action research: Improving the quality of teaching and learning.* Abingdon, UK: Routledge. doi:10.4324/9780203016343

Kember, D., Leung, D. Y. P., Jones, A., Loke, A. Y., McKay, J., Sinclair, K., ... Yeung, E. (2000). Development of a questionnaire to measure the level of reflective thinking. *Assessment & Evaluation in Higher Education, 25*(4), 381–395. doi:10.1080/713611442

Kember, D., McKay, J., Sinclair, K., & Wong, F. K. Y. (2008). A four-category scheme for coding and assessing the level of reflection in written work. *Assessment & Evaluation in Higher Education, 33*(4), 369–379. doi:10.1080/02602930701293355

Kemp, J. (2006). Isn't being a librarian enough? Librarians as classroom teachers. *College & Undergraduate Libraries, 13*(3), 3–23. doi:10.1300/J106v13n03_02

Kenny, N., Berenson, C., Chick, N., Johnson, C., Keegan, D., Read, E., & Reid, L. (2017). *A developmental framework for teaching expertise in postsecondary education.* Paper presented at the International Society for the Scholarship of Teaching and Learning (ISSOTL) Conference, Calgary, Alberta, Canada. Retrieved from http://connections.ucalgary-blogs.ca/files/2017/11/CC3_Teaching-Expertise-Framework-Fall-2017.pdf

Kenny, N., & Evers, F. (2010). Responding to the challenging dilemma of faculty engagement in research on teaching and learning and disciplinary research. *Collected Essays on Learning and Teaching, 3,* 21–26. doi:10.22329/celt.v3i0.3234

Kensington-Miller, B., Renc-Roe, J., & Moron-Garcia, S. (2015). The chameleon on a tartan rug: Adaptations of three academic developers' professional identities. *The International Journal for Academic Development, 20*(3), 279–290. doi:10.1080/1360144X.2015.1047373

Kern, B., Mettetal, G., Dixson, M., & Morgan, R. K. (2015). The role of SoTL in the academy: Upon the 25th anniversary of Boyer's Scholarship Reconsidered. *The Journal of Scholarship of Teaching and Learning,* 1–14. doi:10.14434/josotl.v15i3.13623

Keys, C. W. (1999). Revitalizing instruction in scientific genres: Connecting knowledge production with writing to learn in science. *Science Education, 83*(2), 115–130. doi:10.1002/(SICI)1098-237X(199903)83:2<115::AID-SCE2>3.0.CO;2-Q

Kezar, A. (2001). *Understanding and facilitating organizational change in higher education in the 21st century.* San Francisco, CA: Jossey-Bass.

Kezar, A., Gallants, T., & Lester, J. (2011). Everyday people making a difference on college campuses: The tempered grassroots leadership tactics of faculty and staff. *Studies in Higher Education, 73,* 435–460. doi:10.1353/jhe.2002.0038

Kezar, A., & Sam, C. (2013). Institutionalizing equitable policies and practices for contingent faculty. *The Journal of Higher Education, 84*(1), 56–87. doi:10.1353/jhe.2013.0002

Kim, A., Popovic, C., Farrugia, L., Saleh, S., Maheux-Pelletier, G., & Frake-Mistak, M. (2019, July). On nurturing the emergent SoTL researcher: Responding to challenges and opportunities. *The International Journal for Academic Development*, 8.

Kim, M. K., Kim, S. M., Khera, O., & Getman, J. (2014). The experience of three flipped classrooms in an urban university: An exploration of design principles. *The Internet and Higher Education*, 22, 37–50. doi:10.1016/j.iheduc.2014.04.003

King, H. (2004). Continuing professional development in higher education: What do academics do? *Educational Developments*, 5(4), 1–5.

King, J. (2018). Transformative learning in online college courses: Process and evidence. *International Journal on Innovations in Online Education*, 2(2). doi:10.1615/IntJInnovOnlineEdu.2018028557

King, K. (2009). *Handbook of the evolving research of transformative learning*. Charlotte, NC: Information Age Publishing.

King, S. (2000). *On writing: A memoir of the craft*. New York, NY: Scribner.

Klein, J. H., & Connell, N. A. (2008). The identification and cultivation of appropriate Communities of Practice in higher education. *Communities of Practice: Creating Learning Environments for Educators, 1*, 65-81.

Kleine, K., & McBryar, L. (2009). Preservice teachers experience middle grades curriculum. *Middle School Journal*, 40(3), 28–36. doi:10.1080/00940771.2009.11495584

Knight, P., Tait, J., & Yorke, M. (2006). The professional learning of teachers in higher education. *Studies in Higher Education*, 31(03), 319–339. doi:10.1080/03075070600680786

Koh, J. H. L., Chai, C. S., Wong, B., & Hong, H. Y. (2015). *Design thinking for education: Conceptions and applications in teaching and learning*. Singapore: Springer.

Kolb, A., & Kolb, D. (2005). Learning styles and learning spaces: Enhancing experiential learning in higher education. *Academy of Management Learning & Education*, 4(2), 193–212. doi:10.5465/amle.2005.17268566

Kolb, D. A. (1984). *Experiential learning: Experience as the source of learning and development*. Englewood Cliffs, NJ: Prentice-Hall.

Korthagen, F. A. J., & Kessels, J. P. A. M. (1999). Linking theory and practice: Changing the pedagogy of teacher education. *Educational Researcher*, 28(4), 4–17. doi:10.3102/0013189X028004004

Koster, R. (2004). *A theory of fun*. New York, NY: Paraglyph Press.

Kreber, C. (2006). Developing the scholarship of teaching through transformative learning. *The Journal of Scholarship of Teaching and Learning*, 6(1), 88–109. Retrieved from https://pdfs.semanticscholar.org/ab6d/0db0049f0468bee87ad2b27ce4a20abfda92.pdf

Kreber, C. (2007). What's it really all about? The Scholarship of Teaching and Learning as an authentic practice. *International Journal for the Scholarship of Teaching and Learning*, 1(1). doi:10.20429/ijsotl.2007.010103

Kreber, C. (2013). The transformative potential of the Scholarship of Teaching. *Teaching and Learning Inquiry: The ISSOTL Journal*, 1(1), 5–18. doi:10.20343/teachlearninqu.1.1.5

Kreber, C., & Cranton, P. (2000). Exploring the Scholarship of Teaching. *The Journal of Higher Education*, 71(4), 476–495. doi:10.2307/2649149

Kruger, J., & Dunning, D. (1999). Unskilled and unaware of it: How difficulties in recognizing one's own incompetence lead to inflated self-assessments. *Journal of Personality and Social Psychology*, *77*(6), 1121–1134. doi:10.1037/0022-3514.77.6.1121 PMID:10626367

Kuhn, T. S. (1962). *The structure of scientific revolutions*. Chicago, IL: University of Chicago Press.

Kurtz, G., & Sponder, B. (2010). SoTL in online education: Strategies and practices for using new media for teaching and learning online. *International Journal for the Scholarship of Teaching and Learning*, *4*(1). doi:10.20429/ijsotl.2010.040101

Laiken, M. (2006). Authentic graduate education for personal and workplace transformation. In T. Herrington & J. Herrington (Eds.), *Authentic learning environments in higher education* (pp. 15–33). Hershey, PA: IGI Global. doi:10.4018/978-1-59140-594-8.ch002

Lait, J., Suter, E., Arthur, N., & Deutschlander, S. (2011). Interprofessional mentoring: Enhancing students' clinical learning. *Nurse Education in Practice*, *11*(3), 211–215. doi:10.1016/j.nepr.2010.10.005 PMID:21093376

Lakeland College Faculty Association. (2016). *Collective agreement between the Board of Governors of Lakeland College and the Lakeland College Faculty Association, July 1, 2016 - June 30, 2018*. Retrieved from https://issuu.com/lakelandcw/docs/faculty_collective_agreement_2016-2

Lamott, A. (1994). *Bird by bird: Some instructions on writing and life*. New York, NY: Pantheon Books.

Lancaster, J. W., Stein, S. M., MacLean, L. G., Van Amburgh, J., & Persky, A. M. (2014). Faculty development program models to advance teaching and learning within health science programs. *American Journal of Pharmaceutical Education*, *78*(5), 99. doi:10.5688/ajpe78599 PMID:24954939

Lance, K. C., & Kachel, D. E. (2018). Why school librarians matter: What years of research tell us. *Phi Delta Kappan*, *99*(7), 15–20. doi:10.1177/0031721718767854

Land, R. (2004). *Educational development: Discourse, identity and practice*. Maidenhead, UK: Society for Research in Higher Education & Open University Press.

Larsson, M., Mårtensson, K., Price, L., & Roxå, T. (2017). Constructive friction? Exploring patterns between educational research and the scholarship of teaching and learning. *Proceedings of the EuroSoTL*, *2017*, 161–165.

Lattuca, L., & Stark, J. (2009). *Shaping the college curriculum academic plans in context* (2nd ed.). San Francisco, CA: Jossey-Bass.

Laurillard, D. (2008). The teacher as action researcher: Using technology to capture pedagogic form. *Studies in Higher Education*, *33*(2), 139–154. doi:10.1080/03075070801915908

Lea, M. R., & Stierer, B. (2011). Changing academic identities in changing academic workplaces: Learning from academics' everyday professional writing practices. *Teaching in Higher Education*, *16*(6), 605–616. doi:10.1080/135625 17.2011.560380

Leathwood, C., & Phillips, D. (2000). Developing curriculum evaluation research in higher education: Process, politics and practicalities. *Higher Education*, *40*(3), 313–330. doi:10.1023/A:1004183527173

LeBlanc, E. J. (2013). Designing interactive eLearning for your students. In R. McBride & M. Searson (Eds.), *Proceedings of Society for Information Technology & Teacher Education International Conference 2013* (p. 684). Chesapeake, VA: Association for the Advancement of Computing in Education.

Leckie, G. J. (1996). Desperately seeking citations: Uncovering faculty assumptions about the undergraduate research. *Journal of Academic Librarianship*, *22*(3), 201–208. doi:10.1016/S0099-1333(96)90059-2

Lee Looi Chng, V., & Coombs, S. (2004). Applying self-organised learning to develop critical thinkers for learning organisations: A conversational action research project. *Educational Action Research, 12*(3), 363–386. doi:10.1080/09650790400200256

Lee, A., & Boud, D. (2003). Writing groups, change, and academic identity: Research development as local practice. *Studies in Higher Education, 28*(2), 187–200. doi:10.1080/0307507032000058109

Lee, A., & McWilliam, E. (2008). What game are we in? Living with academic development. *The International Journal for Academic Development, 13*(1), 67–77. doi:10.1080/13601440701860284

Lee, V. S. (2010). Program types and prototypes. In K. J. Gillespie & D. L. Robertson (Eds.), *A guide to faculty development* (2nd ed.). San Francisco, CA: Jossey-Bass.

Leibler, R. (2000). Stimulating cognitive and ethical development. In K. Taylor, C. Marienau, & M. Fiddler (Eds.), *Developing adult learners: Strategies for teachers and trainers* (pp. 217–220). San Francisco, CA: Jossey-Bass.

Lemke, J. L. (1990). *Talking science: Language, learning and values.* Norwood, NJ: Ablex.

Lengyel, A., Szöke, S., Kovács, S., Dénes Dávid, L., Bácsné Bába, E., & Müller, A. (2019). Assessing the essential pre-conditions of an authentic sustainability curriculum. *International Journal of Sustainability in Higher Education, 20*(2), 309–340. doi:10.1108/IJSHE-09-2018-0150

Liebowitz, B. (2017). The significance of SoTL in the South. *SoTL in the South, 1*(1), 1–3.

Linder, K. E., Elek, E. D., & Calderon, L. (2014). SoTL and the Institutional Review Board: Considerations before navigating the application process for classroom research in higher education. *The Journal of Scholarship of Teaching and Learning, 14*(2), 1–14. doi:10.14434/josotl.v14i2.4217

Lin, Y. P. (2016). The purpose and value of higher education: An economic perspective. *International Journal of Economics and Accounting, 7*(1), 66–73. doi:10.1504/IJEA.2016.076755

Little, C. (2015). The flipped classroom in further education: Literature review and case study. *Research in Post-Compulsory Education, 20*(3), 265–279. doi:10.1080/13596748.2015.1063260

Little, D., & Green, D. A. (2012). Betwixt and between: Academic developers in the margins. *The International Journal for Academic Development, 17*(3), 203–215. doi:10.1080/1360144X.2012.700895

Liu, K. (2015). Critical reflection as a framework for transformative learning in teacher education. *Educational Review, 67*(2), 145–157. doi:10.1080/00131911.2013.839546

Lock, J., Kim, B., Koh, K., & Wilcox, G. (2018). Navigating the tensions of innovative assessment and pedagogy in higher education. *The Canadian Journal for the Scholarship of Teaching and Learning, 9*(1), 1–20. doi:10.5206/cjsotl-rcacea.2018.1.8

Loh, P., Kichaev, G., Gazal, S., Schoech, A., & Price, A. (2018). Mixed-model association for biobank-scale datasets. *Nature Genetics, 50*(7), 906–908. doi:10.103841588-018-0144-6 PMID:29892013

Lowry, P. B., Curtis, A., & Lowry, M. R. (2004). Building a taxonomy and nomenclature of collaborative writing to improve interdisciplinary research and practice. *The Journal of Business Communication, 41*(1), 66-99.

Lowry, L. (1993). *The giver.* Boston, MA: Houghton Mifflin.

Lueddeke, G. R. (2003). Professionalising teaching practice in higher education: A study of disciplinary variation and 'teaching-scholarship'. *Studies in Higher Education, 28*(2), 213–288. doi:10.1080/0307507032000058082

Lundgren, H., & Poell, R. F. (2016). On critical reflection: A review of Mezirow's theory and its operationalization. *Human Resource Development Review*, *15*(1), 3–28. doi:10.1177/1534484315622735

Mackiewicz, J., & Thompson, I. K. (2015). *Talk about writing: The tutoring strategies of experienced writing center tutors*. New York, NY: Routledge.

MacLean, M., & Poole, G. (2010). An introduction to ethical considerations for novices to research in teaching and learning in Canada. *The Canadian Journal for the Scholarship of Teaching and Learning*, *1*(2). doi:10.5206/cjsotl-rcacea.2010.2.7

MacMillan, M. (2015). EBLIP + IL = SoTL. *Brain-work: The C-EBLIP blog*. Retrieved from https://words.usask.ca/ceblipblog/2015/03/24/eblip-il-sotl/

Maheux-Pelletier, G., Marsh, H., & Frake-Mistak, M. (2019). The benefits of writing retreats revisited. In N. Simmons (Ed.), *Critical collaboration communities: Academic writing partnerships, groups, and retreats* (pp. 92–105). Rotterdam: Brill-Sense Publishers.

Major, C., & Palmer, B. (2006). Reshaping teaching and learning: The transformation of faculty pedagogical content knowledge. *Higher Education: The International Journal of Higher Education Research*, *51*(4), 619–647. doi:10.100710734-004-1391-2

Mallon, M., Hays, L., Bradley, C., Huisman, R., & Belanger, J. (2019). The grounded instruction librarian: Participating in the Scholarship of Teaching and Learning. Chicago, IL: Association of College and Research Libraries, a division of the American Library Association.

Manarin, K., & Abrahamson, E. (2016). Troublesome knowledge of SoTL. *International Journal for the Scholarship of Teaching and Learning*, *10*(2), 1–6. doi:10.20429/ijsotl.2016.100202

Manathunga, C. (2006). Doing educational development ambivalently: Applying post-colonial metaphors to educational development? *The International Journal for Academic Development*, *11*(1), 19–29. doi:10.1080/13601440600578771

Mann, K. V. (2016). Reflection's role in learning: Increasing engagement and deepening participation. *Perspectives on Medical Education*, *5*(5), 259–261. doi:10.100740037-016-0296-y PMID:27638389

Marcketti, S. B., & Freeman, S. A. (2016). SoTL evidence on promotion and tenure vitas at a research university. *The Journal of Scholarship of Teaching and Learning*, *16*(5), 19–31. doi:10.14434//josotl.v16i5.21152

Marquis, E., & Henderson, J. (2015). Teaching creativity across disciplines at Ontario universities. *Canadian Journal of Higher Education*, *45*(1), 148–166. Retrieved from http://search.proquest.com/docview/1680769339/

Marquis, E., Holmes, T., Apostolou, K., Centea, D., Cockcroft, R., Knorr, K., ... Karamanis, T. (2017). SoTL Research Fellows: Collaborative pathfinding through uncertain terrain. *The Canadian Journal for the Scholarship of Teaching and Learning*, *8*(3), 1–19. doi:10.5206/cjsotl-rcacea.2017.3.9

Mårtensson, K. (2014). *Influencing teaching and learning microcultures: Academic development in a research intensive university*. Retrieved from http://lup.lub.lu.se/search/ws/files/3403041/4438677.pdf

Mårtensson, K., & Roxå, T. (2016). Working with networks, microcultures and communities. In D. Baume & C. Popovic (Eds.), *Advancing practice in academic development* (pp. 174–187). London: Routledge.

Martensson, K., Roxa, T., & Olsson, T. (2011). Developing a quality culture through the Scholarship of Teaching and Learning. Higher Education Research & Development. *Journal of Higher Education Research and Development Society of Australasia*, *30*(1), 51–62. doi:10.1080/07294360.2011.536972

Mårtensson, K., Roxå, T., & Stensaker, B. (2014). From quality assurance to quality practices: An investigation of strong microcultures in teaching and learning. *Studies in Higher Education, 39*(4), 534–545. doi:10.1080/03075079.2012.709493

Martin, C. L. (2015). Writing as a tool to demonstrate mathematical understanding. *School Science and Mathematics, 115*(6), 302–313. doi:10.1111sm.12131

Martin, J. R. (1992). *English text*. Amsterdam: John Benjamins Publishing Company. doi:10.1075/z.59

Martin, J. R., & Rose, D. (2007). *Working with discourse: Meaning beyond the clause* (2nd ed.). London: Bloomsbury.

Martin, J. R., & Rose, D. (2008). *Genres relations: Mapping culture*. London: Equinox.

Martin, J. R., & White, P. R. (2005). *The language of evaluation*. Basingstoke, UK: Palgrave Macmillan. doi:10.1057/9780230511910

Mathany, C., Clow, K. M., & Aspenlieder, E. D. (2017). Exploring the role of the Scholarship of Teaching and Learning in the context of the professional identities of faculty, graduate students, and staff in higher education. *The Canadian Journal for the Scholarship of Teaching and Learning, 8*(3). doi:10.5206/cjsotl-rcacea.2017.3.10

Maton, K. (2013). Making semantic waves: A key to cumulative knowledge-building. *Linguistics and Education, 24*(1), 8–22. doi:10.1016/j.linged.2012.11.005

Maton, K., & Doran, Y. J. (2017). SFL and code theory. In T. Bartlett & G. O'Grady (Eds.), *The Routledge systemic functional linguistic handbook*. London: Routledge.

Matthews, K. E. (2016). Students as partners as the future of student engagement. *Student Engagement in Higher Education Journal, 1*(1), 1-5. Retrieved from https://journals.gre.ac.uk/index.php/raise

Matthews, K. E. (2017). Five propositions for genuine students as partners practice. *International Journal for Students as Partners, 1*(2). doi:10.15173/ijsap.v1i2.3315

Matthews, K. E., Dwyer, A., Hine, L., & Turner, J. (2018). Conceptions of students as partners. *Higher Education, 76*(6), 957–971. doi:10.100710734-018-0257-y

May, H., & Bridger, K. (2010). *Developing and embedding inclusive policy and practice in higher education*. York, UK: The Higher Education Academy.

McAlpine, L., & Weston, C. (2002). Reflection: Issues related to improving professors' teaching and students' learning. *Instructional Science, 28*(5), 363–385. doi:10.1023/A:1026583208230

McConlogue, T. (2015). Making judgements: Investigating the process of composing and receiving peer feedback. *Studies in Higher Education, 40*(9), 1495–1506. doi:10.1080/03075079.2013.868878

McCormack, C., Vanags, T., & Prior, R. (2014). "Things fall apart so they can fall together": Uncovering the hidden side of writing a teaching award application. *Higher Education Research & Development, 33*(5), 935–948. doi:10.108 0/07294360.2014.890569

McGill, I., & Brockbank, A. (2004). *The action learning handbook: Powerful techniques for education, professional development and training*. New York: Routledge Falmer.

McKenna, M. C., Conradi, K., Lawrence, C., Jang, B. G., & Meyer, J. P. (2012). Reading attitudes of middle school students: Results of a U.S. survey. *Reading Research Quarterly, 47*(3), 283–306. doi:10.1002/rrq.021

McKinney, K. (2004). The Scholarship of Teaching and Learning: Past lessons, current challenges, and future visions. *To Improve the Academy, 22*(1), 3-19.

McKinney, K. (2004). The Scholarship of Teaching and Learning: Past lessons, current challenges, and future visions. *To Improve the Academy, 22*, 3-19.

McKinney, K. (2007). *Enhancing learning through the scholarship of teaching and learning: The challenges and joys of juggling.* Anker Publishing Co.

McKinney, K. (2015, December 7). Is SoTL 'less rigorous' or simply 'different' than other research? The SoTL Advocate [weblog]. Downloaded from https://illinoisstateuniversitysotl.wordpress.com/2015/12/07/is-sotl-less-rigorous-or-simply-different-than-other-research/

McKinney, K. (2006). Attitudinal and structural factors contributing to challenges in the work of the Scholarship of Teaching and Learning. *New Directions for Institutional Research, 2006*(129), 37–50. doi:10.1002/ir.170

McKinney, K. (2007). *Enhancing learning through the Scholarship of Teaching and Learning: The challenges and joys of juggling.* Boston, MA: Anker.

McKinney, K. (2012). Increasing the impact of SoTL: Two sometimes neglected opportunities. *International Journal for the Scholarship of Teaching and Learning, 6*(1). doi:10.20429/ijsotl.2012.060103

McKinney, K. (2012). Making a difference: Application of SoTL to enhance learning. *The Journal of Scholarship of Teaching and Learning, 12*(1), 1–7.

McKinney, K., & Jarvis, P. (2009). Beyond lines on the CV: Faculty applications of their Scholarship of Teaching and Learning research. *International Journal for the Scholarship of Teaching and Learning, 3*(1). doi:10.20429/ijsotl.2009.030107

McLinden, M., Cleaver, E., & Lintern, M. (2018). Developing and promoting a culture of critical enquiry within higher education: some final reflections. In E. Cleaver, M. Lintern, & M. McLinden (Eds.), *Teaching and Learning in Higher Education: Disciplinary Approaches to Educational Enquiry.* London: Sage.

McLinden, M., Grove, M., Green, J., & Birch, A. (2019). Developing and embedding inclusive policy and practice within higher-education institutions. In K. M. Krcmar (Ed.), *The inclusivity gap: Expectations and delivery in higher education.* Aberdeen, UK: Inspired by Learning.

McNeill, K., & Haines, B. (2003). Scholarship of teaching and librarians: Building successful partnerships with faculty. *Georgia Library Quarterly, 39*(4), 4–8.

McNiff, J., & Whitehead, J. (2012). *Action research for teachers: A practical guide.* London, UK: David Fulton Publishers. doi:10.4324/9780203462393

McNiff, L., & Hays, L. (2017). SoTL in the LIS classroom: Helping future academic librarians become more engaged teachers. *Communications in Information Literacy, 11*(2), 366–377. doi:10.15760/comminfolit.2017.11.2.8

Mengel, T. (2016). The Scholarship of Teaching and Learning (SoTL) at Renaissance College (University of New Brunswick): A case study of SoTL at the faculty level. *New Directions for Teaching and Learning, 2016*(146), 39–45. doi:10.1002/tl.20185

Mercer-Mapstone, L., Dvorakova, S. L., Matthews, K., Abbot, S., Cheng, B., Felten, P., & Swaim, K. (2017). A Systematic Literature Review of Students as Partners in Higher Education. *International Journal for Students As Partners, 1*(1). doi:10.15173/ijsap.v1i1.3119

Mery, Y., Newby, J., & Peng, K. (2012). Why one-shot information literacy sessions are not the future of instruction: A case for online credit courses. *College & Research Libraries, 73*(4), 366–377. doi:10.5860/crl-271

Meyer, J. H. F., & Land, R. (2005). Threshold concepts and troublesome knowledge (2): Epistemological considerations and a conceptual framework for teaching and learning. *Higher Education, 49*(3), 373–388. doi:10.100710734-004-6779-5

Meyers, S. A. (2008). Using transformative pedagogy when teaching online. *College Teaching, 56*(4), 219–224. doi:10.3200/CTCH.56.4.219-224

Mezirow, J. (1981). A critical theory of adult learning and education. *Adult Education, 32*(1), 3–24. doi:10.1177/074171368103200101

Mezirow, J. (1991). Transformation theory and cultural context: A reply to Clark and Wilson. *Adult Education Quarterly, 41*(3), 188–192. doi:10.1177/0001848191041003004

Mezirow, J. (1994). Understanding transformation theory. *Adult Education Quarterly, 44*(4), 222–232. doi:10.1177/074171369404400403

Mezirow, J. (2003). Transformative learning as discourse. *Journal of Transformative Education, 1*(1), 58–63. doi:10.1177/1541344603252172

Mezirow, J. (2009). Transformative learning theory. In J. Mezirow & E. W. Taylor (Eds.), *Transformative Learning in Practice: Insights from Community* (pp. 18–33). San Francisco, CA: Jossey-Bass.

Mezirow, J. D. (2006). *Learning as transformation: Critical perspectives on a theory in progress*. San Francisco, CA: Jossey-Bass.

Middendorf, J., & Pace, D. (2008). Easing entry into the Scholarship of Teaching and Learning through focused assessments: The "Decoding the Disciplines" approach. *To Improve the Academy, 26*(1), 53-67.

Miettinen, R. (2000). The concept of experiential learning and John Dewey's theory of reflective thought and action. *International Journal of Lifelong Education, 19*(1), 54–72. doi:10.1080/026013700293458

Miller-Young, J. E., Anderson, C., Kiceniuk, D., Mooney, J., Riddell, J., Schmidt Hanbidge, A., & Chick, N. (2017). Leading up in the Scholarship of Teaching and Learning. *The Canadian Journal for the Scholarship of Teaching and Learning, 8*(2). doi:10.5206/cjsotl-rcacea.2017.2.4

Miller-Young, J. E., Yeo, M., & Manarin, K. (2018). Challenges to disciplinary knowing and identity: Experiences of scholars in a SoTL development program. *International Journal for the Scholarship of Teaching and Learning, 12*(1). doi:10.20429/ijsotl.2018.120103

Miller-Young, J., & Yeo, M. (2015). Conceptualizing and communicating SoTL: A framework for the field. *Teaching & Learning Inquiry, 3*(2), 37–53. doi:10.20343/teachlearninqu.3.2.37

Mitchell, L. N., & Mitchell, E. T. (2015). Using SoTL as a lens to reflect and explore for innovation in education and librarianship. *Technical Services Quarterly, 32*(1), 46–58. doi:10.1080/07317131.2015.972876

Moore, J. (2019, March 23). ISSoTL Conference Pedagogy [Web post]. Retrieved from https://www.issotl.com/issotl-conference-pedagogy

Moore, J., Highham, L., & Sanders, J. (2017). *Evidencing teaching excellence analysis of the Teaching Excellence Framework (TEF2) provider submissions*. York, UK: HEA. Retrieved from: https://www.heacademy.ac.uk/system/files/hub/download/TEF2%20Provider%20Submissions%20Review_2.pdf

Moore, J. L. (2018). Writing SoTL: Going public for an extended audience. In N. L. Chick (Ed.), *SoTL in action: Illuminating critical moments of practice* (pp. 119–126). Sterling, VA: Stylus.

Morahan, P. S., & Fleetwood, J. (2008). The double helix of activity and scholarship: Building a medical education career with limited resources. *Medical Education, 42*(1), 34–44. doi:10.1111/j.1365-2923.2007.02976.x PMID:18181845

Morgan, H., & Houghton, A. (2011). *Inclusive curriculum design in higher education. Considerations for effective practice across and within subject areas.* York, UK: HEA. Retrieved from https://www.heacademy.ac.uk/system/files/resources/introduction_and_overview.pdf

Morris, N. (2015). Providing ethical guidance for collaborative research in developing countries. *Research Ethics Review, 11*(4), 211–235. doi:10.1177/1747016115586759 PMID:26640509

Mount Royal Faculty Association. (2016). *Collective agreement between Mount Royal Faculty Association and the Board of Governors of Mount Royal University, July 1, 2016 - June 30, 2018.* Retrieved from https://mrfa.net/wp-content/uploads/2019/01/MRFA-Collective-Agreement-July-1-2016-to-June-30-2018.pdf

Mullen, C. A. (2005). *The mentorship primer.* New York, NY: Peter Lang.

Muller, P. (2006). Reputation, trust, and the dynamics of leadership in Communities of Practice. *The Journal of Management and Governance, 10*(4), 381–400. doi:10.100710997-006-9007-0

Murray, D. M. (1989). *Expecting the unexpected: Teaching myself--and others--to read and write.* Portsmouth, NH: Boynton/Cook.

Musu-Gillette, L. (2015). *Reading for fun: Using NAEP data to explore student attitudes.* Retrieved October 1, 2019, from https://nces.ed.gov/blogs/nces/post/reading-for-fun-using-naep-data-to-explore-student-attitudes

Myatt, P., Gannaway, D., Chia, I., Fraser, K., & McDonald, J. (2018). Reflecting on institutional support for SoTL engagement: Developing a conceptual framework. *The International Journal for Academic Development, 23*(2), 147–160. doi:10.1080/1360144X.2017.1346511

Namaste, N. B. (2017). Designing and evaluating students' transformative learning. *The Canadian Journal for the Scholarship of Teaching and Learning, 8*(3), 3. doi:10.5206/cjsotl-rcacea.2017.3.5

Nardine, J. (2019). The state of academic liaison librarian burnout in ARL libraries in the United States. *College & Research Libraries, 80*(4), 508–524. doi:10.5860/crl.80.4.508

National Center for Educational Statistics (Ed.). (2018, September 17). *Student groups and trends reports.* Retrieved October 1, 2019, from https://nces.ed.gov/nationsreportcard/groups_trends/

National Education Association. (2018). *Preparing 21st century students for a global society.* Retrieved from National Education Association Web: http://www.nea.org/assets/docs/A-Guide-to-Four-Cs.pdf

National Governors Association Center for Best Practices & Council of Chief State School Officers. (2010). *Common core state standards initiative.* Retrieved December 23, 2010 from http://www.corestandards.org/the-standards/english-language-arts-standards

NCIHE. (1997). *Higher education in the learning society: Main report ("The Dearing Report").* London, UK: Her Majesty's Stationary Office.

Nesi, H., & Gardner, S. (2012). *Genres across the disciplines: Student writing in higher education.* Cambridge, UK: Cambridge University Press.

Neumann, R. (2001). Disciplinary differences and university teaching. *Studies in Higher Education, 26*(2), 135–146. doi:10.1080/03075070120052071

Newton, J. (1997). Opportunities for partnership in quality improvement: Responding to the challenge of teaching quality assessment in Wales. *Quality in Higher Education*, *3*(1), 37–50. doi:10.1080/1353832960030105

Nilson, L. B., & Zimmerman, B. J. (2013). *Creating self-regulated learners*. Sterling, VA: Stylus Publishing.

Nohl, A. M. (2015). Typical phases of transformative learning: A practice-based model. *Adult Education Quarterly*, *65*(1), 35–49. doi:10.1177/0741713614558582

North, S. M. (1984). The idea of a writing center. *College English*, *46*(5), 433–446. doi:10.2307/377047

Ntem, A., & Cook-Sather, A. (2018). Resistances and resiliencies in pedagogical partnership: Student partners' perspectives. *International Journal for Students as Partners*, *2*(1). doi:10.15173/ijsap.v2i1.3372

Nugent, J. S., Reardon, R. M., Smith, F. G., Rhodes, J. A., Zander, M. J., & Carter, T. J. (2008). Exploring faculty learning communities: Building connections among teaching, learning, and technology. *International Journal on Teaching and Learning in Higher Education*, *20*(1), 51–58.

O'Brien, M. (2008). Navigating the SoTL landscape: A compass, map and some tools for getting started. *International Journal for the Scholarship of Teaching and Learning*, *2*(2), 15.

O'Byrne, C., McIntyre, G., Townsend, S., Schonthal, B., & Shephard, K. (2018). Can "pooling teaching tips" be more than "pooling teaching tips"? *Tertiary Education and Management*, *24*(4), 351–361.

O'Flaherty, J., & Phillips, C. (2015). The use of flipped classrooms in higher education: A scoping review. *The Internet and Higher Education*, *25*, 85–95. doi:10.1016/j.iheduc.2015.02.002

O'Mara, L., McDonald, J., Gillespie, M., Brown, H., & Miles, L. (2014). Challenging clinical learning environments: Experiences of undergraduate nursing students. *Nurse Education in Practice*, *14*(2), 208–213. doi:10.1016/j.nepr.2013.08.012 PMID:24063792

O'Neill, M. A., & Palmer, A. (2004). Importance-performance analysis: A useful tool for directing continuous quality improvement in higher education. *Quality Assurance in Education*, *12*(1), 39–52. doi:10.1108/09684880410517423

O'Sullivan, M. (2007). Creating and sustaining Communities of Practice among physical education professionals. *New Zealand Physical Educator*, *40*(1), 10–13.

Oborn, E., & Dawson, S. (2010). Learning across Communities of Practice: An examination of multidisciplinary work. *British Journal of Management*, *21*(4), 843–858. doi:10.1111/j.1467-8551.2009.00684.x

Office of Institutional Planning and Analysis (OIPA). (2019a). *Contract faculty and teaching assistants headcount*. Retrieved from http://oipa.info.yorku.ca/data-hub/quick-facts/quick-facts-contract-faculty-and-tas/

Office of Institutional Planning and Analysis (OIPA). (2019b). *Full-time faculty headcount*. Retrieved from http://oipa.info.yorku.ca/data-hub/quick-facts/quick-facts-full-time-faculty-headcount/

OfS. (2019a). *TEF outcomes*. Retrieved from https://www.officeforstudents.org.uk/advice-and-guidance/teaching/tef-outcomes/#/tefoutcomes/

OfS. (2019b). *Value for money*. Retrieved from https://www.officeforstudents.org.uk/advice-and-guidance/student-wellbeing-and-protection/value-for-money/

OfS. (2019c). *What is the TEF?* Retrieved from https://www.officeforstudents.org.uk/advice-and-guidance/teaching/what-is-the-tef/

OfS. (2019d). *Guidance for providers for TEF year four. Video 1: What is the Teaching Excellence and Student Outcomes Framework*. Retrieved from: https://www.officeforstudents.org.uk/advice-and-guidance/teaching/tef-year-four/guidance-for-providers/

OfS. (2019e). *Graduate earnings data on Unistats from the Longitudinal Education Outcomes (LEO) data*. Retrieved from: https://www.officeforstudents.org.uk/data-and-analysis/graduate-earnings-data-on-unistats/

OfS. (2019f). *TEF Outcomes: The Conservertoire for Dance and Drama*. Retrieved from: https://apps.officeforstudents.org.uk/tefoutcomes2019/docs/submissions/Submission_10001653.pdf

Organisation for Economic Co-operation and Development (OECD). (2008). Tertiary education for the knowledge society: Vol. 1. *Special features: Governance, funding*. Paris, France: OECD.

Organisation for Economic Co-operation and Development (OECD). (2008). Tertiary education for the knowledge society: Vol. 2. *Special features: Equity, innovation, labour market, internationalisation*. Paris, France: OECD.

Orlikowski, W. J. (2002). Knowing in practice: Enacting a collective capability in distributed organizing. *Organization Science, 13*(3), 249–273. doi:10.1287/orsc.13.3.249.2776

Osterman, K., & Kottkamp, R. (2004). *Reflective practice for educators: Professional development to improve student learning*. Thousand Oaks, CA: Corwin Press.

Otto, P. (2014). Librarians, libraries, and the Scholarship of Teaching and Learning. *New Directions for Teaching and Learning, 2014*(139), 77–93. doi:10.1002/tl.20106

Paivio, A. (1986). *Mental representations: A dual coding approach*. Oxford, UK: Oxford University Press.

Palloff, R. M., & Pratt, K. (2001). *Lessons for the cyberspace classroom: The realities of online teaching*. San Francisco, CA: Jossey-Bass.

Palloff, R., & Pratt, K. (1999). *Building learning communities in cyberspace: Effective strategies for the online classroom*. San Francisco, CA: Jossey-Bass.

Parker, J. (2008). Theory of SoTL: Translating international perspectives. In *Proceedings of The London Scholarship of Teaching and Learning 7th International Conference 2008* (pp. 171-176). London: City University London.

Parkin, D. (2017). *Leading learning and teaching in higher education: The key guide to designing and delivering courses*. Abingdon, UK: Routledge.

Pascale, R. T., & Athos, A. G. (1981). *The art of Japanese management*. London: Allen Lane. doi:10.1016/0007-6813(81)90032-X

Patel, F., & Lynch, H. (2013). Glocalization as an alternative to internationalization in higher education: Embedding positive glocal learning perspectives. *International Journal on Teaching and Learning in Higher Education, 25*(2), 223–230. Retrieved from https://eric.ed.gov/?id=EJ1016539

Payette, P. R., & Brown, M. K. (2018). Gathering mid-semester feedback: Three variations to improve instruction. *IDEA Paper #67*.

Pearce, C., & Conger, J. (2002). *Shared leadership: Reframing the hows and whys of leadership*. Thousand Oaks, CA: SAGE Publications.

Pelger, S., & Larsson, M. (2018). Advancement towards the Scholarship of Teaching and Learning through the writing of teaching portfolios. *The International Journal for Academic Development, 23*(3), 179–191. doi:10.1080/1360144X.2018.1435417

Penuel, W. R., Fishman, B. J., Yamaguchi, R., & Gallagher, L. P. (2007). What makes professional development effective? Strategies that foster curriculum implementation. *American Educational Research Journal*, *44*(4), 921–958. doi:10.3102/0002831207308221

Peters, K., McInnes, S. & Halcomb, E. (2015). Nursing students' experiences of clinical placement in community settings: A qualitative study. *Collegian*, *22*(2), 175-181.

Peters, M. A. (2008). Academic Writing, Genres and Philosophy. *Educational Philosophy and Theory*, *40*(7), 819–831. doi:10.1111/j.1469-5812.2008.00511.x

Petraglia, J. (1998). *Reality by design: The rhetoric and technology of authenticity in education*. Mahwah, NJ: Lawrence Erlbaum Associates. doi:10.4324/9781410601254

Phillips, R., McNaught, G., & Kennedy, C. (2012). *Evaluating e-learning: Guiding research and practice*. New York, NY: Routledge. doi:10.4324/9780203813362

Pollock, E., Chandler, P., & Sweller, J. (2002). Assimilating complex information. *Learning and Instruction*, *12*(1), 61–86. doi:10.1016/S0959-4752(01)00016-0

Poole, G. (2013). Square one: What is research? In K. McKinney (Ed.), *The Scholarship of Teaching and Learning in and across the disciplines*. Bloomington, IN: Indiana University Press.

Poole, G., & Simmons, N. (2013). The contributions of the Scholarship of Teaching and Learning to quality enhancement in Canada. In G. Gordon & R. Land (Eds.), *Quality enhancement in higher education: International perspectives* (pp. 118–128). London: Routledge.

Poole, G., Taylor, L., & Thompson, J. (2007). Using the Scholarship of Teaching and Learning at disciplinary, national, and institutional levels to strategically improve quality of post-secondary education. *International Journal for the Scholarship of Teaching and Learning*, *1*(2), 3. doi:10.20429/ijsotl.2007.010203

Porter, S., & Whitcomb, M. (2005). Non-response in student surveys: The role of demographics, engagement, and personality. *Research in Higher Education*, *46*(2), 127–152. doi:10.100711162-004-1597-2

Potter, M. K., & Wuetherick, B. (2015). Who is represented in the teaching commons?: SoTL through the lenses of the arts and humanities. *The Canadian Journal for the Scholarship of Teaching and Learning*, *6*(2), 2. doi:10.5206/cjsotl-rcacea.2015.2.2

Potter, M., & Kustra, E. (2011). The relationship between scholarly teaching and SoTL: Models, distinctions, and clarifications. *International Journal for the Scholarship of Teaching and Learning*, *5*(1). doi:10.20429/ijsotl.2011.050123

Power, E. J., & Handley, J. (2019). A best-practice model for integrating interdisciplinarity into the higher education student experience. *Studies in Higher Education*, *44*(3), 554–570. doi:10.1080/03075079.2017.1389876

Probert, B. (2014). *Why scholarship matters in higher education*. Australian Government Office for Learning and Teaching.

Prosser, M. (2008). The Scholarship of Teaching and Learning: What is it? A Personal View. *International Journal for the Scholarship of Teaching and Learning*, *2*(2). doi:10.20429/ijsotl.2008.020202

Pytash, K. (2013). Secondary preservice teachers' development of teaching scientific writing. *The Association for Science Teacher Education.*, *24*(5), 793–810. doi:10.100710972-013-9338-z

Raj Adhikari, D. (2010). Knowledge management in academic institutions. *International Journal of Educational Management*, *24*(2), 94–104. doi:10.1108/09513541011020918

Rath, A. (2002). Action research as border crossing: Stories from the classroom. In N. Lyons & V. LaBoskey (Eds.), *Narrative inquiry in practice: Advancing the knowledge of teaching* (pp. 146–160). New York, NY: Columbia College Press.

Raven, M., & Rodrigues, D. (2017). A course of our own: Taking an information literacy credit course from inception to reality. *Partnership. The Canadian Journal of Library and Information Practice and Research, 12*(1).

Rawn, C. D., & Fox, J. A. (2017). Understanding the work and perceptions of teaching-focused faculty in a changing academic landscape. *Research in Higher Education, 59*(5), 591–622. doi:10.100711162-017-9479-6

REF. (2019). *What is the REF?* Retrieved from https://www.ref.ac.uk/about/what-is-the-ref/

Reinke, J., Muraco, J., & Maurer, T. W. (2016). The state of the Scholarship of Teaching and Learning in family science. *Family Science Review, 10*; Advance online publication.

Rice, R. E. (1992). Towards a broader conception of scholarship: The American context. In T. Whiston & R. Geiger (Eds.), *Research and higher education: The United Kingdom and the United States* (pp. 117–129). Buckingham, UK: SRE and Open University Press.

Richlin, L. (2001). Scholarly teaching and the scholarship of teaching. *New Directions for Teaching and Learning, 2001*(86), 57–68. doi:10.1002/tl.16

Richlin, L., & Cox, M. D. (2004). Developing scholarly teaching and the Scholarship of Teaching and Learning through faculty learning communities. *New Directions for Teaching and Learning, 2004*(97), 127–135. doi:10.1002/tl.139

Rienties, B., Brouwer, N., & Lygo-Baker, S. (2013). The effects of online professional development on higher education teachers' beliefs and intentions towards learning facilitation and technology. *Teaching and Teacher Education, 29*(1), 122–131. doi:10.1016/j.tate.2012.09.002

Robertson, D. (2013). *Australian Design 2013: Issues and concerns in the Design professions.* Melbourne, Australia: Design Institute of Australia PN034 (Issue B). Retrieved July 17, 2019 from https://www.design.org.au/documents/item/127

Roblyer, M. D., & Edwards, J. (2000). *Integrating educational technology into teaching* (2nd ed.). Saddle River, NJ: Prentice Hall.

Rockoff, J., & Lockwood, B. (2010). How and why middle schools harm student achievement. *Education Next*, (Fall): 68–77.

Rodgers, C. (2002). Defining reflection: Another look at John Dewey and reflective thinking. *Teachers College Record, 104*(4), 842–866. doi:10.1111/1467-9620.00181

Roehl, A., Reddy, S. L., & Shannon, G. J. (2013). The flipped classroom: An opportunity to engage millennial students through active learning strategies. *Journal of Family and Consumer Sciences, 105*(2), 44–49. doi:10.14307/JFCS105.2.12

Rose, D., & Martin, J. R. (2012). *Learning to write, reading to learn: Genre knowledge and pedagogy in the Sydney School.* London: Equinox.

Rose, D., & Martin, J. R. (2014). Intervening in contexts of schooling. In J. Flowerdew (Ed.), *Discourse in context* (pp. 273–300). London: Bloomsbury.

Rosenblatt, L. (1960). Literature: The reader's role. *English Journal, 49*(5), 304. doi:10.2307/810700

Rose-Wiles, L. M., & Hofmann, M. A. (2013). Still desperately seeking citations: Undergraduate research in the age of web-scale discovery. *Journal of Library Administration, 53*(2-3), 147–166. doi:10.1080/01930826.2013.853493

Rossett, A. (2002). Waking in the night and thinking about e-learning. In A. Rossett (Ed.), *The ASTD e-learning handbook* (pp. 3–18). New York, NY: McGraw-Hill.

Rosslyn, F. (2004). The emotional background to learning: A university experience. *Emotional & Behavioural Difficulties*, *9*(1), 70–76. doi:10.1177/1363275204041964

Rothery, J., & Stenglin, M. (1997). Entertaining and instructing: Exploring experience through story. In F. Christie & J. R. Martin (Eds.), *Genre and institutions: Social practices in the workplace and school* (pp. 231–263). London: Cassell.

Roth, W.-M., & Lee, Y.-J. (2006). Contradictions in theorizing and implementing communities in education. *Educational Research Review*, *1*(1), 27–40. doi:10.1016/j.edurev.2006.01.002

Rowland, S. (2001). *Higher education: Purposes and roles*. Conference paper: British Educational Research Association Annual Conference, University of Leeds. Retrieved from www.leeds.ac.uk/educol/documents/00001915.doc

Rowland, S. (2002). Overcoming fragmentation in professional life: The challenge for academic development. *Higher Education Quarterly*, *56*(1), 52–64. doi:10.1111/1468-2273.00202

Roxå, T., & Mårtensson, K. (2013). *Understanding strong academic microcultures: An exploratory study*. Retrieved from https://www.lunduniversity.lu.se/lup/publication/246cf361-3a33-47df-8fad-c21ec704fb4d

Roxå, T., & Mårtensson, K. (2009). Significant conversations and significant networks—Exploring the backstage of the teaching arena. *Studies in Higher Education*, *34*(5), 547–559. doi:10.1080/03075070802597200

Roxå, T., & Mårtensson, K. (2015). Microcultures and informal learning: A heuristic guiding analysis of conditions for informal learning in local higher education workplaces. *The International Journal for Academic Development*, *20*(2), 193–205. doi:10.1080/1360144X.2015.1029929

Roxå, T., Olsson, T., & Mårtensson, K. (2008). Appropriate Use of Theory in the Scholarship of Teaching and Learning as a Strategy for Institutional Development. *Arts and Humanities in Higher Education*, *7*(3), 276–294. doi:10.1177/1474022208094412

Roy, D., Borin, P., & Kustra, E. (2007). Assisting curriculum change through departmental initiatives. *New Directions for Teaching and Learning*, *112*(112), 21–32. doi:10.1002/tl.295

Ryan, M. E., & Ryan, M. (2012). Theorising a model for teaching and assessing reflective learning in higher education. *Higher Education Research & Development*, 1–20. doi:10.1080/07294360.2012.661704

Ryman, S. E., Burrell, L., Hardham, G., Richardson, B., & Ross, J. (2009). Creating and sustaining online learning communities: Designing for transformative learning. *International Journal of Pedagogies and Learning*, *5*(3), 32–45. doi:10.5172/ijpl.5.3.32

Saalman, E. (2018). *How do teachers reflect upon their teaching in teaching portfolios? – Analysis of teachers' portfolios at seminars on how to document your pedagogical qualifications and skills at the chalmers university of technology*. Paper presented at the International Symposium on Project Approaches in Engineering Education, Brasilia, Brazil.

Sabagh, Z., & Saroyan, A. (2014). Professors' perceived barriers and incentives for teaching improvement. *International Education Research*, *2*(3), 18–40. doi:10.12735/ier.v2i3p18

Sanacore, J., & Palumbo, A. (2010). Middle school students need more opportunities to read across the curriculum. *The Clearing House: A Journal of Educational Strategies, Issues and Ideas*, *83*(5), 180–185. doi:10.1080/00098650903583735

Savini, C. (2011). An alternative approach to bridging disciplinary divides. *Writing Lab Newsletter*, *35*(7-8), 1–5.

Schleppegrell, M. J. (2004). *The language of schooling: A functional linguistics perspective*. Mahwah, NJ: Lawrence Erlbaum Associates. doi:10.4324/9781410610317

Schoenbach, R., Greenleaf, C., & Murphy, L. (2012). *Reading for understanding : How reading apprenticeship improves disciplinary learning in secondary and college classrooms*. San Francisco, CA: Jossey-Bass, A Wiley Imprint.

Schön, D. (1987). *Educating the reflective practitioner: Toward a new design for teaching and learning in the professions* (1st ed.). San Francisco, CA: Jossey-Bass.

Schön, D. A. (1983). *The reflective practitioner: How professionals think in action*. New York, NY: Basic Books.

Schroeder, C. (2007). Countering SoTL marginalization: A model for integrating SoTL with institutional initiatives. *International Journal for the Scholarship of Teaching and Learning*, *1*(1), 15. doi:10.20429/ijsotl.2007.010115

Schuetz, P. (2002). Instructional practices of part-time and full-time faculty. *New Directions for Community Colleges*, *118*(118), 39–46. doi:10.1002/cc.62

Schulman, L. S. (1988). *American educational research in education*. Washington, DC: American Educational Research Association.

Schulman, S. (2012). Argumentation step-by-step: Learning critical thinking through deliberate practice. *Teaching Philosophy*, *35*(1), 41–62. doi:10.5840/teachphil20123514

Schwartz, B. M., & Haynie, A. (2013). Faculty development centers and the role of SoTL. *New Directions for Teaching and Learning*, *2013*(133), 101–111. doi:10.1002/tl.20079

Scott, A., Jerome, K., & Thomson, S. (2001) Orientating Design Education: Implementing an orientation field trip as an introduction to design education. In V. Popovic, T. Kim, (Eds.), *Proceedings ICSID Educational Seminar 2001*, (pp. 62-68). Seongnam City, South Korea: Academic Press.

Secret, M., Leisey, M., Lanning, S., Polich, S., & Schaub, J. (2011). Faculty perceptions of the Scholarship of Teaching and Learning: Definition, activity level and merit considerations at one university. *The Journal of Scholarship of Teaching and Learning*, *11*(3), 1–20.

Segalla, M. (2008). Publishing in the right place or publishing the right thing: Journal targeting and citations' strategies for promotion and tenure committees. *European Journal of International Management*, *2*(2), 122–127. doi:10.1504/EJIM.2008.017765

Shaw, N., Rueckert, C., Smith, J., Tredinnick, J., & Lee, M. (2017). Students as partners in the real world: A whole-institution approach, a whole of institution case study. *International Journal for Students as Partners*, *1*(1). doi:10.15173/ijsap.v1i1.3079

Sheesley, D. F. (2001). Burnout and the academic teaching librarian: An examination of the problem and suggested solutions. *Journal of Academic Librarianship*, *27*(6), 447–451. doi:10.1016/S0099-1333(01)00264-6

Shephard, K., Rogers, T., & Brogt, E. (in press). Impacts of engaging in research into teaching and learning on academics' conceptions of their development as teachers and on the role of academic developers. *The International Journal for Academic Development*.

Shreeve, A. (2011). Joining the dots: The Scholarship of Teaching as part of institutional research. *Higher Education Research & Development*, *30*(1), 63–74. doi:10.1080/07294360.2011.536973

Shulman, L. S. (1993). Teaching as community property: Putting an end to pedagogical solitude. *Change: The Magazine of Higher Education, 25*(6), 6-7. Doi:10.1080/00091383.1993.9938465

Shulman, L. S. (2000). Inventing the future. In P. Hutchings (Ed.), *Opening lines: Approaches to the Scholarship of Teaching and Learning*. Retrieved from http://www.carnegiefoundation.org/elibrary/inventing-future-opening-lines-approaches-scholarship-teaching-and-learning

Shulman, L. (2001). From Minsk to Pinsk: Why a Scholarship of Teaching and Learning? *The Journal of Scholarship of Teaching and Learning*, 48–53.

Shulman, L. S. (1986). Those who understand: Knowledge growth in teaching. *Educational Researcher*, *15*(2), 4–14. doi:10.3102/0013189X015002004

Shulman, L. S. (1987). Knowledge and teaching: Foundations of the new reform. *Harvard Educational Review*, *57*(1), 1–22. doi:10.17763/haer.57.1.j463w79r56455411

Shulman, L. S. (2005). Signature pedagogies in the professions. *Daedalus*, *134*(3), 52–59. doi:10.1162/0011526054622015

Shusterman, N. (2007). *Unwind*. New York: Simon & Schuster Books for Young Readers.

Siemens, G., & Long, P. (2011). Penetrating the fog: Analytics in learning and education. *EDUCAUSE Review*, *46*(5), 30–32.

Simmons, N. (2009). Personal reflection: Playing for SoTL impact: A personal reflection. *International Journal for the Scholarship of Teaching and Learning*, *3*(2), 30. doi:10.20429/ijsotl.2009.030230

Simmons, N. (2011). Mapping a mirage: Documenting the Scholarship of Teaching and Learning. *Collected Essays on Learning and Teaching*, *1*, 2. doi:10.22329/celt.v1i0.3170

Simmons, N. (Ed.). (2016). *The Scholarship of Teaching and Learning in Canada: Institutional impact. New Directions in Teaching and Learning, 146*. San Francisco, CA: Jossey-Bass; doi:10.1002/tl.20192

Simmons, N., Abrahamson, E., Deschler, J. X., Kensington-Miller, B., Manarin, K., Morón-García, S., & Renc-Roe, J. (2013). Conflicts and configurations in a liminal space: SoTL scholars' identity development. *Teaching & Learning Inquiry*, *1*(2), 9–21. Retrieved from https://journalhosting.ucalgary.ca/index.php/TLI/article/view/57382/43155

Simmons, N., & Marquis, E. (2017). Defining the Scholarship of Teaching and Learning. *The Canadian Journal for the Scholarship of Teaching and Learning*, *8*(2), 1–5. doi:10.5206/cjsotl-rcacea.2017.2.2

Simmons, N., & Taylor, K. L. (2019). Leadership for the Scholarship of Teaching and Learning: Understanding bridges and gaps in practice. *The Canadian Journal for the Scholarship of Teaching and Learning*, *10*(1), 2. doi:10.5206/cjsotl-rcacea.2019.1.7995

Simpson, D., Fincher, R. M. E., Hafler, J. P., Irby, D. M., Richards, B. F., Rosenfeld, G. C., & Viggiano, T. R. (2007). Advancing educators and education by defining the components and evidence associated with educational scholarship. *Medical Education*, *41*(10), 1002–1009. doi:10.1111/j.1365-2923.2007.02844.x PMID:17822412

Simulation. (2019). Retrieved from https://dictionary.cambridge.org/dictionary/english/simulation

Smetkowski, B., Conway, K., & Starrett, D. (2009). SoTL, CASTL, and the CSTL at Southeast Missouri State University: A symbiotic relationship. *Transformative Dialogues*, *3*(1), 1–15.

Smith, E. R., Calderwood, P. E., Storms, S. B., Lopez, P. G., & Colwell, R. P. (2016). Institutionalizing faculty mentoring within a Community of Practice model. *To Improve the Academy*, *35*(1), 35-71.

Smith, R. (2008). *Conquering the content*. San Francisco, CA: Jossey Bass.

Snooks, M. K., Neeley, S. E., & Williamson, K. M. (2004), 7: From SGID and GIFT to BBQ: Streamlining midterm student evaluations to improve teaching and learning. *To Improve the Academy, 22,* 110-124.

Soffer, T., & Nachmias, R. (2018). Effectiveness of learning in online academic courses compared with face-to-face courses in higher education. *Journal of Computer Assisted Learning, 34*(5), 534–543. doi:10.1111/jcal.12258

Solis, M., Miciak, J., Vaughn, S., & Fletcher, J. M. (2014). Why intensive interventions matter: Longitudinal studies of adolescents with reading disabilities and poor reading comprehension. *Learning Disability Quarterly, 37*(4), 218–229. doi:10.1177/0731948714528806 PMID:25378799

Sorcinelli, M. D. (2002). Ten principles of good practice in creating and sustaining teaching and learning centers. *A guide to faculty development: Practical advice, examples, and resources,* 9-23.

Sozer, E. M., Zeybekoglu, Z., & Kaya, M. (2019). Using mid-semester course evaluation as a feedback tool for improving learning and teaching in higher education. *Assessment & Evaluation in Higher Education,* 1–14.

Spillane, J. (2005, June). Distributed leadership. *The Educational Forum, 69*(2), 143–150. doi:10.1080/00131720508984678

Squire, K., & Johnson, C. (2000). Supporting distributed Communities of Practice with interactive television. *Educational Technology Research and Development, 48*(1), 23–43. doi:10.1007/BF02313484

Srivastva, S., & Cooperrider, D. (1990). *Appreciative management and leadership: The power of positive thought and action in organizations.* San Francisco, CA: Jossey-Bass.

Stabile, C., & Ritchie, W. F. (2013). Clarifying the differences between training, development, and enrichment: The role of institutional belief constructs in creating the purpose of faculty learning initiatives. *New Directions for Teaching and Learning, 2013*(133), 71–84. doi:10.1002/tl.20047

Stefani, L., & Baume, D. (2016). "Is it working?" Outcomes, monitoring and evaluation. In D. Baume & C. Popovic (Eds.), *Advancing practice in academic development.* London: Routledge.

Steinert, Y., Mann, K., Centeno, A., Dolmans, D., Spencer, J., Gulula, M., & Prideaux, D. (2006). A systematic review of faculty development initiatives designed to improve teaching effectiveness in medical education: BEME Guide No. 8. *Medical Teacher, 8*(6), 497–526. doi:10.1080/01421590600902976 PMID:17074699

Stes, A., & Van Petegem, P. (2011). Instructional development for early career academics: An overview of impact. *Educational Research, 53*(4), 459–474. doi:10.1080/00131881.2011.625156

Stevenson, C. B., Duran, R. L., Barrett, K. A., & Colarulli, G. C. (2005). Fostering faculty collaboration in learning communities: A developmental approach. *Innovative Higher Education, 30*(1), 23–36. doi:10.100710755-005-3293-3

Stierer, B., & Antoniou, M. (2004). Are there distinctive methodologies for pedagogic research in higher education? *Teaching in Higher Education, 9*(3), 275–285. doi:10.1080/1356251042000216606

Stigler, J., & Hiebert, J. (1999). *The teaching gap: Best ideas from the world's teachers for improving education in the classroom.* New York, NY: Free Press.

Stockley, D., & Balkwill, L. L. (2013). Raising awareness of research ethics in SoTL: The role of educational developers. *The Canadian Journal for the Scholarship of Teaching and Learning, 4*(1), 7. doi:10.5206/cjsotl-rcacea.2013.1.7

Street, B. V. (2005). Recent applications of new literacy studies in educational contexts. *Research in the Teaching of English, 39*(4), 417–423. Retrieved from https://login.cyrano.ucmo.edu/login?url=https://search-proquest-com.cyrano.ucmo.edu/docview/215345525?accountid=6143

Strober, M. (2011). *Interdisciplinary conversations: Challenging habits of thought.* Stanford, CA: Stanford University Press.

Suddaby, R. (2010). Editor's comments: Construct clarity in theories of management and organization. *Academy of Management Review*, *35*(3), 346–357.

Suleman, F. (2018). The employability skills of higher education graduates: Insights into conceptual frameworks and methodological options. *Higher Education*, *76*(2), 263–278. doi:10.100710734-017-0207-0

Sullivan, G. M., & Artino, A. R. Jr. (2013). Analyzing and interpreting data from Likert-type scales. *Journal of Graduate Medical Education*, *5*(4), 541–542. doi:10.4300/JGME-5-4-18 PMID:24454995

Summers, M. (1982). Philosophy of science in the science teacher education curriculum. *European Journal of Science Education*, *4*(1), 19–27. doi:10.1080/0140528820040104

Sutherland, K. A. (2018). Holistic academic development: Is it time to think more broadly about the academic development project. *The International Journal for Academic Development*, *23*(4), 261–273. doi:10.1080/1360144X.2018.1524571

Sutherland, K. A., & Grant, B. (2016). Researching academic development. In C. Popovic & D. Baume (Eds.), *Advancing practice in academic development* (pp. 187–206). London: Routledge.

Svinicki, M. D. (2012). Who is entitled to do SoTL? *International Journal for the Scholarship of Teaching and Learning*, *6*(2). doi:10.20429/ijsotl.2012.060202

Swanson, K. W., & Kayler, M. (2010). Faculty development and adult learning: A model for transforming higher education. *International Journal for the Scholarship of Teaching and Learning*, *4*(1). doi:10.20429/ijsotl.2010.040116

Szenes, E. (2011). *Unpublished 3x3 model for Business in the Global Environment course*. University of Sydney.

Szenes, E., Tilakaratna, N., & Maton, K. (2015). The knowledge practices of critical thinking. In M. Davies & R. Barnett (Eds.), *The Palgrave handbook of critical thinking in higher education* (pp. 573–591). New York, NY: Palgrave Macmillan. doi:10.1057/9781137378057_34

Tanda, R., & Denham, S. A. (2009). Clinical instruction and student outcomes. *Teaching and Learning in Nursing*, *4*(4), 139–147. doi:10.1016/j.teln.2009.01.002

Tanggaard, L. (2007). Learning at trade vocational school and learning at work: Boundary crossing in apprentices' everyday life. *Journal of Education and Work*, *20*(5), 453–466. doi:10.1080/13639080701814414

Taylor, E. W. (1997). Building upon the theoretical debate: A critical review of the empirical studies of Mezirow's transformative learning theory. *Adult Education Quarterly*, *48*(1), 34–59. doi:10.1177/074171369704800104

Taylor, K. (2000). Teaching with developmental intentions. In *Learning as Transformation: Critical Perspectives on a Theory in Progress* (pp. 229–252). San Francisco, CA: Jossey-Bass.

Taylor, K. L. (2010). Understanding the disciplines within the context of educational development. *New Directions for Teaching and Learning*, *122*(122), 59–67. doi:10.1002/tl.398

Teague, G., Anfara, V. Jr, Wilson, N., Gaines, C., & Beavers, J. (2012). Instructional practices in the middle grades. *NASSP Bulletin*, *96*(3), 203–227. doi:10.1177/0192636512458451

TEQSA Guidance Note Scholarship. (2017). (Version 2.3). Retrieved from https://www.teqsa.gov.au/sites/g/files/net2046/f/guidance-note-scholarship-v2-3.docx?v=1508129079

TEQSA. (2017). *Higher Education Standards Framework (Threshold Standards) 2015—TEQSA Contextual Overview Version 1.1*. Canberra, Australia: Tertiary Education Quality and Standards Agency.

TEQSA. (2018). *Guidance Note: Scholarship (Version 2.5_2, 12 December 2018)*. Canberra, Australia: Tertiary Education Quality and Standards Agency.

The American Library Association ALA. (n.d.). *Library education and licensing*. Retrieved from http://www.ala.org/aasl/about/ed/recruit/license

Thomas, S. (2011). Broadening conceptions of what constitutes knowledge and evidence in SoTL. *International Journal for the Scholarship of Teaching and Learning, 5*(1). doi:10.20429/ijsotl.2011.050125

Thompson, N., & Pascal, J. (2012). Developing critically reflective practice. *Reflective Practice, 13*(2), 311–325. doi:10.1080/14623943.2012.657795

Tierney, A. M. (2016). *More than just a teaching fellow: The impact of REF and implications of TEF on life science teaching-focused academics in UK HEIs (Unpublished doctoral dissertation)*. Durham, UK: University of Durham. Retrieved from http://etheses.dur.ac.uk/11826/

Tight, M. (2018). Tracking the Scholarship of Teaching and Learning. *Policy Reviews in Higher Education, 2*(1), 61–78. doi:10.1080/23322969.2017.1390690

Tilakaratna, N., & Szenes, E. (2017). The linguistic construction of critical "self-reflection" in social work and business. In P. Chapell & J. Knox (Eds.), *Transforming Contexts: Papers from the 44th International Systemic Functional Congress*. Academic Press.

Tilakaratna, N., & Szenes, E. (2019). (Un)critical reflection: Uncovering hidden. In C. Winberg, S. McKenna, & K. Wilmot (Eds.), *Building knowledge in higher education: Enhancing teaching and learning with legitimation code theory*. London: Routledge.

Tinto, V. (2015). Through the eyes of students. *Journal of College Student Retention, 19*(3), 254–269. doi:10.1177/1521025115621917

Tonidandel, S., King, E., & Cortina, J. (2018). Big data methods: Leveraging modern data analytic techniques to build organizational science. *Organizational Research Methods, 21*(3), 525–547. doi:10.1177/1094428116677299

Tracey, D., & Morrow, L. (2012). *Lenses on reading: An introduction to theories and models* (2nd ed.). New York, NY: The Guilford Press.

Trepanier, L. (2017). SoTL as a subfield for political science graduate programs. *Journal of Political Science Education, 13*(2), 138–151. doi:10.1080/15512169.2016.1227264

Tri-council, P. S. (1998). *Ethical conduct for research involving humans/Medical Research Council of Canada, Natural Sciences and Engineering Research Council of Canada, Social Sciences and Humanities Research Council of Canada*. Ottawa: Medical Research Council of Canada. Retrieved from http://science-catalogue.canada.ca/record=2649284~S6

Trigwell, K. (2012). Scholarship of Teaching and Learning. In L. Hunt & D. Chalmers (Eds.), University teaching in focus: A learning-centred approach (pp. 253 267). London, UK: Routledge. doi:10.4324/9780203079690-15

Trigwell, K. (2013). Evidence of the impact of Scholarship of Teaching and Learning purposes. *Teaching & Learning Inquiry, 1*(1), 95–105. doi:10.20343/teachlearninqu.1.1.95

Trigwell, K., Martin, E., Benjamin, J., & Prosser, M. (2000). Scholarship of teaching: A model. *Higher Education Research & Development, 19*(2), 155–168. doi:10.1080/072943600445628

Truong, H. (2016). Integrating learning styles and adaptive e-learning system: Current developments, problems, and opportunities. *Computers in Human Behaviour, 55*(B), 1185-1193.

Tsoukas, H., & Chia, R. (2002). On organizational becoming: Rethinking organizational change. *Organization Science, 13*(5), 567–582. doi:10.1287/orsc.13.5.567.7810

United States National Research Council. (2012). Discipline-based education research: Understanding and improving learning in undergraduate science and engineering. In S. R. Singer, N. R. Nielsen, & H. A. Schweingruber (Eds.), *Committee on the status, contributions, and future directions of discipline-based education research. Board on Science Education, Division of Behavioral and Social Sciences and Education.* Washington, DC: The National Academies Press.

University of Central Missouri College of Education Faculty. (2018). *College of Education guidelines for promotion/ tenure.* Retrieved from https://www.ucmo.edu/offices/general-counsel/university-policy-library/academic-policies/promotion-and-tenure-college-guidelines/coe-promotion-tenure-2018.pdf

University of Western Ontario Faculty Association. (2014). *Faculty collective agreement between the University of Western Ontario and the University of Western Ontario Faculty Association, July 1, 2014 - June 30, 2018.* Retrieved from https://www.uwo.ca/facultyrelations/pdf/collective_agreements/faculty.pdf

Vadeboncoeur, C., Townsend, N., Foster, C., & Sheehan, M. (2016). Variation in university research ethics review: Reflections following an inter-university study in England. *Research Ethics Review, 12*(4), 217–233. doi:10.1177/1747016116652650

Vallance, R. J. (2005). Research ethics: Reforming postgraduate formation. *Issues in Educational Research, 15*(2), 193–205.

Van Beveren, L., Roets, G., Buysse, A., & Rutten, K. (2018). We all reflect, but why? A systematic review of the purposes of reflection in higher education in social and behavioral sciences. *Educational Research Review, 24*, 1–9. doi:10.1016/j.edurev.2018.01.002

Van Gelder, T. (2005). Teaching critical thinking: Some lessons from cognitive science. *College Teaching, 53*(1), 41–48. doi:10.3200/CTCH.53.1.41-48

Vander Kloet, M., Frake-Mistak, M., McGinn, M. K., Caldecott, M., Aspenlieder, E. D., Beres, J. L., ... Gill, A. (2017). Conditions for contingent instructors engaged in the Scholarship of Teaching and Learning. *The Canadian Journal for the Scholarship of Teaching and Learning, 8*(2). doi:10.5206/cjsotl-rcacea.2017.2.9

Varghese, J., Faith, M., & Jacob, M. (2012). Impact of e-resources on learning in biochemistry: First-year medical students' perceptions. *BMC Medical Education, 12*(1), 21–30. doi:10.1186/1472-6920-12-21 PMID:22510159

Veeck, A., O'Reilly, K., MacMillan, A., & Yu, H. (2016). The use of collaborative midterm student evaluations to provide actionable results. *Journal of Marketing Education, 38*(3), 157–169. doi:10.1177/0273475315619652

Vescio, V., Ross, D., & Adams, A. (2008). A review of research on the impact of professional learning communities on teaching practice and student learning. *Teaching and Teacher Education, 24*(1), 80–91. doi:10.1016/j.tate.2007.01.004

Vygotsky, L. S. (1980). *Mind in society: Development of higher psychological processes.* Harvard, MA: Harvard University Press. doi:10.2307/j.ctvjf9vz4

Walczyk, J. J., Ramsey, L. L., & Zha, P. (2007). Obstacles to instructional innovation according to college science and mathematics faculty. *Journal of Research in Science Teaching, 44*(1), 85–106. doi:10.1002/tea.20119

Walkington, J. (2005). Becoming a teacher: Encouraging development of teacher identity through reflective practice. *Asia-Pacific Journal of Teacher Education, 33*(1), 53–64. doi:10.1080/1359866052000341124

Walls, J., Carr, A., Kelder, J.-A., & Ennever, E. (2018). Engaging in the "course efficiency" discussion: National drivers and local responses. *Journal of Further and Higher Education*; Advanced Online Publication.

Walters, W. H. (2016). Faculty status of librarians at US research universities. *Journal of Academic Librarianship, 42*(2), 161–171. doi:10.1016/j.acalib.2015.11.002

Wang, F., & Hannafin, M. J. (2005). Design-based research and technology-enhanced learning environments. *Educational Technology Research and Development, 53*(4), 5–23. doi:10.1007/BF02504682

Wardle, E. A., & Mayorga, M. G. (2016). Burnout among the counseling profession: A survey of future professional counselors. *Journal of Educational Psychology, 10*(1), 9–15.

Webb, A. S. (2019). Navigating the lows to gain new heights: Constraints to SoTL engagement. *The Canadian Journal for the Scholarship of Teaching and Learning, 10*(2). doi:10.5206/cjsotl-rcacea.2019.2.8173

Webb, A., Wong, T., & Hubball, H. T. (2013). Professional development for adjunct teaching faculty in a research-intensive university: Engagement in scholarly approaches to teaching and learning. *International Journal on Teaching and Learning in Higher Education, 25*(2), 231–238. Retrieved from http://www.isetl.org/ijtlhe/index.cfm

Weimer, M. (2006). *Enhancing scholarly work on teaching and learning: Professional literature that makes a difference.* San Francisco, CA: Jossey-Bass.

Welch, M. (1999). The ABCs of reflection: A template for students and instructors to implement written reflection in service-learning. *NSEE Quarterly, 25*(2), 1, 23–25. Retrieved from https://digitalcommons.unomaha.edu/slceeval/16

Weller, S. (2011). New lecturers' accounts of reading higher education research. *Studies in Continuing Education, 33*(1), 93–106. doi:10.1080/0158037X.2010.516744

Weller, S., Domarkaite, G., Lam, J., & Metta, L. (2013). Student-faculty co-inquiry into student reading: Recognizing SoTL as pedagogic practice. *International Journal for the Scholarship of Teaching and Learning, 7*(2), 1–16. doi:10.20429/ijsotl.2013.070209

Welsh, J., & Metcalf, J. (2003). Cultivating faculty support for institutional effectiveness activities: Benchmarking best practices. *Assessment & Evaluation in Higher Education, 28*(1), 33–45. doi:10.1080/02602930301682

Wendt, J. (2013). Combating the crisis in adolescent literacy: Exploring literacy in the secondary classroom. *American Secondary Education, 41*(2), 38–48.

Wenger, E. (2011). *Communities of Practice: A brief introduction.* Academic Press.

Wenger, E. (1999). *Communities of Practice: Learning, meaning, and identity.* Oxford, UK: Cambridge University Press.

Wenger, E. (2000). Communities of Practice and social learning systems. *Organization, 7*(2), 225–246. doi:10.1177/135050840072002

Wenger, E. (2010). Communities of Practice and social learning systems: The career of a concept. In C. Blackmore (Ed.), *Social learning systems and Communities of Practice* (pp. 179–198). London, UK: Springer. doi:10.1007/978-1-84996-133-2_11

Wenger, E. C., & Snyder, W. M. (2000). Communities of Practice: The organizational frontier. *Harvard Business Review, 78*(1), 139–146. PMID:11184968

Wenger, E., McDermott, R. A., & Snyder, W. (2002). *Cultivating Communities of Practice: A guide to managing knowledge.* Boston, MA: Harvard Business Press.

Wenger, E., McDermott, R., & Snyder, W. (2002). *Cultivating Communities of Practice.* Boston, MA: Harvard Business School Press.

Werder, C., & Otis, M. M. (2010). *Engaging student voices in the study of teaching and learning.* Sterling, VA: Stylus.

Werder, C., Thibou, S., & Kaufer, B. (2012). Students as co-inquirers: A requisite threshold concept in educational development. *Journal of Faculty Development, 26*(3), 34–38.

Westerheijden, D., Stensaker, B., & Rosa, M. (2007). *Quality assurance in higher education: Trends in regulation, translation and transformation* (Vol. 20). Berlin, Germany: Springer Science & Business Media. doi:10.1007/978-1-4020-6012-0

Weston, C. B., & McAlpine, L. (2001). Making explicit the development toward the scholarship of teaching. *New Directions for Teaching and Learning, 86*(86), 89–97. doi:10.1002/tl.19

Wiersema, M., & Bantel, K. (1992). Top management team demography and corporate strategic change. *Academy of Management Journal, 35*(1), 91–121.

Wiggins, G., & McTighe, J. (2005). *Understanding by design* (2nd ed.). Alexandra, VA: ASCD.

Wignell, P., Martin, J. R., & Eggins, S. (1989). The discourse of geography : Ordering and explaining the experiential world. *Linguistics and Education, 1*(4), 359–391. doi:10.1016/S0898-5898(89)80007-5

Williams, A., Verwood, R., Beery, T., Dalton, H., McKinnon, J., Strickland, K., ... Poole, G. (2013). The power of social networks: A model for weaving the Scholarship of Teaching and Learning into institutional culture. *Teaching & Learning Inquiry, 1*(2), 49–62. doi:10.20343/teachlearninqu.1.2.49

Wine, L. D. (2016). School librarians as technology leaders: An evolution in practice. *Journal of Education for Library and Information Science, 57*(2), 207–220. doi:10.3138/jelis.57.2.207

Winter, J., Turner, R., Spowart, L., Muneer, R., & Kneale, P. (2017). Evaluating academic development in the higher education sector: Faculty developers' reflections on using a toolkit resource. *Higher Education Research & Development, 36*(7), 1503–1514. doi:10.1080/07294360.2017.1325351

Witman, P. D., & Richlin, L. (2007). The status of the Scholarship of Teaching and Learning in the discipline. *International Journal for the Scholarship of Teaching and Learning, 1*(1), 14. doi:10.20429/ijsotl.2007.010114

Wolff, C., Rod, A. B., & Schonfeld, R. C. (2016, April 4). *Ithaka S+R US faculty survey 2015.* Retrieved from http://www.sr.ithaka.org /publications/ithaka-sr-us-faculty-survey-2015/

Wong, A. C. K. (2016). Considering reflection from the student perspective in higher education. *SAGE Open*, 1–9. doi:10.1177/2158244016638706

Wood, E. J. (1990). Biochemistry is a difficult subject for both student and teacher. *Biochemical Education, 18*(4), 170–172. doi:10.1016/0307-4412(90)90123-6

Woodhouse, R. A., & Force, K. (2010). Educational development websites: What do they tell us about how Canadian centres support the Scholarship of Teaching and Learning? *The Canadian Journal for the Scholarship of Teaching and Learning, 1*(1). doi:10.5206/cjsotl-rcacea.2010.1.4

Wood, P., & Cajkler, W. (2018). Lesson study: A collaborative approach to scholarship for teaching and learning in higher education. *Journal of Further and Higher Education, 42*(3), 313–326. doi:10.1080/0309877X.2016.1261093

Wright, M. C., Lohe, D. R., & Little, D. (2018). The role of a center for teaching and learning in a de-centered educational world. *Change: The Magazine of Higher Learning, 50*(6), 38–44. doi:10.1080/00091383.2018.1540826

Wrigley, C., Bucolo, S., & Straker, K. (2016). Designing new business models: Blue sky thinking and testing. *The Journal of Business Strategy, 37*(5), 22–31. doi:10.1108/JBS-04-2015-0041

Wuetherick, B., & Yu, S. (2016). The Canadian teaching commons: The Scholarship of Teaching and Learning in Canadian higher education. *New Directions for Teaching and Learning, 2016*(146), 23–30. doi:10.1002/tl.20183

Wu, X. (2017). Higher education, elite formation, and social stratification in contemporary China: Preliminary findings from the Beijing College students panel survey. *Chinese Journal of Sociology, 3*(1), 3–31. doi:10.1177/2057150X16688144

Wu, X. V., Enskär, K., Heng, G. N. D., Pua, L. H., & Wang, W. (2016a). The perspectives of preceptors regarding clinical assessment for undergraduate nursing students. *International Nursing Review, 63*(3), 473–481. doi:10.1111/inr.12272 PMID:27100137

Wu, X. V., Enskär, K., Pua, L. H., Heng, D. G. N., & Wang, W. (2016b). Development and psychometric testing of Holistic Clinical Assessment Tool (HCAT) for undergraduate nursing students. *BMC Medical Education, 16*(1), 1–9. doi:10.118612909-016-0768-0 PMID:27658587

Wu, X. V., Wang, W., Pua, L. H., Heng, D. G., & Enskar, K. (2015). Undergraduate nursing students' perspectives on clinical assessment at transition to practice. *Contemporary Nurse, 51*(2-3), 272–285. doi:10.1080/10376178.2016.1163232 PMID:26956057

Young, K., James, K., & Noy, S. (2016). Exploration of a reflective practice rubric. *Asia Pacific Journal of Cooperative Education, 17*(2), 135–147. Retrieved from https://www.ijwil.org/files/APJCE_17_2_135_147.pdf

Young, P. (2006). Out of balance: Lecturer's perceptions of differential status and rewards in relation to teaching and research. *Teaching in Higher Education, 11*(2), 191–202. doi:10.1080/13562510500527727

Zibrowski, E., Weston, W., & Golszmidt, M. (2008). I don't have time: Issues of fragmentation, prioritization, and motivation for education scholarship among medical faculty. *Medical Education, 42*(9), 872–878. doi:10.1111/j.1365-2923.2008.03145.x PMID:18715484

Zimmerman, B. J., & Kitsantas, A. (2007). A writer's discipline: The development of self-regulatory skill. In Studies in writing, Volume 19, writing and motivation (pp. 51-69). Oxford, UK: Elsevier.

Zimmerman, B., & Martinez-Pons, M. (1990). Student differences in self-regulated learning: Relating grade, sex, and giftedness to self-efficacy and strategy use. *Journal of Educational Psychology, 82*(1), 51–59. doi:10.1037/0022-0663.82.1.51

About the Contributors

Rachel C. Plews currently works as an educational developer in Western Switzerland. Her work with faculty members supports ongoing professional development with teaching and learning workshops, as well as individual consultations. Her research interests include technology in education, self-directed learning, and faculty development. Prior to moving to Switzerland, Rachel completed her doctoral studies at Teachers College, Columbia University, from which she holds an Ed.D. in Adult Learning and Leadership. She earned a M.Ed. in Teaching, Learning, & Technology from Lehigh University, and she has taught various undergraduate courses in education and hospitality programs. Rachel is a graduate of the School of Hotel Administration at Cornell University and worked in sales and marketing before moving into higher education.

Michelle Amos has more than two decades of experience in reading education, working with learners from sixth grade through adult, specializing in meeting the needs of students with a range of learning challenges. She earned her BA in English and MSE in English Secondary Education Instruction and Curriculum from the University of Florida and her MA in Reading Specialist and Ed.D in Adult Learning and Leadership from Teachers College, Columbia University. Dr. Amos' areas of research include supporting Scholarship of Teaching and Learning through Communities of Practice, the use of technology by English Language Learners, identifying supportive methods of online instruction, and the impact of cognitive bias on reading comprehension in an increasingly polarized media environment.

* * *

Dianne Ashbourne is an educational developer at the University of Toronto Mississauga. She has a MA in Educational Studies from the University of British Columbia where she focused on higher education and research methodology. In her role as educational developer, Dianne coordinates the Teaching & Learning Collaboration and consults with faculty, instructors, and graduate students on a range of pedagogical projects aimed at enhancing student learning. She is particularly interested in the potential for educational developers to support interdisciplinary collaboration and to act as a guide for emerging SoTL researchers as they navigate a new field.

Andy Birch is an Associate Director of Academic Practice at the University of the West of England, Bristol. His current work focuses on digital learning and digital accessibility, reflecting and building on expertise gained in earlier roles where he managed large cross-institutional digital projects including a Virtual Learning Environment (VLE) review and the adoption of lecture recording technologies. A retired police officer with a diverse background including many years as an operational traffic motorcyclist, and later specialising in people development and diversity training, Andy is interested in organisational culture and how knowledge is exchanged in large institutions.

Erik Brogt is Associate Professor (Reader) of Academic Development in the Learning Evaluation & Academic Development team at the University of Canterbury, New Zealand. He obtained an MSc in Astronomy from the University of Groningen and a PhD in Teaching and Teacher Education from the University of Arizona. Erik's research interests are the pedagogical thinking of expert practitioners who become teachers of the profession, the interactions between educational developers and teachers, and teaching and learning of subject disciplines.

Mark Brooke is Senior Lecturer at the Centre for English Language Communication, National University of Singapore. He currently designs and teaches undergraduate academic writing courses combining Sociology of Sport and English for Academic Purposes. In sport sociology, he has authored a book with Common Ground Research Networks, Champaign, Illinois, entitled Case Studies in Sport Socialisation; he has also published in journals such as Sport in Society, Communication & Sport, and the Asia-Pacific Journal of Health, Sport and Physical Education. He has also co-authored a book on academic literacy development entitled a Practical Guide to Project-Based Learning with World Scientific Publishing, Singapore. In the academic literacy field, he predominantly investigates practical classroom applications of Systemic Functional Linguistics and Legitimation Code Theory (LCT). He has published multiple studies on these themes in journals such as Reflective Practice; Teaching in Higher Education; The European Journal of Applied Linguistics and TEFL and the Asian Journal of the Scholarship of Teaching and Learning.

Andrea Carr is Deputy Principal (Education) and Associate Dean Learning and Teaching at University College at the University of Tasmania. Andrea has extensive expertise in designing, delivering and evaluating curricula in higher education. She has been recognised for contributions to learning and teaching at the University of Tasmania and nationally. Andrea was awarded an Office of Learning and Teaching citation for outstanding contributions to student learning for leading collaborative curriculum development and learning programs in 2015. Andrea has published in the field of learning and teaching and has held and/or partnered several institutional and national learning and teaching grants.

Elizabeth Cleaver is Director of Learning and Teaching at the University of the West of England, Bristol, where she leads the Academic Practice Directorate - the University's central hub for the support, development and enhancement of learning, teaching, teaching and curricula. Over a career spanning 25 years she has taught, written and researched in a variety of roles and settings. Her early academic career was in the discipline of sociology where she specialised in the area of youth transitions to adulthood (early work is published in the name Kenyon). Following a six year spell outside the HE sector undertaking local and central government funded policy research and evaluation, she returned to higher education in 2008. This most recent stage of her career has focused on providing strategic leadership in learning, teaching and academic development. Elizabeth is a Principal Fellow of the Higher Education Academy (PFHEA).

Maurizio Costabile graduated from the Flinders University of South Australia with Honours in Biochemistry and Cell biology and completed a PhD in Immunology at the University of Adelaide. He has been an academic at the University of South Australia for 21 years. He teaches Biochemistry and Immunology to undergraduate students in first and second year. He is research active in both the laboratory setting as well as undertaking educational research. He is also a research degree coordinator for Masters and PhD students during their candidature. With an increasing interest in educational strategies to improve student learning, he has recently transitioned to a teaching focussed academic role.

Joseph Crawford is a leadership and curriculum researcher who strives for rigorous theory, measurement, and evaluation practice. He has provided conceptualizations for the authentic leader and follower, and published on best practice methodology for scale development.

Morgan Ely is a 5th generation educator and a firm believer in the thought that it is imperative to never stop learning. She earned her BS in Education and MSE in Curriculum & Instruction at the University of Missouri - Columbia and her EdS in Reading from UCM. After teaching middle schoolers for 9 years, she joined the Literacy faculty at UCM. In addition to being a Royals fan, she enjoys spending time with her family and reading in her spare time.

Lisa Fedoruk received her PhD in Adult Learning from the University of Calgary in 2018. Previously, she obtained her MEd from the University of Calgary, and BEd from the University of Alberta. Dr. Fedoruk is an educational development consultant at the Taylor Institute for Teaching and Learning at the University of Calgary. She collaborates with colleagues, faculty, postdoctoral scholars and students to guide and support post-secondary teaching and learning. As a faculty member she is a facilitator for workshops, programming and resource development related to the Taylor Institute's Certificates in University Learning and Teaching, and Teaching Assistant Orientation. Dr. Fedoruk is a board member on the University of Calgary's Conjoint Faculties Research Ethics Board, acting as a liaison between SoTL researchers and ethics protocols.

Rachel Fitzgerald (SFHEA) is a Senior Lecturer in Curriculum & Learning Design at Queensland Institute of Technology, Brisbane. A former senior lecturer (business) and a head of online programmes in the UK, her research is focused on educational technology and the design of sustainable, authentic curriculum.

Mandy Frake-Mistak, PhD, is an educational developer at the Teaching Commons at York University, in Toronto, Ontario, Canada. Having taught at numerous universities across Southwestern Ontario, her extensive teaching experience informs her everyday work as she leads initiatives related to the Scholarship of Teaching and Learning, higher education policy, course design, and the Instructional Skills Workshop. She is an active member within the educational developer community serving in numerous executive capacities. She has been chair of the Council of Ontario Educational Developers, currently in a past-chair role, secretary of the Educational Developers Caucus, and is the chair of the Accreditation Committee of the Educational Developer Caucus.

Jennifer C. Friberg is the Cross Endowed Chair in the Scholarship of Teaching and Learning and Professor of Communication Sciences and Disorders at Illinois State University in Normal, Illinois, USA. Her teaching focuses on the topics of child language development and disorders. Research interests include student learning outside the traditional classroom environment, the impact of SoTL advocacy, and application of SoTL in varied learning contexts. Friberg is a founding editorial board member for Teaching and Learning in Communication Sciences & Disorders, editor for Gauisus (an internal publication), and co-created and manages the SoTL Advocate weblog. Friberg is a Fellow of the American Speech-Language-Hearing Association and has been awarded over a dozen teaching awards over the course of her career in higher education. Friberg currently serves as the co-chair of the Advocacy & Outreach Committee for the International Society for the Scholarship of Teaching and Learning.

Jane Friedman is a professor of Mathematics. She has research interests in mathematics education, voting theory, combinatorics, and statistical modelling.

Sherry Fukuzawa is an Assistant Professor, Teaching Stream, and Associate Chair in the Department of Anthropology at the University of Toronto Mississauga. She has a PhD in Biological Anthropology from the University of Toronto where she was a contingent instructor for many years. Dr. Fukuzawa's research focuses on technological innovations in teaching and community engaged learning. She has presented at several conferences and published widely on her virtual mystery custom web-tool and technological use in problem-based learning. Dr. Fukuzawa is particularly passionate about inclusive education through the acceptance of different ways of knowing in the Academy. She is a Fellow with the Center of Community Partnerships at the University of Toronto, and a co-investigator on a Connaught Community Partnership Grant with the Mississaugas of the Credit First Nation. Dr. Fukuzawa was recently awarded a teaching excellence award for sessional instruction at the University of Toronto Mississauga.

Kristi Giselsson has a First Class Honours Degree in English Literature and a PhD within the discipline of Philosophy. Her PhD thesis (later published as a book, Grounds for respect: Particularism, universalism, and communal accountability, 2012) critically assessed past and present formulations of – and challenges to – the concept of a common humanity, providing a new conceptualisation of what it might mean to be human and the grounds needed in order to justify respect for others. Her research interests include Moral and Political Philosophy, the intersection between literature and philosophy, and the Scholarship of Teaching and Learning.

Robert Hallis is a professor lf library services and Fine Arts librarian at the University of Central Missouri. He provides face-to-face instruction, flipped instruction, and embeds instructional modules in BlackBoard. Most recently, he teaches a newly developed credit course in managing information, "Truth, Lies, and Managing Information," and taught sections of this course embedded within learning communities. He has presented at state and regional conferences on flipping library instruction, integrating library instruction in Blackboard, immersing students in hands-on activities during library instruction, and using critical thinking in leading students beyond the library databases.

Lauren Hays, PhD, is an Assistant Professor of Instructional Technology at the University of Central Missouri. Previously, she was the instructional and research librarian at MidAmerica Nazarene University in Olathe, KS where she enjoyed teaching and being a member of her institution's Faculty Development

Committee. She has co-presented at the annual conference for the International Society for the Scholarship of Teaching and Learning and was the 2017 speaker on SoTL for the Association of College and Research Libraries' Student Learning and Information Literacy Committee's Midwinter Discussion. Her professional interests include SoTL, teaching, information literacy, educational technology, library and information science education, teacher identity, and academic development. On a personal note, she loves dogs, traveling, and home.

Henk Huijser is a Senior Lecturer, Curriculum and Learning Design in the Learning and Teaching Unit at Queensland University of Technology. Henk is Senior Fellow of the Higher Education Academy, and he has worked in various academic development positions in Australia, China and the Middle East for close to 15 years. He has published widely on a range of topics related to learning and teaching in higher education. For more information please refer to: https://orcid.org/0000-0001-9699-4940.

Alisa Hutchinson is an e-learning specialist whose interests include formative assessment, qualitative research methods, scholarship of teaching and learning, creativity, and professional identity development.

Jenna Kammer, Ph.D., is an Assistant Professor of Library Science in the Library Science and Information Resources program within the School of Professional Education and Leadership at the University of Central Missouri. Prior to working as a professor, Jenna was a librarian and an instructional designer.

Jo-Anne Kelder is Senior Lecturer, Learning and Teaching Quality with the College of Health and Medicine, University of Tasmania. She is currently on secondment as Senior Lecturer, Curriculum Innovation and Development with the University's Academic Division. She has been responsible for a number of operational and strategic projects for quality assurance of curriculum and enhancing student experience, as well as research to develop staff capability and practice in curriculum evaluation and scholarship. She has been recognised for contributions to teaching and learning with four teaching awards and in national projects. She is a Joint Fellow of the inaugural Australian Council of Deans of Science Fellowship (2019).

Bernadette Knewstubb is an adjunct research fellow, School of Education, Victoria University of Wellington and independent consultant in higher education research.

Maxine Lintern is Associate Dean for the Faculty of Business, Law and Social Science at Birmingham City Universitym with responsibility for research and enterprise. An experienced lecturer and researcher, her background is in medical biochemistry and neurophysiology. Maxine has strategic and operational oversight of research and enterprise across the Faculty. She is the Chair of the Faculty Research Committee, and oversees research governance, Doctoral School operations, and development for early career researchers. Maxine also has responsibility for strategic development and operational implementation of research and enterprise links to learning and teaching development, including advances in curriculum design, and creating opportunities for transdisciplinary research. Maxine's broad research interests include teaching interactively to large groups, strategic implementation of enquiry-based learning, haptic feedback in pain management, the impact of science in law decision making and the role of simulation in learning. She is a member of The Physiological Society and is a Principal Fellow of the Higher Education Academy.

Judith Liu is a Professor in the Department of Sociology and a faculty liaison in the Mulvaney Center for Community, Awareness and Social Action. Her research focuses on women and AIDS, education in the People's Republic of China, mentoring, community engagement, and service-learning.

Geneviève Maheux-Pelletier, PhD, is a seasoned educator with 20 years of experience in the post-secondary sector, including eight years on a full-time professorship and additional teaching experience at universities in the United States and France. She is currently the interim director of the Teaching Commons at York University in Toronto, Canada, where she previously served as an educational developer. Her practice and scholarship evolve around experiential learning and evidence-based educational development. She is an active member of the Educational Developer Caucus, having received two grants for projects aimed at developing resources in French and building capacity for the delivery of the Instructional Skills Workshop, a widespread peer-based teaching development model lesser known at French-Canadian universities. She also serves on the editorial board of the Canadian Journal for the Scholarship of Teaching and Learning as well as on the Board of Directors with the Society for the Teaching and Learning in Higher Education.

Heidi Marsh, as the Director of Scholarship of Teaching and Learning at Humber College, is responsible for building and fostering a culture of scholarly inquiry across the institution. In this role, she helps to empower faculty to conduct SoTL research in their classrooms and disseminate their findings. With a background in cognitive and developmental psychology, Heidi's research interests include metacognition, educational development, and learning environments. Currently, she also serves as the Editor-in-Chief for the Journal of Innovation in Polytechnic Education.

Mike McLinden is Professor in Education at the School of Education, University of BIrmngham. With over 25 years' experience of teaching in schools and Higher Education (HE) he has extensive experience as a teacher, university lecturer, researcher and senior manager. He is co-Director of the Vision Impairment Centre for Teaching and Research (VICTAR) at the University of Birmingham and programme lead for the professional development courses in vision impairment education. Mike's pedagogical research interests are focused on equitable participation for students with disabilities and the development of 'research-informed' pedagogical practice through integrated critical enquiry. Mike was conferred the status of 'Principal Fellow of the Higher Education Academy' (PFHEA) in June 2013.

Lindsay McNiff received her Master of Information degree from the University of Toronto in 2012 and her Master of Arts in Creative Writing and English Literature in 2006 from the University of Windsor. She is currently the Learning and Instruction Librarian at Dalhousie University in Halifax, Nova Scotia, where she is also liaison librarian to the Centre for Learning and Teaching, the Department of English, and the School of Information Management. She also teaches graduate courses in the Master of Information program at Dalhousie University, and in 2019 she was the inaugural winner of the Dalhousie Faculty of Management Part-time Teaching Award. Her work concerns approaches to library instruction, and she is also interested in LIS education and reading in the context of academic libraries.

Kathryn Meldrum is a learning advisor and educational developer at James Cook University located in Cairns, Far North Queensland, Australia. After an academic career, primarily as a teacher educator, she moved to supporting colleagues as a facilitator of professional development. In a higher education context where technology enhanced learning (TEL) is continuing to evolve, supporting colleagues to embrace it as well as build sustainability in practice is becoming increasingly important. As a passionate initiator and supporter of innovative curriculum design she supports academic colleagues to achieve this and embrace TEL in their own contexts.

Deanna Meth (PFHEA) is a Senior Lecturer in Curriculum & Learning Design whose practice currently focuses on curriculum development in Creative Industries disciplines, including transdisciplinary and authentic design curricula, and growing and sustaining communities of learning and practice. She has also led strategic projects in learning, teaching, and research in universities in the UK and South Africa. These experiences are reflected in her broad research interests, which include high-level policy, strategy and institutional analysis, curriculum development and student engagement.

Moriah Meyskens is a Clinical Professor of Management, Law & Ethics in the School of Business at the University of San Diego. Her scholarship is focused on social ventures, strategic alliances, and entrepreneurship. She has conducted a multi-year study on the impact of social venture competitions on learning.

Kiara Mikita received her PhD in Sociology from the University of Calgary in 2016. In 2017, she was hired as the inaugural Postdoctoral Scholar at the Taylor Institute for Teaching and Learning (TI) at the University of Calgary. She is currently an Educational Development Consultant at the TI and the Coordinator of the Teaching and Learning Grants Program, and consults with academic staff about their scholarship of teaching and learning and research ethics. Dr. Mikita also works as a researcher and educator about sexual violence in the local community, writing, presenting, and helping develop curriculum in teaching and learning about sexual violence for students, professionals, and the broader community.

Laetitia Monbec is a Lecturer at the CELC, National University of Singapore, where she coordinated the ES1103 English for Academic Purposes module for several semesters. She now coordinates an "Ideas and Exposition" module on colour theory, meaning and practice. Her research interests focus on academic literacy, socio semiotics, multimodality, Systemic Functional Linguistics and Legitimation Code Theory. Her doctoral research concerned writing across the disciplines and investigated transfer from an English for Academic Purposes module to a range of disciplinary contexts. Recent publications include an article in the Special Issue commemorating Michael Halliday in the Journal of English for Academic Purposes and a methodological paper for qualitative pedagogical research in the Asian Journal of Scholarship of Teaching Learning (AJSoTL).

Perla Myers is a professor of Mathematics at the University of San Diego and enjoys doing K-12 community engagement as an outreach initiative of the university. Perla is passionate about achieving equity in education and diversifying the Science, Technology, Engineering, and Mathematics (STEM) fields.

Fiona Rawle has a PhD in Pathology and Molecular Medicine and is the Associate Dean, Undergraduate, at the University of Toronto Mississauga, and an Associate Professor, Teaching Stream, in the Dept. of Biology. Her research focuses on public communication of science, science education, and the science of learning. She has received numerous awards focused on teaching, including the University of Toronto's President's Teaching Award. Dr. Rawle is also a member of the University of Toronto's TIDE group (Toronto Initiative for Diversity & Excellence), through which she gives lectures and workshops on unconscious bias, equity, and diversity.

Tracy Rogers is a Teaching Fellow at the Higher Education Development Centre, University of Otago. Her research interests include academic development for tutors and demonstrators, reciprocal peer observation of teaching, teaching culture, and gender and education. Her doctoral research investigated the various sources of support that enable materially-disadvantaged Cambodian schoolgirls to overcome various hurdles to their education. Current projects include metacognitive awareness training for sessional teaching staff, and enhancing teaching culture through voluntary, non-judgemental peer observation of teaching.

Holly Russell is a manager of curriculum and learning design within the Learning and Teaching Unit at Queensland University of Technology. She has worked on whole of course transformation for degrees in law, justice and urban development. Her research interests include authentic learning and assessment, experiential learning, enabling key partnerships in curriculum design and design thinking as a framework for teaching problem solving and collaboration.

Tara Ceranic Salinas is a Professor of Business Ethics and the current Steber Professor in the School of Business at the University of San Diego. Her research focuses on understanding what motivates ethical behavior and has been published in the Journal of Applied Psychology and the Journal of Business Ethics. It has also been presented at a variety of international conferences. She is the President-Elect for the International Association for Business and Society and she reviews for various academic conferences and journals.

Lauren Scharff is the Director for the Scholarship of Teaching and Learning Program and Professor of Behavioral Sciences at the U.S. Air Force Academy, where she has worked since 2008. Prior to that she was a professor of Psychology at Stephen F. Austin State University where she worked beginning in 1993. She completed her Ph.D. in Human Experimental Psychology in December, 1992 from the University of Texas at Austin. Courses taught include introductory psychology, leadership, research methods, biopsychology, and perception, and she has won several teaching awards. Her current research focuses on a variety of topics within SoTL, with a focus on metacognitive instruction and the science of learning. Dr. Scharff is past president of the Southwestern Psychological Association and served as the United States Regional Vice President for the International Society for the Scholarship of Teaching and Learning (2016-2019). She is co-creator of the award-winning Improve with Metacognition website.

Sandra Sgoutas-Emch is the Director of the Center for Educational Excellence and a Professor of Psychological Sciences at the University of San Diego. Her scholarship focuses on health, community engagement and SoTL.

Kerry Shephard researches higher education. He conceptualise this as a part of the discipline of Education, but with a focus on the functioning of universities and on the nature of learning within this domain. He has a background in a different discipline and his present disciplinary perspective (substantially developed in the past 19 years) was influenced by, and is grounded in, his prior 25 years of research and teaching as a biologist. Kerry thinks of higher education as a field of enquiry, as a discourse and as a community of practitioners defined by the diverse backgrounds of its contributors and this sets it aside from other fields within Education. Kerry's area of interest lies particularly in the affective domain of attitudes, values, dispositions and behaviours.

Anabel Stoeckle is a PhD candidate in Sociology and works as a consultant in the Office for Teaching & Learning at Wayne State University, Detroit, MI. Anabel researches current evidence-based teaching practices and facilitates teaching and pedagogy workshops such as assessment, diversity, evidence-based learning methods, and instructional technologies. She also co-facilitates the bi-weekly Pedagogy Journal Club, conducts the MAP (Midterm Assessment Program), and is a trained classroom observer for the STEM fields using COPUS (Classroom Observation Protocol for Undergraduate STEM). Anabel has been teaching introductory sociology classes at WSU for five years. As a novice instructor, she has learned many teaching methods at the OTL herself.

Namala Tilakaratna is a Lecturer at the Centre for English Language Communication (CELC) at NUS where she coordinates an NUS University Town (UTown) writing module on discourses of national identity. Her research and teaching interests include Systemic Functional Linguistics and Legitimation Code Theory (LCT). She is an associate member of the LCT Centre for Knowledge-building at the University of Sydney. She has a co-authored a chapter (with Dr Eszter Szenes and Professor Karl Maton) in the Palgrave Handbook of Critical Thinking in Higher Education and has a forthcoming co-authored book chapter (with Dr Eszter Szenes) on reflective writing assignments in Building Knowledge in Higher Education: Enhancing teaching and learning with LCT by editors C. Winberg, S. Mckenna and K. Wilmot. She is the Principal Investigator in a Teaching Enhancement Grant from the Centre for Development of Teaching and Learning at NUS for enhancing critical reflection writing in the discipline of nursing in collaboration with co-authors Dr Mark Brooke and Ms Laetitia Monbec, and colleagues from the Alice Lee Centre for Nursing Studies, Drs Lydia Lau, Vivien Wu, and Ms Chan Yah Shih.

Hayley Timms has a BA (Hons) in Professional Communication from the University of South Australia. She has worked in the Higher Education sector for over 21 years and has been in Online Educational Design for over 12 years. Her aim is to raise student and staff engagement (internal and online) through innovative teaching practices, increased activities, constructive feedback, flexibility, continuity, and most importantly, sustainability. Her expertise is in online teaching with a particular interest in simulation. Hayley has also been a casual academic for several years teaching Children's Literature and Global Experience: Professional Development, which has given her insight into the practical applications of teaching and empowering pedagogy in an online environment.

Andrea S. Webb received her Ph.D. in Curriculum Studies from the University of British Columbia in 2015. Prior to joining the Faculty of Education at UBC in 2008, Dr. Webb spent a decade as a secondary school teacher. In 2013, she joined the program advisory for the International Program for the Scholarship of Educational Leadership: UBC Certificate on Curriculum and Pedagogy in Higher Education and became the co-chair in 2019. She writes and presents widely on issues related to the Scholarship of Teaching and Learning, Threshold Concepts, and Teacher Education.

Siobhan Williams is the program administrator of the Teaching Innovation Fund at Humber College, where she helps guide faculty through the process of conducting their own SoTL research from ideation and design to dissemination. Along the way, she helps faculty with planning their research projects and with data collection and analysis. Siobhan's background in Marine Biology and climate science informs her evidence based approach to supporting and conducting research. Her research interests include faculty development, and in her role she also contributes to departmental teaching and learning research activities, including studies of faculty and student experiences with new teaching tools.

Vivien Wu is an Assistant Professor at Alice Lee Centre for Nursing Studies, Yong Loo Lin School of Medicine, National University of Singapore. Vivien has been a central committee member in the Centre for Healthcare Simulation (CHS) at National University of Singapore. She has facilitated simulation-pedagogical workshops for local and international medical and nursing clinicians. Her research interests focus on four major areas: Intergenerational Programs to promote Healthy Ageing in the Community; Chronic Disease Management for patients and caregivers; Professional development of the Healthcare Workforce; and Nursing Education. Vivien has published over 20 peer-reviewed papers in international refereed journals and book chapters. Vivien has served as editorial board reviewer for four International Nursing Journals. She has been awarded with Ministry of Education Tertiary-Research Fund (MOE-TRF) in 2017 for the Healthcare Workforce Professional Development study, Research Grant for Doctoral Studies by Institute of Adult Learning, Singapore in 2014. She is a recipient of grants from the National University of Singapore (NUS), Centre for Teaching & Learning (CDTL) and the Sigma Theta Tau International Honor Society of Nursing (Upsilon Eta Chapter) in 2014 to support the research studies on clinical assessment for Undergraduate Nursing Education. Currently, she has obtained Mind-Science Centre Seed Grant, NUS in 2019 to work on the collaborative project that focuses on the intergenerational project to promote healthy aging in the community in Singapore. In addition, Vivien has been awarded with Ministry of Health-Health Science Research Grant to work on project to enhance self-management of chronic conditions (stroke, chronic heart failure) for patients and caregivers.

Laura Zizka, with more than 20 years of international teaching experience, has been a faculty member at EHL since 2002. As an Assistant Professor, she teaches Business Communication, Academic Writing, and Crisis/Strategic Communication to undergraduate and graduate students as well as coaching Student Business Projects and undergraduate theses. Since 2017, Dr. Zizka has begun teaching similar courses online in the Blended MBA (EHL). Since completing her PhD in Management, Dr. Zizka has presented papers at education, hospitality, and management conferences and published papers on various communications topics linked to both higher education and the workplace. Her main research areas include communications, higher education, hospitality management, Science, Technology, Engineering, and Maths (STEM) education, and Corporate Social Responsibility (CSR)/sustainability actions, initiatives, and reporting. She is also interested in the gaps between higher education and the workplace.

Index

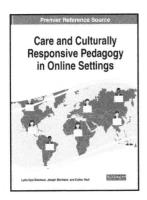
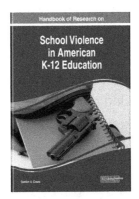

Ensure Quality Research is Introduced to the Academic Community

Become an IGI Global Reviewer for Authored Book Projects

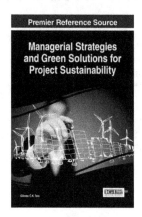

The overall success of an authored book project is dependent on quality and timely reviews.

In this competitive age of scholarly publishing, constructive and timely feedback significantly expedites the turnaround time of manuscripts from submission to acceptance, allowing the publication and discovery of forward-thinking research at a much more expeditious rate. Several IGI Global authored book projects are currently seeking highly-qualified experts in the field to fill vacancies on their respective editorial review boards:

Applications and Inquiries may be sent to:
development@igi-global.com

Applicants must have a doctorate (or an equivalent degree) as well as publishing and reviewing experience. Reviewers are asked to complete the open-ended evaluation questions with as much detail as possible in a timely, collegial, and constructive manner. All reviewers' tenures run for one-year terms on the editorial review boards and are expected to complete at least three reviews per term. Upon successful completion of this term, reviewers can be considered for an additional term.

If you have a colleague that may be interested in this opportunity,
we encourage you to share this information with them.

IGI Global Proudly Partners With eContent Pro International

Receive a 25% Discount on all Editorial Services

Editorial Services

IGI Global expects all final manuscripts submitted for publication to be in their final form. This means they must be reviewed, revised, and professionally copy edited prior to their final submission. Not only does this support with accelerating the publication process, but it also ensures that the highest quality scholarly work can be disseminated.

English Language Copy Editing

Let eContent Pro International's expert copy editors perform edits on your manuscript to resolve spelling, punctuaion, grammar, syntax, flow, formatting issues and more.

Scientific and Scholarly Editing

Allow colleagues in your research area to examine the content of your manuscript and provide you with valuable feedback and suggestions before submission.

Figure, Table, Chart & Equation Conversions

Do you have poor quality figures? Do you need visual elements in your manuscript created or converted? A design expert can help!

Translation

Need your documjent translated into English? eContent Pro International's expert translators are fluent in English and more than 40 different languages.

Email: customerservice@econtentpro.com   www.igi-global.com/editorial-service-partners